E   *au*

EASTERN AFRICAN STUDIES

Abdul Sheriff
Slaves, Spices & Ivory in Zanzibar
Integration of an East African Commercial Empire into the World Economy
1770–1873

Tabitha Kanogo
Squatters & the Roots of Mau Mau 1905–1963

David W. Throup
Economic and Social Origins of Mau Mau 1945–1953

Bruce Berman & John Lonsdale
Unhappy Valley
Clan, Class & State in Colonial Kenya*

Bethwell A. Ogot & Christopher Ehret
*A History of Early Eastern Africa**

* *forthcoming*

Economic & Social Origins of Mau Mau 1945–53

David Throup
Bye-Fellow
Magdalene College, Cambridge

James Currey
LONDON

Heinemann Kenya
NAIROBI

Ohio University Press
ATHENS

James Currey Ltd
54b Thornhill Square
Islington
London N1 1BE, England

Heinemann Kenya
Kijabe Street, PO Box 45314
Nairobi, Kenya

Ohio University Press
Scott Quadrangle
Athens, Ohio 45701, USA

British Library Cataloguing in Publication Data

Throup, David
Economic & social origins of Mau Mau,
1945–1953. —— (Eastern African studies).
1. Kenya —— Politics and government
I. Title   II. Series
967.6'203   DT433.575
ISBN 0–85255–023–5
ISBN 0–85255–024–3 Pbk

Library of Congress Cataloging-in-Publication Data

Throup, David.
Economic & social origins of Mau Mau.
Bibliography: p.
Includes index.
1. Agriculture and state —— Kenya —— History —— 20th century.
2. Kenya —— Economic conditions —— To 1963. 3. Kenya —— Social
conditions. 4. Kenya —— Politics and government —— To 1963. 5. Squatters
—— Kenya —— History —— 20th century. 6. Mau Mau —— History.
7. Kikuyu (African people) —— History —— 20th History. I. Title. II. Title:
Economic and social origins of Mau Mau.
HD2126.5.T48   1987   307.3'36   87–12387
ISBN 0–8214–0883–6
ISBN 0–8214–0884–4 (pbk.)

Typeset in 10/11pt Baskerville by Colset Private Limited, Singapore

To my parents

P73623

Contents

Contents

Four

The Problems of Kikuyu Agriculture

63

Five

The Kikuyu Squatter Problem

91

Six

Olenguruone

120

Seven

The Peasant Revolt: Murang'a, 1947

139

Contents

Eight
Outcast Nairobi
171

Nine
A Change of Direction:
The Agricultural Department's Abandonment of Communalism
203

Ten
The Drift to Mau Mau
224

Eleven
Conclusion
237

Maps, Graphs and Tables

MAPS

GRAPHS

TABLES

Preface and Acknowledgements

One of the pleasures of historical research is the debt one incurs to people in all walks of life – many of whom will probably never read the finished book that they have helped to produce. That is particularly true in the case of a book like this on the social and economic origins of the Mau Mau movement in Kenya, which has taken eleven years to produce and which has involved research in both Britain and Kenya.

In October 1976, I first arrived in Nairobi with the vague idea of doing research while teaching at the *Banda* school. I am grateful to the late J.A.L. Chitty and to Douggie and Patricia Dalrymple for employing a totally inexperienced master and for introducing me to Kenya, while providing time for me to visit the archives. When I returned to Cambridge in September 1979, my research was funded by a grant from the Department of Education and Science and the Smuts Memorial Fund helped to finance another visit to Kenya from July 1980 to September 1981. In 1982–83 I was the holder of the Holland Rose Studentship in Commonwealth History of the University of Cambridge and in January 1984, I was elected to a Bye-Fellowship at Magdalene College, while the Leverhulme Trust awarded me a post-doctoral Study Abroad Studentship which enabled me to return to Kenya from February 1984 to January 1986 to undertake more research. I would like to express my gratitude to all these bodies.

During the last decade many friends have provided accommodation and intellectual sustenance. For their help in Nairobi I would especially like to thank Hugh and Jo Cowie, who welcomed me into their home for twelve months in 1980 to 1981; Glyn Davies, who did the same in 1984; and David and Margaret Pearson and Jan de Graaf, who solved my housing problems for shorter periods on several occasions. Richard and Jenny Davenport-Hines looked after me when I was working in the Public Record Office in Kew in 1979–80 and have done so on several occasions since, while Dave and Angie Anderson, Edward Chandler, James Thorne and Joanna Innes – old undergraduate friends – have sustained my endeavours. More recently, Joe and Janet Miller have welcomed me to the University of Virginia as Visiting Assistant Professor.

Preface and Acknowledgements

Various friends in Nairobi helped to retain my sanity by diverting me from the archives or have provided stimulating company in them. I would particularly like to thank my neighbours – Mary Anne, Tara and Petra Fitzgerald and Kate Macintyre – who used to ferry me in to town; and Susanne Mueller, Simon Myambo, Robert Bates, Michael Schatzberg, John Nordin, Barbara Grosh, Luise White and Jennifer Widner for their company in the archives. Jennifer Widner shared with me not only her knowledge of modern Kenyan politics and a 'hunt for Kimathi' in Nyeri but also introduced me to the charms of New Haven, Washington D.C. and New York on my first visit to America. She and the others have endured far too many of my monologues on Kikuyu history.

The staff of the Public Record Office at Kew; the Kenya National Archives, especially Mr Richard Ambani, who has an amazing ability to find misplaced files; and the Cambridge University Library have made this work possible. Janet Seeley and her colleagues at the African Studies Centre in Cambridge have introduced me to the delights of word processing and have kept me supplied with a steady stream of books and articles on Mau Mau which had escaped my attention. I would also like to take this opportunity to thank my colleagues in the History Department at the University of Nairobi to which I was attached as a research associate in 1980–81 and 1984–86 for showing such an interest in my research, especially Godfrey Muriuki, A.I. Salim, Atieno Odhiambo, Karim Janmohammed and Mwangi wa Githumo. I would also like to pay tribute to the memory of Dr Neville Chittick, the former Director of the British Institute in Eastern Africa, who encouraged me to use the Institute's facilities and always welcomed me to Nairobi, despite my strange interests in twentieth century Kenya instead of the *Shirazi* coast.

The Master and Fellows of Magdalene College, Cambridge, by electing me to a Bye-Fellowship provided me with a perfect home, where I could work in a friendly, productive and humane environment. For the privilege of being a 'Magdalene man', I am most grateful. I would particularly like to thank my fellow historians – Ronald Hyam, Eamon Duffy, Julian Hoppet, John Patterson and Jonathan Scott – for their encouragement and friendship.

Many people have read earlier drafts of chapters in this book – and indeed of some chapters which have been discarded, perhaps to appear in a second volume on *The Political Origins of Mau Mau* – and have offered valuable comments. I would like to thank Polly Bide, Ronald Hyam, John Iliffe, John Overton who also helped to produce the maps, Anne Thurston, Nicholas Westcott and the undergraduate members of the 1985–86 Saturday morning Mau Mau seminar, who over the course of forty hours forced me to change many of my opinions. David Fieldhouse and Richard Rathbone have followed my work with interest for many years and were incisive examiners of my doctoral thesis on 'The Gover-

Preface and Acknowledgements

norship of Sir Philip Mitchell in Kenya, 1944 to 1952'. Selina Cohen has been a far more efficient editor than I have been author and has provided me with information on Kenyatta's Moscow period.

I am also most grateful to three participants – Sir Michael Blundell, who became the leader of the European Elected Members in the Legislative Council in 1952; Desmond O'Hagan, who served as District Commissioner in Murang'a from 1945–47, and then in the Secretariat before returning to Central Province as Provincial Commissioner in 1952 at the onset of Mau Mau; and Bildad Kaggia, the leader of the Clerks' and Commercial Workers' Union and member of the Mau Mau *Muhimu* – for reading and commenting at length upon my manuscript and for their kind hospitality during my frequent visits.

My debts – intellectual and personal – to David Anderson, Richard Waller and John Lonsdale, who began to supervise my work more years ago than he would care to remember, are beyond number. Their knowledge and enthusiasm for Kenya history have been an inspiration and their encouragement and patient criticism of my work has shown me how history ought to be written although I am acutely aware how far I have fallen short of their example. It should perhaps be emphasised here that there is no such thing as a 'Cambridge interpretation' of Kenya's history or a 'Cambridge school'. David, Richard and John have been my strongest critics. As such they have helped to produce this book and are largely responsible for any virtues it may have, but they should not be held responsible for its failings.

Finally, I would like to thank my long suffering parents, who have endured my protracted absences from home and who have sustained me with encouragement throughout this lengthy enterprise. This book is dedicated to them.

Charlottesville
Virginia

Abbreviations

PRO   *Public Record Office*
Cab.   Cabinet
CO   Colonial Office
WO   War Office

KNA   *Kenya National Archives*
Ag.   Department of Agriculture
C&I   Department of Commerce and Industry
CNC   Chief Native Commissioner
CP   Central Province
CS   Chief Secretary
DC   District Commissioner
DO   District Officer
FH   Fort Hall (Murang'a)
GH   Government House
KBU   Kiambu
Lab.   Department of Labour
MAA   Member for African Affairs
MAC/KEN Murumbi Archive Collection/Kenya deposit
MKS   Machakos
NKU   Nakuru
NRK   Narok
NYI   Nyeri
PC   Provincial Commissioner
RVP   Rift Valley Province

Other abbreviations
ADC   aide-de-camp
Afr.   Africa
Brt.Emp. British Empire
CBE   Commander of the British Empire

Abbreviations

CID	Criminal Investigation Department
CIGS	Chief of the Imperial General Staff
CMG	Companion of the Order of St Michael and St George
CMS	Church Missionary Society
CSM	Church of Scotland Mission
CVO	Commander of the Royal Victorian Order
DSO	Distinguished Service Order
EACA	East Africa Court of Appeal
FCS	Fellow of the Chemical Society
FRIC	Fellow of the Royal Institute of Chemistry
GBE	Knight Grand Cross of the British Empire
GCMG	Knight Grand Cross of St Michael and St George
KBE	Knight Commander of the British Empire
KC	Kings Counsel
KCB	Knight Commander of the Order of the Bath
KCVO	Knight Commander of the Royal Victorian Order
Kt.	Knight
LND	Land Number
LO	Land Office
MBE	Member of the Order of the British Empire
MC	Military Cross
MRCVS	Member of the Royal College of Veterinary Surgeons
Mss.	Manuscripts
OBE	Officer of the Order of the British Empire
PC	Privy Councillor
RAF	Royal Air Force
RH	Rhodes House
RMA	Royal Military Academy
RMC	Royal Military College

Glossary of African Words

K = Kikuyu   Sw. = Swahili

Agikuyu na Worjoria Wao	a co-operative of licensed egg exporters
ahoi	tenants at will, plural of *muhoi* (K)
Anake a Forty	the Forty Group, a criminal gang
askari	soldier (Sw.)
athamaki	elders of the *mbari* (K)
baraza	meeting/title of a newspaper (Sw.)
bibi	wife, wives (Sw.)
Dini ya Jesu Kristo	Church of Jesus Christ (Sw.)

Dini ya Kaggia	Church of Kaggia (Sw.)
Dini ya Msambwa	Church of Msambwa/ancestral spirit of the Bukusu (Sw.)
duka	shop (Sw.)
githaka	plot of land belonging to a sub-clan (K)
itura	land (K)
karing'a	pure, strict, orthodox (K)
kiama	council (K)
Kifagio	broom – 'times of troubles' (K)
kipande	labour pass (Sw.)
liguru	land authority (Luhya)
majengo	shanty town (Sw.)
mbari	sub-clan (K)
Mihiriga	nine main Kikuyu clans or agricultural supervisory committees, plural of *Muhirig'a* (K)
Muhimu	Mau Mau Central Committee
Muhirig'a	one Kikuyu clan, or agricultural supervisory committee
muhoi	tenant-at-will, singular of *ahoi* (K)
murumati	trustee of *mbari* land (K)
muthoni	relation-in-law (K)
mwathi	ancestor (K)
ndungata	in-law (K)
ngwatio	communal labour (K)
njahi	pigeon pea
Njuri Ncheke	land authority (Meru)
nyimbo	hymns (K)
pombe	beer (Sw.)
posho	maize meal (Sw.)
Sauti ya Mwafrika	newspaper of the Kenya African Union, literally Voice of Africa (SW.)
shamba	cultivated plot, smallholding (Sw.)
tembo	kind of beer (K)
Uhuru	independence, freedom (Sw.)
utui	land authority (Kamba)
wananchi	people, citizens, the masses (Sw.)
Watu wa Mungu	False Prophets, lit. Men of God (Sw.)
wimbe	finger millet (Sw.)

One

The Economic and Social Origins
of Mau Mau

Rather than attempting to identify a metropolitan grand strategy for the
end of empire in Africa, in this book I try to argue that it would be more
rewarding to abandon such Euro-centric blinkers and to place the policy
makers of the Colonial Office within the context of Africa, the continent
with which they have to deal despite their limited knowledge of the complex social, economic and political context which confronted administrators in the front line. This study, therefore, seeks to investigate the process
of policy formation through the eyes of the local policy makers – the
colonial governors, the Secretariats, the field administrators, and the
various technical departments which dealt directly with Africans. These
men were far more important for the future of Africa than the remote
theorists in Whitehall. Recent studies of the Colonial Office in the 1940s
have over-emphasised the importance of the 'Official Mind' for the
history of decolonisation. This concentration on Whitehall has distorted
our understanding of the process of colonial administration and decolonisation by concealing the different, often conflicting, aims of the various
layers of the 'colonial state'.[1]

This story of Kenya in the decade before the outbreak of the Mau Mau
Emergency attempts to present a more integrated view of imperial
government as well as to examine the social and economic causes of the
Kikuyu revolt. It is a contribution not only to the historiography of Kenya
but also suggests that it is only by investigating the various strands of the
interwoven historical processes of decolonisation that we can hope to comprehend its true complexity. The historiographical triptych of imperial
policy, the international context, and the peripheral experience has to be
reassembled and analysed as a unified whole. All three parts of the picture
were important. No one strand alone can begin to portray the process of
decolonisation for it is the linkages between these political arenas which
provided the crucial element in the story.

In order to understand the process of decolonisation one must start with a discussion of the specificity of the colonial state. This study, therefore, begins with an investigation of the ambitions and policies of the various layers of the colonial state in Kenya. Whitehall, colonial governors and their Secretariats all had a profound impact on Africa, but the men in the field from lowly District Officers to senior Provincial Commissioners, not to mention the often forgotten technical services (particularly the agricultural, veterinary and labour departments) were often more important and frequently in conflict with the colonial administrative cadre.

The mandarins of the Colonial Office or governors and their Secretariats may have believed they ruled Africa, but in reality District Commissioners, agricultural officers and chiefs were far more important. They embodied the colonial state to most Africans – not the remote, unknown figures in the territorial or metropolitan capitals. It must also be remembered that the subconscious prejudices of these grassroots' administrators were often as important, as far as Africans were concerned, as the conscious policy decisions taken higher up the colonial hierarchy. Frequently, policies devised in Whitehall or Nairobi made little impression on the ingrained prejudices of policy implementers in the field. This study will attempt to justify these sweeping statements by examining the evolution of post-war policies in Kenya. It seeks to show how the aims of the Colonial Office, which were largely determined by the international climate and Britain's weak economic position in the late 1940s, were transformed by the political realities of Kenya. By combining traditional 'imperial' history, with its emphasis on the high politics of the official mind in the Colonial Office or in Government House, with the new peripherally focused African historiography, one can appreciate more fully the complexity of the problems which confronted not only British administrators but African politicians as they sought to construct their nationalist coalitions.[2]

The Kenyan settlers had made substantial economic and political advances during the last years of the war when Britain's African colonies were called upon to maximise production following the Japanese conquest of South East Asia. Whitehall, for example, had been alarmed in 1942 at the spectre of South African hegemony in East Africa, particularly in Kenya. Consequently, as the allied forces advanced towards victory, the Colonial Office reconsidered its pre-war policies and determined to reassert metropolitan authority in Kenya by instilling new life into the Duke of Devonshire's moribund 1923 declaration of African paramountcy.[3]

The new governor, Sir Philip Mitchell, was selected to undertake this task. He had secured a reputation as a pro-African administrator in Tanganyika and Uganda during the 1920s and 1930s. Mitchell's governorship was a failure for two reasons. First, he was reluctant to antagonise the settlers because he considered that any attempt to reduce their newly secured power would damage the colony's ambitious development plans. The future of East and Central Africa after 1945, under the Colonial Office's strategy of multiracialism, was posited upon the continued presence of a thriving European community, which would guarantee political stability, attract metropolitan investment into the region, and also act as the economic dynamo for industrial expansion since in the immediate future the settlers would provide the main consumers for the new secondary industries which, it was hoped, would absorb landless Africans from the reserves into wage employment.

Secondly, Mitchell was a proconsul of the old, pre-war school. He was an ardent defender of 'indirect rule'. Indeed his reputation had been founded upon his skilful introduction of the system into Tanganyika as Sir Donald Cameron's energetic adviser on African affairs. The new governor therefore had little sympathy for the Colonial Office's post-war plans to co-opt African politicians. Thus, despite the fact that in Kenya's acephalous, segmentary, lineage societies chiefs were British appointees, during Mitchell's eight years in office, the Kenyan government became dependent upon such antiquated allies. With little political legitimacy or influence, the chiefs became increasingly dictatorial, thereby further alienating their people. In contrast, the emerging African politicians remained excluded from the decision-making processes. Without any influence on official policy, they became increasingly intemperate. In consequence, their hopes of incorporation became even more remote. Their followers became disillusioned and abandoned advocates of constitutional politics, turning in desperation to the militants who became influential inside the nationalist movement.[4]

It was against this background of stymied African political advance and growing militancy that the colonial administration in Kenya evolved the policies that are examined here. The problems of Kikuyu agriculture both in the reserves and among the squatter communities on settler farms in the Rift Valley preoccupied Mitchell and his colleagues. We shall examine the development of agricultural policy in the Kikuyu reserves and follow the fate of the squatter farm labourers in the European enclave of the 'White Highlands' with particular attention since the government's failure to solve these problems lay at the heart of Mau Mau. The squatter communities, in particular, were confronted after the war by a drastic reduction in their cultivation and stock-holding rights without any commensurate increase in wages.[5]

The government's agricultural policies and political grand strategy, formulated partly by Mitchell and partly in Whitehall, were transformed by the field administration and the chiefs into an attack on those members of the emerging African élite who had not secured incorporation. These rivals of the chiefs for power and access to the pork-barrel of the colonial state had perforce turned to politics (in the 1930s to the Kikuyu Central

Association and after 1946 to the Kenya African Union) to force open the doors to the corridors of power. Their attempts to attract attention on both occasions backfired and ensured that their ambitions were denounced as illegitimate, subversive of the moral economy of 'Merrie Africa'. These attacks after the war on the political ambitions of the emerging proto-capitalists among the Kikuyu marked a return to the policies of the 1920s, when the settlers had also been politically influential.

The depression of the early 1930s, however, had created a fiscal crisis for the colonial state in Kenya, which forced the government to promote African peasant production in order to finance its bureaucracy and to ensure the survival of the settler farming community through subsidies until international commodity prices rose in the late 1930s. This encouragement of African individualism progressed even further during the war, when Kenya's exports were required to reduce the dollar deficit. Schemes for soil conservation and cattle destocking in the reserves were postponed and African entrepreneurs were encouraged to increase production regardless of the long-term effects on soil fertility. This decade, denounced after the war as an era of 'land-mining', came abruptly to an end when the Kenyan government began in 1944 to formulate its post-war policies in consultation with European settler leaders. The danger of erosion provided Kenya's settlers with a potent weapon with which to persuade the government in Nairobi and the Colonial Office to move against the economic base of their rivals, the emerging African capitalists and their representatives in the Kenya African Union and the banned Kikuyu Central Association.[6]

Policies formulated in the Colonial Office were subtly transformed by the local district administration and the chiefs into an attack on their political rivals in the Kenya African Union, who were struggling to emerge as an alternative indigenous élite. This belated attempt to forestall the emergence of African capitalism generated fierce resistance among the African élite, especially in Kikuyuland where these processes were most advanced. It coincided, moreover, with the disruptive effects on the peasantry of what Lonsdale and Low have described as 'the second colonial occupation'. For the first time ordinary Africans, cultivating their maize *shambas*, encountered administrative interference. Agricultural instructors and the chiefs ordered them to cultivate cassava and millet as security against famine, instead of the multi-purpose cash crop wattle, or maize which was more easily grown and prepared than the drought resistant new crops.[7]

Three mornings every week, peasant women were compelled to labour on communal terracing or grass-planting campaigns. Frequently they had to neglect their own plots in order to provide unpaid labour on the holdings of the chiefs and their wealthy supporters. Compulsion, not persuasion, was the hallmark of the first phase of the post-war agricultural betterment campaign, despite the Nairobi Secretariat's attempts to revive traditional land authorities such as the *Mihirig'a* among the Kikuyu, the *Njuri Ncheke* in Meru, or the Kamba *utui*. In fact, despite the advice of anthropologists, these bodies had never held executive power over the peasantry and their prestige had atrophied during 50 years of colonial rule.[8]

This second colonial occupation of the reserves was spearheaded by the chiefs, whose position became increasingly invidious. The colonial régime began to assess the loyalty and efficiency of its intermediaries by calculating the miles of terracing constructed in each location. The communal terracing campaign rapidly came to be perceived as the key indicator of social and economic progress. In the more advanced reserves, such as Kikuyuland, a new generation of chiefs were appointed after the war – school teachers, agricultural instructors, district headquarters' clerks. Long serving chiefs with established support among their people were replaced by younger men, willing to follow unquestioningly the orders of District Commissioners and agricultural officers. These new men had few claims to political power and were to prove less effective as intermediaries than the previous generation of African 'collaborators'. By 1947 peasant resistance was widespread.[9]

Following the Peasant Revolt, the agricultural department belatedly realised that compulsory terracing had alienated the rural population. Gradually the department adopted a new policy which sought to reward those who co-operated and built broad-based terraces, with permission to grow high-value cash crops such as coffee, tea and pineapples. By 1952, considerable areas had already been planted to such crops in Meru and Embu, but in Nyeri less than two per cent of peasant families had established coffee trees and in Murang'a fewer than one in 200 households were cultivating these remunerative new crops, which had hitherto been reserved for the European settlers. In Kiambu, in contrast, pineapple cultivation had been sponsored and sisal cultivation encouraged by the Agricultural Officer and the Administration in Machakos. Elsewhere, the field administration was reluctant to abandon compulsory labour and to return to the free enterprise policies of the 1930s and the war years, which it considered had increased social differentiation and threatened the traditional moral economy and, therefore, the fabric of peasant society. Officials consequently refused to switch once more to encouraging Kikuyu entrepreneurs, many of whom were enthusiastic supporters of the Kenya African Union or the Kikuyu Central Association, which were in conflict with the paternalist traditions of the district administration. The agricultural department's new strategy, therefore, made the least progress in those areas where the second colonial occupation had aroused the strongest African opposition, such as the Kikuyu heartlands of Murang'a and Nyeri. It was in these areas that communal terracing had most seriously eroded the authority of the chiefs and had alienated the peasantry. Thus although agricultural officers, such as Jack Benson in Meru and Leslie Brown in Embu, had recognised the need to secure African support for the betterment campaign by rewarding them with valuable cash crops, the field administration in the Kikuyu reserves remained reluctant to foster greater individualism, which they feared would exacerbate the problems created by increasing social differentiation. Individualism, they considered, would further undermine the cohesion of Kikuyu society and destroy customary social controls. Compulsion, therefore, continued to dominate the agricultural campaign in Kiambu, Murang'a and Nyeri, because the administration failed to recognise the need to broaden the colonial régime's narrow collaborative base. Thus, by 1952 the colonial order had become dangerously exposed in the Kikuyu reserves and the new generation of chiefs, appointed after the war, had squandered their political legitimacy.[10]

In many respects, of course, these new chiefs were very similar in education and background to the local leaders of the Kenya African Union and the Kikuyu Central Association, who were their strongest critics. Yet, despite Andrew Cohen's strategy of political incorporation, devised for the Gold Coast and Nigeria, African politicians in a settler colony such as Kenya, particularly at the district level, remained as firmly excluded from political and economic influence as before the war. They had, however, greater expectations. The field administration in Kenya (the infantrymen of the Colonial Service) failed to respond to the uncertain hints which percolated from Whitehall. African criticisms, however well founded or moderate, were deemed to be disruptive; subversive of the established order in the reserves. Some politicians deliberately attempted to stir up opposition to the chiefs, but official intransigence ensured that the district administration's fears became self-fulfilling. African politicians in Kenya, unlike their West African counterparts, or Kenya's settlers, could not break into the colonial corridors of power. Not all Africans, however, were excluded. The chiefs were securely entrenched at the local level, but the epithet 'politician' aroused the enmity of the administration and precluded the incorporation of Kenyatta and the Kenya African Union.[11]

The disruptive effects of the second colonial occupation enabled the activists of the Kenya African Union, under Kenyatta's leadership, to mobilise a popular constituency among the peasantry in opposition to the chiefs and communal terracing. The development of this confrontation is examined in detail in Murang'a District, the historic heartland of the Kikuyu, where Local Native Councillor James Beauttah, the chairman of the district branch of the Kenya African Union, clashed with Chief Ignatio Morai, the government's leading supporter. During the second half of 1947, the terracing campaign was disrupted throughout Murang'a.

Several attacks were made on Chief Ignatio and Beauttah was arrested. Similar opposition to terracing and compulsory cattle dipping developed in Kiambu and Nyeri, the two other Kikuyu districts, until by September 1947, the government's authority appeared to be about to collapse throughout Kikuyuland.[12]

Meanwhile, the 200,000 Kikuyu squatters on settler farms had also been antagonised by the spate of post-war district Council orders, which regulated their stock and cultivation rights. Led by the Naivasha District Council, the main settler dairy and beef farming areas had introduced rules to end the disease threat posed to their grade cattle by squatter-owned stock. Settler cereal farmers and the large plantations were more cautious. They depended heavily upon squatter labour for sowing and harvesting their crops and feared serious disruption of their labour supply if draconian new restrictions were introduced. All settler farmers, however, were united in the fear that African resident labourers might secure squatters' rights under English law to the land they occupied on European-owned farms. Many squatter families had resided on the same farm since before the First World War, when they had been enticed by European farmers, short of capital and labour to develop their properties, to work in return for as much land as they wanted to graze their stock and to cultivate, in contrast to conditions in the already crowded reserves, where they were also subject to the exactions of the chiefs and their headmen and to taxation.

The Second World War had been a period of prosperity, as much for the squatters as for the peasants in the Reserves. Many settler farmers had been absent in the armed forces and the European district councils in the White Highlands had been cautious about antagonising their African labour in the midst of the hostilities once the British government, in December 1941, had urged Kenya to maximise production and had provided financial incentives to break new land and guaranteed prices. During the war, therefore, the squatters had been largely left alone and had been able to increase their own production for the black market at inflated war-time prices. Until the post-war squeeze, squatter family incomes had compared favourably with those in the Kikuyu reserves and the squatter option had enjoyed one last brief period of comparative prosperity. With the end of the war the situation changed. Squatter cultivation was restricted to two and a half acres per wife, while the number of sheep and goats they were permitted was drastically reduced, and all males over the age of sixteen were required to work 270 days per annum – virtually a full working year. During 1946, these new measures provoked fierce opposition, particularly in the Naivasha, Aberdares and Nakuru district council areas. The following year, discontent spread to the Uasin Gishu and Trans Nzoia, and to Abaluhya and Elgeyo squatters as well as to the Kikuyu, following the introduction of compulsory destocking of squatter cattle. In these western districts of the White Highlands, Elijah Masinde's Dini ya Msambwa provided a potent focus of resistance and was a portent of things to come among the Kikuyu – Mau Mau, which was to secure a strong following among dispossessed Kikuyu squatters.[13]

Relations between the former Kikuyu resident labourers at Olenguruone, the prototype African settlement scheme on the Mau escarpment above the White Highlands, and the remaining Kikuyu squatters in Naivasha and Nakuru were extremely close. In theory, the settlement had been designed to accommodate former Kikuyu squatters, who had been forced out of the White Highlands by the 1937 Resident Native Labour Ordinance, but in practice most of the residents of Olenguruone had been forcibly repatriated from Maasailand by the district administration in Narok during 1940–41. Most of them had, indeed, once been squatters, but they had arrived at Olenguruone in a belligerent mood, having been expelled from the more attractive ecological environment at Il Melili and Nairage Ngare. Thus, when the government attempted to enforce the settlement's agricultural rules in 1943, it encountered fierce resistance. Eventually, in September 1946, the residents had to be threatened with eviction and, after a three-year legal battle, were finally expelled in January 1950. Olenguruone was a running sore for the Kenyan government throughout the 1940s. Its Kikuyu residents introduced a new oath in 1942–43, which was administered to young men, women and children and not simply to the leaders, as with traditional Kikuyu oaths to ensure communal solidarity. This rapidly spread to the Kikuyu squatters on neighbouring farms, who were resisting the new district council regulations. Olenguruone thus became the centre of political subversion throughout the Rift Valley and established close ties with discontented squatters at Soysambu, Naivasha and Limuru. This chain of radical contacts provided the organisational framework for the development in the White Highlands, where one in four of the total Kikuyu population lived, of what came to be known as Mau Mau.[14]

The capital, Nairobi, was the other seed-bed of political militancy. While many squatters and peasants had prospered from the high commodity prices during the war, Kenya's urban population, particularly in Mombasa and Nairobi, lived on, or in many cases below, the official poverty line. Wages trailed behind inflationary price increases. Yet thousands of new migrants flocked to the capital and Mombasa throughout the 1940s. Between 1941 and 1948, Nairobi's population grew by 17 per cent each year. Many of these urban migrants after 1945 were former squatters, who had been squeezed off European farms, or Kikuyu *ahoi* (tenants) from Central Province, who had lost their small plots with the commoditisation of production and land. Senior lineages, like the settler farmers, cast off their dependent junior lineages and tenants and intensified their own commercial cultivation. Reinforced by increasing population pressure, the development of capitalist relations undermined the moral economy of Kikuyu society, destroying the 'traditional' land law, as the Kikuyu élite asserted their exclusive occupation rights and demanded the introduction of individual title. In this process of increasing social differentiation, the rights of subsidiary categories, such as *ahoi* and *ndungata*, who during the nineteenth century had enjoyed an unquestioned· access to land for cultivation, were devalued as land became a scarce resource. Customary law was required to perform discriminatory functions for which it had not been devised. Litigation increased since both claimants had perfectly legitimate cases, but while the emerging 'class' of land accumulators justified their acquisitions in terms of English land law, the junior lineages and *ahoi* sought to defend their rights according to pre-colonial Kikuyu customs. The delineation of fixed Reserve boundaries, the alienation of land to European settlers and increased social differentiation, however, had transformed the internal structure and social hierarchy of *mbari* (sub-clans) and endowed the *aramati* (or trustees) with enhanced authority. These internal pressures increased dramatically during the 1940s, when population growth in the Kikuyu reserves reached three per cent per annum, at the same moment as the war-time commodities boom and remittances from soldiers in the King's African Rifles provided the additional income which financed a land scramble. As competition for land increased and commodity prices rose, bribing Native Tribunals and investment in litigation became an economically sensible use of accumulated income for rich peasants and traders and other members of the Kikuyu élite.[15]

Those who lost out in this scramble, and were dispossessed, were compelled to become wage labourers (perhaps on their former land) either for settler farmers or for the successful Kikuyu litigants from the senior lineages. Others sought refuge in Nairobi with friends or relatives, who had already been attracted by the high wages which seemed to be offered. The Kikuyu came to dominate life in the capital's African locations, the informal sector and crime. In particular, the provision of housing abysmally failed to keep pace with the influx despite an unprecedented municipal house-building programme for Africans from 1939 to 1947. African earnings, however, were so low that housing had to be provided at sub-economic rents, which placed a mounting burden on settler rate payers who became increasingly discontented. After the war prices continued to rise, unemployment grew and crime became a serious problem in Nairobi. By September 1947, when the peasants' revolt against enforced agricultural change was at its height in the Kikuyu reserves and farming in the White Highlands was gradually beginning to recover from two years' disruption by discontented squatters, the administration virtually lost control over the African locations of Nairobi to Kikuyu armed gangs and the militants of the African Workers' Federation. Demands for a general strike attracted much support after the detention of the trade union leader, Chege Kibachia, and the shooting two weeks later by the police of Kikuyu workers at Uplands.[16]

Despite the introduction of legislation to allow for tighter control over the influx of people into the capital and to remove unemployed labourers and unlicensed hawkers, and new measures to increase the presence of the police and the administration in the African locations, there was little improvement in the situation. Those who were expelled from the city soon drifted back. In 1950, the Kikuyu street gangs remained firmly in control of African Nairobi. By this date, they had established close links with the militant Kikuyu politicians and trade unionists who had risen to prominence since 1947, most notably Fred Kubai and Bildad Kaggia. Encouraged by Makhan Singh, a self-avowed although rather undogmatic Asian communist, Kubai and Kaggia organised the general strike of May 1950 and severely disrupted the capital. Armoured cars patrolled the African locations and tear gas was used for the first time in Kenya to disperse the belligerent crowds of strikers on the streets of Pumwani and Shauri Moyo in the heart of the African residential area. When the strike was defeated after ten days and the strike leaders, including Kubai and Makhan Singh, arrested, the Nairobi militants had to reassess their syndicalist strategy and, after careful deliberation, decided to switch from their strategy of confrontation and trade unionism to one of political action, the infiltration of the constitutional nationalist movement, the Kenya African Union, and the mass oathing of the capital's Kikuyu under-class of criminals, prostitutes, taxi drivers, vagrants and casual labourers.[17]

Once they had seized control of the Nairobi branch of the Kenya African Union from the constitutionalists and had ousted Tom Mbotela, Kenyatta's deputy, from the branch chairmanship, the trade union militants quickly established alliances with other radicals in the reserves and the White Highlands. In September 1951, they felt strong enough to challenge Kenyatta's leadership and when their attempt to capture control of the Kenya African Union's national executive committee was thwarted, they contemplated leaving the movement and establishing a more radical organisation as Nkrumah had done two years earlier in the Gold Coast. From September 1951 until the declaration of the Emergency by the Colonial government on 20 October 1952, the militants, secure in their own Nairobi bailiwick, challenged Kenyatta's authority and became increasingly influential, raising the stakes in the political contest. Unlike Kenyatta and the leaders of the banned Kikuyu Central Association, who provided his most stalwart supporters, the Nairobi militants and their rural associates, a generation younger, were prepared to use force to undermine the settlers' hegemony.[18]

The Mau Mau movement, as it was called by the government, was an alliance between three groups of discontented Kikuyu: the urban unemployed and destitute; dispossessed squatters from the White Highlands; and poor peasants, tenants and members of the junior lineages of *mbari* (sub-clans) in the Kikuyu reserves who had endured the second colonial occupation, particularly the communal terracing campaign, at the moment they were being transformed into a landless rural proletariat as the senior lineages attempted to establish their exclusive access to land. The post-war agricultural betterment campaign, as it was conceived by Whitehall and the Secretariat in Nairobi, disrupted Kikuyu rural society and helped to destroy the political legitimacy of the chiefs, the essential intermediaries of the colonial system of control. Under the leadership of the Nairobi militants, who had established close links with the armed bands of Kikuyu thugs, these desperate elements among the Kikuyu, in the Reserves and on the European farms in the Rift Valley as much as in Nairobi, accepted violence as their last resort. They were convinced that they had nothing to lose and much to gain from a campaign of terror.[19]

By January–February 1952, violence had already reached serious proportions. Cattle on settler farms were hamstrung in large numbers and standing crops and haystacks were set on fire, particularly in the Nanyuki area immediately to the north of the Nyeri Reserve. Chiefs were attacked and agricultural instructors and police informers locked in their huts and burnt to death. Six months before the declaration of the Emergency, Othaya Division in Nyeri had become, like the African locations of Nairobi, a virtual Mau Mau republic where African officials and tribal police rarely went alone. The situation deteriorated rapidly after the retirement of Sir Philip Mitchell as governor in May 1952, during the four-month interregnum before his successor, Sir Evelyn Baring, arrived in Kenya at the end of September. Pressure from the settler community on the interim Governor, Henry Potter, to declare an Emergency and to detain those African political leaders who were considered to be behind the campaign of violence, became intense. Late in August, Potter sought permission from Whitehall to ban meetings of the Kenya African Union and to introduce legislation to control the vernacular press and freedom of movement in the Kikuyu areas. The Chief Native Commissioner and the Attorney General were despatched to London for consultation early in September to persuade a doubtful Colonial Office that the situation in Kenya was as bad as Potter's despatches had portrayed and to reinforce the case for drastic measures. The rapid deterioration in the political situation in Kenya during August and September 1952 astounded Whitehall. Under Mitchell, they had been given little inkling of the depth of Kikuyu alienation and, consequently, Potter's first warnings outlining the growing crisis had been dismissed as alarmist.[20]

When the new governor, Sir Evelyn Baring, arrived on 30 September, he was confronted by Potter and the Secretariat with extremely pessimistic reports and with carefully prepared plans for the declaration of an Emergency and the detention without trial of the colony's nationalist politicians. The assassination of Chief Waruhiu on 7 October, on his way home from a meeting with the governor, when Baring had been in the colony for only nine days, seemed to confirm the warnings of Potter and the district administration in Kikuyuland and compelled the new governor to accept their ill-considered solution. Like Mitchell, his predecessor, who had been captured in 1945 by his advisers in the Secretariat and had abandoned the Colonial Office's co-optive strategy for multiracialism, Baring in his first three weeks was persuaded to accept the Secretariat's interpretation of events. Denied time to consider the crisis, he failed to perceive the political divisions inside the Kenya African Union and the wide gap between Kenyatta and the militants, and denied himself the opportunity of incorporating Kenyatta, the moderate constitutional politician, and the chance to isolate the Nairobi militants and their rural allies from the peasantry. The remaining seven years of his governorship were to be spent paying for this error.[21]

Notes

1. Such an approach has already been attempted by several authors. R.F. Holland, *European Decolonization, 1918–1981*; J.A. Gallagher, *Decline, Revival and Fall of the British Empire*; J.M. Lee, *Colonial Development and Good Government*, pp. 1–206; J.M. Lee and M. Petter, *The Colonial Office, War and Development Policy*, pp. 49–256; R.D. Pearce, *The Turning Point in Africa, passim*, and R.F. Holland and G. Rizvi, (eds), *Perspectives on Imperialism and Decolonization*, particularly the essays by Holland, pp. 165–86 and J. Darwin, pp. 187–209. The following articles suffer from the same weakness, J.M. Lee: 'Forward Thinking and War', pp. 64–79; R.D. Pearce, 'Governors, Nationalists and Constitutions in Nigeria, 1935–1951' pp. 289–307; R.E. Robinson, 'Sir Andrew Cohen', pp. 353–63; and R.E. Robinson, 'Andrew Cohen and the Transfer of Power in Tropical Africa', pp. 50–72.

2. For a detailed assessment of Whitehall's strategy, see R.D. Pearce, *The Turning Point in Africa*, pp. 132–205; R.E. Robinson, 'Sir Andrew Cohen', pp. 353–63; and 'Andrew Cohen and the Transfer of Power in Tropical Africa', pp. 50–72. A more critical view of Cohen can be found in J.W. Cell, 'On the Eve of Decolonisation', pp. 235–57. The views of the field administration have been investigated by B.J. Berman in his unpublished thesis, 'Administration and Politics in Colonial Kenya', pp. 57–71, 113–60, 217–404. See also Berman, 'Bureaucracy and Incumbent Violence', pp. 143–75; and his unpublished paper, 'Provincial Administration and the Contradictions of Colonialism'.

3. G. Bennett, 'Settlers and Politics in Kenya, up to 1945', pp. 265–332, remains the standard account of European settler influence in Kenya. For a more radical critique of settler power, see E.A. Brett, *Colonialism and Underdevelopment in East Africa*; or R.M.A. van Zwanenberg, *Colonial Capitalism and Labour in Kenya, 1919–39*, pp. 1–35. B.J. Berman's thesis, 'Administration and Politics in Colonial Kenya', pp. 163–204 assesses settler pressure on the administration and Secretariat.

Economic and Social Origins of Mau Mau

4. CO 533/543/38086/5 (1945–47), 'Kikuyu Petitions', Mitchell to Gater, November 1946; CO 533/543/38086/38 (1948), 'Kikuyu Petitions: Kikuyu Central Association', Rankine to Creech Jones, 28 December 1948; CO 533/543/38086/38 (1949), 'Kikuyu Petitions: Kikuyu Central Association', Mitchell to Creech Jones, 28 February 1949; and CO 533/537/38672 (1947–48), 'Memorandum from the Kenya African Union', Mitchell to Creech Jones, 11 February 1947.

5. CO 533/549/38232/15, 'European Settlement: Squatters', Wyn Harris, 'A Discussion of the Problem of the Squatter', 21 February 1946; KNA Lab 9/309, 'Resident Labourers General: Report of the Ad Hoc Committee, 1946–50', Hyde-Clarke's 'Policy on Resident Labour' for Cavendish-Bentinck, 5 March 1947; and Lab 9/1071, 'Resident Labourers Ordinance: The Problem of the Squatter: Ad Hoc Committee, 1946–48', draft statement of policy for Cavendish-Bentinck's committee, prepared by E.M. Hyde-Clarke and J.H. Martin.

6. Mitchell's views on the Kenya African Union and the Kikuyu Central Association can be found in CO 533/543/38086/5 (1945–47), 'Kikuyu Petitions', Mitchell to Creech Jones, 1 December 1945, November 1946, and 20 January 1947; CO 533/540/38032 (1949), 'Legislative Council', Mitchell to Creech Jones, 11 December 1948; and CO 533/543/38086/38 (1948), 'Kikuyu Central Association', Rankine to Creech Jones, 28 December 1948.

7. J.M. Lonsdale and D.A. Low, Introduction in Low and Smith, *History of East Africa*, pp. 1–63.

8. KNA DC/NYI 2/1/20, 'Mr Humphrey's Report on South Nyeri, 1944–47'; CO 852/662/19936/2 (1945–46), 'Soil Erosion: Kenya', H.E. Lambert and P. Wyn Harris's memorandum on 'Policy in Regard to Land Tenure in the Native Lands of Kenya'; and CO 852/557/16707/2 (1946), 'Land Tenure Policy: Kenya', especially the report of the Soil Conservation Committee to the District Commissioner Central Kavirondo, 18 August 1945; and H.E. Lambert, 'Policy in Regard to the Administration of the Native Lands – Note for Discussion', 10 July 1946.

9. See Chapter 7 *infra*.

10. B.J. Berman's thesis, 'Administration and Politics in Central Kenya', p. 361–7, 372–98; KNA DC/FH 1/26, 'Fort Hall Annual Report, 1947', pp. 2–6 and DC/FH 4/6, 'Chiefs and Headmen, 1937–54', for attacks on the Murang'a chiefs; and MAA 8/68 'Chief Waruhiu, 1948–52', *passim*, for Kiambu.

11. KNA MAA 7/49, 'Chiefs and Headmen: Discipline, 1942–46'; MAA 7/320, 'Chiefs Engaged in Commerce, 1948'. For examples of chiefs who became successful businessmen, see G. Kitching, *Class and Economic Change in Kenya*, pp. 297–311, where nine of the fourteen case studies were chiefs. See also J.M. Lonsdale's unpublished paper, 'African Elites and Social Classes in Colonial Kenya' pp. 10–13; and B.E. Kipkorir, 'The Educated Elite and Local Society', pp. 255–68.

12. KNA DC/FH 1/26, 'Fort Hall Annual Report, 1947', p. 6: Ag 4/451, 'Fort Hall Safari Diaries, 1948–51', entries for 2–6 March and 6–10 July 1948; and MAA 8/106, 'Intelligence Reports: Mumenyereri, 1947–50', extract for 1 December 1947.

13. T.M.J. Kanogo's, 'The History of Kikuyu Movement into the Nakuru District of the White Highlands, 1900–63', pp. 245–379; F. Furedi, 'The Social Composition of the Mau Mau Movement in the White Highlands', pp. 492–504; M. Tamarkin, 'Mau Mau in Nakuru', pp. 228–37; B.A. Ogot, 'Politics, Culture and Music in Central Kenya', pp. 277–86; KNA Secretariat 1/2/2, 'Nyanza Province, 1949–50', P. Wyn Harris to the Executive Council, 12 October 1949; and A. Wipper, 'Elijah Masinde', pp. 157–81.

14. C.G. Rosberg and J. Nottingham, *The Myth of Mau Mau*, pp. 243–4, 248–59; and F. Furedi's unpublished paper, 'Olenguruone in Mau Mau Historiography'.

15. KNA DC/FH 1/26, 'Fort Hall Annual Report, 1947', pp. 1–6, 15; DC/FH 1/27, 'Fort Hall Annual Report, 1948', pp. 1–2, 4–5, 11; MAA 8/68, 'Chief Waruhiu, 1948–52'; and CO 852/557/16707/2 (1946), 'Land Tenure Policy: Kenya', H.E. Lambert's

13

memorandum on 'Policy in regard to Administration of the Native Lands – Note for Discussion', 10 July 1946.

16. KNA Secretariat 1/12/8, 'Labour Unrest: Intelligence Reports, Central Province, 1947', C. Penfold to P. Wyn Harris, 29 August, 3, 24 and 25 September and 10 October 1947; and M. Singh, *History of Kenya's Trade Union Movement*, pp. 154–60.

17. J. Spencer *KAU*, pp. 202–32; B. Kaggia, *Roots of Freedom*, p. 79; KNA Lab 9/87, 'Labour Troubles: Nairobi, 1950'; and *East African Standard*, 17 February 1951.

18. Interview with Bildad Kaggia, 21 January 1985; KNA DC/FH 1/31, 'Fort Hall Annual Report, 1952', pp. 1–6, 11–18; Ag 4/410, 'Central Province and Districts: Annual Agricultural Reports, 1952', G. Gamble's Nyeri District Report; and F.D. Corfield, Historical Survey of the Origins and Growth of Mau Mau, Cmd. No. 1030 (London and Nairobi, 1960), pp. 124–6.

19. B. Kaggia, *Roots of Freedom*, pp. 113–15; and KNA Mss. 324.296762, Eliud Mutonyi Wanjie, 'Mau Mau Chairman', pp. Ii–J4.

20. CO 822/437, 'Proposals to Deal with the Disturbances Arising from the Activities of the Mau Mau Secret Society: Kenya', J. Whyatt to P. Rogers, 2 September 1952; CO 822/436, 'Activities of the Mau Mau Secret Society: 29 July–25 October 1952', H.S. Potter to P. Rogers, 17 August 1952 and Press Office Handout 203, 29 August 1952.

21. CO 822/443, 'Proclamation of a State of Emergency', E. Baring to O. Lyttelton, 10 October 1952; and CO 822/447, 'Reports on the Mau Mau Situation by the Commissioner of Police, Kenya', 16 October 1952–1 April 1953.

Two

The Metropolitan Perspective
and the View from Nairobi

The official mind

During the scramble for Africa, Whitehall had perhaps responded coherently to the disintegration of informal empire once the imperialism of free trade had proved only too successful for the continued stability of Britain's allies on the periphery, but by the time the formal empire began to disintegrate, the Colonial Office had spawned a host of local sub-imperialists in every Secretariat with their own ambitions and rivalries. Superficially, the aims of the old official mind in Whitehall and the new ones in the colonies appeared to be the same. Both agreed that they should attempt to ensure that the colonies attracted as little international attention as possible. This study of Kenya from the war to the outbreak of Mau Mau in 1952, however, will show that the centre and the periphery had different policies. Consequently, although the Colonial Office and the Kenyan government considered that they were working together, by the time policies reached the district level they bore little resemblance to Whitehall's strategy for incorporating Africans into the political process.[1]

The prisms through which the Colonial Office, the Nairobi Secretariat and the field administration viewed Kenya produced different impressions of reality. No one image was correct; all contained elements of truth. While the Colonial Office had to withstand the pressures of world opinion and the reproofs of the Treasury, and recognised that Britain's diminished status required that African nationalism should be directed into constitutionalist paths before it attracted adverse attention to Britain's imperial trouble spots, the field administration, by contrast, looked at events from a local, not an international, perspective. The Secretariat and Sir Phillip Mitchell, the governor, stood mid-way between these extremes and tried to reconcile the contradictions between their instructions from Whitehall and the daily political pressures from the settlers, the African chiefs and the field administration against their rivals, the African politicians. In Kenya and the other colonies in which there were large settler communities, the metropolitan and peripheral official minds had contradictory priorities and consequently the Kenyan state, which enjoyed considerable autonomy, did not always carry out Whitehall's instructions.[2]

The world from Whitehall

Britain in 1945 was exhausted; the United States seemed about to retreat into economic, if not military, isolationism; India and South East Asia were in turmoil; and the Russians had advanced deep into central Europe. World opinion had also moved sharply against the imperial powers since the 1930s. The new United Nations provided an arena for Britain's critics to condemn colonialism. Moreover, Britain's economic decline meant that she could no longer afford to carry the burden of a major power. Even if delusions of grandeur remained in the Foreign Office, she did not have the economic resources to compete with the new superpowers, both of which were ideologically hostile to the British empire. Although the spectre of American interference in colonial affairs had receded since the anxious days of 1942 and the dispute over the Atlantic Charter, the future did not bode well. Even Australia could not be relied upon to oppose plans for the internationalisation of the colonies under the suzerainty of the United Nation's Trusteeship Committee. The collapse of Malaya, Singapore and Burma and the acquiescence of the people of South East Asia to Japanese rule irreparably damaged Britain in the eyes of American opinion, But perhaps even more important, this debacle had destroyed the imperialists' own self-confidence. Britain's psychological commitment to empire was never quite the same.[3]

After the war the metropolitan mind wanted to keep the colonies quiet. The West Indies in the late 1930s; South East Asia during the post-war battles for independence in the Dutch East Indies, Vietnam and Malaya; and India almost continuously, showed a distressing inability to keep out of the world's headlines. Race riots, the catastrophic famine in Bengal and military disaster had all embarrassingly exposed Britain's imperial pretensions. It seemed that Africa was about to follow, unless the Colonial Office learnt from its lessons in the West Indies and the uninspired example of the India Office, and moved decisively to institute social and constitutional reforms. Thus, Lord Hailey, O.G.R. Williams and finally Andrew Cohen, attempted to devise plans for controlled political devolution which, it was hoped, would incorporate the emerging African nationalists into the colonial state. The Colonial Office was preparing to make a pre-emptive bid to direct African nationalism, unlike Indian, into constructive constitutionalist activity. In India, Whitehall had lagged behind events; in Africa, the Colonial Office was determined to lead the way. In addition, Whitehall was deeply influenced by the social welfare ethos of Beveridge's Britain, especially as it seemed to provide a new weapon with which to keep the 'natives' quiet.[4]

Professor Robinson has called this growing self doubt and reluctance to carry the white man's burden in Africa 'the moral disarmament of African Empire'. He has observed that:

> By 1947 the trustees in the person of Arthur Creech Jones and officials like Andrew Cohen had come to believe that the tropical African empire should be dismantled in stages within the next two decades . . .[since] colonial governments during the inter-war years had proved incapable of supplying the necessary dynamic and therefore in their opinion, 'self-government was better than good government'. . . They prepared to hand over their tasks to nationalists and achieve the purpose of trusteeship by other means. The long frustration in defending the ethic contributed much to the fall of African empire, in changing the mind of the imperial bureaucracy. The generation of consuls between the wars remoralised the empire so far beyond their capacity to live up to expectations that they demoralised the belief in empire of the post-war generation to come.[5]

This is an arresting interpretation of decolonisation in Africa, but was it quite so simple? Did the inter-war years really destroy Britain's will to rule in Africa as Robinson has suggested or was it, as Berque has suggested for the Maghreb and Iliffe for Tanganyika, that Africans became increasingly disillusioned with the economic advantages of colonialism? And in Britain's case was not the decision to withdraw as quickly as possible primarily determined by the blow the imperial psyche had suffered in Malaya and India, when subjugated peoples had shown themselves to be indifferent in the struggle between Britain and Japan rather than by any moral disarmament in the African colonial service?[6] Robinson has also failed to recognise the paradox that the lessons Whitehall had learnt in the white settler colonies of central and eastern Africa during the 1920s and 1930s had only undermined Whitehall's will to rule in the settler-less colonies of West Africa. The effects of any moral disarmament of African empire were not as straightforward as he would have us believe. The Colonial Office's co-optive strategy was essentially devised for colonies like the Gold Coast and Nigeria, where an educated élite had existed for many years and vigorous political movements had clearly emerged. In the east and central African colonies, such as Kenya, the future was less clear.[7]

In the dark days of May 1943, when American criticism of empire had been at its height, a Cabinet Committee pondering the fate of the colonies had declared that:

> Many parts of the Colonial Empire are still so little removed from their primitive state that it must be a matter of many generations before they

are ready for anything like full self-government. There are other parts inhabited by people of two or more different races, and it is impossible to say how long it will take to weld together these so-called plural communities into an entity capable of exercising self-government.[8]

This does not sound like moral disarmament. The Cabinet clearly did not envisage any rapid withdrawal. Moreover, the late Jack Gallagher has shown that the Second World War intensified rather than weakened Britain's commitment to empire. The war years did not produce any mass conversion to anti-imperialism, even in the rank and file of the Labour Party, while among the leadership, Attlee and Bevin, and even Cripps, proved to be just as sound defenders of Britain's imperial heritage as Churchill and Eden.

Ronald Hyam has pointed out that, before 1914, the Colonial Office had been well aware that it was impossible to translate the political decisions of the metropolitan mind into political practice in the colonies. In the age of the telegraph, Whitehall had simply acted as 'the final arbiters of empire, but they knew that they had no executive or enforcing power'. By 1945, this awareness of their limitations had disappeared and the metropolitan official mind attempted directly to control the periphery and to dictate policy. The colonies were to be bound together and a grand strategy of decolonisation implemented. This had disastrous consequences when the second colonial occupation disrupted Africa after the war. Now disturbances in one area, mediated through the official mind in Whitehall, had profound effects throughout the empire. Thus even Kenya could not remain completely untouched by Andrew Cohen's reactions to the Accra riots of February 1948.[9]

Cohen's five-phase strategy of decolonisation sprang from the same roots as Professor Robinson's wider moral disarmament. Despondent at the lack of development in the colonies, both economic and political, and alarmed at the spectre of nationalist protests which would attract international condemnation of British imperialism, the Colonial Office wanted to incorporate African political activists into the constitutional process. In West Africa it was apparent that the 'native' rulers would have to be ditched, except perhaps in the backwaters of northern Nigeria where the emirs seemed to be as powerful as ever, and a new alliance established with the educated élite of the towns and the primary school graduates of the provinces.[10] In east and central Africa, the settlers stood in the way of any attempt to incorporate the emerging African politicians, who represented the interests of a less well-established group of traders, commercial farmers and teachers. These men, it was believed, were not a serious challenge to colonial rule, unlike the lawyers and established cocoa farmers of the west, with their university degrees and tradition of active politics. In the east, the Colonial Office was more concerned that the settlers would destroy the present calm with their demands for self-government of dominion status. Such provocative suggestions would arouse African opposition and attract unfavourable attention to the settler colonies, where racial discrimination and the privileged status of the settlers invited condemnation. Whitehall was only too acutely aware that in Kenya and the Rhodesias, Africans were living in over-crowded reserves while their former land was being farmed by a small number of British settlers. If American and Russian anti-imperialists were not to have a field-day at Britain's expense, with untold consequences for the alliance with America, metropolitan authority had to be reasserted and the settlers reduced to a less powerful position inside the colonial corridors of power.[11]

The metropolitan mind, however, was divided between the colonialists and the 'little Englanders'. While the Colonial Office wanted to promote African interests and to use the new Colonial Development and Welfare Act to increase social welfare, the Treasury and the domestic ministries were concerned that the colonies should serve British interests. With an uncovered external debt of £2,879 million in 1945, Britain's economic position was unprecedentedly difficult. It quickly emerged that Creech Jones was a political lightweight in the Cabinet and could not defend the interests of the colonies against the exactions of the Board of Trade and the Ministry of Food. Africa was a world far removed from the usual preoccupations of government ministers and evoked little interest. Even Cripps and Strachey, who had held advanced views on colonial affairs, became preoccupied with domestic British politics. The government's electoral survival after all depended on the British voter. Thus, the British housewife's margarine supply was more important than the plight of the Tanganyikan peasant.[12]

The empire had emerged from the war over-stretched, much criticised and, above all, economically vulnerable. To finance the campaign, £1,118 million of overseas investments had been sold, but during the last year of the war Britain's food and raw material imports had amounted to over £2,000 million, of which only £800 million had been covered by exports. Existing gold and convertible currency reserves covered only one-sixth of her short-term debts. These problems were exacerbated by the sudden cancellation of land–lease by the United States on 21 August 1945. Throughout the immediate post-war years Britain's economic position remained perilous. The premature decision under American pressure to restore free convertibility in September 1947 cost Britain one-quarter of her hard-earned foreign reserves in only three weeks. Consequently the demands upon the colonies to maximise their hard currency earnings were intensified, fuelling further discontent.[13]

Despite the rhetoric of the Colonial Development and Welfare Act, these harsh economic realities dictated the Attlee government's colonial policies. Paradoxically, the theories of 'capitalist imperialism' only reflected British rule in most of tropical Africa when the Christian

Socialist, Stafford Cripps, was Chancellor of the Exchequer and the former Marxist, John Strachey, Minister of Food. Ostensibly the second colonial occupation was couched in the language of humanitarian social welfare thinking, but Britain's economic position prevented the Labour Party from fulfilling its promises of welfare state colonialism as had been advocated by the party's Imperial Advisory Committee and Creech Jones when he had been head of the Fabian Colonial Bureau. In fact, Africa was increasingly forced to subsidise the expansion of the welfare state in Britain, and the development measures which were undertaken were carefully devised to serve Britain's immediate interests.[14]

The correspondence of the Colonial Office's Economic Department clearly shows how Britain's perilous financial position, particularly her serious deficit on trade with the United States, was throughout the immediate post-war years a crucial determinant of plans for African economic and social development. As far as the Treasury, the Board of Trade or the Ministry of Food were concerned, the Colonial Office was Sydney Caine, not Creech Jones or Cohen. Caine was an economist and carried into the Colonial Office the inflexible *laissez-faire* ideology of a Treasury mandarin. It was hardly surprising that he clashed with the social welfare humanitarianism propounded by Arthur Lewis, Evan Durbin and Sir Bernard Bourdillon on the Colonial Economic Advisory Committee, and with Sir Philip Mitchell in Nairobi. As the economic crisis deepened, Caine's judgement became increasingly influential, if only because he could assuage a ruffled Treasury. His *laissez-faire* policies were cheap and did not commit the British taxpayer to endless subventions to colonial social welfare projects, or promote secondary industrialisation and commodity processing, which might have conflicted with established British industries. Moreover, this free market approach to economic development ensured that the flow of cheap raw materials continued unabated for Britain's post-war reconstruction and to reduce the dollar deficit.[15]

After the war Britain continued to hold sterling balances in London and used them to fund her trade deficit with the United States and to finance Britain's recovery. David Fieldhouse has estimated that between 1946 and 1951, while the colonies received a mere £40.5 million under the Colonial Development and Welfare Act, colonial sterling balances in London rose from £760 million to £920 million, and another £93 million was held for the West African marketing boards. Throughout the Attlee government's period in office funds flowed from the dependent empire to Britain as the periphery was exploited to serve metropolitan interests. Thus Fieldhouse points out, when international demand for tropical commodities was buoyant for the first time since the 1920s, when colonial governments were clamouring for increased investment in direct production as well as social welfare schemes, and when there was a pent-up demand for British exports among ordinary Africans following seven years of war, the metropole could not deliver the goods. Africa would have to wait until her resources had enabled the British economy to recover. Only then would Africans receive their cotton piece-goods and the benefits of their increased production. Until then inflation and continued neglect would be their only reward. Britain not Africa came first.[16]

The Colonial Office and the Kenyan settlers

The Cabinet and the Colonial Office considered Kenya to be one of the empire's plural communities. Europeans, Asians and Arabs had all settled in the colony and considered themselves to have as much right to live in Kenya as the Africans. In 1945, it appeared to be unthinkable that these immigrant populations would be abandoned within less than two decades to African rule. Rather, the war-time Cabinet and its Labour successor hoped that European settlers would provide the 'steel frame' or 'cornerstone' of a new multiracial Kenya, in which the settlers would exert an influence incommensurate with their small numbers.[17]

South East Asia, especially French Indo-China and the Dutch East Indies, however, were soon to show that European settlers, even large-scale plantation capital, were a political nuisance, complicating the process of nationalist co-option.[18] This proved to be equally true in Kenya and the Rhodesias. It was already evident that settlers were less efficient than African cash-crop cultivators, and were always demanding preferential rights; while, politically, they represented the unacceptable face of imperialism, with their plans for self-government. They did, however, have the ability to appeal to a residual patriotism, particularly among the unreconstructed imperialists of the Tory right. This was to prove a great political asset.[19]

During the war, the settlers in Kenya had prospered as never before from the increased demand for their agricultural exports. By 1942, a major transformation had occurred in the world economy, ending the long years of restricted demand for East Africa's produce and marking the beginning of a new era of commodity shortages. Even the internal market expanded as the European population of the three mainland colonies trebled with the arrival of Italian prisoners of war and Polish refugees. The allied forces in the Middle East were also fed Kenyan wheat, maize and vegetables. Moreover the Japanese advance into the Philippines and Java benefited the sisal plantations (Kenya's most important export crop) by reducing British and American supplies of hard fibres from 530,000 to 245,000 tons, half of which came from East Africa. The prosperity of the European farming community was ensured by the preferential terms they were guaranteed by the settler-controlled Agricultural Production and Settlement Board which organised the war-time campaign for maximum production. The high guaranteed prices for settler maize and new breaking and clearing grants to encourage production resulted in a dramatic increase in maize cultivation from 80,000 acres in 1941 to 131,563 acres four years later, while wheat production rose from 103,000 to 184,500 acres by 1945.[20]

This economic security coincided with a period of greater settler political influence. During the 1930s, the Kenyan administration had suffered a decade of retrenchment and, on the outbreak of war, one-third of the field administration were absorbed into the armed forces and a mere skeleton force was left to police the reserves.[21] These military demands upon an already stretched administrative cadre forced the Kenyan government to incorporate settler agencies, such as the Kenya Farmers' Association, into the colonial state, especially in the economic sector. This use of settler organisations to oversee the marketing mechanism meant that by 1945 the settlers had become much more powerful. The reason why Kenya proved so difficult to control during the 1940s was that Mitchell found it virtually impossible to dislodge the settlers from their newly secured political and constitutional redoubts. Even after the war the field administration was called upon to supply men to help the army administer Somaliland and Eritrea and had insufficient staff to operate the new production and supply agencies which were left in the control of the local settlers. After the war, therefore, they were firmly entrenched in these positions and had been conceded far more authority over the economy than they had ever enjoyed in pre-war Kenya.[22]

As early as 1942 the Colonial Office had perceived that the presence of an over-mighty settler community was the fundamental problem in Kenya. The settlers, it was feared, would hinder African political and economic development and distort the colony's economy. Even if Whitehall had not yet realised that settlers and Kikuyu were on a collision course, it had, unlike the Kenyan Secretariat, recognised that their rival ambitions might soon become a dangerous source of conflict. In June 1942, Viscount Cranborne, the Secretary of State, had recorded his

> Extreme disquiet about the situation that is developing in East Africa. Since the formation of the Supply and Civil Defence Council in April, a step which was taken by the Government of Kenya without any consultation with the Colonial Office, things seemed to have moved at an increasingly rapid rate. There is ample evidence that the white inhabitants, both official and unofficial, are taking matters into their own hands, and that the Council is taking the form of a Cabinet, arrogating to itself the power to take decisions without any reference home, and increasingly intolerant of any guidance from the Colonial Office . . . It seems to me that immediate action is necessary if the position is to be held. If we dally, we shall be faced with what is in effect a white self-governing Dominion, backed by the whole force of white public opinion.[23]

His sentiments were echoed throughout the Colonial Office. Sir Arthur Dawe, one of the Assistant Under-Secretaries, for example, was prompted to contrast the settlers to twelfth-century barons who had 'constructed strong bulwarks against the power of the central government' in their campaign to secure effective control over Kenya. Whitehall was so concerned about the advances which the settlers had secured that they reassessed their policies during the inter-war years.[24]

When one analyses the history of Kenya during these years it is difficult not to conclude that the Devonshire declaration of African paramountcy of 1923 had been fatally undermined by a succession of secretaries of state and governors who had allowed the settlers to have their way throughout the 1920s and 1930s. The one exception was Sir Joseph Byrne, who had been governor during the depression, from 1931 to 1937. Dawe lamented that

> The policy of the home authorities has been one of appeasement and conciliation. With the lesson of 1923 in mind they, i.e. we, appear, in general, to have avoided any head-on clash with the settlers. . . .The fitful advocacy of the native point of view in England does not appear to have opposed any effective obstacle, to the steady pressure, which, quietly upon the spot, the settlers have been able to bring to bear on the local Government.[25]

It is striking that the governors of Kenya had been singularly subservient to settler aspirations and correspondingly unsuccessful in asserting metropolitan authority. Part of their failure was rooted in the fact that Nairobi, more than any other African governorship, was a political appointment. Of the fourteen governors, only five were appointed from inside the Colonial Service and, during the inter-war years, this ratio had fallen to one in five. Northey and Brooke-Popham were military men; Grigg was a politician; while Coryndon had worked for Rhodes's British South Africa Company in the Rhodesias and Swaziland. Of the governors of Kenya, only Byrne had been willing to stand up to the settlers, much to the dismay of his Chief Secretary, Henry Moore, who had been caught in the cross-fire. Throughout his term as governor from 1940 to 1944, therefore, Moore had been determined to avoid a confrontation with the Kenyan Europeans.[26]

Dawe and Cranborne were particularly concerned that 'the move towards settler domination has been much speeded up by the war'. Although the Colonial Office recognised that it was inevitable that settler farmers and businessmen would have to be enlisted to operate the network of boards and controls which were required for the war effort, Whitehall was alarmed that the Kenyan settlers would

> . . . look beyond these immediate necessities and see in the war a chance of quickening up the processes which, for a generation, have

been working in the direction of the White Dominion . . . To the settlers these events must appear as a further example of the beneficient working of evolution in their affairs. They must hope that this desirable piece of war-time machinery will prove to be the engine of policy which by its unobtrusive working will make the White Dominion an accomplished fact, beyond the power of the British Government to modify.[27]

South African expansion also concerned the Colonial Office. The presence of white South African troops in Kenya during the Ethiopian campaign and their continued passage through Kenya to the Libyan front, it was feared, had made a marked impression on the settlers. There were, it was believed in London, 'strong elements among the British in Kenya, who see in South Africa the ally which will enable them to break away from the trammels of Westminister and Downing Street. They are turning to this powerful ally to safeguard themselves against the rising black tide and the menace of British native policy'.[28] Undoubtedly the South African government was cautiously fostering this attitude and General Smuts seized every opportunity to improve contacts with East Africa where South African representatives became increasingly active. The Johannesburg mining interests were also keen to establish closer control over the mineral and agricultural wealth of central and eastern Africa. Certainly many settlers in Kenya looked to South Africa as a counterweight to the new Labour government in Britain. Alfred Vincent, the leader of the European elected members of the Kenyan Legislative Council and a prominent Nairobi businessman, was an admirer of Smuts and was eager that South Africa should establish closer economic ties with Kenya. Although the spectre of South African expansionism was exaggerated, it did arouse serious concern in Whitehall. Indeed one of the reasons for Mitchell's appointment as governor was that he had close ties with South Africa through his wife and had a farm near Grahamstown where he spent his holidays. Mitchell's contacts, it was thought, among the Cape Town and Durban liberal establishment might be useful if pressure had to be brought discreetly upon Smuts to divert South African ambitions from Kenya.[29]

In 1945 the Colonial Office was determined to recapture some of the ground that had been lost since Sir Joseph Byrne's departure in 1937. Settler power was becoming an embarrassment. Although it had been possible in 1923 to allow the Europeans in Southern Rhodesia to gain control over an overwhelmingly African country, this was impossible in the new international environment. The settlers' demands for self-government were becoming a diplomatic embarrassment. Organisations such as the Fabian Colonial Bureau and the Anti-Slavery Society had been particularly critical of the continued exclusion of Africans from the European enclave of the White Highlands despite the crisis of overcrowding in the reserves. No-one in Whitehall, except Harold Macmillan, was willing to grasp the thorn. In 1942, after only a few months at the Colonial Office, and unencumbered by any previous knowledge of Africa, he had reached the radical conclusion that the settlers would have to be bought out and the Kikuyu allowed to settle on collective farms in the White Highlands. This went too far for the Whitehall establishment. The cautious Colonial Office chose instead to 'sandbag' the settlers from behind and to sap their strength by using their overweening ambitions to pull them down.[30]

The view from Nairobi

The official mind in Nairobi, however, was little influenced by the global problems which preoccupied the metropolitan mind. American and Russian condemnations cut little ice in 'darkest Africa' and were easily dismissed as meddling interference. Ostensibly the Nairobi Secretariat also wanted to keep things quiet, but while the Colonial Office saw Kenyan settlers as the essential problem, the Secretariat and the field administration were preoccupied by the Kikuyu. These pre-war administrators, conditioned by Kenya, necessarily did not have the global view of Whitehall or possess Andrew Cohen's ability to devise bold strategies, bordering on genius. The only problem with Whitehall's plan was that Mitchell, whom they had selected to become governor because they thought he shared their broad vision, having so sucessfully disarmed American criticism of British rule in the Pacific, proved to have a limited imagination. He was quickly converted to the myopic concerns of his Secretariat and showed little zeal for a confrontation with the settlers. Mitchell abandoned Whitehall's bold innovations and side-stepped the fundamental problem of settler hegemony.

After the war the sheer scale of the colonial presence increased dramatically, particularly in Kikuyuland. Between 1945 and 1957 the number of administrative officers increased from 117 to 213, while another 30 temporary District Officers and 150 district assistants were recruited during the Emergency. The expansion of the technical departments was even more dramatic. The agricultural department increased from 298 in 1945 to 2,519 in 1958 and the veterinary department grew from 291 to 892. The effect of this second colonial occupation upon the African cultivator was profound. Between 1945 and 1952 the total staff employed in the agricultural campaign in Central Province grew more than tenfold and, by the declaration of the Emergency, numbered more than 3,000. By 1952, the colonial state was stronger than ever before and was penetrating to new depths.[31]

The field administration's commitment to the preservation of a mythical, egalitarian, communal Africa, which had been the basis of indirect rule, the official ideology of British Africa during the 1920s and

1930s, had been strengthened by modern anthropological research, emphasising the communal solidarities of pre-colonial Africa. Indirect rule had initially emerged as much from fiscal constraint as administrative design, since neither the Colonial Office nor the territorial governments had the funds to intervene in African life. African progress, therefore, had necessarily had to be 'organic'. Increasingly, however, it appeared as though this administrative expedient was in fact a valuable mechanism of social control. After 1945, many members of the field administration in Kenya were alarmed that the traditional social linkages were being destroyed by the growth of 'irresponsible' individualism as the forces of economic competition undermined the power of the elders and the chiefs and increased pressure on the soil. By 1945, anthropological research had given these prejudices against African entrepreneurs a veneer of scientific respectability, which enabled the administration to justify resistance to Whitehall's plans to incorporate the emerging traders and school teachers, who were in the vanguard of increasing social differentiation. The field administration transformed the second colonial occupation from a social welfare campaign into an outright attack, designed to hinder these proto-capitalists. Social engineering was to be undertaken more blatantly than ever before to bolster the existing rural order and to entrench the authority of the chiefs and 'traditional' elders.[32]

The African proto-capitalists, however, were also stronger than before the war, and the new Kenya African Union provided them with leaders to present their case to the Secretariat and, if necessary, the Colonial Office and the United Nations. During the depression of the 1930s, the government actively encouraged African production to preserve the fiscal base of the colonial state and, during the war, to supply the allied forces in the Middle East, regardless of the long-term consequences on soil fertility or African communalism. Although Spencer has pointed out that Africans received lower prices for their crops than the settlers, and squatters were supposedly forced to sell their produce to their employers who then resold it to the government marketing board at a higher rate, in fact, African cultivators bypassed the official purchasing mechanism and sold their crops on the Black Market. Official returns, the historian should be aware, provide little guide to the quantities of African produce sold. Most lay concealed from view.[33]

The African proto-capitalists after 1945 were clamouring to enjoy the rewards of government patronage. These demands, of course, clashed with the determination of the field administration to obstruct the development of individualism because of the dangers of increasing social differentiation in the reserves. After the war, however, neither side was willing to back down and a clash between the paternalist administration and the emerging African entrepreneurs, especially in Central Province among the Kikuyu where this process was most advanced, was perhaps inevitable, as in the Gold Coast.[34] District Commissioners were determined to support their allies, the government-appointed chiefs, and to bolster their authority whenever it was attacked by the emerging African politicians. The politicians represented the traders and cash-crop cultivators who resented the preferential treatment bestowed upon the chiefs and their supporters when wattle and trading licences were issued. They were simply dismissed as irresponsible 'agitators' by the administration, which refused to recognise that they had widespread support.[35]

With the growth of a ramifying bureaucracy, the field administration had become isolated from African opinion and spent more and more time preparing reports and memoranda. Provincial Commissioners' meetings, which in the 1920s provided the vital link between policy and action, became increasingly anodyne and restricted to approved topics based on prepared memoranda. No longer were they rent by bitter disputes between Provincial Commissioners defending 'their people'. This bureaucratisation of the Colonial Service also isolated the District Commissioners and lowly District Officers.[36] Increasingly the administrative system ruled out direct consideration of what was happening in the reserves in favour of abstract policy, formulated in the Secretariat, despite the warnings of Shirley Victor Cooke and Clarence Buxton that they were becoming dangerously divorced from African reality.[37] During the 1940s, the Secretariat became obsessed with the technical aspects of its job. This retreat into theory was reinforced by Mitchell, who saw himself as a social technician who wanted to interfere in African society to preserve what he believed to be its surviving egalitarianism, and to prevent the emergence of an exploitative clique of capitalist accumulators. Unfortunately, given the administration's limited understanding of pre-colonial Africa, this social engineering was extremely dangerous, especially as the administration had become isolated from ordinary Africans. This bureaucratisation was only reversed after 1952, when manpower was rushed into Kikuyuland to contain Mau Mau and a belated attempt was made to return to the more primitive, but effective, grassroots administration. But by then it was far too late.[38]

Notes

1. R.F. Holland, *European Decolonization*, *passim*, provides the most useful example of this genre but see also J. Gallagher, *The Decline, Revival and Fall of the British Empire*, pp. 141–3. J.M. Lee and M. Petter, *The Colonial Office, War and Development Policy*, pp. 49–256 and R.D. Pearce, *The Turning Point in Africa*, pp. 132–205 are the most notable examples of this historiographical pre-occupation with the official mind of Whitehall. A more critical view of Cohen can be found in J.W. Cell, 'On the Eve of

Decolonisation', pp. 235–57. The attitude of the field administration has been investigated in B.J. Berman's thesis, 'Administration and Politics in Colonial Kenya,' pp. 57–71, 113–60, 217–404. See also Berman, 'Bureaucracy and Incumbent Violence', pp. 143–75, and his unpublished paper, 'Provincial Administration and the Contradictions of Colonialism'.

2. G. Bennett, 'Settlers and Politics in Kenya'. pp. 256–332, remains a standard account of European settler influence in Kenya. For a more radical critique of settler power see E.A. Brett, *Colonialism and Underdevelopment in East Africa, passim*.

3. W.R. Louis, *Imperialism at Bay*, pp. 512–73; C. Thorne, *Allies of a Kind*, pp. 202–48, 596–604; and J.M. Lee and M. Petter, *The Colonial Office, War and Development Policy*, pp. 101–14, 231–42. See also R. Storry, *Japan and the Decline of the West in Asia*, pp. 1–13; and B.W. and L.Y. Andaya, *A History of Malaysia*, pp. 247–54. Even the Kenyan settlers noted the Colonial Office's loss of morale after the fall of Malaya and Singapore: see the editorial in *East African Standard*, 16 July, 1943. The metropolitan political mind reacted swiftly to the blow and determined to replenish lost supplies from the Far East by developing Africa, while the African Colonies were kept quiet with promises of increased political participation after the war. See especially the following debates: 6 May 1942, *Hansard*, House of Lords, vol 122, cols. 889–940; 24 June 1942, *Hansard*, House of Commons, vol 380, cols. 2004–2119 (this was the first debate in the Commons on colonial affairs since June 1939) and 13 July 1943, *Hansard*, House of Commons, vol 391, cols. 48–151. Copies of these debates were sent to the Kenya Secretariat; see KNA CS2/7/36, 'Colonial Office: Reorganisation of Administration of the Colonial Empire'.

4. First the Morley–Minto constitution of 1909, then the Montagu–Chelmsford proposals of 1918, and finally the 1935 India Act and the 1937 Indian Provincial elections had been designed to incorporate 'moderate' Indian nationalists into the political processes of the colonial state and to transform them into collaborators. In India, at the centre at least, this had failed, and the Congress had remained intact, if not untarnished. A similar strategy had also been attempted in Egypt; J. Darwin, *Britain, Egypt and the Middle East*, pp. 49–137.

5. R.E. Robinson, 'The Moral Disarmament of African Empire', p. 101.

6. J. Berque, *French North Africa*, pp. 232–80; J. Iliffe, *A Modern History of Tanganyika*, pp. 342–80; and J. Forbes Munro, *Africa and the International Economy*, pp 150–74. See also N.J. Westcott's unpublished thesis, 'The Impact of the War on Tanganyika', pp. 107–86, and R. von Albertini, *Decolonization*, pp. 158–75.

7. R.E. Robinson, 'Non-European Foundations of European Imperialism', p. 122. There were a series of suggestions after the war to transform Kenya into a major military base to safeguard British interests in the Middle East, Africa and the Indian Ocean, and to treble the settler population. For the progress of these schemes see CO 537/1233/13012/24 (1945–46), 'Defence East Africa: The Development of Mombasa as a Major Port and Base'; CO 537/1230/13011 (1946) (Part II), 'Bases for British Forces in Kenya: Road Construction in Equatorial Africa'; CO 537/1883/94023/3 (1946), 'Defence of East Africa: Construction of a Base'. The Kenyan government also spent £1.6 million during these years attracting Europeans to settle in Kenya, CO 533/534/38232 (1944) and (1945), 'European Settlement Scheme'.

8. Quoted in J. Gallagher, *The Decline, Revival and Fall of the British Empire*, pp. 142–3.

9. R. Hyam, 'The Colonial Office Mind', p. 31 and R.D. Pearce, *The Turning Point in Africa*, pp. 188–202, outline Cohen's reaction.

10. D. Austin, *Politics in Ghana*, pp. 1–102 for a detailed account. R. Rathbone, 'The Government of the Gold Coast after the Second World War', pp. 209–18; R.E. Robinson, 'The Progress of Provincial Councils in the British African Teritories', pp. 59–62, 63–4. M. Crowder, *West Africa Under Colonial Rule*; and J. Miles, 'Rural Protest in the Gold Coast' provide useful insights into politics in British West Africa during the inter-war years. See also J.B. Bell, *On Revolt*, pp. 72–9, 92–106, which contrasts decolonisation in the Gold Coast and Kenya.

11. Mitchell's views on the Kenya African Union and the Kikuyu Central Association can be found in CO 533/543/38086/5 (1945-57), 'Kikuyu Petitions'; CO 533/540/38032 (1949), 'Legislative Council' and CO 533/543/38086/38 (1948), 'Kikuyu Central Association'. See also CO 967/56 (1942), 'Memorandum and Record of meetings with Sir Henry Moore to discuss the war effort in East Africa and the Political and Economic Situation in Kenya as a Result of the War', Cranborne to Gater, 18 June 1942.

12. H. Thomas, *John Strachey*, pp. 245-6; Scott Newton, 'Britain, the Sterling Area and European Integration', pp. 163-80; and P. S. Gupta, *Imperialism and the British Labour Movement*, pp. 309-25. A most useful overview is to be found in P. Kennedy, *The Realities Behind Diplomacy*, pp. 315-69.

13. D.J. Morgan, *The Official History of Colonial Development: Developing British Colonial Resources*, pp. 177-308. Morgan, however, underestimates Britain's exploitation.

14. KNA Secretariat 1/11/41, 'Balance of Trade with USA, 1947-49', and Secretariat 1/4/3, 'Trade and Commerce: The Colonial Empire and the Economic Crisis, 1948'. The centralisation of the marketing of colonial produce is evident from CO 852/650/19879/65 (1946). 'Marketing of Colonial Produce: British Colonial Exports 1939-45', Memorandum by F.V. Meyer. For Mitchell's opinions see CO 852/650/19879/62 (1944). 'Marketing of Colonial Produce – Primary Produce: Note by Sir P.E. Mitchell' and Caine's memorandum of 4 July 1944, in the same file. See also CO 852/650/19879/64 (1944), 'Marketing of Colonial Produce: Future of Agricultural Prices'; CO 852/650/19879/64 (1945), 'Marketing of Colonial Produce: Future of Agricultural Prices'; and J.M. Lee and M. Petter, *The Colonial Office, War and Development Policy*, pp. 78-84.

15. CO 852/588/19260 (Part 1) (1944). 'Planning of Economic and Social Development'; for Caine's exasperation with Mitchell, see CO 852/608/19643/1 (1944), 'Sisal: East Africa', memorandum from Caine to Clauson, 8 June 1945; and CO 852/650/19879/62 (1944), 'Marketing of Colonial Produce and Primary Produce Markets: Note by Sir P.E. Mitchell', minutes by Caine and Clauson on 4 July 1944. RH Mss. Afr. r. 101 entry for 29 November, 1944, contains Mitchell's account in his diary of his first meeting with Caine.

16. Review article by D. K. Fieldhouse of 'The Official History of Colonial Development' in the *English Historical Review*, vol. 97 (1982), pp. 386-94.

17. CO 533/534/38232 (1945), 'European Settlement Scheme' and RH Mss. Afr. r. 101, 1 November 1944, for Mitchell's advocacy of multiracialism.

18. M.C. Ricklefs, *A History of Modern Indonesia*, pp. 200-21; and R. Jeffrey (ed.) *Asia, The Winning of Independence, passim*.

19. G. Wasserman, *Politics of Decolonization*; and E.A. Brett, *Colonialism and Underdevelopment in East Africa*, for the inter-war years. D.K. Kennedy's unpublished thesis, 'A Tale of Two Colonies' and P. Mosley's thesis, 'The Settler Economies' provide some interesting insights and contrasts. For Mitchell's reactions to settler political demands, see CO 533/558/38688 (1947), 'Local Political Developments', Mitchell to Cohen, 26 February and 8 March 1947; and CO 822/114/46523 (Part 1) (1946), 'Closer Union', Mitchell to Gater, 19 March 1946, when he observed: 'If . . . the Elected Members can get it into their heads once and for all, first, that this (Col 191) is not a wicked plot by the present Government to destroy them, and secondly, that nobody of any party in the United Kingdom will for one moment tolerate a state of affairs in which a handful of European politicians, with an electorate of a few thousand voters, have over-riding political power in this or any other African Colony, then I think they will talk sense. Francis Scott, of course, still goes about talking of self-government for Kenya, or at least for the Highlands, by which he means of course, self-government based on an electorate composed only of those members whose names are in Debrett, if one might put it so. But he is, to be quite frank, a very prejudiced man.' For the reactions of the Tory right-wing in a slightly later period, D. Goldsworthy, *Colonial Issues in British Politics*, pp. 24-35, 169-202, 279-316; D. Horowitz, 'Attitudes of British Conservatives Towards

Decolonization in Africa', pp. 9–26; and his unpublished thesis, 'Attitudes of British Conservatives Towards Decolonization in Africa during the Period of the Macmillan Government'.

20. N.J. Westcotts's unpublished paper, 'The Politics of Planning and the Planning of Politics', pp. 4–9; and his thesis, 'The Impact of the Second World War on Tanganyika', pp. 62–3; and KNA Secretariat 1/1/12, 'Maize Control and Food Shortage, 1942–44'; CO 852/641/19785/1 (1944), 'East African Maize'; CO 533/535/38551/1 (1944–46), 'Food Shortage Appointment of Commission of Enquiry'; and Food Shortage Commission Evidence, p. 84; and Kenya Department of Agriculture Annual Report (1944) p. 11. See also I.R.G. Spencer, 'Settler Dominance, Agricultural Production and the Second World War in Kenya', p. 503, and D.M. Anderson and D.W. Throup, 'Africans and Agricultural Production in Colonial Kenya'; pp. 327–45.

21. A.H.M. Kirk-Greene, 'The Thin White Line', p.27; and B.J. Berman's unpublished thesis, 'Administration and Politics in Colonial Kenya', p. 68. Between 1931 and 1939 the Kenyan administration fell from 140 to 114, and the total European staff of the Kenyan government declined from 1,531 to 1,398, with a low of 1,252 between 1933 and 1935. The largest cutback was in the Public Works' Department where the number of Europeans fell from 207 to 87. See also KNA Defence 9/88, 'Analysis of Man Power, 1940–45', Sir H. Moore to Legislative Council, 13 November, 1940.

22. The notion of 'incorporation' is taken from K. Middlemas, *Politics in Industrial Society*, pp. 18–23. For its application to Kenya see J.M. Lonsdale's unpublished paper, 'The Growth and Transformation of the Colonial State in Kenya', p. 8, where he observes: 'The problem of competition between private interests could be solved only by extending the principle of delegated authority from production and marketing to supply as well, so that farmers and businessmen rationed themselves. The new functions of government passed, if for no other reason than that the apparatus of control was too large for the colony's slender Secretariat, into the hands of those who lived by making commercial assumptions about the future. By the end of the war, and in imitation of the British organisation of the war economy, settler farmers had captured the whole apparatus of production quotas and credit on the Highlands.' For acknowledgements of the administration's loss of control see CO 967/56 (1942), 'Memorandum and Record of Meeting with Sir Henry Moore to Discuss the War Effort in East Africa and the Political and Economic Situation in Kenya as a Result of the War', and CO 533/536/38598 (1945–46), 'Kenya: Staff Position', Mitchell to Creasy, 30 December 1944.

23. CO 967/56 (1942), 'Memorandum and Record of Meeting with Sir Henry Moore to discuss the War Effort in East Africa and the Political and Economic Situation in Kenya as a Result of the War', especially Cranborne to Gater, 18 June 1942.

24. CO 967/57/46709 (1942), 'Sir Arthur Dawe's Memorandum on a Federal Solution for East Africa and Mr Harold Macmillan's Counter-Proposals'.

25. *ibid.* Dawe, however, also observed that 'the main point to be kept in mind by the British Government is the difficulty that they would be in if matters were carried to the ultima ratio of physical force. The lesson of 1923 is always there and the settlers would be a much sterner proposition now than they were at that time. It is possible now that many of the British officials would come out on their side, which would not have happened in 1923.'

26. A.H.M. Kirk-Greene, 'The Progress of Pro-Consuls'; pp. 190–1; and his *A Biographical Dictionary of the British Colonial Governor*, p. 51. For details of a governor's duties and selection, see A.H.M. Kirk-Greene, 'On Governorship and Governors in British Africa', pp. 210–57. A brief assessment of Kenya's inter-war governors can be found in the Biographical Appendix *infra*. See also CO 967/56 (1942), 'Memorandum and Record of Meeting with Sir Henry Moore to Discuss the War Effort in East Africa and the Political and Economic Situation in Kenya as a Result of the War' and RH Mss. Afr. r. 101, Mitchell's diary entry 24 November 1944, for his view of Moore's relations with Oliver Stanley.

27. CO 967/57/46709 (1942), 'Sir Arthur Dawe's Memorandum on a Federal Solution for East Africa and Mr Harold Macmillan's Counter-Proposals', Sir Arthur Dawe to Sir George Gater, 27 July 1942.

28. *ibid.*

29. CO 537/5922 (1950), 'Liaison with the South African Government by Kenya Unofficials'. See also Legislative Council Debates, 2nd Series, vol. xx (1944–45), third Session, 4 January 1945, cols. 472–500 and *East African Standard*, 5 January 1945.

30. CO 822/114/46523 Part 1 (1946), 'Closer Union', Mitchell to Gater, 19 March 1946. R.E. Robinson, 'The Moral Disarmament of African Empire', pp. 86–102 analyses this transition. CO 533/537/38608 (1944–46), 'Land Policy: Memorandum by the Anti-Slavery Society'; and CO 533/558/38690 (1947), 'Fabian Society'. For Macmillan's proposal see CO 967/57/46709 (1942), 'Sir Arthur Dawe's Memorandum on a Federal Solution for East Africa and Mr Harold Macmillan's Counter-Proposals'.

31. A.H.M. Kirk-Greene, 'The Thin White Line', p. 32. and B.J. Berman's unpublished thesis, 'Administration and Politics in Colonial Kenya', pp. 415–52.

32. C. Cagnolo, *The Akikuyu*; A.C. Hollis, *The Nandi*; J.G. Peristiany, *The Social Organization of the Kipsigis*; and W.S. and K. Routledge, *With a Prehistoric People*, to mention only the most well known. For a critique of western anthropology see T. Asad (ed.), *Anthropology and the Colonial Encounter*; J. Tosh, *Clan Leaders and the Colonial Chiefs in Lango*, pp. 1–6. L.S.B. Leakey's most recently published three-volume work, *The Southern Kikuyu before 1903*, (London, 1977), suffers from the same weaknesses. For an anthropologist's view see L. Mair, 'Anthropology and Colonial Policy', pp. 191–5.
    The concept of 'indirect rule', which was introduced from its Lugardian fastness in Nigeria during the 1920s and 1930s into Tanganyika, Sierra Leone, Nyasaland and Northern Rhodesia should perhaps be seen as the ex-centric counterpart to Gallagher's metropolitan retreat to informal empire; see J. Gallagher, *The Decline, Revival and Fall of the British Empire*, pp. 99–129; and R.D. Pearce, *The Turning Point in Africa*, pp. 7–11 and 154–9.
    The District Administration's attitude towards social engineering in Kikuyuland can be discerned from KNA DC/FH 1/24, 'Fort Hall Annual Report, 1945', pp. 13–16; DC/FH 1/25, 'Fort Hall Annual Report, 1946', pp. 7–9, 19–24; and DC/FH 1/26, 'Fort Hall Annual Report, 1947', pp. 5–6, for a few examples from one district out of many. See also B.J. Berman, 'Bureaucracy and Incumbent Violence' pp. 143–77.

33. Although the term 'proto-capitalist' may be inelegant, it captures the contest between the settlers and the Kikuyu élites to become Kenya's first local capitalists. See J.M. Lonsdale's unpublished paper, 'The Growth and Transformation of the Colonial State in Kenya' and E.A. Brett, *Colonialism and Underdevelopment in East Africa*, pp. 165–212. G. Kitching, *Class and Economic Change in Kenya*, pp. 297–311 provides 14 brief biographical case studies.
    G. Kitching, *Class and Economic Change in Kenya*, pp. 70–3, has some sensible observations on the difficulty of using district agricultural production figures. These crude totals mislead perhaps more than they reveal. For one example see KNA DC/FH 1/23, 'Fort Hall Annual Report, 1944', pp. 6–7. Only 1,400 bags out of an estimated surplus of 30,000 were sold to the Maize Control.

34. J.M. Lonsdale's unpublished paper, 'The Growth and Transformation of the Colonial State in Kenya' pp. 13–14. For the Gold Coast see R. Rathbone, 'Businessmen in Politics', pp. 391–401.

35. CO 533/54 38086/5, 'Kikuyu Memorials and Petitions' (1945–47). For the reaction of the field administration see KNA DC/FH 1/26, 'Fort Hall Annual Report, 1947' pp. 1–5.

36. KNA Secretariat 1/2/2, 'Nyanza Province, 1949–50', Memorandum by P. Wyn Harris, 13 July 1949, about arson in Trans Nzoia. This report by the Chief Native Commissioner followed complaints by two Legislative Councillors, Major Keyser and S.V. Cooke that the North Nyanza administration had lost control in Kitosh and had

allowed the *Dini ya Msambwa* to mount an anti-European campaign. Wyn Harris pointed out that North Nyanza with a population of over 600,000 was twenty times the size of the Seychelles, and twice that of Zanzibar, or of Mitchell's former governorship in Fiji. Every day the District Commissioner received fifty letters, and twenty more as chairman of the Local Native Council. The district's European staff consisted of one District Commissioner, three District Officers, one district welfare officer and one district revenue officer. There were three African assistant administrative officers, eight Asian and forty African clerks. Each month the cashiers' office made over 500 payments, amounting to 150,000 shillings, and received 420 payments quite apart from the Local Native Council, which had an annual revenue of £107,000 and an expenditure of £104,000. The District Commissioner was burdened by the following administrative tasks: policy; secret correspondence; government circulars and publications; political records; agriculture; public health; veterinary affairs; education; buildings and roads; control of revenue; African local government; chiefs and headmen; mines; monthly and annual reports; staff discipline and establishment. He acted as the chairman of the district team and the Local legislation committee, prepared the estimates; supervised postings; forests; and the registration of births, deaths and marriages.

The District Officers were equally busy. One of them had the following duties: secretary of the district team; liquor licences; furniture; transport licences; plots in townships and trading centres; supervising the African location; applications for motor vehicles; arms and ammunition; the issuing of *kipande*; meteorological records; trading licences; control of commodities; food rationing; sugar distribution; wildlife; and also acted as the secretary of the township committee and supervised the local cooperative societies. By the late 1940s, life as an administrator in Africa was almost as desk bound as in Britain.

37. *ibid* and RH Mss. Brit.Emp. s. 390, Box 3, File 4, Item 3, ff.1-4, C.E.V. Buxton to Mitchell, 15 August 1948; and KNA MAA 8/102, 'Intelligence and Security: Miscellaneous Press Cuttings, 1948-50'. *East Africa News Review*, 22 January 1948.

38. B.J. Berman's unpublished thesis, 'Administration and Politics in Colonial Kenya', pp. 415-52.

Three

The Character and Policies
of Sir Philip Mitchell

The Colonial Office and Sir Philip Mitchell

Mitchell was chosen to become governor because of his vast experience of East Africa. He seemed to be the ideal choice to reassert metropolitan authority. A blunt, unattractive, fat, little man, without any social graces, Mitchell was on paper the best man for the job and had a wide knowledge of the problems he would find in Kenya. He had served as Chief Native Commissioner and Chief Secretary in Tanganyika, as governor of Uganda and, for the first two years of the war, was based in Nairobi as deputy chairman of the East African Governors' Conference, where he co-ordinated the war effort against the Italians in Ethiopia and Somalia. His brief tour of duty as governor of Fiji and High Commissioner in the Western Pacific from 1942 to 1944 confirmed his high reputation in Whitehall. He had been appointed at a difficult moment when Anglo–American relations had been strained. Many Americans had wanted to establish international or regional trustees to administer the recaptured territories rather than return them to their former colonial rulers. Mitchell had quickly resolved these problems and had demonstrated such a zeal to promote economic development in Fiji that the Americans had become reconciled to British imperialism in the area.[1] The Colonial Office hoped that he would reproduce these successes in Kenya and heal the bitter racial divisions. Ever since the visit of the young Margery Perham to Tanganyika in 1929, Mitchell's reputation as the able administrator who had implemented Sir Donald Cameron's plans for 'native authorities' in the most successful implanting of the ideology of 'indirect rule', had been high. As Miss Perham's influence in the Colonial Office grew, Mitchell's career flourished. In 1944, her authority was at its zenith, overriding the muted opposition of Sir Arthur Dawe and of the discredited Colonial Office establishment of the 1930s to his appointment.[2]

33

Whitehall wanted a forceful personality not only to reassert metropolitan authority, but also to implement new development policies to promote African production. Throughout the empire, since the West Indian disturbances of the late 1930s, there had been a new emphasis on development as the essential prerequisite for political advance. Under the influence of Malcolm MacDonald and Lord Moyne, the old trusteeship tradition had been transformed into a positive programme to ensure economic diversification, which would enable 'the agricultural slums of the colonial empire' to finance improved social services from a sound economic base. Whereas the inter-war ideology of indirect rule, or in Kenya the more direct supervision of the prefectoral field administration, had emphasised the need for organic, evolutionary development in the reserves, the new philosophy required a shift towards positive administration and a more interventionist role for both the technical departments and the District Officers.[3]

In Kenya, the Colonial Office's strategy to reassert metropolitan authority and to encourage African economic and political advance, failed and ended in the debacle of Mau Mau for three reasons. First, the settlers were more securely entrenched than the Colonial Office had considered possible. Secondly, African problems, both in the reserves and in the towns, were much more serious than had been anticipated and, thirdly, Mitchell failed because he was not up to his job. He was an indirect ruler of the inter-war years, ill-equipped to cope with the complex rivalries between settler, Asian and Kikuyu accumulators. The Colonial Office was trying to fight post-war problems with pre-war weapons. Mitchell's panicky despatches from the field simply played into the hands of the settlers and the Nairobi Secretariat, whose aims were different from those of Whitehall.

Mitchell's governorship can be divided into three distinct periods. This periodisation, however, is more a reflection of how Mitchell wanted to be perceived by the Colonial Office and of his changing relationship with metropolitan policy makers, than of the situation in Kenya. From his first year in office until his breakdown in December 1945 Mitchell was a clever alarmist, constantly bombarding the Colonial Office with lengthy despatches about the dreadful conditions he had discovered and the appalling disorganisation of the Kenyan administration. His spate of proposals was, of course, designed to convince Whitehall that he was fulfilling their instructions and thoroughly shaking up the moribund Secretariat and field administration.[4]

The second period overlaps slightly with the first, beginning in mid-1945 with Mitchell's proposals for the reorganisation of the Secretariat and of the agricultural department and continuing until the end of 1947. These were the years of 'Mitchell the doer'. Preparatory planning had been completed, the Secretariat had been mobilised for action and extension services had been expanded. The government's deck had been cleared for action. Resistance, he warned Whitehall, was inevitable. Until ordinary cultivators had perceived that terracing and the agricultural betterment campaign were for their benefit, the local agitators would gain considerable support for a brief period. The depth of opposition to compulsory cattle dipping in South Nyeri in 1946 and to terracing in Murang'a and Kiambu during 1947, clearly suprised Mitchell, but his confidence did not wane. After 1948, he was confident that the measures were beginning to be accepted and that peasant agriculture would soon be transformed. During his last four years as governor, Mitchell became a 'passive optimist'. Tenacity would see the government through. Eventually the militants would be discredited and ordinary Africans would be convinced that the administration, not the rabble-rousers of the Kenya African Union, had their best interests at heart.[5]

Mitchell was an intensely ambitious man. He knew that he was at the peak of his career and desperately wanted to perpetuate his reputation as a distinguished colonial ruler. His speedy diagnosis, which events later proved to be seriously flawed, was carefully designed to make the maximum impression in Whitehall. While Sir John Hathorn Hall quietly got on with a similar task in Uganda, Mitchell was acutely conscious of his political image and won all the plaudits. By 1948, he had successfully convinced himself, as well as the Colonial Office, that his strategy was working. He therefore agreed, in 1949, to accept another term as governor and turned down the opportunity of a retirement festooned with honours. This passive optimism, however, was itself a reflection of Mitchell's declining powers. Mentally, physically and spiritually he was exhausted throughout his last term, from which he emerged as an administrative dinosaur, a remnant from the era of indirect rule, increasingly out of touch with the Colonial Office's plans for local government reform and controlled African political advance.[6]

After 1947, isolated in Government House, Mitchell lost touch with reality. As peasant discontent and urban unrest were politicised, he refused to acknowledge that the administration was losing control, obstinately insisting that a few alarmist reports were untypical and unduly exaggerated. Meanwhile, the government lost its sense of direction and ultimate purpose and increasingly came to react simply on a day-to-day basis without any overall strategy. As the district administration's fire brigade rushed from crisis to crisis, Mitchell and the Secretariat failed to realise that the conflagration was getting out of control and that their attempted social engineering was fanning the flames.

Mitchell's policies for Kenya

When Mitchell arrived in Nairobi on 12 December 1944, the problems seemed rather different than when assessed in Whitehall. The field administration and the Secretariat insisted that unrestrained individualism in the reserves was producing serious erosion, undermining the authority of the chiefs and destroying the traditional moral economy.[7]

The settlers were also demanding that the squatters in the White Highlands be converted into a passive agricultural labour force, tied to the European farms and deprived of their cattle and smallholdings. Only then would the squatter threat to the safety of the White Highlands disappear. Meanwhile, in Nairobi and Mombasa, urban Africans were becoming increasingly restless and were showing alarming signs of resorting to crime and politics. The official mind in Nairobi was preoccupied with these issues rather than with reducing the influences of the settlers.[8]

The new governor found an exhausted, understaffed administration both in the provinces and the Secretariat. Within three weeks of his arrival, as the Colonial Office had hoped, he had embarked upon a fundamental reorganisation of the government machine. Before the end of 1944 he had decided that the financial secretary, the conservator of forests, the director of public works, the commissioner for lands and settlement, three of the four Provincial Commissioners and the directors of agriculture and veterinary services would all have to retire. At the same time, many men lower down the bureaucracy were told that they could not expect to rise any higher under Mitchell. The governor informed Whitehall that men over 45 were exhausted in the tropics and needed replacing if Kenya was to embark upon the drastic development needed to solve its problems.[9]

These draconian measures created much resentment inside the government. In the short term they confirmed Mitchell's reputation in the Colonial Office; but in the longer term they were to have disastrous consequences on his understanding of the deteriorating situation in the Kikuyu areas. No-one in the Secretariat or field administration had the courage to oppose Mitchell's social engineering or to warn about the dangers of growing administrative isolation. In fact, no Kenyan governor since Girouard (1909–1912) had had such an easy time with the Secretariat.[10] In the 1930s, the anti-settler Joseph Byrne had faced considerable opposition, but throughout Mitchell's governorship neither Rennie nor Rankine, his two Chief Secretaries, had the guts or the ability to stand up to him. Whereas Rennie, who had already spent six years in office under the 'settlers' nominee' Brooke-Popham and the cautious Moore, simply wanted to escape to a governorship of his own,[11] Rankine was a Mitchell protégé and his rise in Uganda occurred under Mitchell's patronage as governor. He had accompanied him in 1939 to Nairobi as assistant secretary to the Governors' Conference and followed him to Fiji as assistant Colonial Secretary. Apart from a two-year term as Colonial Secretary in Barbados, from 1945 to 1947, Rankine's career from cadet in Uganda to Resident in Zanzibar progressed under the watchful eye of his benign patron, Philip Mitchell. From 1947 to 1952, therefore, as the situation in

Kikuyuland and Nairobi deteriorated, the crucial position of Chief Secretary, which involved vetting all information that reached the governor and serving as head of the Development and Reconstruction Authority, was occupied by a Mitchell acolyte who was completely overawed by his chief.

The settlers capture Mitchell

When he had been in the colony for only 18 days, Mitchell reported to Oliver Stanley that the war-time advances in settler power would have to be acknowleged and proposed that the most prominent of the settler politicians, Ferdinand Cavendish-Bentinck, become an official member of the Legislative and Executive Councils. Mitchell explained that the 'processes which have brought about the present state of affairs in respect of Cavendish-Bentinck are of a kind which I do not think it would be either wise or practicable to put into reverse'.[12] He was already functioning virtually as Minister of Agriculture. During the war he had come to dominate the agricultural sector of the economy and had served as a member of the East African Supply Council, as well as on its executive board and production executive committee. He had also been chairman of the Kenya Agricultural Production and Settlement Board, Controller of Stock Feed and Fertilisers, a member of the Highlands and the Land Advisory Boards, Timber Controller, and chairman of the Kenya and East African Publicity Associations. He was also a member of both the Kenya Legislative and Executive Councils and was leader of the European Elected Members. To oust Cavendish-Bentinck from his war-time positions, Mitchell warned, would provoke vociferous settler opposition and seriously damage Whitehall's multiracial strategy. The governor argued that there was no alternative but to institutionalise Cavendish-Bentinck and to temper his anti-African sentiments with government responsibility, although he had to confess to Whitehall that 'I would have been happier if he had emerged straw in hair and dung on boots from a farm and had no political past'. Cavendish-Bentinck's appointment as member for Agriculture and Natural Resources, Mitchell realised, was bound to provoke African and Asian criticism.[13]

Cavendish-Bentinck's appointment was part of a major reorganisation of the Secretariat to prepare it for the demands of the post-war development campaign. Mitchell proposed reducing the excessive burden on the Chief Secretary by introducing a member system into the Executive Council, whereby members would be responsible for specific departments in an embryonic ministerial structure. The volume of work and its increasingly technical nature, he informed the Colonial Office, made it impossible for even the most industrious Chief Secretary to control the expanding government machine. The present arrangement, whereby all problems in the Secretariat had to go through the Chief Secretary before they reached the governor or the Executive Council, was creating a serious bottleneck in the government not only of Kenya but of many other large colonies. Mitchell's appointment of Cavendish-Bentinck as Member for Agriculture and Charles Mortimer, the former Commissioner for Local Government, as Member for Health and Local Government, was hailed by Andrew Cohen in the Colonial Office as the first attempt to restructure colonial governments. It confirmed Whitehall's belief that Mitchell was a dynamic reformer, especially as he suggested that Rennie, the Chief Secretary, should be appointed director of the Development and Reconstruction Authority and should oversee the second colonial occupation in Kenya. Whitehall's fascination with government efficiency, however, obscured the crucial fact that Mitchell had effectively conceded the settlers' war-time gains and had abandoned the Colonial Office's plans for a metropolitan invasion, which would reduce the settlers to a subordinate position, and allow greater African participation in political affairs.[14]

In reality, Mitchell had quickly been captured by the local administration and the settlers. This meant that African advance would be conditional upon settler agreement. Although Mitchell still hoped to create a multiracial society, he had nothing to offer Africans except increased government interference in the reserves and modest social reforms in the cities, and they were soon alienated from colonial rule. His policies were merely palliatives, since his early concession to the settlers precluded any root and branch reforms.

Mitchell's agricultural policies in Kikuyuland and the White Highlands

Humanitarian and mission organisations in Britain had for many years been critical of the exclusion of Africans from the White Highlands. The Aborigines Protection Society, for example, protested to Oliver Stanley in 1944 that the Africans in Kenya were crowded into 30 million acres, while a mere 1,890 Europeans occupied nearly 11 million acres, of which they actually cultivated only half a million. The Colonial Office, however, rejected these estimates of land distribution. Three years later the Communist Party's colonial expert, Sam Aaronovitch, alleged that during the 1930s, on settler farms of over 2,000 acres, on average only 269 acres were actually cultivated. In support of his statement he quoted the Kenya Land Commission's report which noted that, in 1934, only 11.8 per cent of the alienated White Highlands, which had an area of 10,345 square miles, was under cultivation, while 40.7 per cent was grazing land for stock, 20 per cent occupied by African squatters, and 27.5 per cent was completely unused. Similar criticisms were often made by left-wing opinion in Britain, which condemned the fact that the settlers, who formed less than

0.25 per cent of the population, should control nearly one third of the best agricultural land, while Africans were crowded into the exhausted reserves, which were suffering from continuous cultivation and overstocking.[15]

These problems had been exacerbated by the war-time drive to maximise production, regardless of the effects on the reserves. Many agriculturalists and members of the field administration feared that the damage to the soil structure and the organic harmonies of 'tribal' life had been irreparable. Sir Harold Tempany, the Colonial Office's chief agricultural adviser, shared these fears and recommended a drastic remedy. He reported in July 1946, after a brief visit to Kenya, that 'to put the matter quite plainly, from what I saw of the position, Kenya will never be able to solve its land problems satisfactorily until the findings of the Carter Commission have once more been thrown into the melting pot'.[16]

After protracted deliberations, the Kenya Land Commission had decided, in 1934, that the area of the Kikuyu reserves should be increased by a mere 21,000 acres. The Commission also recommended that the restored land should not be distributed among the *mbari*, which had been dispossessed at the beginning of the century, but handed over to the British-created Local Native Councils, which were controlled by the District Commissioner and used to benefit the whole district.[17] This, of course, had meant that the only people who had really benefited had been the collaborators of the local élite – the chiefs, Local Native Councillors and their supporters. The dispossessed *mbari* had remained uncompensated. As a final insult, the Commission also confirmed the sanctity of the European enclave in the White Highlands and excluded Africans from ever owning land in this vast area of eleven million acres. Two million Africans in overcrowded Central Province, therefore, looked with mounting anger upon the 2,000 settlers who occupied so large a proportion of the best farming land in the colony.[18]

Mitchell, the social engineer, felt confident that he could solve these problems, especially as the new Colonial Development and Welfare Act seemed to have removed the financial limitations which had hindered previous governments. The war, however, had exacerbated rather than healed Kenya's divisions and the new confidence and prosperity of both settlers and African cultivators had increased political expectations and rivalry. Social engineering alone could do little to diminish the frustration of many Africans. The agricultural crisis in the reserves and the squatter problem in the White Highlands were symptoms, not causes, of Kenya's divisions.

The Colonial Office's plan to reassert metropolitan authority and to create a tolerant multiracial society satisfied no one. The divisions were already too great; settlers and Africans could not be reconciled. The settlers, for example, demanded immediate self-government and insisted

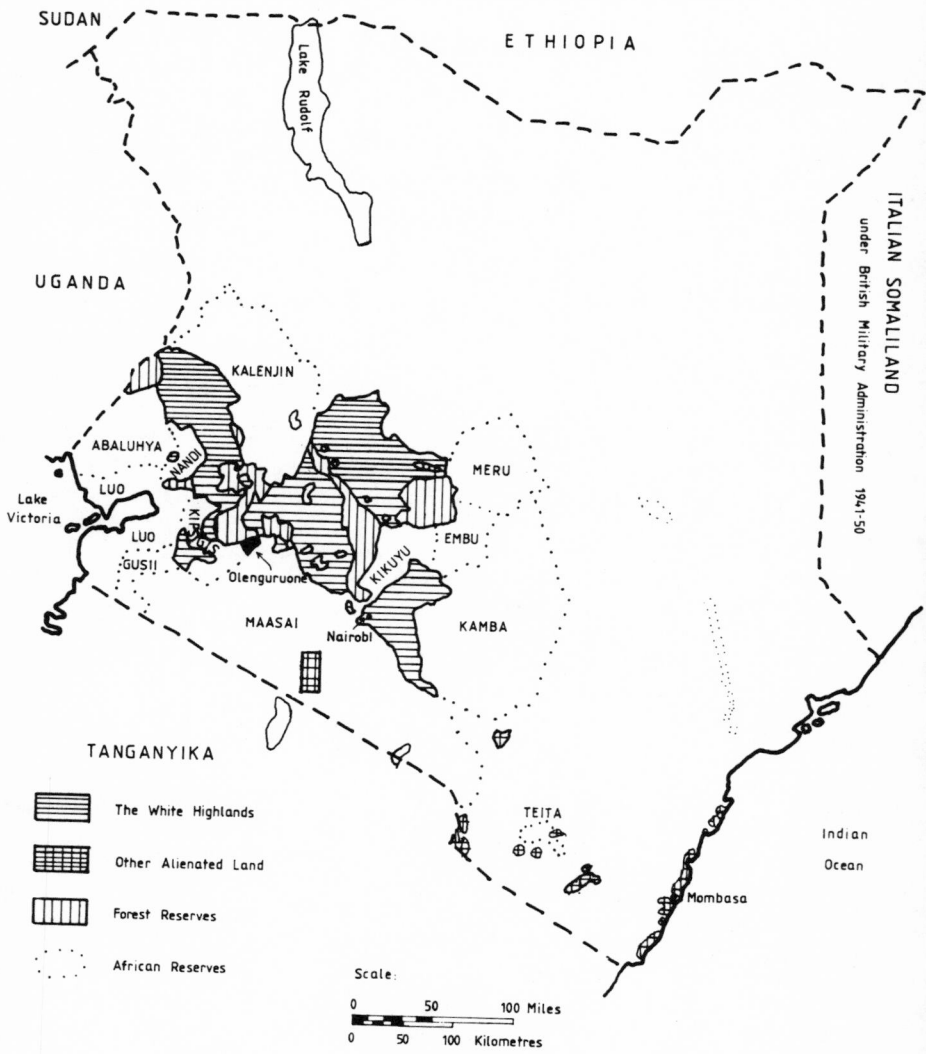

Map 3.1: *Kenyan Tribes and Alienated Areas*

on the White Highlands remaining a European enclave, while Africans demanded land and greater political involvement. It should have been evident to Mitchell that African political and economic aspirations could only be met by overturning the whole political economy of Kenya. In 1942, Macmillan had recognised that a serious peasant revolt was inevitable within ten years unless the settlers were ditched or bought out of the White Highlands and replaced by Kikuyu peasants organised in collective farms. A new arrangement between the government and the settlers' enemies, the Kikuyu proto-capitalists, was, he had warned essential. Time was running out.[19]

Whitehall and the Nairobi government unfortunately failed to appreciate that, for the landless Africans who had lost their *githaka* in Kiambu or Nyeri at the beginning of British rule and been forced to become squatters, sometimes on the same land as they had occupied, continued exclusion from the White Highlands was a constant indictment of colonial rule. Political activists, therefore, were able to undermine the government's attempts to restructure African agriculture simply by claiming that the land was being prepared for alienation to another wave of settlers. The full dimensions of African opposition to the White Highlands policy were never really understood by Mitchell and his advisers.[20]

Although the governor privately disagreed with the decisions of the Carter Land Commission, he thought it was essential to defend its report in order to reassure the settlers. To question the inviolable nature of the 1934 settlement was to open a Pandora's box of political conflict and, Mitchell believed, to destroy any chance of persuading the bitterly divided races of Kenya to co-operate and to work towards their mutual benefit. Mitchell considered that his 'task as Governor of Kenya in 1945 is to get on with the business on the basis of that settlement and on the assumption that it is authoritative and final'. Along with Cohen in Whitehall, he considered that to open the White Highlands to Africans would prove a false solution to the fundamental problems of African agriculture. Unless African farming techniques were changed, to transfer European farms to Africans would merely result in the destruction of the soil fertility of an even greater area. What was needed was not more land, but improved farming methods which would restore nutrients to the soil and land consolidation, particularly in Central Province.[21]

Mitchell did, however, hope that certain marginal changes in the delineation of the White Highlands might be negotiated without antagonising the settlers or undermining their faith in the integrity of the government. Creech Jones, who became the Secretary of State in October 1946, invariably adopted a more critical view of the settlers than either his advisers in the Colonial Officer or the governor. When he first heard of Mitchell's decision to defend the Carter Land Commission settlement he had insisted that:

I think . . . that while it may be expedient to build the case on the Carter Commission it would be unfortunate from my point of view if the impression were conveyed that this was a final and inflexible allocation of lands which could not permit of any adjustment either as a result of population needs or subsequent political development. I want to avoid any suggestion that the European Highlands are absolutely reserved when later it may be necessary to make room for some forms of African settlement.[22]

Yet this was exactly the suggestion Mitchell wished to give the settlers. Slowly, the governor and his ally in the Colonial Office, Cohen, persuaded Creech Jones to accept their view. It took them less than a year. When the Secretary of State's former colleagues in the Fabian Colonial Bureau complained, in 1947, that they 'were unaware that the present British Government stood by the findings of this Commission . . .', he replied that the continued presence of a large settler community was essential if African development was rapidly to progress. Creech Jones informed them that:

The African land problem is less one of the distribution of existing land . . . than of the use to which the lands are being put . . . It is hardly a case that a solution to the Africans' large and complex problems can be found in the Highlands marked for European settlement . . . The African land problem needs primarily to be attacked by the great campaign of resettlement, improved agriculture and water supplies.[23]

Cohen and Mitchell had won; Creech Jones, completely captured by the official mind, abandoned his opposition to the Kenya Land Commission's settlement. Kenyan Africans, however, did not.

Despite his reputation in Tanganyika and Uganda as an advocate of peasant production and a critic of the settlers, in Kenya it had required little persuading by the settler politicians and the Secretariat to convince Mitchell that European farming offered the most effective means to develop the colony and to increase production to meet the world's commodity shortages. He was soon convinced that the threat of erosion was so serious that any attempt to increase peasant production would irreparably destroy the fertility of the soil with disastrous consequences for rural Africans. In fact the reverse happened. By foreclosing the peasant option and by evicting the squatters from the settler farms in the Rift Valley, Mitchell destroyed any chance of creating a multiracial society in Kenya.

The continued dominance of the settlers, however crucial they were for financing African development and enticing foreign investment to Kenya, effectively hamstrung the government's agricultural campaign in the Kikuyu reserves. The colonial authorities were entrapped in an impossible situation. To open up the White Highlands would destroy political stability (the essential prerequisite for economic development in both the settler and the African sectors of the economy) by provoking settler opposition; whereas failure to abandon the Kenya Land Commission would merely provoke peasant protest and destroy, by another means, the political equilibrium needed if Kenya was to attract new investment.[24]

With the exception of Macmillan, no-one in the Colonial Office or Kenyan government realised that, in the long run, the seemingly more dangerous option of ditching the settlers and accommodating moderate African leaders afforded the greater assurance of Kenya's future stability. Instead, post-war policies for Kenya were based on the fatal premise that it was politically impossible to ditch the settlers. Apart from Macmillan's flight of fancy, the alternative was never seriously considered. The settlers remained stronger than before the war. The government never seriously attempted to solve the problem of how it should reconcile the small, but politically powerful, European community's interests with the demands of the increasingly confident and articulate African élite.

Mitchell's paternalism

The governor misguidedly reassured the Colonial Office that settler and African interests were compatible. The harmonious mixing of Polynesians, Indians and Europeans in Fiji had made a profound impression on him and his diaries show that Mitchell had been inspired to attempt to recreate this tolerant atmosphere in Kenya.[25] This multiracial strategy in which the settlers were to provide the 'steel-frame' for African progress, lulled Whitehall into a false optimism and convinced them that a confrontation could be avoided. This was completely incorrect. Mitchell and the Secretariat, however, were convinced that their development plans were dependent upon British settlement. The settlers' presence would attract investment and demonstrate Britain's long-term commitment to the region. Moreover the settlers and local Asians would provide the stable internal demand for the new processing and import substitution industries the government hoped to encourage. These, in turn, would generate the economic expansion necessary to provide the revenue for the post-war social engineering projects in the reserves.[26]

Mitchell proved to be far less radical than many settlers had feared and shared the field administration's prejudices against African politicians and traders. He believed in the myth of the organic nature of African society. The governor, like his senior colleagues, was a second not third generation colonial ruler; a man of the indirect rule era. Mitchell had entered the Colonial Service in Nyasaland in 1913 and had served in the area disrupted by the Chilembwe rising; Rennie, the Chief Secretary, had entered the Ceylon service in 1920; Thornley had gone to Tanganyika in 1930; while Wyn Harris and Troughton had spent the whole of their careers in Kenya. Such men found it impossible to adjust, as Whitehall could, to the emergence of African nationalism and failed to respond to the growing demands for African paramountcy and the clamour for the abrogation of the Carter Land Commission and the opening up of the White Highlands.[27]

Mitchell was personally hostile to African politicians. Even a comparatively moderate figure like Kenyatta, he considered, was a dangerous demagogue, merely out to further his own career at the expense of the African masses, who needed the protection of many years of British rule before they could be safely entrusted with greater political power.[28] To paraphrase Churchill, he had not become a governor to preside over the dissolution of the British empire. Mitchell firmly believed that 'ignorant agitators' had to be kept in their place. Centuries would be required before the ordinary African could be entrusted to their unscrupulous mercy. Africa was only beginning the journey to civilization, which had taken 2,000 years in Europe. With British aid and direction, he considered, Africa could advance quickly along the path of civilization:

> I am not one of those who say because it has taken Europe two thousand years it must necessarily take that time for Africans; but it is barely two thousand weeks since Africans had not even an alphabet, let alone any means of writing, no transport except their wives' backs or heads; no plant except arrows, spears, hoes and digging sticks; no common language (they have not yet); no government other than small tribal authorities, and no industries – in fact, since they were in a condition of which, as far as I know, there is no record in England – for when Caesar landed 'The English' were centuries ahead of Africans in 1880 or '90. I have no doubt that it will be possible in much less than two thousand years to bring Africa to the condition of . . . Europe; but *some* sense of historical time values is surely not an unreasonable postulate.[29]

If Britain withdrew too soon, he prophesied that Africa would degenerate to the level of independent Liberia or Ethiopia. Mitchell had first-hand knowledge of conditions in Ethiopia, having served briefly as chief political adviser to the Middle East Command under Field Marshall Wavell, with responsibility for the administration of the areas recently captured from the Italians. Haile Selassie's régime had confirmed his opinion that Africa was not yet ready for independence and that to withdraw would be to betray Britain's duty and to leave the ordinary African to the exploitation of a corrupt élite. The 'white man's burden' still had its advocates in the late 1940s.

In consequence, the governor failed to satisfy rising African expectations and few concessions were made to their new economic importance. Although Eliud Mathu was appointed to the Legislative Council in October 1944 to represent African interests, this was a small advance.

Usually African opinion was not consulted or was provided by the chiefs. The administration knew little about the realities of rural African life and even less about the plight of the urban residents of Pumwani or the *majengo* of Mombasa.[30] The African traders and commercial farmers who wanted to share in government patronage were dismissed as middlemen, prospering on the backs of the peasantry, and were never acknowledged as legitimate representatives of indigenous capitalism.[31] The field administration and the Secretariat remained convinced that only the chiefs represented ordinary Africans. Their authority was, therefore, strengthened. A new generation of chiefs, more sympathetic to Mitchell's interventionist policies, was appointed to explain and enforce the agricultural campaign. Thus, while the settler-controlled district councils and farmers' associations were securing new powers and were being incorporated into the state's decision making to an extent they had never achieved before the war, the new African organisations, the Kenya African Union, the Central Province Wattle Growers' and Producers' Association and their political leaders, Eliud Mathu, and later Jomo Kenyatta, remained excluded from participation in the formulation of new policies because of the paternalist assumptions of the official mind about the structure and future coherence of African society.[32]

The continued neglect of the African politicians while popular political consciousness was growing transformed Mathu's client relationship with the government. From his nomination to the Legislative Council until Kenyatta's return from exile in Britain in September 1946, Mathu had been the leading African politician. To the government and chiefs he seemed a reliable representative of the new generation of constitutionalist politicians, who, it was hoped, would replace the discredited Kikuyu Central Association. Kenyatta's return, however, forced Mathu to become increasingly critical of the government and its allies, the chiefs, otherwise he would have lost his popular following and credibility as an independent political force. He had to move closer to Kenyatta and attempt to improve relations with the Kikuyu Central Association in order to ensure his political survival.[33] This move to the left, of course, discredited him in the eyes of Mitchell. Mathu had always had his critics. Carey Francis, the influential headmaster of the Alliance High School, for example, had earlier attempted to convince the Secretariat that Mathu was unreliable. During 1947, his critics became increasingly numerous; a host of police and field administration reports about Mathu's subversive contacts eventually persuaded Mitchell that he could not be trusted.[34] No African, therefore, was appointed to the Executive Council, which continued to be dominated by the settlers and their supporters inside the Secretariat. Counting Cavendish-Bentinck and Sir Charles Mortimer as settlers disguised as officials, five of the eleven members on the central body of the Kenyan state were settlers during the post-war years. Such a body could hardly be expected to challenge the settlers' privileged status in the political economy of Kenya.[35]

The Kenyan government saw the settlers, not as an obstacle to African advance but as the agents of further progress. Mitchell, for example, believed that:

> It is of the greatest importance . . . for the future well being and prosperity of the native people that there should be a vigorous and well established British settlement in these Highlands, for without it there is no hope of successfully overcoming the immense problems which confront us . . . The British people in East Africa are the key-stone of the arch.[36]

The governor reported that, 'so far from this state of agricultural slum existence being due to white settlement . . . the only known palliative is White Settlement, industry or mining', since 'an ignorant man and his wife with a hoe are a totally inadequate foundation for an enlightened state of society'.[37] Cohen in the Colonial Office concurred. He and Mitchell agreed that the proposed £1.6 million European settlement scheme was essential for Kenya's future and they reassured Creech Jones, persuading him that: 'Increased white settlement must be looked at not as a thing in itself, but as an integral part of the Kenya development programme and is necessary in order to provide the increased financial and economic resources without which African social development cannot proceed.'[38] Without Cohen's help, Mitchell would have found it extremely difficult to persuade the Colonial Office to approve this large grant, which marked the abandonment of Byrne's peasant strategy and increased the economic power of the settlers. Mitchell and Cohen, however, considered that this European presence would strengthen Kenya's stability and facilitate its development into a fully multiracial society and ally of Britain.

Mitchell's anti-Asian prejudices prevented him from recognising that small-scale Asian enterprises might have generated a larger multiplier effect on the Kenyan economy and absorbed a much larger unskilled workforce than the capital-intensive multinational corporations the government was attempting to attract. This would have enabled the government to resettle families from the reserves as urban employment opportunities expanded. Colin Leys has argued that Asian capital would have provided a more effective means of generating industrial expansion and has pointed out that, despite official disapproval, at the time of Independence Asians owned nearly three-quarters of the private non-agricultural assets of the colony, and over 67 per cent of locally-owned industrial concerns employing more than 50 people. By the early 1950s, there was no more room for expansion in real estate and trading, which had attracted Asian capital, and it began to invest in the secondary processing and manufacturing sectors, which the government wished to encourage.[39]

In contrast, multinational companies regarded their Kenyan interests as peripheral and reinvested their profits in Britain. Indeed these companies were only willing to invest in Kenya after they had received assurances of protection and special privileges.[40] The multinationals' presence, however, had a political as well as a purely economic purpose. The settlers had vociferously supported the government's attempts to attract them because they appeared to guarantee the continuation of the settler community and would provide jobs for the next generation. International capital offered the settlers their only opportunity to become Kenya's first national bourgeoisie. Without its support they would be squeezed between Asian and African entrepreneurs. The settlers believed that the multinationals would tighten the links between Britain and Kenya, guarantee Kenya's continued colonial status and protect their dominant position. Events, however, were to show that British capital, like the metropolitan official mind, had a global vision and was willing to sacrifice the dependent Kenyan settlers for a new world strategy of informal rather than formal empire, that would now be called neo-colonialism. This, however, only became apparent in the late 1950s. Ten years earlier, the settlers' position in Kenya had seemed secure. Kenya, it had appeared, was about to become the strategic centre of a retreating empire, with the settlers as the core.[41]

Thus, instead of being the bogey destroying every effort to improve race relations, the Kenyan settlers came to be seen as an essential element in the economic and political development of Kenya. Whitehall's commitment to African advance wavered. Advance there was to be, or so Whitehall hoped, but it was to be at a pace that would not unduly alarm the settlers. After 1946, following the planned British withdrawal from India and Palestine, the presence of a prosperous settler community was deemed essential for the strategic security of Africa and for the dollars the settler exports contributed to embattled sterling. The presence of the growing settler population, therefore, made the future of Kenya much more problematic than that of the Gold Coast or Nigeria. Indeed, with the withdrawal from India in 1947 and from Palestine in 1948, and with mounting Egyptian demands for British withdrawal from Suez, Kenya seemed likely to become the fulcrum of British defence strategy not only in Africa, but in the Middle East and Indian Ocean, providing a secure base for a British rapid-deployment force. The Cabinet, for example, seriously contemplated transforming Mackinnon Road near Mombasa into a major base. Stores began to be moved to Kenya. Creech Jones accepted, without any qualms, plans to quadruple the settler population in Kenya, and to transform it into a second Southern Rhodesia. More than £120 million was to be spent, mainly in Kenya, on these military preparations in East Africa.[42] Until Britain's financial problems and government retrenchment compelled a reassessment, the soldier settlement scheme had seemed likely to be only the first of many schemes to strengthen the

British presence in Kenya. The retreat from empire was not without its repercussions in the remaining colonies. British withdrawal from India and the Middle East clearly made the retreat from Kenya, in the long term, much more difficult and, in the short term, strengthened the settlers' bargaining position.

Closer union

Another political factor, which alienated African opinion, was the government's confusing behaviour during the Closer Union controversy. Mitchell and Whitehall had hoped to achieve four objectives with their proposals in 'Colonial 191'; Closer Union would improve inter-territorial co-operation, dilute settler influence in Kenya, enhance metropolitan power and point the way towards the evolution of a multiracial political system in Kenya and the other East African colonies. In consultations with the Colonial Office while *en route* from Fiji to Kenya, Mitchell revitalised the Closer Union proposals.[43] He began by increasing their scope while making them more acceptable to Africans and Asians and to the Labour Party at home. Instead of being a device to entrench settler power, Closer Union was redesigned to restore metropolitan authority and to create a bulwark against South African expansionism. Kenyan settlers, he hoped, would still support the new proposals because they fulfilled one of their old ambitions, but they would also prove acceptable to the other races who were to be given an equal number of seats as the settlers on the Central Assembly. This was the first example of Mitchell's attempts to obscure the racial divide and to appear as all things to all men.[44]

The new scheme was much simpler than his predecessor's plans for complete integration. It was also specifically designed not to antagonise opponents of Closer Union and was presented as 'a natural growth from the existing state of affairs'. Health, education, labour and African affairs – the issues that most interested Africans – were to remain territorial responsibilities. Industrial development, the railways, fiscal policy, research, agricultural investigations, Mitchell was convinced could only be effectively tackled on a co-ordinated East African basis. He also hoped that Kenya's racial divisions might be reduced under the moderating influence of the two other territories. The Closer Union proposals, therefore, were Mitchell's most important attempt to reduce the overweening influence of the Kenyan settlers.[45]

By the time of the Governors' Conference meeting in August 1945, Mitchell, who had taken careful soundings of settler opinion, was already beginning to doubt that the proposed equal racial composition of the Central Assembly would prove acceptable to the Kenyan Europeans. He therefore attempted to make the Assembly more acceptable to them, not at the expense of African or Asian members, but by introducing an electoral college to select the Europeans. This would have enabled the Kenyan settlers to secure extra representation at the expense of Tanganyikan and Ugandan Europeans. After nine months in Nairobi, Mitchell realised that, as it stood, 'Colonial 191' would prove unacceptable and he struggled to make it more presentable without changing the vital principle of equal unofficial representation for the three major races.[46] He had the difficult task not only of reassuring Africans and Asians, but also of gaining the confidence of the vociferous European population in Kenya. This had proved more difficult than he had anticipated. Settler suspicion of the Colonial Office's new man, especially after the return of the Labour government, was deeply entrenched.[47] At the crucial moment, Mitchell fell ill and, from December 1945 until March 1946, the delicate negotiations were left in the hands of Chief Secretary Rennie, who was a much less subtle political operator than Mitchell.[48]

In December 1945, when 'Colonial 191' was finally published, settler opposition erupted against the proposals, although the hue and cry did have the advantage of ensuring unanimous African and Asian support. The settlers, however, feared that the Labour government was 'determined to take away the power of the Europeans in Kenya'. These suspicions undermined Mitchell's attempts to create a less racially divisive atmosphere. Alfred Vincent, the settlers' political leader, for example, demanded an immediate unofficial majority on the Kenya Legislative Council as 'the only means by which we can stop this fooling around by the Colonial Office'. Yet, despite this apparently irreconcilable divide, Rennie as acting governor still believed that:

> Equal territorial and unofficial representation on any East African Council form the only possible foundation on which post-war programmes of social, cultural and material development can be safely built, if these East African territories are to progress harmoniously . . . All three communities in East Africa as a whole are inter-dependent and no one of them can prosper without the co-operation of the other two. All must advance together.[49]

The settler politicians, however, were committed too deeply for them to extricate themselves without help.

After their visit to East Africa in August 1946, in an abortive attempt to solve the deadlock, Creech Jones and Andrew Cohen, as well as the three governors, became even more convinced that a scheme similar to 'Colonial 191' was essential.[50] The revised proposals embodied in 'Colonial 210', as far as the Colonial Office and the East African governments were concerned, maintained the principle of equal racial representation, although there was now to be one member from each racial group per territory instead of two.[51] In addition, the territorial Legislative Councils were to choose one extra unofficial member for the Assembly. The Colonial Office hoped that this would prove acceptable to all three races while it would enable the composition of the Central Assembly to be modified as Africans gained greater representation at the territorial level. Racial fluidity would replace rigidity.

'Colonial 210' was not devised, as has frequently been suggested, by the Colonial Office as a sell-out to settler pressure. The racial composition of the unofficials on the Central Assembly clearly proved that equal racial representation was preserved. 'Colonial 210' simply presented the Assembly in a more attractive way to Kenyan settlers by restricting the power of the High Commission and subordinating its revenue to the control of the territorial Legislative Councils. The Colonial Office and the governors never anticipated that this would arouse African and Asian opposition. Mitchell, indeed, still feared that the scheme had not gone far enough to appease the settlers.[52] Creech Jones was willing to take a hard line: 'I am not unduly alarmed at the danger of precipitating a major political crisis. It is the European settler method in Kenya of asserting their claim to a degree of political dominance and of showing resentment. Whatever privilege they may have had in the past cannot be perpetuated much longer.'[53] The Secretary of State was evidently less apprehensive of creating a political storm with the settlers than Sir Philip Mitchell.

The new proposals, however, encountered African and Asian opposition because the official announcement emphasised that four unofficial members were to be elected from each territory. Since Africans and Asians knew that they were only to be given one seat each, they jumped to the conclusion that the other two members were to be settlers. In contrast, 'Colonial 191' had made it appear as if there were to be equal unofficial representation of the three main races and had hidden the additional European members among the representatives to be nominated by the High Commission.[54] Thus 'Colonial 210' heightened African suspicions. Although '210' retained the essential core of '191', in the racially divided arena of Kenyan politics, myth proved to be more powerful than reality. By miscalculating in the original proposals how much reassurance the Kenyan settlers required before they would support Closer Union, both British and Kenyan governments appeared to have conceded the racial equality promised in '191' because of intense settler pressure, although they were simply seeking to reassure the settlers rather than to abandon their promises to the Africans and Asians. The Closer Union crisis, which lasted from December 1945 to March 1948, was the first of a series of cases of the Kenyan government trying to appeal to both Africans and settlers, but merely succeeding in arousing the suspicion of both communities and alienating the authorities even further from the Africans.

The Closer Union controversy also marked an important change in metropolitan attitudes to the settlers, particularly on the part of Creech Jones and Andrew Cohen. Creech Jones had the reputation, from his days as chairman of the Fabian Colonial Bureau, of being a noted sympathiser with African criticism of colonial rule. As Under-Secretary and, after October 1946, as Secretary of State for the Colonies, however, he seemed to be a completely different figure, totally subservient to his official advisers.[55] His East African journey in the summer of 1946 encouraged this dramatic change. This visit made an equally profound impression upon Andrew Cohen, his chief adviser on East African affairs, who, the following year, became Assistant Under-Secretary for Africa; a position of crucial importance not only for the future of Kenya but for decolonisation throughout British Africa. Cohen had the most creative mind in the Colonial Office and possessed a dynamic personality and willpower equalled by few other bureaucrats.[56] After a brief visit to Central Africa as private secretary to Sir John Maffey in the late 1930s, Cohen had returned to Whitehall disillusioned with the morality of empire. Like Creech Jones he was determined to transform the imperial relationship into a force for African development, but this did not mean African political power in the settler colonies. Cohen was concerned primarily to create self-sustaining nations with sound economic bases. He had, therefore, been quickly convinced by Mitchell that the settlers offered the most effective way of improving conditions for the African masses in colonies like Kenya. Thus, despite their initial distrust of the Kenya settlers, both Creech Jones and Cohen were more susceptible to their views than appeared at first sight. After prolonged discussions with Mitchell and the settlers' political leaders, they returned to London with a much more sympathetic appreciation of the settlers' role in Kenyan life and its future economic progress.[57] As had happened to Mitchell in the first months of 1945, the political and economic realities of Kenya forced them to modify their previous inclination to side with African demands. Although no-one realised it at the time, this was a vital turning point. The British government's new proposals on Closer Union, contained in 'Colonial 210', were significant not because of what they had to say about economic integration but because they marked a turning point in the subconscious assumptions of the two most influential men in the Colonial Office. The Kenya African Union's meagre chance of rewriting the rules of Kenyan politics had been lost before Kenyatta appeared on the scene. His return in September 1946 simply confirmed the settlers' dominant influence, not only in Nairobi but also in London. Exposed to the political situation in Kenya, Creech Jones's and Cohen's preconceived opinions had begun slowly to change.[58]

Their visit and several despatches from Mitchell over the previous 18 months highlight the reasoning of the official mind as it came to grips with the intractable political realities of settler intransigence. Slowly the Colonial Office realised that the reform of African empire would be extremely difficult to implement in those colonies that had actually provoked this reassessment – Kenya and the Rhodesias. By the end of 1946, any thoughts the Labour Party may have had of transferring some power to the African élite in Kenya in the same way as in the Gold Coast had been dispelled; the presence of the settler community precluded such a step. Indeed, the excesses of left-wing rhetoric had increased the settlers' intransigence. The price of abandoning the settlers appeared to be too high in terms of political uproar, economic chaos and lost confidence.[59]

Sir Philip Mitchell and the rationale of the Kenyan official mind

Within less than three years, the agricultural campaign in the three Kikuyu Districts, the attempt to remove the threat of squatter accumulation which was undermining the heart of the settler economy by expelling squatter cattle from the White Highlands, and the government's failure to tackle Nairobi's acute social problems, had all helped to alienate Africans from the colonial régime. The impact of Mitchell's policies was most acute upon the Kikuyu, the largest 'tribe' in the colony. The government's agricultural development programme was particularly disruptive in the three overcrowed Kikuyu reserves. The Kikuyu formed nearly two-thirds of the total squatter community, with an even larger proportion in the Naivasha, Nakuru and Aberdares district council areas, where the new anti-squatter rules were' most severe. In Nairobi, approximately 55 per cent of the total population were Kikuyu.[60] The Kikuyu and the government thus clashed over post-war Kenya's three most explosive problems. Moreover, it was the Kikuyu politicians who dominated the fledgling trade unions and the Kenya African Union, while Kikuyu businessmen and commercial farmers provided the greatest threat to the economic hegemony of the settlers.[61] When the Mitchell government failed to incorporate them into the political process, to reward them with a share in government patronage or to provide new economic opportunities, many Kikuyu were driven into militant opposition to the colonial order. By 1952, many of them had turned in desperation to open revolt in the Mau Mau rebellion. Why did the government fail to react and not attempt to prevent the development of violent opposition among the Kikuyu to colonial rule? Why was the situation allowed to deteriorate so far?

The Kenyan authorities and settlers placed the blame for these troubles on Jomo Kenyatta, whom they denounced as a communist agitator. It appeared inconceivable that anyone else could have masterminded the protests. After all, Kenyatta was the avowed leader of the main African political movement – the Kenya African Union. In 1960, the official Corfield report on 'the origins and growth of Mau Mau' still contended that Kenyatta had controlled Mau Mau. It declared:

> Land had already become a political issues, but it did not become a burning issue until the return of Jomo Kenyatta to Kenya at the end of

1946 . . . Jomo Kenyatta and his associates saw all too clearly that the exploitation of land hunger was a sure way of furthering their own ends of uniting the Kikuyu against the Government in general, and the settled European farmer in particular.[62]

This campaign, Corfield alleged, had been organised through the Kikuyu Central Association and the Kikuyu Karing'a Educational Association which, he believed, Kenyatta controlled as part of the web of contacts centred on the Githunguri Teachers' Training College. This educational movement, with Githunguri and Kenyatta at the centre and the Karing'a schools and the African Orthodox Church in the localities, provided the organisation through which Kenyatta had allegedly fostered the spread of Mau Mau.

Kenyatta was thus seen as the evil genius in whom the various strands of Kikuyu subversion met. The independent schools, the Teachers' Training College, age-group organisations, ex-soldiers' associations, the trade unions, the Kikuyu Central Association and the Kenya African Union, all looked to him as their ultimate leader and, it appeared to the offical mind, only he could unite these movements into a formidable challenge to the colonial state. He appeared particularly insidious to many settlers because his long sojourn in Britain and his contacts with the Labour Party had made him as adept as themselves at bypassing the Kenyan government when he wanted to put pressure on the metropolitan state. Kenyatta refused to accept the rules of the Kenyan political game of the previous 50 years, whereby only the settlers had direct access to the counsels of Whitehall and Westminister.[63]

Kenyatta all too easily fitted the Kenyan government's need for a scapegoat; a brilliant, evil mastermind who could employ traditional witchcraft and modern anthropology to terrify the Kikuyu into revolt, while tying the colonial authorities' iron fist by skilful manipulation of the humanitarian sentiments of the Labour left and of missionary opinion in Britain. Corfield expressed this settler alarm when he castigated Kenyatta for manipulating British support with his references to

> . . . the word democracy, as this word was dearly respected by left-wing sympathizers in the United Kingdom. He also had a full knowledge and understanding of the psychology of the Kikuyu and was able to blend the technique of revolution, undoubtedly learnt while he was in Russia, with an appeal to superstition and to the strong sense of tribal destiny which the Kikuyu possessed.[64]

Such views were not simply the product of Corfield's bilious view of Africans, but were typical of European attitudes in Kenya, not only among the settlers but also in the field administration and the Secretariat.

The Kenyan authorities never realised that they were out of touch with African opinion. The field administration, for example, had become desk-bound and was dependent on the colonial chiefs for most of its information about what people really thought. The chiefs, of course, used this control over government information to discredit their own political rivals in the Kenya African Union, who thereupon became increasingly disillusioned with constitutionalist politics. The Special Branch's concentration on preserving the political *status quo* also coloured the reports of African political activity that reached the Secretariat and prevented the central bureaucracy from understanding what was really happening in the reserves and the White Highlands.[65]

Both the White Highlands and African Nairobi were areas in which the colonial state was peculiarly weak, as power had been devolved to the settler-controlled district and municipal councils. This division of responsibility between settler institutions and the field administration had created a serious gap in the government's defences and reduced its ability to monitor and suppress opposition. The social transformation which followed the war was, however, especially acute in these same two areas where settler and African Kenya were inextricably interlinked.[66] The Kenyan government, therefore, failed not only to appreciate the depth of the discontent which simmered beneath the surface, but critically misread the warning signs of violence among the squatters on the settler farms, the urban unemployed in Pumwani and Shauri Moyo, and among the peasantry in the Kikuyu reserves. The problems were compounded by the field administration's prejudices against the emerging proto-capitalists and the Kenya African Union, which distorted the reports they forwarded to the Secretariat and the governor and obscured the complex struggles beneath the surface of popular African politics.

Mitchell and the field administration were convinced, until the end, that their strategy had worked. The year 1947 was one disaster, when the second colonial occupation began to provoke sustained resistance. But the administration saw this unpopularity as something that had to be endured for a brief period before Kikuyu society could be restructured. Ignorant protests from self-seeking politicians cut little ice.[67] They were inevitable in the short run, before the benefits of the agricultural development programme filtered down to the *wananchi*. Although 1948 was a difficult year, opposition seemed to be less vociferous. In 1949, when Mitchells's term as governor was renewed for another three years, it seemed to him and his advisers in the Secretariat that the tide had at last turned. By 1950 or 1951, the governor believed that his programme was on course, tackling land degradation and reducing social tension in the reserves. The soil had been saved from the depredations of the greedy land-miners, and was being protected and replenished for the future prosperity of the ordinary African.[68]

In fact by 1950, the grand design with which he had arrived in Nairobi in 1944, intending to wrest control of the colonial state from the settlers and to create in Kenya the contented multiracial society he believed he had governed in Fiji, had collapsed into chaos. Instead of striving to achieve set goals, the weary governor was reduced to responding on an *ad hoc* basis to every problem that passed over his desk. Grand strategy was dead; tactical survival was all that remained. His poor health made it impossible for Mitchell to maintain his original punishing régime of tours throughout the colony.[69] After his serious illness in the middle of the Closer Union furore over 'Colonial 191', when he was incapacitated from December 1945 to March 1946, his energies were noticeably diminished. Although the stream of correspondence to the Colonial Office continued in full spate, the constant round of district tours he had undertaken during his first year, was drastically cut. During his last three years as governor after 1949, he was virtually a prisoner in Nairobi, seldom venturing into the districts, tied to Government House by his heart condition and utter exhaustion.[70]

Instead of instilling enthusiasm into the field administration by his forceful presence, Mitchell became isolated; an aloof figure, little known to the new generation of District Commissioners. For example, while O'Hagan, who had been District Commissioner in Murang'a from 1945 to 1947 before moving to the Secretariat, remembers the dynamic governor of the first years, his friend and colleague Kennaway, who was the District Commissioner in Kiambu during the early 1950s, recalls a totally different man, devoid of any interest in the problems of the district.[71]

One abiding passion did, however, survive Mitchell's decline; his intense personal ambition. A solitary, unapproachable man, who found it difficult to make friends and extremely easy to provoke lasting personal enmity, Mitchell was driven by fiercely competitive instincts, whether at work or in his leisure. He had to be outstanding, whether it was governing Kenya or fishing for trout. Indeed it was reported that he had only married his wife, a South African open golf ladies' champion, because she was the first woman to have defeated him. Mitchell's constant desire was to excel and to leave his imprint upon what he believed to be the *tabula rasa* of Africa and the African mind.[72]

As the complexities of Kenya ground him down by their sheer intractability, Mitchell's nerve snapped and his health collapsed. Although he managed to conceal this from the Colonial Office when it renewed his appointment in 1949, the Kenyan governor between 1949 and 1952 was a mere shadow of his former self, but the ambition remained. If Sir Arthur Richards could get to the House of Lords, then so could he. Well aware of his reputation in the Colonial Office as the most dynamic of the African governors, Mitchell clung on, impervious to administration and settler warnings about the imminence of a widespread Kikuyu revolt. The governor became increasingly reluctant to heed advice as the political situation deteriorated and his energies were sapped. He showed a remarkable ability to ignore events and opinions that contradicted his preconceived view. While in 1948, when Clarence Buxton and Canon Capon had first warned him of the serious situation among the Kikuyu, it might have been true that the tensions were no more serious than an experienced governor like Mitchell had encountered many times before in his long career, this was no longer true after 1950.[73] But as Mitchell's term of office drew to a close, he became reluctant to contemplate the possibility of a widespread rebellion and closed his mind to all the evidence that was presented, obstinately refusing to acknowledge that the situation had changed in case it endangered his reputation and let slip the peerage. By 1952, he was already an exhausted, shuffling, ill figure; a remnant from the age of indirect rule. He had succeeded for too long and survived too well into an uncongenial time. This was his tragedy; and Kenya's.

Notes

1. C. Thorne, *Allies of a Kind*, pp. 259, 371-2, outlines the tensions in the Anglo–American alliance in the Pacific when Mitchell became governor of Fiji in 1942. For Mitchell's view of Nimitz and the American commanders see RH Mss. Afr. r. 101, Mitchell's diary entry for 29 August 1944, the day before he received the cable from the Colonial Office offering him the governorship of Kenya.

2. CO 822/114/46523 (1944), 'Closer Union', minute by Dawe, 4 December 1944 for his unenthusiastic response to Mitchell and his proposals. For Margery Perham's view of Mitchell see her *East African Journey*, pp. 17, 42, 56; and her *Colonial Sequence*, vol. 1, pp. 12-33 for an account of his work in Tanganyika. A.H.M. Kirk-Greene, 'Margery Perham and Colonial Administration', pp. 122-43 provides a brief introduction to her career.

3. D.J. Morgan, *The Official History of Overseas Development*, vol. 1, pp. xiv-xvii, 23-34, 64-99, 185-239; and J.M. Lee, *Colonial Development and Good Government*, pp. 13-18, 41-53, 111-39, 172-88. See also J.M. Lee, 'Forward Thinking and War', pp. 64-79; and CO 852/588/19260 (Part 1) (1944), 'Planning of Economic and Social Development', Economic Advisory Committee questions to Oliver Stanley and memorandum by W.A. Lewis, 14 September 1944.

4. CO 533/536/38598 (1945-46), 'Kenya: Staff Position', and CO 533/537/38628 (1945), 'Grouping of Agricultural Departments', for a host of examples.

5. CO 533/557/38672 (1947-48), 'Memorandum from the Kenya African Union', Mitchell to Creech Jones, 11 February 1947; and CO 533/556/38664 (1946-47), 'Land Policy', Half Yearly Report on Soil Conservation in Fort Hall, June 1946, and T. Hughes Rice to A.B. Cohen, 3 August 1946; and P.E. Mitchell's published despatch, *Agricultural Policy in African Areas*, 1951.

6. CO 533/557/38672 (1947-48), 'Memorandum from the Kenya African Union', P.E. Mitchell to the Kenya African Union, March 1948; CO 533/543/38086/38 (1949), 'Kikuyu Petitions: Kikuyu Central Association', Mitchell to Creech Jones, 28 February 1949; CO 533/557/38678/1 (1947-48), 'African Land Settlement: Olenguruone', A.B. Cohen, 14 July 1947; CO 533/557/38678/1 (1949) 'African Land

The Character and Policies of Sir Philip Mitchell

Settlement: Olenguruone', I.D. Robertson, 28 November 1949; and P.E. Mitchell, *Agricultural Policy in African Areas, passim*. See also CO 533/537/38646 (1945), 'Proposals for the Reorganization of the Administration', A.B. Cohen, 10 August 1945.

7. KNA Secretariat 1/1/12, 'Report of the Joint Agricultural and Veterinary Services Sub-committee of the Development Committee', pp. 6–15; CO 852/662/19936/2 (1945–46), 'Soil Erosion: Kenya', N. Humphrey, 'The Relationship of Population to the Land in South Nyeri'; and H.E. Lambert and P. Wyn Harris, 'Memorandum on Policy in Regard to Land Tenure in the Native Lands of Kenya'; and Legislative Council Debates, Second Series, vol. xx, 1944–45, 3rd Session, 30 November 1945, speech by Cavendish-Bentinck, columns 328–330.

8. KNA Lab 9/97, 'Association of District Councils, 1941–53', conference 12–13 September 1944; Lab 9/10, 'Labour: Squatters in Forest Areas, 1944–50', Agricultural Production and Settlement Board to Chief Secretary, 17 March 1945; and Lab 9/316, 'Resident Labour: Naivasha Country Council, 1941–59', meeting 27 October 1945. For an African view see K.J. King and R.M. Wambaa, 'The Political Economy of the Rift Valley', pp. 201–8.

9. CO 533/537/38628 (1945), 'Grouping of Agricultural Departments'; and CO 533/536/38598 (1945–46), 'Kenya Staff Position', Mitchell to Creasy, 30 December 1944. This is also based upon conversations with Desmond O'Hagan, 24 April and 10–11 June 1981 in Nairobi; and T.H.R. Cashmore, 21 and 28 October 1982 in London.

10. G.H. Mungeam, *British Rule in Kenya*, pp. 208–73. See also R. Hyam, '*The Colonial Office Mind*', p. 47, which provides another parallel between Girouard and Mitchell: 'The need for a stronger governor in the Kenya trouble-spot was obvious; the new man must not be swayed by the settlers. The office thought it had found one who met all its requirements for grip and capacity, energy and pro-African enthusiasm – Sir Percy Girouard, who had upheld African interests well in Nigeria and shown aversion to military adventurers and swashbucklers. His appointment proved to be a colossal miscalculation. It was a major turning-point in the wayward evolution of Kenya, enabling the settlers to entrench themselves in a way far removed from official intention.' This was to be equally true of Mitchell.

11. Interviews in Nairobi with M.H. Cowie, 8 July 1981; H. Kennaway, 4 September 1979; and Clive Salter, 11 March 1981. See also RH Mss. Brit.Emp. s. 390, Box 3, File 4, Item 3, ff. 32–9, C.E.V. Buxton's memoranda on the Emergency. These are undated, but internal evidence suggests that they were probably written in February or March 1953. Interview in Ferndown, Dorset, with C.O. Oates, 20 June 1983.

12. CO 533/536/38598 (1945–46), 'Kenya: Staff Position', Mitchell to G. Creasy, 30 December 1944; and CO 533/537/38628 (1945), 'Grouping of Agricultural Departments'. C.O. Oates, who was acting deputy director of agriculture in 1944, recalled that the agricultural department lost more than half its manpower during the war and had to recruit settlers as agricultural officers, (interview 20 June 1983).

13. CO 533/537/38628 (1945), 'Grouping of Agricultural Departments' Mitchell to Creasy, 18 February 1945.

14. CO 533/537/38646 (1945), 'Proposals for the Reorganisation of the Administration', Cohen's minute, 10 August 1945. For his earlier opposition to Mitchell's proposals see his note of 2 March 1945.

15. CO 533/537/38608 (1944–46), 'Land Policy: Memorandum by the Anti-Slavery and Aborigines Protection Society', letter to Stanley, 5 May 1944. See also S. and K. Aaronovitch, *Crisis in Kenya*, p. 74.

16. CO 533/534/38313 (1946), 'Alienation of Crown Land outside Townships', Tempany's minute, 27 July 1946.

17. R.M. Breen's unpublished thesis, 'The Politics of Land', pp. 81–91.

18. C.G. Rosberg and J. Nottingham, *The Myth of Mau Mau*, pp.153–5, 223–5; and B.A. Ogot, 'Politics, Culture and Music in Central Kenya', pp. 277–86. See also Maina wa

57

Kinyatti's controversial collection of Mau Mau *nyimbo* (hymns), *Thunder from the Mountains*, pp. 14–46, for various songs lamenting the lost lands.

Harold Macmillan's warnings of a peasant revolt if the Kikuyu were not given more land are in CO 967/57/46709 (1942), 'Sir Arthur Dawe's Memorandum on a Federal Solution for East Africa and Mr Harold Macmillan's Counter-Proposals', dated 15 August 1942.

19. CO 822/114/46523 (1946), 'Closer Union', Vincent's opening speech at the Electors' Union Conference, 24 January 1946; and Mitchell to Creech Jones, 11 May 1946.

20. C.G. Rosberg and J. Nottingham, *The Myth of Mau Mau*, pp. 223–5; and B.A. Ogot, 'Politics, Culture and Music in Central Kenya', pp. 227–82. See also CO 533/534/38232 (1945), 'European Settlement Scheme', Mitchell to George Hall, 11 September 1945.

21. *ibid*, Mitchell to Creasy, 30 May 1945. See also CO 533/536/38557 (1945), 'Development and Welfare Schemes', Sessional Paper no. 2 of 1945, Interim Report on Development, 4 June 1945; and CO 533/553/38557/8 (1947–48), 'General Aspects of the Agrarian Situation in Kenya', Despatch 44 of 1946 to Hall, 17 April 1946. The constitutionalist leaders of the Kenya African Union, Gichuru and Mathu, also initially accepted this view: see CO 533/537/38672 (1946), 'Memorandum by the Kenya African Union', forwarded by the Secretariat, 17 August 1946.

22. CO 533/534/38232 (Part II) (1945), 'Land Use and Settlement in Kenya', Creech Jones's comments, 26 September 1945.

23. CO 533/558/38690 (1947), 'Fabian Society', Creech Jones to Hinden, 22 May 1947; and CO 533/557/38678 (1948–49), 'African Land Settlement', Creech Jones to Hinden, 16 August 1949.

24. Mitchell considered that a confrontation with the settlers would be politically and economically disastrous: CO 533/558/38678/2 (1949), 'African Land Settlement-Kamba', Mitchell to Cohen, 7 September 1949. See C.G. Rosberg and J. Nottingham, *The Myth of Mau Mau*, pp. 198–203, for their assessment of Mitchell's multiracialism.

25. RH Mss Afr. r. 101, Mitchell's diary, 1 November 1944; P.E. Mitchell, *African Afterthoughts*, p. 211; and R.A. Frost, 'Sir Philip Mitchell', pp. 535–53, and his book, *Race against Time*, pp. 45–64. For Mitchell's optimistic hopes see CO 533/537/38628 (1945), 'Grouping of Agricultural Departments', Mitchell to Stanley, 9 March 1945.

26. CO 533/534/38232 (1945), 'European Settlement Scheme', Mitchell to Stanley, 19 March 1945. By 1948 non-African direct taxation was producing 18 per cent of Kenya's government revenue, compared to only 7 per cent from African hut and poll tax. Twenty years earlier these proportions had been reversed with 2 per cent from non-African and 31 per cent from African sources; see D.A. Low and A. Smith, *History of East Africa*, vol. 3, pp. 603–4.

27. Mitchell had served briefly in July 1914, in the area which was at the centre of the Chilembwe rising the following year, and had been confronted with a serious famine. See P.E. Mitchell, *African Afterthoughts*, pp. 27, 248–50. G.A. Shepperson and T. Price, *Independent African*, provide a definitive account.

28. CO 533/540/38032 (1949), 'Legislative Council', Mitchell to Creech Jones, 11 December 1948; CO 533/543/38086/5 (1945–57), 'Kikuyu Petitions and Memorials', Mitchell to Gater, November 1946; CO 533/543/38086/38 (1949), 'Kikuyu Central Association', Mitchell to Creech Jones, 28 February 1949; and CO 533/545/38091/10 (1944–47), 'Labour Registration and Identification', Rennie to Creech Jones, 11 May 1947.

29. CO 533/549/38232/15 (1946–47), 'European Settlement: Squatters', Mitchell to Creech Jones, 14 April 1947.

30. KNA MAA 7/491, 'Administration Policy: Urban Areas Nairobi, 1945–47'; MAA 8/22, 'Municipal African Affairs Officer: Correspondence, 1947–50'; and CO 533/558/38715 (1948), 'Municipal African Affairs Annual Report', reveal all too

clearly the Administration's ignorance of urban Africa. KNA Lab 9/1775, 'Survey of African Housing in Mombasa, 1946-47'; and Lab 9/1751, 'African Housing: General', provide grim evidence of the appalling housing conditions in the African locations of Mombasa and Nairobi. For details of the cost of living for urban Africans see the evidence in Lab 9/1841, 'Trade Disputes Tribunal, 1947'.

31. KNA MAA 7/14, 'Fort Hall African Merchants' Association, 1950'; C&I 6/782, 'Trading by Africans, 1946-50'; and Ag 4/77, 'Wattle Cooperative Societies, 1947-51'. For the administration's attitude to African commercial farming, see CO 852/662/19936/2 (1945-46), 'Soil Erosion: Kenya', N. Humphrey's report on South Nyeri, pp. 19-20; and KNA MAA 6/13 and 14, 'Committee on Agricultural Credit for Africans, 1949-50'.

32. CO 533/543/38086/5 (1945-47), 'Kikuyu Petitions', Mitchell to Gater, November 1946, and to Creech Jones 20 January 1947; CO 533/545/38091/10 (1944-47), 'Labour: Registration and Identification', Rennie to Creech Jones, 11 May 1947; CO 533/543/38086/38 (1949), 'Kikuyu Central Association Petitions and Kikuyu Grievances', Mitchell to Creech Jones, 28 February 1949; CO 537/3588/38696 (1947-48), 'Activities of Mathu', shows the government's increasing suspicion of Mathu and the Kenya African Union following Kenyatta's return in September 1946.

33. CO 537/3588/38696 (1947-48), 'Activities of Mathu'; and J. Roelker, *Mathu of Kenya*, pp. 89-106.

34. KNA MAA 8/8, 'Intelligence Reports: Confidential Information', C.M. Johnston to Provincial Commissioner, Central, 18 May 1947; and Director of Intelligence to the Chief Native Commissioner about Mathu's contacts with Kenyatta, 7 August 1947.

35. The Executive Council consisted of seven ex-officio members, including Cavendish-Bentinck as member for Agriculture and Natural Resources and Sir Charles Mortimer as member for Health and Local Government; three Europeans nominated 'unofficials' including the missionary, Archdeacon L.J. Beecher, who was appointed to represent African interests, and A.B. Patel, the senior Asian Legislative Councillor. In 1952 Mathu was finally appointed the first African member of the Executive Council, although the first African to be appointed a minister was B.A. Ohanga in 1954. See G. Bennett, *Kenya*, p. 137; and D.A. Low and A. Smith (eds), *History of East Africa*, vol. 3, pp. 558-9 for a brief outline of the evolution of the Kenya Legislative and Executive Councils.

36. CO 533/534/3823A (Part 1) (1945), 'European Settlement Scheme', Mitchell to Stanley 19 March 1945.

37. CO 533/553/38557/8 (1947-48), 'General Aspects of the Agrarian Situation in Kenya', despatch no. 44 of 1946, Mitchell to Hall, 17 April 1946.

38. CO 533/534/38232 (Part II) (1945), 'Land Use and Settlement in Kenya', draft despatch prepared by Cohen, February 1946, to Anti-Slavery and Aboriginal Protection Society.

39. C. Leys, *Underdevelopment in Kenya*, pp. 44-5, 119-21.

40. N. Swainson, *The Development of Corporate Capitalism in Kenya*, pp. 116-24, 130-69. See also KNA C&I 6/331, 'East African Industrial Council, 1942-60'; C&I 6/418, 'Kenya Canners Ltd., 1948-51'; C&I 6/457, 'British Standard Portland Cement Co. Ltd., Bamburi, 1951-56'; C&I 6/333, 'Agenda and Papers: East African Industrial Council, 1948-53'; C&I 6/332, 'East African Industrial Council, 1942-49'; C&I 6/638, 'Secondary Industries: Committee to Advise on Industrial Siting, 1949-50'; C&I 6/683, 'Secondary Industries: Fiscal Policy Committee on Drawbacks of Custom Duty, 1949-50'; and C&I 6/374, 'Secondary Industries: Allocation of Industrial Plots, 1946-49', for various disputes over protection, siting and government guarantees.

41. CO 537/1233/13012/24 (1945-46), 'Defence East Africa: Mombasa as a Major Port and Base', Bevin to G. Hall 21 January 1946; CO 537/1883/94023/3 (1946), 'Defence of East Africa: Construction of a Base', East Africa as a Base (501 Mission) 26 November 1946; CO 537/4711 (1948-49), 'African Conference: Address by

Montgomery'. Three files of the East African High Command also contain interesting information, WO 276/251 'Visit C.I.G.S.: Defence Policy Discussions'; WO 276/9, 'East African Command: Defence Services Sub-committee'; and WO 276/10, 'East African Governors' Conference, 1947'. See also CO 968/94/6/13023/24 (1945), 'Defence Middle East: Imperial Security and Location of British Troops', Cabinet Paper, Minister Resident in the Middle East, 2 July 1945.

42. CO 537/1883/94023/3 (1946), 'Defence of East Africa: Construction of a Base'. The expenditure was to be spread over six years. The War Office was to provide £64 million; the RAF £22 million; the Admiralty £20 million; and the three mainland colonial governments a total of £24 million.

43. RH Mss. Afr. r. 101, Mitchell's diary, 23 November to 5 December 1944; and CO 822/114/46523 (1944), 'Closer Union', minutes of Mitchell's meeting with Stanley, Gater, Devonshire and Creasy, Seel and Edmonds on 29 November 1944; and Dawe's minute on Constitutional Questions in East Africa.

44. *ibid*, and CO 822/114/46523 (1945), 'Closer Union', Memorandum from East African Governors' Conference, 14 February 1945; and Mitchell to Stanley, 15 March 1945. For Mitchell's private commitment to multiracialism see CO 533/536/38599/4 (1945 and 1946), 'Education: Admission of Mixed Blood Children to European Schools'.

45. CO 822/114/46523 (1944), 'Closer Union', minute of meeting in Colonial Office with Mitchell on 28 November 1944; and CO 822/114/46523 (1945), 'Closer Union', Mitchell to Creasy 7 September 1945; and meeting with Creech Jones 24–25 October 1945.

46. CO 822/114/46523 (1945), 'Closer Union', Mitchell to George Hall, 6 September 1945; and meeting with Creech Jones, 24–25 October 1945. See also Vincent to Gater 17 October 1945, for Kenya settler opinion.

47. CO 822/114/46523 (Part I) (1946), Rennie to Gater, 6 February 1946, enclosing Vincent's speech at the opening of the Electors' Union Conference on 24 January 1946. For the Labour Party's opposition to Closer Union during the war, see CO 822/114/46523 (1944), 'Closer Union', Note on the Position as at 1 March 1944; Edmonds's memorandum of 4 April 1944; and Stanley to Moore 12 April 1944. Contrast these with Creech Jones's minute of 4 October 1945 in CO 822/114/46523 (1945).

48. RH Mss. Afr. r. 101, Mitchell's diary 2 December 1945, and 9 to 14 December 1945, for the governor's physical exhaustion and eventual collapse. The White Paper on Closer Union was published on 12 December. See CO 822/121/46523 (1947), 'Closer Union', Mitchell to Creech Jones, 18 April 1947, for an example of Rennie's lack of subtlety as a politician.

49. CO 822/114/46523 (1946), 'Closer Union', Rennie to Hall, 6 March 1946.

50. *ibid*. Cohen to Gater, 10 September 1946, about the meeting with the three mainland governors at Dar-es-Salaam on 11 August 1946, and with the Kenyan Secretariat on 22 August, to discuss 'The Necessity for the Early Establishment of Constitutional Backing for East African Inter-Territorial Machinery'.

51. CO 822/121/46523 (1947), 'Closer Union', especially M.J. Davies to the India Office, 19 May 1947; and Cohen's note to the Indian government in June 1947. A more orthodox interpretation of the controversy can be found in N.J. Westcott, 'Closer Union and the Future of East Africa', pp. 83–4.

52. CO 822/114/46523 (1946), 'Closer Union', Cohen to Gater, 10 September 1946 for his views on the public reaction to the proposed composition of the Central Assembly; and CO 822/121/46523 (1947), 'Closer Union', C.D.W. Anderson, proprietor of the *East African Standard* to Cohen, 10 June 1947.

53. CO 822/114/46523 (1946), 'Closer Union', Creech Jones's minute, 20 September 1946.

54. CO 822/121/46523 (1947), 'Closer Union', Cohen's memorandum, June 1947.

55. Mbiyu Koinange was becoming increasingly critical of the Labour government; see

The Character and Policies of Sir Philip Mitchell

CO 533/547/38132/465, 'Visit of Mr Koinange to the United Kingdom', especially Koinange to Creech Jones, 24 June 1947.

56. RH Mss, Afr. r. 101, Mitchell's diary, 20 July to 22 August 1946 and CO 822/114/46523 (1946), 'Closer Union', especially European Elected Members' meeting with Creech Jones in August 1946; and Cohen's long report to Gater of 10 September 1946. Favourable appraisals of Cohen are R.E. Robinson, 'Sir Andrew Cohen', pp. 353–63; and his 'Andrew Cohen and the Transfer of Power in Tropical Africa'. See also R.E. Robinson, 'The Journal and the Transfer of Power', pp. 255–8 and A.B. Cohen's own *British Policy in Changing Africa*. Unfortunately this says nothing about his visit to East Africa in 1946, but pp. 51–3 provide some insights into its effect on his thinking.

57. CO 822/114/46523 (1946) 'Closer Union', and CO 822/121/46523 (1947), 'Closer Union', provide evidence for this gradual 'mellowing' of Creech Jones and Cohen towards the Kenyan settlers. It is apparent, of course, that the Colonial Office was giving something away to assuage the fears of the Europeans in Kenya in 'Colonial 210'. It should, however, be emphasised that this was not, as has hitherto been believed, the principle of equal racial representation on the Central Assembly. '210' instead attempted to reassure the Kenyan settlers by reducing the powers of the central bureaucracy in the High Commission, and by granting a veto on the expansion and funding of the High Commission to the territorial Legislative Councils, where, of course, in Kenya there was a strong settler lobby.

58. CO 533/558/38690 (1947), 'Correspondence with Fabian Society', Creech Jones to Hinden 22 May 1947; and CO 533/556/38664/2 (1947), 'Land Policy: Memorandum by the Labour Party on Land Utilization and Settlement'. These all show how far Creech Jones's opinions had been changed by his journey to East Africa. This had been his first visit to Kenya, and only his second to Africa. He was also slowly being 'captured' by the Colonial Office.

59. R.D. Pearce, *The Turning Point in Africa*, pp. 177–9, for a brief discussion of Mitchell's attempt to persuade the Colonial Office that their West Africa strategy would fail in the settler colonies. See also CO 533/534/38232 (1945), 'Land Use and Settlement in Kenya', Mitchell to Stanley, 19 March 1945, for an early defence of the Kenyan settlers.

See also RH Mss. Afr. r. 101, Mitchell's diary, 29 October to 14 November 1947, for his account of the African Governors' Conference in London, especially the entry for 10 November, where he recorded: 'We conferred all day, largely on dry theoretical ideas of Colonial self-government, totally divorced from the realities of the present day. The C.D. has got itself into a sort of mystic enchantment and sees visions of grateful, independent Utopias beaming at them from all round the world, as if there was – yet – any reason to suppose that any African can be cashier of a village council for three weeks without stealing the cash. It is uphill work, but we bludgeoned them pretty severely from both sides, although the West Africans, other than Milverton, are a silent lot. There is really no understanding whatever of contemporary realities in the C.O. – Creech blathered a good deal.'

60. CO 533/549/38232/15 (1946–47), 'European Settlement: Squatters', J.H. Martin's report, 'The Problem of the Squatter: Economic Survey of Resident Labour in Kenya', 24 February 1947.

61. N. Swainson, *The Development of Corporate Capitalism in Kenya*, pp. 173–82; and J.M. Lonsdale's unpublished paper, 'The Growth and Transformation of the Colonial State in Kenya', pp. 6–14.

62. F.D. Corfield, *The Origins and Growth of Mau Mau*, pp. 18 and 51.

63. RH Mss. Brit.Emp. s. 390, Box 3, File 4, Item 3, ff. 1–4, C.E.V. Buxton to Mitchell 15 August 1948; and Mss. Afr. s. 596, 'European Elected Members' Organisation', File 38 (A)/1, 'Mau Mau 1947–55', Executive Committee of the Electors' Union, 26 October 1946; and memorandum by Major C.E.V. Buxton on Kikuyu Associations,

February 1947, and Kendall Ward, 'The Rise of Mau Mau: European Warnings', 17 March 1953.

64. F.D. Corfield, *The Origins and Growth of Mau Mau*, p. 52.

65. N.S. Carey Jones, *The Anatomy of Uhuru*, p. 84.

66. See Chapters 4 and 6 *infra*.

67. CO 533/543/38086/5 (1945–47), 'Kikuyu Petitions', Mitchell to Gater, November 1946; CO 533/543/38086/38 (1948), 'Kikuyu Petitions: Kikuyu Central Association', Rankine to Creech Jones, 28 December 1948; CO 533/543/38086/38 (1949), 'Kikuyu Petitions: Kikuyu Central Association', Mitchell to Creech Jones, 28 February 1949; and CO 533/557/38672 (1947–48), 'Memorandum from Kenya African Union', Mitchell to Creech Jones, 11 February 1947.

68. P.E. Mitchell's published despatch, 'Agricultural Policy in African Areas' (1951); and CO 533/5/38678, 'African Soil Improvements, 1948–50'.

69. Interviews with Sir Michael Blundell, Noel Kennaway, Clive Salter and Mervyn Cowie, and N. Farson, *Last Chance in Africa*, p. 45.

70. Sir Michael Blundell and Mervyn Cowie. See also RH Mss. Afr. r. 101, Mitchell's diary for regular references to exhaustion and ill health. KNA CS 2/5/6, 'Speeches Miscellaneous by Governor, 1940–49'; CS 2/5/37, 'Addresses by Governor Mitchell, 1947–48'; and RH 4/346, 'Governor Mitchell's Speeches, 1948–52' show that Mitchell made most of his speeches to Europeans in Nairobi and rarely ventured into the African reserves. CS 2/5/7, 'Addresses by the Governor in Central Province, 1940–49' contains only one entry for the Mitchell era, when the governor visited Meru in May 1949. It should, however, be pointed out that Mitchell continued to go fishing in the trout streams of the Aberdares and Mount Kenya.

71. Interviews with Noel Kennaway and Desmond O'Hagan.

72. For a more sympathetic portrait see N. Farson, *Last Chance in Africa*, pp. 18–19, 28–35, 47–52, which Mitchell had persuaded him to write. RH Mss. Afr. r. 101, Mitchell's diary, 1 September 1947, contains Mitchell's account of a meeting to arrange Farson's trip to Kenya later that year.

73. RH Mss. Afr. s. 596, 'European Elected Members' Organisation' File 38(A)/1, Kendall Ward, 'Mau Mau, 1947–55'; Mss. Brit.Emp. s. 390, Box 3, File 4, Item 3, ff. 1–4, Buxton to Mitchell, 15 August 1948; and two memoranda about the Emergency by Buxton, ff. 32–9. See also (cont.) KNA DC/FH 1/30, 'Fort Hall Annual Report, 1951', pp. 1–2, 14; MAA 8/102 'Intelligence and Security: Press Cuttings, 1948–50'; MAA 8/106, 'Intelligence and Security: Mumenyereri, 1947–50'; MAA 8/109, 'Intelligence and Security: Daily Chronicle, 1947–49'; and MAA 8/68, 'Intelligence: Chief Waruhiu, 1948–1952' for a series of warnings from the Special Branch and settlers about the deteriorating position in the reserves and for militant African attacks on the colonial régime.

Four

The Problems of Kikuyu Agriculture

In the 1930s, the Kenyan government became concerned by reports of serious land degradation in the reserves. The agricultural department had begun closely to follow the anti-erosion measures which were being devised in the United States and South Africa. In 1938, for instance, Colin Maher, the head of the recently established soil conservation unit in the department, was sent to America to study their techniques and South African experts were asked to advise on the worst affected areas, Ukambani and Baringo.[1]

During the depression and even more so during the war, however, regardless of its effects on soil fertility, Africans were encouraged to maximise production to bolster the finances of the colonial state and to supply the troops. Norman Humphrey's report on South Nyeri in 1944 and the arrival of Mitchell, who considered himself an expert on African agriculture, marked another shift in the Nairobi official mind as the Secretariat became alarmed once again about the situation in the reserves, especially in Machakos, where there were serious food shortages between 1942 and 1944. Humphrey's alarmist report reinforced the administration's opposition to African individualism and strengthened its commitment to defending a mythical, egalitarian 'Merrie Africa' against the encroachment of cash-crop cultivators and small traders who supported the Kenya African Union. This was a futile strategy which not only attempted to reverse a process of increasing differentiation, dating back at least to the late nineteenth century, but also failed to recognise that the second colonial occupation was encouraging individualism and social differentiation. The administration and initially the agricultural department, however, after the war ignored these African realities and attempted to bolster communal authority by reviving the traditional power of the *Muhirig'a* elders among the Kikuyu, and by strengthening the *Njuri Ncheke* in Meru. These supposedly traditional institutions, it was planned, would supervise the post-war agricultural campaign in the reserves.[2]

Official perceptions of crisis before 1945

In the late 1930s, several reports warned the Kenyan authorities that the African reserves faced a serious ecological crisis. The most obvious damage could be seen in Ukambani and Baringo, but the problem was not confined to the semi-arid pastoral reserves. The situation was even more serious in the densely-populated Kikuyu districts where once fertile land was being destroyed by constant cultivation and grazing following the abandonment, through population pressure, of shifting cultivation. Already the population density in the central zone between 4,500 and 6,000 feet was over 500 to the square mile.[3]

For five months every year, from March to May during the long rains, and again during the short rains in November and December, torrential downpours cascaded down the steep ridges and washed away the precious topsoil into the overflowing rivers. Streams and rivers became dark brown as the floods swept the soil downstream. The agricultural department warned that resolute action was immediately required to stem the loss or the Kikuyu reserves would soon be destitute. These reports convinced the Secretariat that the ecological crisis of the Kikuyu reserves was the most crucial issue facing the Kenyan government.

When the depression began to recede in the late 1930s, the government became increasingly concerned about land degradation in the pastoral reserves. Colin Maher prepared a series of reports on Baringo, Machakos and East and West Pokot, which emphasised the rapid growth of erosion and ecological collapse. In Machakos and the agricultural reserves, pasture land was being reduced, destroying the balance between arable and pastoral elements in the economy, as population growth and the demand for cash crops increased pressure on the commonage. But while arable land expanded at the expense of the pastoral commonage, the number of cattle using the commonage for grazing also expanded dramatically. This pressure on the various sectors of the rural economy exacerbated the ecological problems in the more arid reserves.[4] In 1929, the Hall Agricultural Commission had already recognised that erosion in Machakos was extremely serious. A decade later Maher and Barnes estimated that between 37 and 75 per cent of the land in Machakos needed to be closed to grazing and, in 1938, the South African agriculturalist, Professor I.B. Pole-Evans had reported that: 'The reserve as shown to me was a most distressing sight. It was a shambles . . . most of the topsoil had gone and the subsoil was rapidly following suit. Sheet erosion and gully erosion were eating the land away in almost every direction. The grass cover had almost entirely disappeared.'[5] Machakos attracted the most concern because of its large population. The spectre of a major famine in the pastoral reserves haunted the government in Nairobi, following the serious food shortages which had occurred in the pastoral reserves in the early 1930s.

The Problems of Kikuyu Agriculture

After the dislocation during the conquest and the First World War, the population of Kenya had grown rapidly after the early 1920s. By the late 1930s, the Kenyan government was convinced that the situation in Kikuyuland and in certain pastoral areas had reached crisis proportions. The first attempts to combat the problem were ill advised, beginning with the Machakos destocking campaign in 1938. Against the advice of the administration, compulsory culling was introduced and the stock was disposed of at the nearby Liebigs processing factory at Athi River. This merely united African opposition and undermined the reputation of the local administration and the Kamba chiefs. A few years earlier, in Baringo, the agricultural department's grass-planting scheme had proved equally ineffective because of lack of investment and supervision during the depression.[6]

These measures to prevent erosion, however, clashed with the government's need during the depression to encourage African production (regardless of the ecological effects on the reserves or on African communalism) to offset the declining fiscal returns from the settler sector. This process was carried further during the war. Kikuyu wattle and vegetable growers and Abaluhya maize cultivators prospered; the war was not a period of increasing African disillusionment with colonial rule, despite the grumblings about import shortages and discriminatory crop prices. Funds were available for the larger producers to acquire new land at the expense of the marginal lineages and poor peasants, who lacked the resources to increase commodity production.[7]

The quantitative evidence for increased African production is less clear than for the settlers. The district export figures are haphazard and African production fluctuated considerably with the weather. But official figures unduly exaggerate the variations. African cultivators did not attempt to compete with the settlers but restructured the local terms of trade to their own advantage by producing not for the settler-controlled marketing boards but for the black market where prices were far above those offered by the Maize Control. The Kikuyu, for example, during the droughts of 1942–45, switched their sales from official channels to the more remunerative black market in Ukambani. District Commissioners lamented that only a fraction of Kikuyu production appeared at the marketing boards' inspection centres. In Murang'a only 1,400 out of an estimated 30,000 surplus bags of maize were sold to the Government Control.[8]

Black market goods from South Nyeri followed three main routes: into Murang'a via Karatina and then into Ukambani; through the Aberdares forest to Nanyuki; and to Rumuruti and Thomson's Falls. These were pre-colonial trade routes. The black market was in fact organised on a similar basis to local inter-tribal trade in the late nineteenth century, which continued underground throughout the colonial era. The field administration had only come near to controlling this hidden trade network in the late 1920s, but with the depression it had once again become an extremely important adjunct to the maintenance of the peasant option against settler pressure. It allowed African accumulators to circumvent the restrictions imposed on them by their settler rivals and to consolidate their own position in the reserves. Even when the rains failed, as in May 1944, and Murang'a needed to import maize, large quantities were still exported at high prices to Machakos, while cheap imports were bought from Embu and Nyeri. As the District Commissioner observed: 'Viewed by the cold light of business morals the Kikuyu had brought off a notable and meritorious coup – he had sold in the highest and bought in the lowest market.'[9] When the movement of maize was banned in 1945, large quantities were transported by lorry at night to Ukambani. These shipments far outnumbered the mere 1,169 bags which were sold to the Maize Control for £4,000. In Kambu, supposedly a grain deficit area, the assistant agricultural officer complained in 1947 that 'the urban population are living entirely on Kiambu maize and buying but little of their rationed mixed meal and the farm labour forces augment their rations as they like. It is a traffic that is impossible to stop owing to our network of roads'.[10] Every day Kikuyu women carried their loads into the African locations of Nairobi where they fetched higher prices than if sold to the government. In August 1945, an estimated 700 to 1,000 bags of charcoal a day were transported into the capital. These exports were so remunerative that wattle in southern Kiambu was rarely permitted to reach maturity but was chopped down to sell as charcoal and firewood in Nairobi, Thika and Ruiru. Nairobi Africans depended on the black market for their supplies and, throughout the war, African traders thrived, accumulating funds to invest in new shops or lorries when these became available. The District Commissioner in Murang'a was convinced that greater changes had occurred in Kikuyuland during the war than ever before.[11]

The failure of the maize harvest in 1942, and the resulting famine in marginal Ukambani, focussed government attention once more on the agricultural problems of the reserves. The famine strengthened the opponents of African production and seemed to demonstrate the need to transform agricultural practices in the reserves. During the last two years of the war, new plans were devised for immediate application as soon as equipment and supervisors could be obtained. Meanwhile a few ameliorative measures were undertaken. During 1943–44, 23,000 acres were terraced in Central Province and 26,000 closed to grazing; but these were temporary palliatives. The agricultural department warned that more drastic action was required to prevent erosion. The 1944 Soil Conservation report, for example, warned that at the current rate of progress it would take 200 years to protect the province. Economic collapse was inevitable unless peasant incomes were increased and investment in agriculture facilitated. Land alienation, the demarcation of fixed Kikuyu reserves (in the 1920s) and population growth, had all destroyed the traditional system of shifting cultivation. Now the Kikuyu were unable to abandon their exhausted plots for virgin land; pressure on *shambas* was increasing; fallows were shorter and in the more heavily-populated areas were virtually nonexistent. Even when yields dropped because the soils were exhausted, the old plots were not abandoned; instead new areas on steep hillsides were opened for cultivation to fill the deficiencies created by the declining fertility of the main *shambas*. These slopes in the bracken zone were particularly susceptible to erosion. The problem was compounded by the fact that the land had to provide school fees, clothing and government taxes in the changing world of rural Africa.[12]

Medical evidence showed that Kikuyu health was deteriorating as the intake of animal protein declined. During the war, 90 per cent of recruits for the army had had to be rejected because they were suffering from malnutrition. The army's medical advisor, Dr T.F. Anderson, considered that much less milk and meat were being consumed than in 1900 and the calcium-rich traditional crops, *wimbe* and *njahi*, had become scarce and expensive. He reported, 'the loss of *wimbe* is a grave misfortune. It could have been offset only by the introduction of milk into the diet, but that has not occurred . . . As a result calcium deficiency is a fact'. The administration blamed the spread of individualism at the expense of communal values for the abandonment of these traditional crops for more easily cultivated and remunerative crops like maize and wattle, which were now the main sources of income for most Kikuyu families.[13]

Both maize and wattle had been introduced 20 years earlier by the colonial authorities and had been eagerly adopted because they were easy to grow.[14] But after 1945 the agriculturalists denounced them for exhausting the nitrogen content of the soils. Maize, it was belatedly discovered, was an unsuitable crop for most of Central Province, where uncertain rainfall guaranteed a good harvest in only one year in three. The agricultural department, therefore, attempted to restrict cultivation to the long rains, especially in Machakos and Kitui where the rainfall averaged less than 30 inches per annum, and strenuous efforts were made to popularise the traditional Kikuyu food crop, *wimbe*, whose once dominant place in African diets had been usurped by maize.[15] Yet, despite these endeavours, maize remained the staple food crop during both harvests and provided considerable income in Kikuyuland from black market sales to Ukambani. Although the rainfall in Machakos was unsuitable for maize, successive harvest failures merely ensured that even greater acreages were planted in a desperate attempt to ensure that at least some food would be harvested.[16] This desire for edible crops with a secure market value for the surplus had also resulted in the French bean replacing cow peas and *njahi* and English potatoes being grown instead of the more resilient sweet potato. The agricultural department bemoaned that 'once again an exportable crop has advanced at the expense of an older one, grown solely for food'. Despite attempts by the Local Native Councils to enforce compulsory planting of famine reserve crops such as cassava and yams, the acreages declined.[17]

The field administration blamed the emerging commercial cultivators and small traders rather than population growth and the collapse of shifting cultivation for the ecological crisis. Greed, it was suggested, and the spread of selfish individualism at the expense of the communal solidarities of pre-colonial Africa had undermined the harmonious balance between Africans and their land. Only by restoring the authority of the indigenous land authorities could the land-miners be checked and the people's long-term interests in the soil be protected.[18]

Sir Philip Mitchell shared this distaste for the proto-capitalists in the reserves, whom he denounced as exploiters of ordinary Africans. He too sought to restore 'the organic balances' of African society, although he recognised that there was an urgent need to transform agricultural practices. Shortly after his arrival, Mitchell had gone on a tour of Ukambani and had returned deeply perturbed. The eroded hillsides, failed crops and malnutrition had so disturbed the governor that he had proposed an agricultural 'D Day'. He informed Oliver Stanley, the Secretary of State, that Kenya faced serious problems because of the declining fertility of the land after continuous cultivation. The colony was 'heading for a really shocking disaster. Unless we get onto the job in a really large scale [way] with a determination and consistency, in ten years time there will be a million landless people'.[19] The governor castigated his predecessors for their failure to devise a coherent agricultural policy. Action seemed to have been left to the idiosyncracies of individual District Commissioners without any continuity or co-ordination. He complained, 'I can't think how they can have existed all these years without having thought out their land administration at all, and without any attempt at getting the Administration and the Departments to shoot at the same target.'[20] This was symptomatic of Mitchell's alarmist strategy to convince Whitehall that he was energetically tackling Kenya's problems. During this first year, he bombarded the Colonial Office with a barrage of proposals, warning that Kenya's stability could only be assured by resolute action to solve the problems created by peasant cultivation. He was confident that, as an expert on peasant agriculture, he could transform the situation.[21]

Norman Humphrey's proposals

The most influential agriculturalist in Kenya during the first years after the war was Norman Humphrey. His writings, which were typical of the gloomy pessimists, exerted a profound influence on the government. During 1944, Humphrey and Hughes Rice had studied South Nyeri in the north of Kikuyuland. They discovered that since the last detailed agricultural survey by Fazan in 1931, the population density had increased from 463 to 542 per square mile; average smallholdings had fallen from 8.09 to 6.71 acres; and Humphrey predicted that they would decline to 5.22 acres by 1955, when only half the land would be under crops. Mathira Division, the most densely-populated part of the district, already only just managed to grow enough maize to feed its population and there was no surplus for export. The area was seriously overstocked because grazing land was being used for cultivation. There would have been a serious food shortage but for the money earned from selling crops to the dried-vegetable factory at Karatina, and for the remittances from *askari* and migrant workers in Nairobi and the White Highlands, which amounted to £250,000 a year. If these conditions spread, the government would face social collapse in Kikuyuland.[22]

Humphrey's report reflected contemporary thinking about the low carrying capacity of Africa's soils. Investigations by agriculturalists in Northern Rhodesia, based on careful analyses of soil types and vegetation, had instilled this belief into agriculturalists throughout British Africa. Humphrey adopted their excessively strict criteria for assessing carrying capacity and consequently underestimated how many people could stay in Nyeri without exacerbating land degradation.[23]

He wanted to ensure that Africans enjoyed an adequate diet and a household income of not less than £20 per annum, compared to a mere 60 shillings. Humphrey calculated that this target income could only be generated on holdings over twelve acres, more than double the size of most existing *shambas*.[24] After 1948, Leslie Brown proved that household incomes could be raised to £100 per annum on smallholdings of between seven and ten acres by growing high-priced cash crops such as coffee and tea. Unfortunately, until peasant opposition became evident in 1947, the agricultural campaign was based on Humphrey's reports, which had failed to appreciate that the only way to tackle rural immiseration was to challenge the settlers' monopoly on the cultivation of the most remunerative crops. The Swynnerton Plan in the 1950s showed that Brown's scheme offered the only chance to restructure peasant agriculture without provoking serious opposition. Humphrey, however, accepted that only European farmers should grow tea and coffee and accepted the differentiated price structure for African-grown cereals. Thus, instead of encouraging the government to continue with its peasant production strategy of the 1930s, which had promoted commercial cultivation in the reserves, Humphrey proposed that many Africans should be moved to new settlement areas, which the government had neither the time, the land, the money, nor the manpower to develop. Nyeri, he argued, was incapable of providing a subsistence standard of living for its present population. According to his calculation, one in two families would have to move because the land could only accommodate 15,360 families compared to the existing 29,271. A mass exodus was required to rest the land and to restore soil fertility in order to avert social collapse.[25]

Humphrey's temporary solution to Nyeri's problems was to undertake a massive reafforestation programme – planting over 350,000 acres. This was to provide employment for those whose *shambas* were being left to regenerate for three years. A search was also to be conducted to find suitable settlement sites. Attention was, therefore, diverted from persuading the peasantry to adopt new agricultural methods and drought-resistant crops. The government hoped that some magical panacea would be discovered for the problems of erosion and African discontent. The Tana and Juba Valleys, Trans Mara and Makueni were all carefully investigated as suitable resettlement areas, but only Makueni was deemed appropriate, although several smaller schemes were also approved. The alternative strategy of attempting to educate the population to follow approved techniques of 'sound' land use was dismissed as too slow, since it was considered that immediate action was essential. Consequently the palliative anti-erosion measures were introduced without the understanding or support of the peasantry. This was a fatal error.[26]

The settlements proved equally unsuccessful; even the largest at Makueni had absorbed only 664 families, at a cost of £18,340, by the end of 1952. This was only a small fraction of the people who supposedly had to be moved from Machakos. It had also quickly become apparent that African peasants with limited capital were incapable of developing the semi-arid lands on which all the new settlements were situated. In Makueni, for example, each family needed 120 acres compared with the five-acre plots they had cultivated in their former locations. It would, therefore, have required 1,680,000 acres (2,625 square miles) – the equivalent of 30 per cent of the alienated White Highlands – to accommodate the surplus families from South Nyeri on similar marginal land in Laikipia. The best farming land in Kenya was already occupied; Kikuyuland and Nyanza were densely-populated African reserves; the only uninhabited areas had irregular rainfall and were totally unsuited to intensive peasant cultivation. All the potential resettlement sites were in areas with an average rainfall of less than 20 inches per annum and needed extensive irrigation. Their soils were unsuitable, with low organic matter, slightly acid in reaction and low in bases and phosphates. The natural vegetation was a thorn and scrub grassland with much bare soil exposed for sheet and gully erosion. The optimistic expectation that thousands of African families could be resettled outside the reserves or the White Highlands was a complete fallacy. Even where suitable land was available, such as in the Shimba Hills near the coast, the overcrowded peasant cultivators of nearby Teita obstinately refused to leave their homes.[27]

Humphrey's alarmist reports, however, had reinforced the widely-held view that erosion had reached crisis proportions. He had warned that 'unless radical reforms are introduced, the land and the people of South Nyeri face disaster within the next decade'. Immediate action was needed to ensure that new systems of land tenure and cutivation were adopted. Even compulsion, he acknowledged, might have to be used as a last resort, although he recognised that 'used by itself, its lessons will be grudgingly learnt, and it must lead to still more compulsion over an ever-widening field, until by sheer excess it breaks down in utter failure'.[28] Humphrey himself had perceived that if the agricultural campaign was to succeed, then the people must understand what the government was doing and why. But at the same time he emphasised that immediate action was required and had conceded that force might have to be used. Thus was the seed of disaster planted.

The paternalist administration decided that the most effective way to gain popular support was to work through the traditional African land authorities – the *Muhirig'a* elders in Kikuyuland, the *Liguru* among the Abaluhya, the *Utui* in Kamba and the *Njuri Ncheke* in Meru. Osborne, the enterprising District Commissioner in Murang'a during the last years of the war, had dramatically increased terracing and anti-erosion work by using the local *Muhirig'a*. During the first six months of 1945, only 377 miles of narrow-based terraces had been constructed, but with the help of the *Muhirig'a* this increased to 3,051 miles during the second half of the year. The administration considered that this remarkable change of attitude towards soil conservation had been achieved by reviving the precolonial land authorities, which had been suppressed but not destroyed by 50 years of British rule. The successes of Murang'a, it was believed, proved that the traditional elders still exerted considerable influence, despite the supposed growth of unrestrained individualism among the Kikuyu.[29]

Humphrey proposed giving full recognition to these indigenous authorities so that support could be mobilised for the terracing and agricultural betterment campaign. This plan was considered by H.E. Lambert, the government's advisor on African land tenure, and Percy Wyn Harris, who was then Provincial Commissioner for Central Province and was therefore responsible for Kikuyuland and Ukambani. Their 'Memorandum on Policy in Regard to Land Tenure in the Native

Lands of Kenya' largely accepted Humphrey's assessment of the problems facing the reserves and endorsed his fear of individualism and increasing differentiation.[30] They also agreed that the traditional communal controls over the land should be strengthened as the basis for post-war development. Wyn Harris and Lambert explained that the advantage of the 'untouched native system' was that it preserved a stable equilibrium between the interests of the community and the rights of the individual. British rule, they declared, had disturbed this balance, weighting the scales in favour of individualism which had helped destroy the traditional controls. These, they feared, would soon be completely destroyed and it would then be impossible to use indigenous institutions to protect the land. Wyn Harris and Lambert therefore recommended that every effort should be made to preserve 'the spiritual conception of community'. Chiefs and the Local Native Councils were no real substitute for accepted African authorities because they were foreign impositions and did not command popular respect. By relying upon such arms of government, the possibilities of mobilising popular support, which were still provided by the traditional authorities, might be irredeemably lost.

The prejudices of the field administration and the Secretariat against the African 'proto-capitalists' blinded them to the fact that the indigenous land authorities' remaining power would vanish as soon as they became associated with the government's terracing campaign; they would soon become identified as merely another government-controlled institution like the supposedly traditional Tribunal Elders. The administration failed to recognise that anyone who supported the second colonial occupation and greater interference in African society would lose African support. It also failed to understand that the *Muhirig'a* elders were as much involved in the race for more land and struggle for economic resources as the rest of the Kikuyu people. They were not neutral observers of the development of capitalist relations of production, committed to the preservation of an egalitarian Kikuyu communalism, but active participants in the growth of individualism, which the administration so condemned.[31]

The official mind and the myth of 'merrie Africa'

These recommendations, of course, strongly appealed to Mitchell, the indirect ruler, striking deep chords in his experience. In Tanganyika in the 1920s, he had been instrumental in uncovering and reviving Native Authorities, which were to provide the new framework for British rule. The proposals of the Kenya Secretariat also accorded with the thinking of the Colonial Office's advisory committe on African land tenure. Its chairman, the arch-mandarin Lord Hailey, a former governor of the Punjab and of the United Provinces who, after his retirement from the Indian Civil Service had become an expert on African administration and land tenure, also considered that the essential problem was 'how to ensure that the community retains the power to guard against the harmful consequences of the growth of individual rights in land, while at the same time not impeding the development of such rights, under proper control by the community, to the extent that they are an essential concomitant of economic or social progress'. [32] Consequently, requests from 'progressive' African farmers for loans were refused. Both the Kenyan government and the Colonial Office were convinced that any concession to the mounting pressure for individual rights would be against the communal interest and would be bound to end in the disaster of peasant indebtedness as in India. [33]

In his secret war-time study, *Native Administration and Political Development in British Tropical Africa*, Lord Hailey had warned that certain developments could already be discerned in 'native' land ownership which would create a serious problem for governments throughout the continent. He observed that quite apart from the question of land alienation to Europeans which had aroused opposition in Kenya and Northern Rhodesia, there were:

. . . problems of another character connected with the land, which, though they have not yet been a source of friction, remain as a potential cause of trouble for the future. They are those which relate to the legal definition of title in the lands occupied by natives and of the tenures under which they are held. The treatment of these questions will demand decisions of general policy affecting most of the African dependencies. If individual land rights are allowed to grow up in a form which involves a system under which the relations of landlord and tenant are regulated only by market competition, we may have to face all the social and political evils consequent on the existence of large bodies of rackrented tenants. If, again, no legal restraint is placed on the use of the land as a basis of credit, the African Colonies may in time see the growth of widespread agricultural indebtedness, such as now constitutes so grave a menace in many of our Eastern dependencies.

No one can fail to regret that the British administration did not at an earlier date foresee the necessity for providing against the development of these conditions in rural India. Their existence has not only been inimical to agricultural progress, but has proved a potent source of social division and one of the main causes of political unrest. Those provisions could have been made with relative ease at an early period of our administration, before rights based on European conceptions of law and novel to Indian practice, had assumed the character of vested interests. But to-day it is estimated that no less than twenty-five million persons classified as agricultural workers are landless, and agricultural indebtedness is estimated to amount to £675,000,000. [34]

Thus the lessons of India weighed heavily on the official mind, not only in Whitehall but throughout Africa. For the best of reasons the field administration throughout British Africa had imbibed the orthodoxies of contemporary anthropology with the ideology of indirect rule and had adopted its commitment to the preservation of what were believed to be traditional African communal values. Under the influence of Malinowski and Evans-Pritchard and the British anthropological tradition of structural-functionalism, during the 1930s and 1940s the Kenyan administration saw itself as the defender of the egalitarian values of pre-colonial 'Merrie Africa'. This myth was to prove very difficult to destroy. Thus, as government intervention in African societies penetrated to greater depths and became increasingly demanding during the second colonial occupation after the war, the provincial administration earnestly believed that the campaign was a final attempt to prevent the collapse of African communalism and the disintegration of the traditional ordering of rural society.[35]

Both the Secretariat and the provincial administration were trapped within this stereotype of African life. African towns were regarded as an anomaly, dangerously disruptive of the hierarchy of communal Africa. So entrenched was this belief that urban Africans were categorised as 'detribalised'; selfish individuals who had abandoned the communalism of rural life. The peripheral official mind, especially the field administration, was resolutely opposed to the idea that urban expansion might provide the best way to ease the population burden on the reserves.[36]

There were also certain practical difficulties as well as ideological prejudices. The administration's control over the African locations of Nairobi was weak, partly because responsibility was shared with the settler-controlled Municipal Council.[37] In addition, Nairobi's African population was already expanding faster than the government could supply new accommodation or employment. When the first official census was taken in 1948, it was discovered that the population had increased nearly eightfold in the previous 25 years. Moreover, this rapid urban expansion had not noticeably eased the problems of rural overcrowding in the reserves. The southern locations of Kiambu, around Dagoretti, had indeed become suburbs of the capital. While Nairobi's workforce remained unskilled, wages were too low for them to bring their families to live in the capital. Wives and children were, therefore, left in the reserves to cultivate as best they could their small *shambas* without the advantages of male labour. Margaret Hay and Mike Cowen have shown that in Kowe in Central Nyanza and in South Nyeri, the families of migrant labourers had fallen behind in the rural scramble for more land and new resources, and had been forced to sell land and to seek work on the plots of their more prosperous neighbours. As rural differentiation increased, it was usually the families of low-paid migrant workers who formed the emerging 'class' of poor peasants with less than three acres of land. Nairobi and the smaller towns did not provide any panacea for the problems of the reserves while urban wages remained at subsistence levels.[38]

The Problems of Kikuyu Agriculture

However, the Kenyan government's plans to transform African agriculture and to inculcate improved farming techniques in order to raise peasant standards of living were also flawed because the administration's commitment to change African society was halfhearted. Agricultural reform required a traumatic transition. To have ensured its success, the administration would have had to abandon its alliance with the chiefs and forge a new arrangement with the emerging 'class' of rich peasants and traders, who resented the privileged position the chiefs and their supporters enjoyed with preferential access to the resources of the Local Native Councils and government patronage. In the past, the more radical of these 'outsiders' had supported the now banned Kikuyu Central Association. Indeed, by the act of opposing the chiefs, they had identified themselves to the administration as untrustworthy 'agitators'.[39] Most District Commissioners, particularly in Kikuyuland where the divisions between the chiefs and the politicians had been acute since the days of Thuku's Young Kikuyu Association in the early 1920s, found it impossible to reconcile themselves to Whitehall's plans to incorporate the more moderate political 'outsiders'. Aspiring businessmen, like Andrew Ng'ang'a and James Beauttah in Murang'a, were often prominent leaders of the local Kikuyu Central Association and, therefore, stood condemned by their past indiscretions and could not be supported in preference to loyal chiefs who had performed such stalwart service.[40] Indeed, the administration was convinced that such men and their supporters, who were constantly pestering the district headquarters for new licences or seeking new business opportunities, were the people who were responsible for the increasing differentiation in the reserves, which was undermining Africa's egalitarian communalism. Young men, it was lamented, no longer showed respect for the elders, chiefs, or indeed the government.[41]

Only romantically inclined Englishmen, escaping from the pressures of life in industrial Britain, could have failed to realise that this idealised image of African communalism was a delusion and have attempted to foist upon the Kikuyu a system of land law that bore little resemblance to their traditions.[42] All levels of the peripheral official mind – District Commissioners, the Secretariat, even initially, the agricultural department – failed to perceive that the peasantry in Central Province had always been intensely independent, jealous of its neighbours and mindful of the chance to prosper at their expense. In particular, the administration failed to recognise that the second colonial occupation primarily benefited those who were closely associated with the colonial power structure, the chiefs and their supporters; while the 'outsiders' became increasingly frustrated at their exclusion. The prejudices of the field administration became more explicit when it had more resources with which to reward the collaborators than during the inter-war era.

75

Petty traders and commercial cultivators were denounced as disruptive 'agitators', insidiously undermining the fabric of peasant life. Thus, the supporters of the banned Kikuyu Central Association and the more cautious Kenya African Union were further alienated. The administration and the agricultural department also failed to recognise that their reliance on the chiefs and the Mihiriga elders to mobilise communal labour for the agricultural betterment campaign was antagonising the peasantry. There was a contradiction in government policy. Although the administration wanted to strengthen communalism, the second colonial occupation was also designed to transform African agriculture, the basis of rural life. As we have seen, Humphrey even wanted to remove thousands of people from the reserves. Such social engineering inevitably had a profound effect on ordinary Africans and seriously disrupted their lives.[43]

The chiefs and elders seized the new resources, which the government provided after the war, to enhance their own economic power. Increased funds became available; remunerative cash crops were supplied for them to grow and technical staff provided to advise on how to make the most of these new opportunities. Despite the administration's intentions, therefore, the second colonial occupation increased the disparities between the favoured few and the African masses. Whatever the government may have believed it was doing, the chiefs were active participants in the contest for resources in the reserves. During the 1930s, they had effectively discredited the Kikuyu Central Association and monopolised the political weapon of controlled access to the district administration to serve their own interests. After the war, they attempted to destroy the new challenge to their authority posed by the Kenya African Union and to undermine the economic independence of their rivals, the traders and commercial farmers, who supported the new movement. This attempt to intimidate the opposition backfired as the exactions of the second colonial occupation drove the peasantry into the arms of the political activists.[44] The field administration, however, remained oblivious of this conflict. The chiefs had only too successfully mesmerised it into believing that the aspiring 'men in trousers' were undermining the stability of the colonial state, when, in fact, most of them in the first years after the war desired to be co-opted. As events were to prove, the chiefs' monopolising of access to government patronage was a much greater threat to peace in the reserves. Nevertheless, until 1947 and the emergence of widespread opposition to terracing and the authority of the chiefs, the administration had pressed ahead with its communalist strategy, blind to the realities of Kikuyu society.[45]

As a result, the Kenyan government failed to consider other possible approaches. Harold Macmillan had proposed, in 1942, that Soviet-style collective farms should be established in the White Highlands, onto which the 'surplus' population from the over-crowded reserves could be moved.[46] The provincial agricultural staff in Nyanza were also experimenting with the establishment of group farms from contiguous smallholdings, which were to be operated on a communal basis. This scheme, of course, fitted more closely than Macmillan's with the field administration's commitment to the preservation of African communalism and was thoroughly investigated. In marked contrast, any suggestions for harnessing African individualism, as the Kenya African Union demanded, such as introducing government loans for 'progressive' farmers, were dismissed with great hostility. In theory, the government remained totally opposed to the creation of a 'class' of rich peasants who could absorb the growing number of landless Africans as wage labourers.[47]

This opposition to peasant entrepreneurs was a decisive break with the government's strategy during the 1930s, when the agricultural department had encouraged African production in the face of a contracting settler economy. Then, small cultivators had not been regarded as a protected species and the extension services had actively encouraged large African cash-crop growers, whom they had hoped would subsidise the failing settlers, to emerge as a 'class' of proto-capitalists.[48] But after the war, these same large-scale African wattle and maize growers were attacked by their rivals for government patronage – the settlers and the chiefs – who convinced the field administration and the Secretariat that the proto-capitalists were merely irresponsible land-miners, destroying the fertility of the reserves, while exploiting their fellow Africans.[49] The administration therefore became committed to reviving the traditional land authorities. They were to supervise the use of *ngwatio* (communal) labour on terracing and other anti-erosion projects, which were designed to encourage improved farming while preserving the holdings of small-scale peasant cultivators. The problem with this approach was that the Kikuyu reserves were not static or changeless, but had undergone dramatic changes which had undermined the position of women in the household division of labour and had increased social differentiation. The clock could not be put back.[50]

African realities

Let us briefly investigate what had happend in Kikuyuland. Lineage ties had grown weaker and *mbari* had begun to question the rights of *ahoi* and their descendants to cultivate. It was argued that only members of the senior lineage, directly descended from the *githaka*'s founder, were entitled to occupy the land. During the first 50 years of British rule, Kikuyu attitudes to land had been transformed. With British examples of outright ownership before them, the status of the *ahoi*, who had traditionally had rights to the usufruct of the land, diminished while that of the *muramati* and the direct heirs of the *githaka* founder was strengthened. This process had been carried furthest in Kiambu. This district, immediately to the north of Nairobi, had attracted immigrants from Murang'a and Nyeri, who used it as a suburb for commuting to the capital. It was also the Kikuyu district in which the greatest proportion of land had been alienated for European settlement. The example, therefore, of British notions of individual ownership had been extremely strong. Another reason for the growth of individual land claims in Kiambu stemmed from the history of pre-colonial Kikuyu expansion into the area. This had created a distinctive attitude towards the control and cultivation of land among the southern Kikuyu, which had predisposed them to adopt British land law with its notion of individual ownership. Thus, by 1945, Kikuyu attitudes to land use were far removed from the field administration's belief in African communalism.[51]

In 1933, in their evidence to the Kenya Land Commission, the Kikuyu delegates from Kiambu claimed to have traditionally followed a system of individual land ownership. They claimed they had bought their land from the Ndorobo hunter–gatherers, who had lived in the forests into which the Kikuyu penetrated as they had moved south during the nineteenth century.[52] This was, perhaps, to overstate their case, but it was a more accurate view of Kiambu traditional land law than the field administration's obsession with egalitarian communalism. Since the colonial conquest there had gradually emerged new, more strictly-defined categories of land ownership and differentiation between the rights of *githaka* holders, who had developed an individualist conception of ownership, and the *ahoi* and *ndungata*, who had sunk to the status of mere tenants – a position entirely alien to pre-colonial Kikuyu land law.[53] In his discussion of the settlement of Kiambu by the southern Kikuyu in the last third of the nineteenth century and their relations with the original Ndorobo occupants of the land, Kitching has perceptively observed that:

. . . any attempt by the historian to determine whether the original transfers were 'really' a form of rent or a form of land purchase is based on a false premise. For in the pre-colonial situation, conditions were such that the people involved had no need of such concepts because the distinction they embodied was otiose. Land was abundant. People to work it and to defend the people and livestock upon it were scarce. Hence in the 'typical' situation there was no reason for second comers to suppose that they would be asked to leave and no incentive for first comers of pioneers to make such a request. The land which they all occupied was available to be put to the limited range of uses then open. This substantive situation would have been all that mattered to them. It only became necessary to distinguish between land 'owned' and land 'rented' when land became a commodity as a result of relative scarcity, and this itself came about through a change of land use . . .

and through the increasing commoditisation of agricultural production.[54]

Increasing social differentiation had already, therefore, been accepted by the Kikuyu and was reflected in the transformation of their traditional land law and the emergence of a concept of individual ownership.

Since the beginning of the century the elders of the *mbari*, led by the *athamaki*, had asserted control over the distribution of land. In these new conditions the sons of junior wives and the descendants of *ahoi* and *ndungata* felt increasingly insecure. Land their fathers had regarded as their own was taken away as the rewards of commodity production became evident. Wattle was an ideal crop for the aspiring Kikuyu entrepreneur since, once planted it required little cultivation and possessed a variety of uses. The leather industry wanted the tannin, or it could be sold for charcoal, or as wood for building. Members of *mbari*, therefore, who did not belong to the senior lineages were dispossessed and replaced by wattle plantations. When they protested to the Native Tribunals, they discovered that these were packed with the chiefs' and other prominent government supporters' friends. Thus the reputation of the courts deteriorated until by the late 1940s they had been totally discredited and were regarded as tools of the local élite.[55]

The field administration refused to co-opt this emerging group into a restructured patronage network and chose to depend upon its old allies, the chiefs and their clients. The settlers also encouraged the growing antagonism of the district officials to these African accumulators. Chiefs, settlers and the district administration all realised that the proto-capitalists of the Kenya African Union posed a serious challenge to their authority. Thus the requests of the African commercial farmers and traders, who were not supporters of the chiefs, for a greater share of government patronage were rejected. Kenya's post-war agricultural campaign was based upon the futile attempt to revive the traditional land authorities as a medium for government intervention. Instead of attempting to use the growth of individualism and the development of capitalist relations to promote new agricultural techniques and to engender support for the government-sponsored campaigns to prevent erosion, the administration vainly attempted to resist them by appeals to a mythical communal past.[56]

From 1945 until 1947 the policy seemed to have worked in Murang'a, where Osborne had first encouraged the *Muhirig'a* to organise terracing. The *ngwatio* communal-labour system was expanded dramatically during 1946 and constructed an astounding 7,086 miles of narrow-base terraces, protecting more than 24,000 acres. During the first six months of 1947, Murang'a produced 43 per cent of the total number of terraces completed in Central Province. Between July 1945 and July 1947, under

Table 4.1: *Narrow-based Terraces Constructed in Central Province 1944 to 1947[57]*

	July–Dec 1944	Jan–June 1945	July–Dec 1945	Jan–June 1946	July–Dec 1946	Jan–June 1947	July–Dec 1947
Meru:							
Miles	212	95	503	130	208	20	306
Acres	2,650	n.a.	n.a.	550	2,095	n.a.	2,290
Embu:							
Miles	426	n.a.	802	978	555	663	827
Acres	5,321	4,344	3,362	5,514	1,975	2,596	4,565
Nyeri:							
Miles	200	184	453	100	554	888	977
Acres	2,493	n.a.	n.a.	692	1,385	2,220	3,420
Murang'a:							
Miles	42	377	3,051	3,448	3,620	2,611	918
Acres	527	n.a.	11,700	11,467	12,711	9,137	3,107
Kiambu:							
Miles	882	554	888	1,000	831	1,012	1,555
Acres	11,025	n.a.	n.a.	3,520	2,907	3,591	5,443
Machakos:							
Miles	228	220	367	567	939	762	1,233
Acres	2,800	n.a.	n.a.	2,851	4,885	3,835	6,222
Kitui:							
Miles	n.a.	25	768	97	104	125	246
Acres	n.a.	n.a.	n.a.	354	523	625	1,228

the direction of the District Commissioner, Desmond O'Hagan, and T. Hughes Rice, the local agricultural officer, Murang'a built more terraces than South Nyeri, Meru, Machakos and Kitui Districts combined.[58] Table 4.1 shows the total number of miles of terracing dug and the acreages protected from erosion in Central Province during the half-yearly periods from July 1944 to December 1947.

In contrast with several districts, Osborne and O'Hagan in Murang'a had collaborated closely with the technical departments and the local chiefs. A district team was established to organise the campaign. This consisted not only of the local administration but also of the representatives of the various technical departments, such as the local agricultural, veterinary and education officers, as well as several chiefs, African councillors and some nearby settler coffee farmers. Murang'a's successes had been helped by the fact that Hughes Rice, the local agricultural officer, had helped Humphrey prepare his report on conditions in South Nyeri in 1944 and had been instrumental in devising the new policy of using *ngwatio* labour and reviving the *Muhirig'a*. He energetically directed the agricultural aspects of the campaign, while

O'Hagan, who became the District Commissioner in 1945, ensured that the chiefs actively enforced the new soil conservation rules and kept a close watch on their location's progress at terracing. This close collaboration ensured that Murang'a did not suffer from the disputes over policy which disrupted progress in Machakos and Embu, where the local agricultural officers were dubious of the new approach.[59]

These successes simply confirmed the Secretariat in the belief that the *Mihiriga* elders were the best people to prevent land degradation in Kikuyuland. The strategy of 'indirect rule' seemed to have fulfilled their expectations. Creech Jones was greatly impressed by the progress that had been achieved in Murang'a when he toured the area in August 1946 and asked Hughes Rice to prepare a memorandum for him, outlining how this dramatic growth of 'popular' support for conservation had been achieved. Neither Creech Jones, nor the agriculturalists sent by Whitehall to investigate conditions in Kenya, had realised, any more than the Kenyan Secretariat or field administration, that they were sitting on a volcano of pent-up rural frustration and discontent. The figures of terraces dug, live wash-stop planted and acreages protected, blinded them to the realities of peasant opposition to the compulsory labour required for the agricultural campaign.[60]

Although the betterment programme was supposed to persuade the peasantry to adopt new crop rotations, more suitable for areas with uncertain rainfall and to build compost pits and cattle sheds, it appeared to many Kikuyu cultivators that the new agricultural strategy consisted of little more than compulsory terracing two mornings every week. Most people continued to plant maize rather than millet or cassava, which required a much higher input of labour and more land – both scarce resources among the overcrowded Kikuyu. For most people in 1947, the agricultural campaign had not produced any positive returns, such as high-value cash crops, which might have encouraged them to persevere with terracing. Disillusionment was spreading and centres of opposition were emerging in what the administration considered to be its most successful district – Murang'a.[61]

Notes

1. John Saul and Roger Woods, 'African Peasantries', pp. 103-13, have provided a useful working definition, which can be applied to the Kikuyu: 'Peasants are those whose ultimate security and subsistence lies in their having certain rights in land and in the labour of family members on the land, but who are involved, through rights and obligations, in a wider economic system which includes the participation of non-peasants'. See the recent special issue 'Kenya: the Agrarian Question', of the *Review of African Political Economy*, no. 20, January–April 1981, for the current debate between

The Problems of Kikuyu Agriculture

Michael Cowen and Apollo Njonjo, and their supporters; and E.R. Wolf, *Peasants*, (Englewood Cliffs, New Jersey, 1966), for an interesting introduction to the question by a social anthropologist.

For details of the ecological crisis in Baringo, Ukambani and Pokot see J.F. Munro, *Colonial Rule and the Kamba* pp. 189-246; D.M. Anderson's unpublished thesis, 'Herder, Settler and Colonial Rule pp. 217-60; KNA MAA 7/604, 'Surveys: Dr. Stanner: The Kitui Kamba, 1943-50'; and C. Maher's unpublished report, 'Soil Erosion and Land Utilisation in the Kamasia'.

2. DC/NYI 2/1/20, 'Mr Humphrey's Report on South Nyeri, 1944-47', C. Tomkinson to Information Officer, 3 July 1945; CO 852/662/19936/2 (1945-46, 'Soil Erosion: Kenya', H.E. Lambert and P. Wyn Harris's memorandum on 'Policy in Regard to Land Tenure in the Native Lands of Kenya'; and CO 852/557/16707/2 (1946), 'Land Tenure Policy: Kenya', especially the report of the Soil Conservation Committee to DC Central Kavirondo, 18 August 1945; and H.E. Lambert, 'Policy in Regard to the Administration of the Native Lands – Note for Discussion', 10 July 1946.

3. For details of population densities in Murang'a see DC/FH 5/1 (Dep 1) 'District Team Fort Hall, 1949-52'. See also DC/FH 1/27, 'Fort Hall Annual Report, 1948; Appendix D, to compare population estimates based on poll and hut tax returns and the actual returns of the first African census in 1948. A survey of locations 4, 5, 8, 11, 13 and 15 in Murang'a revealed that average-sized holdings varied with altitude: under 4,000 feet they were 13.5 acres; 4–5,000 feet – 10.4 acres; 5,000–5,500 feet – only 4.3 acres; 5,500–6,000 feet – 4.0 acres; 6,000–6,500 feet – 4.9 acres; and over 6,500 feet – 7.6 acres.

4. J.F. Munro, *Colonial Rule and the Kamba*, pp. 189-223; and D.M. Anderson's thesis, 'Herder, Settler and Colonial Rule', pp. 141-63.

5. DC/MKS 10A/29/1, Barnes's Memorandum on Soil Erosion, p. 6; C. Maher, 'Soil Erosion and Land Utilisation in the Ukamba Reserve', p. 16; and I.B. Pole-Evans, 'Report of a Visit to Kenya', p. 4.

6. J.F. Munro, *Colonial Rule and the Kamba*, pp. 225-46; R.L. Tignor, *The Colonial Transformation of Kenya* pp. 331-54; and J.R. Newman's *The Ukamba Members Association*, pp. 7-18; and KNA GH/505, 'Soil Erosion: Destocking, Liebigs, 1938-50'.

7. G. Kitching, *Class and Economic Change in Kenya*, pp. 108-30.

8. KNA DC/FH 1/23, 'Fort Hall Annual Report, 1944', pp. 6-7; DC/FH 1/29, 'Fort Hall Annual Report, 1950', p. 10. Andrew Ng'ang'a, first chairman of the district's Kenya African Union branch, led the opposition to the monopoly of the government marketing boards. See KNA PC/CP 8/5/4, 'Fort Hall Merchants', protest to Provincial Commissioner, 31 October 1950, 21 March 1951, and 11 May 1951, and reply from Cavendish Bentinck, 5 February 1951.

9. See KNA Ag 4/118, 'Provincial Agricultural Handing Over Reports, 1942-51', Nyeri Marketing Report, 15 January 1951 for complaints that agricultural officers had to spend far too much time overseeing local Maize Control and curtailing the black market; and Handing Over Report South Nyeri, 3 March 1947, for· details of smuggling and the black marketeers favoured routes.

10 KNA Ag 4/381, 'Kiambu Monthly Agricultural Reports, 1940-49', July–September 1947.

11 KNA Ag 4/220, 'Wattle Rules and Marketing, 1942-46', G.J. Gollop, Assistant Agricultural Officer, Kiambu, to acting Senior Agricultural Officer, Kiambu, 21 August 1945; and Ag 4/381, 'Kiambu Monthly Agricultural Reports, 1940-49', January–June 1948; C&I 6/782, 'Trading by Africans, 1946-50', T.C. Colchester, Municipal Native Affairs Officer to Rennie, November 1944; C. Tomkinson, PC Central, to Rennie, 6 October 1945; and F.R. Stephen to A. Hope-Jones, 23 August 1946. See also DC/FH 1/23, 'Fort Hall Annual Report, 1944', p. 2, and DC/FH 1/24, 'Fort Hall Annual Report, 1945', pp. 1-2, 34-6.

82

12. CO 852/662/19936/2 (1945–46), 'Soil Erosion: Kenya', 1944 Soil Conservation Report.
13. *ibid.*, N. Humphrey, 'The Relationship of Population to the Land in South Nyeri', paragraphs 22 and 28; KNA Ag 4/488, 'Monthly Agricultural Reports Central Province, 1940–47', January–March 1945 and 1946; and Secretariat 1/1/13, 'Native Welfare in Kenya, 1944', A.M. Champion, 'Review of Present Conditions in the Native Areas', pp. 3–6 and 39; Dr Philip, 'Nutrition in Kenya'. In the main cash-crop areas of eastern Buganda household income and labour have also been invested in the cultivation of inedible cash crops. This has produced a decline in dietary standards and the population have become dependent upon cassava as their main source of protein.
    Humphrey's report on South Nyeri was excessively alarmist. The work of M.P. Cowen, especially his unpublished papers, 'Concentration of Sales and Assets' and 'Patterns of Cattle Ownership and Dairy Production' have recently shown that milk remained a staple element in the diet in Nyeri.
14. For a defence of controlled wattle growing see Ag 4/220, 'Wattle Rules and Marketing, 1942–46', Senior Agricultural Officer, Central, 26 July 1944. M.P. Cowen has argued that wattle was of crucial importance to the success of the peasant option because it enabled the middle peasantry to preserve a household mode of production and provided an antidote to the prohibition on African coffee planting. See Cowen's unpublished thesis, 'Capital and Household Production', pp. 189–99, 205–11.
15. KNA Ag 4/488, 'Monthly Agricultural Report Central Province, 1940–47, Lyne Watt to Director of Agriculture, October–December 1944 and January–March 1945; DC/FH 3/1, 'Reports on the Kikuyu by Miss J.M. Fisher, 1950–52', paragraphs 181–262; and CO 852/662/19936/2 (1945–46), 'Soil Erosion: Kenya', N. Humphrey, 'The Kikuyu Lands: the Relationship of Population to the Land in South Nyeri, (Nairobi, 1945), paragraphs 25–29; and B.D. Bowles, 'Underdevelopment in Agriculture in Colonial Kenya' pp. 195–213.
16. KNA Ag 4/125, 'Annual District Agricultural Reports, Central Province 1951', Machakos District Agricultural Annual Report, 1951.
17. CO 852/662/19936/2 (1945–46), 'Soil Erosion: Kenya', N. Humphrey, 'The Relationship of Population to the Land in South Nyeri', paragraph 27; and KNA Ag 4/118, 'Provincial Agricultural Handing Over Reports, 1942–51', Embu, August 1945; and Kitui, April 1951.
18. CO 852/662/19936/2 (1945–46), 'Shifting Erosion: Kenya', N. Humphrey, 'The Relationship of Population to the Land in South Nyeri', paragraphs 19–24; and KNA DC/NYI/2/1/20, 'Mr Humphrey's Report on South Nyeri, 1944–47', W. Lyne Watt to Director of Agriculture, 27 October 1944.
19. CO 533/537/38628 (1945), 'Grouping of Agricultural Departments', P.E. Mitchell to G. Creasy, 27 February 1945, and to O. Stanley, 15 March 1945. For Mitchell's comments on African agriculture, see CO 533/553/38557/8 (1947–48), 'General Aspects of the Agrarian Situation in Kenya', Despatch no. 44 of 1946 to Hall, 17 April 1946.
20. CO 533/537/38628 (1945), 'Grouping of Agricultural Departments', Mitchell to Stanley, 15 March and 26 May 1945.
21. CO 533/537/38646 (1945), 'Proposals for the Reorganization of the Administration'; CO 533/553/38557/8 (1947–48), 'General Aspects of the Agrarian Situation in Kenya', Despatch no. 44 of 1946 to Hall, 17 April 1946; and CO 852/662/19936/2 (1945–46), 'Soil Erosion: Kenya', for the most important correspondence files.
22. N. Humphrey's most influential reports were subsequently published as *The Kikuyu Lands* and *The Liguru and the Land*. For the 1931 survey, see S.H. Fazan, 'An Economic Survey of the Kikuyu Reserves'; Kenya Land Commission, Evidence and Memoranda, vol. i, paragraphs 971–1039. See also Fazan's minority recommendations in the 'Report of the Committee on Land tenure in Kikuyu

The Problems of Kikuyu Agriculture

Province, 1929'. G. Kitching, *Class and Economic Change in Kenya*, pp. 35-9, 115-20 has an interesting discussion of these reports. See also CO 852/662/19936/2 (1945-46), 'Soil Erosion: Kenya', N. Humphrey, 'The Relationship of Population to the Land in South Nyeri', paragraphs 1-10. Estimates of remittances from *askari* can be found in KNA DC/FH 1/23, 'Fort Hall Annual Report, 1944', p. 26 and DC/FH 1/24, 'Fort Hall Annual Report, 1945', p. 38. Murang'a contributed 1,806 men to the armed forces, who sent home the following sums: 1942 - 114,000 shillings; 1943 - 388,000 shillings; 1944 - 781,000 shillings; 1945 - 976,000 shillings. In 1944-45 remittances from African *askari* exceeded the total revenue of central government poll tax and Local Native Council rates in the district, or the total value of Murang'a's exports through official channels, excluding wattle, which in 1945 amounted to approximately £50,000 out of a total of £93,000. The money sent back to the reserves by migrant labourers is unknown, but probably considerably enhanced the sums received from *askari*.

23. These beliefs in the ecological fragility of African soils were not wrong, but the colonial agricultural departments institutionalised the reports and exaggerated the dangers involved. W. Allan, *Studies in African Land Usage in Northern Rhodesia*; C.G. Trapnell and J.M. Clothier, *The Soils, Vegetation and Agricultural Systems of North-Western Rhodesia* and C.G. Trapnell, 'Ecological Methods in the Study of Native Agriculture', pp. 491-4. J. McCracken, 'Experts and Expertise in Colonial Malawi', pp. 104-5, 108-14 has similar observations to make for the agricultural department in Nyasaland. For the pastoral reserves of Kenya, D.M. Anderson's thesis, 'Herder, Settler and Colonial Rule', pp. 141-64 and 'Depression, Dust Bowl, Demography and Drought', pp. 321-43, contain most useful assessments of official attitudes. I am grateful to Dr Anderson for many interesting discussions on this topic.

24. CO 852/662/19936/2 (1945-46), 'Soil Erosion: Kenya', N. Humphrey, 'The Relationship of Population to the Land in South Nyeri', paragraphs 9 and 41-7. Humphrey estimated that total export earnings amounted to only 57 shillings per family per annum. The Kenya Department of Agriculture's memoranda to the East African Royal Commission contain some useful insights into the evolution of official thinking: 'Report on Agrarian Policy for Dealing with Population Increase: Land Tenure and Fragmentation in Kenya' (1951); and 'The Agricultural Problems and Potential of the African Lands of Kenya', 23 February 1952. I am grateful to Dr J.M. Lonsdale for lending me xeroxes of these reports.

    For the first signs of Brown's new approach see KNA Ag 4/419, 'Agricultural Development and Maintenance of Soil Fertility: The Growing of High Priced Crops, 1933-51', J.T. Moon to Director of Agriculture, 5 February 1948; and L.H. Brown to DC Embu, 6 February 1948; and Ag 1/1079, 'Soil Erosion Native Areas, 1946-54', L.H. Brown, Provincial Agricultural Officer to Director of Agriculture, 20 August 1951, for a discussion of the planning of arable areas for peasant farmers. See also Ag 4/502, 'Agricultural Reports Central Province, 1942-55'; Ag 4/328, 'Annual Agricultural Report Central Province, 1951'; Ag 4/125, 'Annual Agricultual Reports, Central Province Districts, 1951'; Ag 4/410, 'Central Province and Districts Annual Agricultural Reports, 1952'; and Ag 4/118, 'Provincial Agricultural Handing Over Reports, 1942-51', Embu Handing Over Report, February 1951.

    Brown believed that it was possible in Central Province to establish balanced smallholdings which could carry 1,000 people to the square mile and perhaps 2,000 near Nairobi. Nevertheless, in 1952 he considered that only 5 per cent of the population followed 'sound agricultural' techniques, such as paddocking and rotational grazing and cultivation. See his letter to *East African Standard*, 17 April 1953; and RH Mss. Afr. s. 596, 'European Elected Members Organisation', 38(A)/1, 'Mau Mau 1947-55', for his views on Kikuyu agricultural practices.

25. R.J.M. Swynnerton, *A Plan to Intensify the Development of African Agriculture in Kenya*; and A. Thurston's draft manuscript, 'The Intensification of Smallholder Agriculture in

84

Kenya', pp. 38, 50–2, 97–104, 118–19. See also CO 852/662/19936/2 (1945–46), 'Soil Erosion: Kenya', N. Humphrey, 'The Relationship of Population to the Land in South Nyeri', Appendix A. For the official account of the rehabilitation and resettlement campaigns, African Land Development Board, *African Land Development in Kenya 1946–55*.

26. For estimates of the value of these new crops see KNA Ag 4/410, 'Central Province and District Annual Agricultural Reports, 1952', Appendix D.

27. African Land Development Board, *African Land Development in Kenya 1946–55*; pp. 38–44; KNA DC/MKS 14/3/2, 'Machakos Gazeteer, 1890–1957', pp. 31–50; and Ag 1/732, 'Land: African Settlement Board: Simba, Kibwezi, Chuyulu and Teita Areas, 1946–55', minutes of the meeting with the Provincial Commissioner, 10 April 1948, to discuss land and water conservation in the Teita Hills; and DC Teita–Taveta 3/32, 'Development in the Reserves: Teita Betterment Scheme, 1948–50', A.W. Thompson, Shimba Hills Survey, 24 January 1950. I am grateful to Simon Myambo for these references and for a tour of the terracing work in Teita.

28. CO 852/662/19936/2 (1945–46), 'Soil Erosion: Kenya', N. Humphrey, 'The Relationship of Population to the Land in South Nyeri', paragraph 55. See also CO 533/538/38005/29 (1947), 'Land Commission: Native Lands Trust Board', minute by P. Wyn Harris, 9 August 1947.

29. CO 852/557/16707/2 (1946), 'Land Tenure Policy: Kenya', especially the report of the soil conservation committee under Archdeacon Owen to DC Central Kavirondo, 18 August 1945. See also N. Humphrey, *The Liguru and the Land*; CO 852/662/19936/2 (1945–46), 'Soil Erosion: Kenya', H.E. Lambert and P. Wyn Harris, 'Memorandum on Policy in Regard to Land Tenure in the Native Lands of Kenya'; KNA DC/FH 1/24, 'Fort Hall Annual Report, 1945', pp. 7–8; and Ag 4/512, 'Fort Hall Monthly Agricultural Reports, 1940–49', reports for January–March 1945 and October to December 1945.

30. CO 852/662/19936/2 (1945–46), 'Soil Conservation: Kenya', H.E. Lambert and P. Wyn Harris, 'Memorandum on Policy in Regard to Land Tenure in the Native Lands of Kenya'. See also CO 852/557/16707/2 (1946), 'Land Tenure Policy: Kenya'. Lambert was the author of two noted books on the Kikuyu, *Systems of Land Tenure in the Kikuyu Land Unit* and *Kikuyu Social and Political Institutions*.

31. As late as 1954 the District Commissioner in Machakos was still defending communalism and hindering the emergence of African entrepreneurs and commercial farmers. See B.J. Berman's unpublished thesis, 'Administration and Politics in Colonial Kenya', pp. 308–27. The gradual evolution of official thinking can be followed in KNA MAA 7/842, 'Provincial Commissioners' Meetings, 1945–51'; MAA 6/13 and 14 'Reports of the Committee on Agricultural Credit for Africans, 1949–50'; and MAA 9/959, 'Credit to Africans Ordinance, 1941–59'.

The rivalry between the chiefs and the alternative élite is evident in DC/FH 1/26, 'Fort Hall Annual Report, 1947', pp. 4–5, 17–18; Ag 4/77, 'Wattle Cooperative Societies, 1947–51'; Ag 4/220, 'Wattle Rules and Marketing, 1942–46'; and C&I 6/782 'Trading by Africans, 1946–50'.

32. Lord Hailey, *Native Land Tenure in Africa*, p. 13. For the attitudes of the Kenyan administration see M.P.K. Sorrenson, *Land Reform in the Kikuyu Country*, p. 56; and KNA MAA 6/13, 'Report of the Committee on Agricultural Credit for Africans, 1949–50', meeting 29 October 1949. Mitchell endorsed this view, and observed that '. . . in fact, outright ownership by ignorant and often avaricious small farmers is the most disastrous thing that can happen to land anywhere as examples all over the world prove.' LO/LND 30/2/2, Mitchell to Rennie, 25 April 1945. For similar comments in Whitehall see CO 852/557/16708 (1945), 'Land Tenure Panel', Colonial Office to the Colonial Social Science Research Council, 28 December 1944; and M. Perham, *East African Journey*, pp. 17, 42–6, 56; and her *Colonial Sequence, 1930–1949*, pp. 12–33.

33. KNA MAA 6/13 and 13, 'Reports of the Committee on Agricultural Credit for

The Problems of Kikuyu Agriculture

Africans, 1949–50'; MAA 9/959, 'Credit to Africans Ordinance, 1941–59'; and MAA 7/842, 'Provincial Commissioners' Meetings, 1945–51', 12 April 1945.

34. Lord Hailey, *Native Land Tenure in Africa*, p. 13.
35. L. Mair, 'Anthropology and Colonial Policy', pp. 191–5; D.H. Johnson, 'Evans-Pritchard, the Nuer, and the Sudan Political Service', pp. 231–46; and T. Asad (ed.), *Anthropology and the Colonial Encounter*, passim. For relations between anthropologists and the administration in Kenya, KNA MAA 7/604, 'Surveys by Dr W.E.H. Stanner: The Kitui Kamba, 1943–50'; and I. Schapera, 'Some Problems of Anthropological Research in Kenya Colony', p. 14, quoted in J.M. Lee, *Colonial Development and Good Government*, pp. 86–98. B.J. Berman's unpublished thesis, 'Administration and Politics in Colonial Kenya', pp. 119–39, analyses the attitude of the Kenyan field administration. See also P.E. Mitchell's foreword to R.O. Hennings, *African Morning*, p. 9; and J.M. Lonsdale, 'European Attitudes and African Pressures', p. 142.
36. For the opinions of the 'detribalised' élite in Nairobi see KNA MAA 2/5/223, 'Nairobi Advisory Council, 1946–49', especially T.G. Askwith's memorandum on the Advisory Council, 1 September 1948; and MAA 7/491, 'Administration Policy: Urban Areas Nairobi, 1945–47', F. Khamisi to Rennie, 10 September 1945; and meeting in Secretariat, 28 November 1945, when Khamisi, Mathu and Odede met the Deputy Chief Secretary, the Chief Native Commissioner, the Mayor, the Commissioner for Local Government and the Provincial Commissioner Central Province. For Mitchell's attitude, see CO 533/549/38232/15 (1946–47), 'European Settlement: Squatters', Mitchell to Creech Jones, 14 April 1947.
37. KNA Lab 9/99, 'Labour Efficiency Survey, Kenya and Uganda Railways and Harbours: Northcott Report, 1946–49'; and MAA /22, 'City African Affairs Officer: Correspondence, 1947–50', clearly show the depth of African discontent in Nairobi. This culminated in the general strike of May 1950, for which see Lab 9/87, 'Labour Troubles: Nairobi, 1950'. For Mombasa see CO 533/545/38091/6 (1947 and 1948), 'Labour: Strikes and Disturbances'; CO 533/534/38091/13 (1947), 'Labour: A Social and Economic Survey of Mombasa'; KNA Lab 9/1835, 'Mombasa Strikes, 1937–46'; Lab 9/1841, 'Trade Disputes Tribunal, 1947'; and Lab 9/1775, 'A Survey of African Housing in Mombasa, 1946–47'. A. Hake, *African Metropolis*, pp. 19–63, provides an account of African life in the capital. See also J. Bujra, 'Women entrepreneurs of Early Nairobi', pp. 213–34; N. Nelson, 'How Women and Men Get By'; and R.M.A. van Zwanenberg, 'History and Theory of Urban Poverty in Nairobi', pp. 165–203.
38. G. Kitching, *Class and Economic Change in Kenya*, pp. 82–94, 121–30; M.J. Hay's unpublished thesis, 'Economic Change in Luoland: Kowe, 1890–1945', pp. 204–32; J.M. Fischer, *Anatomy of Kikuyu Domesticity and Husbandry*, pp. 237–54, 261–85; and several unpublished articles by M.P. Cowen, especially, 'Differentiation in a Kenya Location', p. 20; M.P. Cowen and K. Kinyanjui, 'Some Problems of Class Formation in Kenya', M.P. Cowen and F. Murage, 'Notes on Agricultural Wage Labour in a Kenya Location'; M.P. Cowen and F.Murage, 'Wattle Production in the Central Province'; and M.P. Cowen's unpublished thesis, 'Capital and Household Production'.
39. KNA MAA 2/5/146, 'Kenya African Union, 1948–52'; Secretariat 1/12/8, 'Labour Unrest: Intelligence Reports Central Province, 1947'; and B.J. Berman's thesis, 'Administration and Politics in Colonial Kenya', pp. 378–404. See also DC/FH 1/26, 'Fort Hall Annual Report, 1947', pp. 1–6; DC/FH 1/27, 'Fort Hall Annual Report, 1948', pp. 1–5; and DC/KBU 1/43, 'Kiambu Annual Report, 1952', pp. 1–4.
40. KNA DC/FH 1/26, 'Fort Hall Annual Report, 1947', pp. 1–6; DC/FH 1/27, 'Fort Hall Annual Report, 1948', pp. 1–5; and DC/FH 1/30, 'Fort Hall Annual Report, 1951', pp. 1–2.
41. CO 852/557/16707/2 (1946), 'Land Tenure Policy: Kenya', H.E. Lambert, 'Policy in Regard to Administration of the Native Lands – Note for a Discussion', 10 July 1946; CO 852/662/19936/2 (1945–46), 'Soil Erosion: Kenya', H.E. Lambert and P.Wyn Harris, 'Policy in Regard to Land Tenure in the Native Lands of Kenya'; and CO

86

The Problems of Kikuyu Agriculture

852/557/16708 (1945), 'Land Tenure Panel', Colonial Office to Colonial Social Science Research Council, 28 December 1944.

42. H.E. Lambert's *Systems of Land Tenure in the Kikuyu Land Unit*, should be compared with L.S.B. Leakey, *The Southern Kikuyu before 1903*, vol. 1, which shows an acute consciousness of the differences between the Metume (the Kikuyu from north of the River Chania) and the Karura (those from the south, in Kiambu).

In his thesis Berman has characterised the administration's views as those of an aristocratic conservative élite: '. . . an anti-urban, anti-materialist and anti-bourgeois response of the traditional landed rural class to modern industrial society'. He claims that these views were preserved in the Kenyan administration 'long after their influence had begun to wane in Britain', pp. 105–6. Berman adopted these ideas from S. Barrington Moore, *The Social Origins of Dictatorship and Democracy*, pp. 491–6, and C.F. Behrmann's unpublished thesis, 'The Mythology of British Imperialism', which he cites.

The most influential advocate of such ideas was Lord Hailey; see his four-volume survey of *Native Administration in the British African Territories*. For a discussion of Hailey's influence see R.D. Pearce, *The Turning Point in Africa'* pp. 42–67; and his secretary, Sir Frederick Pedler's account, 'The Contribution of Lord Hailey to Africa', pp. 267–75.

43. C.G. Rosberg and J. Nottingham, *The Myth of Mau Mau*, pp. 188–234; and KNA MAA 2/5/146, 'Kenya African Union, 1948–52', for many examples of the Kenyan government's refusal to incorporate African politicians.

44. KNA MAA 7/320, 'Chiefs Engaged in Commerce'; and complaints in Ag 4/77, 'Wattle Cooperative Societies, 1947–51', James Warrego, Secretary of the Central Province Wattle Growers' Association to the Agricultural Officer, Kiambu, 20 August 1948; and the meeting at Ruiru with the District Commissioner, 2 March 1949. For opposition to terracing, Secretariat 1/12/8, 'Intelligence: Mumenyereri, 1947–50', letter from Mrs M.W. Gathaku, published in Mumenyereri, 29 September 1947, about events in Location 13 in Murang'a; and the letters from B.K. Ruhia, 27 October 1947; and Benjamin Mang'uru, 3 November 1947.

45. KNA DC/FH 1/25, 'Fort Hall Annual Report, 1946', pp. 3–7; and DC/KBU 1/36, 'Kiambu Annual Report, 1945', pp. 13–15. See also Ag 4/118, 'Provincial Agricultural Handing Over Reports, 1942–51', South Nyeri, 12 February 1945; and T. Hughes Rice to C.D. Knight in Murang'a, March 1947; Ag 4/147, 'Fort Hall Agricultural Annual Report, 1945'; Ag 4/381, 'Kiambu Monthly Agricultural Reports, 1940–49'; Ag 4/512, 'Murang'a Monthly Agricultural Reports, 1940–49'; and Ag 4/539, 'Reconditioning: Central Province, 1934–48'.

46. CO 967/57/46709 (1942), 'Sir Arthur Dawe's Memorandum on a Federal Solution for East Africa and Mr Harold Macmillan's Counter-Proposals', Macmillan to Gater, 15 August 1942. For other collectivisation schemes, see C. Maher, 'Peasantry or Prosperity?' and KNA Ag 1/1065, 'Soil Erosion Native Areas, 1943–46', C. Maher's 'Agricultural Changes as Alternatives to Disaster in the Native Reserves'; Secretariat 1/1/13, 'Native Welfare in Kenya', A.M. Champion's 'Review of Present Conditions in the Native Areas, 1944', pp. 42–44. Champion, a former Provincial Commissioner, considered that collective farming was more 'in keeping with native communal ideas of land cultivation . . . and also it is only by some such method that optimum production can be obtained from the soil. The possibility of introducing such a system with a minimum disturbance to native society should be one of the prime considerations of the social anthropologists', whom he wished the government to appoint.

Mitchell also favoured collective farming and considered that African peasant societies needed 'some form of organization which will do what the peasant cannot do for himself . . . In the two greatest areas where the peasant system survives, e.g. in India and China, the picture is one of extreme poverty and recurring economic disasters. There is no reality behind the belief that the African peasant farmer can do for himself what other (and often better) farmers have done elsewhere, if only he is given

The Problems of Kikuyu Agriculture

more land and help with communications and markets'. For Hailey's comments on this despatch, see CO 852/557/16707/2 (1946), 'Land Tenure Policy: Kenya', 13 May 1946.

47. African Land Development Board's report on African Land Development in Kenya, 1946–55, pp. 6–7; KNA Ag 1/1065, 'Soil Erosion Native Areas, 1943–46', especially C. Maher, 'Notes on a Visit to South Kavirondo and to Nyakatch, Central Kavirondo', 3 January 1945 and 'Agricultural Changes as Alternatives to Disaster in the Native Reserves'. See also Maher's 'Notes on Estimates for the Development of the Native reserves' to D.L. Blunt, 1 June 1945, in the same file. For A.M. Champion's report see Secretariat 1/1/13, 'Native Welfare in Kenya', A.M. Champion, 'Review of Present Conditions in the Native Areas, 1944'; and DC/NYI/2/1/20, 'Mr Humphrey's Report on South Nyeri, 1944–47', Lyne Watt to Director of Agriculture, 27 October 1944; and C. Tomkinson's interim comments on development to Rennie, 14 May 1945.

Lyne Watt blamed the uncontrolled spread of wattle cultivation for the growth of rampant individualism, and favoured a communal development programme to reverse this trend. He was completely opposed to encouraging a few selected progressive smallholders. Tomkinson also considered that 'unless it is to be Government policy to encourage the evolution of the big landowner and employer of labour, it will be necessary for such men to be made to realise that they must reorientate themselves on clan lines sufficiently to ensure their conformation to sound land usage'. This, of course, marked the escalation of the conflict between the administration and its allies, the chiefs, in their political and economic struggle with those aspiring entrepreneurs who supported the Kenya African Union and the Kikuyu Central Association.

48. C. Leys, *Underdevelopment in Kenya*, pp. 33–62; E.A. Brett, *Colonialism and Underdevelopment in East Africa*', pp. 288–95, 300–5; and J.M. Lonsdale's unpublished paper, 'African Elites and Social Classes in Colonial Kenya', pp. 10–14.

49. KNA Ag 4/77, 'Wattle Cooperative Societies, 1947–51', G.J. Gollop to DC Kiambu, 18 December 1948; Ag 4/80, 'Agricultural Conferences and Meetings, 1933–51', Conference of Senior Agricultural Officers, 10–11 June 1946; Secretariat 1/1/12, 'Report of the Joint Agricultural and Veterinary Services Sub-Committee of the Development Committee'; and Secretariat 1/1/13, 'Native Welfare in Kenya', A.M. Champion, 'A Review of the Present Conditions in the Native Areas, 1944'. By 1949 the district team in Murang'a contained three settlers, see DC/FH 5/1 (Dep 1), 'District Team Fort Hall, 1949–52'. See also DC/NYI/2/1/20, 'Mr Humphrey's Report on South Nyeri, 1944–47'; DC/NYI 2/2/4, 'Mr Humphrey's Report on Agriculture in South Nyeri, 1945'; and DC/NYI 2/1/16, 'Development and Welfare Planning, 1944–48' for further examples of the post-war commitment to preserving African communalism. These topics were debated in the Legislative Council in November 1944; see Legislative Council Debates, Second Series, vol. 20, (1944–45), Third Session, Mrs V. Watkins, 23 November 1944, cols. 139–49; D.L. Blunt, Director of Agriculture, cols. 203–17; R. Daubney, Director of Veterinary Services, cols. 217–22; W.F.O. Trench, cols. 238–49; and F.W. Cavendish-Bentinck, who six months later was appointed Member for Agriculture, 30 November 1944, cols. 323–36.

50. KNA DC/FH 3/1 'Reports on the Kikuyu by Miss J.M. Fisher, 1950–52', paragraphs 181–262; and G. Kitching, *Class and Economic Change in Kenya*, pp. 82–94 and 121–130.

51. G. Kitching, *Class and Economic Change in Kenya*, pp. 282–97. See also L.S.B. Leakey, *The Southern Kikuyu before 1903*, vol. 1, pp. 105–27; and KNA DC/NYI/2/1/20, 'Mr Humphrey's Report on South Nyeri, 1944–47', C. Tomkinson to Information Officer, 3 July 1945. Calculations of average-sized landholdings revealed that these had fallen to 4.83 acres per family, plus 3.87 acres of communal grazing, compared to the agricultural department's estimated minimum of 8 acres arable and 6 acres grazing. Maher considered that there were 11,500 too many families in Kiambu. The *ahoi*

The Problems of Kikuyu Agriculture

system of clientage had collapsed and many people were already being employed at low wages by large landowners. See Ag 4/392, 'District Agricultural Annual Report, Kiambu, 1948'. In the 'suburban' area, population densities were over 1,000 to the square mile. Gollop, the Assistant Agricultural Officer, reported that in this area the Kikuyu 'are largely parasitical on Nairobi. They have no interest in the land other than as a dwelling place for their families and there they leave their wives to scratch what they can from the soil by methods both primitive and destructive, while they themselves, ply their multifarious trades, often dishonest, in Nairobi . . . Here is needed stern and drastic action to stop a rape of the land that is criminal to the highest degree, and what is worse must to future generations spell poverty and bankruptcy. No doctor's diagnosis is needed here but the surgeon's knife and that quickly before the patient dies. These locations should receive firm handling in 1949'. By 1948, in contrast to when Fazan had done his report in 1929, both the actual and available cultivated land per household was less than in Nyeri or Murang'a, and over these years the population increase in Kiambu was double that of Murang'a (4.4 per cent), and treble Nyeri's (3.0 per cent). See G. Kitching, *Class and Economic Change in Kenya*, pp. 199–20 for a detailed assessment of these changes.

52. G. Kitching, *Class and Economic Change in Kenya*, pp. 288–97; H.E. Lambert, *Systems of Land Tenure in the Kikuyu Land Unit*, pp. 23–5, 79, 87, 95–109, 152–3; and L.S.B. Leakey, *The Southern Kikuyu before 1903*, vol. 1, pp. 89–104.

53. L.S.B. Leakey, *The Southern Kikuyu before 1903*, vol. 1, pp. 105–27, outlines the *githaka* system and the circumstances under which *mbari* land could be divided, the rights of a *muthami* or resident tenant, a *muhoi* or tenant-at-will, and a *muthoni* or relation-in-law. Basically the *githaka* was the land cleared by one individual, who left his home *mbari* or sub-clan to seek more land on the Kikuyu frontier. These landholdings varied in size from 50 acres to perhaps 20 square miles. The man who cleared the land or 'bought' it from the Dorobo became the *mwathi* or *githaka* controller, with absolute rights to the land. When he died the *githaka* continued to be named after him and became the property of all his male descendants, who formed a new *mbari*, under the leadership of a trustee, the *murumati*, who was usually the eldest son of the former *mwathi*. Sometimes the *mwathi* had come from one of the wealthier families in his original *mbari* and sought more land for his stock, but normally it was members of the junior lineages who left either to search for land to establish their own *githaka* or to become *ahoi* or tenants-at-will of richer landholders. In either case once they had left their *mbari* and had relinquished their cultivation rights, the *murumati* and the *kiama*, or council, would allocate their land to another member of the *mbari*. The *muhoi* originally merely cultivated the land of a neighbouring *mwathi* in exchange for a portion of his crops, but did not actually live on the new *githaka*; while the *muthami* or resident tenant was required to pledge his services to the landowner but did not pay any rent, and could only be evicted under Kikuyu law if the land was needed for the *mwathi*'s own family. Often he hoped to consolidate his position and to marry a member of the *mwathi*'s family or to have one of his sons or daughters do so. He would then become a *muthoni* or relation-in-law, who could only be evicted with great difficulty. All tenants were traditionally safeguarded from unreasonable eviction by the custom that the land a tenant had cleared and cultivated had to be allowed to lie fallow and to revert to bush before it could be used for cultivation by the *mwathi*. G. Kitching, *Class and Economic Change in Kenya*, pp. 288–97 provides an extremely lucid assessment of the effects of the development of capitalist relations upon Kikuyu land law and concept of 'ownership'.

54. G. Kitching, *Class and Economic Change in Kenya*, p. 290; see also M.P. Cowen and F. Murage's unpublished paper, 'Wattle Production in the Central Province, p. 63.

55. A. Thurston's draft manuscript, 'The Intensification of Smallholder Agriculture in Kenya', p. 75. For an African view see KNA MAA 8/102, 'Intelligence and Security: Press Cuttings, 1948–50', letter from E.N. Samson published in *Mucemanio*, 3 July 1948.

56. For a detailed study of the formation of the anti-Kikuyu Central Association coalition see D.M. Feldman's unpublished thesis, 'Christians and Politics', pp. 202–301; and J.M. Lonsdale's unpublished paper, 'African Elites and Social Classes in Colonial Kenya', pp. 7–13.

The administration's attitude to individualism can be found in CO 852/662/19936/2 (1945–46), 'Soil Erosion: Kenya', H.E. Lambert and P. Wyn Harris, 'Policy in Regard to Land Tenure in the Native Reserves of Kenya'; CO 852/557/16707/2 (1946), 'Land Tenure Policy: Kenya', Soil Conservation committee to DC Central Kavirondo, 18 August 1945; and H.E. Lambert, 'Policy in Regard to Administration of the Native Lands – Note for Discussion', 10 July 1946; KNA Ag 4/491, 'Nyeri Reconditioning Report, 1944–46', Secretariat circular no. 64, 22 May 1946; Ag 4/80, 'Agricultural Conferences and Meetings, 1933–41', conference of Senior Agricultural Officers 10–11 June 1946; Ag 4/330, 'Provincial Agricultural Newsletters, 1939–51', September 1949, Group Farming in Nyanza; and Hughes Rice on Youth Conference in Central Province, in February 1950 issue; and Ag 4/539, 'Reconditioning Central Province, 1934–48', PC Central to Chief Native Commissioner, 7 March 1945; and Secretariat circular no. 3 on 'Soil Conservation in the Reserves', 24 April 1945.

57. Table 4.1 was compiled from the following sources: KNA Ag 4/147, 'Fort Hall Agricultural Annual Report, 1945'; Ag 4/358, 'Monthly Agricultural Report, Embu, 1945–49'; Ag 4/381, 'Kiambu Monthly Reports, 1940–49'; Ag 4/512, 'Fort Hall Monthly Agricultural Reports, 1940–49'; Ag 4/539, 'Reconditioning Central Province, 1934–48'.

58. KNA Ag 4/539, 'Reconditioning Central Province, 1934–48', Soil Conservation reports, July–December 1945; January–June 1946; July–December 1946; and January–June 1947. See also Ag 4/512, 'Fort Hall Monthly Agricultural Report, 1940–49'; Ag 4/147, 'Fort Hall Annual Agricultural Report, 1945'; DC/FH 1/24, 'Fort Hall Annual Report, 1945', pp. 7–9; DC/FH 1/25, 'Fort Hall Annual Report, 1946', pp. 6–7; and DC/FH 1/26, 'Fort Hall Annual Report, 1947', pp. 1–4, 15.

59. CO 533/537/38628 (1945), 'Grouping of Agricultural Departments', Mitchell to Creasy, 18 February 1945; CO 533/537/38646 (1945), 'Proposals for the Reorganization of the Administration', Mitchell to Stanley, 5 June 1945; DC/FH 5/1 (Dep 1), 'District Team Fort Hall, 1949–52'; and DC/FH 2/1, 'Fort Hall Production Sub-Committee Meetings, 1931–52'. A. Thurston's draft manuscript, 'The Intensification of Smallholder Agriculture in Kenya', pp. 66–9, provides some examples of dissension and departmental rivalry. Relations between the agricultural and veterinary departments were particularly strained according to C.O. Oates, the former Provincial Agricultural Officer in Nyanza and the Rift Valley; interview in Dorset, 20 June 1983. See also KNA Ag 4/80, 'Agricultural Conferences and Meetings, 1933–51', Agricultural Officer, Embu, 29 July 1947; Agricultural Officers' meetings, 11 August 1947, and 8–9 April 1948; L.H. Brown, 21 August and 26 October 1948 to Senior Agricultural Officer, Nyeri; and the Provincial Agricultural Officers' meeting on 9 June 1950; Ag 4/518, 'Reconditioning Central Province, 1948–51, Soil Conservation report, Central Province, January–June 1948, especially the entry for Machakos; and G.M. Roddan to F.W. Cavendish-Bentinck, 31 August 1948; and Ag 4/392, 'District Annual Agricultural Reports, 1948', the Embu report.

60. CO 533/556/38664 (1946–47), 'Land Policy', T. Hughes Rice to A.B. Cohen, 3 August 1946.

61. KNA Ag 4/125, 'Central Province Agricultural Annual Reports, 1951'; Ag 4/410, 'Central Province and Districts Agricultural Annual Reports, 1952'; and Ag 4/451, 'Fort Hall Safari Diaries, 1948–51', clearly demonstrate the continued emphasis upon terracing.

Five

The Kikuyu Squatter Problem

'I have received information that squatter labour is pouring into the forest reserve, where the conditions are probably so attractive as to make this a squatters' paradise, and a haven of refuge. Land; land; land; nice fresh virgin land, is their cry; little or no work for their *bibis*; sheep filling their bellies with good green luscious grass; firewood quite handy; *pombe* brewing galore – who will visit us in the forest at night . . . Utopia has been discovered; Bacchus reigns peacefully, or noisily; no horrid police to disturb us; very handsome profits from vegetables and potatoes; and enough to spare for our dear indolent brethren; thereby saving them the dreadful prospect of work.'[1]

This complaint from an Aberdares farmer was typical of the wave of anti-squatter feeling which swept the White Highlands after the war. It contained elements of truth; although squatter life was never so idyllic, it was better than staying in the reserves. Squatters during the previous 30 years had enjoyed access to more land, had owned more stock and cultivated larger *shambas* than their relatives in Central Province. According to official estimates, squatter household incomes of 1,000 shillings a year from wage labour, stock and crops, were not uncommon during the war. The peasant option seemed to be even more successsul among the squatters on European farms than in Central Province.[2]

This success explains why the settlers were so eager after the war to restrict squatter cultivation and small stock and to eliminate their cattle. The squatter option had become a serious threat to the privileged economic status of the settlers. The squatters seemed to be gaining ground, gnawing away from the inside of the settler enclave in the White Highlands. African accumulation was strongest among the Kikuyu, who dominated the squatter communities in Naivasha, Nakuru and the Aberdares. It was in these three district councils, on the borders of Kikuyuland, that the post-war confrontation between settlers and squatters was most intense.[3]

The Kenyan government was deeply divided over the squatter problem. Under pressure from the chiefs and the African Local Native Councils, the field administration strongly opposed any attempt to expel squatter stock into the reserves as the European district councils demanded, supported by the local government department. The labour department, under the able leadership of Wyn Harris and Hyde-Clarke, bcame a particularly forceful critic of the new anti-squatter orders. These divisions within the official mind ensured that the evolution of squatter policy was protracted and painful. By 1947, however, it appeared as though a five-stage policy for the controlled evolution of squatters into wage labourers over a generation had been agreed, but it was never introduced because of the opposition of Cavendish-Bentinck, the member for agriculture, and Mortimer, the member for health and local government, who were sympathetic to the settlers' cause. Until the declaration of the Emergency in October 1952, the settler-controlled district councils were allowed to devise their own policies with only minimal supervision from the Secretariat, despite the protests of Hyde-Clarke, the Labour Commissioner. In August 1950, the last semblance of control by the Nairobi government was abandoned and squatter policy was left to the Association of District Councils. Henceforth the district councils were to moderate themselves.[4]

Squatter versus settler accumulation

The squatters typified Kenya's problem – the clash between two forms of accumulation, Kikuyu and settler. Between 1905 and 1920 their interests had seemed compatible. Under-capitalised European farmers had needed cheap African labour to develop their farms. Squatter cattle provided milk and manure, helped to prevent bush regeneration and kept pastures sweet for European stock. In contrast to the early settlers, the first squatters were over-capitalised, that is they had too many stock to remain in crowded Kikuyuland. During the nineteenth century aspiring Kikuyu had abandoned the security of their *mbari* to search for more land on the frontier of Kikuyu expansion. The term *ahoi*, which has been used to describe many of the squatters, was not a social category for the landless poor but a legal concept, defining the terms on which they had gained access to the land of a different *mbari*. Often, therefore, the people who became *ahoi* were not the landless, but wealthy cattle owners who required additional grazing land beyond the resources of their *mbari*. After 1905, when expansion to the south was closed by the alienation of land to European settlers, the Kikuyu turned westwards into the sparsely-populated Rift Valley to work on the European farms which had been alienated from the Maasai.[5]

This arrangement worked well for both sides until the 1920s when high commodity prices enabled the settlers to diversify into cattle and sheep. For the first time, the interests of the two communities clashed and the settlers, fearful of the diseases carried by squatter stock began to force them off their farms. Squatter cultivators, however, had also increased cultivation during the First World War and, in Naivasha and Nakuru, had prospered. They too in the 1920s had bought cattle and small stock and did not wish to lose their grazing rights.[6]

During the 1920s the squatters encountered stringent new controls. 'Kaffir farming' agreements, whereby under-capitalised settlers had allowed squatters to rent land for cash or payments in kind, without requiring any labour, had been prohibited under the Resident Native Labour Ordinance of 1918. The 1920s provided both sides with a fore-taste of what would happen 20 years later. Squatter stock were seized and Africans retaliated by maiming settler cattle and burning crops. But just when a clash appeared inevitable, the collapse of international commodity prices in the depression undercut settler prosperity. Many settlers had to abandon their farms and most had to retrench and go back to an earlier stage of accumulation and to a symbiotic relationship with their squatters. In contrast, the depression provided squatters with further opportunities as peasant production was encouraged to bolster the fiscal base of the state. As before the First World War, the race between settler and squatter accumulators once again favoured the squatters.[7]

The economic depression of the 1930s removed the threat of intensive European farming for more than a decade. Many settlers farming marginal land in areas such as Solai, Sotik and Machakos could survive only by resorting to illegal 'kaffir farming' agreements with squatters and Africans in the neighbouring reserves, who wanted to graze their cattle on less exhausted pastures. Along sections of the border between the Tugen Reserve and Nakuru District, 90 per cent of farms were abandoned at the height of the depression.[8]

Large parts of the White Highlands were 'colonised' by squatters. In 1931, the *East African Standard* reported that only 2,828,000 acres of a total area of 6,847,000 acres of land which had been alienated to settlers were actually under crops or being grazed. Another 1,850,000 acres were occupied by squatters. Other estimates suggested that the squatters were occupying an even larger proportion of the so-called White Highlands. Maasai cattle were grazing pastures on unoccupied farms on the Mau escarpment, and the Nandi were trespassing into the Uasin Gishu.[9]

At this crucial juncture the Kenyan government decided, after a certain amount of wavering, not to abandon the settlers to their fate. It hedged its bets and vainly attempted to help settler farming through the crisis, by providing loans from the government-controlled Land Bank, at the same time as it encouraged African production. The agricultural department also encouraged the settlers to diversify from maize monoculture into mixed farming with dairy and stock herds. This failure to choose between the settlers and the Kikuyu, although no one appreciated it at the time, was the beginning of the end for Kikuyu squatters. After 1935 a violent confrontation between settler and Kikuyu accumulators, both in the reserves and the White Highlands, was almost inevitable. In the late 1930s the settlers were already trying to claw back their advantages and to prevent the squatters gaining *de facto* rights to land in the White Highlands. They knew that if squatters' rights under English law were conceded then the game would be over, since during the depression the government had clearly shown its ambiguous commitment to Kenya as a 'White Man's Country' and its willingness to back the winning side, be it African or European.[10]

Thus in the late 1930s, when the depression had receded and agricultural prices had improved, the settlers once again moved against squatter stock and attempted to undermine the peasant option in the reserves by arousing fears among the administration that the irresponsible land-mining of their African competitors was exacerbating erosion and land degradation. By 1939, the rallying cry of 'the White Highlands in danger' and the conservation card had almost won the game. The settlers had secured the right to dictate their own rules in the contest with the squatters under the 1937 Resident Native Labour Ordinance, which transferred responsibility for controlling squatters to the settler district councils. Meanwhile the focus of the agricultural department's erosion phobia was successfully diverted from the White Highlands to the neighbouring African reserves.[11]

The war, however, intervened just as the squatters were beginning to feel threatened. The real reversal of fortunes in the late 1930s was thus masked until 1945, as both sides profited from the new demand for Kenya's products and the high prices they were able to command. War-time prosperity, however, ensured that when the battle resumed the ensuing crisis would be even worse than had seemed likely in the late 1930s, since both the settler and African economies had expanded and both sides had more to lose than before the war.[12]

When the district councils moved against the squatters in 1945, eliminating small stock and reducing cultivation to two acres per family, the settlers encountered the opposition of a revamped labour department, which warned of the crisis that would be created in the reserves if thousands of squatter stock were forced out of the White Highlands. The labour department attempted to rewrite the terms of the 1937 Ordinance and to reassert central control over the autonomous district councils. It soon discovered, however, like the Colonial Office, that the settler-controlled institutions, such as the district councils, had become firmly incorporated into the colonial state during the war. Both the settlers and the Secretariat saw the department's campaign as a threat to the newly-established accord between state and settlers.[13]

Settler divisions

Settler farmers were deeply divided over the future of squatter labour. Under-capitalised settlers, struggling to survive on marginal land, often connived with their squatters to avoid the Resident Native Labour Ordinance, which had banned 'kaffir farming' at the insistence of the prosperous settlers who had the resources to develop their farms and who had invested on large herds of expensive high-grade cattle. This division became less important during the Second World War, when virtually all European farmers flourished under the guaranteed purchasing agreements with the Ministries of Supply and Food. In this transformed economic environment, settler confidence in Kenya's future as a 'White Man's Country' was restored. During the late 1940s, however, the division became acute once more. Even in the early days of European settlement, the interests of cereal farmers and the plantation sector, which depended on squatter labour, had conflicted with those of the dairy and stock farmers, who were determined to eliminate squatter cattle and small stock from the White Highlands, regardless of the possible disruption of the labour supply. As early as 1908, the stockmen had formed their own Pastoralist Association to represent their interests against those of the settler maize and wheat farmers. After 1945 the stock farmers and their supporters among the prosperous mixed farmers pushed through the district councils' new restrictions on squatter cultivation and stock, which were a source of tick-borne diseases, such as East Coast Fever, and Black and Red Water Fever. By the late 1920s, Rinderpest and Bovine Pleuro-Pneumonia had almost been eliminated in the White Highlands but remained enzootic in the surrounding reserves. Undipped squatter cattle, which were continually being moved between the reserves and the controlled settler areas, were undoubtedly a possible source of infection.[14]

The coffee, tea and pyrethrum plantations, and the commercial maize and wheat farmers, in contrast, all required large quantities of seasonal labour to help with planting and harvests. They encouraged squatters to remain on their farms and allowed them to cultivate small *shambas* and to graze their stock, so that a dependent labour force could easily be tapped when required. Initially the cereal farmers and planters endorsed the stricter post-war regulations. They also feared that their resident labourers might acquire 'squatters' rights' to the land they occupied under English law. But as squatter opposition became apparent and there was a spate of strikes and refusals to reattest on new contrasts, many maize, wheat and pyrethrum growers became increasingly concerned about their threatened harvests. These farmers began to reconsider and to doubt the wisdom of the stringent new regulations. Thus the survival of one group of settlers seemed to threaten the destruction of the other.[15]

This harsher attitude towards the squatters first became evident at a two-day conference of District Council Production Committee representatives in June 1944. Under the chairmanship of Cavendish-Bentinck, the delegates demanded an end to the recruitment of squatters and pressed for the adoption of an agreed policy. The government, they insisted, must take the initiative and put its own house in order by extending the new district council orders to cover the 19,000 squatters who lived in the forests and evaded local controls. Three months later, a conference of district council chairmen declared the existing orders too 'generous' and agreed to strive to eliminate all squatter stock from the White Highlands within five years. The resident labourer, they decided, should be replaced by 'properly paid labour which should not be bribed by allowing it to cultivate and keep stock for gain'. Despite the reservations of certain chairmen about the speed, a motion was adopted that they would begin to remove all squatter stock immediately. These conferences in 1944 marked the beginning of a new phase during which the district councils started to introduce more restrictive regulations under pressure from the dairy and stock interests.[16]

These new orders, however, soon revealed divisions in the settler community and ensured that intense political disputes over the future of squatters occurred in several districts in the decade after the war. Map 5.1 shows the complexity of district council politics and emphasises the varying importance of particular interests with their conflicting views of squatters. Previous historians have ignored these divisions within the settler farming community and have underestimated the labour department's difficulties in trying to co-ordinate the various local options into a coherent policy.[17]

Let us briefly investigate these conflicting economic interests among the settlers in three district councils; Nyanza, Naivasha and the Trans Nzoia. The Nyanza District Council was particularly plagued by the conflicting interest of its settler population. The district ranged from prosperous tea estates at Kericho, owned by metropolitan capital, to poor scrub farmers, surviving on maize monoculture in Sotik. Nyanza, therefore, lacked a unified attitude to squatters. There was always strong opposition to new regulations because the settlers lacked the homogeneous agricultural structure of Naivasha or Nakuru. In Nyanza particular interests could invariably be safeguarded by securing exemptions under the local option clause of the 1937 Ordinance.[18] Naivasha, by contrast, was relatively united. It was the one district which had attempted to impose new restrictions during the war and, over the next few years, consistently adopted the most intransigent attitude to the squatters. The settlers were a relatively homogeneous group of small mixed farmers. Situated on the borders of both the Kikuyu and Maasai reserves, many settlers were financially heavily committed to dairy and stock farming and had built up large herds of high-grade cattle, which were particularly susceptible to the diseases they believed were carried by squatter cattle. Whereas in most other districts the cereal farmers were a powerful lobby in support of squatter rights and opposed any measure that threatened to antagonise over half their labour force, in Naivasha the dairy and stock farmers completely dominated the council and were able to ride roughshod over the few defenders of the resident native labourers. In this European cattle-farming area the fear of diseased squatter stock proved far more powerful than the danger of disrupting the harvest by antagonising the squatters. The Naivasha District Council therefore provided the leadership, throughout the period, for the anti-squatter campaign and set the pace for the other councils to follow.[19]

Even in Naivasha, certain farmers in the semi-arid region on the floor of the Rift Valley considered the Council's 1945 proposal to reduce squatter sheep from 40 to 15 too drastic. It would force virtually all squatters to leave the area and seriously disrupt their labour supply. During the summer of 1945, while the new order was being considered in the Secretariat, several farmers warned of the dire consequences it would have. This opposition was centred on Elmenteita and the Kedong Valley, areas with low rainfall, where the squatters depended on their sheep in years of drought and crop failure. Crops had failed for the last three years and earlier, in 1945, famine relief had been distributed. Both the squatters and the local farmers complained that it was unfair that these areas, with an average rainfall of only 24 inches per annum, which was only enough to grow irregular crops of poor-quality maize, should receive the same regulations as in wetter parts of Naivasha. Squatters on Lord Delamere's feudal estate at Soysambu insisted on keeping 40 sheep. Both 1944 and 1945, they pointed out, had been bad years when they had been unable to reap any harvest and their families had survived only by selling sheep. Their continued existence was imperilled by the district council's limitation of squatter stock to a maximum of 15 sheep. These problems of survival were particularly acute on stock farms that provided little work for women or other opportunities to diversify squatter household incomes. Unfortunately stock farms were concentrated in exactly those semi-arid areas where squatter families most needed alternative sources of money or food. During 1944 and 1945 many squatters had left Soysambu to seek work on farms where they could be assured of harvesting enough food to satisfy their families, and the manager was extremely concerned that many more would leave if sheep numbers were reduced as proposed by the new order. The Naivasha Council, however, supported by the majority of dairy and stock farmers, refused to back down, despite pressure from the labour department and mounting squatter protests.[20]

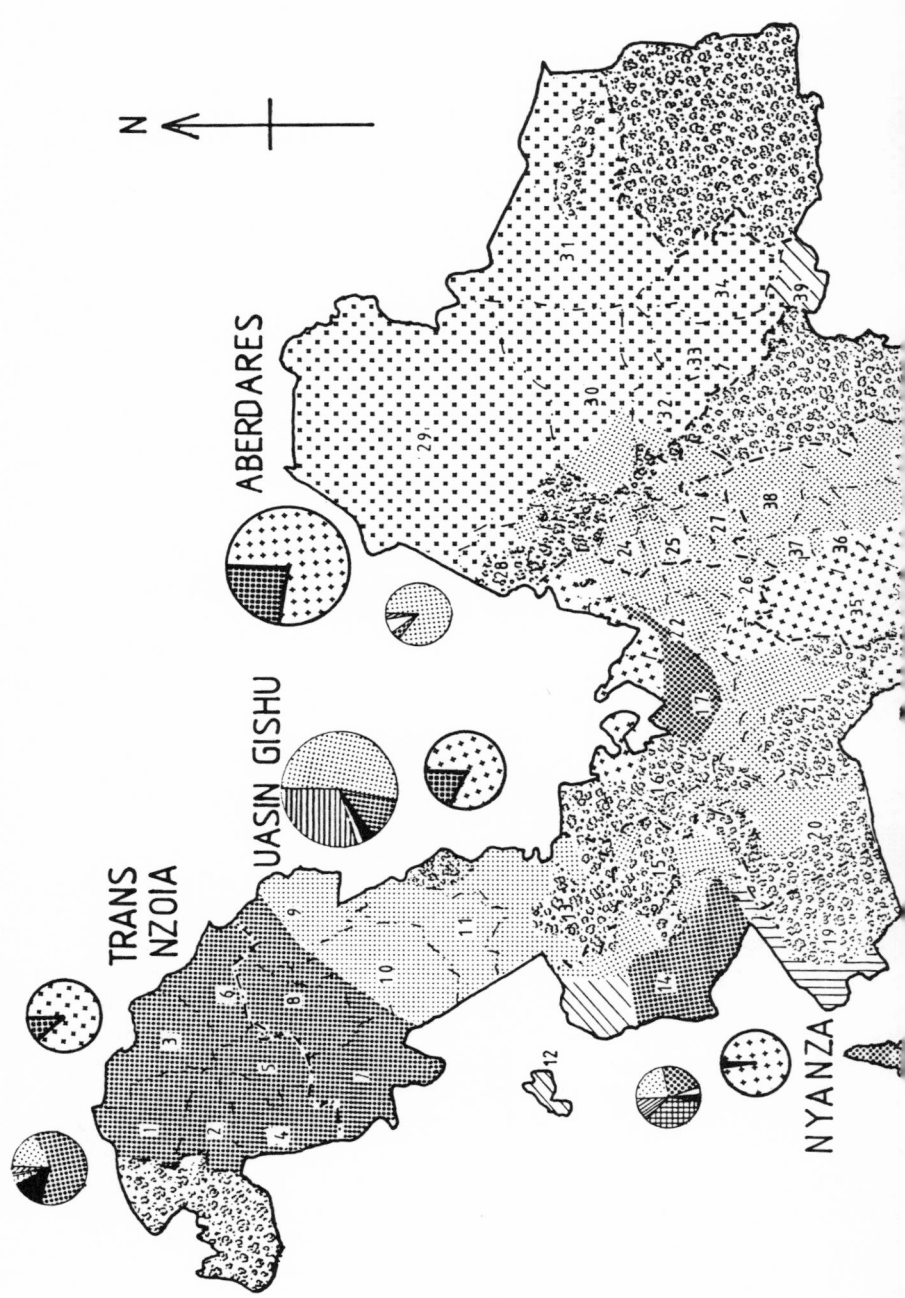

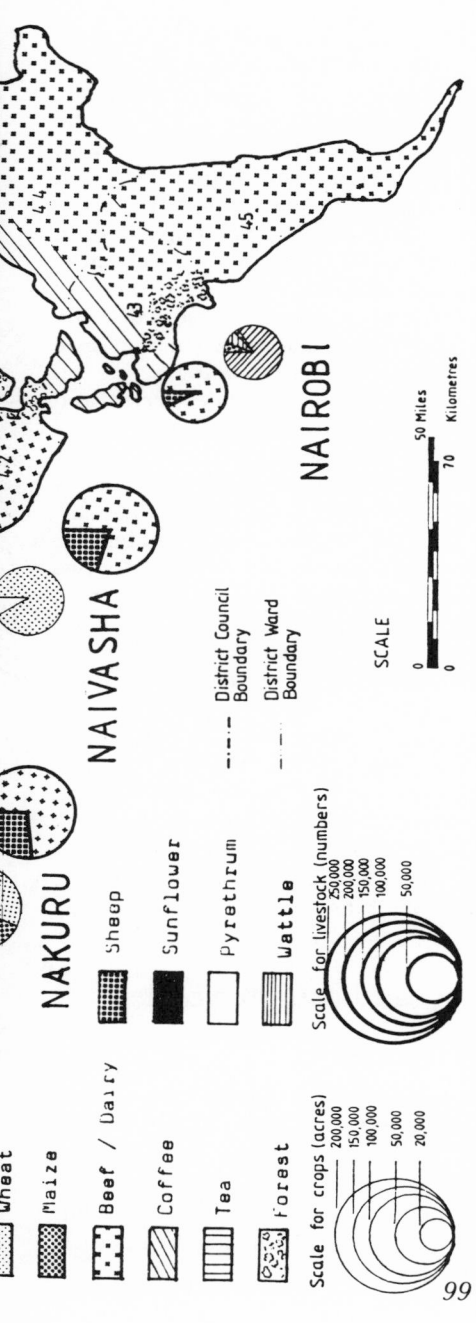

Wheat

Maize

Beef / Dairy

Coffee

Tea

Forest

Sheep

Sunflower

Pyrethrum

Wattle

Scale for crops (acres)
200,000
100,000
50,000
20,000

Scale for livestock (numbers)
250,000
150,000
150,000
100,000
50,000

NAKURU

NAIVASHA

NAIROBI

--- District Council Boundary

---- District Ward Boundary

SCALE

0   50 Miles
0   70 Kilometres

99

District Council Ward Production Committee Areas

1 NNW Trans Nzoia
2 NW Trans Nzoia
3 NE Trans Nzoia
4 WSW Trans Nzoia
5 SSW Trans Nzoia
6 SE Trans Nzoia
7 Turbo
8 Soy/Hoey's Bridge
9 Moiben

10 Eldoret
11 Elgeyo Border
12 Nandi
13 Kipkabus
14 Lumbwa/Songhor
15 Londiani
16 Eldama Ravine
17 Rongai
18 Sotik

19 Kericho
20 Mau/Molo
21 Njoro
22 Solai
23 Subukia
24 Thomson's Falls
25 Ol Joro Orok
26 Mereroni
27 Ol Kalou

28 Marmanet
29 Rumuruti
30 Leshau
31 Nanyuki
32 Aberdares
33 Moyo Ridge
34 Naro Moru
35 Elmenteita
36 Lower Gilgil

37 Upper Gilgil
38 Ol Bolossat
39 Nyeri
40 Naivasha
41 N. Kinangop
42 S. Kinangop
43 Nairobi
44 Thika
45 Machakos

Map 5.1: *Settler Districts and Land Use*

In Trans Nzoia, by contrast, the council was eventually forced to reconsider. By the beginning of 1946, many maize and pyrethrum farmers had already become seriously concerned about what effect the council's order would have on their labour supply. Within a month of the regulations being introduced, the district council found itself faced with strong opposition from the settlers as squatter resistance grew. A special meeting of the council failed to resolve the disagreements, as the hardliners proposed that if the order made the labour situation impossible on certain farms, then the district council should insist on the government reintroducing conscription to ensure that the district's valuable food crops were harvested. The opponents of the order, however, insisted that any attempt to reduce squatter stock would seriously disrupt production since resident labourers provided 40 per cent of the labour force.[21]

This dispute was a struggle, as in the other districts, between cereal and dairy farmers. Of the 102 farmers who voted for the elimination of squatter stock in the poll organised by the district council, 42 did so primarily out of fear of the threat posed by African stock to their dairy herds, while of the 63 votes cast against the order, 38 stated that they saw the orders as guaranteed to exacerbate the existing shortage of labour. They proposed that the operation of the regulations be postponed for two years until the world food crisis had eased and Kenya's labour pool increased. Defeated in the council by six votes to five, the maize and pyrethrum farmers continued to protest and eventually forced the council to postpone the reduction of squatter cattle for 18 months until 1 June 1947.[22]

By 1946, maize and wheat farmers, the plantations and even some cattle ranchers in the more arid areas, were concerned by the repercussions of the new draconian limitations on squatter stock and cultivation, which had been pushed through the district councils by the dairy and stock lobby, which did not depend on squatter labour. A cleavage had emerged within settler ranks as African, particularly Kikuyu, opposition increased and the threat of large-scale disruption of production became increasingly apparent.[23]

The labour department and squatter policy

The Kenyan official mind did not have a squatter policy. Indeed as will become apparent, different sections of the colonial state held fundamentally opposed views. The member for local government, for example, soon emerged as a firm ally of the settler district councils in their fight to impose stricter controls. At the centre of this dispute inside the Secretariat stood the labour department. Throughout the war, although it had enforced the new orders, the department had taken little part in the formulation of policy. When bitter opposition emerged among the squatters in Naivasha and Nakuru, the department felt increasingly frustrated by the councils' utter disregard of its warnings.[24]

For the first five years after the Colonial Office had belatedly approved the new Resident Native Labour Ordinance in 1940, the reconstituted labour department had left the district councils to grope towards their different solutions to the squatter problem, but, as the anti-squatter lobby began to force the pace at the end of the war, the labour department felt compelled to intervene. As early as April 1945, Wyn Harris, the Labour Commissioner, had seen the dangers involved and had warned the Chief Secretary that 'the problem of the squatter is going to be one of the most serious problems of this country, and it has already assumed in certain areas unmanageable proportions'. The Labour Commissioner understood the fears of many settler farmers about squatters acquiring land rights inside the White Highlands and the disease threat posed by squatter stock, but he warned that the new district council orders would antagonise the resident labourers and their families and create violent opposition.[25]

The labour department was especially concerned about the draconian restrictions proposed in Naivasha. The department vigorously opposed the order inside the Secretariat and attempted to persuade the Council to reconsider and to allow squatters in the more arid zones to keep 30 or 40 sheep. When the Council rejected this advice, the Labour Commissioner informed the Commissioner for Local Government of his formal opposition to the proposed reductions. Wyn Harris urged a gradual reduction, which would enable the squatters and their employers to adjust and to increase the wage component of household incomes. Despite these protests from the department, which was responsible for enforcing the district councils' orders, the Standing Committee for Local Government in Rural Areas – a settler-dominated body – approved the restrictions on 27 October 1945.[26]

Following this rejection of its advice, the labour department began to devise its own squatter policy. This, however, proved to be an extremely difficult task, since the 1937 Ordinance had transferred power over resident labourers from central government to the district councils. The Secretariat was therefore extremely reluctant to interfere with council affairs in case this precipitated one of Kenya's famed political storms, since to tamper with settler privileges, especially those established by statute, was to play with fire. Settler power had been consolidated during the war. We have seen how the acute manpower shortage forced the government to co-opt settlers to serve in the state bureaucracy. This wartime acceptance of the district councils' responsibility for squatters meant that, after 1945, the labour department had to compete against accepted settler authorities for control over the policy. The war and the 1937 Ordinance had both fundamentally shifted the political balance of power and transformed the district councils into 'governing institutions' with a legitimate right to influence, and even sometimes to dictate, the direction of government action. By 1945 it was widely accepted within the Kenyan government that these settler institutions, rather than the labour department, should determine squatter policy. The department had become no more than the executive arm of the district councils and was expected simply to enforce their orders.[27]

Following the refusal of the district councils and the Standing Committee to heed its warnings, the labour department launched a campaign to force the Secretariat to reconsider or, if this could not be achieved, to transfer responsibility for controlling squatters from the department either to the field administration or to the agricultural department. The Labour Officer at Nakuru warned that if the Nakuru and Naivasha orders were introduced, they would have a catastrophic effect on squatter household incomes. While settlers had profited from the high commodity prices during the war, squatter wages had remained static at eight shillings per 30-day ticket, and they had relied upon selling their stock and vegetables from their *shambas* to satisfy their subsistence requirements. The new orders, he pointed out, were specifically designed to reduce this additional income but did not compensate the squatter families with higher wages or increased rations. Consequently, squatters who had been a comparatively prosperous group of Africans were being squeezed into destitution by the district council regulations.[28]

Wyn Harris was so alarmed by the growth of squatter resistance in Naivasha and the spectre of widespread food shortages among the squatters, who accepted new contracts, that he took independent action and instructed the attestation officers not to issue new contracts unless wages in the semi-arid zones were increased to at least twelve shillings per ticket and squatters given two pounds of *posho* for every day worked. These measures at least ensured that those who reattested were not threatened by starvation. The Labour Commissioner complained that the district councils did not realise the consequences of their restrictions. While their long-term aim to change the squatter into a wage labourer was correct, they were moving far too rapidly. Squatters would not disappear overnight if their stock and cultivation rights were removed. The only result would be chaos and serious resistance. Progress towards stricter control had to be slow, spread over perhaps one or two generations rather than one or two years as some district councils envisaged.[29]

Wyn Harris and his successor Hyde-Clarke both persistently reiterated that squatter wages must be increased to offset reductions in stock and crops. Squatters, Wyn Harris observed in November 1945, often made profits from selling stock of 50 shillings per month; 30 shillings was common. This vital source of income, one of the attractions that originally encouraged squatters to leave the reserves for the White Highlands, was being destroyed. The Nakuru order, for example, would reduce these earnings by half to 25 shillings per month, with the result that squatter family budgets would decline by one-third unless male wages were increased from between eight to twelve shillings per 30-day ticket to at least 30 or 40 shillings. Even this dramatic increase would merely preserve the *status quo*. Until the district councils realised this crucial fact and raised squatter wages in an attempt to offset the effects of their more stringent controls of land use, squatter opposition would continue. Wyn Harris therefore urged the government to assert its authority and to refuse to sanction further reductions in squatter rights.[30]

Eventually the Labour Commissioner persuaded Rennie, who was acting as governor during Mitchell's absence in South Africa, to agree to squatters being compensated with higher wages for reduced stock and crops. He also succeeded in obtaining a respite during which the Secretariat would reconsider the Naivasha order. Cavendish-Bentinck, the member for agriculture, was appointed chairman of an interim committee to consider squatter policy.[31]

Cavendish-Bentinck's committees on squatter policy

Cavendish-Bentinck recognised that the district councils had acted precipitately; after neglecting the squatter problem for years, he observed, the 'local authorities have now taken the bit in their teeth and are all vying with each other in passing regulations which are far too drastic and which do not in any way conform to any general plan'. The committee first met on 14 March 1946 to discuss a detailed report by Wyn Harris. Part one presented a factual review of the question and analysed squatter household incomes. The second part, entitled 'An Approach to the Solution', contained the dramatic statement that the 250,000 squatters simply could not be reabsorbed into the African reserves. Any discussion of the possible options, Wyn Harris declared, had to begin with the recognition that 'it must be accepted that the majority of these families are on the farms for good'. This, of course, was diametrically opposed to the settlers' desire to end the threat of resident labourers acquiring squatters' rights on their farms.[32]

The labour department reported that it had discovered that squatter household incomes were even higher than it had estimated. Wyn Harris explained that they should aim to create a contented wage labourer, 'who regards his labour as his main means of livelihood, but whose efficiency, and indeed, the general economy of the country makes it impossible to pay the wage we know to be necessary for his reasonable standard of living'.[33] Investigations in Naivasha had revealed that in the Kinangop, a high, wet area, where the settler dairy farms were concentrated, average squatter family incomes had amounted to 1,200 shillings per annum, and one household had even earned 3,700 shillings. In the lower zone, where the stock farms were situated, average annual incomes were still above 700 shillings. Indeed the lowest figure the labour department discovered in the whole district was 274 shillings. Average squatter household annual incomes in neighbouring Nakuru District could be broken down as in Table 5.1 below.[34]

Table 5.1:   Squatter Household Earnings in Nakuru District in 1946

	Shillings per household per annum
Earnings from cultivation	374
Income from selling sheep	120
Male earnings from ticket labour	90
Earnings by women and children	46
Total earnings	630

This amounted to over 50 shillings per month per household which was more than many urban workers received. These figures, of course, were only estimates acquired in unsettled times when squatter distrust of government was at its height. Nevertheless, they provide the most detailed estimates available of squatter incomes and had a profound impact on the labour department's thinking. Both Wyn Harris and Hyde-Clarke realised that total squatter household earnings would have to be safeguarded and wages raised as quickly as possible. Few settlers had yet realised that squatters earned such considerable sums from their *shambas* and stock. The Labour Commissioner summed up the problem to the committee: 'Farmers regard the resident labourer as cheap labour. He is not, he receives in total wages far more than the ordinary monthly or migrant labourer.'[35] It was therefore inevitable that the district council orders, which had all failed to take account of squatter earnings apart from wage labour, would provoke unrest. Squatter households were earning far more from the black economy than they did by working for settlers. As occupation and stock rights were reduced, the squatters and their families, Wyn Harris emphasised, would have to be compensated. The question was how much could the settler economy afford?

The labour department proposed that total family incomes should not fall below 480 shillings per annum. According to its calculations, this could be assured without threatening the profitability of settler agriculture, since wages only needed to be raised to 12 shillings per month. This would amount to 120 shillings per annum, while earnings by wives and children from farm labour should produce another 150 shillings per annum. Produce grown on squatters' *shambas* would contribute another 90 shillings and food provided by employers would be equivalent to another 120 shillings. The department was optimistic that this 50 per cent increase in the basic wages could be offset by greater productivity.[36]

From this stage onwards progress became extremely slow as the forces of opposition gathered inside the Secretariat to resist the new policy. Cavendish-Bentinck's interim committee had first met to discuss Wyn Harris's statement of squatters on 14 March 1946. There was then a delay of a year while more precise information was gathered on squatter household incomes and, for the first three months of 1947, the Secretariat was preoccupied by the Mombasa general strike. It was therefore not until 3 March 1947 that Cavendish-Bentinck's committee reconvened. So far it had taken nearly a year to confirm Wyn Harris's memorandum.[37]

The new Labour Commissioner, Meredyth Hyde-Clarke, proposed that squatters should be seen as part of the interrelated agrarian problems confronting Kenya. The African reserves were already overpopulated and overstocked and were incapable of absorbing large numbers of dispossessed squatters with their stock. Settler farmers, he insisted, must be persuaded that it was in their interests to keep Africans in the White Highlands as a contented labour supply. Hyde-Clarke outlined a five-phase strategy for creating a contented African population in the White Highlands while ending its dependence on the land. According to this analysis, Africans in the reserves were still at phase one, being totally dependent on the land for their livelihood, while the squatters had advanced to stage two and were partially dependent upon wage labour although cultivation and stock still provided their main source of income. Stage three, which had now been reached, required a gradual continuation of this trend with squatters becoming less dependent on the land and more on wages, until they had reached a position similar to that of the Scottish crofter. Stage four carried this process even further, until the labourer received his income almost entirely in wages and had only a small vegetable plot akin to the cottage labourer. Stage five, the ultimate aim of the process, was the creation of completely dependent wage labourers, without any access to land.[38]

Essentially the move to stage three – the crofter – which was taking place in the White Highlands was the most difficult change, requiring the reduction of squatter cultivation and stock. The labour department considered that this transformation had been made more difficult than necessary by the precipitate action of certain district councils, which seemed to be attempting to jump straight from stage two – the squatter – to stage four without any increase in squatter wages. This foolhardy course inevitably provoked serious opposition and profoundly increased African suspicions of all attempts to wean them away from dependence on the land. According to the labour department, the crofter phase ought to last a generation, during which time the squatters' wives and children could be coaxed into working at least six months a year. The reduction of African holdings to one acre of cultivation and sufficient land to graze ten sheep or two cattle would enable large portions of the White Highlands to be returned to the settler for intensive occupation. This redistribution of land, it was believed, would itself enable the settlers to pay higher wages to their squatters. This would enable a further reduction in African plots and facilitate the progression to stage four. This evolution from the crofter to the cottage labourer phase should be gradual rather than precipitated by convulsive changes in African life. Workers would live on the settler farms and markets, schools, welfare centres and shops would be established in 'villages'. Increased efficiency would enable higher wages to be paid, which would further reduce reliance on land, until in the fifth phase Africans would live in these villages, working as craftsmen or farm labourers, without any access to land.[39]

When the squatter policy committee met on 7 May 1947 to consider Hyde-Clarke's proposals, it agreed that the squatter problem was primarily another aspect of Kenya's agrarian crisis. It also acknowledged that it was politically impossible to send large numbers of dispossessed squatters back to the reserves. Any such attempt would create grave social and economic distress. Squatters must, therefore, either remain 'under control' in the White Highlands or be absorbed in secondary industries in the towns. This statement was a decisive victory for the labour department over its settler critics. It was the first unambiguous assertion by the government that the squatter problem would not go away and could not simply be resolved by moving disgruntled Africans back to the over-crowded reserves. If the squatter was to disappear, he and his family would have to be transformed into fully-paid agricultural labourers, capable of living on their farm wages. The solution to the problem, it seems to have been acknowledged, lay in the White Highlands themselves, and with increased investment and modernisation by the settlers, rather than in new draconian restrictions. At last, it appeared, a policy had been agreed by the Secretariat. Provided the official mind remained united it would be able to force the district councils to moderate their moves against squatters.[40]

The retreat of the Trans Nzoia district council

Let us briefly examine how the combined opposition of the cereal and pyrethrum farmers, the labour department and the field administration in North Nyanza and Nandi was able to force one of the more divided district councils – Trans Nzoia – to reconsider its anti-squatter legislation. Trans Nzoia was the maize granary of East Africa, producing nearly half the settler crop in Kenya, while the neighbouring African reserve, North Nyanza, was the main African producer. During 1946 and 1947 there was a serious shortfall in maize supplies to the central Supply Board and, in February 1946, the Maize Controller had recommended that maize rations, the staple African diet, would have to be cut in the towns from two to one and a half pounds. When the government finally agreed in July, the supply position had become even more desperate. The Trans Nzoia's new restrictions upon squatters would have further disrupted supplies of maize, not only in Trans Nzoia, when the squatters refused to reattest under the new regulations, but also in North Nyanza, which would have had to reabsorb 20,000 cattle and thousands of squatter families, who would have consumed a large proportion of the district's surplus maize crop, which was usually exported. Any further reduction in maize supplies might have had serious repercussions in Nairobi and Mombasa where discontent was growing over the lack of food.[41]

The new Labour Commissioner, Hyde-Clarke, was extremely perturbed that the situation in Trans Nzoia and North Nyanza might become the same as in Naivasha, where the district council's restrictions had produced widespread strikes among farm labourers and mounting violence. He suggested that Trans Nzoia should follow the example of its neighbours in Uasin Gishu, who had introduced what the labour department regarded as the least oppressive of the spate of new orders. Like the labour department's own proposals, it was designed gradually to replace squatters with casual labour. Squatter cattle were gradually to be absorbed into the reserve over a five-year period. The ultimate aim of the Tranz Nzoia regulations was the same, but the labour department and the field administration felt that they were trying to move too quickly.[42]

As we have seen, widespread opposition from the maize and pyrethrum farmers won a postponement of the order until July 1947. This, however, compounded the dangers since the dairy farmers had insisted that, over the following 18 months, squatter cattle would not simply be reduced in number but completely eliminated from the district. This 'compromise' between the settler factions was guaranteed to provoke mass resistance by the squatters and was likely to create serious discontent in North Nyanza. The labour department and field administration protested that no regard had been given to the squatters' interests. The timing of the exodus, for example, had been fixed to serve the settlers rather than to diminish the plight of the squatters' families. The local Labour Officer insisted on the date of the moves coinciding with the African planting season. The end of June, proposed by the district council, was totally unsatisfactory; maize would be at the beginning of its growth cycle; there would be no crops in the reserves to tide the squatters over until they could break new land and secure their harvest. This would take at least six months.[43]

During July and August 1947, Vaughan-Philpott, the chairman of the Trans Nzoia District Council, held discussions with Hyde-Clarke and T.C. Colchester, the secretary for local government, to devise a more acceptable solution. The Labour Commissioner reiterated his view that a gradual reduction was the only way to avoid serious disruption of the labour supply and squatter resistance. He pointed to the situation in

Naivasha as a warning of the dangers of rapid destocking and cautioned that if the Trans Nzoia order were submitted to the governor, the labour department would vigorously oppose its passage through the Executive Council. The government, he informed the hardliners, would under no circumstances contemplate introducing conscription to solve the labour crisis which would ensue. He urged the council to reconsider and to follow its neighbours in the Uasin Gishu, who had adopted a policy of gradual destocking, whereby the number of squatters with cattle were to be reduced by 20 per cent per annum. If only one-fifth of squatters on every farm lost their stock each year, this would sufficiently limit the number of cattle flowing into the reserves to enable them to be absorbed. Equally, if some squatters refused to accept the new regulations they could be dismissed without totally disrupting the labour supply since only a proportion would have to leave every year, and the gaps could be filled with casual labour before the next stage of the controlled reduction began. Hyde-Clarke suggested that squatters' contracts should be allowed to expire rather than be terminated, as the council had suggested, at a specific time. This would further reduce the threat of disruption, since the movement of squatters back to the reserves would become a continuous flow. Serious dislocation in both the Trans Nzoia and the reserves would be prevented and a further fall in the colony's food supply circumvented.[44]

Eventually the council agreed to phase its elimination of squatter stock over a four-year period. It was also persuaded, at the prompting of the District Commissioner for North Nyanza, to meet the North Nyanza chiefs at Kakamega to discuss how they could minimise the effects of the expulsion on the reserves. The chiefs also agreed to encourage disgruntled squatters to remain as farm labourers in the Trans Nzoia without their cattle. Thus the labour department and the field administration, supported by a large number of apprehensive maize farmers, successfully forestalled the growth of squatter resistance and persuaded the district council to reconsider.[45]

Opposition in the Secretariat

Meanwhile the labour department's opponents in the Secretariat had become increasingly vociferous. Both Mortimer, the member for Health and Local Government, who was nominally responsible for district council affairs and therefore for squatters, and Cavendish-Bentinck, who was firmly embedded inside the government, were unwilling to antagonise the district councils. These key officials were both settlers in disguise. Mortimer's father had been a prominent settler politician and mayor of Nairobi, while Cavendish-Bentinck was a former leader of the European Elected Members in the Legislative Council and a settler nominee on the Executive Council. They had been extremely embarrassed by the labour department's campaign and feared that it would destroy the good relations between the government and the settlers, which they deemed essential if the government was to secure settler politial support for its social engineering schemes in the reserves. The fight against the Labour Department's squatter policies, therefore, continued inside the Secretariat. Cavendish-Bentinck and Mortimer were particularly adept at using delaying tactics to prevent further consideration of the department's proposals.[46]

It was now two years since Wyn Harris, exasperated by Cavendish-Bentinck's delaying strategy, had tried to shift responsibility for enforcing squatter controls to the agricultural department. It was, he had informed Cavendish-Bentinck, a problem 'concerned to a very much greater degree with the proper utilisation of land, which is your responsibility, rather than with the proper utilisation of man power, which is perhaps mine'.[47] Wyn Harris had argued that the labour department was destroying its reputation among Africans by being identified as the enforcer of the hated new regulations. The agricultural department, however, had no desire to become associated with the anti-squatter orders while it was attempting to gain African support for its agricultural campaign in the reserves. Cavendish-Bentinck did not want to take over executive responsibility for squatter affairs or to be exposed to settler and squatter criticism. He realised that, as a former settler politician, he would have provided an ideal target for Kenyatta and for left-wing criticism in Britain if he appeared to be leading the anti-squatter campaign. He preferred instead to play a spoiling role, hamstringing the labour department's attempts to reduce the authority of the district councils from the anonymity of the Secretariat. The labour department, therefore, remained trapped in the invidious position of having to enforce district council orders with which it wholeheartedly disagreed.[48]

By June 1949, relations between Hyde-Clarke and Cavendish-Bentinck had become so strained that the Labour Commissioner was not even consulted over the preparation of a new memorandum on squatters for the Executive Council discussions. When Hyde-Clarke discovered the meeting had taken place, he furiously demanded that responsibility for squatters be immediately transferred from his department. The squatters, he declared, were an agricultural problem which should be controlled as part of the proposed agrarian legislation. He pointed out that the Executive Council's decision the previous day to approve raids to seize excess stock from squatters in Nairobi district clearly demonstrated the oppressive nature of squatter control and that this was undermining African trust in his department which was supposed to protect African interests. Since the Executive Councils's squatter sub-committee no longer contained any representative from the labour department, the situation was now completely ludicrous.[49]

Nothing, however, actually happened. The district councils'

dominance became even more entrenched with the formation of a resident labour sub-committee of the standing committee for Local Government in Rural Areas on 4 July 1949 and the announcement, in August, that resident labour inspectors, although members of the labour department, would henceforth come directly under the control of the district councils. Scrutiny of the memorandum on squatters, which was presented to the Executive Council in January 1950, clearly reveals how little progress had been made since 1946 in enforcing the labour department's strategy on the councils. Meanwhile squatter opposition had spread from Naivasha throughout the White Highlands. If anything, the department's influence was less than at the end of the war. In February 1950, the governor himself intervened to ensure that the authority of the settler-dominated Standing Committee for Local Government in Rural Areas should not be infringed. The settlers' infiltration into the heart of the colonial state had ensured that they had been able to block any proposals to reduce their power. The final *dénouement* came in August 1950, when the district councils unilaterally decided to seize complete control over squatter affairs. Major Sharpe, the chairman of the Aberdares Council, with the support of the six other district council representatives on the central co-ordinating committee successfully resolved to disband this consultative committee and to transfer discussion of resident native labour regulations to the Association of District Councils. Henceforth the district councils were to scrutinise their own orders. The attempt to formulate a uniform squatter policy acceptable to different sectors of settler agriculture, the field administration in the reserves and the labour department, was abandoned. After 1950, each district council was allowed to devise its own squatter policies according to the relative strength of the pastoral and arable interests in each particular area. Soon there was a proliferation of local options as the councils abandoned the attempt to reconcile these conflicting interests; by 1952 there were no less than 14 local options in the Nyanza District Council area alone. This plethora of local variations made the labour department's task of enforcement virtually impossible, while the constant alteration of regulations inflamed the squatters.[50]

The growth of squatter resistance

By November 1946, more than 3,000 Kikuyu squatters in Naivasha, Nakuru and the Aberdares had refused to reattest and had been forced to leave the White Highlands.[51] Many of them congregated at Limuru just inside the Kikuyu reserve. On 21 and 22 November 1946, large numbers of them travelled to Nairobi and demonstrated outside the Secretariat, insisting that they would not go away until they had seen the Chief Native Commissioner, the head of the field administration. When a meeting eventually took place at Kiambu on 30 December 1946, with the Provincial and District Commissioners and Hyde-Clarke, the dispossessed squatters protested against the settlers having seized their land at the beginning of the century and demanded that they be resettled on their original *githaka* in Kiambu. The squatters' campaign continued. On the evening of 1 February 1947, for example, a group of 30 squatters broke into the grounds of Government House and confronted a startled Mitchell. They complained that their wives and families in Limuru were starving and insisted on knowing why they had been forced off their small *shambas* when the settlers already had such large farms. Many of their families, they declared, had worked on settler farms for 30 years, had completely lost contact with Kikuyuland and had nowhere to go. The governor, of course, refused their demand for land in Kiambu and urged them to reattest, if only for 12 months, until the authorities could investigate the problem. They had, the governor declared, brought their troubles upon themselves, by abandoning their homes and *shambas* when the new district council regulations were introduced, without any thought of how they would survive.

Throughout 1947, petitions flowed from the Kikuyu Highlands Squatters' Association in Limuru to the Secretary of State, complaining about the Kikuyu's plight and urging the Colonial Office to intervene to save them from the settler-controlled Kenyan government. Mitchell, however, advised Whitehall that they must not waver since 'any weakening in this attitude at the present time would inevitably lead to the belief that Africans could occupy the European lands with impunity and a very dangerous situation would be created'.[52] In other words, the sanctity of the White Highlands must remain inviolate and the authority of the Kenyan government and the settler-controlled district councils upheld.

In Naivasha, Nakuru and the Aberdares, where the vast majority of squatters were Kikuyu, the labour department could do little to protect them from the onslaught of a united settler community after the war. We have noted that these three districts were comparatively homogeneous communities of heavily capitalised dairy and stock farmers, who were determined to get rid of all squatter-owned stock from their farms. Between 1945 and 1947 the settlers successfully fought and defeated their Kikuyu economic rivals, using their privileged access to the corridors of power to manipulate the colonial state.[53]

During the first months of 1947, squatter discontent spread. Abaluhya, Elgeyo and Nandi squatters, as well as the Kikuyu, had realised that the district council orders threatened their continued prosperity and, in desperation, had turned to violence as a final act of resistance. Arson and cattle maiming enabled the politically powerless to voice their opposition to the new restrictions which were destroying their way of life. By the end of 1947, the intransigent behaviour of the district councils had irreparably damaged the labour department's gradualist strategy to transform the squatter into a contented and productive wage labourer. September 1947 had seen the virtual collapse of Mitchell's original policies. The government's agricultural campaign in the reserves, based on terracing, had alienated the Kikuyu peasantry and Nairobi seemed to be on the verge of a general strike. Meanwhile, in the White Highlands squatter discontent was causing acute alarm not only in Naivasha and Nakuru, where many were still refusing to reattest under the new regulations, but also in the Uasin Gishu and the Aberdares, where within six weeks there were strikes on 14 farms. Many Trans Nzoia settlers, such as S.H. Powles and A.C. Hoey, two of the district's largest landowners, were also extremely concerned about the possibility of the troubles spreading to their area when the new district council order, reducing squatter cattle by one-third, came into operation on 1 January 1948. If all squatter stock were to be removed in a three-stage operation by 1 April 1950, the overcrowded Nandi and North Nyanza reserves would have to absorb large numbers of squatter-owned cattle. It was estimated, for example, that the total number of cattle in the Nandi reserve would increase by more than 50 per cent, from 175,000 to 275,000, with disastrous consequences for the ecological balance of the reserve.[54]

By the end of 1947, Kikuyu squatters from the Naivasha, Nakuru, Aberdares and Nairobi district council areas had been forced to admit defeat. Unlike the Kalenjin or Abaluhya squatters, they could not pressurise the settler farmers by threatening to return to the reserves, since most had abandoned their *githaka* land three decades earlier when they had moved to the White Highlands. The Kikuyu squatters therefore had three options. Some began to move into the Uasin Gishu and Trans Nzoia, where the squatter option was still possible. Others returned in frustration to Central Province, where they became a focus of discontent. The vast majority, however, realising that a return to Kikuyuland was pointless, remained on the settler farms, embittered and waiting to be politicised. Once again the settlers seemed to have got their way and had forced the government to approve measures about which many members of the administration and the labour department had serious reservations. It appeared to many squatters that constitutionalist African politicians of the élitist Kenya African Union made little headway against the entrenched influence of the settlers. The moderates became increasingly discredited as their constituents turned in desperation to the militant advocates of violent resistance to what they denounced as 'settler rule'.[55]

After 1947 the Kikuyu squatters waited, preparing to get their own back on their settler overlords. By 1949/50, the situation was already very tense. Those squatters who had reattested were being attacked and large numbers of the radicals were abandoning the farms and vanishing into the forests. The deteriorating labour supply was already beginning to concern the Naivasha resident labour committee. In the neighbouring Aberdares

District Council, Major L.B.L. Hughes complained that when squatters refused to reattest 'it is a very rare occurrence that new labour applies to take their place, unless first class land, usually the very best on the farm is made available for their cultivation'.[56]

Squatter resistance in the area was led by Mwangi Mukea and, until his arrest, the administration seemed on the verge of losing control. As in the Uasin Gishu, where Elijah Masinde's *Dini ya Msambwa* was active, resistance took the form of religious millenarianism. Former squatters in Naivasha joined the *Dini ya Jesu Kristo*, with its message that the White Highlands belonged to Africans and its prophecy that the Europeans would soon be driven out of Kenya. Rumours of a secret organisation called Mau Mau, which would unite the Kikuyu and drive out the settlers, began to circulate. The District Commissioner, R.D.F. Ryland, was so concerned that he held six anti-Mau Mau *barazas* in Naivasha during August 1950, which were attended by hundreds of squatters. Between 1950 and 1952, physical intimidation increased among the squatters with the spread of oathing from Olenguruone on the Mau escarpment, an area radicalised by a ten-year conflict over the government's agricultural regulations. Oath administrators from Nairobi had also been active around Limuru, where many former Naivasha squatters had taken refuge. Oathing had also spread to the resident labourers on the settler farms in North and South Kinangop. Underground opposition was gaining strength. Africans opposed to Mau Mau were attacked and several mutilated bodies were discovered. Beneath the surface calm of the White Highlands discontent seethed.[57]

The district councils' policies of compulsory destocking and drastic reductions in squatter cultivation had produced a violent backlash. By 1952, the labour department's squatter inspectors had been completely discredited in African eyes, because of the district councils' intransigence, and had become identified as the oppressive arm of the settler-controlled state. Mau Mau support was strongest exactly where the reductions in squatters' rights had been most severe – among the Kikuyu resident labourers of the Aberdares, Nakuru and, above all, Naivasha areas.[58]

Notes

1. KNA Lab 9/320, 'The Resident Labourers' Ordinance: Aberdare District Council, 1944-51', Major L.B.L. Hughes to DC Naivasha, 16 March 1949.
2. Contrast the estimates of squatter household incomes in CO 533/549/38232/15 (1946-47), 'European Settlement: Squatters', Wyn Harris's 'A Discussion of the Problem of the Squatter', 21 February 1946; and J.H. Martin, 'The Problem of the Squatter: Economic Survey of Resident Labour in Kenya', 24 February 1947; with CO 852/662/19936/2 (1945-46), 'Soil Erosion: Kenya', N. Humphrey, 'The Relationship of Population to the Land in South Nyeri', paragraph 9.

3. KNA Lab 9/316, 'Resident Labour: Naivasha County Council, 1941-59'; Lab 9/320,'
    The Resident Labour Ordinance: Aberdares District Council, 1944-51; Lab 9/317,
    'Resident Labour: Nakuru, 1945-53'.

Ethnic Orgins of Squatters in the White Highlands in 1945

	Luo, Gusii & Luhya	Kipsigis	Nandi	Kikuyu	Kamba	Others	Total
Nairobi	252	nil	nil	11,675	18,620	96	30,643
Naivasha	24	166	50	22,136	79	227	22,682
Nakuru	687	929	106	36,383	87	300	38,492
Aberdares	24	392	5	19,622	11	218	20,272
Uasin Gishu	3,843	898	16,723	3,709	4	4,907	30,084
Trans Nzoia	8,946	431	1,800	754	nil	5,811	17,742
Nyanza	822	9,582	4,295	6,754	nil	24	21,477
Forests	66	52	nil	21,143	8	114	21,383
Total	14,664	12,450	22,979	122,176	18,809	11,697	202,775

The table is based on information from CO 533/549/38232/15 (1946-47), 'European Settlement: Squatters', J.H. Martin, 'The Problem of the Squatter: Economic Survey of
Resident Labour in Kenya', 24 February 1947.

4. KNA Lab 9/310, 'Resident Labourers' General: Ordinance Committee, 1949-50',
    meeting of the central co-ordinating committee, 9 August 1950; and minute by the
    Secretary of Health and Local Government, 28 August 1950.
5. F. Furedi, 'The Kikuyu Squatters in the Rift Valley', pp. 179-83; K.J. King and R.M.
    Wambaa, 'The Political Economy of the Rift Valley', pp. 193-209; and T.M.J.
    Kanogo's unpublished thesis, 'The History of Kikuyu Movement . . .', especially
    pp. 74-87, 113-17. See also her unpublished articles, 'The Kikuyu Squatter Pheno-
    menon in the Nakuru District of the Rift Valley', and 'Comparative Analysis of Aspira-
    tions of the Kikuyu, Luo and Luhya Workers in the White Highlands', pp. 3-9; G.
    Kitching, *Class and Economic Change in Kenya*, p. 294; and Report of the Kenya Land
    Commission: Evidence and Memoranda, vol. 1, (London, 1934, Cmd. 4556), pp.
    167-70, 589-92, 885-7.
6. T.M.J. Kanogo's thesis, 'The History of Kikuyu Movement . . .', pp. 149-224; and
    R.M.A. van Zwanenberg, *Colonial Capitalism and Labour in Kenya*, pp. 210-74.
7. KNA Lab 9/594, 'Resident Native Labour Ordinance: Operation and Application of
    Ordinance, 1940-48'; and CO 533/549/38232/15 (1946-47), 'European Settlement:
    Squatters', P. Wyn Harris, 'A Discussion of the Problem of the Squatter', 21 February
    1946; and J.H. Martin, 'The Problem of the Squatter: Economic Survey of Resident
    Labour in Kenya', 24 February 1947.
8. D.M. Anderson's unpublished thesis, 'Herder, Settler and Colonial Rule', pp. 130-1,
    202.
9. *East African Standard*, 11 and 12 September 1931, quoted in R.M.A. van Zwanenberg,
    Colonial Capitalism and Labour in Kenya, p. 216; CO 533/537/38608 (1944-46), 'Land
    Policy: Memorandum by the Anti-Slavery and Aboriginal Protection Society', note to
    Oliver Stanley, 5 May 1944; and CO 533/556/38664/2 (1947), 'Land Policy:
    Memorandum by the Labour Party on Land Utilization and Settlement', Morgan
    Philips to Creech Jones, 4 March 1947.
10. P. Mosley's thesis, 'The Settler Economies', pp. 178-80. For the Land Bank's role in
    the post-war years see CO 533/542/38071 (1945-47), 'Land and Agricultural Bank';
    and CO 533/534/38232 (1945), 'European Settlement Scheme', Mitchell to Creasy, 30

May 1945; and meeting of B.F. Macdona and A.B. Cohen, 11 May 1945; J.M. Lonsdale's unpublished paper, 'The Growth and Transformation of the Colonial State in Kenya', pp. 1-8. The campaign by the settlers to foreclose the squatter option paradoxically, in the long term, brought the end of European farming in Kenya.

11. M.G. Redley's unpublished thesis, 'The Politics of a Predicament', pp. 175-202, 239; Y.P. Ghai and J.P.W.B. McAuslan, *Public Law and Political Change in Kenya*, pp. 130-1, 202.

12. S. Stichter, *Migrant Labour in Kenya*, pp. 128-9; K.J. King and R.M. Wambaa, 'The Political-Economy of the Rift Valley', pp. 201-2; and T.M.J. Kanogo's unpublished thesis, 'The History of Kikuyu Movement . . .', pp. 294-338.

13. KNA Lab 9/309, 'Resident Labour General: Report of Ad Hoc Committee, 1946-50', Hyde-Clarke's memorandum on Resident Labour Policy, undated, but probably March 1947; Lab 9/316, 'Resident Labour: Naivasha County Council, 1941-59', P. Wyn Harris to T. Colchester, Commissioner for Local Government, 29 September 1945; and to Rennie, Chief Secretary, 16 February 1946; and Resolution of the Council, 21 February 1946; Lab 9/326, 'Resident Labour: Trans Nzoia, 1945-57', P. Wyn Harris to the acting Chief Secretary, 12 November 1945, Chairman Trans Nzoia Council's letters, 14 August 1946 and 14 May 1947; Lab 9/749, 'Nyeri Production and Manpower Committee, 1946-52', Kenya Information Office, release no. 435, on the Labour Commissioner's speech at Naro Moru on 28 August 1946; Lab 9/1071, 'Resident Labourers Ordinance: The Problem of the Squatter: *Ad Hoc* Committee, 1946-48', E.M. Hyde-Clarke to the Member for Labour, 16 June 1949 and E.M. Hyde-Clarke to Rennie, 17 September 1946; and MAA 8/124, 'Central Coordinating Committee for Resident Labour, 1947-51', minutes of the meeting on 7 May 1947; Lab 9/598, 'Resident Labour: Trans Nzoia, 1943-56'; Lab 9/326 'Resident Labour: Trans Nzoia, 1945-57'. See also Lab 9/310, 'Resident Labour General: Ordinance Committee, 1949-50', Cavendish-Bentinck to Assistant Secretary for Agriculture, 28 June 1950.

14. KNA Lab 9/316, 'Resident Labour: Naivasha County Council, 1941-59', Soysambu Estate to P. Wyn Harris, 26 April 1945; Lab 9/326, 'Resident Labour: Trans Nzoia, 1945-57', Council minutes, 23 October 1946; and F.R. Bancroft to Commissioner for Local Government, 7 November 1946; and Lab 9/598, 'Resident Labour: Trans Nzoia, 1943-56', A.C. Hoey to F.W. Cavendish-Bentinck, 12 February 1946; and protest from R.W. Buswell, February 1947 and Council minutes, 23 October 1946; and R.L. Tignor, *The Colonial Transformation of Kenya*, pp. 310-23.

15. This was especially true in Trans Nzoia. Lab 9/326, 'Resident Labour: Trans Nzoia, 1945-57' and Lab 9/598, 'Resident Labour: Trans Nzoia, 1943-56' contain a large number of petitions from cereal and plantation farmers against the district council order, and reports of bitter meetings of the divided council.

16. KNA Lab 9/97, 'Association of District Councils, 1941-53', report of the Councils' conference on 26-27 June 1944; and the meeting on 12-13 September 1944. See also Lab 9/10, 'Labour: Squatters in Forest Areas, 1944-50', S.J. Pinney to the Conservator of Forests, 11 October 1944.

17. Furedi, Kanogo, King and van Zwanenberg have largely ignored these important divisions among the European settler farming community and have treated them as an undifferentiated conglomerate. In fact, settler farmers were extremely divided and had diametrically opposed attitudes towards squatters.

18. KNA Lab 9/331, 'Resident Labour: Nyanza District Council, 1946-53'; and Lab 9/304, 'Resident Labour: General Correspondence', provides a detailed list of the various district council orders as of 21 June 1945.

19. KNA Lab 9/316, 'Resident Labour: Naivasha County Council, 1941-59'.

20. *ibid*, Manager of Soysambu Estate, Elmenteita, to the Secretary for Local Government, 26 April 1945; W.O. Townsend to C.E. Mortimer, 22 December 1945 and P. Wyn Harris to C.E. Mortimer, 31 December 1945.

21. KNA Lab 9/326, 'Resident Labour: Tranzs Nzoia, 1945-57', debate of the Trans

Nzoia District Council, 27 February 1946; and Lab 9/598, 'Resident Labour: Trans Nzoia, 1943-56', A.C. Hoey to F.W. Cavendish-Bentinck, 12 February 1946.

22. KNA Lab 9/326, 'Resident Labour: Trans Nzoia, 1945-57', T.L. Bolton, Chairman of the Council, to the Commissioner for Local Government, 14 May 1947; and the minutes of the special meeting of the district council and the Trans Nzoia Association with Hyde-Clarke, 26 May 1947, for subsequent developments in the battle.

23. KNA Lab 9/1071, 'Resident Labourers Ordinance: The Problem of the Squatter: *Ad Hoc* Committee, 1946-48', Hyde-Clarke to Rennie, 17 September 1946; and Hyde-Clarke's memorandum on squatters, dated 7 May 1947.

24. KNA Lab 9/309, 'Resident Labourers' General: Report of *Ad Hoc* Committee, 1946-50', Hyde-Clarke to the Member for Labour, 16 June 1949; Lab 9/316, 'Resident Labour: Naivasha County Council, 1941-59', P. Wyn Harris to T. Colchester, Commissioner for Local Government, 29 September 1945; W.O. Townsend to C.E. Mortimer, 22 December 1945; and P. Wyn Harris to C.E. Mortimer, 31 December 1945; Lab 9/326, 'Resident Labour: Trans Nzoia, 1945-57', P. Wyn Harris to T. Colchester, 12 April 1946; and Hyde-Clarke to T. Colchester, 2 July 1946; Lab 9/598, 'Resident Labour: Trans Nzoia, 1943-56', Marchant, the Chief Native Commissioner to C.E. Mortimer, 29 July 1946; and Lab 9/1071, 'Resident Labourers Ordinance: The Problem of the Squatter: *Ad Hoc* Committee, 1946-48', Hyde-Clarke to Rennie, 17 September 1946.

25. KNA Lab 9/304, 'Resident Labourers: General Correspondence', Wyn Harris to Rennie, 12 April 1945; Lab 9/97, 'Association of District Councils, 1941-53', P. Wyn Harris to Rennie, 3 November 1945; Lab 9/316, 'Resident Labour: Naivasha County Council, 1941-59', Wyn Harris to the Commissioner for Local Government, 29 September 1945; and to C.E. Mortimer, 31 December 1945; and to Rennie, 16 February 1946; Lab 9/326, 'Resident Labour: Trans Nzoia, 1945-47', Wyn Harris to acting Chief Secretary, 12 November 1945; Lab 9/331, 'Resident Labour: Nyanza District Council, 1946-53', Wyn Harris to the Attorney General, 7 November 1945; and CO 533/549/38232/15 (1946-47), 'European Settlement: Squatters', P. Wyn Harris, 'A Discussion of the Problem of the Squatter', 21 February 1946.

26. KNA Lab 9/316, 'Resident Labour: Naivasha County Council, 1941-59', P. Wyn Harris to the Commissioner for Local Government, 29 September 1945; protest from Soysambu Estate, 26 April 1945; W.O. Townsend to C.E. Mortimer, 22 December 1945; and Wyn Harris to Mortimer, 31 December 1945. See also Lab 9/97, 'Association of District Councils, 1941-53', Wyn Harris to Rennie, 3 November 1945; Lab 9/97, 'Association of District Councils, 1941-53', Wyn Harris to C.E. Mortimer, the Commissioner for Local Government, 29 September 1945; and the memorandum prepared for the Executive Council, dated 5 February 1946.

27. KNA Lab 9/594, 'Resident Native Labour Ordinance: Operation and Application of the Ordinance, 1940-48'. See also Y.P. Ghai and J.P.W.B. McAuslan, *Public Law and Political Change in Kenya*, pp. 95-6. Lab 9/316, 'Resident Labour: Naivasha County Council, 1941-53'; Lab 9/326, 'Resident Labour: Trans Nzoia, 1945-57'; Lab 9/317, 'Resident Labour: Nakuru, 1945-53' provide many examples of district councils taking independent action against the advice of the labour department.

28. KNA Lab 9/1071, 'Resident Labourers Ordinance: The Problem of the Squatter: *Ad Hoc* Committee, 1946-48', Hyde-Clarke to Rennie, 17 September 1946; and Hyde-Clarke to the Committee, 7 May 1945; Lab 9/749, 'Nyeri Production and Manpower Committee, 1946-52', Kenya Information Office, release no. 435, about the Labour Commissioner's speech at Naro Moru on 28 August 1946; Lab 9/317, 'Resident Labour: Nakuru, 1945-53', W.O. Townsend to Wyn Harris, 11 November 1945; and Hyde-Clarke to Rennie, September 1946. See also CO 533/549/38232/15 (1946-47) 'European Settlement: Squatters', Wyn Harris, 'A Discussion of the Problem of the Squatter', 21 February 1946; and J.H. Martin, 'The Problem of the Squatter:

Economic Survey of Resident Labour in Kenya', 24 February 1947, for detailed estimates of squatter household incomes.

29. KNA Lab 9/316, 'Resident Labour: Naivasha County Council, 1941–59', Wyn Harris to Rennie, 16 February 1946; and to the Labour Officer, Nakuru, 20 March 1946; and CO 533/549/38232/15 (1946–47), 'European Settlement: Squatters', Wyn Harris, 'A Discussion of the Problem of the Squatter', 21 February 1946.

30. KNA Lab 9/317, 'Resident Labour: Nakuru, 1945–53', Hyde-Clarke to Rennie, September 1946; and Lab 9/749, 'Nyeri Production and Manpower Committee, 1946–52', Kenya Information Office, release no. 435, 28 August 1946; and Lab 9/316, 'Resident Labour: Naivasha County Council, 1941–59', Wyn Harris to Rennie 16 February 1946; and C.H. Thornley to Marchant, the Chief Native Commissioner, 22 February 1946. See also the protest from the Naivasha district council at the decision, 21 February 1946.

31. KNA Lab 9/1071 'Resident Labourers Ordinance: The Problem of the Squatter: *Ad Hoc* Committee, 1946–48', Hyde-Clarke to Rennie, 17 September 1946; and MAA 8/124, 'Central Coordinating Committee for Resident Labour, 1947–51', Hyde-Clarke to Cavendish-Bentinck, 3 March 1947, for the campaign behind the establishment of the *Ad Hoc* Committee.

32. KNA Lab 9/598, 'Resident Labour: Trans Nzoia, 1943–56', Cavendish-Bentinck to A.C. Hoey, 15 February 1946; and CO 533/549/38232/15 (1946–47), 'European Settlement: Squatters', Wyn Harris, 'A Discussion of the Problem of the Squatter', 21 February 1946.

33. CO 533/549/38232/15 (1946–47), Wyn Harris, 'A Discussion of the Problem of the Squatter', 21 February 1946.

34. CO 533/549/38232/15 (1946–47), 'European Settlement: Squatters', Wyn Harris, 'A Discussion of the Problem of the Squatter', 21 February 1946. For other estimates of squatter household earnings, see KNA 9/309, 'Resident Labourers General: Report of *Ad Hoc* Committee, 1946–50', Hyde-Clarke's Policy on Resident Labour for Cavendish-Bentinck, 5 March 1947.

35. CO 533/549/38232/15 (1946–47), 'European Settlement: Squatters', Wyn Harris, 'A Discussion of the Problem of the Squatter', 21 February 1946. See also KNA 9/749, 'Nyeri Production and Manpower Committee, 1946–52', Kenya Information Office, release no. 535, 28 August 1946.

36. KNA Lab 9/1071, 'Resident Labourers Ordinance: The Problem of the Squatter: *Ad Hoc* Committee, 1946–48', draft statement of policy for Cavendish-Bentinck's committee, prepared by Hyde-Clarke and J.H. Martin, dated 5 March 1947.

37. For the origins of the *Ad Hoc* Committee, see KNA MAA 8/124, 'Central Coordinating Committee for Resident Labour', Hyde-Clarke to Cavendish-Bentinck, 3 March 1947.

38. KNA Lab 9/309, 'Resident Labourers General: Report of *Ad Hoc* Committee, 1946–50' Hyde-Clarke's 'Policy on Resident Labour', 5 March 1947; and Lab 9/1071, 'Resident Labourers Ordinance: The Problem of the Squatter: *Ad Hoc* Committee, 1946–48', draft statement of policy discussed by Cavendish-Bentinck's committee, 7 March 1947.

39. *ibid.*

40. KNA Lab 9/1071, 'Resident Labourers Ordinance: The Problem of the Squatter: *Ad Hoc* Committee, 1946–48', draft statement of policy discussed by Cavendish-Bentinck's committee, 7 March 1947.

41. KNA Lab 9/748, 'Naivasha District Council Labour Committee, 1944–47', meeting 14 May 1946; Lab 9/598, 'Resident Labour: Trans Nzoia, 1943–56', PC Rift Valley to the Chief Native Commissioner, 2 March 1945; and Wyn Harris to the acting Chief Secretary, 12 November 1945; and Lab 9/1835, 'Mombasa Strikes, 1937–46', Mombasa Monthly Intelligence Report, September 1942; and P. de V. Allen to the

acting governor, Rennie, 15 October 1942.

42. KNA Lab 9/598, 'Resident Labour: Trans Nzoia, 1943–56', Chief Native Commissioner to C.E. Mortimer, 29 July 1946; and Wyn Harris to Mortimer, 19 February 1947. See also Lab 9/326, 'Resident Labour: Trans Nzoia, 1945–47', Labour Officer, Kitale to Hyde-Clarke, 2 August 1946; and Hyde-Clarke to the Commissioner for Local Government, 30 August 1946; and to C.E. Mortimer, 25 November 1946.

43. Lab 9/326, 'Resident Labour: Trans Nzoia, 1945–47', Wyn Harris to Colchester, 12 April 1946; Hyde-Clarke to Commander Vernon of the Trans Nzoia District Council, 26 July 1946; the Labour Officer, Kitale to Hyde-Clarke, 2 August 1946; and T. Colchester, the Commissioner for Local Government to Hyde-Clarke, 21 August 1946.

44. Lab 9/326, Vaughan-Philpott's memorandum on resident labour, 14 August 1946; and the minutes of the special meeting between Hyde-Clarke and the district council and the Trans Nzoia Association, 26 May 1947.

45. Lab 9/326, minutes of the special meeting between Hyde-Clarke, the District Council and the Trans Nzoia Association, 26 May 1947. For petitions to be excluded from the council order by cereal farmers see KNA Lab 9/598, 'Resident Labour: Trans Nzoia, 1943–56'.

46. KNA Lab 9/1071, 'Resident Labour Ordinance: The Problem of the Squatter: *Ad Hoc* Committee, 1946–48', Hyde-Clarke to Rennie, 17 September 1946; Hyde-Clarke to Cavendish-Bentinck, 18 March 1948 and 2 July 1948.

47. KNA Lab 9/309, 'Resident Labour General: Report of *Ad Hoc* Committee, 1946–50', Labour Department to Cavendish-Bentinck, 3 March 1947.

48. *ibid*, Hyde-Clarke to Member for Labour, 16 June 1949. See also Lab 9/310, 'Resident Labourers General: Ordinance Committee, 1949–50', Cavendish-Bentinck to the Assistant Secretary of Agriculture, 28 June 1950.

49. KNA Lab 9/310, 'Resident Labour General: Report of *Ad Hoc* Committee, 1946–50', Hyde-Clarke to Member for Labour, 16 June 1949. For further details see Lab 9/1071, 'Resident Labour Ordinance: The Problem of the Squatter: *Ad Hoc* Committee, 1946–48', memorandum to the Executive Council on the disposal of surplus stock in the Nairobi District, 8 June 1949; and Lab 9/309, 'Resident Labour General: Report of *Ad Hoc* Committee, 1946–50', Hyde-Clarke to Member for Labour, 16 June 1949.

50. KNA MAA 8/124, 'Central Coordinating Committee for Resident Labour, 1947–51', Cavendish-Bentinck's 'Resident Labour in Kenya: Outline of Policy', drafted 15 February 1949. This should be contrasted with CO 533/549/38232/15 (1946–47), 'European Settlement: Squatters', Wyn Harris, 'A Discussion of the Problem of the Squatter', 21 February 1946; and KNA Lab 9/1071, 'Resident Labour Ordinance: The Problem of the Squatter: *Ad Hoc* Committee, 1946–48', Hyde-Clarke's proposals, discussed on 7 May 1947. See also Lab 9/310, 'Resident Labourers General: Ordinance Committee, 1949–50', F.W. Cavendish-Bentinck to the Assistant Secretary for Agriculture, 28 June 1950; and KNA Lab 9/304, 'Resident Labour General Correspondence', provisions of District Councils' Orders; Lab 9/312, 'Resident Labour Provincial Coordinating Committees, 1950', the second meeting of the Nyanza Coordinating Committee, 6 May 1950; and the first meeting of the Kericho committee, 20 February 1950. See also Lab 9/331, 'Resident Labour: Nyanza District Council, 1946–53', comprehensive order, 5 October 1951.

51. KNA DC/NKU 1/5, 'Nakuru–Naivasha–Ravine District Annual Reports', (1946) pp. 3, 7–8; and (1947) Annual Report, pp. 25–6. F. Furedi, 'The Social Composition of the Mau Mau Movement in the White Highlands', pp. 492–7; and T.M.J. Kanogo's thesis, 'The History of Kikuyu Movement . . .', pp. 360–8.

52. CO 533/549/38232/15 (1946–47), 'European Settlement: Squatters', Mitchell to Creech Jones, 19 February 1947; and CO 533/543/38086/38 (1946–47), 'Petitions: Kikuyu Grievances', Samuel K. Gikami to Creech Jones, 16 July 1947; and Kikuyu Squatters to the Chief Justice of Kenya, 2 September 1947.

53. KNA Lab 9/316, 'Resident Labour: Naivasha County Council, 1941–59'; Lab 9/320, 'Resident Labourers Ordinance: Aberdare District Council, 1944–51'; Lab 9/317, 'Resident Labour: Nakuru, 1945–53'; and Lab 9/10, 'Labour: Squatters in Forest Areas, 1944–50'.

54. KNA Lab 9/1071, 'Resident Labourers Ordinance: The Problem of the Squatter: *Ad Hoc* Committee, 1946–48', Labour Officer, Eldoret, to the Labour Commissioner, 29 January 1948. See also Lab 9/325, 'Reduction of Resident Labour Stock, 1950–57', PC Nyanza to Cavendish-Bentinck, 3 April 1952.

55. Lab 9/320, 'Resident Labourers Ordinance: Aberdare District Council, 1944–51', A.R. Swift, Labour Officer at Thomson's Falls, to Hyde-Clarke, 18 October 1946; and Lab 9/317, 'Resident Labour: Nakuru, 1945–53', J.D. Stringer to the Chief Native Commissioner, 25 November 1946; and the reports by W.O. Townsend, dated 12 September 1946, and A.R. Swift, dated 13 November 1947; RH Mss. Afr. s. 1121, S.H. Powles's diary 10 July 1947. KNA Lab 9/598, 'Resident Labour, Trans Nzoia, 1943–56' contains complaints from other settlers, especially A.C. Hoey to F.W. Cavendish-Bentinck, 12 February 1946; and Lab 9/771, 'Labour Control: Agricultural, 1946–47', G. Walker to Hyde-Clarke, 15 October 1946. See also Lab 9/1071, 'Resident Labourers Ordinance: The Problem of the Squatter: *Ad Hoc* Committee, 1946–48', Labour Officer, Eldoret, to the Labour Commissioner, 29 January 1948; and Lab 9/325, 'Reduction of Resident Labour Stock, 1950–57', PC Nyanza to Cavendish-Bentinck, 3 April 1952.

56. KNA MAA 8/125 'Reports Principal Labour Officer, 1947–48', report for February 1947, quoted in F. Furedi's unpublished paper, 'Olenguruone in Mau Mau Historiography', p. 4; Lab 9/320, 'Resident Labourers Ordinance: Aberdare District Council, 1944–51', A.R. Swift to Hyde-Clarke, 18 October 1946. See also Lab 9/317, 'Resident Labour: Nakuru, 1945–53'; and Lab 9/316, 'Resident Labour: Naivasha County Council, 1941–59', and MAA 8/124, 'Central Coordinating Committee for Resident Labour, 1947–51', A.T. Wise, Registrar of Native Societies, to Hyde-Clarke, 13 March 1947; Secretariat 1/12/8, 'Labour Unrest: Intelligence Reports, Central Province, 1947', report 20 February 1947; and CO 533/543/38086/38 (1946–47), 'Petitions: Kikuyu Grievances', Samuel K. Gikami to Creech Jones, 16 July 1947; and the government's reply, dated 14 November 1947; and Lab 3/41, 'Resident Labour: Squatters', police report, September 1946; and F. Furedi, 'Social Composition of the Mau Mau Movement in the White Highlands', pp. 492–7, for details of the gathering at Naivasha. Lab 9/317, 'Resident Labour: Nakuru, 1945–53', A.T. Wise to the Labour Commissioner, 25 July 1946, reports the attempt at mediation with discontented squatters by Joseph Kinyua, the Secretary of the Kenya African Union branch at Nakuru, and recounts the hostile treatment he received. Lab 9/337, 'Resident Labour: Forest Areas, 1947–50', Hyde-Clarke to Wyn Harris, 5 April 1949; and F.J. Hart, Labour Officer, Thomson's Falls, to Divisional Forest Officer, 25 August 1949, contains details of plans to reward Johnson Kaya, the President of the local branch of the Kenya African Union, for mediating in squatter disputes. See also F. Furedi, 'The Development of Anti-Asian Opinion among Africans in Nakuru District', pp. 347–58.

57. KNA Lab 9/320, 'Resident Labourers Ordinance: Aberdare District Council, 1944–51', Major L.B.L. Hughes to DC Naivasha, 16 March 1946, for protest about the lax supervision of forest squatters employed by the Forest Department and private sawmills.

58. KNA Lab 9/1071, 'Resident Labourers Ordinance: The Problem of the Squatter: *Ad Hoc* Committee, 1946–48', Hyde-Clarke to Rennie, 17 September 1946; and Hyde-Clarke to the Member for Labour, 16 June 1949; F. Furedi, 'The Social Composition of the Mau Mau Movement in the White Highlands', p. 499; and T.M.J. Kanogo's thesis, 'The History of Kikuyu Movement . . .', pp. 337–8, 366–75.

Six

Olenguruone

The fate of the prototype African settlement at Olenguruone on the western Mau escarpment was of profound importance for the development of Mau Mau. The 4,000 people who were moved into the area in 1941 were mainly former Kikuyu squatter families who had left the White Highlands to pursue the peasant option as 'interpenetrators' in Maasailand. By 1944, they had already created a centre of militant opposition to the government's agricultural campaign and transformed the traditional Kikuyu oaths into a powerful device for guaranteeing communal solidarity. They are credited with having introduced what subsequently became the first Mau Mau oath. Throughout the 1940s Olenguruone provided inspiration to Kikuyu militants in the White Highlands and set an example of unconditional resistance to the colonial régime, which has been celebrated in several Mau Mau *nyimbo*.[1]

From the beginning Olenguruone had little chance of success. This was because the majority of the people who were moved into this prototype settlement were not squatters who had refused to accept the new restrictions imposed by the district councils, but Kikuyu cultivators who had been farming in Maasailand where they had discovered new opportunities for the peasant option. They loathed having to move to the bleak environment, high on the Mau escarpment, where they realised they would be unable to grow their normal crops.[2]

By October 1946, the Olenguruone residents were locked in battle with the colonial state, which was trying to evict them for failing to follow the settlement's agricultural rules. They developed close contacts with the Kikuyu squatters in the Nakuru and Naivasha districts and with the Kikuyu Highlands Squatters' Association in Limuru.[3] The new oath of unity, which had been introduced in 1944, quickly spread among the Kikuyu squatter communities throughout the White Highlands. Meanwhile, as the eviction plans became bogged down in legal technicalities in the Kenya Supreme Court and the Court of Appeal for Eastern Africa, the administration and the legal department began to blame each other for their respective failures to deal with the Olenguruone 'agitators'.[4] The Olenguruone Kikuyu insisted that they were *githaka* rightholders and that the government was not entitled to interfere with their *shambas*. After eight years of resistance morale in the settlement was very low; by 1949 it had become apparent that the government intended to expel all the dissidents. The evictions and mass arrests at Olenguruone between January and March 1950 were, however, counter-productive and merely confirmed the Olenguruone resistors' position in the pantheon of Kikuyu heroes and provided further ammunition to the militants.[5]

The foundation of the settlement

Much of the agricultural department's post-war development programme, we have noted, was based upon Norman Humphrey's contention that vast numbers of people would have to be resettled on newly-cleared land or absorbed with their families into permanent urban employment, before land degradation could be tackled. During the first three years after the war a series of ecological and geological surveys were undertaken and several potential settlements were scrutinised. It was hardly surprising, therefore, that the progress of the prototype African settlement at Olenguruone, high on the western slopes of the Mau escarpment, was closely watched and considered of vital importance to the success of the new strategy.[6]

The Colonial Office had initially refused to sanction the transfer of responsibility for resident labour legislation to the settler-controlled district councils, as proposed in the 1937 Resident Native Labour Ordinance, until the Kenyan authorities established a settlement for those squatters who refused to accept the tighter restrictions imposed on squatter cultivation and stock during the *Kifagio* in the late 1930s. After a three-year delay, the Secretary of State reluctantly approved the Ordinance, but only when he was assured that the Kenyan government had excised 33,000 acres from the Maasai Reserve and the South West Mau Forest, on which to establish a settlement for former Kikuyu squatters who had refused to reattest and had been expelled from settler farms.[7] Such families, who had often been away from the Kikuyu reserves for 30 years, had lost their *githaka* rights and were now completely landless and threatened with destitution. Many had left Kikuyuland voluntarily to search for better conditions in the White Highlands; others had been forced off their land when it had been alienated to Europeans. In moving to the Rift Valley they had abandoned their lineage ties in the reserves to take advantage of the new opportunities that opened up in the White Highlands between 1904 and 1913, when the British removed the Maasai from their traditional northern grazing grounds and opened the area for European and, unwittingly, Kikuyu settlement.[8]

Olenguruone

The Colonial Office believed that Olenguruone would serve two purposes. Firstly, it would enable the Kenyan government to minimise squatter opposition to the new regulations governing squatter contracts (which was anticipated once the new Ordinance transferred squatter legislation to the district councils) because Olenguruone would absorb the more obdurate squatters who refused to accept the new regulations without causing trouble in Kikuyuland. But secondly, and more importantly, the settlement at Olenguruone was designed to enable Whitehall to assuage humanitarian criticism in Britain about another concession to Kenya's settlers.[9] Events, however, turned out very differently. Once reassured and armed with information to withstand left-wing criticism, Whitehall quickly lost interest in Olenguruone and turned its attention to the pressing problems of mobilising the colonies' war effort. The Kenyan government was therefore able to use Olenguruone for other purposes.

Instead of resettling squatter families that had been evicted from European farms during the *Kifagio*, Olenguruone was used to accommodate those Kikuyu who had settled in Maasailand. During the 1920s and 1930s more than 4,000 Kikuyu had abandoned the White Highlands and began to cultivate at Il Melili and Nairage Ngare in north Narok. They established economic alliances with prominent local Maasai, who, as pastoralists, were willing to allow these enterprising Kikuyu cultivators as much land as they wanted in return for food and labour.[10] By 1937, many settler farmers around Elburgon, on the other side of the Mau escarpment, were already becoming concerned in case this new settlement in Maasailand provided a more attractive option to their squatters and encouraged others, whose stock rights were being curtailed in the White Highlands.[11] This would have severely impaired the settlers' supplies of labour. By the late 1930s, these farmers' protests and complaints about Kikuyu interpenetration relayed by the field administration in Maasailand, had persuaded the Secretariat to remove these 'undesirables' and to resettle them at Olenguruone with other former Kikuyu squatters who had come directly from European farms.[12]

The concept of interpenetration had a long and tarnished history, but, by the late 1930s, the field administration had begun to discuss it in a more constructive manner. The administration in Maasai, however, had remained resolutely opposed to the idea. When, in the late 1930s, it recognised that interpenetration would soon become official policy, it was determined to undertake one last drive to expel the Kikuyu interlopers. In 1936, Clarence Buxton, who was then Officer-in-Charge in Maasai, had attempted to clear Il Melili and Nairage Ngare. Olenguruone provided his successor with one last opportunity to clear Narok before interpenetration became accepted and the Maasai administration was stuck with unwanted Kikuyu interlopers.[13]

The choice of Olenguruone as the site for the new settlement was therefore a compromise between the forestry department and the Maasai Rift Valley administration. It was an isolated place that nobody wanted where discontented Kikuyu could be 'abandoned' without, it was thought, any danger of spreading dissent. It soon, however, proved to be a singularly inauspicious site for the first African settlement, becoming notorious as the 'Sherwood Forest' of western Kenya and an important staging post on the stock-theft routes.[14]

The situation was made even worse when the Kikuyu refused to leave their smallholdings in Maasailand.[15] Consequently the first families were not moved into Oleguruone until 1941, by which time the administration was being stretched by the war against the Italians in Ethiopia and was unable to assert its authority. The ex-squatters were able to disregard the settlement's rules when they were belatedly promulgated in 1942. By then many families had already started to cultivate large acreages and refused to obey the new regulations.[16]

The geographical and administrative roots of failure

Olenguruone was completely unsuitable for a settlement of peasant cultivators. The four main valleys all had extremely steep slopes covered with dense bamboo and trees. The ridges between the main rivers were broken by deep ravines, densely covered with bamboo, and swift streams. Any cultivation or movement was extremely difficult. The climate was equally unsuitable for peasant agriculture. The rainfall appeared to be good, averaging more than 80 inches per annum, but it fell unevenly in violent downpours between April and October, often turning into hailstorms which damaged the crops. Frost also hindered cultivation and night temperatures averaged only 40°F. Sunshine in the rainy months was confined to a brief spell in the early morning. Consequently, in contrast to most of Central Province and the White Highlands, only one crop a year could be grown at Olenguruone.[17]

The hilly terrain was another major obstacle to the development of the settlement and made the construction of internal roads financially prohibitive. During the rainy season, from May to September, most of the slopes in the cultivated area were too steep and slippery for the ex-squatters' mules and donkeys to move about. All communication to the north-west and south-east was virtually impossible throughout the year because of the difficulty of crossing the ridges and four main rivers, which all flowed from the north-east to the south-west. These long radial lines of communication added considerably to the cost of marketing produce. Even the two main roads out of Olenguruone were usually impassable during the rainy season. The official line of access ran over the Maasai Mau and through the Elburgon Forest Reserve, along a sawmill road to Elburgon. Although some attempts were made to improve it, in bad weather it was impassable since it climbed to 10,000 feet and meandered over several hills. The alternative route, along district council and farm roads through the Marindas and Keringet estates, took a better alignment and avoided steep hills, but was not chosen as the official road to Olenguruone because the local settlers feared that diseased stock would constantly be moving across their land.[18]

When cultivation regulations were finally introduced in 1942, the Olenguruone Kikuyu refused to accept any attempt to restrict their *shambas* to a maximum of eight acres per family or to limit their stock to seven cattle.[19] Their leader, Samuel Koina Gitebi, insisted that the Officer-in-Charge in Maasai had assured them, in the presence of Senior Chief Koinange and Chief Josiah Njonjo, that they could hold Olenguruone on *githaka* terms without any restrictions or agricultural regulations, as compensation for their *githaka* in Kiambu, which had been alienated to European settlers. If this was untrue, he asked, why had everyone allowed into Olenguruone been carefully vetted by the Kiambu Local Native Council's representative, Chief Njonjo, to ascertain which of the Kikuyu in Maasailand had originally been *githaka* holders and were, therefore, eligible for land in the settlement?[20]

By attempting to restrict Olenguruone to former *githaka* holders and by refusing to accept the claims of former *ahoi* and other 'tenants' the government had in fact created the impression that this land was being given to them without any conditions in compensation for their alienated *githaka* and was to be held on *githaka* terms. The Olenguruone Kikuyu, therefore, refused to accept the belated settlement rules. Gitebi defended this interpretation in a petition to the King and alleged that:

> A totally new set of laws was introduced in 1943 based on the Government's failure to honour the previous agreed terms . . . The Kenya Government alleged that we have refused to obey the laws of the settlement but have never shown precisely what clause of the said laws we have violated. We were admitted to Olenguruone Settlement on the terms and conditions agreed upon and satisfactory to Government in January 1940.[21]

As early as June 1942, three months before the promulgation of the Native Settlement Areas (Olenguruone) (No 2) Rules, Gitebi had complained that the administration was attempting to regulate cultivation on the *shambas* which, he insisted, were held on *githaka* terms and, therefore, should not be subject to any kind of government interference.[22] When the settlement rules were eventually issued and translated into Kikuyu, discontent escalated. The dispute over whether they held *githaka* rights of exclusive ownership, or were *ahoi* and merely occupied the land under conditional tenure, became so serious that the Chief Native Com-

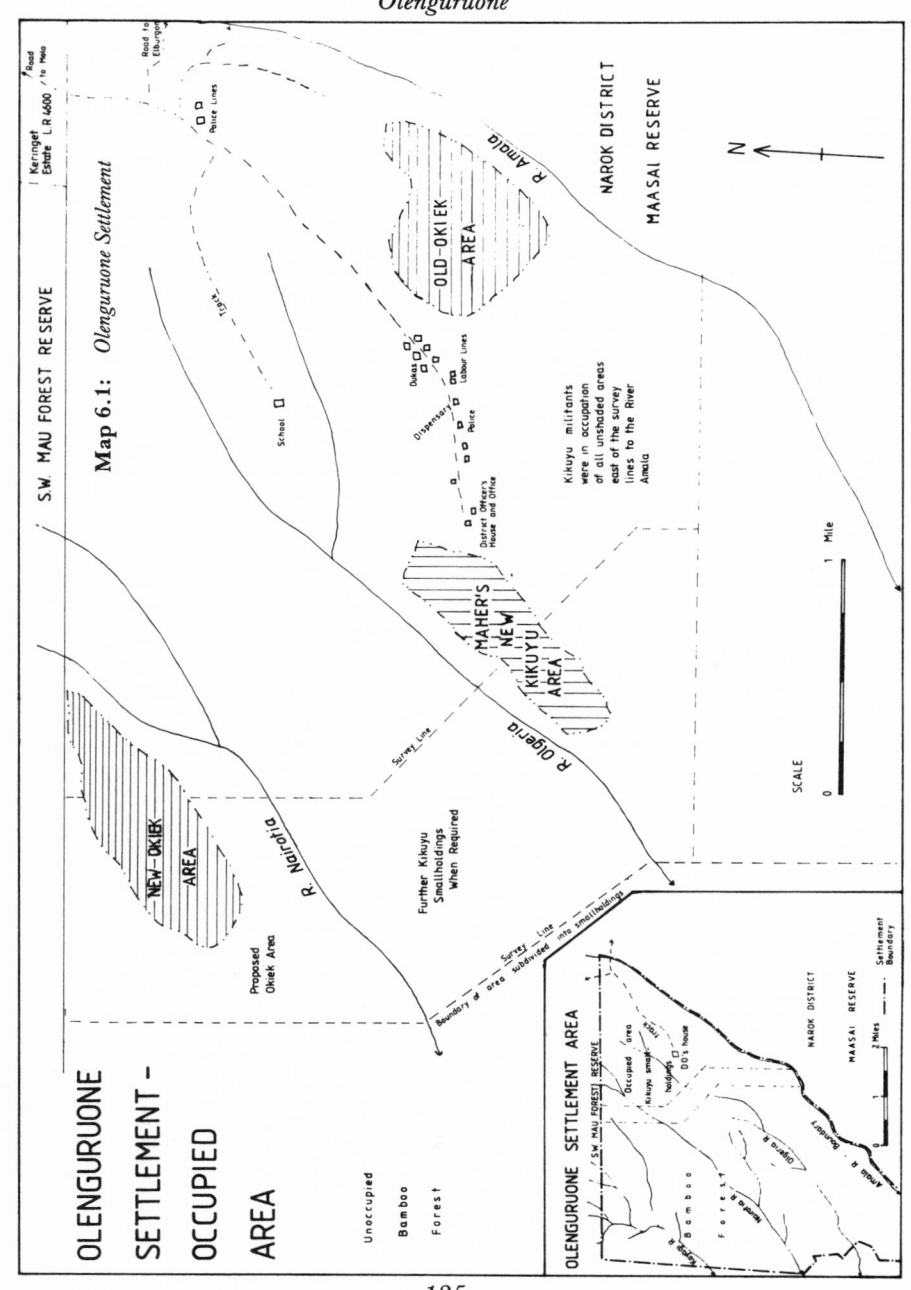

Map 6.1: *Olenguruone Settlement*

missioner eventually held a *baraza*, on 21 June 1943, to resolve the disagreement. This was attended by 200 Kikuyu and 20 Okiek elders who protested that they were not *ahoi*, as they had been described in the Kikuyu version of the settlement rules. They demanded to be treated like the Kikuyu who had been moved to Lari and Kerita and who had been compensated for their lost land with new *githaka*, insisting that Bailward, the Officer-in-Charge in Maasai, had promised them in 1940 that Olenguruone would be held on *githaka* terms.[23]

The Chief Native Commissioner, however, remained adamant, arguing that as trespassers in Maasailand they had already received extremely generous treatment by being allowed to go to Olenguruone. He warned them that they held their *shambas* on the government's terms: they were in fact *ahoi* and would be dispossessed if they did not obey the settlement rules and the instructions of the Settlement Officer. When their own customs were incompatible with the regulations, they would have to give way. They would be required to conserve soil fertility, and the eight-acre plots which had been allocated could not be subdivided, according to the partible inheritance customs of the Kikuyu, but would have to be passed intact to one heir.[24]

Following this declaration of the government's hard line many Kikuyu refused to sign their occupation permits and started a policy of active non-co-operation.[25] All orders from the Settlement Officer and Agricultural Department staff were ignored; experimental agricultural work was hindered; and rules about crop rotation and maize cultivation were disregarded, as was the prohibition against burning grass to clear new *shambas*. This campaign of disobedience continued throughout 1944 and 1945; government threats of eviction were met by virulent opposition and communal oathing to ensure unity.[26]

Maher's agricultural regulations

Meanwhile, the government was becoming extremely concerned about the rapid decline in soil fertility. By 1944 this had become so serious that the settlement could no longer feed itself.[27] Between 1943 and January 1946, conditions were allowed to drift because the administration lacked the manpower to enforce the rules. With the end of the war, as plans were being prepared for other new settlements, it suddenly became imperative for Olenguruone to be brought under control and the cultivation rules enforced, in order to demonstrate to future settlers at Makueni or the Shimba Hills that opposition would not be tolerated.[28] Robertson in the Colonial Office observed that 'the present agitation is purely for political motives and . . . if the Government gives way in this case, the large scale African Settlement Schemes which are planned for the future will be prejudiced'.[29] His superior, Andrew Cohen was even more determined to reassert control at Olenguruone, and warned that:

There is a vital issue at stake here – the willingness . . . of Africans to accept conditions of proper land control in schemes for settlement . . . A determined campaign is being coordinated in Kenya at the moment, under the leadership of Jomo Kenyatta, to encourage Africans everywhere to resist attempts to improve the condition of the land. If this campaign succeeds the bad consequences will be incalculable. [30]

Early in 1946, therefore, Colin Maher, the head of the Soil Conservation Unit, was despatched to investigate conditions and to suggest how the administration could regain control. Able though he undoubtedly was, Maher had little sympathy for traditional African agricultural practices; he strictly adhered to his 'scientific' preconceptions about tropical agriculture and completely disregarded Kikuyu land-use practices. In his zeal to propagate the gospel of soil conservation, Maher based his programme on what he believed was agriculturally desirable rather than on what was possible in the face of outright opposition. Like many agricultural officers, Maher had been greatly impressed by Allan and Trapnell's work in Northern Rhodesia and was obsessed with the belief that, through close investigation of the vegetation, soils and climate, it was possible to determine the exact human and stock-carrying capacities of specific areas. [31] Maher was the most vociferous advocate of this approach in Kenya and, like Humphrey, obstinately refused to recognise that, even in relatively small areas like Olenguruone, it was exceedingly difficult to determine with any precision the fertility of the soil or its powers of regeneration. Indeed, given the climatic conditions and the nitrogen-deficient soils at Olenguruone, Maher's recommendations were probably more destructive than the Kikuyu's shifting cultivation he so condemned. The Olenguruone Kikuyu in fact utilised their land in a highly efficient manner, well adapted to meet the difficult conditions of their inhospitable *shambas* high on the Mau escarpment. After their experiences in the White Highlands and among the pastoral Maasai, they concentrated primarily on stock keeping rather than on growing poor crops of maize and wheat. Unlike Maher, who remained inflexibly committed to his preconceived views about sound agricultural practice, which bore little resemblance to the realities of Olenguruone, the Kikuyu were willing to adapt to fit in with the environment. By turning to pre-colonial Kikuyu practices of shifting cultivation in a mixed farming rotation of stock and crops, the Olenguruone Kikuyu maximised the economic potential of the area and minimised the danger of land degradation. The government, however, failed to recognise this simple fact and endorsed Maher's recommendations. [32]

Maher proposed a radical reorganisation of the settlement, with every household having five acres of arable land on slopes of less than 20 per cent, a further three acres under permanent grass and four acres of communal grazing for every smallholder. This total of 12 acres, he pointed out, was 'considerably in excess of that available in the Kikuyu Reserves'.[33] This formula, however, failed to take account of the fact that only one crop a year could be grown in the harsh environment at Olenguruone. Maher also recommended that no more than two and a half acres per household be allowed under cultivation at any given moment, that initially land should be cultivated continuously for no more than four years and then, after three years complete rest under planted grass, for no more than three years at a stretch. These two and a half acres, he considered, could supply both cash and food crops. The remaining five and a half acres and the four acres of communal grazing should be used to keep eight or nine high-grade cattle or the equivalent number of sheep. All the grassland, temporary and permanent, private or communal, Maher suggested, ought to be divided into paddocks and grazed in rotation using grazing permits. He even suggested building all the houses in the settlement on a single contour. Everyone at Olenguruone was to be compelled to follow this new agricultural plan and the settlement was to be dramatically reformed. Every plot was to be resurveyed and those on steep slopes closed within two years. Once the new *shambas* had been demarcated, the Olenguruone Kikuyu would have to build terraces and follow agricultural regulations. During this interim period, however, Maher made a fatal concession to expedite the clearing of bamboo from the proposed smallholdings. He agreed to let those who were to be moved cultivate as large an area as they wished. This undermined all the attempts to enforce his recommendations, for once settled and allowed to cultivate as much land as they could clear, the Kikuyu refused to reduce their *shambas* to eight acres.[34] The government resorted to force and opposition escalated.

The growth of Kikuyu opposition

On 16 October 1946, Major F.W. Carpenter, the District Commissioner in Nakuru, who had taken over responsibility for Olenguruone from the Maasai administration the previous month, held another *baraza* attended by over 700 Kikuyu, at which he reiterated the government's interpretation of their status.[35] He did, however, announce two new major government concessions. Junior wives of polygamous households were to be granted their own *shambas* and married sons of Olenguruone residents, who had illegally entered the settlement, were to be allowed to remain, to be treated as separate families and to be given their own five-acre *shambas*. These concessions were warmly welcomed, but the crowd angrily refused to accept impartible inheritance on the grounds that it would leave younger sons landless and with a bleak future. Carpenter then presented them with the blunt alternative of either accepting the conditions or being evicted. The District Commissioner remained optimistic that the new arrangements and the threat of eviction would win the majority over to the government's side and undermine the authority of the militants. The concessions, however, had come too late to reduce the Olenguruone residents' determination to uphold their *githaka* rights.[36]

Meanwhile the troubles had attracted widespread attention throughout the White Highlands and in Central Province. Messengers left the settlement to seek support or to hide on neighbouring farms and they spread their new oath to Kikuyu Central Association activists throughout the Rift Valley, using Lord Delamere's Soysambu estate as a staging post on their journeys to Kiambu. Close ties were created between the settlement and the Kikuyu squatters, who were fighting the new district council regulations and were already in a militant mood.[37] Gitebi, the Olenguruone leader, was well known among the squatter political activists as one of the founders of the Kikuyu Central Association in the Rift Valley, which he had joined at Limuru in 1928. He was particularly well known at Soysambu where he had opened a Kikuyu *Karing'a* school in the 1930s.[38]

In April 1946, when nearly the whole settlement had taken the oath – and not simply the elders as is traditional for Kikuyu oaths – Gitebi led several hundered supporters on a 150-mile march from Olenguruone to Kiambu to discuss their problems with Senior Chief Koinange and Eliud Mathu and to spread the new oath among discontented squatters in Nakuru and Naivasha. Resistance to the district council's new regulations spread rapidly throughout the White Highlands.[39] The day before Creech Jones, then Under Secretary of State for the Colonies, was due to arrive in the district in August 1946, the Soysambu squatters went on strike and refused to reattest under the new Naivasha resident labour rules.[40] The District Commissioner explained that, in taking 'full advantage of the power of oath-swearing, many hundreds of squatters were induced not to re-attest in the hope that either farming would be paralysed or District Councils' Resident Labour legislation jettisoned.'[41] In September, the Olenguruone Kikuyu helped organise a secret meeting on a Naivasha farm at which 700 squatters from 33 farms and the Kikuyu at the settlement were represented.[42] This was the climax of the initial resistance to the new squatter orders. In 1947 militancy diminished, primarily because the district councils had started to evict those who refused to accept the new contracts and loss of employment was too great a risk for most squatters, who had nowhere to go. By February 1947, the Nakuru Labour Officer was already confidently reporting that he had 'formed the opinion that the back of the Squatter Resistance movement had been broken and there were indications of a more general willingness to attest'.[43]

Kikuyu solidarity at Olenguruone, in contrast, remained unshaken. Even Mbote wa Karamba, one of the four government-appointed headmen, organised a petition against evictions, which was sent to Kenyatta who had recently returned from England and, when the settlement leaders were ordered to report to the District Commissioner at Nakuru, they set out instead to visit Kenyatta at Githunguri.[44] On 15 February 1947, a large crowd gathered outside the Settlement Office, shouting that the Settlement Officer must go and that Europeans should leave Kenya. The Chief Native Commissioner, Wyn Harris, was extremely alarmed by the protests, which he saw as 'a climax of disobedience, defiance and non-co-operation extending since 1942', and blamed the resistance on 'unscrupulous political agitators' who were using Olenguruone as a device to force the government to re-open the questions solved once and for all by the Kenya Land Commission. He complained:

> It is clear from the recent history of the Olenguruone Settlement, that the whole of the basis of the Settlement is now being used by certain Kikuyu as a political pawn against Government in the claim for the return of alienated land in the Kiambu area, and that neither improved conditions within the Settlement itself nor the generous concessions recently announced to the settlers at the *baraza* held by the District Commissioner, Nakuru, on 16 October, 1946, even when fully implemented, will in any way alter their claim now being put forward that they, the settlers, hold the land freehold and that Government has no right to interfere in any way or even to enforce rules of good farming.[45]

Finally on 22 March 1947, the Provincial Commissioner informed the non-co-operators that they must obey or leave Olenguruone within 14 days. At this threat, the crowd of 400 started to walk away. The Provincial Commissioner shouted at the retreating figures that, as they had failed to fulfil the conditions on their permits, he was now formally giving them notice to leave and any crops planted after 22 March would be destroyed.[46]

These threats merely strengthened Kikuyu solidarity and united legal and illegal residents against the government. When 25 leaders were summonsed, they refused to attend the magistrate's court and went into hiding among squatters on nearby farms. Tension grew. The Kikuyu *Karing'a* school committee, for example, decided that if they were forced out, they would burn down the school they had built rather than leave it for the government. After ten weeks, however, nothing had happened and the Kikuyu were still in residence. Each failure by the government to fulfil its threats convinced the residents that it would never carry out the evictions. Moreover, when the men who had fled the settlement in March began to return, they reported that they had been unenthusiastically received in Kiambu. The cool reception and the over-crowded conditions came as rather a shock to those who had never lived in the Kikuyu reserves. Until this visit, most had little idea of what conditions were like in Kikuyuland and were astonished to discover that many of the agricultural rules they were fighting against were rigorously applied in Kiambu. They returned to Olenguruone determined not to leave. Now they not only objected to the agricultural rules, but were also alarmed by their insecurity of tenure and feared that, even if they accepted the government's demands, they could still be evicted.[47]

In fact the 50 residents served with evictions were saved by the Attorney General, who advised the District Commissioner that the notices would not stand up in court. This was the first of several legal errors by the administration and relations between the Department of African Affairs and the Attorney General's chambers were soon extremely strained, because of what the administration considered the lawyers' over-cautious adherence to legal proprieties. Morgan, the Provincial Commissioner, was furious at this interference and started to blame the Attorney General and the cancellation of the eviction orders for 'all our present troubles'. This failure by the government to take any action bolstered confidence in the settlement that the evictions would never take place. On 22 March 1947, they had been given two weeks to leave, but by mid-July virtually all the men had returned and the new season's planting was well under way.[48]

Meanwhile, the African Settlement and Land Utilization Board, the agricultural department, the administration and the legal department were all blaming each other for Olenguruone's failure.[49] No-one was willing to acknowledge that the whole scheme had been a catastrophe from the beginning. Not only had force had to be used to compel the residents to leave Maasailand, but it was now apparent that the area was totally unsuited to peasant cultivation. R.B. Malcolmson, acting as lawyer for the Kikuyu, delighted in exposing these deficiencies and the bitter divisions within the government at hearings in the magistrate's court at Nakuru.[50]

The legal proceedings were long and involved, moving between the Kenyan Supreme Court and the East African Court of Appeal on intricate points of law over Kikuyu rights to appeal under Section 348(2) of the Criminal Procedure Code.[51] These legal arguments delayed further evictions for nearly a year until March 1948, when 22 cattle and 78 sheep, belonging to the first four appellants, were seized. After a brief period of shock, Kikuyu defiance quickly reasserted itself. Fox, the Settlement Officer, in fact warned: 'To date the defiant attitude remains unbroken and it cannot be said that we have made our point or any point. There are high hopes abroad that Government will once again step down from the first show of determined action.'[52] Morgan, the Provincial Commissioner, also considered that the prosecutions had simply increased Kikuyu morale and that the residents 'are quite convinced that we are not prepared to throw them out.' The government did however act and, between 30 July and 5 August 1948, after a 16-month delay, the huts and *dukas* of those who had been individually prosecuted were destroyed.[53]

Even this did not shake the confidence and resolve of the Olenguruone Kikuyu. Although most of the men in the settlement prudently vanished when the demolition parties arrived with 40 policemen, the women met them with shouts of derision. Gathungu Kunga's wives mocked the labourers and Gitebi's wife personally 'thanked' Inspector Potgieter for destroying the rats and bugs in her hut. Njoroge Waweru, even more defiant, hammered a note to the door of his abandoned house. His defiance provides an interesting insight into the residents' political under-standing of government and demonstrates the willingness of some Kikuyu militants at Olenguruone to contemplate the use of force to overthrow colonial domination. Waweru warned:

> I want to inform you British, that you are not to spoil the boundaries of Olenguruone *shambas*. If you just think since you came to Kenya you have never seen an African with a gun. I am the one to inform you that the Kikuyu have more power than you have with guns. Just wait until the year 1949 you will have to be sorry for the rules which you are giving us now and when it will be my turn to order you in the same way.[54]

The administration had simply succeeded in transforming the Olenguruone Kikuyu into desperate militants and had got nowhere in its attempts to enforce what it considered to be sound agricultural practices.

Buttery, the new District Officer, maintained that the problems stemmed largely from the government's unwillingness to invest sufficient funds to develop the settlement. He told Wyn Harris, the Chief Native Commissioner, in May 1948, that Maher's plan could be implemented only if Olenguruone were allocated £250,000 over the next five years and given the necessary staff, equipment and enthusiastic residents. With its climate and isolated situation the settlement would succeed only if the government were willing to lavish considerable sums on ensuring that it worked.[55]

The expulsion of the Olenguruone Kikuyu

When the Court of Appeal for Eastern Africa gave its judgement against the Olenguruone residents on 20 February 1949, the Chief Native Com-missioner introduced legislation empowering the administration to evict everyone without a valid residence permit, to impound all property and livestock and to destroy or sell huts and crops. The Kikuyu militants, however, warned the government that: 'our hardships have undoubtedly become noticeable to our fellow Africans elsewhere in the country. . . Today many of them very much fear and doubt the Government's real intention in the schemes for the settlement of Africans in selected areas under supervision'.[56] These were perceptive warnings. The Kamba, at Makueni, and the Teita, who were to be resettled in the Shimba Hills, were watching events at Olenguruone closely and might have reacted with alarm at any mass eviction. Paradoxically, this was the converse of the government's concern that other settlements might become contaminated unless an example were made at Olenguruone of those refusing to accept the settlement rules. Whichever way it turned, the government could not extricate itself from Olenguruone without severely damaging the African settlement programme.[57]

After further delays the government eventually acted. Early in the morning of 28 October 1949, shops in the centre of the settlement were destroyed and by the 30th, 900 cattle and 2,500 sheep had been seized. Two days later the first 18 houses were demolished and 100 acres of maize cut down. By 3 December all the original huts had been destroyed and burnt, but many Kikuyu had built temporary bivouacs and more than 2,200 people still refused to leave. Some had cunningly hidden maize, peas and potatoes from the police search parties and were living in hollows in the ground, protected by temporary bamboo roofs.[58]

As the evictions continued, the Special Branch intercepted a letter to Gitebi, the Olenguruone leader, from the leader of the Bataka Party in Uganda, Semakula Mulumba, who, to avoid detention following the riots in April 1949 had fled to London, where he had been welcomed by the Communist Party and by Mbiyu Koinange. In the letter, Mulumba urged Gitebi to continue the fight against the settlers who had confiscated their land.

Confidence among the Olenguruone Kikuyu was, however, crumbling. During the first few days of January 1950, another 100 families set out on foot for Elburgon to take refuge with squatter friends. The District Officer in Nakuru, it had been announced, was to be empowered to act as a magistrate and to hear cases at Olenguruone. When the first cases were heard in mid-January, the accused played into the government's hands by refusing to pay their 100-shilling fines. This enabled the administration to despatch them *en masse* to Bl Yatta – an inhospitable, arid area in northern Ukambani. On 1 February, 90 cases were heard and thereafter, until the middle of March, there were twice-weekly arrests of some 50 people who were sentenced to imprisonment at the Yatta Detention Camp. By 3 March, after a final major drive, Olenguruone was almost cleared. But as they left, the Kikuyu sought one last revenge; they spread arsenic over the pastures of the few residents who had co-operated and followed the agricultural rules. This parting blow eloquently testified to their bitterness and determination to fight for *githaka* land on *githaka* terms.[59]

The government optimistically believed the struggle was over and hoped that Olenguruone would quickly be forgotten, but in reality it was only the beginning of Kikuyu opposition to continued British rule and the privileged position of the European settlers. One incident in the last days of Olenguruone demonstrated the depth of popular feeling in Central

Province and the impact the struggle had made on the Kikuyu people. On 17 January 1950, the first batch of convicted Olenguruone residents had been despatched to the Yatta Detention Camp, via Karatina and Thika. When they arrived at Karatina, itself a centre of opposition to colonial rule in which the radicals were particularly influential, the prison cortège stopped to refuel and was immediately surrounded by crowds of inquisitive people who, on discovering they were the martyrs of Olenguruone, mobbed the prison vans and had to be driven back. All subsequent convoys to the Yatta followed a different route, carefully avoiding Kikuyuland in case there should be an attempt to release these heroes of the *wananchi* in transit.[60]

The depth of popular support for the residents is further demonstrated by the important role given to Olenguruone in several Mau Mau *nyimbo*. One of the most interesting of these was composed by former prisoners at the Yatta Detention Camp. It shows that a sophisticated political awareness developed in the settlement and that the Mau Mau radicals were committed to wider goals in their struggle for 'land and freedom'. The *nyimbo* declared that:

> There was great wailing in Olenguruone
> Even as we collected together belongings
> The enemy had scattered about.
> The enemy was telling us:
> Hurry up, quick.
> Are you forgetting you are criminals.

Chorus

> *We will greatly rejoice*
> *The day Kenyan people*
> *Get back their land.*

> We are being oppressed all over this land.
> Even our homes have been destroyed.
> And our bodies have been exploited.
> But do not be afraid.
> Because we are heading for a great victory.

> The British came from Europe
> In order to oppress our people
> Since then they have continued oppressing us.
> *Ngai*, when will they go back to Europe?

> We shall continue to suffer for our freedom;
> We shall continue struggling
> For the return of our stolen land.
> You British know that though you detain us
> For demanding our land and freedom,
> Kenya is ours for ever and ever.[61]

Whatever the administration had hoped, the struggle would go on.

Notes

1. C.G. Rosberg and J. Nottingham, *The Myth of Mau Mau*, pp. 243-4, 248-59. See also F. Furedi's unpublished paper, 'Olenguruone in Mau Mau Historiography', and his 'The Social Composition of the Mau Mau Movement in the White Highlands', p. 495; and T.M.J. Kanogo, 'Rift Valley Squatters and Mau Mau', p. 245.

2. For details of the climate and growing season at Olenguruone see KNA PC/RVP 6A/1/17/2, 'Olenguruone, 1948-50', J.F.D. Buttery, 'Report on Olenguruone Settlement', December 1948.

3. C.G. Rosberg and J. Nottingham, *The Myth of Mau Mau*, pp. 254-5; and F. Furedi's unpublished paper, 'Olenguruone in Mau Mau Historiography', pp. 3-5. For details of the Kikuyu Highlands Squatters Landowners' Association, see CO 533/543/38086/38 (1946-47), 'Petitions: Kikuyu Grievances', Samuel K. Gitebi to Creech Jones, 16 July 1947; and KNA Secretariat 1/12/8, 'Labour Unrest: Intelligence Reports, Central Province, 1947', report 20 February 1947.

4. KNA PC/RVP 6A/1/17/2, 'Olenguruone, 1948-50', Criminal Appeals Supreme Court, Nairobi, nos. 252, 253, 254 and 255 of 1948. *Decisions of the Court of Appeal for Eastern Africa*, vol. xv, 1948, pp. 118-120 (15, EACA, 118), criminal appeals, nos. 22, 23 and 24 of 1948; and *Decisions of the Court of Appeal for Eastern Africa*, vol. xvi, 1949, pp. 95-8 (16, EACA, 95), criminal appeals, nos. 178, 179, 180 and 181 of 1948; and I. Rosen and F. de F. Stratton, *A Digest of East African Criminal Case Law*, p. 229.

5. Maina wa Kinyatti, *Thunder from the Mountains*, pp. 53-6; and F. Furedi's unpublished paper, 'Olenguruone in Mau Mau Historiography', pp. 2-6.

6. KNA DC/NKU 6/2 'Olenguruone, 1947-50', Rennie to Creech Jones, 27 June 1947; and CO 533/577/38678/1 (1947-48), 'African Land Settlement: Olenguruone Settlement', I.D. Robertson', 11 July 1947; and A.B. Cohen, 14 July 1947.

7. KNA DC/NKU 4/1, 'Olenguruone Settlement', acting Native Courts Officer to Eric Davies, 8 March 1950; and memorandum for the Executive Council, 2 March 1950.

8. T.M.J. Kanogo's unpublished thesis, 'The History of Kikuyu Movement . . .', pp. 73-89.

9. See CO 533/641/38223, 'Kenya: Resident Native Labour Ordinance', minute dated 12 October 1936, for Whitehall's attitude to the 1937 Ordinance.

10. KNA DC/NKU 4/1, 'Olenguruone Settlement', Memorandum to the Executive Council, 2 March 1950. The decision to remove Kikuyu interpenetrators from Maasailand was promulgated in Government Notices, 832 and 1,030 of 1940, and 522, and 523 of 1941. See also DC/NRK 1/1/3, 'Narok Annual Reports', for 1939, pp. 4, 6, 20, 23; 1940 Report, pp. 3, 6; and 1941 Report, pp. 3, 10, for evidence of the Maasai administration's eagerness to remove the Kikuyu from Il Melili and Nairage Ngare. I am grateful to Richard Waller for many insights into the thinking of the field administration in Maasailand.

11. KNA PC/RVP 6A/1/3/1, 'Kikuyu in the Rift Valley Province', copy of letter from Elburgon farm manager to Officer-in-Charge, Maasai, 7 September 1936.

12. F. Furedi's unpublished article, 'Olenguruone in Mau Mau Historiography', pp. 1-2.

13. KNA DC/NRK 2/1/1, 'Handing Over Reports, Narok District, 1946-59', A.N. Bailward to R.A. Wilkinson, October 1946; and DC/NRK 1/1/3, 'Narok Annual Reports' for 1939, 1940 and 1941.

14. I am indebted for this information to Richard Waller.

15. KNA PC/RVP 6A/1/17/2, 'Olenguruone 1948-50', S.K. Gitebi to C.R. Attlee, 5 October 1949; and to HM King George VI, 19 December 1949.

16. For conflicting views on the Olenguruone rules, contrast KNA DC/NKU 4/1, 'Olenguruone Settlement', acting Native Courts' Officer to the Executive Council, 2 March 1950, and Gitebi's protests in PC/RVP 6A/1/17/2, 'Olenguruone, 1948-50', 5 October and 19 December 1949.

17. KNA PC/RVP 6A/1/17/2, 'Olenguruone, 1948–50', J.F.D. Buttery, 'Report on the Olenguruone Settlement', December 1948 for climatic and topographical details.
18. *ibid.*
19. *ibid*, S.K. Gitebi to C.R. Attlee, 5 October 1949; and to HM King George VI, 19 December 1949.
20. KNA DC/KBU 4/9, 'Olenguruone Settlement, 1940–44', C. Tomkinson, PC Central to DC Narok, 23 July 1940; and A.N. Bailward, Officer-in-Charge Maasai to DC Kiambu, 16 March and 17 April 1944.
21. KNA PC/RVP 6A/1/17/2, 'Olenguruone, 1948–50', S.K. Gitebi to HM King George VI, 19 December 1949.
22. *ibid.* This letter contained a detailed history of the settlement from the ex-squatters' perspective. See also the correspondence in DC/KBU 4/9, 'Olenguruone Settlement, 1940–44', to H.E. Lambert, DC Kiambu, in 1942.
23. KNA PC/RVP 6A/1/17/1, 'Olenguruone, 1946–48', notes on the Olenguruone *baraza*, 21 June 1943. Bailward's view is found in his letter to Rennie, 10 July 1946. For details of Lari and Kerita see M. Omosule's unpublished paper, 'An Assessment of the Role of the Kenya Land Commission Report', pp. 9–10, 17–28.
24. KNA PC/RVP 6A/1/17/1, 'Olenguruone, 1946–48', notes on the Olenguruone *baraza*, 21 June 1943.
25. F. Furedi's unpublished article, 'Olenguruone in Mau Mau Historiography', p. 2.
26. KNA DC/NKU 4/1, 'Olenguruone Settlement', acting Native Courts' Officer to Executive Council, 2 March 1950; and to Eric Davies, the Chief Native Commissioner, 8 March 1950. For the importance of the Olenguruone oath, see T.M.J. Kanogo, 'Rift Valley Squatters and Mau Mau', p. 245.
27. See comments in PC/RVP 6A/1/17/2, 'Olenguruone, 1948–50', J.F.D. Buttery, 'Report on Olenguruone', December 1948; and his extracts from the Agricultural Officer, C.D. Knight's 1943 report. See also R.D.F. Ryland's comments to the Secretary for Commerce and Industry, 2 July 1948, about the food situation in the settlement.
28. CO 533/557/38678/1 (1947–48) 'African Land Settlement: Olenguruone Settlement', I.D. Robertson, 11 July 1947; and A.B. Cohen, 14 July 1947.
29. *ibid*, I.D. Robertson, 11 July 1947.
30. *ibid*, A.B. Cohen, 14 July 1947.
31. The most influential reports included W. Allan, *Studies in African Land Usage in Northern Rhodesia*, and C.G. Trapnell and J.M. Clothier, *The Soils, Vegetation and Agricultural Systems of North-Western Rhodesia*, and Trapnell's article, 'Ecological Methods in the Study of Native Agriculture'.
32. KNA PC/RVP 6A/1/17/1, 'Olenguruone, 1946–48', Maher's report on Olenguruone, 22 January 1946; and the meeting of the Olenguruone sub-committee of the African Settlement Board, 19–20 February 1946. See also PC/RVP 6A/1/17/2, Olenguruone, 1948–50', for J.F.D. Buttery's comments on Maher.
33. PC/RVP 6A/1/17/1, 'Olenguruone, 1948–50', Maher's report, 22 January 1946.
34. *ibid.* Maher calculated that the residents would be able to generate the following income: 1.5 acres of wheat, or 12 bags, @ 20/- each, equals 240/-; half an acre of beans with maize interplanted, yields 2 bags @ 20/- each; and half an acre of potatoes, yields 20 bags @ 3/- each, equals 60/-. Total income of 340/-.
35. PC/RVP 6A/1/17/1, 'Olenguruone, 1946–48', minutes of F.W. Carpenter's *baraza* at Olenguruone on 16 October 1946.
36. *ibid.* For the background to these concessions see African Settlement Board to the Chief Native Commissioner, 5 July 1946; and A.N. Bailward to Rennie, 10 July 1946.
37. F. Furedi's unpublished paper, 'Olenguruone in Mau Mau Historiography', pp. 3–4; C.G. Rosberg and J. Nottingham, *The Myth of Mau Mau*, pp. 255–6.
38. C.G. Rosberg and J. Nottingham, *The Myth of Mau Mau*, p. 254.
39. In February 1946, Senior Chief Koinange, Chief Josiah Njonjo, Chief Waruhiu Kungu

and Eliud Mathu had presented a report on Olenguruone to the Kiambu Local Native Council. This severely criticised the government and declared that the Olenguruone Kikuyu held their land on *githaka* terms. See KNA PC/RVP 6A/1/17/1, 'Olenguruone, 1946–48', report of the committee chaired by Senior Chief Koinange, 14 February 1946. For the government's response, see E.L. Brooke Anderson, Chairman African Settlement and Land Utilisation Board, to PC Rift Valley, 10 October 1946.

40. KNA Lab 9/601, 'Resident Labour General, 1942–45', Hyde-Clarke to Mitchell, June 1946; and DC/NKU 1/5, 'Nakuru–Naivasha–Ravine Annual Report, 1946', p. 2.
41. KNA DC/NKU 1/5, 'Nakuru–Naivasha–Ravine Annual Report, 1946', p. 6.
42. KNA Lab 9/1071, 'Resident Labourers Ordinance: The Problem of the Squatter: *Ad Hoc* Committee, 1946–48', reports of Kenya African Union meeting at Naivasha, 17 November 1946, by M.S. Athumani and J. Kariuki.
43. Quoted by F. Furedi in his unpublished article, 'Olenguruone in Mau Mau Historiography', p. 4.
44. KNA PC/RVP 6A/1/17/1, 'Olenguruone, 1946–48', D.L. Morgan, acting PC Rift Valley, to Rennie the Chief Secretary, 3 February 1947.
45. *ibid*. Wyn Harris to D.L. Morgan, 17 March 1947.
46. KNA DC/NKU 6/2, 'Olenguruone, 1947–50', Wyn Harris to Olenguruone Kikuyu, 25 March 1947 and D.L. Morgan to P. Wyn Harris, 8 May 1948.
47. KNA PC/RVP 6A/1/17/1, 'Olenguruone, 1946–48', report by the District Commissioner R.D.F. Ryland, on the prosecution of four Olenguruone residents, 19 May 1947; and the Kikuyu Karing'a school committee to DO Olenguruone, 21 May 1947.
48. *ibid*, A. Crabb for acting Chief Native Commissioner to D.L. Morgan, 31 May 1947 and R.D.F. Ryland, DC Nakuru to D.L. Morgan, 11 July 1947. Morgan's comment was written in the margin.
49. *ibid*, C.O. Oates, Provincial Agricultural Officer, to S. Fox, District Officer, Olenguruone, 9 October 1947.
50. KNA PC/RVP 6A/1/17/2, 'Olenguruone, 1948–50', J.F.D. Buttery, 'Report on Olenguruone', December 1948; KNA DC/NKU 1/5, 'Nakuru–Naivasha–Ravine Annual Report, 1947', p. 15; and DC/NKU 6/2, 'Olenguruone, 1947–50', R. Black Malcolmson to Creech Jones, 2 May 1947.
51. The magistrate was entitled to hear the cases under the Minor Cases Procedure and Section 197 of the Criminal Procedure Code if the sentence imposed did not exceed one month's imprisonment or a £5 fine. For details of the legal debate see KNA PC/RVP 6A/1/17/2, 'Olenguruone, 1948–50', Criminal Appeals Supreme Court, Nairobi, nos. 252, 253, 254 and 255 of 1948. *Decisions of the Court of Appeal for Eastern Africa*, vol. xv, 1948, pp. 118–20, (15, EACA, 118), criminal appeals, nos. 22, 23 and 24 of 1948; and *Decisions of the Court of Appeal for Eastern Africa*, vol. xvi, 1949, pp. 95–8 (16, EACA, 95), criminal appeals, nos. 178, 179, 180 and 181 of 1948.
52. KNA PC/RVP 6A/1/17/1, 'Olenguruone, 1946–48', S. Fox's report on action taken to remove four plot holders, and huts and crops, 18 March 1948.
53. *ibid*, D.L. Morgan to Wyn Harris, 8 May 1948. See also J.F.D. Buttery's first report to the African Settlement and Land Utilisation Board, 7 May 1948, in PC/RVP 6A/1/17/2, 'Olenguruone, 1948–50'.
54. KNA DC/NKU 6/2 'Olenguruone, 1947–50', R.D.F. Ryland, DC Nakuru to J.F.D. Buttery, DC Olenguruone, 14 July 1948; D.V. Kapila's protest to the Chief Native Commissioner, 3 August 1948; and J.F.D. Buttery to R.D.F. Ryland, 3 August 1948.
55. KNA PC/RVP 6A/1/17/2, 'Olenguruone, 1948–50 , J.F.D. Buttery, 'Report on Olenguruone', December 1948. One should perhaps consider that if the government took its claims seriously then the prototype African agricultural settlement should have been worth more than the miserly £10,000 which was spent during the ten years of its existence, especially when it was prepared to spend £80,000 on the new European primary school at Nakuru.
56. *ibid*, Olenguruone Kikuyu to Wyn Harris, the Chief Native Commissioner, 26 June

1949. For details of the new legislation see Wyn Harris, Chief Native Commissioner to D.L. Morgan, 7 June 1949.

57. KNA Lab 9/339, 'Labour Squatters: Olenguruone Settlement, 1945–51', P. Wyn Harris to D.L. Morgan, 17 March 1947.

58. KNA DC/NKU 6/2, 'Olenguruone, 1947–50', J.F.D. Buttery to D.L. Morgan, PC Rift Valley, 31 October 1949 and 7 November 1949. See also J.F.D. Buttery's situation report, 3 December 1949.

59. *ibid*, J.F.D. Buttery to R.D.F. Ryland, DC Nakuru, 16 November 1949, enclosing an intercepted letter from S. Mulumba to S.K. Gitebi, dated 11 November 1949. A.F. Sagar, District Officer, Olenguruone, to DC Nakuru, 16 January 1950 and P.H. Jones DO Nakuru, who had gone to Olenguruone as an assistant magistrate to hear the cases, to Provincial Commissioner, Rift Valley, 16 January 1950 and 21 January 1950.

60. *ibid*, A.F. Sagar, DO Olenguruone to DC Nakuru, 21 January 1950.

61. Maina wa Kinyatti, *Thunder from the Mountains*, pp. 55–6. It would appear that Maina wa Kinyatti has transposed these tape-recorded 'Mau Mau hymns' into Marxist idiom, distorting the complex ideology of Kikuyu peasant resistance.

Seven

The Peasant Revolt: Murang'a, 1947

The second colonial occupation severely disrupted Kikuyu society and undermined the position of colonial chiefs. This chapter places the peasant revolt in Murang'a during 1947 and 1948 within the wider context of the alienation of the Kikuyu and the origins of Mau Mau. We have seen how the government endeavoured to revive the traditional land authorities and to prevent the development of commercial farming and a local entrepreneurial élite which, it was feared, would produce greater social differentiation and undermine the fabric of Kikukyu culture and social order.[1] The competition for government patronage, however, continued to grow, and the commercial farmers and traders came increasingly to resent the privileged access of the chiefs to the rewards of the colonial state. Meanwhile, the administration and agricultural department's post-war policies, with their over-reliance on communal terracing, had alienated the peasantry and severely weakened the government-appointed chiefs. As the agricultural campaign gathered momentum, many of the older chiefs were replaced by a new clique of modernisers, who could be relied upon to support the new policies. But by dismissing the older chiefs, the administration weakened the ties of clientage between the chiefs and their people, just when the agricultural betterment campaign had increased popular opposition on the colonial régime. The administration's reliance on compulsory terracing created a latent constituency for the men of violence, who began to organise a campaign against the chiefs in the African press and to raise popular political consciousness. The effects of this political mobilisation upon the chiefs, the field administration and the Secretariat are briefly considered. The new Chief Native Commissioner, Wyn Harris, who had been Provincial Commissioner in Central Province until early in 1947, was unable to convince the legal department of the seriousness of the deteriorating situation in Kikuyuland.[2] The chapter concludes with a brief assessment of the factional divisions among the African political activists and their supporters.

The growth of popular discontent

It has become fashionable to suggest that increasing social differentiation in Kiambu, Murang'a and Nyeri was the crucial factor, if not indeed according to some historians the only factor, behind growing opposition by 'the poor peasants' to the chiefs and other collaborators with British rule. Such an interpretation is not wrong – poor peasants, *ahoi* and other members of junior lineages in Kikuyu sub-clans were squeezed and even 'proletarianised' as the cost of an acre of land rose from 100 goats in 1939 to 1,000 in 1952 – but it is only a partial explanation for the growth of popular discontent in the Kikuyu reserves between 1945 and 1952.[3]

The new generation of Kikuyu radical historians has correctly discerned that the process was not quite so simple as was once believed. *Ahoi* and the other Kikuyu 'tenants' were expropriated not only by the chiefs and their clients but also by the aspiring traders and cash-crop cultivators, who provided the backbone of support for the underground Kikuyu Central Association and the constitutionalist Kenya African Union under Kenyatta's leadership after June 1947.[4] Support for the political militants in the Kikuyu reserves was also a function of the effects of the post-war agricultural development programme and the massive influx of technical advisers, which amounted to a second colonial occupation almost as disruptive in its consequences for the ordinary African digging in his *shamba* as the first. While some chiefs attempted to insulate their people from the new demands of the agricultural and veterinary departments, others were more concerned with retaining the favour of the district administration and with safeguarding their privileged access to government patronage. Such chiefs zealously enforced the new soil-conservation regulations and communal terracing, and alienated their people. The following study of Murang'a in central Kikuyuland shows a close correlation between the locations in which the chiefs pushed terracing in the late 1940s and the centres of Mau Mau support in the early 1950s. As early as 1947, the government's agricultural policies had aroused such widespread opposition that they were undermining the foundations of the colonial state.[5]

'Mere events' ought not to be entirely subsumed within *la longue durée* of internal social differentiation among the Kikuyu, if we are to uncover the complexity of the past. This chapter charts the course of local events, 'the mere dust' of history, and it therefore places proportionately less weight than much recent work upon the underlying social processes.[6] The problems created by increasing differentiation, however, exemplified by the estates of over 150 acres acquired by chiefs such as Muhoya and Nderi in Nyeri, were obviously an important source of discontent. One index of this mounting frustration is the increase in court fees from land cases from £13,000 in 1949 to £24,000 only two years later.[7] But this alone does not adequately explain the dynamics of peasant opposition to the chiefs. The social strains were indeed there, but popular frustration needed a catalyst if it was to be transformed into violent resistance. In Murang'a and the other Kikuyu districts, the overt government intervention of the post-war terracing campaign and the host of new agricultural regulations focused resentment against the chiefs and enabled the rural radicals, with the help of the more politically-experienced urban militants, such as Mwangi Macharia in Murang'a or the Forty Group in Nyeri, to mobilise popular discontent and to organise a determined and protracted challenge to the chiefs and their allies in 1947 and 1948.[8]

The aims of the agricultural campaign

Norman Humphrey's reports on Nyeri and Machakos so alarmed the Nairobi Secretariat that it became convinced of the need for immediate action to avert an agricultural crisis in the Kikuyu reserves. It was feared that 'land-mining', continual cultivation and over-stocking had drastically impaired soil fertility. Various solutions were canvassed, most of which were based on the need for an intensive communal terracing campaign.[9] Only a few agricultural officers, such as Jack Benson in Meru, argued that a more effective approach would be to reward those Africans who adopted better farming techniques by allowing them to grow high-value cash crops. The encouragement given to these schemes, however, was dwarfed by the mobilisation of the peasantry in the terracing campaign.[10]

Chiefs competed to ensure that their location headed the district terracing figures and to retain official approval. Successful chiefs – that is, those who most rigorously enforced terracing and agricultural improvements upon their reluctant locations – were rewarded with wattle trading licences and schools to distribute among their supporters. Increasingly the administration came to assess a chief's performance in terms of how many miles of terracing had been dug.[11]

Colin Maher, the head of the Soil Conservation Unit, was responsible for this emphasis on terracing. He shared the fears of Humphrey and Lambert, and believed that remedial action was urgently required to prevent further destruction of the soil. Maher did, however, warn that terracing should be only one aspect of the land rehabilitation programme, which ought also to include strip cropping, paddocking of cattle and bracken clearing to open pastures. He insisted that terracing alone would prove inadequate to reverse agricultural decline and stressed the need for an integrated campaign to restructure the whole ethos of peasant cultivation.[12] As at Olenguruone, the administration knew what it wanted to do but, despite the Colonial Development and Welfare Act, it had neither the manpower, equipment nor finance to follow Maher's proposals. His perfectionist schemes were dangerous; both at Olenguruone and in Central Province, the best proved to be the enemy of the good. Theoretically, his integrated development plans followed the most recent theories about land use, crop rotations and anti-erosion measures, but, until the Swynnerton Plan of the 1950s, the over-stretched Kenyan agricultural department never had the capacity to implement them as a complete programme of reform. Instead, Assistant Agricultural Officers, pushed by the field administration, were forced to select one or two elements from the package and to stress these at the expense of balanced development, which Maher had insisted was essential. Usually this meant selecting the key feature of Maher's recommendations, which in Central Province was the construction of narrow-base terraces to catch the run-off on the upper slopes of the ridges. These required much hard, compulsory labour, which soon provoked popular opposition. Other elements of Maher's original plan, which had been designed to win support for the campaign, were ignored.[13] The administration and the Secretariat believed that such schemes would merely encourage 'excessive individualism' which was blamed for 'land-mining' and erosion. Humphrey, for example, had observed that in Nyeri: 'Individualism, indeed, is running riot and it is certain it is being carried so far that the future is fraught with danger if it continues uncontrolled.'[14] While the administration remained so resistant to any attempt to increase African production of remunerative crops, individual agricultural officers could make little headway, especially as the settlers were determined to destroy the peasant option, which they saw as a serious threat to their economic dominance. The settlers were determined that the cultivation of coffee, tea and pyrethrum should remain a European monopoly.[15]

Even within the agricultural department, this liberal, co-optive approach had many opponents, the most prominent of which were Hughes Rice, who served as Assistant Agricultural Officer in Nyeri, Murang'a and Machakos between 1944 and 1952, and J.T. Moon, the Provincial Agricultural Officer. Both refused to countenance any concessions to African opposition to terracing and contended that any signs of weakening resolve would endanger the progress already achieved and ensure that the communal campaign would disintegrate. Maher's perceptive warnings about excessive reliance on terracing were therefore ignored and compulsion came increasingly to dominate the agricultural campaign.[16]

To be effective, however, terraces had to be built on the contour, along a whole ridge. This meant that they had to cross several *shambas* belonging to different households. Popular opposition was soon aroused, for terracing not only required exhausting work, but also reduced the land available for cultivation. Philip Rimington, who became Assistant Agricultural Officer in Murang'a in 1949, recalled that terrace drains and run-offs were three feet wide and that when the excavated earth was piled up, either above or below them, no less than four to six feet of land was lost for every three-foot drop between the contour terraces. This provoked bitter resentment and, with the advantage of hindsight, he now considers that 'you've got to have some give and take, and you've got to adapt your terracing to the needs and lives and existence, I think. You just don't really bulldoze through the whole of a person's smallholding, which is in fact what we did do. And that is really where I think we sort of came unstuck'.[17] Leslie Brown was another convinced opponent of excessive terracing. In an interview just before his death in 1980, he recalled the resentment narrow-base terracing had created:

> They were undesirable in that they were relatively laborious to dig and required constant maintenance as natural erosion tended to fill them very quickly. They were, however, insisted upon by Colin Maher, senior soil conservation engineer, as policy – a profound error which could not be rectified until I became more senior and I and other officers fought the policy successfully.[18]

He also considered that the district administration was responsible for much of the opposition to terracing because:

> The Administration . . . liked to regard soil conservation as a punishment, and when some location was backward over tax paying and given to drunkeness and crime I was often required to go and lay on some soil conservation there. I usually made a token effort to do some but this was obviously an unsound point of view which should not have prevailed and I usually paid as little as possible attention to such requests as I could.[19]

Unfortunately, not all agricultural officers were so wise. While such attitudes prevailed among the field administration it was inevitable that terracing would eventually provoke resistance.

Although Maher's original programme had attempted to foster popular support for terracing by rewarding the co-operators with cheap manure and improved stock, once the campaign began, practical limitations on supervisory manpower, equipment and finance, distorted the aims, so that the reality experienced by Kikuyu and Kamba peasants was very different from the idealistic expectations of Maher and the Secretariat. Out in the maize *shambas*, compulsion dominated official thinking and attempts to win popular acceptance were at best half-hearted. By the time the campaign had percolated down to the ordinary African, it bore little resemblance not only to Maher's grandiose plan, but also to Lambert's or Wyn Harris's conception of a revitalised *Muhirig'a*.[20]

The rewards of chiefship

Throughout the 30 years between the outbreak of the First World War and the end of the Second, Kikuyu chiefs controlled the rewards of government patronage in the reserves through the Local Native Councils. Grants for ploughs or carts, new varieties of seed for cash crops, and preferential access to grade cattle were all used by the chiefs to enrich themselves and their supporters. Colonial chiefs could not afford to antagonise all their people, otherwise they would have ceased to command respect, so they all attempted to consolidate their position by the use of patronage to reward their immediate *mbari*.[21]

The chiefs' privileged access to the 'pork-barrel' of the colonial state, however, aroused resentment among aspiring cash-crop cultivators and traders who were excluded from government patronage. By the late 1920s, these ambitious outsiders had emerged as the leaders of the Kikuyu Central Association and challenged the chiefs' monopoly of power and rewards.[22] At the same time, many poor peasants were being forced to become migrant labourers or to sell their land to the emerging African élite to survive. Such people identified the chiefs as their exploiters. These processes were intensified during the war and the Mitchell era, when those who had surplus to extract profited as never before from the high prices offered on the black market. During these years social differentiation became increasingly apparent. While the chiefs and their allies prospered, poor peasants dependent on earnings from wage labour suffered from the high rate of inflation. Moreover, African traders who were known to oppose the chiefs found it virtually impossible to restock their shops or acquire spare parts to keep their lorries or *posho* mills functioning, for the district administration had left the distribution of rationed commodities largely to the chiefs.[23]

The chiefs also alienated the returning *askari*. In the political and economic rivalries of Kikuyuland, the ex-*askari* quickly discovered that a six-year absence, however socially prestigious, put them at a political disadvantage. Denied special representation on the Native Tribunals and the Local Native Councils, they saw the chiefs and the elders consolidating their control of government patronage. The *askari* were not given licences for trading or permits for shops; these went to the chiefs and their clients.[24]

In fact the administration was attempting to ensure that the new businesses were well run, viable concerns. The much-resented regulation limiting the number of shops to one for every 400 inhabitants, for example, was designed to protect the welfare of established traders and to ensure that newcomers did not waste their money competing with experienced businessmen. But to those who were refused licences – and they were in the majority – it simply provided further evidence of the domination of rural life and the suffocation of new business rivals by the established coterie around the chiefs. Aspiring African entrepreneurs were convinced that new financial opportunities were being restricted to acquiescent supporters of the chiefs and of the *status quo*. By 1947, when their savings had been dissipated or lost on ill-considered business ventures, the ex-*askari* were ready to add their voices to the growing chorus of peasant protest.[25]

The colonial régime in Central Province after 1945 was simply incapable of admitting all those who wanted to share in the rewards of state patronage. Unless the colony's whole political economy was fundamentally restructured and the privileged position of the European settlers abandoned, which Sir Philip Mitchell never comtemplated, the administration had no option but to restrict the number of Africans who could be incorporated on a first-come-first-served basis. Thus only the chiefs and their supporters were allowed to share in the pickings from Kenya's controlled economy, while requests from the emerging alternative élite had to be rejected. James Beauttah, for example, founder of the Kenya Automobile Association (a cartel of African bus owners), and Andrew Ng'ang'a, leader of the *Agikuyu na Worjoria Wao* (a co-operative of licensed egg exporters), who were in the vanguard of indigenous capitalism, became disgruntled and turned to political action. As Vice-President of the Kenya African Union in Central Province and secretary of the Murang'a district branch respectively, these men soon became noted opponents of the chiefs and, therefore, of the chiefs' allies in the district administration.[26]

The chiefs discovered after the war that it was increasingly difficult to satisfy both the administration and their people. Whereas in the inter-war years the position had provided many opportunities for capital accumulation through the manipulation of government and Local Native Council grants, after 1945 the administration made new demands on the chief, while the agricultural campaign aroused widespread opposition and considerably increased the risks of being a chief. Tenure of office became less secure and many chiefs were ignominiously dismissed for failing to enforce the new agricultural regulations.[27] This, of course, reduced the financial attractions of the post. In the 1920s and 1930s, a newly-appointed chief could confidently expect to have at least ten years in which to restructure the local trade networks to enrich himself and his supporters and to direct development funds into particular *mbari*, but after 1945 a new chief had virtually no time in which to exploit his position and to channel government money into his area. Instead he had immediately to begin to worry about defending his newly-gained authority as the political contest in the locations gathered momentum. The agricultural betterment campaign and soil terracing had to be enthusiastically supported, regardless of their divisive effects, if the chief was to retain official approval and to remain in office. As the men in the middle, the chiefs were under intense pressure from both the district administration, on the one hand, and their political opponents and increasing numbers of ordinary Africans, on the other.[28]

After the war, under Mitchell's drive to improve African agriculture, a chief was expected to instigate a social revolution in peasant life instead of being left to preside over his location and to ensure that the tax was paid and peace preserved, as had been the case during the inter-war years. For the first time the peasant quietly cultivating his *shamba* felt the full force of government intervention. At this critical juncture, however, the government decided to replace many of the pre-war generation of chiefs with younger, better-educated men, who would energetically support the agricultural campaign and 'modernise' their locations.[29] But these changes exacerbated the problems created by the campaign, for these new men often lacked popular support and had not yet established ties of clientage with which to withstand widespread opposition. They could only fall back on the government and the use of force to compel obedience.[30]

Until 1935 Murang'a was divided into two divisions; Maragua–Tana in the north and Chania–Maragua in the south, with 22 and 15 locations respectively. Between 1912, when the Political Record Books began, and 1935, Murang'a District had a total of 84 different chiefs; 54 in Maragua–Tana and 30 in Chania–Maragua, who served an average of nine years in the north and eleven in the south.[31] The post-war generation of chiefs, however, rarely survived this long, as can be seen from Table 7.1.[32]

Table 7.1: *Murang'a Chiefs 1944 to 1953*

Location	Chief	Dated appointed	Reasons for departure
1	Ndungu Kagori	1933	Served throughout
2	Njiri Karanja	1912	Retired old age; succeeded by son
	Kigo Njiri	1951	
3	Reuben Gachau	1927	Dismissed
	Mwangi Wambico	1949	Dismissed
	Samuel Githu	1953	
4	Kimani wa Thuo	1913	Dismissed for corruption
	Raphael Munyori	1946	Dismissed, but said to have resigned
	Paulo Mungai	1952	
5	Joseph Kangethe	1932	Dismissed
	Jibsam Mwaura	1945	Appointed African Administration

	Kuria Kinyanjui	1947	Dismissed
	Jibsam Mwaura	1951	
6	Karanja wa Kibarabara	1923	Dismissed for corruption
	Dishon Meri wa Wandia	1945	
7	Waweru Kehia	1932	Resigned old age
	Erastus Njeroge	1946	
8	Muriranja Mureithi	1908	Died alcoholism
	Ignatio Morai	1944	
9	Wakomo Muthenyi	1921	Resigned ill health
	Joshua Kogi	1945	
10	Sila Karimu	1936	Dismissed
	Aram Muhari Karema	1948	Dismissed
	Evan	1952	
11	Joseph Wanjie	1940	Retired honourably 1954, served throughout Mitchell era
12	Joel Michuki	1939	Succeeded his father who had been chief since 1908
13	Parmenas Mockerie Githendu	1936	Dismissed; became leader KISA
	Paulo Kiratu	1948	Dismissed
	Ben Jacob	1953	
14	Munyoroku Ndurwa	1941	Dismissed
	Pharis Kariuki	1943	Dismissed
	Wilson Morangi	1949	
15	Kigwaine Kamaru	1924	Resigned ill health
	Peterson Kariuki	1946	

The brief biographical studies in Table 7.1 point to some of the problems the post-war chiefs faced as they attempted to straddle the divide between the government and their people and to meet the demands imposed by the new interventionist policies. Only one of the earliest generation of chiefs, Njiri Karanja of Location 2, managed to survive in the Mitchell era. His former colleagues were dismissed or 'retired' and even Njiri was criticised for taking too little interest in terracing. Kimani wa Thuo of Location 4 and Karanja wa Kibarabara of Location 6 were replaced; they had taken to drink but were eventually dismissed when they were found to be trading the sugar ration and holding unauthorised land hearings. Corrupt old Muriranja Mureithi in Location 8 died of chronic alcoholism and was replaced by the dynamic Ignatio Morai.[33]

Even most of the first generation of Christian chiefs, who were appointed in the 1920s and early 1930s, failed to satisfy the stringent new requirements and were retired. Mwangi Wambico, for example, replaced

Reuben Gachau in Location 3 in 1949. The new chief was closely identified with the administration, having served as a clerk in the District Commissioner's office from 1945 until he was appointed chief. Wambico, however, failed to compel his people to dig terraces. Despite a warning from the District Commissioner early in 1951 that he must 'get round his location or else', he devoted most of his energies to developing his large wattle plantation rather than controlling his location. Finally he was replaced by his friend, Samuel Githu, an energetic young trader whom the administration hoped would prove a more forceful personality and control the location more effectively.[34]

In neighbouring Location 4, Raphael Munyori, who had replaced the disgraced Kimani wa Thuo, also failed and resigned on 16 October 1952, only four days before the declaration of the Emergency. On his appointment Munyori had been a popular choice, having recently secured a large majority in his election as vice-president of the Kandara Tribunal. Initially, he administered his location with great vigour and successfully put an end to illicit *tembu* brewing in Muruka, a notoriously bad spot where Nubian gin distilling was rampant, but by 1949 he had lost interest in soil conservation. Despite having been selected to attend one of the chiefs' courses at Kabete, Kimani's enthusiasm diminished as he gradually realised how deep rooted opposition was to the new interventionist government policies. By February 1952, the District Commissioner was complaining that Kimani did 'less than the minimum' and that 'the Administration could achieve nothing in Location 4'.[35]

In Location 5, Jibsam Mwaura, another former district clerk, resigned after only two years of service as a chief and his successor, Kuria Kinyanjui, was dismissed as ineffective in 1951. Aram Muhari Karema, who replaced Chief Sila Karimu in Location 10, also survived for only four years; while Paulo Kiratu, who succeeded the wily Parmenas Mockerie Githendu in Location 13 in 1948, was replaced in 1953. Location 14 was the worst in the district and between 1937 and 1952 had five different chiefs. Only Joseph Wanjie in Location 11, and Joel Michuki in Location 12, managed to cling to office throughout the Mitchell years.[36]

This rapid turnover of chiefs was a reflection of the more stringent criteria employed by the government during the second colonial occupation to measure progress. Chiefs who failed to produce impressive terracing statistics, for example, were condemned as inefficient and in the new interventionist atmosphere after the war, were dismissed. The field administration became much less sensitive to African opposition and pressed ahead with its agricultural theories about carrying capacity and crop rotations, ignoring signs of discontent. This arrogant attitude was not confined to Murang'a. Two cautious Nyeri chiefs, who had served with distinction for many years, were now criticised for obstructing the

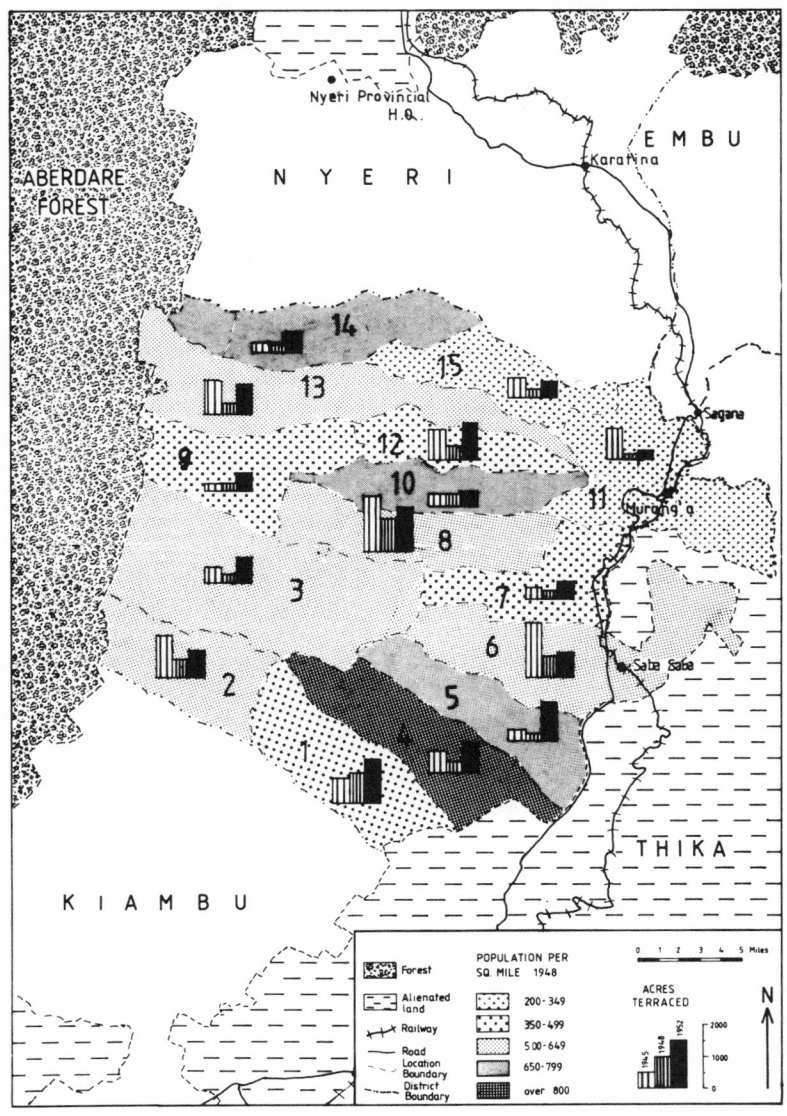

Map 7.1: *Population Density and Terracing in Murang'a*

Muhirig'a elders and for being too concerned with their own popularity.[37] Some Murang'a chiefs were also reluctant to push their people too far and realised that the new agricultural programme was generating bitter discontent. Chief Sila of Location 10 was one such sceptical old man of the pre-war generation of chiefs. Although he was regarded as the best farmer in the whole district, eager to adopt new techniques and crops, he ruled his location with great caution and did not push terracing too hard.[38]

Another chief who wished to remain on good terms with his people was Parmenas Mockerie Githendu, the best known and, in African political circles, the most influential of the Murang'a chiefs. Like Sila he was a member of the old school and refused to ruffle his location with over-zealous enforcement of terracing and soil conservation rules. As a longstanding member of the Kikuyu Central Association he was, unlike most chiefs, still close to the political activists and, as the administration was forced to admit, remained 'popular in his location since he makes little effort to enforce soil conservation measures'.[39] In 1931, the Kikuyu Central Association in Murang'a selected Parmenas to accompany Kenyatta to Britain to present evidence before the Joint Select Committee on Closer Union. He briefly attended Ruskin College, Oxford, before returning to Kenya in 1933 and was appointed chief three years later. Almost from the start he failed to fulfil the administration's expectations. The steep slopes of Mathioya in his location continued to be cultivated despite repeated orders to the contrary from the District Commissioner. Osborne, the District Commissioner in Murang'a throughout the war, however, astutely recognised that Parmenas was a popular chief and reported, 'I would only recommend his dismissal as a last resort. In spite of his deterioration he appears to command a large measure of general support.[40] This wise advice was ignored and, in 1948, Parmenas was dismissed, only to re-emerge as a prominent local politician and leader of the Kikuyu Independent Schools' Association throughout Murang'a. In his new position he soon became an even greater irritant to the district administration.

These chiefs realised that the terracing programme was alienating their people. Some of the older generation, like Kimani wa Thuo, Karanja wa Kibarabara and Wakomo Muthenyi, understood this opposition. However corrupt they might have been, unlike the new generation of chiefs who replaced them they did share the ambitions and suspicions of the ordinary Kikuyu peasant.[41] Even although they used their position to enrich themselves and exploited their people, over the course of 20 or 30 years as chiefs they established a complex network of obligations for favours rendered. Their long years in power had placed them at the centre of an intricate matrix of political antennae, penetrating deep into location life. They shared the thoughts of their peasant neighbours and quickly perceived the dangers involved in the post-war soil conservation drive.

Their obstinacy, tantamount to downright obstructionism, was an inarticulate condemnation of the agricultural campaign, which should have provided a potent warning to the field administration. The government, however, was not interested in warnings and pressed ahead regardless of the consequences. Mitchell himself insisted that the campaign must continue with 'a firm refusal to be rattled'.[42]

The growth of Kikuyu opposition

Discontent continued to lurk below the surface. The peasantry distrusted European intervention and failed to understand the need for the host of new regulations restricting cultivation near streams or on hillsides. Many suspected that, once the terraces had been completed, their land would be alienated to Europeans under the soldier settlement scheme. Garbled versions of Humphrey's reports spread through the reserves with the alarming news that thousands of families were to be dispossessed and thrown off their land. Since little attempt was made to explain the need for terracing, the arrival of agricultural department levellers to measure contour lines aroused further dismay.

The first resistance came from former soldiers who objected to communal labour and stopped their wives digging terraces.[43] Initially this was simply another step in their drive to secure special recognition from the chiefs and the administration, but the protest escalated into a wider anti-terracing campaign. Encouraged by local political activists, the former *askari* broadened their campaign early in 1946 by using the vernacular press to condemn female communal labour on the terraces. Popular disillusionment with terracing and the chiefs had not, however, become sufficiently pervasive to evoke a wide enough response and their campaign soon faltered. By the end of 1946, the District Commissioner, Desmond O'Hagan, was optimistic that the Kikuyu had finally realised the benefits of soil conservation.[44]

Between October and December 1946, more than 2,000 acres were protected each month in Murang'a and, over the year, approximately 7,000 miles of terraces were dug, more than double the figure for 1945. It was this sustained drive that destroyed Kikuyu acceptance of the colonial régime. Early in July 1947, Knight, the new Assistant Agricultural Officer, noted that 'only constant pressure keeps work going'. He failed, however, to draw the logical conclusion that the peasantry had been alienated and opposed these interventionist agricultural polices. The pressure to keep the campaign going, of course, was provided by the chiefs and the Native Tribunal elders. Both propaganda and force were used, and locational rivalry was encouraged to promote terracing. In an attempt to motivate the chiefs and their people, monthly lists of work completed in each location were sent round to be read out at *barazas*. So intense was the competition to do well among the new generation of chiefs, that some even published lists of the terracing done in each sub-location in order to stimulate their headmen and levellers on to greater efforts.[45]

The revolt when it came, only a fortnight after Knight's belated recognition that all was not well, completely destroyed Murang'a's famed system of *ngwatio* (communal labour). The year of disaster, 1947, had started extremely well. In January, 1,839 acres were terraced and this high level was sustained until July, but on Sunday 20 July, the Murang'a branch of the Kenya African Union held a meeting. This meeting, which was attended by over 10,000 people, was the first to be held in the district since Kenyatta had become President of the Kenya African Union on 1 June 1947, and he was the guest speaker. Kenyatta began by praising the soil-conservation campaign, emphasising to the crowd how important it was for erosion and declining fertility to be halted. The meeting, however, had become increasingly restless. They had come to hear him denounce, not praise, the terracing campaign. As the meeting progressed Kenyatta became aware that he was in danger of losing his audience and began to criticise certain aspects of the agricultural policy, particularly the reliance on female labour to dig terraces. The meeting finally resolved that no women should be compelled to join the *ngwatio* labour gangs. Until then the vast majority of the communal terracing workforce had been female. The resolution, therefore, was a direct challenge to the agricultural campaign and to the authority of the chiefs and the district administration.[46]

The following morning virtually no women turned out to work and only a few old men could be found digging terraces. By the middle of August even they had abandoned the slopes and all communal work had ceased. To prevent total collapse, the District Commissioner issued an order early in August that *shambas* would, in future, be individually measured and that prosecutions would follow unless terraces were dug by each cultivator within 15 days. It was hoped that this individualist approach and heavy fines would rekindle interest in *ngwatio* communal work, but by this time the chiefs' political opponents had mobilised peasant opposition to terracing and had proclaimed that 'the people were determined to have no more terracing at any price'.[47] In September, only 187 acres were protected and the agricultural campaign had totally collapsed. The greatest resistance had come from the north of the district, where the Kikuyu Central Association had always been strongest, around the Church Missionary Society stations at Kahuhia and Weithaga, and especially from the locations of Chiefs Ignatio, Joel and Joshua. Although the sharp steps taken by the government produced a small revival in October and November, when some 334 acres were terraced, the women still refused to return to work and the communal strategy had to be abandoned in favour of the allocation of specific tasks to each household.[48]

The Peasant Revolt: Murang'a, 1947

Compulsory female labour provided the government's critics with an easy target, for emotive appeals could be made to world opinion which was ignorant of the fact that, in Kenya, the main burden of cultivation and hard physical labour usually fell upon the women. The political activists were to prove adept at embarrassing the administration with appeals to the International Labour Organisation and the United Nations. The Secretariat quickly recognised that they had been outsmarted and warned the field administration that the use of compulsory female labour could not be defended by the British delegation to the International Labour Organisation. The administration, however, pointed out that there was simply no alternative but to use Kikuyu women to dig terraces.[49]

When the district administration attempted to enforce terracing, violence erupted. An Agricultural Instructor was assaulted in Location 12, terraces were destroyed in Locations 8 and 9 , and some Tribunals showed signs of refusing to convict 'malcontents'. Nevertheless, the chiefs prosecuted no less than 607 people in October alone for refusing to comply with agricultural orders. Meanwhile, Murang'a's share of Central Province's terracing fell in the first half of the year from 43 per cent to a mere 15 per cent and the work done by each cultivator was of a much lower quality than under the *ngwatio* method.[50]

Following the collapse, J.T. Moon, the Provincial Agricultural Officer, attempted to absolve his department of responsibility and blamed unscrupulous agitators for deceiving the peasantry with promises of less work. Similar excuses were made by the district administration, which blamed young militants from Nairobi and the local leaders of the Kenya African Union, such as Beauttah and Gideon Macharia. Coutts, the new District Commissioner who had taken over just before the disturbances did, however, recognise that popular discontent with the despotic rule of the chiefs might lie behind the trouble. Unfortunately he blamed the older generation of chiefs. He reported:

> . . . there can be no doubt that the people have a good deal on their side. The age of the old type of despot has definitely gone and no longer are the Kikuyu prepared to accept orders without questioning the right of the person to give them or the validity of the order itself. This is of course universal and merely a symptom of the birth of liberty.[51]

This may have been true, but the crucial factor was overlooked. The people were rebelling not against 'the old type of despot', but against the new generation of educated chiefs who were convinced supporters of the agricultural campaign. Resistance was concentrated in their locations and directed against them, not against the surviving representatives of the old style of chieftainship.

The previous District Commissioner, O'Hagan, had dimly perceived this before he was promoted to the Secretariat, in May 1947, because of his successes in Murang'a. He observed that 'land reclamation measures in a location depend entirely on the energy and powers of leadership of its chief. General support and encouragement are not enough, the chief as chairman of his location team must be the moving force directing operations and this can only be achieved by hard work, great energy and much enthusiasm'.[52] It was hardly surprising then that, when the storm broke, it was the newly-appointed zealous young chiefs who proved incapable of controlling the protest. The 'agitators' made least impression in Locations 1 and 2, where Ndungu Kagori and Njiri Karanja, of the older generation, had been chiefs since 1932 and 1912 respectively. In these locations in the extreme south of the district, the women were already beginning to resume terracing early in 1948, while in Chief Ignatio's former model Location 8, the soil conservation campaign was still badly disrupted.[53] Let us now look in greater detail at events in the locations controlled by the post-war generation of chiefs, such as Ignatio Morai.

Kikuyu chiefs and the peasant revolt

Chief Ignatio Morai was a former schoolmaster at the Mogoire Roman Catholic school and a devout Christian. He became chief in 1944 on the death of the notorious old Muriranja wa Mureithi. As an apostle of modernisation, who had improved his own smallholding – applying manure, enclosing his land, dipping his cattle and building terraces – Ignatio was not simply a 'collaborator', but firmly believed in the benefits that would result from the agricultural campaign. As a leading exponent of the new programme and a strict enforcer of the conservation regulations, he alienated many people in his location and was an easy target for the Kikuyu Central Association to single out for attack. As chairman of the Local Native Council's Agriculture Sub-committee, he was known to be the administration's most loyal supporter in Murang'a and had become a personal enemy of the local leaders of the Kenya African Union, especially James Beauttah, who led the opposition on the council to the chiefs. Ignatio was also politically exposed because the people in Location 8 had for many years endured the tyranny of his predecessor and had little sympathy for the colonial régime. Even Muriranja's old cronies failed to support Ignatio, for he had turned them out of their positions and denied their long-accustomed access to state patronage.[54]

During his first three years as chief, Ignatio was remarkably successful in mobilising his people to dig terraces. While old Chief Kigwaine in Location 15 managed to complete only 44,704 yards of terraces in 1946, Ignatio's produced 357,214 yards, almost eight times Kigwaine's figure and the second highest total in the district.[55] Before the revolt, the District Commissioner reported that Ignatio was:

. . . one of the most outstanding Kikuyu chiefs. He was in all respects the best Chief in the District. He is a great leader, is highly intelligent and is very popular with his people. His location has led the way in land reclamation measures . . . As Chairman of the Local Native Council Standing Committee for Agriculture, he played a leading part in persuading the people throughout the District to adopt better farming methods.[56]

With the revolt, however, this view rapidly changed. Early in 1948, when the agricultural officer went around Location 8 on safari, he discovered that Ignatio's own sub-location was more recalcitrant than the areas supervised by his headmen. Knight was surprised to find this and recorded: 'I hesitate to say that Chief Ignatio is losing his grip but this is the only location in which no communal work of any kind is being done and he cerainly does not 'go places' as he used to do nor does he seem to have much idea of what is, or is not, being done in his location.'[57] Ignatio's failure stemmed from his previous success. His remarkable terracing figures had been secured at the expense of growing popular discontent. The supposed revitalisation of the *Muhirig'a* and use of *ngwatio* labour, and the establishment of location and sub-location councils to advise the chiefs, had not concealed from the peasantry the fact that government demands had become far more onerous. The Kikuyu Central Association seized upon the dislike of terracing and consolidated its support before challenging the power of the new chiefs and the administration over the agricultural campaign.[58]

Chief Ignatio, who had been singled out for attack, initially fought back. One month after Kenyatta's visit to Murang'a, Ignatio accused Beauttah at the Local Native Council session on 21 August 1947, of 'nurturing evil counsels against him and further of stirring up trouble in his location'. Shortly afterwards he banned all political meetings in his location. The local Kenya African Union leaders responded by encouraging opposition to terracing and by calling a meeting in Location 8 for Sunday 24 August, where, supported by Councillor Isaak Gathanju, Beauttah demanded Ignatio's dismissal.[59]

Ignatio responded immediately by arresting Beauttah, Gathanju and two other political activists, Mwangi Macharia and Mwangi Thomas, for organising an illegal meeting. While on bail awaiting trial, Beauttah attempted to mobilise further opposition against Ignatio, issuing posters calling for a demonstration outside the courtroom on the grounds that he and his colleagues were being prosecuted for standing up for the people in their anti-terracing protests. On the day of the trial vast crowds gathered outside the District Commissioner's office. When the four heroes were sentenced to six weeks hard labour and each fined 100 shillings, the crowd became violent. Threats were made against Chief Ignatio, and an armed guard had to be placed on his village. On the evening of Sunday 28

September 1947, a riot occurred near the village and the guards shot into the crowd, killing one man and injuring another as they sought to protect the chief. After this incident, a levy-force of 24 Kenyan policemen, under the command of a European Inspector, were stationed at Kahuro to maintain order.[60]

Mwangi Macharia had also been active before his trial, stirring up opposition against terracing and the chiefs in the three most northerly locations of Chiefs Joel, Joshua and Parmenas. Even after his imprisonment these locations remained centres of resistance. When Macharia was released in November 1947, he had considerable success in arousing further opposition. He also improved contacts between his supporters in Murang'a, the Nairobi militants in the Forty Group and the trade unions, which, in the early 1950s, quickly spread the first Mau Mau oaths throughout the district. Macharia had emerged as a prominent figure in the African Workers' Federation during the general strike in Mombasa in January 1947. After being deported from Mombasa he was instrumental in forming the Federation's Nairobi branch before returning to his home district to organise opposition to the Murang'a chiefs.[61]

Ignatio was not the only new chief to encounter opposition. Chiefs Kimani, Waweru and Kigwoine had all retired in 1946. Their replacements were young, educated men, who were enthusiastic supporters of the second colonial occupation. Since replacing Chief Waweru in September 1946, Erastus Njeroge transformed Location 7 into a centre of terracing by producing the highest terracing figures in Murang'a, with 366,556 yards of communal work. Even before Kenyatta's meeting on 20 July 1947, however, there had been growing clandestine activity in his location by the Kikuyu Central Association. In June, for example, some Maragua residents had alleged that Njeroge had fined and imprisoned some women, and impounded their goats, for refusing to dig terraces. Subsequently the District Commissioner discovered that over-zealous *Muhirig'a* elders, probably with the chief's approval, had indeed been using force to ensure that their location headed the Murang'a soil-conservation league. Erastus, like most of the new chiefs, believed that the administration's main criteria for judging his success was the effectiveness of the terracing programme.[62] The chiefs and elders were convinced that their continuation in office depended upon the progress made with terracing and that the administration would turn a blind eye as to how exactly it was achieved. Ambitious headmen knew that if the chief failed they stood a good chance of succeeding to his position with its control over local patronage. The chiefs, headmen and *Muhirig'a* elders therefore became obsessed with terracing and failed to recognise that they were alienating the peasantry and driving them towards the political activists.[63]

The year 1948 was a quieter one in Murang'a, but the District Commissioner feared further trouble. He warned that: 'it appears as though there is a slow revival of political activity which unless directed into safer channels may result in about one year's time in another upheaval perhaps of greater magnitude than the last'.[64] Kikuyu acceptance of the colonial state and its most conspicuous representative, the chief, he recognised, would never be the same again in Murang'a. The situation had still not returned to normal. The women's revolt was not over. At the beginning of the year, for example, only Chief Ndungu in Location 1 had persuaded his women to return to work. When the Local Native Council tried to force a return in March 1948, serious resistance was provoked.

On 14 April 1948, more than 2,000 women from Location 15 appeared outside the District Commissioner's office chanting opposition to the new order. The following month they refused to participate in the grass-planting campaign, which had become an annual ritual for the whole community. These demonstrations forced Chief Peterson wa Kariuki, who had hitherto kept a low profile, to take firm action and to order specific women to plant grass. When they refused, he promptly had them arrested. When news of the arrests spread round the location, a large crowd of women assembled on 4 May and marched on the district headquarters, brandishing sticks and shouting abuse against the chief and the district administration. Tribal police had to be used to break up the demonstration and large numbers were arrested. When their cases were heard before the Native Tribunal on 8 May, another large crowd of angry women descended on the district headquarters and were only driven back by police truncheons. Murang'a gradually returned to normal, but discontent continued to simmer below the surface and suspicion of the chiefs and the agricultural department continued. The *wananchi* needed little provocation to erupt once more.[65]

The growth of resistance in Central Province and the reaction of the official mind

Although the problems created by the administration's obsession with narrow-base terracing were most severe in Murang'a, where the *ngwatio* system had originated and where the steep slopes made erosion particularly acute, the two other Kikuyu districts suffered similar disturbances. In Nyeri during 1946 there had been violent opposition to compulsory cattle dipping. Both the District Commissioner and Chief Nderi, who was an enthusiastic supporter of the policy, were attacked. The District Commissioner eventually had to advise the Executive Council that there would be serious trouble throughout the district unless the compulsory order was revoked.[66]

The Peasant Revolt: Murang'a, 1947

Kiambu was also disrupted by political protests in 1947.[67] As in Murang'a, it took two years for the peasantry to become thoroughly alienated by the government's interventionist polices. The worst affected areas, as in Murang'a, were the locations of those chiefs most closely identified with the new agricultural campaign. Chief Waruhiu's Githunguri division was badly disrupted. This had appeared to be the most progressive area. The Chura *Muhirig'a* had even rivalled Murang'a in using indigenous authorities to mobilise the peasantry for terracing.[68] As in Murang'a, the opposition was led by the area's Local Native Councillor. His election early in 1947 should have provided a warning that all was not well, but, as in Murang'a, this danger signal went unnoticed. Other signs of growing discontent were available. Wangige cultivators had refused to stop cultivating along the riverbanks. At the other end of Kikuyuland, at Karatina in Nyeri, cultivators destroyed the irrigation channels on the war-time dried-vegatable project when the government refused to turn it into an African co-operative. The administration, however, regarded these disturbances as individual incidents and failed to realise that they were the first signs of a general revolt against the second colonial occupation and the authority of the chiefs.[69] As a result, the provincial administration and the agricultural and veterinary departments had been ill prepared for the onslaught, which erupted in all three Kikyu districts in 1947.

In December 1946, the new Provincial Commissioner, Wyn Harris, had warned that 'the outward sign of unrest among Africans is a pernicious African press, increased activities of the known political agitators and opposition to many forms of Government activity in the Reserves, particularly if it is directed by Europeans or Chiefs'.[70] This, however, overlooked the crucial fact that it was the new development measures that were alienating the Kikuyu. Instead of attempting to reduce discontent, Wyn Harris adopted an intransigent attitude and insisted that all opposition must be defeated and agricultural reforms forced through. He proposed that the technical departments explain the need for the conservation campaign at *barazas* and ordered the field administration to gain the support of the leaders of African opinion, such as the officials of the traders' and farmers' associations. Unfortunately, instead of reducing fears of renewed land alienation, the agricultural campaign intensified African suspicions.

Wyn Harris attempted to bolster the chiefs by empowering them to ban political meetings, including gatherings of the Kenya African Union, under the Native Authority Ordinance of 1937.[71] In 1947, this Ordinance became the symbol of the chiefs' power and the focus of many attacks by the vernacular press and African politicians. The first critical article appeared in the Asian newspaper, the *Daily Chronicle*, which was sympathetic to the radical critics of British colonialism. It denounced the dictatorial powers of the chiefs, particularly Ignatio Morai, and alleged that 'the chief was gathering wool round the eyes of his immediate supervisors and the people could not do anything as long as he was in power'.[72] As the government's leading supporter in Murang'a, Ignatio had to endure sustained press criticism. The *Daily Chronicle* even alleged that Ignatio had deliberately ordered the shooting at Kahuro. Although the newspaper published an apology two months later, after a Commission of Enquiry, this did little to offset the harm that had been done to the chief's reputation.

The African newspaper, *Mumenyereri*, also denounced the chief for arresting Councillors Beauttah and Gathanju, who had merely been protecting their constituents from Ignatio's tyranny. Under the Native Authority Ordinance, the paper complained, the people had no redress against the arbitrary acts of the chiefs. One editorial protested:

> We, the public, demand the power to remove any Chief who becomes unpopular and power to say that a certain member of any Council cannot be ejected from any Council just because there is some difference between him and the President of the Council. If the public had power Mr James Beauttah and Isaak Gathanju would not leave the Fort Hall Local Native Council.[73]

This press campaign against prominent chiefs continued throughout 1947 and 1948.[74]

By July 1948, Wyn Harris, who had become the Chief Native Commissioner, was extremely alarmed. The newspaper attacks on Chief Ignatio were only the most scurrilous part of an organised campaign against everyone closely identified with the government. Four Kiambu chiefs, for example, were also denounced in the African press and, by mid-1948, a total of seven cases had been brought to court against prominent chiefs. While the campaign in Murang'a concentrated on Chief Ignatio and in Nyeri on Chief Muhoya, who had supported compulsory dipping at the height of its unpopularity in 1946, Chief Waruhiu endured the most attacks in Kiambu – both physical and verbal.[75] These three chiefs were the administration's most loyal supporters in their districts and were enthusiastic advocates of the post-war agricultural campaign. All three were devout Christians and noted opponents of the independent schools and churches. If they could be discredited then the other chiefs would have been seriously intimidated.

The first case against Waruhiu alleged he had destroyed a plantation of 400 wattle trees while imposing compulsory terracing. Despite strenuous attempts by Wyn Harris to ensure his acquittal, the judgement in the magistrate's court went against him. Even before his appeal was heard, a second case was brought against the chief for wrongful imprisonment. The administration feared the chief would again be found guilty, which would further undermine his authority and encourage complaints against other chiefs.

Protesting to the Attorney General about the impartial behaviour of the magistrate, Wyn Harris warned that 'from the Administrative point of view it is essential that Waruhiu's authority should be upheld as these cases are beginning to break the hearts of our better chiefs as they feel they have not got the support of government in keeping peace and good order in their districts'.[76] Despite such pressure, the Attorney General insisted on prosecuting Waruhiu and refused to invoke the Public Officer Protection Ordinance to safeguard the chief. The government's lawyers again refused to give way to the field administration's practical problems. The Solicitor General considered that Waruhiu was guilty and insisted that the law should proceed even if it meant discrediting the administration's main supporter in Kiambu. Chiefs, he argued, should no longer be allowed to behave like petty tyrants; a new era had dawned and responsible, educated Africans were entitled to be protected from wrongful arrest.

The split between the legal department (with its pristine notions of legal propriety more appropriate to the Inns of Court than to the African reserves) and the field administration forced Wyn Harris to warn the governor of the crisis in Kikuyuland and of the imminent collapse of the chiefs' authority. The Chief Native Commissioner informed the governor that 'the effects have been disastrous on our attempts to govern native areas'. The legal department, he complained, did not realise that the allegations against Waruhiu were part of a careful campaign to discredit the chiefs. Wyn Harris reminded Mitchell that two years before he had warned District Commissioners that, 'Individual attacks on chiefs alleging all sorts of malpractices are likely to be the next phase of those dissident elements who desire to make profit from indiscipline in the native areas.'[77] He informed the governor that the charges against Waruhiu were clearly designed to humiliate the chief and to destroy his colleagues' confidence in the government. 'I submit that before very long we will have no single chief, no tribal police or other authority running the risk of finding themselves held up to ridicule by the masses while Government feebly looks on.'[78] The colonial government, he declared, should not simply 'stand idly by while one of our most devoted servants is prosecuted on a criminal charge for doing what he conceived to be his duty'. Desirable though it might be in Britain, unquestioning adherence to legal propriety was impossible in Africa. Collaborators had to be protected from the African peasantry when the British increased their demands on Africa during the second colonial occupation. The Attorney General's refusal to withdraw the prosecution and to tarnish his department's legal integrity in order to help unpopular chiefs, marked an imporant step towards the disintegration in Kenya of Ronald Robinson's 'non-European foundations of European imperialism'.[79]

Although the charges against Chief Waruhiu were of most concern to the administration, there were several similar cases. For example, Chief Makimei, who helped the police break the strike at Uplands, had thereby 'incurred the odium of many dissident elements in his location' when several of the strikers had been shot. Wyn Harris admitted that Makimei was a very different character from the god-fearing Waruhiu and had been lucky, a few years earlier, to have escaped a manslaughter charge. Nevertheless, he insisted, 'the fact is that he has stood loyally by Government, at great personal risk to himself and incurred the dislike of many fellow Kikuyu'. Wyn Harris considered that the chief must be supported. When Makimei was finally convicted of 'grievous assault' the district administration was so concerned about the possible effect on other Kiambu chiefs that it paid Makimei's £50 fine and the further £40 awarded as compensation to his victim.[80]

These divisions between the field administration and the Attorney General did not, as Berman has argued, stem from the administration's frustration at its supremacy being challenged by the influx of specialist staff, or from any fear that the generalists were being supplanted by the technical departments. The District Commissioners remained 'king of the castle' and presided over district policy and politics. It was the District Commissioners who chaired the district committees established by Mitchell and who had the ear of the Secretariat, which was recruited from the same élite Colonial Service cadre. Indeed, many of the troubles caused by the second colonial occupation occurred because the Secretariat was only too willing to listen to the field administration, with its belief in the organic communalism of Kikuyu society, rather than to the more subtle agricultural department which, after the debacle of 1947, wanted to encourage African cash-crop production as a reward for those who adopted new agricultural methods. By 1950, the agricultural department was convinced that the new strategy provided the only way of transforming Kikuyu agriculture without provoking massive resistance, but the field administrators only became convinced by the outbreak of Mau Mau, which the agriculturalists had wanted to avoid.[81]

Even within the field administration there were profound disagreements about how to respond to the African politicians. Walter Coutts, who was the District Commissioner in Murang'a at the height of the peasant revolt, had only recently replaced O'Hagan when the troubles began. He was a liberal, anxious to establish good relations with the local Kenya African Union leadership and to relax the tight reins of control favoured by his predecessor. Paradoxically the strict conservative, Desmond O'Hagan, with his paternalist policies, was acknowledged to have been a popular District Commissioner. Even his greatest opponent, the wily James Beauttah, recalled 30 years later that O'Hagan had helped African traders and had tried to improve social welfare. With a conservative like O'Hagan, the Kenya African Union and the underground

Kikuyu Central Association knew where they stood and how far they could go.[82] If they stepped out of line, they were well aware that the full might of government would have immediately descended upon them. At the same time the chiefs were equally confident, under O'Hagan, that the District Commissioner would always back them up, in public at least. Coutts, however, thought that O'Hagan had been too strict and believed that constructive criticism from the educated Africans in the Kenya African Union should be encouraged. This encouraged the Kikuyu politicians to experiment to see what concessions they could extract from the new District Commissioner and undermined the confidence of the chiefs. Both O'Hagan and Coutts, however, failed to recognise that the agricultural campaign was destroying popular acquiescence in the colonial régime.[83]

The politicisation of the Kikuyu reserves

The terracing campaign highlighted the dependence of the colonial state in Kenya upon the chiefs and African collaborators. After 50 years of British rule the Kikuyu chief had become as securely established as his counterparts in Tanganyika. By the late 1940s, the distinction between direct and indirect rule was otiose. The disturbances in north Pare in 1945 and 1946, and in Sukumaland during the early 1950s, demonstrated that it was not simply the Kikuyu chiefs who were undermined by the second colonial occupation's disruptive impact on African societies.

Dr Iliffe has shown, in his discussion of the *Mbiru* crisis in Upare, that these post-war protests marked an important step forward in rural Africa in the evolution of political consciousness. Although the peasants in Kikuyuland and the Usambaras had identified a single grievance – compulsory terracing or graduated taxation – the techniques of opposition showed a new sophistication and marked the beginning of a new era of more militant opposition to British rule.[84] In Kikuyuland, the terracing campaign provided urban radicals, such as Mwangi Macharia and the Forty Group, with an issue around which to mobilise their popular constituency in the reserves, with whose support they could challenge their enemies, the chiefs. This politicisation of the Kikuyu peasantry also enabled the militants, with their close contacts with Nairobi, to undermine the authority of the more radical of the old-style activists of the illegal Kikuyu Central Association. The moderates in both organisations, in contrast, wanted to co-operate with the district administration and to be co-opted into the political nation so that they could get access to government patronage.[85]

Throughout Kikuyuland, the demands imposed on the peasantry by the agricultural campaign had eaten away the foundations of colonial control. The chiefs had been completely discredited. When the ordinary

Kikuyu finally protested, the political activists and the vernacular press turned on their rivals. Under this barrage of criticism, the chiefs became a more united political force and fought back, attacking the Kenya African Union, which they saw as the main centre of opposition to their domination of rural Africa. The chiefs sought every opportunity to bolster their own position by maligning the African politicians. This, of course, accorded well with the thinking of the field administration, which had little time for these upstart 'agitators' who were threatening the organic hierarchy of Kikuyu society. The District Commissioners then forwarded this distorted information to the Secretariat, where it was received as an accurate assessment of politics at the district level. In fact it was a political weapon in the chiefs' struggle to preserve their power and economic dominance. Neither the chiefs nor the administration were neutral observers of the political struggle in the reserves; both were interested parties in the growing conflict with the alternative élite which supported Kenyatta and the Kenya African Union.[86]

Thus, despite its arduous fight, the Kenya African Union could not shake the field administration's alliance with the chiefs. Indeed, as the chiefs came under attack they moved closer to the district administrators, who were equally determined to keep the terracing campaign functioning. Compulsory terracing was, therefore, both the major weakness and the greatest strength of the chiefs. Although the agricultural campaign had alienated the peasantry, the attacks of the Kenya African Union made it easy for the chiefs as a political class to strengthen their alliance with the administration and to discredit their political rivals who were seeking incorporation into the political nation. The protests failed because the chiefs tightened their control over the locations and launched a counter-attack on the political activists. For example, Chief Ignatio moved against James Beauttah, Murang'a's most prominent member of the Kenya African Union, who symbolised the alliance between the supposedly constitutionalist politicians and the 'subversive' Kikuyu Central Association.[87] To many chiefs, and increasingly to many government officials, the two organisations appeared to be virtually identical. After 1947, the Secretariat and Sir Philip Mitchell came to share this view and became suspicious of virtually all African politicians, including the moderates on the Legislative Council. The troubles in Murang'a during 1947 helped destroy Mitchell's hopes of a multiracial Kenya and drove him further into an alliance with the European settlers. This had disastrous consequences after 1950.

During the anti-terracing campaign, therefore, Macharia and the Forty Group successfully widened the divisions between the local politicians and their rivals, the chiefs, and prevented any compromise with the administration. Instead, they laid the foundations of a political alliance between the rural poor – disposed *ahoi* and poor peasants – who were being squeezed off their land and compelled to become wage labourers on the chiefs' and rich peasants' *shamba*, on the one hand, and the unskilled migrant workers and unemployed of 'outcast' Nairobi, on the other.[88] The struggle in Central Province during 1947 and 1948 marked the beginning of a new era in Kikuyu politics. The power of the constitutionalist élite diminished under the onslaught of the militants as the contradictions in their tenuous alliance with the Kikuyu poor became increasingly apparent. The aspiring traders and commercial farmers, from whom the local leadership for the Kenya African Union and earlier of the Kikuyu Central Association had been recruited, were in fact among the most conspicuous of the exploiters of the *ahoi* and poor peasant households. Only for a brief period in the late 1940s, when the chiefs had seemed about to topple from favour, had their mutual antipathy to the chiefs overcome their own internal divisions. With the failure of the anti-terracing campaign the alliance disintegrated and the militants became less active until the early 1950s, when they resurfaced as leaders of Mau Mau.[89]

Notes

1. CO 852/662/19936/2 (1945–46), 'Soil Erosion: Kenya', N. Humphrey, 'The Relationship of Population to the Land in South Nyeri', paragraphs 19–21; and H.E. Lambert and P. Wyn Harris, 'Policy in regard to Land Tenure in the Native Lands of Kenya', paragraph 62.
2. KNA MAA 8/68, 'Chief Waruhiu, 1948–52', P. Wyn Harris to Basil Hobson, 30 July 1948; and P. Wyn Harris to P.E. Mitchell, undated, but probably August 1948.
3. L. Cliffe, 'Nationalism and the Reaction to Enforced Agricultural Change in Tanganyika during the Colonial Period', pp. 17–23; J.M. Lonsdale, 'Some Origins of Nationalism in East Africa', pp. 131–6; and M.P.K. Sorrenson, *Land Reform in the Kikuyu Country*, pp. 105–9, provided many insights in the late 1960s which are in danger of being forgotten. Sorrenson, for instance, warned that there was no simple correlation between wealth and collaboration, or 'marginalisation' and rebellion. Too many recent studies have lost sight of the actual events and have forced Mau Mau into their favoured typology of peasant resistance. See Maina wa Kinyatti, 'Mau Mau', pp. 287–310; and his introduction to the collection of Mau Mau *nyimbo*, *Thunder from the Mountains*, pp. 1–8.
4. D. Mukaru-Ng'ang'a, 'Mau Mau, Loyalists and Politics in Murang'a', pp. 365–83; and his thesis, 'Political History of Murang'a', pp. 69–73.
5. KNA DC/FH 1/26, 'Fort Hall Annual Report, 1947', pp. 1–6, 14–15.
6. The most vociferous representatives of this radical Kikuyu school are Maina wa Kinyatti, 'Mau Mau', pp. 287–310; and D. Mukaru-Ng'ang'a, in his thesis, 'Political History of Murang'a'. This interpretation has been popularised by Ngugi wa Thiong'o in his novels, and in the historical passages in *Detained*.
7. See A. Thurston's draft manuscript, 'The Intensification of Smallholder Agriculture in Kenya', p. 75.

The Peasant Revolt: Murang'a, 1947

8. KNA DC/FH 1/26, 'Fort Hall Annual Report, 1947', pp. 1–6; MAA 8/106, 'Intelligence Reports: Mumenyereri, 1947–50', C. Penfold, Director of Intelligence, to P. Wyn Harris, 10, 18, 20 and 21 October 1947. See also MAA 8/132, 'Law and Order: Legal Matters, 1947–51', P. Wyn Harris to Foster-Sutton, Attorney General, 25 November 1947, for attempts by the field administration to bolster the power of the chiefs.

9. CO 852/662/19936/2 (1945–46), 'Soil Erosion: Kenya', N. Humphrey, 'The Relationship of Population to the Land in South Nyeri', paragraphs 1–10 and 42–54.

10. A. Thurston's draft manuscript, 'The Intensification of Smallholder Agriculture in Kenya', pp. 24–30, 39–60; KNA Ag 4/419, 'Agricultural Development and the Maintenance of Soil Fertility: The Growing of High Priced Crops, 1933–51', J.T. Moon to Director of Agriculture, 5 February 1948; and L.H. Brown to DC Embu, 6 February 1948. See also Ag 4/125, 'Annual Agricultural Reports: Central Province, 1951', and contrast J.P. Benson's report for Meru with those from Murang'a and Nyeri.

11. KNA DC/FH 4/6, 'Chiefs and Headmen, 1937–54', *passim*; and Ag 4/451, 'Fort Hall Safari Diaries, 1948–51', especially the tours to Location 2, 17–21 February 1948; Location 8, 2–6 March 1948; Location 7, 9–13 March 1948; and Location 6, 5–8 April 1948.

12. KNA Ag 4/518, 'Reconditioning: Central Province, 1948–51', Colin Maher to Director of Agriculture, 30 November 1948; and the comments of J.T. Moon to the Director of Agriculture, 10 December 1948, in reply to Maher's criticisms.

13. *ibid.* See also KNA Ag 4/539, 'Reconditioning: Central Province, 1934–48', Colin Maher to the Senior Agricultural Officer, Nyanza, 28 January 1946.

14. CO 852/662/19936/2 (1945–46) 'Soil Erosion: Kenya', N. Humphrey, 'The Relationship of Population to the Land in South Nyeri', paragraph 21.

15. KNA Ag 4/419, 'Agricultural Development and the Maintenance of Soil Fertility: The Growing of High Priced Crops, 1933–51', J.T. Moon to Director of Agriculture, 5 February 1948; and Carolyn Barnes's thesis, 'An Experiment with African Coffee Growing in Kenya', pp. 161–4.

16. KNA Ag 4/539, 'Reconditioning: Central Province, 1934–48', T. Hughes Rice to J.T. Moon, 20 May 1946; and Ag 4/518, 'Reconditioning: Central Province, 1948–51', J.T. Moon, 3 February 1950.

17. A. Thurston's draft manuscript, 'The Intensification of Smallholder Agriculture in Kenya', pp. 46–7.

18. *ibid*, p. 48.

19. *ibid.*

20. For details of how the campaign impinged upon the peasant in his maize *shamba*, see KNA Ag 4/451, 'Fort Hall Safari Diaries, 1948–51', *passim*; and MAA 8/106, 'Intelligence Reports: Mumenyereri, 1948–51', Mrs M.W. Gathaku's letter in *Mumenyereri*, 29 September 1947; Johnson Maina Joshua's speech at Njumbii school, Location 13, Murang'a, reported in the same issue; and B.K. Ruhia's letter in *Mumenyereri*, 27 October 1947.

21. G. Kitching, *Class and Economic Change in Kenya*, pp. 188–99. For the rise of the *athomi* see unpublished papers by M.P. Cowen, 'Differentiation in a Kenya Location', *passim*; and G.C.M. Mutiso, 'The Creation of the Kitui Asomi'.

22. D.M. Feldman's thesis, 'Christians and Politics', pp. 160–224.

23. KNA MAA 7/49, 'chiefs and Headmen: Discipline, 1942–46'; and MAA 7/320, 'Chiefs Engaged in Commerce, 1948', for the problems this sometimes created. In Murang'a the clan elders supervised the rationing of sugar in each *itura*, see DC/FH 1/24, 'Fort Hall Annual Report, 1945', p. 9. For examples of chiefs who became successful businessmen, see G. Kitching, *Class and Economic Change in Kenya*, pp. 297–311, where nine of the fourteen case studies were chiefs; J.M. Lonsdale's

unpublished 'African Elites and Social Classes in Colonial Kenya', pp. 10-13; and B.E. Kipkorir, 'The Educated Elite and Local Society', pp. 255-68.

24. KNA Ag 4/77, 'Wattle Cooperative Societies, 1947-51', James Warnegi, Secretary, Central Province Wattle Growers' Association to G.J. Gollop, Agricultural Officer, Kiambu, 20 August 1948; C&I 6/782, 'Trading by Africans, 1946-50', especially Edward Karanja's complaint to the Secretariat, 27 May 1946; D. O'Hagan to A.C.M. Mullins, 17 October 1946; and A.C.M. Mullins to G.M. Rennie, 15 November 1946.

25. KNA DC/FH 1/25, 'Fort Hall Annual Report, 1946', pp. 9-10; and C&I 6/782, 'Trading by Africans, 1946-50', D. O'Hagan to A.C.M. Mullins, acting PC Central Province, 17 October 1946.

26. KNA DC/FH 1/24 'Fort Hall Annual Report, 1945', pp. 4-7; and John Spencer, *James Beauttah*, pp. 55-8, 64-76. See also E.S. Atieno Odhiambo, 'Seek Ye First the Economic Kingdom', pp. 223-51 for similar problems in Nyanza.

27. KNA DC/FH 4/6, 'Chiefs and Headmen, 1937-54', *passim*, contains detailed comments about every Murang'a chief; DC/FH 1/24 to 1/31, 'Fort Hall Annual Reports, 1945-52' all contain two or three pages about the behaviour of the chiefs.

28. KNA DC/FH 1/25, 'Fort Hall Annual Report, 1946', pp. 19-22; Ag 4/392, 'District Agricultural Annual Reports: Central Province, 1948', Fort Hall Agricultural Report, 1948, in which C.D. Knight observed: 'Terraces are extremely unpopular with African farmers, chiefs, Instructors, Officers and Native Tribunals, and at the present rate of digging, the end is not in sight and never will be. It behoves us to put on our thinking caps and try to design a method of completing the work rapidly so that other, more interesting avenues to Agricultural Progress may be explored. The word Agriculture is becoming associated in the public mind with nothing but digging terraces and the nauseating affluvium is bringing this Department into disrepute. The sooner we can stop terracing as our main effort and get moving in the direction of better farming the better.' See also Ag 4/118, 'Provincial Agricultural Handing Over Reports, 1942-51', especially the South Nyeri Handing Over Report, 3 March 1947.

29. See comments by P.S. Osborne in KNA DC/FH 1/23, 'Fort Hall Annual Report, 1944', p. 11; and by D. O'Hagan in DC/FH 1/24, 'Fort Hall Annual Report, 1945', p. 14. T. Hughes Rice, who served as agricultural officer in South Nyeri, Murang'a and Machakos during the Mitchell era, commented in 1944 that 'the location's best manure is the Chief's footsteps', see Ag 4/113, 'South Nyeri Monthly Agricultural Report, 1938-49', entry for July-September 1944.

30. KNA DC/FH 1/26, 'Fort Hall Annual Report, 1947', pp. 1-6, provides the official view. See also MAA 8/105, 'Intelligence Reports: Radio Posta, 1947-48', C. Penfold to P. Wyn Harris enclosing editorial, 16 October 1947, and Intelligence reports of the meetings in Nairobi of the Nyeri Reformed Kikuyu Society on 11 October and of the Forty Group on 12 October 1947. The Chief Native Commissioner's grave concern is evident in MAA 8/68, 'Chief Waruhiu, 1948-52', *passim*.

31. R.L. Tignor, *The Colonial Transformation of Kenya*, pp. 68-72.

32. Table 7.1 is based on material from KNA DC/FH 1/23 to 1/31, 'Fort Hall Annual Reports, 1944-52'; DC/FH 2/1(b), 'Fort Hall Handing Over Reports, 1929-60', J.H. Clive to P.S. Osborne, July 1944; P.S. Osborne to D. O'Hagan, April 1945; and F.A. Loyd to J. Pinney, August 1953; and DC/FH 4/6, 'Chiefs and Headmen, 1937-54', *passim*.

33. KNA DC/FH 4/6, 'Chiefs and Headmen, 1937-54', *passim*; and DC/FH 1/24, 'Fort Hall Annual Report, 1945', pp. 13-14, which presents the official view; while a more critical account can be found in MAA 8/108, 'Intelligence: Daily Chronicle, 1947-49', C. Penfold to P. Wyn Harris, 16 October 1947.

34. KNA DC/FH 4/6, 'Chiefs and Headmen, 1937-54', reports for Location 3.

35. *ibid*, reports for Location 4.

36. KNA DC/FH 2/1(b), 'Fort Hall Handing Over Reports, 1929–60', F.A. Loyd to J. Pinney, 20 August 1953, has some interesting comments on Michuki who was a rich man, who had many wives and much land. He tended to spend too much time on his own business interests and was never a strong chief. After the declaration of the Emergency, Location 12 was subdivided.

37. The two cautious old chiefs were Njaakio of Aguthi Location and Mutheithia of Mathira. KNA Ag 4/491, 'Nyeri Reconditioning Reports, 1944–46', entry for 8 August 1945, for comments on Aguthi; and Ag 4/518, 'Reconditioning: Central Province, 1948–51', J.A. Gardner's soil conservation report for July–December 1948.

38. KNA DC/FH 1/25, 'Fort Hall Annual Report, 1946', p. 21.

39. *ibid*, pp. 21–22; and KNA DC/FH 1/26, 'Fort Hall Annual Report, 1947', p. 6, where O'Hagan observed: 'The foibles of Clarence are, I regret to say, applicable to Parmenas – false, fleeting, perjured, but he out-does Clarence in one respect in that he is continuously (not once) drowning himself in a butt of Malmsey and coming up for more. Chief Parmenas Githendu is a super problem. He has the education, the ability and a hold on his people, but he continuously refuses to do the job. He is now a complete sponge and must soon be replaced.'

40. KNA DC/FH 4/6, 'Chiefs and Headmen, 1937–54', entry for Parmenas, 7 April 1945. For his early life see Parmenas Githendu's contribution to M. Perham (ed.), *Ten Africans*. KNA DC/FH 1/28, 'Fort Hall Annual Report, 1949', pp. 22–3 chronicles his subsequent career as a prominent figure in the Kikuyu Independent Schools' Association.

41. KNA DC/FH 4/6, 'Chiefs and Headmen, 1937–54', *passim*. The District Commissioners repeatedly expressed frustration at the backwardness of the older generation of chiefs.

42. P.E. Mitchell's despatch, 'Agricultural Policy in African Areas', p. 15. See also CO 537/4317/14322/10 (1949), 'Communism in the Colonies: East Africa', P.E. Mitchell to Creech Jones, November 1949.

43. KNA Ag 4/451, 'Fort Hall Safari Diaries, 1948–51', *passim*.

44. KNA DC/FH 1/25, 'Fort Hall Annual Report, 1946', pp. 6–7 and KNA MAA 2/5/223, 'Nairobi Advisory Council, 1946–49', meeting of the Advisory Council, 3 June 1946, for resolution condemning compulsory female labour on terracing.

45. KNA Ag 4/512, 'Fort Hall Monthly Agricultural Reports, 1940–49', C.D. Knight's report, April–June 1947.

46. KNA DC/FH 1/26, 'Fort Hall Annual Report, 1947', pp. 1–7; and Secretariat 1/12/8, 'Labour Unrest: Intelligence Reports, Central Province, 1947', C. Penfold, Director of Intelligence, to P. Wyn Harris, 22 July and 25 July 1947. These reports contain a detailed account of Kenyatta's speech and the resolutions passed at the meeting. See also KNA Ag 4/512, 'Fort Hall Monthly Agricultural Reports, 1940–49', report for January–June 1948 and DC/FH 3/1, 'Reports on the Kikuyu, 1950–52', paragraphs 181–262 for an assessment of the importance of female labour.

47. KNA DC/FH 1/26, 'Fort Hall Annual Report, 1947', p. 1.

48. KNA Ag 4/392, 'District Annual Agricultural Reports, 1948', Fort Hall Report.

49. KNA DC/FH 1/26, 'Fort Hall Annual Report, 1947', p. 1; and MAA 8/106, 'Intelligence Reports: Mumenyereri, 1947–50', C. Penfold to P. Wyn Harris, 16, 18, 20 and 21 October 1947.

50. KNA Ag 4/512, 'Fort Hall Monthly Agricultural Reports, 1940–49', July–September 1947 and KNA Ag 4/518, 'Reconditioning: Central Province, 1948–51', J.T. Moon's report on soil conservation, July–December 1947.

51. KNA DC/FH 1/26, 'Fort Hall Annual Report, 1947', pp. 2–3, 5–6.

52. KNA DC/FH 1/25, 'Fort Hall Annual Report, 1946', pp. 19–20.

53. KNA DC/FH 1/27, 'Fort Hall Annual Report, 1947', p. 1, and Ag 4/451, 'Fort Hall

Safari Diaries, 1948–51', contrast the report on Location 2, 17–21 February 1948, with the one for Location 8, 2–6 March 1948.

54. The administration's high regard for Ignatio is apparent throughout the Annual Reports. For a particularly effusive reference see KNA DC/FH 1/26, 'Fort Hall Annual Report, 1947', p. 6.

55. KNA Ag 4/512, 'Fort Hall Monthly Agricultural Reports, 1940–49', table in C.D. Knight's report for April–June 1947.

56. KNA DC/FH 1/25, 'Fort Hall Annual Report, 1946', p. 20.

57. KNA Ag 4/451, 'Fort Hall Safari Diaries, 1948–51', entry for 2–6 March 1948. For a more favourable view of Ignatio after the peasant revolt see the entry for 6–10 July 1948.

58. The Forty Group denounced terracing at a large meeting in Nairobi on 11 October 1947, see KNA MAA 8/105, 'Intelligence Reports: Radio Posta, 1947–48', extracts from Radio Posta for 16 October 1947, and the comments of C. Penfold to P. Wyn Harris.

59. KNA DC/FH 1/26, 'Fort Hall Annual Report, 1947', p. 2. See also KNA 8/106, 'Intelligence Reports: Mumenyereri, 1947–50', extract from *Mumenyereri*, 1 December 1947, for an African view of the conflict between Chief Ignatio and James Beauttah.

60. KNA DC/FH 1/26, 'Fort Hall Annual Report, 1947', pp. 2–3; MAA 8/105, 'Intelligence Reports: Radio Posta, 1947–48', C. Penfold to P. Wyn Harris, 31 October 1947; and MAA 8/108, 'Intelligence: Daily Chronicle', C. Penfold to P. Wyn Harris, 16 October 1947.

61. KNA Secretariat 1/12/8, 'Labour Unrest: Intelligence Reports, Central Province, 1947', C. Penfold to P. Wyn Harris, 25 August, and 3 September 1947. See also MAA 8/109, 'Intelligence and Security: African Workers' Federation, 1947–48', C. Penfold to P. Wyn Harris, 25 November 1947, for a report of Macharia's speech to the African Workers' Federation, Nairobi branch, on his release from gaol. For details of Macharia's career after his deportation from Mombasa, see KNA Secretariat 1/12/8, 'Labour Unrest: Intelligence Reports, Central Province, 1947', C. Penfold to P. Wyn Harris, and M. Singh, *History of Kenya's Trade Union Movement*, vol. 1, pp. 165, 270–1, 281, 293. Macharia was finally detained in May 1950 during the Nairobi general strike, of which he became the chief organiser following the arrest of Makhan Singh and Fred Kubai.

62. KNA Ag 4/512, 'Fort Hall Monthly Agricultural Reports, 1940–49', C.D. Knight's report for April–June 1947; Ag 4/392, 'District Agricultural Annual Reports, 1948', Fort Hall Report, especially the section on soil conservation; and Ag 4/518, 'Reconditioning Central Province 1948–51', Soil Conservation report for Fort Hall, January–June 1949. See also MAA 8/106, 'Intelligence Reports: Mumenyereri, 1947–50', extracts from *Mumenyereri*, 29 September 1947.

63. KNA DC/FH 1/25, 'Fort Hall Annual Report, 1946', pp. 6–7. See also the comments by several District Commissioners in DC/FH 4/6, 'Chiefs and Headmen, 1937–54', *passim*.

64. KNA DC/FH 1/27, 'Fort Hall Annual Report, 1948', pp. 1–2.

65. *ibid*, and J. Spencer, *James Beauttah*, pp. 82–3; and KNA DC/FH 1/30, 'Fort Hall Annual Report, 1951', p. 1.

66. KNA Ag 4/538, 'South Nyeri Agricultural and Veterinary Committee, 1946–48', Nyeri Local Native Council meeting, 29 September 1946; Ag 4/107, 'Veterinary Department: Central Province Annual Reports, 1940–53', Nyeri Annual Veterinary Report, 1946; and Secretariat 1/27/1, 'Animals: Diseases Control – Dipping, 1946', A.C.M. Mullins, acting PC Central, to G.M. Rennie, 26 September 1946; and report from the Superintendent of Police, Nyeri, 26 September 1946.

67. KNA DC/KBU 1/38, 'Kiambu Annual Report, 1947', pp. 1–5.

The Peasant Revolt: Murang'a, 1947

68. KNA Ag 4/539, 'Reconditioning: Central Province, 1934–48', V.A. Maddison, acting Provincial Commissioner, to F.W. Cavendish-Bentinck, June 1947.
69. KNA DC/FH 1/26, 'Fort Hall Annual Report, 1947', *passim*; and DC/KBU 1/38, 'Kiambu Annual Report, 1947', *passim* clearly show how the field administration continued to think in parochial terms.
70. KNA MAA 8/68, 'Chief Waruhiu, 1948–52', P. Wyn Harris to all District Commissioners, Central Province, 'Directive on the African Political Situation, Central Province', 11 December 1946.
71. *ibid*. See also KNA MAA 8/132, 'Law and Order: Legal Matters, 1947–51', Foster-Sutton to P. Wyn Harris, 29 October 1947; and P. Wyn Harris to all Provincial Commissioners, 28 November 1947.
72. KNA MAA 8/108, 'Intelligence and Security: Daily Chronicle', *Daily Chronicle*, 16 October 1947. A useful account of the African press at this time is F. Gadsden 'African Press in Kenya', pp. 515–35 which contains a detailed appendix of the African newspapers published between 1945 and 1952. The *Daily Chronicle* was, however, an Asian newspaper, published partly in English and, despite its title, partly in Gujerati.
73. KNA MAA 8/106, 'Intelligence Reports: Mumenyereri, 1947–50', C. Penfold to P. Wyn Harris, 10 December 1947, enclosing extracts from *Mumenyereri*, 1 December 1947.
74. KNA MAA 8/68, 'Chief Waruhiu, 1948–52', *passim*, for attacks on Kiambu chiefs; and DC/FH 1/26, 'Fort Hall Annual Report, 1947', pp. 2–6, for cases in Murang'a; and KNA MAA 8/68, 'Chief Waruhiu, 1948–52', P. Wyn Harris to Basil Hobson, 30 July 1948.
75. *ibid,* and P. Wyn Harris to H.E. Stacey, 22 November 1948; KNA DC/FH 1/26, 'Fort Hall Annual Report, 1947', pp. 2–6; and Secretariat 1/27/1, 'Animals: Diseases Control – Dipping, 1946', A.C.M. Mullins to G.M. Rennie, 26 September 1946. See also MAA 8/106, 'Intelligence Reports: Mumenyereri, 1947–50', *Mumenyereri*, 12 April 1948; and N.F. Kennaway, DC Kiambu, to P. Wyn Harris, 3 May 1948.
76. KNA MAA 8/68 'Chief Waruhiu, 1948–52', P. Wyn Harris to P.E. Mitchell, undated, but probably August 1948; and to Basil Hobson, 30 July 1948.
77. *ibid*, Basil Hobson to P. Wyn Harris, 12 August 1948; and to all District Commissioners, Central Province, 'Directive on the African Political Situation, Central Province', 11 December 1946.
78. *ibid*, P. Wyn Harris to P.E. Mitchell, undated, but probably August 1948.
79. R.E. Robinson, 'Non-European Foundations of European Imperialism', pp. 132–40.
80. KNA MAA 8/68, 'Chief Waruhiu, 1948–52', Shapley, Barnet, Archer and Co. (Solicitors) to N.F. Kennaway, DC Kiambu, 27 August 1948.
81. KNA MAA 6/13, 'Report of the Committee on Agricultural Credit for Africans, 1949–50', H.E. Lambert's memorandum submitted to the African Affairs' Committee, 8 November 1948; nd the various memoranda submitted by District Commissioners and agricultural officers. See also B.J. Berman's thesis, 'Adminstration and Politics in Colonial Kenya', pp. 303–36.
82. Interviews with D. O'Hagan in Nairobi, 24 April and 10–11 June 1981; and KNA DC/FH 1/25, 'Fort Hall Annual Report, 1946', *passim*.
83. KNA DC/FH 1/25, 'Fort Hall Annual Report, 1946', pp. 3 and 7; Ag 4/118, 'Provincial Agricultural Handing Over Reports, 1942–51', Fort Hall Handing Over Report, T. Hughes Rice to C.D. Wright, March 1947; and Ag 4/539, 'Reconditioning: Central Province, 1934–48', V.A. Maddison, acting PC Central to F.W. Cavendish-Bentinck.
84. J. Iliffe, *A Modern History of Tanganyika*, pp. 494–6, 503–7, 510–14; I.N. Kimambo, *Mbiru*, pp. 7–27; and A. Maguire, *Towards Uhuru in Tanzania*, pp. 107–41.
85. KNA MAA 8/109, 'Intelligence and Security: African Workers' Federation, 1947–48', C. Penfold to P. Wyn Harris, 16 December 1947, for early reports of discontent with

Kenyatta's leadership. For Kenyatta's increasing political isolation, see B. Kaggia, *Roots of Freedom*, pp. 81-2; and P. Abrahams, 'The Blacks', pp. 58-9. See also MAA 8/102, 'Intelligence and Security: Press Cuttings – Miscellaneous, 1948-50', C. Penfold to P. Wyn Harris, 16 June 1948, for reports of a meeting at James Gichuru's house of Kikuyu moderates, who were dissatisfied with Kenyatta's leadership of the Kenya African Union and Githunguri Teacher Training College.

86. B.J. Berman's thesis, 'Administration and Politics in Colonial Kenya', pp. 361-7, 372-98; and J.M. Lonsdale's unpublished 'African Elites and Social Classes in Colonial Kenya', pp. 10-13. The government's changing atitude to Mathu and the other African Legislative Councillors can be followed in CO 537/3588/38696 (1947-48), 'Activities of Mathu', *passim*; and CO 533/543/38086/38, 'Petitions by the Kikuyu Central Association: Kikuyu Grievances', P.E. Mitchell to Creech Jones, 28 February 1949. This new hostility is particularly apparent in KNA MAA 8/8, 'Intelligence Reports: Confidential Information, 1946-47', C.M. Johnston, DC Meru, to V.A. Maddison, 18 May 1947; and DC/FH 1/26, 'Fort Hall Annual Report, 1947', pp. 5-6.

87. KNA DC/FH 1/26, 'Fort Hall Annual Report, 1947', pp. 2-3.

88. KNA MAA 8/109, 'Intelligence and Security: African Workers' Federation, 1947-48', C. Penfold to P. Wyn Harris, 16 December 1947; MAA 8/105, 'Intelligence Reports: Radio Posta, 1947-48', C. Penfold to P. Wyn Harris, 24 October 1947, reporting meetings of the Nyeri Reformed Kikuyu Society in Nairobi on 11 October 1947, and of the Forty Group Friendly Union on 12 October 1947, which reveal the close ties between the Nairobi militants and political discontent inthe three Kikuyu districts. Mwangi Macharia's career in Mombasa, Nairobi and Murang'a between January 1947 and his detention in May 1950 provides one notable example.

89. The years 1948 and 1949 were comparatively quiet in Kikuyuland. See KNA DC/FH 1/27 and 1/28, 'Fort Hall Annual Reports, 1948 and 1949', *passim*; John Spencer, 'Kenya African Union and Mau Mau', pp. 203-18; and C.G. Rosberg and J. Nottingham, *The Myth of Mau Mau*, pp. 270-4.

Eight

Outcast Nairobi

Although African discontent was clearly growing in the Kikuyu reserves and the Rift Valley, it was in the towns, especially in the capital which had a population of over 100,000 by 1952, that it really threatened to erupt into violent conflict. During the war, for example, there were eight strikes in Mombasa and labour relations deteriorated drastically in Nairobi as the growth in population far outspaced the provision of new housing. Wages fell behind the high levels of inflation, which persisted throughout the 1940s, and competition for jobs increased as Nairobi's African population trebled between 1939 and 1952. As a result, there were growing numbers of unemployed and vagrants who depended on crime and the informal sector to eke out a meagre subsistence.[1] In Pumwani, the largest of Nairobi's locations, 14 men slept in a room, four to a bed, with the rest on the floor. They were the fortunate ones; many had to sleep in the open, or bed down in parked buses or under the verandas along River Road.[2]

The Secretariat decided to introduce a system of local consultation in the African locations under pressure from the African élite and agreed to build model estates. Unfortunately, these were too expensive for ordinary workers and placed a heavy burden of subsidised rents on the Municipal Council, much to the annoyance of European ratepayers. African Nairobi came low down on the Secretariat's list of priorities. As advocates of indirect rule, the Administration had little understanding of what it considered 'de-tribalised' urban Africans. Consequently, between 1947 and 1954, the presence of the administration and the police was extremely weak in the locations, which were abandoned to the control of the political militants and their allies among the Kikuyu-dominated street gangs, who terrorised the Luo and Abaluhya inhabitants of the city.[3] This freedom from government interference enabled the radicals to establish secure headquarters in Nairobi, from where they controlled the introduction of the Mau Mau oaths into the Kikuyu reserves and the

White Highlands, and organised concerted political action against the colonial state and moderate African politicians.[4]

The administration of African Nairobi

By 1947, the government's policies had provoked bitter resentment throughout Kikuyuland, the White Highlands and in the new settlement at Olenguruone, but perhaps the greatest failure of control had occurred in the back streets and hovels of the African locations of Nairobi. During the second half of 1947, it became increasingly apparent that the rule of law had collapsed in Pumwani and Shauri Moyo. The situation in African Nairobi was threatening to undermine the colonial régime at its heart, as violence and crime grew unchecked.

Just how complete the militants' control over the capital was, can be seen from a report to the CID by the Superintendant of African Locations, the moderate Kenya African Union leader, Tom Mbotela. It was, he warned:

> . . . common knowledge that armed gangs [move] around the African Locations and its outskirts at night . . . and the law abiding resident is afraid to go abroad at night. The number of assaults and threats to persons at night is on the increase . . . [while] the number of police patrols available in the locations are afraid to tackle these people, and they cannot be blamed.[5]

Askwith, the Municipal African Affairs Officer, agreed with the report and himself complained to the Nairobi Superintendant of Police that there was 'a definite tendency towards mob-rule in the Native Locations'. The small, easily-controlled African population of the inter-war years had burgeoned into an unruly mass of over 100,000, many of whom were scornful of British rule. Askwith warned that they were on the brink of a violent confrontation with the governnment. He told the police that 'Africans have now adopted an attitude of opposition to local and central Government which is very much more than a civil disobedience campaign. When the enforcement of laws or by-laws is attempted, physical and sometimes armed opposition is encountered. This will continue so long as the African knows that there is no real force behind the enforcement'.[6] When for example, the police had attempted to arrest illegal brewers at Marurani, they had been driven off by local Africans and their prisoners forcibly released. By the time the police had returned with rifles and bayonets, the culprits had vanished. At night armed gangs waylaid people with impunity and terrorised the locations. They were even beginning to infiltrate into the poorer Asian residential area of Eastleigh. Gangs of unemployed Kikuyu were roaming the streets in groups of 30, armed with pangas and knives. So effective was this reign of terror that incidents were rarely reported. Askwith informed the police that 'I have come to the conclusion that the lawlessness is part of a carefully conceived plan to bring the wheels of Government to a standstill by creating conditions of anarchy'.[7] In his opinion, 'the passing of laws which cannot be enforced is a waste of time'. The situation in Pumwani and most of the other locations had reached such a critical state that only large bodies of police, operating in military fashion, could be successful against such formidable opponents, and he called for 200 policemen to be transferred from the Northern Province to help re-establish control. Drastic action was essential before a crime wave hit the central business district and the European and Asian suburbs of the capital.

Both Askwith and Mbotela singled out Maina Heron, an unemployed Kikuyu from Ziwani, as the ringleader of the gangs and named him as the organiser of the infamous Forty Group. Originally from Murang'a, Heron was one of the main illegal traders in European beer and controlled prostitution in Ngara, where most of his gang lived and where he hired out African women to the local Asians. Each member of the group, Askwith alleged, received a salary of 30 shillings a month 'for the sole purpose of causing trouble and to do anything against law and order'.[8] The Forty Group was not simply a criminal gang but had close links with several African political organisations, such as the Nyeri Reformed Kikuyu Society, which the authorities believed was a front for the Group and for other advocates of violent confrontation.[9]

Following the detention in August 1947 of Chege Kibachia, the leader of the African Workers' Federation, and the shooting by the police in September of Kikuyu strikers at Uplands, the situation in the capital became extremely tense.[10] Police agents in the Forty Group warned the Special Branch that, at a meeting in Kariakor early in October 1947, it had been decided that all Europeans should be driven out of Kenya and that preparations were being made to attack prominent African supporters of the colonial government, such as Chief Johanna of Nyeri.[11] The government became increasingly concerned about its ability to retain control of Nairobi should a general strike break out. After the January 1947 strike in Mombasa, the Kenyan government carefully reconsidered its plans for resisting concerted strike action throughout the colony and established an emergency committee under the chairmanship of the member for law and order. Careful preparations were made to entrain police, troops and emergency labour from the northern frontier to likely trouble spots and to stockpile emergency supplies of food and essential materials. Throughout September and October 1947, discontent simmered and threatened to erupt into violent confrontation in Nairobi and the three Kikuyu districts, where the anti-terracing agitation was at its height. Tension increased when reports reached Nairobi of a general strike sweeping through Tanganyika, which had started among the dockers of Dar-es-Salaam.[12]

In Nairobi, preparations were made to introduce an emergency rationing system for meat, wood and petrol. The capital, however, consumed some 3,000 lbs of meat a day and even if the government had requisitioned all the available cold-storage space, it could only have maintained supplies for five days at the ordinary rate of consumption. Wood and fuel supplies were another serious problem. Householders were requested to increase their supplies, but the two leading bakeries each consumed one ton of wood a day and neither of them could store more than three tons. Three days supply of petrol were stored at Nairobi, Nakuru, Kisumu and Eldoret and, should the railway be disrupted, it was planned to restrict petrol supplies in the capital to three garages, where only doctors, transporters of essential supplies and those doing vital work were to be supplied. The Inland Revenue Department was to be responsible for all emergency distribution. Consumption of tinned milk, invalid and infant food, and canned foodstuffs in general were monitored and issue-permits printed in case the situation deteriorated rapidly.[13] Clearly the government viewed the threat of a general strike and civil disturbances in Nairobi with grave concern, but why had this crisis arisen, and why had it been allowed to escalate to such serious proportions? Let us consider these questions.

The presence of the field administration and of the police in African Nairobi was very weak. The capital, like the White Highlands, had largely been left to the control of the settler-dominated Municipal Council, which showed little interest in the appalling social problems of the African parts of the city. The Council and its European electorate only became interested in the locations when African discontent or crime threatened to spill over into the European business area or suburbs. With only one policeman to every 1,000 inhabitants, the authorities could do little to preserve control or to combat crime in the locations, even when the newly-constructed police station at Shauri Moyo was completed after the war. The Commanding Officer, James Juma, who was one of the few African Inspectors, and his force of five policemen, were overwhelmed by the scale of the organised crime and violence they discovered.[14]

The crux of the trouble in Nairobi was that the Municipal Council failed to decide how to deal with the African areas. Unable to decide whether the locations should be controlled by tribal associations with a hierarchy of chiefs and headmen, as in the reserves, or by a European-style system of local government, the Municipal Council wavered between the two options. Half believing in the myth of detribalised urban Africans while constantly being reminded of the authority of the tribal associations, the council and the government failed to evolve an effective system of control. The appointed African Advisory Council was not an effective democratic African local government with any independent authority, while proposals for government-appointed chiefs were rejected. Thus the authority of the colonial state was weakest at the very centre, among the poor of outcast Nairobi.[15]

As we have seen, the communalist prejudices of the administration had disastrous consequences in the Kikuyu reserves, but in Nairobi, amidst the complex ethnic *mélange* of the African locations, the tribal associations might have provided the most effective mechanism of social control. This had been recognised at the end of the war by Tom Askwith, the experienced Municipal African Affairs' Officer, who was on secondment to the council from the field administration. He had decided that government control over African Nairobi had already deteriorated so far during the war that the introduction of the full panoply of rural government, based on the various tribal associations, was essential. Impressed by the ability of the leaders of the associations to police the locations and to control fighting on VJ Day, and their enthusiasm for repatriating vagabonds and prostitutes, he concluded that the municipal authorities should acknowledge their corporate influence and foster their development into an effective system of tax collection and urban control.[16]

Although these proposals were initially accepted by the Provincial Commissioner of Central Province, they infuriated the African élite serving on the Nairobi Advisory Council, which had been established in 1939. This small but articulate section of the African population, led by Francis Khamisi, the General Secretary of the Kenya African Union, and the Abaluhya political activist, W.W.W. Awori, condemned the proposals as a retrograde measure designed to preserve ethnic suspicions in order to facilitate a 'divide and rule' policy. Instead of relying on tribal solidarities, as did most urban Africans, the élite representatives on the Advisory Council wished to secure their own incorporation into the colonial state and to be recognised as full participants in the political life of colonial Nairobi, with their own members on the Municipal Council. They would settle for nothing less than being themselves appointed to the posts of Assistant Municipal African Affairs Officer, Municipal Welfare Officer, and African Superintendents in each location to preside over the locational councils and control the allocation of accommodation. Their denunciation of Askwith's proposals was so vociferous that they forced the Chief Native Commissioner to reconsider and to devise a more democratic system of consultation, more in line with the Colonial Office's strategy of greater African political participation.

Only a few administrators, such as Askwith, recognised that most Nairobi Africans were still enmeshed in ethnic rivalries and were not yet ready to enter the democratic multi-tribal future espoused by the Kenya African Union and the African Advisory Council. The aspirations of the élite were completely unrealistic, given the tribal particularisms of the vast majority of the capital's African population, however 'progressive' they may have appeared to the liberal conscience. The Forty Group and

Mau Mau were to show that most urban Africans could only be mobilised by appeals to tribal solidarity and cultural specificities. Askwith had correctly perceived that control could only be achieved by appealing to the same forces. The élite, however, feared official recognition of the tribal associations' power, as this would mean that their own influence would be diminished and their incorporation blocked. Khamisi therefore protested that Nairobi Africans were not divided by tribalism and claimed that any attempt to establish 'Native Authorities' in the capital in a modified system of indirect rule would fail. When Mathu, Khamisi and Odede met Surridge and Askwith in November 1945 to discuss the future organisation of the locations, they successfully persuaded the officials to abandon the idea of reinforcing the power of the tribal associations and to introduce a ward structure, dividing the locations into three areas, Kaloleni–Shauri Moyo, Kariokor–Ziwani–Starehe, and Pumwani, rather than along ethnic divisions.[17]

After the war the power of the African élite grew considerably. Tom Mbotela was appointed Assistant Superintendent of Locations and authorised to collect rents and to allocate quarters on the advice of locational housing committees, which also selected the members of the African Advisory Council. This enjoyed considerable patronage, including deciding on who should be given resident or visitor passes. The Native Tribunals, which were composed of other prominent Africans, were empowered to hear cases under the municipal bylaws dealing with hawkers, vehicles for hire, public rickshaws, dead bodies, firearms and casual labour.[18] By 1946 certain members of the élite had become accepted by the government as valuable allies and co-opted on a personal basis into the political structure. Muchohi Gikonyo, for example, was nominated to the Central Commodity Distribution Board, where he used his position to benefit his friends and relations, successfully securing a license to run a tea stall for his brother on his demobilisation from the army. Gikonyo, a Murang'a Kikuyu, along with Khamisi was also appointed to the Municipal Council and occupied the important post of chairman of the Advisory Council's trade sub-committee. The following list of the active members of the Advisory Council reveals how strong the control of the moderates was and how successful they had been in forcing the government to incorporate them into the decision-making process.[19]

The list also reveals that the Kikuyu, who formed approximately 55 per cent of the capital's African population, were seriously under-represented among the influential officeholders on the Advisory Council, while the people from the Coast, who after the Second World War comprised only a small proportion of the total population, were extremely influential. Francis Khamisi, Tom Mbotela and Jimmy Jeremiah, who were possibly the three most influential members of the Advisory Council, all came from Coast Province, as did Maulidi Jasho. In contrast, only two of the

Table 8.1: *Senior Officials of the African Advisory Council, Nairobi, 1946*

African Members nominated by the Advisory Council to the Municipal Council	Francis Khamisi and Muchohi Gikonyo
Vice Chairman of the Advisory Council	Jimmy Jeremiah
Secretary of the Advisory Council	Tom Mbotela
Chairman Finance Sub-Committee	Francis Khamisi
Chairman of Trade Sub-Committee	Muchohi Gikonyo
Chairman of Welfare Sub-Committee	Tom Mbotela
Chairman New School Sub-Committee	Francis Khamisi
Chairman Native Affairs Sub-Committee	Jimmy Jeremiah
Sub-Committee on Unemployment and Crime	Tom Mbotela Muchohi Gikonyo Edward Mwangi Maulidi Jasho Jimmy Jeremiah Albert Awino Dedan Githegi *et al.*
Chairman Education Sub-committee	Dedan Githegi
Assistant Municipal African Affairs Officer	Dedan Githegi 16 votes Tom Mbotela 9 votes
Assistant African Welfare Officer	Justo Obwa

leaders, Muchohi Gikonyo and Dedan Githegi, were Kikuyu, while Justo Obwa, the Assistant African Welfare Officer was an Abaluhya. Thus the leaders of the African Advisory Council were isolated by class and ethnicity from the mass of illiterate unskilled Kikuyu, who formed by far the largest element in African Nairobi.[20]

The blocking by the élite of the Municipal Welfare Officer's attempts to establish an effective administrative presence in the African parts of the capital in alliance with the tribal associations, left the locations to the mercy of political gangs, which controlled organised crime and prostitution and intimidated the law-abiding African population. Gang warfare and crime were the most visible manifestations of African discontent with slum conditions, rampant inflation and growing unemployment. As early as January 1945, the rising crime wave was already causing such concern among the settlers that Mrs Olga Watkins moved an emergency debate in the Legislative Council. While Mrs Watkins and the other settler politicians emphasised the need for more effective policing and called for severer penalties, the two members representing African interests, Eliud Mathu and Archdeacon Beecher, stressed the social causes of crime. For them the crime wave 'is the outcome of social and economic disturbances . . . in so far as the African and crime is concerned we must look beyond the apparent circumstances and see that he is affected as a criminal by his social and economic circumstances'.[21] Whatever the causes of discontent and crime, the administration, its settler critics and the African moderates identified the crime wave as the most important problem to be tackled. In December 1948, Tom Mbotela, for example, considered that the rule of law had collapsed in 'outcast Nairobi' and drew an alarmist, but prescient, comparison with the anti-British revolt in Malaya which had just begun.[22] Let us examine the social and economic roots of African discontent in Nairobi.

Nairobi's housing crisis

Migrant labourers, separated from their families in the reserves and living in the towns for a few months at a time, provided a major barrier to increased efficiency in both industry and peasant agriculture. Returning home to the reserves at frequent intervals, the migrant labourer quickly forgot his newly-acquired skills and had to re-enter the urban world at the bottom, while his wife, alone on the family *shamba*, found it equally impossible to cultivate the new cash crops and became increasingly in debt to her richer neighbours and compelled either to sell some land or to become a hired labourer at crucial moments in the agricultural cycle. Trapped in this cycle of poverty, the migrant-labour question seemed, to the official mind, to provide a recipe for certain disaster unless a stabilised, efficient urban community could be created. Increased productivity would enable higher wages to be paid, which would allow the urban worker to bring his family to live in the city, which would, in turn, break the vicious circle of the migrant labourers' dependence on the reserves and periodic absences from the industrial economy.[23]

The Secretariat and field administration were even more concerned about Nairobi's housing shortage. Throughout the 1940s the number of new inhabitants grew rapidly, increasing by 17 per cent per annum.[24] In these circumstances the provision of new housing failed to keep pace. Although the government and the Municipal Council built new African locations near the industrial area, conditions deteriorated as dispossessed squatters and *ahoi* from the reserves flocked to Nairobi for employment, and sought refuge in the slums of Pumwani and in the shanty-towns, which had sprung up beyond the municipal boundaries at Dagoretti, Ngata Rongai and Quarry. It was not that the government and municipality failed to take any action, but rather that they were overwhelmed by the tidal wave of new urban immigrants. In the 20 years before the outbreak of the Second World War, the government and council had provided accomodation for nearly 4,500 Africans but had demolished Pangani, the shanty-town built by the capital's first African inhabitants at the beginning of the century. Between 1939 and 1947, state provision of housing for Africans in Nairobi nearly doubled. During the war a further 2,100 quarters were completed and in the first two years of Mitchell's governorship this was increased by another 2,219. New estates were built at Makongeni in 1940, Ziwani in 1943, Kaloleni in 1944, and at Marurani in 1946. Meanwhile accommodation was extended at Starehe, Shauri Moyo and Pumwani.[25]

Nevertheless, by 1947 the housing shortage in the capital was desperate. The government calculated that the African locations were grossly overcrowded, with at least 28 per cent more people than they were supposed to contain. Pumwani, the oldest, for example, had 375 people to the acre compared to the approved density of 225. Although it was the most overcrowded location, it was also by far the largest, containing over one-third of Nairobi's Africans. The labour department feared that the problem was even worse than the official figures had revealed, since many people had probably evaded the housing census through fear of being expelled as illegal residents or unemployed vagrants. The department estimated there might be another 13,000 people, who were being sheltered by friends in the area, who had not appeared on the official census which had recorded a total population of 15,000 for the location.[26] In the other locations, directly controlled by the municipality or Railway Administration, conditions were not quite so overcrowded. Many of these estates had been recently built and had higher public-health standards than the early locations, such as Kariokor, where the barrack-like conditions were grotesque. But even in the new locations conditions were cramped, especially as most accommodation housed at least 20 per cent more people than had been planned. Table 8.2 provides some index of the dreadful overcrowding which even those Africans who were sufficiently fortunate to have a roof over their heads had to endure.[27]

By 1947 it had become apparent that the government and municipality could not keep pace with the demand for housing. Each year the deficit of 26,000 beds was increased by another 10,000. To remove this shortage would have cost over £1,500,000, and would have required an expenditure of another £600,000 each year to house the continuing influx. Already the administration estimated that 82,000 Africans were living in housing designed to accommodate only 54,000. Two-thirds of them were staying in the African locations which were supposed to contain a maximum of 33,000, and Pumwani, the most decrepit area, contained somewhere between 15,000 and 28,000 people instead of the approved maximum of only 9,000. Another 4,000 people had nowhere to live, and were sleeping on verandas, in the streets, or in parked buses. Meanwhile a large shanty-town had developed in the swamp to the east of the commercial centre of the capital and unauthorised villages were springing up on farms to the east of the town. Somalis were renting shacks in Eastleigh and peri-urban settlements, like Kariobangi, which had been a thorn in the flesh of the administration for 20 years, were growing alarmingly.[28]

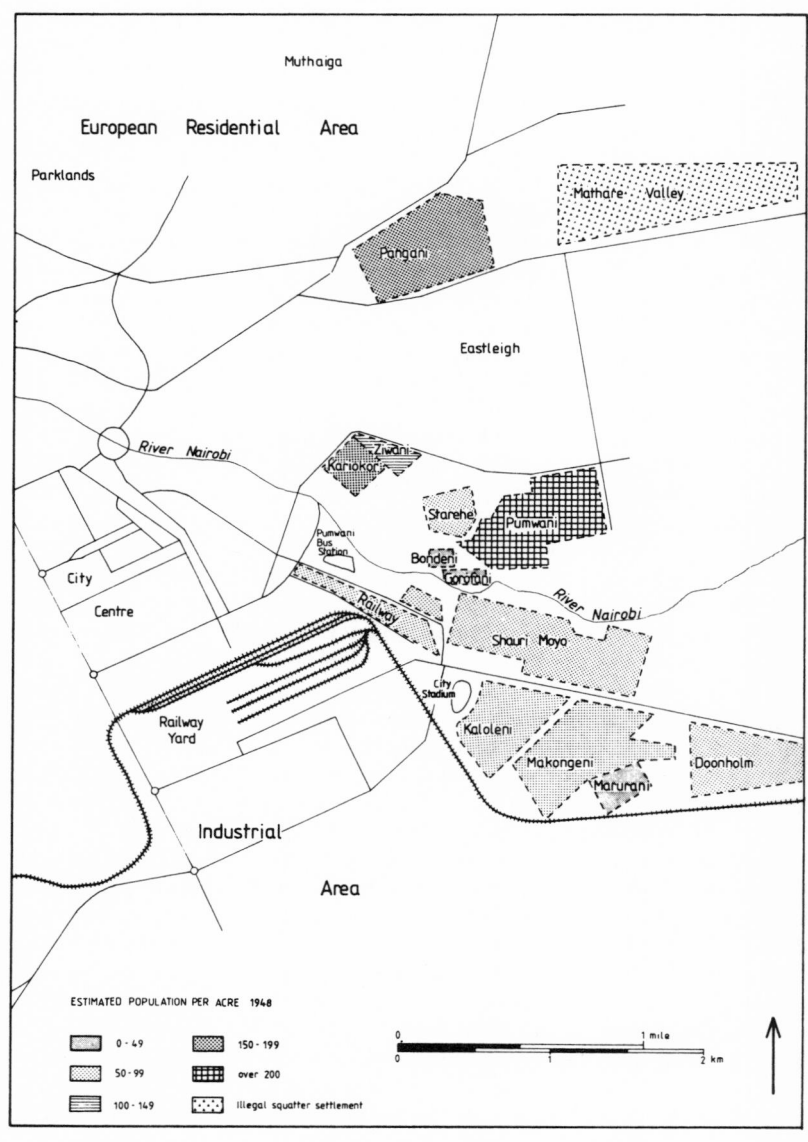

Map 8.1: *Population Densities of the African Locations of Nairobi*

Table 8.2: *Population Density Estimates for the African Locations of Nairobi in 1948*

Location	Date built	Quarters	Acreage	Theoretical Capacity	Theoretical Number per acre	Actual Number Accommodated	Actual Accommodated per acre	% Over-crowding
Government Built Accommodation:								
Railway Old Lhandies	Pre 1930	2,391	80	9,082	68	10,373	77	14
Government Starehe	Pre 1930	157	53	2,505	47	2,755	52	10
	1942	103						
	1944	82						
	1946	99						
Kariokor	1931	929	10	1,534	153	1,841	184	20
Shauri Moyo	1938	1,020	39	3,225	83	3,708	95	15
	1945	30						
Railway Makongeni	1940	1,200	54	n.a.	n.a.	n.a.	n.a.	n.a.
	1946	270						
	1947	336						
Ziwani Lodging Houses	1942	120	2	240	120	264	132	10
Ziwani	1943	163	18	1,928	107	2,121	118	10
	1944	202						
	1945	80						
Kaloleni	1944	102	70	3,196	46	3,516	50	10
	1945	166						
	1946	99						
	1947	245						
Marurani	1946	600	41	1,200	30	1,380	34	17
Pumwani Loan	1946	112	6	496	83	548	91	10
Public Works's Department	n.a.	n.a.	4	358	90	430	108	20
Non-Government Built Accommodation:								
Pumwani	Pre 1930	n.a.	40	9,000	225	15,000	375	66
Private Employers	n.a.	n.a.	5	228	46	228	46	nil
TOTAL		n.a.	422	32,992	78	42,164	100	28

The boom in government house building was unfortunately almost over. Once the 245 houses planned in Kaloleni had been completed, there were no plans to build any more. The only new accommodation for Africans authorised by the government after 1948 consisted of certain small self-help schemes, in which a few Africans were allowed to build their own houses on government land.[29] Despite evidence of urban discontent, the Kenyan government failed to appreciate the seriousness of the housing shortage and its effect on African opinion. Warnings from the field administration and the labour department failed to penetrate the Secretariat, which was preoccupied with the peasant revolt in Murang'a, squatter resistance in the White Highlands, the court cases over Olenguruone and the general strike in Mombasa.

One person who did understand the seriousness of the crisis in Nairobi was Askwith. In his 1948 report he complained that:

> It was disheartening for those concerned with the welfare of Africans in Nairobi . . . to see another year go by with no appreciable progress made in providing even a limited amount of housing for them. To see legitimately employed Africans sleeping under the verandas on River Road, in noisome and dangerous shacks in the Swamp, in buses parked by the roadside, and fourteen to a room in Pumwani, two to a bed and the rest on the floor. To see plans for new housing schemes hang fire month after month for some reason or another, while the number of Africans taking up employment grew and grew.[30]

Such conditions hindered the government's plans to increase industrial productivity and to create a permanent urban labour force, completely dependent on its industrial wages, which would help to reduce the pressure on the land in the over-populated reserves. Askwith became increasingly perturbed by the Municipal Council and Secretariat's complacency over the African housing shortage. The settler politicians were much more concerned about the high cost of improving African accommodation and overlooked the importance of the difficulties that remained. Complaints about excessive expenditure and the growing subsidisation of urban African accommodation were winning an increasingly favourable hearing in the Municipal Council. Askwith lamented what he saw as a complete failure to understand the need to provide cheap housing to improve African health and efficiency at work. Instead of being complacent about the number of new estates that had been built since the beginning of the war, he felt that greater vigour was required 'to retrieve the position at the eleventh hour', because the unprecedented postwar growth in population had created a dangerous shortage of accommodation.

Unfortunately, by 1947 the money available for housing under the Colonial Development and Welfare Act of 1945 was nearly exhausted, although the urban population was still soaring, growing by over 20 per cent from 53,000 in 1945, to 64,000 in 1946, and then to 77,000 in 1947. The government responded by attempting to control the inflow into Nairobi, refusing to sanction labour recruitment unless the employers provided housing. Askwith wanted to go even further and to make the provision of accommodation mandatory for the acquisition of an industrial licence. He also urged the Labour Controller to refuse to sanction permits for industrial expansion unless employers agreed to house their own workers, because the council could not begin to build sufficient accommodation.[31]

The Municipal Council could not carry the financial burden of providing even more African housing estates. It was not simply the problem of finding the initial capital outlay to construct new accommodation, but the accumulating burden of recurrent expenditure required to subsidise rents because of the low level of African wages. If Nairobi Africans were to afford to live in the municipality's new housing estates sub-economic rents had to be charged. Thus, while industry prospered the debt burden of the City Council grew from £587,566 in 1940 to £860,869 at the end of the war, before reaching £2,634,260 four years later; by 1957 municipal borrowing totalled £9,021,836.[32] The Nairobi Chamber of Commerce and many ratepayers viewed this escalating burden with alarm. Ernest Vasey, the mayor, warned the chief secretary that the housing estates would prove inadequate to satisfy rising African expectations long before the loans were repaid.[33] Until employers accepted that wages would have to be increased, the burden of housing the capital's African workforce would fall on the overstretched municipality. Employers joined forces with their staff in opposing the idea of increased rents, for this would have resulted in pressure for higher wages. Employers and Africans insisted that sub-economic housing was essential to Nairobi's industrial sector, but the burden of subsidisation limited the provision of accommodation and placed a severe strain on the financial resources of the council.

One of the reasons for this financial problem was that Nairobi had modelled its African housing on South Africa. Mitchell and several other influential officials and settler politicians had been greatly impressed by the example of the new African estates at Port Elizabeth. Carpenter, the Assistant Labour Commissioner, had been despatched to investigate African housing in South Africa.[34] These schemes, however, ignored the crucial problem that it was impossible to build similar accommodation in Kenya at a cost ordinary African workers could afford to pay. Not only were African wages in South Africa four times higher than in Kenya, but the unit cost of construction in Nairobi was much higher than in Port Elizabeth, since Kenya did not have the industrial base to provide cheap building materials. All the cement and concrete for the Nairobi estates, for example, had to be imported from South Africa because the Portland Cement Company had not yet been enticed to Kenya by the government's offers of protection and several local companies had all failed.[35] The attempts of the government-sponsored East African Industrial Research Board to manufacture tiles and glass in the colony had also proved to be expensive failures, since the high development costs meant that the poor quality finished product was often more expensive than high-quality imports. Another obstacle to cheap housing in Nairobi was that the building industry was dominated by Asian artisans; thus housing for low-income Africans was being built by comparatively well-paid Asians. As a result of these problems the unit cost of accommodation in Kenya was more than double that in South Africa, where the economic rent per room was only 61 shillings. The proportion of total average African incomes taken by rent in Port Elizabeth's new housing estates, therefore, was less than one-eighth that required for similar accommodation in Nairobi. Consequently, while South Africa could charge economic rents for the accommodation, the new Nairobi estates had to be heavily subsidised by the government and the council.[36]

Phillips and Booker, who investigated the causes of industrial discontent in Mombasa after the strikes of August 1945 and January 1947, recommended that rents should form no more than 17 per cent of total household incomes. If this rule had been applied to the new housing estates and there had been no subsidy, it would have meant that nobody earning less than 168 shillings per month could, theoretically, have afforded to live with their families in the new accommodation. The Phillips Report, however, discovered that out of the 13,000 Africans employed in Mombasa, 10,000 earned less than 40 shillings per month, the absolute minimum subsistence income for a single man, while only 300, just over 2 per cent of the workforce, earned over 100 shillings per month or more than 50 cents per hour. The wage structure of the Nairobi workforce was very similar.[37]

Industry, however, refused to increase wages or build housing for its employees while the productivity of the unskilled African labour force remained so low. This meant that the government could not enforce a law requiring employers to provide accommodation for their workers, since this would cripple Kenya's new industries and discourage others from investing in the colony. The Kenyan government's post-war industrialisation strategy depended on attracting multinational corporations to Kenya because of the low wages, which industry saw as a form of economic subsidy almost as important as the government's promises of protection from external competition. This low-wage economy, however, not only placed a heavy burden on the Municipal Council, but also hindered attempts to increase industrial productivity by creating a stable urban workforce, and undermined the government's schemes to reduce overcrowding in the reserves by creating new employment opportunities in the expanding industrial sector.[38]

Careful consideration was given to several ideas for solving these problems. The labour department suggested that the government should strictly enforce Section 31 of the 1937 Employment of Natives Ordinance which placed the burden of housing urban workers upon their employers. This, as we have just seen, was rejected because it would discourage investment and retard Kenya's industrial expansion. Many employers were already complaining about the department's interference and declared that the council's insistence on the construction of permanent structures to house workers would be prohibitively expensive. The most constructive suggestion for escaping this impasse was proposed by Vasey. He suggested the council raise the finances and build the accommodation, while industry subsidise the gap between the sub-economic rents paid by the workers and the full economic rent required by the council to cover its debt payments. The first of these joint estates, called 'Gorofani', was built between Bondeni and the Nairobi River. It consisted of 800 two-storey blocks with three men to a room. These were rented to Nairobi firms on long leases at economic rentals, which, it was hoped, would reduce the costs to both employers and the council.[39]

It was also believed that this solution would enable adjustments to be made when the Africans' incomes increased and their standard of living rose. Thus, as more families abandoned life in the reserves and settled in the towns, as better conditions were required and as wages increased because of higher productivity, the number of individuals per room could be reduced. In the interim, the system ensured that the social burden of the rapid expansion of the city would not simply fall on the Council but would be shared with employers. This would not only reduce the municipality's debts and lessen the rate burden on the settler population, but would also enable new loans to be raised on the incipient Nairobi money market and in London to fund improved social services for the growing population. The first of these was the King George VI Hospital, completed in 1950 and designed to accommodate 650 African and 42 Asian patients, and the enlargement of the capital's water supply, achieved by constructing a second main from the Ruiru Dam and building the Chania Ssasumua Dam at a cost of £750,000. The council and the government also began to build more housing estates, first at Gorofani, and then at Bahati and Mbotela.[40]

This sharing of the burden of uneconomic housing between the council and industry, however, proved to be only a partial solution to the problems and in fact hindered the encouragement of stable African family life in the capital. The urban family remained a rare phenomenon. Only 7,600, or 13 per cent of the total African population in 1946 were women, while a mere 12 per cent were children. The average rent for a room at

Gorofani in the late 1940s was 28 shillings, or over 9 shillings per bed. These high charges meant that only a few, comparatively well-off Africans could afford to bring their wives and children to live in the new estates.[41] The picture the government painted of happy African families sitting on the lawns outside their homes was a propaganda myth to silence its critics in Britain. In reality, employers wanted to house as many workers as possible at the minimum cost and rarely considered what advantages might be gained from creating a contented, stable and more productive workforce.[42]

Few Kenyan industrialists were as far sighted as Lord Faringdon, a left-wing critic of colonial policy who warned in the *East African Standard* that:

A certain number of Africans can, I believe, be absorbed in industry and commerce, but if they are to be so absorbed it must be on the condition that when they are removed from the Reserves they are accompanied by their wives and families who will be able to live with them in the urban areas . . . From this it clearly follows, in my view, that the wages paid to Africans must be adequate to enable them to support their wives and families as well as themselves, which is not at present the case. At the present time the Reserves are subsidising African wages.[43]

Social needs, it appeared, could not be reconciled with economic facts. The political and economic pressures that were driving African families into the urban centres after the war simply exacerbated the problems and ensured that wages remained at subsistence levels, precluding any improvement in labour productivity or in African living conditions.[44]

Another approach considered was an early example of the present-day site-and-service scheme. Since neither the council nor the government could afford to build enough housing in permanent materials to keep pace with the expansion of Nairobi, experiments were undertaken on cheaper semi-permanent materials. Many settlers suggested that the council was in financial difficulties because it wasted its money housing Africans in 'pokey replicas of a European home' instead of using traditional materials. Dressed stone, for example, could be replaced with pressed earth blocks. It was absurd, they argued, to provide every house with doors costing 50 shillings, when this added 50 cents a month to the rent.

The more moderate of these complaints were supported by Askwith, the Municipal Welfare Officer. He too was opposed to cramming Africans into poor European-style housing. Many, he declared, could not afford to furnish their homes and were forced to sleep on cement floors in badly-ventilated conditions, which were ideal for spreading tuberculosis and respiratory diseases. Mud and wattle, he argued, provided a more effective natural discouragement of mosquitoes and bugs. He recommended that only Africans who could afford to live in a European style should be housed in the new estates. The rest should be left to solve the housing shortage by building their own mud and wattle dwellings. This self-help approach would quickly end the artificial shortage of accommodation created by the British-based health regulations of the Municipal Council.[45]

The medical establishment, however, dismissed these proposals and insisted that only the strict enforcement of public-health regulations would prevent plague. Tuberculosis and relapsing fever, the experts argued, were associated with damp floors, inadequate ventilation and poor housing, and would spread rapidly in a shanty-town of mud huts. They pointed out that Kenya's housing regulations fell far below those deemed adequate by scientific opinion and needed to be made more stringent rather than relaxed. The ratepayers, they observed, would be the first to protest if cholera or plague spread to the European suburbs because the Medical Department had reduced its public-health standards in the African locations. Mud and wattle houses were perhaps adequate for the reserves, where homesteads were spread across the countryside, but they were completely unsuitable for the overcrowded African locations in Nairobi, where disease would rapidly spread throughout the population.[46]

Another solution was to encourage Africans to build their own houses provided they reached certain approved standards. Carpenter and the labour department, for example, suggested that the council should provide the land, roads and drains, but that the actual houses should be built by the more prosperous sections of the African community. This idea was enthusiastically supported by the *East African Standard*, which argued that provided the estates were carefully planned, it would be better to allow Africans to build their own houses from cheap materials to an approved standard than to leave them in the urban slums, which undermined every attempt to improve health and to create a contented working class.[47]

Prodded by these ideas, the government granted permission for 600 experimental self-help houses to be built north of the railway to Thika. The government supplied the materials at cost price and precise standards were specified. Supporters of the scheme hoped that it would provide family homes or social security for older Africans who had ceased to work, for they could rent out rooms and remain in the city on their retirement, instead of returning to the reserves. It was hoped that 6,000 beds would be provided by these self-help schemes. They were extremely popular among the wealthier sections of the African community. Within a short time more than 800 people had applied for the first 600 experimental plots. In Pumwani, where Africans had been building their own houses for many years, the government decided to legalise the situation and to grant 40-year leases. The Nairobi Chamber of Commerce and the labour department enthusiastically supported these new developments and urged Kenyans to follow the examples of Elizabethville, Leopoldville and

Bloemfontein, where self-built African housing on permanent foundations had been encouraged for many years. In the long term these had proved much better than the costly urban estates that had been built in Kenya. Many of the new estates were already extremely dilapidated. Marurani was in an appalling condition after less than six years' occupation. As costs continued to rise and the council could no longer afford to meet its self-imposed health standards, the self-help solution to the housing crisis became increasingly popular in official circles and among the ratepayers.[48]

The growth of African discontent

Rural Africans flocked to the capital during the 1940s only to discover that its streets were not paved with gold. Many were unable to find jobs and had to eke out a meagre subsistence in the informal sector as street hawkers or petty criminals for the men, or as illegal brewers or prostitutes for the women.[49] The appalling shortage of accommodation was not the only problem they had to overcome in the alien urban environment. Throughout the 1940s the general retail price index rose much faster than wages. Although the rate of inflation had briefly diminished at the end of the war, after June 1947 it increased dramatically until by June 1948 the retail price index was 20 points higher than it had been 12 months before. Food prices rose particularly sharply as the result of a combination of poor harvests and successful pressure from the European settlers for better producer prices. By March 1948, vegetable prices had risen by nearly 50 per cent, while milk now cost 1 shilling 75 cents instead of 1 shilling 10 cents per gallon. The cost of a bag of *posho* increased by almost 600 per cent between August 1939 and December 1948, rising from 5 to 29 shillings. During this period wages had barely doubled and had returned to their pre-depression levels. In real terms they were still far below wages in the late 1920s.[50]

The official retail price index and the cost of living allowances, which both the government and the railway awarded to their lower-paid workers, seriously underestimated the increase in the cost of living since the beginning of the war. These indices were based only on official prices and did not take account of black market prices. As we have noted, most urban Africans were heavily dependent on the black economy for many commodities, ranging from imported goods to vegetables and firewood from the neighbouring reserves.[51] Graph 8.1 vividly reveals the deteriorating economic situation faced by Africans in Nairobi during the 1940s. In particular, the upswing in inflation during 1947 coincided with a period of increasing political discontent, with growing popular support for the African Worker's Federation in Nairobi and increasing peasant opposition to the terracing campaign in the reserves. There was a close

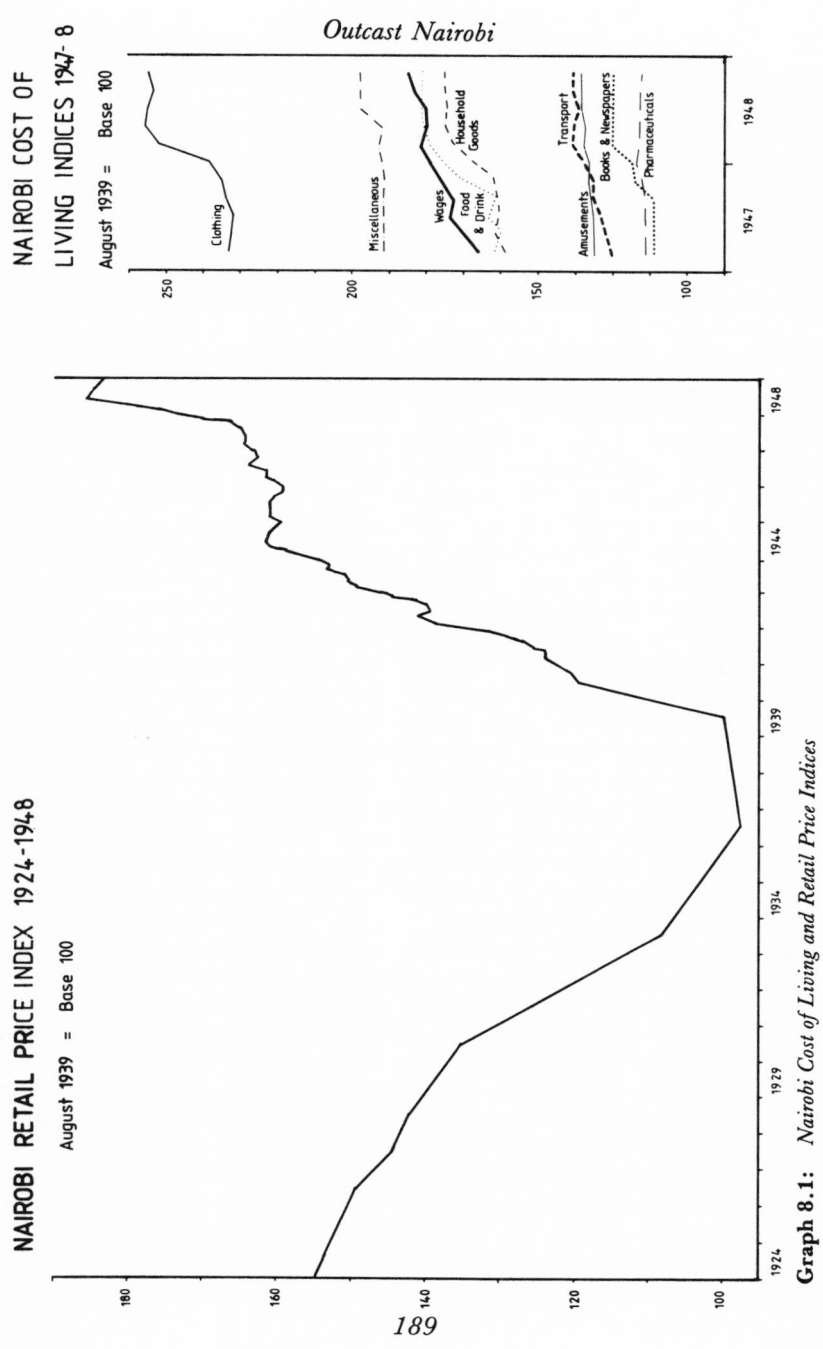

Graph 8.1: *Nairobi Cost of Living and Retail Price Indices*

NAIROBI RETAIL PRICE INDEX 1924-1948

August 1939 = Base 100

NAIROBI COST OF LIVING INDICES 1947-8

August 1939 = Base 100

Outcast Nairobi

Clothing

Miscellaneous

Wages

Food & Drink

Household Goods

Transport

Amusements

Books & Newspapers

Pharmaceuticals

189

correlation between African militancy and the deteriorating economic position of many Africans.[52]

Despite the government's attempts to improve urban housing, the majority of Africans in the capital experienced a marked deterioration in their standard of living. At the same time, *ahoi* and poor peasant families in Central Province, especially in Kiambu, were being squeezed off the land by the growing élite of commercial farmers. Many squatters were also being expelled from the White Highlands. Deprived of their land, these people flocked to Nairobi.[53] Hawking, brewing, prostitution and crime offered these new urban residents their only hope of survival. All these occupations were, however, deemed illegal by the colonial authorities. Thus, the desperately poor were involved in another battle with the state. Already antagonised by their recent loss of land, condemned to an alien urban existence, it was hardly surprising that the Kikuyu poor, who formed more than half of Nairobi's population, vented their dismay in political violence.

As these dispossessed squatters and poor peasants sought refuge in Nairobi, the African locations became even more overcrowded, unemployment increased and inflation mounted. More and more Africans were drawn to the metropolis and trapped within its web of despair. Pushed to the limits of human endurance, the Nairobi poor created their own alternative society in clandestine opposition to the forces of law and order and to the colonial state.[54] The colonial authorities were reduced to impotence and could merely bemoan the collapse of 'tribal values' and 'the sad demoralisation of a part of the indigenous population of the Colony leading to drunkenness, crimes of violence, idleness, dishonesty, theft and many other objectionable things'. They failed to appreciate that growing numbers of Africans had no alternative. In the White Highlands, in the reserves and, above all, in Nairobi, the plight of the majority of Africans had never been so desperate as it was after 1947.[55]

Nairobi Africans, however, were not a homogeneous community united by despair, but were bitterly divided by class and ethnic animosities. The world of the clerk earning 100 shillings per month was entirely different from that of the unskilled labourer, the illegal hawker, or the unemployed vagrant. The African élite demanded equal pay for equal work, a unified African and Asian civil service and the ending of the colour bar. In other words, it emulated the settler communities.[56] The urban poor were preoccupied with the struggle for survival. Condemned to a constant battle for existence, constitutional politics had nothing to offer them, it seemed, but deception.[57] Men like Tom Mbotela and Dedan Githegi, the Assistant Superintendent and Municipal Welfare Officer, were identified as their enemy; stooges of the Europeans.[58]

Class, however, was not the most important divide. Linguistic and cultural differences ensured that tribalism remained the most important influence upon daily life and political allegiances in the locations. Tribal associations not only provided the most effective mechanism of social control, but were also the only rudimentary welfare most Africans encountered. Life in the city intensified rather than diminished ethnic rivalries. Financial assistance, moral welfare, strike money and burial expenses were all provided within the confines of the tribe, or of even more parochial district associations. The 'detribalised' urban African was a myth.[59]

As conditions deteriorated in the face of growing unemployment and rampant inflation, tribal tension increased. In particular, the unemployed and low paid turned to crime to supplement their meagre resources. These criminal gangs were usually comprised of friends from the same area. The *mbari* was as potent a unit of organisation in the city as in the reserves, guaranteeing cohesion and support among the criminal fraternity as in every aspect of African life.[60] Consecrated by an oath, few dared to transgress group solidarity. Social pressure and superstition reinforced each other to ensure that the urban poor tacitly supported the men of violence. The authorities failed to perceive the extent to which the locations had become a distinct world in which law-abiding Africans faced such overwhelming pressures that they were forced to conform to the norms of outcast Nairobi. In consequence the administration and the police were forever complaining that 'it was astonishing to find how often criminals were arrested as unauthorised lodgers and how willingly many Africans offered them hospitality'.[61]

As early as January 1945, this problem had become so serious that Mortimer, who was then the Commissioner for Local Government, introduced an amendment to the Rent and Mortgage Bill to enable the Nairobi Council to expel tenants who broke the housing rules by subletting. Even those convicted of holding illegal liquor parties or tenants occupying family houses while their wives and children were in the reserves could be expelled. The Bill created widespread alarm. Many Africans feared that they would be thrown out of their homes for trivial offences once they were deprived of the protection of the original Ordinance. Archdeacon Beecher explained that many were apprehensive that 'they will be expelled from the municipal housing and will be condemned to that dog kennel existence that these fifteen thousand Africans in Nairobi have to undergo because there is no other housing available for them'.[62]

For these people, the casual labourers, hawkers and unemployed of Nairobi, crime provided the only way of surviving. Living in appalling conditions and in real deprivation, the outcasts of Nairobi resorted to crime. As the largest element in the population, the 30,000 Kikuyu and members of the related Embu and Meru people subjected the 12,000 Nyanza Africans and the 7,000 Kamba to an unending reign of terror. The returning *askari*, who spurned the training courses at Kabete and quickly dissipated their gratuities, the angry squatters expelled from the

European farms in the White Highlands, and the dispossessed *ahoi* of Kikuyuland, sought refuge in Pumwani with few illusions about the harshness of life. Crime paid; crime opened up new avenues for social advancement; it enabled the outcast to gain prestige provided the gangs did not prey upon their own kind and their own kind were defined in strictly tribal terms – kinsmen from the same *mbari* or migrant workers from the same rural location. For the Kikuyu criminal, this did not include the Luo or Abaluhya poor.[63]

Unable to control African Nairobi or to create a stable labour force, the Municipality resorted to pass laws, curfews and removal orders. Since reform and social improvement were too expensive, further legislation restricting the influx of Africans into the town in search of non-existent jobs offered an easy alternative. Municipal bylaws confined Africans to their locations or servants' quarters between ten at night and five in the morning, while visitors were not allowed to remain in the town for longer than 36 hours without employment unless they had a resident's or visitor's permit signed by the town clerk. When the Supreme Court declared these pass laws *ultra vires* in September 1945, new legislation, the Removal of Undesirable Natives Ordinance, had to be rushed through the Legislative Council to preserve the controls. These measures were, of course, bitterly resented by the African population and, in that they failed to tackle the problems responsible for the crime wave and for growing African discontent, were largely ineffective. They provided only another irritant to law-abiding Africans.[64]

Until Operation Anvil, which cleared all the disgruntled Kikuyu out of the capital in 1954, the government never seriously attempted to recover control of Nairobi's locations. The curfew bylaw, for example, did not extend to the locations, where African gangs were freely allowed to prowl the dark alleys, waylaying anyone sufficiently foolish to be about at night. Although 'reputable' Africans were issued with passes for one year, the stigma of these racial laws remained, generating further ill-will between the races. Social, economic and political divisions reinforced the racial barrier. G.R.B. Brown, who succeeded Askwith as Municipal Welfare Officer, warned that, 'to the natural envy felt by the poor for the rich is added the poison of racialism'.[65] Although it was in the workers' interests to reduce the number of unemployed and the mass of surplus labour, Africans resented pass laws and labour controls, such as the *kipande*, as an affront to their personal liberty. Europeans and Asians were not subjected to the humiliation of mass tax-collection checks on their way to work, or of being forced to work wherever the labour exchange directed them rather than being allowed to look for jobs they found congenial. So long as the police viewed all Africans as potential vagrants and criminals, instead of law-abiding members of the community, and while respectable African women continued to be arrested as prostitutes, then the image of government would remain tarnished and trust in the authorities undermined.[66]

In these circumstances, periodic eruptions of frustrated anger were inevitable. After several minor disturbances, the most protracted of which was a 16-day strike by members of the Transport and Allied Workers' Union against the Nairobi Council's taxi-cab bylaws, tension reached crisis point early in 1950 with the introduction of the Essential Services (Arbitration) Ordinance and the Voluntarily Unemployed Persons Ordinance.[67] These new laws reflected growing concern in the government and among the settlers at the inability of the authorities to control the flow of people into the capital. Unemployment had replaced shortages of labour and was blamed for the high crime rate in the capital. The campaign to rehouse the African community in new estates with improved social services, where the administration could keep more effective control than in Pumwani, had palpably failed. Alarmed by the financial cost, the colonial state had drawn back and resorted to its traditional policy of coercion. Reform and social improvement were too expensive; force seemed to be a cheaper option.[68]

The first Vagrancy Ordinance had been passed in 1902, but the new legislation introduced in 1949 was much more Draconian than any previous measure. The Vagrancy (Amendment) Bill of May 1949 empowered the authorities to repatriate anyone who failed to secure permanent employment after three months residence in Nairobi. This was followed by the Voluntarily Unemployed Persons (Provisions of Employment) Ordinance, finally approved in January 1950, which empowered the police to arrest anyone suspected of being a vagrant or unemployed. These powers of arrest were condemned at a mass meeting in the Desai Memorial Hall in Nairobi on Saturday 14 January as forced labour legislation. The following day when the Ordinance came into force, the shop workers section of the Labour Trade Union of East Africa held an even bigger meeting at the Kaloleni Social Hall in the centre of one of the African housing estates and, to the fury of the Kenyan government, sent petitions to the Secretary of State for the Colonies and the United Nations, protesting against the new restrictions.[69]

The Colonial Office also announced that Nairobi would become a city on 30 March 1950. The militant African politicians, led by two prominent trade unionists, Fred Kubai and Bildad Kaggia, decided that this would be an ideal opportunity to focus attention on the plight of urban Africans and called for a boycott of the celebrations. Kubai declared the celebrations 'a mere propaganda trick designed to make it appear to the outside world that democracy was on the march in this country'. Kikuyu opinion was further aroused by rumours that the civic celebrations were merely a plot to enlarge Nairobi at the expense of the Kikuyu reserves. It was reported that 32 square miles of Kiambu were to be added to the new city and that all the Africans were to be moved out to make way for another 12,000 European settlers.[70]

African resentment smouldered until 12 May 1950, when the Essential Services (Arbitration) Ordinance, empowering the government to prosecute workers who went on strike in essential industries, came into force. That morning Nairobi ground to a halt under the impact of the capital's first general strike. Makhan Singh and Fred Kubai, the two most prominent trade union leaders, were both arrested and charged with being officials of an unregistered organisation.[71] The following day another strike leader, Chege Kiburu, was arrested and the government declared the food, oil, power, lighting, posts, railways, roads and ports to be essential industries whose employees were not allowed to go on strike. The government then announced that Kubai had been arrested for the attempted murder of Councillor Muchohi Gikonyo. Gikonyo was the most prominent African to attend the civic celebrations six weeks earlier and narrowly escaped assassination a few days later when three shots were fired while he was closing his shop.[72]

Even before the news of Kubai's arrest on the attempted murder charge had become known, nearly 3,000 Africans were on strike in Nairobi and the police had had to use baton charges to break up crowds in Shauri Moyo. On 18 May, tear gas was used for the first time in Kenya in a pitched battle between demonstrators and the police in Shauri Moyo.[73] By the sixth day of the strike, 75 per cent of the Public Works Department's labour force had joined the strike and only 44 of the Municipal Cleansing Department's staff of 700 were at work, despite an offer of double pay for those who reported for work. The strikers' demands for a 25 per cent wage increase, regular annual increments, free accommodation or a housing allowance, sick leave, 14 days holiday per year and the establishment of a provident fund had been subsumed in a general protest against the deprivation and squalor most Africans had to endure in Nairobi and against government harrassment of the trades union. Kubai's arrest, to most Africans, simply showed the lengths to which the government would go in its unscrupulous campaign against the trade union, which seemed to be the only organisation capable of standing up to the colonial state and protecting the interests of the African masses.[74]

Police wireless cars toured the African locations, relaying information about crowd movements and clusters of demonstrators, and armoured cars were moved opposite the central police station. Demonstrations were concentrated in the Kaloleni Valley where large crowds of unemployed swelled the strikers' ranks. Police Bren-gun carriers and armoured cars patrolled the area, making regular circuits around the location, dispersing the crowds with more tear gas. Aften ten days, when Chege Kiburu was sentenced to eleven months hard labour, the strike remained unbroken. Intimidation of workers increased and some people had their heads shaved. More than 300 people had been arrested and the Public Works Department had dismissed over 100 strikers. Gangs of Kikuyu strikers roamed the streets, particularly the Asian residential areas, assaulting anyone found still at work, while others attempted to ensure total support for the strike in the locations. Most of their victims were Luo or Abaluhya, who flocked to enrol as special constables to deal with the Kikuyu.[75]

The strike revealed the divisions within the African community. This was the crucial flaw in the armour of the Kikuyu militants who dominated the trade unions. While in the cosmopolitan world of Mombasa social discontent had to mobilise the diverse elements in the population in a multi-tribal alliance, in the African locations of Nairobi dissatisfaction was often directed against other Africans. The Kikuyu domination of the locations, particularly Pumwani, meant that in the capital non-Kikuyu came to identify Kikuyu slum landlords as their exploiters. At the same time they were terrorised by the Kikuyu criminal gangs. Consequently the non-Kikuyu in the locations became profoundly sceptical, even hostile, to Kikuyu leadership.[76]

Conclusion

As early as 1947 the police and the administration had already been over-whelmed in Nairobi. Even after the geneal strike on May 1950, the government made little attempt to defeat the armed gangs which terro-rised the locations and used Nairobi as a secure base from which to poli-ticise the discontented peasants in the reserves and the squatters in the White Highlands. Throughout the Mitchell era the administration had little control over events in Pumwani and Shauri Moyo, which provided a haven for the militants. Meanwhile the deplorable accommodation short-age, unemployment and rampant inflation alienated the capital's poor, driving the Kikuyu among them, who formed over half the city's popu-lation, into the arms of Mau Mau.[77]

Only a few months before the general stike, the Labour Commissioner, Hyde-Clarke, delivered a prescient warning to the Legislative Council. He declared that a new African township was urgently needed to house Nairobi's destitute, otherwise 'if we cannot answer this question quickly you can put paid to the question of better output, because relations will deteriorate . . . to such a degree that there will be no question of employ-ment and output. There will be riot and revolutions'.[78] His words went unheeded. Instead the Nairobi general strike confirmed the government in its diagnosis of the problems of the African locations and did not prompt it to reconsider its policy of repression. It failed to use the tribal associations, the only organised bodies in the locations capable of chal-lenging the power of the organised gangs, as a mechanism of social con-trol. The government instead chose to suppress African opposition.

Outcast Nairobi

Makhan Singh and the trade unions were condemned as subversive – as front for agitators who had perverted the infant unions, swamped thei responsible leaders and poisoned the minds of the masses.[79] The goverr ment never paused to ponder whether its own actions could have led th poor of Nairobi to emphasise the primacy of political action. After th general strike, for example, over 2,000 Kikuyu were dismissed and force to join the crowds of unemployed, who could only survive by crime.

Because the governor was aware of the need to promote economi expansion and to improve housing and social services if, to use his ow: words, they were going to stifle the 'communist' influence, he over emphasised the importance of political stability as a prerequisite fo Kenya attracting increased foreign investment.[80] All opposition, there fore, would have to be crushed if Kenya was to develop the economic bas from which the government could finance the increased provision of socia benefits. Although the policy was destined to benefit Africans in the lon; term, in the short term settler opinion and international capital had to b assured of the colony's continuing stability. Once again, the power of th settler community effectively foreclosed any possibility of the governmen seriously attempting to solve the problems of the urban Africans, wh were abandoned to the militants.

Notes

1. KNA Lab 9/1751, 'African Housing: General, 1946–51', memorandum by Josepl Mortimer, Mayor of Nairobi in 1930 and 1937, and father of C.E. Mortimer, Membe for Heath and Local Government, to Town Clerk, Nairobi, 23 February 1948; and CC 533/558/38715 (1948), 'Municipal African Affairs Annual Report', 1947 Report pp. 6–7.
2. KNA Lab 9/1751, 'African Housing: General, 1946–51', T.G. Askwith's report or overcrowding in Pumwani, 30 July 1946.
3. KNA MAA 8/22, 'City African Affairs Officer: Correspondence, 1947–50', Ton Mbotela to Superintendent, CID, Nairobi, 28 October 1947; and T.G. Askwith tc Superintendent, CID, Nairobi, 29 October 1947; and CO 533/558/38715 (1948) 'Municipal African Affairs Annual Report', 1947 Report, p. 4. See also *East African Standard*, 24 May 1950.
4. J. Spencer, *KAU*, pp. 208, 211–13, 221–4, 227–8; and C.G. Rosberg anc J. Nottingham, *The Myth of Mau Mau*, pp. 264–76.
5. KNA MAA 8/22, 'City African Affairs Officer: Correspondence, 1947–50', Ton Mbotela to Superintendent, CID, Nairobi, 28 October 1947.
6. *ibid*, T.G. Askwith to Superintendent, CID, Nairobi, 29 October 1947.
7. *ibid*. See also KNA Secretariat 1/12/6, 'Coast Province: Labour Unrest Corres pondence, 1947', C.R.B. Brown, acting PC Coast to Foster-Sutton, 15 March 1947 about the emergency preparations in Mombasa; and Secretariat 1/12/11, 'Laboui Unrest: Notes on Communications, Supplies and Transport, 1947', *passim*.
8. KNA MAA 8/22, 'City African Affairs Officer: Correspondence, 1947–50', Tom

Mbotela to Superintendent, CID, Nairobi, 28 October 1947. Mbotela had recently been appointed Superintendent of African Locations with responsibility for overseeing the administration of the capital's African housing estates.

9. KNA MAA 8/105, 'Intelligence Reports: Radio Posta, 1947–48', C. Penfold to P. Wyn Harris, 24 October 1947. See also *Radio Posta*, 16 October 1947, for reports of meetings of the Nyeri Reformed Kikuyu Society and the Forty Group in Nairobi; and F. Furedi, 'The African Crowd in Nairobi', pp. 282–5.
10. KNA MAA 8/109, 'Intelligence and Security: African Workers' Federation, 1947–48', for reports from C. Penfold to P. Wyn Harris of African Workers' Federation meetings in Nairobi on 25 October, 8 and 22 November, 14 and 15 December 1947, and 3 January 1948; MAA 8/105, 'Intelligence Reports: Radio Posta, 1947–48', *Radio Posta* editorial, 8 October 1947; and C. Penfold to P. Wyn Harris, 24 October 1947, See also Secretariat 1/12/8, 'Labour Unrest: Intelligence Reports, Central Province, 1947', C. Penfold to P. Wyn Harris, 29 August and 1 September 1947.
11. KNA Secretariat 1/12/8, 'Labour Unrest: Intelligence Reports, Central Province, 1947', C. Penfold to P. Wyn Harris, 9 October 1947.
12. KNA Secretariat 1/12/11, 'Labour Unrest: Notes on Communications, Supplies and Transport 1947', note to the Financial Secretary, J.F.G. Troughton, 2 February 1947 on the maintenance of essential supplies; and Secretariat 1/12/6, 'Coast Province: Labour Unrest Correspondence, 1947', G.R.B. Brown, acting PC Coast, to Foster-Sutton, 26 February and 15 March 1947; and J. Pinney, DC Isiolo, to Chief Native Commissioner, 24 March 1947. For the influence of the Tanganyika general strike, see KNA Secretariat 1/12/12, 'Labour Unrest: Inter-Territorial, 1947', Police Head Quarters, Dar-es-Salaam to Police Head Quarters, Nairobi, 30 September 1947. J. Iliffe, *A Modern History of Tanganyika*, pp. 402–4, provides a brief account of the events of September 1947 in Tanganyika.
13. KNA Secretariat 1/12/11, 'Labour Unrest: Notes on Communications, Supplies and Transport, 1947', note to J.F.G. Troughton, on maintenance of essential supplies, 2 April 1947.
14. KNA MAA 2/5/223, 'Nairobi Advisory Council, 1946–49', meetings of the Crime Committee, 19 and 26 June, and 15 August 1947; and MAA 7/491, 'Administration Policy: Urban Areas, Nairobi, 1945–47', T.G. Askwith to Marchant, Chief Native Commissioner, 9 November 1945, and to G.M. Rennie, 3 December 1945.
15. KNA MAA 7/491, 'Administration Policy: Urban Areas, Nairobi, 1945–47', T.G. Askwith to C. Tomkinson, 22 August 1945; C. Tomkinson to G.M. Rennie, 5 September 1945; T.G. Askwith's memoranda to Tomkinson, Marchant and Rennie, 14 September and 9 November 1945; and the counter-arguments of F. Khamisi, General Secretary of the Kenya African Study Union, to G.M. Rennie, 10 September 1945; and the meeting in the Secretariat between the officials and E.W. Mathu, Francis Khamisi, and F.W. Odede, 28 November 1945.
16. *ibid*, T.G. Askwith to C. Tomkinson, 22 August 1945.
17. KNA MAA 7/491 'Administration Policy: Urban Areas, Nairobi, 1945–47', note by Marchant, the Chief Native Commissioner, 19 September 1945; and by T.G. Askwith, 22 August, 27 October and 9 November 1945.
18. *ibid*. T.G. Askwith's memoranda, 9 November and 17 December 1945.
19. KNA MAA 2/5/223, 'Nairobi Advisory Council, 1946–49', Advisory Council meetings, 3–4 June and 2–3 September 1946.
20. Labour Department Annual Report, 1954, paragraph 30. In December 1953 the Kikuyu, Embu and Meru comprised 46.3 per cent of adult male African workers in Nairobi; the Luo and Abaluhya 27.6 per cent; and the Kamba 18.8 per cent. After Operation Anvil on 25 April 1954 these proportions became 26.7 per cent Kikuyu, Embu and Meru; 35.4 pe cent Luo and Abaluhya; and 25.6 per cent Kamba. The 1962 census figures were: 42.0 per cent Kikuyu; 16.9 per cent Abaluhya; 15.9 per cent Luo; 15.3 per cent Kamba; and others 9.9 per cent.

21. Legislative Council Debates, second series, vol. xx (1944–45), third session, 3 January 1945, cols. 612–649; and 10 January, cols. 651–675. Beecher had once been a student of the noted social pscychologist, Professor Sir Cyril Burt.

22. KNA MAA 2/5/223, 'Nairobi Advisory Council, 1946–49', Advisory Council meeting, 6–7 December 1948.

23. KNA Lab 9/57, 'East African Labour Conference, Entebbe, November 1949', memorandum prepared by the Kenya Labour Department on the stabilisation of labour; and Lab 9/99, 'Labour Efficiency Survey: Kenya and Uganda Railways and Harbours, Northcott Report, 1946–49', E.M. Hyde-Clarke to J.D. Rankine, 25 August and 16 September 1948; and Lab 9/2, 'Address on Labour Policy by Mr Hyde-Clarke, 1946', E.M. Hyde-Clarke, 6 November 1946.

24. CO 533/558/38715 (1948), 'Municipal African Affairs Annual Report', 1947 Report, pp. 6–7.

25. KNA Lab 9/1751, 'African Housing: General, 1946–51', T.G. Askwith to E.M. Hyde-Clarke, 20 November 1947. See also A. Hake, *African Metropolis*, pp. 48–50.

26. KNA MAA 8/22, 'City African Affairs Officer: Correspondence, 1947–50', T.G. Askwith to P.Wyn Harris, 20 November 1947; and Lab 9/1751, 'African Housing: General, 1946–51', T.G. Askwith, Annual Report on African Affairs in Nairobi, 1947, December 1947.

27. This information is taken from KNA Lab 9/1751, 'African Housing: General, 1946–51', T.G. Askwith to E.M. Hyde-Clarke, 20 November 1947.

28. *ibid*, F.W. Carpenter's memorandum on Nairobi housing, 9 March 1948; T.G. Askwith's comments on Joseph Mortimer's memorandum, 23 February 1948; and T.G. Askwith, Annual Report on African Affairs in Nairobi, 1947, December 1947.

29. *ibid*; and T.G. Askwith, Annual Report on African Affairs in Nairobi, 1948, December 1948.

30. *ibid.*

31. *ibid*, T.G. Askwith's comments on Joseph Mortimer's memorandum, 23 February 1948; and to the Town Clerk, Nairobi, 6 February 1947; F.W. Carpenter's memorandum on Nairobi housing, 9 March 1948; and E.M. Hyde-Clarke to Labour Officer, Nanyuki, 10 June 1948.

32. A. Hake, *African Metropolis*, p. 58. See also CO 533/546/38128/4 (1947–48), 'Loans: Requirements of Local Government Authorities', *passim*; and CO 533/547/38128/48 (1948–49), 'Loans: Requirements of Local Government Authorities – Nairobi Municipal Council', P.E. Mitchell to Creech Jones, 8 April 1948.

33. KNA Lab 9/1751, 'African Housing: General, 1946–51', E.A. Vasey to J.D. Rankine, 6 July 1949.

34. *ibid*, E.M. Hyde-Clarke to J.D. Rankine, 17 January 1950; and F.W. Carpenter, quoted in *East African Standard*, 15 September 1950.

35. KNA Lab 9/1751, 'African Housing: General, 1946–51', G.A. Atkinson, Colonial Liaison Officer, Building Research Station, to Colonial Labour Advisory Committee, 26 January 1950. See also H.L. Adams, Secretary for Commerce and Industry, to R.J.C. Howes, Secretary for Health and Local Government, 14 October 1949; and E.M. Hyde-Clarke to C.H. Thornley, Member for Labour, 2 February 1950; and 1949 Kenya Annual Housing Report: and F.W. Carpenter, quoted in *East African Standard*, 15 September 1950. See also KNA C&I 6/457, 'British Standard Portland Cement Co. Ltd.: Bamburi, 1951–56', *passim*; and C&I 6/390, 'Secondary Industry: Cement and Lime, 1943–49', H.L. Adams to East Africa Industrial Council, 11 May 1948; and to P. Wyn Harris, 17 July 1948; and minutes of the meeting of the East Africa Industrial Council, 10 June 1948; and the memorandum presented to the Council on proposals to manufacture cement, 22 September 1948.

36. KNA Lab 9/1751, 'African Housing: General, 1946–51', note by Miss N.M. Deverell, 28 March 1948. For the employers' response see C&I 6/445, 'Secondary Industries: East Africa Industries Ltd., 1949–53', H.W. Howell, of the Commonwealth Develop-

ment Corporation, to A. Hope-Jones, 11 September 1950; and C&I 6/243, 'East Africa Industries Ltd., 1950-57', General Manager's report, April-June 1950.

37. KNA Lab 9/60, 'Labour Conditions and Strikes, 1945-50', L. Silberman's comments on the Phillips Report, 1946, undated.

38. KNA Lab 9/1751, 'African Housing: General, 1946-51', E.M. Hyde-Clarke to J.D. Rankine, 17 January 1950; and to the Inter-African Labour Conference, Elizabethville, July 1950. See also N. Swainson, *The Development of Corporate Capitalism in Kenya*, pp. 116-18; and S.B. Stichter, *Migrant Labour in Kenya*, pp. 130-1.

39. KNA Lab 9/1751, 'African Housing: General, 1946-51', E.M. Hyde-Clarke to Labour Officer, Nanyuki, 10 June 1948. *East African Standard*, 17 August 1950, reported the rival view of the Nairobi Chamber of Commerce, which argued that 'there was definite evidence available that in a large number of cases, after a certain point had been reached, any further increases in wages resulted in a decrease in output or a reduction in working hours'; E.A. Vasey to J.D. Rankine, 6 July 1949; and T.G. Askwith, Report on African Affairs in Nairobi, 1948, December 1948.

40. A. Hake, *African Metropolis*, p. 57.

41. KNA Lab 9/1751, 'African Housing: General, 1946-51', T.G. Askwith to E.M. Hyde-Clarke, 20 November 1947; and E.M. Hyde-Clarke to C.H. Thornley, 2 February 1950; and MAA 8/22, 'City African Affairs Officer: Correspondence, 1947-50', T.G. Askwith to P. Wyn Harris, 20 November 1947.

42. CO 533/558/38715 (1948), 'Municipal African Affairs: Annual Report', contains some interesting propaganda photographs. See also KNA Lab 9/99, 'Labour Efficiency Survey: Kenya and Uganda Railways and Harbours, 1946-49', for the views of Dr C.H. Northcott, formerly Labour Manager of Rowntree and Co. Ltd, who surveyed 6,000 railwaymen in Nairobi; and the comments of E.M. Hyde-Clarke on his report, 25 August and 6 September 1949.

43. *East African Standard*, 10 April 1945.

44. KNA Lab 9/1841, 'Mombasa: Trade Disputes Tribunal, 1947', E.H. Robins's evidence, 17 February 1947; and evidence from Railways and Harbours' staff, 21, 26 and 27 February, and 4 March 1947; and Chege Kibachia of the African Workers' Federation, 29 April 1947, for the problems of surviving on subsistence wages in the urban arena. See also Lab 9/57, 'East African Labour Conference, Entebbe, November 1949', Kenya Labour Department's memorandum on stabilisation; Lab 9/30, 'Colonial Cooperation: African Labour Conference, Elizabethville, July 1950', for a discussion of African housing and sub-economic rents; Lab 9/1751, 'African Housing: General, 1946-51', E.M. Hyde-Clarke to J.D. Rankine, 17 January 1950; and Lab 9/789, 'African Affairs Committee, 1948-52', J.H. Lewis, from the African Settlement and Land Utilisation Board, memorandum on surplus population and the necessity of housing African workers outside the reserves, 14 July 1948; and T.G. Askwith's memorandum on urbanization in Kenya, 23 July 1948, for the government's view of these intractable problems.

45. KNA Lab 9/1751, 'African Housing: General, 1946-51', T.G. Askwith to E.M. Hyde-Clarke, 6 December 1950; and Dr D. Drury, Director of Medical Services, memorandum on African housing standards, 8 December 1947; and T.G. Askwith, recently promoted Commissioner for Community Development, to E.M. Hyde-Clarke, 6 December 1950. See also 'note D75', 'Space and Accommodation Standards for Low Cost Housing in Colonial Territories', May 1949, for the medical establishment's opinion.

46. *ibid*, Dr D. Drury to T.G. Askwith, 30 December 1950.

47. Editorial in *East African Standard*, 15 September 1950.

48. KNA Lab 9/1751 'African Housing: General, 1946-51', E.M. Hyde-Clarke to J.D. Rankine, 17 January 1950; and Lab 9/789, 'African Affairs Committee,

1948–52', meeting on 14 July 1948, to discuss the problem of surplus population and the need for housing African workers outside the reserves. See also F.W. Carpenter, quoted in *East African Standard*, 15 September 1950; and Lab 9/301, 'Problems of Old Age Security, 1943–45', *passim*.

49. S.B. Stichter, *Migrant Labour in Kenya*, pp. 130–1; Janet M. Bujra, 'Women entrepreneurs of Early Nairobi', pp. 213–34; S.B. Stichter, 'Workers, Trade Unions and the Mau Mau Rebellion', pp. 260–75; and N. Nelson, 'How Women and Men Get By', *passim*, for life in African Nairobi from the 1920s to the 1970s.

50. KNA CS 1/8/196, 'Cost of Living Commission: Incoming Correspondence, 1948–49', Director of Statistics, note about the General Retail Price Index, undated, but probably January 1949, and letter from the manager, Kaisugu Tea Estate, to the Commission, complaining about the price of *posho*.

51. KNA MAA 8/22, 'City African Affairs Officer: Correspondence, 1947–50', African Advisory Council to the Central Commodity Distribution Board, 22 June 1948; and Ag 4/381, 'Kiambu Monthly Agricultural Reports, 1940–49', G.J. Gollop, July–September 1947 report.

52. Graph 8.1 has been devised from information in KNA CS 1/8/196, 'Cost of Living Commission: Incoming Correspondence, 1948–49', *passim*. For a more extended treatment of these issues see S.B. Stichter, *Migrant Labour in Kenya*, pp. 130–1; and her 'Trade Unionism in Kenya', pp. 156–58; and KNA MAA 8/109, 'Intelligence and Security: African Workers' Federation, 1947–48'. See also S.B. Stichter, 'The Formation of a Working Class in Kenya', pp. 21–48.

53. G. Kitching, *Class and Economic Change in Kenya*, pp. 119–21, 129–30; and F. Furedi, 'The Social Composition of the Mau Mau Movement in the White Highlands', pp. 492–4. See also KNA DC/KBU 1/36, 'Kiambu Annual Report, 1945', p. 8.

54. KNA MAA 8/22, 'City African Affairs Officer: Correspondence, 1947–50', Tom Mbotela to Superintendent, CID, Nairobi, 28 October 1947; and T.G. Askwith to Superintendent, CID, Nairobi, 29 October 1947. This is equally true of Nairobi today, see Meja Mwangi's novels, *Kill Me Quick* and *Going Down River Road*.

55. KNA Ag 4/330, 'Provincial Agricultural Officers: Newsletters, 1939–51', T. Hughes Rice, February 1950.

56. KNA MAA 8/22, 'City African Affairs Officer: Correspondence, 1947–50', T.G. Askwith to P. Wyn Harris, 30 March 1948; and R. Frost, *Race against Time*, pp. 155–70. See also D. Goldsworthy, *Tom Mboya*, pp. 13–14, for its effect on one Nairobi African.

57. KNA Secretariat 1/12/8, 'Labour Unrest: Intelligence Reports, Central Province, 1947', C. Penfold to P. Wyn Harris, 25 September 1947; and MAA 8/109, 'Intelligence and Security: African Workers' Federation, 1947–48', C. Penfold to P. Wyn Harris, 4 November and 16 December 1947.

58. B. Kaggia, *Roots of Freedom*, pp. 78–82; and M. Singh, *History of Kenya's Trade Union Movement*, vol. 1, pp. 260–1. For Mbotela's view of the militants, see KNA MAA 8/22, 'City African Affairs Officer: Correspondence, 1947–50', Tom Mbotela to Superintendent, CID, Nairobi, 28 October 1947. See also his father's autobiography, J.E. Harris, *Recollections of James Juma Mbotela*, pp. 73–81.

59. KNA MAA 7/491, 'Administration Policy: Urban Areas, Nairobi, 1945–47', T.G. Askwith to C. Tomkinson, 22 August 1945; and CO 533/543/38086/5 (1945–47), 'Kikuyu Petitions and Memorials', Director of Intelligence and Security, Notes on African Unions, 6 November 1945, which lists the most prominent tribal and political associations. K. Little, *West African Urbanization*, pp. 24–65; and N.J. Westcott, 'Erica Fiah', pp. 88–92, provide useful summaries of their role in West Africa and in Dar-es-Salaam.

60. KNA MAA 8/105, 'Intelligence Reports: Radio Posta, 1947–48', C. Penfold to P. Wyn Harris, 24 October 1947, and *Radio Posta*, 16 October 1947. D. Parkin, *The Cultural Definition of Political Response*, pp. 36–44, details why the Luo in Nairobi have congregated in Kaloleni. It should, however, be remembered that this ethnic exclusive-

ness was fostered by the colonial government after Operation Anvil in April 1954, when Kaloleni became an almost exclusively Luo estate, and the Kikuyu, Embu and Meru were concentrated in Bahati. Tom Mboya was one of the few non-Kikuyu to live in Bahati at the height of the Emergency. See D. Goldsworthy, *Tom Mboya*, p. 28.

61. KNA Lab 9/1751, 'African Housing: General, 1946–51', T.G. Askwith, Annual Report on African Affairs in Nairobi, 1947, December 1947.

62. Legislative Council Debates, second series, vol. xx (1944–45), third session, 4 January 1945, Archadeacon L.J. Beecher, col. 505.

63. KNA MAA 7/491, 'Administration Policy: Urban Areas, Nairobi, 1945–47', T.G. Askwith to C. Tomkinson, 22 August 1945; MAA 8/22, 'City African Affairs Officer: Correspondence, 1947–50', T.G. Askwith to Superintendent, CID, Nairobi, 29 October 1947; and Lab 9/87, 'Labour Troubles: Nairobi, 1950', extract from *East African Standard*, 24 May 1950.

64. Legislative Council Debates, second series, vol. xx (1944–45), third session, 4 January 1945, Archadeacon L.J. Beecher, col. 505; KNA MAA 7/377, 'Legislation: Urban Pass Laws, 1946', *passim*; MAA 8/22, 'City African Affairs Officer: Correspondence, 1947–50', minutes of meetings to discuss vagrancy bylaws, 29 June, 9 August, 8 September and 12 October 1948, and 11 January 1949. See also MAA 2/5/223, 'Nairobi Advisory Council, 1946/49', Advisory Council meeting 21–22 January 1946, and the Crime Committee meetings on 19 and 26 June, and 15 August 1947. The meeting of the Advisory Council on 13–14 September 1948, however, expressed its 'thanks to Government for the way in which Bylaws (211 and 212) were being enforced, and congratulated the police on its efforts. It was recommended that the Spiv Squad should concentrate on Kariakor and Shauri Moyo, and the taxi ranks, and should work at night'.

65. KNA MAA 8/22, 'City African Affairs Officer: Correspondence, 1947–50', T.G. Askwith to Superintendent, CID, Nairobi, 29 October 1947; and MAA 2/5/223, 'Nairobi Advisory Council, 1946–49', Crime Committee, 19 and 26 June, and 15 August 1947; and the full Advisory Council meetings, 1–2 March and 13–14 September 1948. G.R.B. Brown's 'Observations on the Nairobi Strike', 23 May 1950, are interesting. When Askwith went on leave to Britain in 1949, before being appointed Commissioner for Community Development, Brown, who had been African Affairs Officer in Mombasa, was transferred to Nairobi to prevent a bid by the Municipal Council to appoint its own man to the post rather than to rely on the secondment of a member of the administration to the staff of the Municipal Council. This issue had caused concern both to the Secretariat and to the Nairobi African Advisory Council before Askwith's departure. See correspondence in MAA 8/22.

66. KNA MAA 7/491, 'Administration Policy: Urban Areas, Nairobi, 1945–47', T.G. Askwith's memorandum on African Grievances, 14 .September 1945. See also CO 533/545/38091/10 (1944–47), 'Labour Registration and Identification, 1944–47', report of the sub-committee of the Labour Advisory Board, December 1946; and comments of G. Orde-Browne, 5 February 1947, for African opposition to the *kipande*.

67. M. Singh, *History of Kenya's Trade Union Movement*, vol. 1, pp. 240–50.

68. With the ending of the building campaign in 1948, the government relied increasingly on the vagrancy laws to resolve Nairobi's social problems. See MAA 8/22, 'City African Affairs Officer: Correspondence, 1947–50', meetings to discuss the relationship between crime, unemployment and vagrancy, 29 June, 9 August, 8 September, and 12 October 1948, and 11 January 1949. See also CO 533/556/38666 (1946–48), 'Removal of Undesirable Natives (Temporary) Legislation', P.E. Mitchell to George Hall, 4 May 1946; and Creech Jones's comments, 2 January 1948.

69. CO 533/566/6 (1950), 'Temporary Removal of Undesirable Natives Legislation', *passim*; and M. Singh, *History of Kenya's Trade Union Movement*, vol. 1, pp. 248–9.

70. *ibid*, pp. 252–3; and *Daily Chronicle*, 7 March 1950; and F.D. Corfield, 'Origins and Growth of Mau Mau', p. 83.

71. KNA Lab 9/87, 'Labour Troubles: Nairobi, 1950', cutting from *East African Standard*, 17 May 1950, giving details of the Essential Services (Arbitration) Ordinance; *Kenya Daily Mail*, 16 May 1950; and M. Singh, *History of Kenya's Trade Union Movement*, vol. 1, pp. 268–71. For details of the trials see M. Singh, pp. 277–86; and *East African Standard*, 24 May 1950, and 30 January, 1, 2, 3, 4, 7, 8, 14 and 17 February 1951.

72. M. Singh, *History of Kenya's Trade Union Movement*, vol. 1, p. 276; and F.D. Corfield, 'Origins and Growth of Mau Mau', p. 89.

73. *The Times*, 19 May 1950, and *East African Standard*, 19 May 1950.

74. M. Singh, *History of Kenya's Trade Union Movement*, vol. 1 pp. 272–7. Contrast with the comments of the Attorney General, K.K. O'Connor, reported in *Daily Herald*, 19 May 1950. When Eliud Mathu tried to speak to the strikers, he was shouted down and accused of being 'a traitor, bribed by Europeans'; see KNA Lab 9/87, report 20 May 1950; *The Times*, 20 May 1950; and *The Observer*, 21 May 1950.

75. *East African Standard*, 23 and 24 May 1950; and F.D. Corfield, 'Origins and Growth of Mau Mau', p. 89.

76. *East African Standard*, 24 May 1950. F. Furedi, 'The African Crowd in Nairobi', pp. 279–88; and S.B. Stichter, 'Trade Unionism in Kenya', pp. 167–72 and 'Workers, Trade Unions, and the Mau Mau Rebellion', *passim* (except p. 260) failed to recognise this fatal flaw in the campaign of the Nairobi militants, who were overwhelmingly Kikuyu.

77. F. Furedi, 'The African Crowd in Nairobi', pp. 285–8; and S.B. Stichter, 'Workers, Trade Unions, and the Mau Mau Rebellion', pp. 266–75; B. Kaggia, *Roots of Freedom*, pp. 79–82, 107–16; J. Spencer, 'Kenya African Union and Mau Mau', pp. 217–18; and C.G. Rosberg and J. Nottingham, *The Myth of Mau Mau*, pp. 269–76.

78. KNA Lab 9/1751, 'African Housing: General, 1946–51', E.M. Hyde-Clarke to J.D. Rankine, 17 January 1950, quoting his speech in the Legislative Council on 21 December 1949. See also MAA 8/22, 'City African Affairs Officer: Correspondence, 1947–50', G.R.B. Brown, 'Observations on the Nairobi Strike', 23 May 1950.

79. F.D. Corfield, 'Origins and Growth of Mau Mau', p. 89; and KNA Lab 9/87, 'Labour Troubles: Nairobi, 1950', *passim*. *The Times*, 26 May 1950, observed that 'the Kenya Government has tried to establish trade unionism on a sound basis among Africans, but has failed through the immaturity of the Africans who have been swayed by propaganda'.

80. KNA Lab 9/87, 'Labour Troubles: Nairobi, 1950', extracts from *Kenya Weekly News*, 26 May 1950; and *Tribune*, 26 May 1950. MAA 8/71, 'Communism, 1948–49', especially the meeting of the Secretariat sub-committee on communist subversion, 10 January 1949; and CO 537/4317/14322/10 (1949), 'Communism in the Colonies: East Africa', for a long report by P.E. Mitchell, November 1949.

Nine

A Change of Direction: the Agricultural Department's Abandonment of Communalism

With the breakdown of the conservation campaign following the peasant revolt, many agricultural officers recognised that many Kikuyu had been alienated by compulsory terracing and began to search for new ways of safeguarding the land. The field administration was sceptical of the new proposals and continued to rely upon the *Muhirig'a* elders and compulsion. Gradually the agricultural department won the argument, and, between 1950 and 1952, the Secretariat reluctantly accepted that progressive cultivators should be rewarded with the right to grow high-value cash crops, which had been restricted to settler farmers. This belated acceptance of African proto-capitalists, however, came too late to gain new support for the colonial state. If positive steps had been introduced in 1945, or even in 1948 after the collapse of the communal campaign, it might have been possible for the colonial régime to broaden its support, but the administration's opposition had delayed the adoption of the new strategy and by 1952 few benefits had filtered down to the Kikuyu peasantry.[1] In Meru and Embu, in contrast, where the district agricultural officers, Jack Benson and Leslie Brown, had experimented with peasant cash-crop production, many Africans by 1952 were already reaping the financial rewards. Consequently, these districts remained comparatively quiet during the Mau Mau Emergency.[2]

Field administration and agricultural department attitudes to the peasant option

In 1945 Tomkinson warned that African commercial cultivators would be forced to obey the *Muhirig'a* and to follow the agricultural regulations. He also reaffirmed that it was the government's policy to oppose the evolution of a class of large landowners, who would employ agricultural labourers.[3] These limitations inevitably slowed down the expansion of Kikuyu participation in the market economy. In addition, the opportunity was spurned to broaden the collaborative base of the colonial state and to incorporate the supporters of the Kenya African Union. Even the liberal minded Wyn Harris failed to realised that the administration's attempt to block the advance of the proto-capitalists and to shore up the authority of the chiefs, while increasing intervention in peasant agriculture, was alienating the people.[4] Until his departure for the Gambia, Wyn Harris remained one of the main supporters of the *Muhirig'a*'s attempt to supervise the agricultural campaign and a convinced opponent of any effort to reverse the communal strategy.

When Mathu and Kenyatta warned the Secretariat in August 1947, at the height of the disturbances in Murang'a, that unless the Settlement Board paid more attention to the criticism of the Machakos Local Native Council, Makueni would become another centre of confrontation between Africans and the government, their advice was ignored.[5] Cavendish-Bentinck had been informed that the African members of the Settlement Board were becoming restless and might resign because of pressure from Kenyatta over section 65 of the Native Lands' Trust Ordinance of 1938, which empowered the Board to oversee the agricultural campaign in the reserves.[6] Initially it seemed as if the protests in Murang'a and Olenguruone had merely strengthened the government's resolve to push ahead with terracing and to support the chiefs and the *Muhirig'a*. Sorrenson has suggested that 'the spirit of social reform which was abroad in Europe, and which in 1945 led to a Labour Government in Britain, was in Africa reinvigorating the ghosts of indirect rule'.[7] After 1947 this began slowly to change. The peasants' revolt destroyed Mitchell's agricultural strategy, not because compulsion was unable to produce a fundamental restructuring of African agriculture – although this was true – but because it had failed to incorporate the proto-capitalists in a wider political alliance, which could prop up the colonial state when the development campaign alienated the peasantry.

After 1947, the agricultural department, led by Leslie Brown, who had been transferred from Nigeria, belatedly attempted to appeal to this emerging élite and to broaden the colonial state's established clients with loans, individual land titles and high-value cash crops.[8] These rewards, they hoped, would provide a more powerful inducement to better farming than compulsion. Unfortunately these were at first minority views, even in the agricultural department. The communalists inside the agricultural department, led by Hughes Rice and the Provincial Agricultural Officer in Central Province, Trevor Moon, resisted Brown's new strategy, but by 1951 Brown had become the most influential agriculturalist in Kenya and Hughes Rice's ideas were discarded. He was then transferred from

Central Province to the backwaters of Nyanza where he could do less harm.[9]

From 1950 until the Emergency was declared in October 1952, the agricultural department and the field administration were locked in battle over the agriculturalists' new strategy.[10] Brown and his colleagues insisted that the peasant revolts in 1947 and 1948 were clear demonstrations of the depth of Kikuyu opposition to the compulsory agricultural betterment campaign, especially communal terracing. To press ahead and to ignore African protests was to ask for trouble; a new, more attractive approach was required, which would lessen suspicions about the second colonial occupation and persuade people voluntarily to adopt the new agricultural methods on their *shambas*. Compulsion had failed; African cultivators would have to be enticed to terrace their land and to reduce their dependence on maize and wattle.[11]

The evolution of a new consensus

Maher, the soil conservationist, had always advocated rewarding those who supported the agricultural betterment campaign.[12] He was now supported by Leslie Brown, who argued that 'progressive' African cultivators who followed the agricultural regulations should be given permission to grow high-value crops, such as coffee and tea, which had previously been restricted to settlers. Brown was determined to improve the tarnished image of the agricultural department among Africans, who had come to equate it with compulsory labour.[13] Brown and Maher were the two most able agriculturalists in Kenya and both were to acquire reputations far beyond the colony for their work and abrasiveness. Neither of them would tolerate opposition or interference from Nairobi. It was, therefore, almost inevitable that the collaboration would be marred by conflict.[14]

This began when Brown criticised the department for its obsession with narrow-base terracing. He advocated broad-base terracing, which although more difficult to construct would provide more permanent defences against erosion and, within a few years, would reduce the burden of communal terracing. Agricultural officers would cease being glorified policemen and would be able to devote their attentions to experiments with improved crops and techniques – tasks to which Brown was then able to devote less than 10 per cent of his time.[15]

At first Brown made little progress, even among his fellow agriculturalists. In February 1950, Trevor Moon, the Provincial Agricultural Officer, was still confident that compulsory narrow-base terracing would succeed. During 1949 the campaign had gathered momentum again and the acreage protected was now 47 per cent higher than in 1948.[16] Even in Machakos, the terracing figures for the last six months of 1949 were 200 per cent higher than they had been for the first half of the year, and

Hughes Rice had reported that in Nyeri nearly all the adult males were now digging terraces. Opposition also appeared to be declining in Murang'a where sub-location targets had been issued. November 1949, saw more than 1,000 acres terraced in a month for the first time since the 1947 disturbances.[17]

In 1950, however, the agricultural headquarters in Nairobi was dramatically reformed. Two assistant directors were appointed from outside Kenya: Roger Swynnerton, whose name was to become synonymous with the encouragement of peasant commodity production, was to supervise all fieldwork and Dr Tom Webster was to co-ordinate planning and research. This reorganisation freed G.M. Roddan, the deputy director, to liaise with the districts and to integrate local initiatives, such as Brown's in Embu, into central policy.[18] Swynnerton's appointment was particularly significant as it provided Brown and his supporters with a powerful defender in Nairobi. Swynnerton had been closely involved with encouraging African coffee and cotton cultivation in Tanganyika and had helped devise the Sukumaland development scheme, the most ambitious development project yet undertaken in East Africa which was designed to encourage African cash-crop cultivation.[19]

Under pressure from Brown and Swynnerton, by May 1951, even Moon was beginning to reconsider his position and to acknowledge that compulsory terracing had largely failed.[20] Swynnerton and Brown had already decided that African support for the conservation campaign would have to be 'bought'. Their new strategy rejected the communalist assumptions of the policy debates of 1944 and 1945 and encouraged individual enterprise. They sought to create a stratum of prosperous smallholders who practised mixed farming rotations and were allowed to grow high-value cash crops on permanent bench terraces, while domestic food crops were concentrated on the ridge tops. Brown confidently estimated that such families would be able to earn a cash income of at least £100 plus subsistence, compared to Humphrey's target figure of between £18 and £20.[21]

These advocates of change in the agricultural department also forced the administration to reconsider its opposition to individual land titles and loans for Africans.[22] Ever since the early 1920s, these issues had provided a rallying cry for all shades of African political opinion, ranging from the chiefs to the Kikuyu Central Association.[23] Until the late 1940s, their demands had been ignored but, as the reassessment of agricultural policy gathered momentum, the administration began to consider the issues more carefully. Any move towards individual titles in Kenya's African reserves should fulfil four aims. It should ensure sound agricultural practices were followed by those who gained individual titles; prevent fragmentation and the emergence of sub-economic holdings; provide security for Africans who wished to buy more land or improve their *shambas by* removing the fear that the land could be redeemed under Kikuyu law without any compensation for improvements; and provide security on which long-term agricultural credit could be based.[24]

When this question was considered in Whitehall in December 1944, the Colonial Office's Committee on African Land Tenure insisted that it was essential 'to ensure that the community retains the power to guard against the growth of individual rights in land, while at the same time not impeding the development of such rights, under the proper control of the community, to the extent that they are an essential concomitant of economic growth or social progress'.[25] Humphrey's investigations in Nyeri in 1944 had convinced many administrators that individualism was already rampant among the Kikuyu and needed to be curtailed if land degradation was to be reversed.[26] The Committee's declaration seemed to justify a strident reassertion of communal authority after the uncontrolled war years. Three years later in a very different climate it could equally be used to justify the new policies of Brown and his colleagues, which recognised the changes in Kikuyu society and, in a reversal of Tomkinson's and Mitchell's policies, attempted to construct a new network of collaborators, who would be dependent upon government loans and technical advice.[27]

Under pressure from the agricultural department and the Kenya African Union a committee was eventually appointed under J.H. Ingham to consider introducing agricultural credit for Africans. Its ponderous interim report of October 1949 highlighted the conflict between the paternalism of the administration and the commitment of certain agriculturalists to a more *laissez-faire* approach. The committee admitted that African agricultural productivity could be increased only by borrowing capital to introduce improved farming techniques, but it also declared: 'At the outset, however, we must state emphatically the dangers inherent in any attempt to make credit available in an agricultural community at that stage of development which the African had reached today.'[28] The difference between Kenya and the various colonies in which government loans had been introduced was that those schemes had been designed to mitigate the evil effects of existing debts to private money lenders who did not exist in Kenya. The committee, therefore, considered that: 'We would be doing the country a permanent disservice were we to advocate the introduction of a widespread scheme of agricultural credit which would result in agriculturalists living permanently in advance of their income and under the continual fear of foreclosure.'[29] The field administration was also concerned about the political dangers associated with loans guaranteed by land – the only property of sufficient value most Africans could offer as security. Foreclosure would involve a political confrontation, as the peasantry would consider it a direct attack on their land rights by the settler-controlled government.[30]

The main problem was that, although the granting of a lease would provide security, Africans could still be evicted if they did not obey the agricultural regulations. Their security was thus far from absolute, especially if the banks were to be allowed to foreclose on defaulters. Most Africans were unwilling to accept a scheme that declared the land they considered their property was only held on a 21 year lease. Mathu, the only African on the Ingham Committee, refused to sign the report since he considered it exaggerated the danger of large-scale defaulting and set interest rates so high that most potential borrowers would be discouraged from applying.[31] Although most agricultural officers favoured the changes, the administration remained apprehensive. Despite the Provincial Commissioners' decision in April 1948 to experiment with special titles in Kiambu, the district where the pressure for individual titles was strongest, no action was taken.[32]

It should be noted, however, that greater acceptance of individualism could be a double-edged weapon. Although it could be used, as Brown and Benson wished, to co-opt the proto-capitalists into the government's alliance and to strengthen the peasant option, it could also be used by the settlers and their supporters in the Secretariat to enforce agricultural reform in an even more draconian manner, completely overriding any African opposition by the threat of mass evictions for those who disobeyed the conservation regulations. The attack on African communalism did not only come from the Kenya African Union and the new co-optive strategy, which was being devised by some local agricultural officers. The settlers and some 'hard men' in the Secretariat, notably R.P. Armitage, the Assistant Secretary for Agriculture, were also beginning to question whether African customs were hindering the progress of the second colonial occupation. They did not want to incorporate the African alternative élite, which supported Kenyatta and the Kenya African Union, but to override opposition to essential conservation measures. The destruction of the land, they argued, would be stopped only when those who refused to accept agricultural orders were evicted. Such an approach, of course, necessitated a fundamental change in attitudes towards African land tenure and a move to individualism.[33]

In a secret report, Armitage reminded his colleagues in the Secretariat and other policy makers that the Kenya Land Commission had proposed that the government should guide tenure from native custom towards individual titles. This attack from the hardliners on African communal land tenure provides a timely reminder that the post-war development campaign had stemmed from an altruistic desire to serve African interests, despite the fact that it had been based upon the paternalist preconceptions of a few key individuals, most notably Mitchell, Wyn Harris, Lambert and Humphrey, rather than upon a premeditated attempt to allow the settlers to destroy the peasant option. These paternalist defenders of African communalism, therefore, by the early 1950s were bring criticised by both the advocates of peasant commodity production – the economic manifestation of Cohen's co-optive strategy – and the pro-settler lobby which feared the emergence of a new group of collaborators who might use the peasant option to undermine the settlers' economic hegemony. Under this combined onslaught, the resistance of the administration to individual titles and consolidation slowly began to diminish.[34]

Eventually, in 1951, the Ingham Committee tentatively proposed establishing a few co-operative credit societies and offering some carefully-monitored loans, issued by the Government Land Bank on the recommendation of district committees composed of the District Commissioner, the local agricultural and veterinary officers and two Africans. Preference, it was suggested, should be given to co-operative societies or to individuals organised in group farms or co-operative credit societies. A few individuals of proven farming ability were also to be eligible, provided their applications were approved by the location council. Should a location earn a bad name for defaulting, then loans would be curtailed and additional funds allocated to areas that repaid promptly. It was hoped that this measure would inculcate a sense of financial responsibility into the location councils and associate them with the scheme. Communal land tenure, however, remained inviolate. Personal character, either individual or collective, had to provide the main proof of security, since both Mitchell and H.E. Lambert refused to countenance any tampering with African communal tenure.[35] This debate over individualism and loans was not confined to Kenya. These challenges to pre-war ideas of 'organic' development had been discussed at the Cambridge Summer School in 1947, and at Jos in Nigeria two years later, but the problems of intellectual adjustment were especially difficult in pioneering colonies like Kenya. Gradually, however, the agriculturalists undermined the confidence of the administration and forced it to consider new options.[36]

Too little, too late: the failure of co-option

The agricultural department's new strategy, however, could only be introduced once most arable land had been terraced. Only then could the positive elements designed to raise African living standards come to the fore, such as mixed farming, crop rotations, enclosure, individual titles and land consolidation. Unfortunately compulsory terracing had destroyed any chance there might have been of gaining new collaborators. After 1945 the administration opposed the peasant option and refused to abandon either its communalist ideology or its alliance with the Kikuyu chiefs.[37] When the agricultural department belatedly began once again to encourage peasant production and to seek an alliance with the entrepreneurial élite of Kikuyuland, it was four years too late. Four years of compulsory terracing had alienated the peasantry and discredited the moderate African politicians who had sought incorporation. The peasant revolt of 1947, which had precipitated the agricultural department's new strategy of greater sensitivity to African opinion, had itself demonstrated the depth of peasant discontent which would have to be overcome in Kikuyuland. By 1947 the Kikuyu reserves were irredeemably alienated from the colonial régime. The changes in agricultural policy were insufficiently dramatic to regain lost ground. The new policy of promoting smallholder production advanced very slowly and by 1952 few Kikuyu had gained any benefits.[38]

The strategy was based upon careful analysis of local vegetation, soils and rainfall patterns to discover which cash and subsistence crops were best suited to a particular area. Brown, who was a trained zoologist as well as an agriculturalist, devised precise zonal agricultural plans during 1951 and 1952.[39] The first priority of these plans was to ensure that each zone was self-sufficient in food, since it was feared that North Nyanza and the Trans Nzoia might soon be unable to meet rising demand.[40] The other feature of the plans was the introduction of high-value cash crops, which would raise average household cash earnings to £100 per annum and also act as an incentive to the adoption of an integrated and sound farming system, since only those cultivators who obeyed the agricultural regulations were to be allowed to grow the new crops.[41]

Essentially Brown was proposing that the Kikuyu proto-capitalists be rewarded with loans, technical advice and new remunerative crops. This, of course, was completely the reverse of the administration's shibboleths. The individualists were now to be courted and rewarded on condition they supported the agricultural betterment campaign. A few 'progressive' farmers were already leading the way. The agricultural department hoped that, as they became increasingly numerous and prosperous, others would be encouraged to co-operate. In Kiambu, for example, one farmer was earning £400 per annum from his ten-acre plot; another received £100 a year from selling carnations to the Nairobi market and £400 from pyrethrum.[42] Brown estimated that it was theoretically possible to earn 5,700 shillings per annum from a six and a half acre plot, with two acres of arable land, three acres grazing, and half an acre of fodder crops, poultry or fruit and, most important, half an acre of coffee.[43] In practice, he set his sights rather lower and aimed to generate £100 surplus income per household per annum.[44] In theory, this appeared to be an ideal solution to 'the roots of rural poverty', which, according to Humphrey's calculations, would admirably suit the average-sized Kikuyu holding. The abandonment of the settlers' monopoly on high-value cash crops, which Humphrey had failed to tackle, appeared to have transformed the economic potential and rewards of the peasant option.

A Change of Direction

Although estimates of the profitability per acre of various crops can be misleading, varying considerably according to the fertility of the soil and climatic conditions, they do demonstrate the dramatic difference between the prices offered for the new cash crops with which the agricultural department could reward collaborators, and the staple crops of the Kikuyu *shamba*. It should, of course, be remembered that the acreages of the new high-price crops were carefully restricted by agricultural officers.

Table 9.1: *Comparative Profitability per acre of Selected Crops in Central Province in 1952*

Tobacco (prepared as snuff)	9,000 shillings
Coffee (maximum)	7,310 shillings
Pineapple	6,230 shillings
Coffee (minimum)	2,150 shillings
Potatoes	1,485 shillings
Pyrethrum (mature)	1,290 shillings
Sisal	784 shillings
Castor Oil Seed	450 shillings
Tobacco (finely cured)	187 shillings
Pyrethrum (immature)	180 shillings and 60 cents
Green Gram	139 shillings and 13 cents
Maize	131 shillings and 35 cents
Beans	121 shillings and 16 cents
Other Pulses	90 shillings and 75 cents
Wattle Bark	87 shillings
Millets	57 shillings and 13 cents

The new strategy was implemented most quickly in Meru and in Embu, where Brown himself had been agricultural officer. In Embu he had ensured that the new approach was introduced earlier and encouraged more assiduously than in other parts of Central Province where the agricultural department was still recovering from the 1947 revolt and had not yet had time to reconsider its policies.[45] The quick adoption of the scheme in Meru sprang from the fact that the district had been the scene of experiments with African coffee growing since 1937. It was, therefore, not a question of starting from scratch, preparing the district for new cash crops, but of expanding the existing plots.[46] Moreover, in Meru the *Njuri Ncheke* had been encouraged to direct agricultural programmes since the 1920s. It was not, therefore, regarded as an alien resuscitation but was acknowledged by the people to have a legitimate right to intervene. Meru Africans, therefore, enjoyed the rewards of the new tactics much earlier than the Kikuyu. By 1952, for example, there

were more than 6,473 coffee growers with 1,822 acres of coffee trees compared to less than 1,000 growers in 1948.[47] Jack Benson, the local agricultural officer, triumphantly observed that:

> My contention that the development of the coffee industry would even-
> tually lead to improved systems of agriculture in those areas where it
> was started are I believe now being justified. The rapid progress
> towards a better system of agriculture which is being developed in
> Chogoria . . . can be attributed largely to the fact that growers, having
> followed our advice on coffee with remarkable success have become so
> confident that they will now follow it in other directions.[48]

Only those cultivators who had built cattle bomas, terraced their land,
and manured their crops had been allowed to plant coffee. The rest had
seen the advantages of co-operation and had begun to adopt some of the
recommended farming techniques in the hope that they too would eventually be rewarded with the privilege of coffee growing. Benson explained
his tactics: 'Those people who are most progressive individually are
assisted to the fullest extent for it is through them that we have been able,
to a slow and increasing extent, to modify useful customs and to weaken
and dispense with the bad ones.'[49] This meant that the Meru peasantry
had quickly perceived that there was a close relationship between acceptance of agricultural regulations and wealth from coffee.

Meru, however, was a large, fertile district, covering 3,740 square
miles. Land was not a scarce resource as among the Kikuyu. Kiambu, for
example, had 20 per cent more people than Meru on less than one-sixth
the area. The struggle for land and possible ecological collapse were much
less acute, therefore, than in Kikuyuland. Of the three Kikuyu districts,
Nyeri was the one where the agricultural officers found it easiest to persuade the district administration to adopt the new strategy. The Nyeri
betterment scheme had originated from the plans of the local agricultural
committee in 1948, and was in many respects the most carefully integrated of the various development plans. It was based upon encouraging
mixed farming throughout the area. Progress, however, varied considerably. While fragmented holdings had largely been consolidated in
Chief Muhoya's location in North Tetu, there were few progressive
farmers in Othaya.[50]

Much of the success of the Nyeri scheme was due to Osborne, who
became District Commissioner after his successful tour in Murang'a. As
early as 1948, he had endorsed plans to introduce coffee, pyrethrum and
tea, and, with the enthusiastic support of his agriculturalists, had
organised marketing and the processing of African co-operative
societies.[51] The district was later divided by Brown into three agricultural
zones based on rainfall and altitude. In the highest zone, which in 1948
was largely uninhabited and covered with bracken, dairy farming and

wattle plantations were encouraged. It was hoped that once this land, which was over 6,000 feet, had been cleared and opened to pasture following a communal grass-planting campaign, it would relieve the population pressure on the overcrowded middle zone, between 4,500 and 6,000 feet, and demonstrate the economic potential of a few well-nourished cows. It was hoped that this would encourage others to introduce paddocking, rotational grazing, stock dipping and controlled breeding. Grass, it was predicted, would prove to be a highly remunerative cash crop, once it had 'metamorphosed' into milk.[52]

The middle zone was the most densely populated part of all three Kikuyu districts, with population densities in some locations of over 600 to the square mile. It was, therefore, the area most urgently in need of a high-value cash crop to relieve pressure on the land. Coffee and commercial fruit growing were to provide the financial incentive to agricultural improvements in these areas. Permission to cultivate these new crops, of course, was initially restricted to those who had already accepted the agricultural department's advice, which usually meant the chiefs and their supporters. Thus, malcontents were still excluded from sharing the district's new prosperity. The new strategy had not yet broadened the base of collaboration in the middle zone. In the lowest, more arid areas, mixed farming, tobacco and rice were to be introduced to stimulate similar farming improvements, but these also had not yet filtered down to the mass of the people.[53]

In theory, the new agricultural campaign coincided for the first time with the ambitions of ordinary Africans and offered them a higher standard of living in return for supporting the colonial order. In practice, however, the campaign was still dominated by terracing, since all these who wished to be considered to grow the new crops had to protect their slopes. Little seemed to have changed. Schools were used to demonstrate better farming methods and to propagate bench terracing. Dotted around the district, existing in all agricultural and climatic zones, they provided a far more extensive system of demonstration centres in which the rewards of co-operation could be clearly shown. The agricultural officer in Murang'a enthusiastically declared that 'all this adds up to the finest form of propaganda imaginable – the impetus from within'. Many parents, however, objected to having to help build the schools' terraces or to provide stock. It seemed to be yet one more infringement of African freedom by the second colonial occupation.[54]

Agricultural progress and the emergence of new collaborators was still very slow. Brown, for example, complained that although in certain locations the proportion of land under sound use was considerably above the general mean, particularly in the Iriaini and North Tetu locations of Nyeri, Chief Magugu's locations in Kiambu and the bracken zone of Murang'a, in most parts of Central Province improvements remained 'pitifully inadequate'. The vast majority of the Province, he reported, was:

> still covered with fragmented holdings run on a primitive shifting culti-
> vation system, which, in less fertile soil, would have brought ruin long
> ago. There are large areas where, as far as the eye can see, the land is
> still one hundred per cent unsoundly used, though various rot stopping
> measures such as narrow base terraces have been put in . . . Progress
> in improved farming is still nowhere near keeping pace with increasing
> population, fragmentation and degeneration.[55]

If the agricultural department could as yet see little return from the new
approach this was even more true of the Africans.

The second colonial occupation had enabled the state bureaucracy to
penetrate to new depths and had profoundly disrupted Kikuyu life. The
following extract from the safari diaries of the agricultural officer in
Murang'a show just how demanding the new agricultural rules were on
the ordinary Kikuyu when the might of the government descended upon
them as never before. In February 1948, he inspected work in headman
Ngure's part of Location 2 near Kirera. He noted:

Kirera: Shocking demonstration of terraces. Mere scratches in the
              ground neither wide nor deep enough. Assistant Agricul-
              tural Instructor Pithon Kamau. Another lot of terraces dug
              by the same group rather worse. Kaptein told to redig all
              immediately and Agricultural Instructor Geoffrey to
              ensure correct size.

Gathanjo: Eight men digging. Work quite fair. Found a young man
              sitting at home so his *shamba* was terraced on the spot
              (Nganga Kareja).

Irati: Nothing doing at all. Told Agricultural Instructor to start
              individual measuring . . . A woman name Wambui
              Gikonyo, a widow, found digging up a good runway near
              the Irati bridge. To be run (i.e. prosecuted) at once and all
              to be grassed in the rains. Njeha Warugi of Gathanje mak-
              ing *tembo*. Headman Ngure says he has permission but very
              much doubt it. The drinking in this sub-location is very
              bad – led by Headman?[56]

Such in-depth pressure continued throughout Mitchell's governorship
and European inspection became increasingly regular. On reading these
agricultural reports of the late 1940s one is struck by how often the Kikuyu
had to redig all the terraces they had so laboriously constructed because of
a mistake by the Assistant Agricultural Instructor. Almost invariably in
the early years of the agricultural betterment campaign the terraces were
incorrectly marked out at the contour and were virtually useless. Until
1950, the expansion in the number of barely trained agricultural staff far

exceeded the ability of the small experienced staff to inspect their work on a regular basis. This meant that when the agricultural officer eventually did manage to get round the locations, he found much of the work had been so badly supervised that it had to be done again.[57] This, of course, further antagonised the peasantry and destroyed their support for the agricultural betterment campaign. By the time there were enough European supervisory staff to keep a close eye on development schemes throughout the district, most of the population had been completely alienated from agricultural development schemes by their previous experiences and were extremely suspicious of anything the government proposed.[58] In 1945 there had usually been only one European agricultural officer per district, who relied on a handful of African assistants, but by 1952 European staff were thick on the ground, interfering in virtually every facet of Kikuyu life.[59]

In Nyeri, for example, there were nine European officers, including the provincial headquarters' staff, by the time the Emergency was declared. In 1952, Embu had ten European agriculturalists, Machakos eleven, Murang'a five, Kiambu four, Meru three, and Kitui only two. The total African staff employed on agricultural work in Central Province had also expanded dramatically since the war. In 1952, the agricultural department employed 373 Africans, the African district councils had 1,199 (with the Development and Reconstruction Authority employing another 429 in the province), the African Settlement and Land Utilization Board 1,053, and the agricultural development programme a mere twelve. By the Emergency, therefore, there were 44 European agriculturalists in Central Province to supervise 3,066 Africans. Meanwhile the staff of the veterinary department had expanded equally dramatically and by 1952 numbered nearly 1,000 in Central Province.[60] This tremendous expansion meant that even the most recalcitrant African could not escape the two technical departments. The agricultural officer in Murang'a, for example, received reports on the smallholding of the Kikuyu Central Association activist, Job Muchuchu, which was condemned for its 'filthy compound and revolting pig styes'.[61] Muchuchu, it is interesting to note, was generally regarded as a successful fruit farmer with carefully cultivated crops of oranges, lemons and custard apples. The agricultural department's increased manpower enabled it to concentrate upon known recalcitrants and to force them to adopt new techniques and to terrace their land, while the veterinary department harassed them until they began to innoculate and cull their cattle.[62]

As Table 9.2 shows, by the early 1950s the demands of the second colonial occupation were far above the levels of 1947, when communal terracing had provoked such virulent opposition:[63]

215

Table 9.2: *Terraces Constructed in South Nyeri, 1945 to 1954*

	Narrow-base Terraces	Bench Terraces
1945	637 miles	nil
1946	654 miles	nil
1947	1,865 miles	nil
1948	c.2,500 miles	nil
1949	c.2,500 miles	nil
1950	3,155 miles	21 miles
1951	3,833 miles	61 miles
1952	3,832 miles	228 miles
1953	1,382 miles	250 miles
1954	1,079 miles	1,452 miles

Brown's strategy of building the more durable bench terraces only really gathered momentum after the declaration of the Emergency. In 1951 and 1952, as far as the Kikuyu peasants were concerned, the agricultural campaign was indistinguishable from the earlier communal approach. So far only known supporters of the colonial régime had been rewarded with the lucrative new cash crops. According to official calculations, the average family income in the middle zone of Murang'a was still only 918 shillings per annum, and 735 shillings in the bracken zone.[64] Although earnings were estimated to have increased fourfold since 1947, in real terms little improvement had occurred and production had ceased to grow. The explanation for this failure to translate the new policy into positive results was that Brown's plans to promote peasant production and to reward collaborators with high-price cash crops had been undermined by the field administration, which had delayed action until it was too late.

Many Local Native Councils had also diverted revenue raised by the agricultural cess to non-agricultural purposes, with less than 25 per cent being ploughed back into agricultural improvements. This obstructionist attitude on the part of District Commissioners and Local Native Councils inevitably meant that development was much slower than it might have been. In Murang'a, for example, in 1952 there were only 383 households allowed to grow coffee, while in Kiambu the first seedlings were not even planted until April 1953. The same was true for tea and pyrethrum. By 1952, only 779 acres of pyrethrum had been planted in Central Province and the African tea crop was even smaller – a mere 35 acres in Nyeri, expected to increase to 500 acres by 1958 when it would still amount to less than 3 per cent of the district's total agricultural area.[65] Thus, although the agricultural department theoretically abandoned compulsory communal terracing and adopted the strategy of encouraging peasant cultivation of high-priced cash crops in an attempt to encourage individualism rather than vainly attempting to preserve Africa's mythical communal-

A Change of Direction

ism, this remained effectively hidden from the Kikuyu. This time, when their anger boiled over again, their reaction proved far more violent than in 1947. Whatever Mitchell may have reported to Whitehall, in reality the situation in the Kikuyu reserves was still deteriorating and the peasantry had become thoroughly disillusioned with the second colonial occupation, which seemed to be entrenching the economic domination of the chiefs and their cronies. The Kikuyu masses remained obdurately opposed to agricultural change. Coercion had merely increased the influence of the political activists and produced violent attacks upon the chiefs, headmen and agricultural instructors, who were the most exposed representatives of the colonial state.[66]

Notes

1. KNA Ag 4/125, 'Annual Agricultural Reports: Central Province Districts, 1951', C.D. Knight's Fort Hall report; T.B. Spence's Kiambu report; and T. Hughes Rice's Machakos report; Ag 4/328, 'Annual Agricultural Report; Central Province, 1951', passim; and Ag 4/410, 'Central Province and Districts: Annual Agricultural Reports, 1952', especially L.H. Brown's Provincial report; and G. Gamble's Nyeri report.
2. KNA Ag 4/125, 'Annual Agricultural Reports: Central Province Districts, 1951', J.P. Benson's Meru report; Ag 4/118, 'Provincial Agricultural Handing Over Reports, 1942-51', H.B. Ambrose's Embu handing over notes, 15 October 1951; and Ag 4/410, 'Central Province and Districts: Annual Agricultural Reports, 1952', L.H. Brown's Provincial report; T.R. Golding's Embu reports; and V.E.M. Burke's Meru report. See also A. Thurston's draft manuscript, 'The Intensification of Smallholder Agriculture in Kenya', pp. 26-8, 52-60; and the African Land Development Board's Report on African Land Development in Kenya 1946-55, pp. 93-104. For details of discontent in Meru see J.T.S. Kamunchuluh, 'The Meru Participation in Mau Mau', pp. 196-206.
3. KNA DC/NYI 2/1/20, 'Mr Humphrey's Report on South Nyeri, 1944-47', C. Tomkinson's interim report on development to G.M. Rennie, 14 May 1945.
4. CO 852/662/19936/2 (1945-46), 'Soil Erosion: Kenya', H.E. Lambert and P. Wyn Harris, 'Policy in Regard to Land Tenure in the Native Lands of Kenya', passim; and KNA MAA 8/68, 'Chief Waruhiu, 1948-52', P. Wyn Harris to all District Commissioners, Central Province, 'Directive on the African Political Situation, Central Province', 11 December 1946.
5. KNA MAA 8/20, 'African Settlement: Teita Hills, Makueni, Ukamba Land Unit and Lambwe Valley, 1947-51', minutes of the meeting of the African Settlement and Land Utilisation Board, 13 June 1947; the second quarterly report of the African Settlement and Land Utilisation Board on Makueni, 20 June 1947; the resolution of the Machakos Local Native Council on Makueni, 13 August 1947; and R.J.C. Howes to A.C.M. Mullins, Provincial Commissioner, Central, 13 August 1947. See also CO 533/556/38668 (1946-47), 'African Resettlement', F.W. Cavendish-Bentinck to A.B. Cohen, 25 January 1947.
6. CO 533/538/38005/20 (1947), 'Land Commission: Native Lands Trust Board', minutes of the meeting of the Executive Council, Kenya, 25 August 1947; and

217

F.W. Cavendish-Bentinck to R.P. Armitage, Secretary for Agriculture, 26 August 1947.

7. M.P.K. Sorrenson, *Land Reform in the Kikuyu Country*, p. 58.

8. KNA MAA 6/13, 'Report of the Committee on Agricultural Credit for Africans, 1949-50', interim report of J.H. Ingham's committee, 29 October 1949; MAA 6/14, 'Committee to Make Recommendations on Agricultural Credit for African Farmers, 1949', report of the Colonial Economic Advisory Committee, forwarded by Creech Jones, 6 March 1947; minutes of preliminary meetings of the Ingham Committee, 2 May, 11 July, 8 August and 1 September 1949. Ag 4/80, 'Agricultural Conferences and Meetings, 1933-51', minutes of the meeting of Central Province Agricultural Officers, 18-19 October 1948; Ag 4-419, 'Agricultural Development and the Maintenance of Soil Fertility: The Growing of High Priced Cash Crops, 1933-51', J.T. Moon to D.L. Blunt, Director of Agriculture, 5 February 1948; and L.H. Brown to R.E. Wainwright, 6 February 1948; and Ag 4/125, 'Annual Agricultural Reports: Central Province Districts 1951', J.P. Benson's Meru report.

9. For Hughes Rice's approach see KNA Ag 1/1079, 'Soil Erosion Native Areas, 1946-54', T. Hughes Rice's memorandum, 'Soil Conservation Organisation in Fort Hall as Adapted from the Indigenous *Ngwatio* System', February 1947; and Ag 4/330, 'Provincial Agricultural Officer: News Letters, 1939-51', T. Hughes Rice's report in the February 1950 issue of the youth conference in Nyeri on 1-2 September 1949.

10. KNA DC/FH 1/29, 'Fort Hall Annual Report, 1950', pp. 1, 11-12; MAA 7/842, 'Provincial Commissioner's Meetings, 1945-51', minutes of meeting with D. Rees-Williams, Under Secretary of State for the Colonies, 29 April 1948; and MAA 6/13, 'Report of the Committee on Agricultural Credit for Africans, 1949-50', H.E. Lambert's memorandum on land titles, 8 November 1948. See also M.P.K. Sorrenson, *Land Reform in the Kikuyu Country*, pp. 60-71.

11. KNA Ag 4/80, 'Agricultural Conferences and Meetings, 1933-51', District Agricultural Officers Conference at Kisumu, 29-30 August 1949; and Central Province Agricultural Officers Conference, 11-12 October 1949.

12. KNA Ag 4/539, 'Reconditioning: Central Province, 1934-48', C. Maher to Senior Agricultural Officer, Nyanza, 28 January 1946; Ag 1/1065, 'Soil Erosion: Native Areas, 1943-46', A.C. Maher to G.M. Rennie, 'Agricultural Changes as Alternatives to Disaster in the Native Areas', undated; A.C. Maher's memorandum on the aims of soil conservation planning, 6 March 1945; and A.C. Maher to D.L. Blunt, 'Notes on Estimates for the Development of the Native Reserves', 1 June 1945. See also Maher's dispute with the Nyanza administration over discontent in Kitosh, North Nyanza, with the demands imposed on the peasantry by the terracing campaign, in Ag 1/1074, 'Soil Erosion: Nyanza Province, 1946-52', A.C. Maher to D.L. Blunt, 3 February 1947; D.L. Blunt to F.W. Cavendish-Bentinck, 14 February 1947.

13. KNA Ag 4/518, 'Reconditioning: Central Province, 1948-51', L.H. Brown to J.T. Moon, 15 December 1949; Ag 4/358, 'Monthly Agricultural Reports: Embu District, 1945-49', L.H. Brown's Half-Yearly report, January-June 1949; AG 4/392, 'Central Province Districts Agricultural Annual Reports, 1948', L.H. Brown's Embu report; and Ag 4/80, 'Agricultural Conferences and Meetings, 1933-51', minutes of the meeting of Agricultural Officers, Central Province, 18-19 October 1948.

14. For details of Maher's career, and especially his difficult relations with his superiors, see his personal file, KNA Ag 2/274, 'A.C. Maher: Agricultural Officer, 1929-52', *passim*. Maher resigned from the Kenya Agricultural Service at the earliest possible opportunity, on 30 June 1950, when he was 45, and retired to his farm on the Kinangop. Brown, in contrast, rose to become Chief Agriculturalist in Kenya.

15. KNA Ag 4/80, 'Agricultural Conferences and Meetings, 1933-51', L.H. Brown to J.T. Moon, 21 August, 1948, and 26 October 1948. Brown estimated that he spent 74 hours per month on routine administration and only three hours on experimental work.

218

A Change of Direction

See also Ag 4/518, 'Reconditioning: Central Province, 1948–51', L.H. Brown to J.T. Moon, 15 December 1949; and Ag 4/392, 'Central Province Districts Agricultural Annual Reports, 1948', L.H. Brown's Embu report. Maher never became reconciled to bench terracing, see Ag 1/1079, 'Soil Erosion Native Areas, 1946–54', A.C. Maher to S. Gillett, 30 November 1948; J.T. Moon to S. Gillett, 10 December 1948; and memorandum on bench terracing by Mr Hill, Assistant Agricultural Officer, Fort Hall, December 1948; and Ag 4/518, 'Reconditioning: Central Province, 1948–51', A.C. Maher to J.T. Moon, 12 January 1950.

The alternative methods of terracing propounded by Maher and Brown are illustrated below.

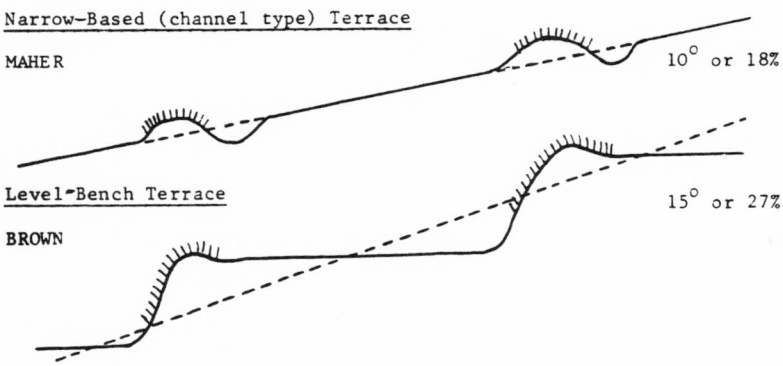

Narrow–Based (channel type) Terrace

MAHER   10° or 18%

Level–Bench Terrace   15° or 27%

BROWN

Source: D.B. Thomas, 'Some Observations on Soil Conservation in Machakos District, with special reference to terracing', Institute of Development Studies, Occasional Paper No. 27, 1978.

16. KNA Ag 4/518, 'Reconditioning: Central Province, 1948–51', J.T. Moon to S. Gillett 3 February 1950; and E.H. Windley to F.W. Cavendish-Bentinck, 'Central Province Soil Conservation Report, July–December 1949'.
17. *ibid*. E.H. Windley to F.W. Cavendish-Bentinck, 'Central Province Soil Conservation Report, July–December 1949'.
18. KNA Ag 4/80, 'Agricultural Conferences and Meetings, 1933–51', minutes of the Provincial Agricultural Officers' meeting, 9 June 1950.
19. A. Thurston, 'The Intensification of Smallholder Agriculture in Kenya', pp. 87–9, G.A. Maguire, *Towards Uhuru in Tanzania*, *passim*, provides a detailed history of the political consequences of agricultural development in Sukumaland.
20. KNA Ag 4/518, 'Reconditioning: Central Province, 1948–51', J.T. Moon to S. Gillett, 8 May 1951; and Ag 4/328, 'Annual Agricultural Report: Central Province, 1951', especially J.T. Moon's subsection on soil and water conservation.
21. KNA Ag 4/502, 'Annual Agricultural Reports: Central Province 1942–55', Agricultural Education Report, Fort Hall, 29 December 1952, for details of L.H. Brown's speech to the conference of primary school teachers, 1–6 December 1952.
22. KNA MAA 6/13, 'Report of the Committee on Agricultural Credit for Africans, 1949–50', *passim*; and MAA 6/14, 'Committee to Make Recommendations on Agricultural Credit for African Farmers, 1949', minutes of committee meetings, 2 May, 11

A Change of Direction

July, 8 August and 1 September 1949; and D. O'Hagan, 11 October 1949; and M.P.K. Sorrenson, *Land Reform in the Kikuyu Country*, pp. 60–71.

23. C.G. Rosberg and J. Nottingham, *The Myth of Mau Mau*, pp. 43, 93–4. See also D.M. Feldman's thesis, 'Christians and Politics', pp. 219–24, for details of the business activities of the early political activists.

24. KNA MAA 6/13, 'Report of the Committee on Agricultural Credit for Africans, 1949–50', H.E. Lambert's memorandum on African Land Titles to the African Affairs Committee, 8 November 1948.

25. CO 852/557/16708 (1945), 'Land Tenure Panel', Minutes of the meeting of the Colonial Social Science Research Council to discuss African land tenure, forwarded to Kenya, 28 December 1944. See also KNA MAA 6/14, 'Committee to Make Recommendations on Agricultural Credit for African Farmers, 1949', Creech Jones to P.E. Mitchell, 6 March 1947.

26. CO 852/662/19936/2 (1945–46), 'Soil Erosion: Kenya', N. Humphrey, 'The Relationship of Population to the Land in South Nyeri', paragraphs 19–24; and KNA DC/NYI 2/1/20, 'Mr Humphrey's Report on South Nyeri, 1944–47', N. Humphrey to D.L. Blunt, 'A Preliminary Report on Agricultural Conditions in South Nyeri', 22 September 1944; W. Lyne Watt to D.L. Blunt, 27 October 1944; and C. Tomkinson to G.M. Rennie, 14 May 1945.

27. KNA MAA 6/13, 'Report of the Committee on Agricultural Credit for Africans, 1949–50', *passim*; and Ag 1/1079, 'Soil Erosion: Native Areas, 1946–54', G.S. Cowley, Provincial Agricultural Officer, Rift Valley, to S. Gillett, 20 August 1951.

28. KNA MAA 6/13, 'Report of the Committee on Agricultural Credit for Africans, 1949–50', paragraph 3, 29 October 1949.

29. *ibid*, paragraph 4. See also KNA MAA 6/14, 'Committee to Make Recommendations on Agricultural Credit for African Farmers, 1949', Creech Jones to P.E. Mitchell, 6 March 1947, enclosing report by the Colonial Economic Advisory Committee on short and long-term credit; and memorandum by Sir Malcolm Darling, formerly of the Indian Civil Service, undated.

30. KNA MAA 6/13, 'Report of the Committee on Agricultural Credit for Africans, 1949–50', H.E. Lambert's memorandum to the African Affairs' Committee on African Land Titles, 8 November 1949.

31. *ibid*. Lambert observed: 'Although in actual fact the method of setting apart and lease would give an absolute security to the individual, as long as he behaved himself, it is not surprising that he feels some doubt about it, and fears a snag somewhere, when he is told that the land, which in his eyes (and those of all his tribe) belongs to him entirely for his lifetime and thereafter to his sons is now (by way of giving him a better title to it) offered to him on a lease of twenty-one or thirty-three years only.' See also E.W. Mathu's minority report and his memorandum on land titles in the African Land Units, 1 July 1949.

32. M.P.K. Sorrenson, *Land Reform in the Kikuyu Country*, pp. 61–71.

33. CO 533/538/38005/20 (1947), 'Land Commission: Native Lands Trust Board', R.P. Armitage's report, 'Land Management and Utilisation in Kenya', August 1947. For an outright attack on Armitage's proposals, see P. Wyn Harris to F.W. Cavendish-Bentinck, 9 August 1947.

34. M.P.K. Sorrenson, *Land Reform in the Kikuyu Country*, pp. 61–71; and KNA MAA 8/25, 'African Affairs' Committee: Minutes, 1948–52', meetings 3 November; and 4 November 1948; 13 April 1949; 4 August 1949; 5 October 1950; and 15 March 1951.

35. KNA MAA 6/13, 'Report of the Committee on Agricultural Credit for Africans, 1949–50', paragraphs 12–21; and H.E. Lambert's memorandum on land titles to the African Affairs' Committee, 8 November 1949; and CO 533/553/38557/8, 'Colonial Development and Welfare Schemes' (1947–48), P.E. Mitchell to George Hall, 17 April 1946, later published as 'General Aspects of the Agricultural Situation in Kenya'. See also M.P.K. Sorrenson, *Land Reform in the Kikuyu Country*, p. 60.

36. R.O. Hennings, Secretary for Agriculture, 'Some Trends and Problems of African Land Tenure in Kenya', pp. 122–34; Lord Hailey, 'The Land Tenure Problem in Africa', pp. 3–7; and his revised edition of *An African Survey*, pp. 775–811. See G.B. Masefield, 'Farming Systems and Land Tenure', pp. 8–14; C.K. Meek, 'Some Social Aspects of Land Tenure in Africa', pp. 15–21; C.W. Rowling, Adviser on Land, Nigeria, 'An Analysis of Factors Affecting Changes in Land Tenure in Africa', pp. 21–8; and H.H. Fosbrooke, Senior Government Sociologist, Tanganyika, 'Public Opinion and Changes in Land Tenure', pp. 28–36. See also C.K. Meek, 'The Amsterdam Land Tenure Symposium', pp. 113–14; KNA Ag 4/330, 'Provincial Agricultural Officer: News Letters, 1939–51', G.F. Clay, the Agricultural Adviser to the Secretary of State, address to the Cambridge Summer School, 11 September 1948, reprinted in the monthly newsletter, April 1949.
37. CO 852/557/16707/2 (1946), 'Land Tenure Policy: Kenya', H.E. Lambert's report on 'Central Kavirondo Land Tenure', 29 August 1946; CO 852/662/19936/2 (1945–46), 'Soil Erosion: Kenya', N. Humphrey, 'Relationship of Population to the Land in South Nyeri', and H.E. Lambert and P. Wyn Harris, 'Policy in Regard to Land Tenure in the Native Lands of Kenya'. See also KNA DC/FH 4/6, 'Chief and Headmen, 1937–54'.
38. KNA DC/FH 1/26, 'Fort Hall Annual Report, 1947', pp. 1–6, 15; MAA 8/106, 'Intelligence Reports: Mumenyereri, 1947–50', C. Penfold to P. Wyn Harris, 16 October, 18 October and 20 October, 10 and 19 November, and 10 December 1947.
39. KNA Ag 4/118, 'Provincial Agricultural Handing Over Reports, 1942–51', L.H. Brown to J.T. Moon, Central Province Handing Over Report, 5 December 1950; and L.H. Brown's Handing Over Notes, Embu, 8 February 1951. For the subsequent implementation of the zonal plan in Nyeri, see Ag 4/387, 'A Review of the Cash Crop Situation, 1960–66', *passim.*
40. Humphrey had first pointed to this alarming possibility in CO 852/662/19936/2 (1945–46), 'Soil Erosion: Kenya', N. Humphrey, 'The Relationship of Population to the Land in South Nyeri', paragraphs 6 and 54. See also CO 533/553/38557/8 (1947–48), 'Colonial Development and Welfare Schemes', P.E. Mitchell to George Hall, 17 April 1946, 'General Aspects of the Agricultural Situation in Kenya'.
41. KNA Ag 4/518, 'Reconditioning: Central Province, 1948–51', J.T. Moon to S. Gillett, 8 May 1951; Ag 4/502, 'Annual Agricultural Reports: Central Province, 1942–55', L.H. Brown, Department of Agriculture Report, 1952, p. 2; DC/NYI 7/1, 'Nyeri District Programme of Work, 1951', *passim*; and Ag 4/125, 'Annual Agricultural Reports: Central Province and Districts, 1951', J.P. Benson's Meru report. For attempts to stimulate peasant production, see Ag. 4/118, 'Provincial Agricultural Handing Over Reports, 1942–51', Major G.O. Hughes to C.A.B. Thurburn, Handing Over Report, Marketing Officer, Nyeri, 15 January 1951.
42. KNA Ag 4/410, 'Central Province and Districts: Annual Agricultural Reports, 1952', T.B. Spence's Kiambu District report; and L.H. Brown's Central Province report, for details of the earnings of various African progressive farmers.
43. KNA Ag 4/502, 'Annual Agricultural Reports: Central Province, 1942–55', L.H. Brown quoted in the Agricultural Education Report, Fort Hall, 29 December 1952.
44. These estimates of comparative profitability per acre have been adapted from KNA Ag 4/410, 'Central Province and Districts: Annual Agricultural Reports, 1952', L.H. Brown's Central Province Report, Appendix D. Ag 4/330, 'Provincial Agricultural Officer: News Letters, 1939–51', November–December 1950 issue contains similar estimates from North Nyanza.
45. KNA Ag 4/80, 'Agricultural Conferences and Meetings, 1933–51', L.H. Brown to J.T. Moon, 21 and 26 August 1948; and minutes of the meetings of Central Province Agricultural Officers, 18–19 October 1948; 3–4 February 1949; and 19–21 October 1949; Ag 4/118, 'Provincial Agricultural Handing Over Reports, 1942–51', L.H. Brown's Embu Handing Over Notes, 8 February 1951; and Ag 4/392, 'Central

Province Districts' Annual Agricultural Reports, 1948', L.H. Brown's Embu Report. Brown did, however, continue with the terracing campaign, see Ag 4/358, 'Monthly Agricultural Reports: Embu District, 1945–49', reports for July–September 1947; January–June 1948; and January–June 1949.

46. KNA Ag 4/392, 'Central Province Districts' Annual Agricultural Reports, 1948', J.P. Benson's Meru report: Ag 4/125, 'Annual Agricultural Reports: Central Province Districts, 1951', J.P. Benson's Meru report; and Ag 4/410, 'Central Province and Districts: Annual Agricultural Reports, 1952', V.E.M. Burke's Meru report.

47. KNA Ag 4/410, 'Central Province and Districts: Annual Agricultural Reports, 1952', V.E.M. Burke's Meru report, Appendix ii, Annual Report of the Coffee Officer, Embu. These 6,473 growers represented 9 per cent of the total male population of the district or approximately 30 per cent of the family heads living within the approved coffee-growing areas. Coffee exports from Meru totalled £40,000, the largest single item in the district's external earnings. It was intended to double the coffee area over the next two years. See also Ag 4/125, 'Annual Agricultural Reports: Central Province Districts, 1951', J.P. Benson's Meru report for information on the high quality of Meru coffee. For a detailed study of agricultural change in Meru, see F.E. Bernard, *East of Mount Kenya.*

48. KNA Ag 4/392, 'Central Province Districts' Annual Agricultural Reports, 1948', J.P. Benson's Meru report.

49. *ibid.*

50. KNA Ag 4/410, 'Central Province and Districts: Annual Agricultural Reports, 1952', L.H. Brown's Central Province report; and G. Gamble's Nyeri District report; and RH Mss.Afr.s. 596, 'European Elected Members' Organisation', 38(A)/1 'Mau Mau, 1947–55', file 55, 'Kikuyu and Mau Mau: The Land'; and a letter from L.H. Brown, published in *East African Standard,* 17 April 1953.

51. KNA Ag 4/419, 'Agricultural Development and Maintenance of Soil Fertility: The Growing of High Priced Crops, 1933–51'; DC/NYI 7/1, 'Nyeri District Programme of Work, 1951', *passim*; and Ag 4/392, 'Central Province Districts' Annual Agricultural Reports, 1948', T. Hughes Rice's Nyeri report.

52. KNA Ag 4/410, 'Central Province and Districts: Annual Agricultural Reports, 1952', L.H. Brown's Central Province report; and G. Gamble's Nyeri District report; and Ag 4/419, 'Agricultural Development and Maintenance of Soil Fertility: The Growing of High Priced Crops, 1933–51', L.H. Brown's memorandum, 6 February 1948.

53. KNA Ag 4/419, 'Agricultural Development and Maintenance of Soil Fertility: The Growing of High Priced Crops, 1933–51', L.H. Brown, 6 February 1948. See also Ag 4/387, 'A Review of the Cash Crop Situation 1960-66', undated memorandum on the cash crop zones of Nyeri; Ag 4/518, 'Reconditioning: Central Province 1948–51', E.H. Windley to F.W. Cavendish-Bentinck, 13 January 1950; and Ag 4/410, 'Central Province and Districts: Annual Agricultural Reports, 1952', G. Gamble's Nyeri District report.

54. KNA Ag 4/80, 'Agricultural Conferences and Meetings, 1933–51', C.D. Knight's memorandum on 'The Development of Smallholdings', undated, but probably June 1950; and Ag 4/330, 'Provincial Agricultural Officer: News Letters, 1939–51', T. Hughes Rice's report on the Nyeri Youth Conference in the February 1950 issue.

55. KNA Ag 4/410, 'Central Province and Districts: Annual Agricultural Reports, 1952', L.H. Brown's Central Province report.

56. KNA Ag 4/451, 'Fort Hall Safari Diaries, 1948–51', C.D. Knight's report of his tour around Location 2, 17–21 February 1948.

57. KNA Ag 4/451, 'Fort Hall Safari Diaries, 1948–51' *passim*, especially Knight's comments on Assistant Agricultural Instructor Gacheru and Kapitein Kahega Kimani of Location 2, in his report of 17–21 February 1948; and on Assistant Agricultural Instructors Ngunjiri Kibugu, Macharia and Grishon of Location 8, in his report dated 2–6 March 1948.

A Change of Direction

58. KNA MAA 8/106, 'Intelligence and Security: Mumenyereri, 1947–50', C. Penfold to
P. Wyn Harris, 16 and 27 October 1947; and Secretariat 1/12/8, 'Labour Unrest: Intelligence Reports, Central Province, 1947', Provincial Intelligence Report no. 2, 1947, 18 March 1947.
59. KNA Ag 4/410, 'Central Province and Districts: Annual Agricultural Reports, 1952', L.H. Brown's Central Province report. By 1952 the number of European agricultural staff consisted of one Provincial Agricultural Officer, two Assistants, nine District Agricultural Officers, and 32 Assistant Agricultural Officers. There were also four African Assistant Agricultural Officers, 734 Agricultural Instructors, 484 Assistant Agricultural Instructors and 121 Produce Inspectors.
60. KNA DC/NYI 2/1/16, 'Development and Welfare Planning, 1944–48', R. Daubney, Director of Veterinary Services, 'Post-War Development for the Veterinary Department', 22 August 1944; and Ag 4/107, 'Veterinary Department: Annual Reports, 1940–53', passim.
61. KNA Ag 4/451, 'Fort Hall Safari Diaries, 1948–51', C.D. Knight's report of his tour through Location 5, 20–23 January 1948 and his report on Location 2 for comments on the extensive farming activities of the Kikuyu Central Association activist, Petro Njuguna, who grew mulberries, raspberries, figs, avocado pears, mangos, custard apples, Cape tomatoes, plums, peaches and apples for the Nairobi market.
62. KNA Ag 4/102, 'Veterinary Monthly Reports: Central Province, 1943–50', A.E. Dorman to F.W. Ashton, 'Veterinary Handing Over Report, Nyeri', 11 November 1946; and F.W. Ashton's report, March 1947; and Ag 4/107, 'Veterinary Department: Annual Reports, 1940–53', F.W. Ashton's 'Nyeri Annual Report, 1946'; R.A. Hammond's 'Central Province Annual Report, 1945', N. King's 'Nyeri Annual Report 1949' and A.E. Dorman's 'Nyeri Annual Report, 1951'.
63. KNA Ag 4/113, 'South Nyeri: Monthly Agricultural Reports, 1938–49', passim; and African Land Development in Kenya 1946–55: Report by the African Land Development Board, pp. 81–2.
64. KNA Ag 4/502, 'Annual Agricultural Reports: Central Province, 1942–55', C.D. Knight's estimates of agricultural income per taxpayer, 15 April 1953. Contrast the estimates from Embu, Machakos, Nyeri and Kiambu with L.H. Brown's target of £100 in 'Agricultural Education Report, Fort Hall', 29 December 1952; and Ag 4/410, 'Central Province and Districts: Annual Agricultural Reports, 1952', L.H. Brown's Central Province report.
65. KNA Ag 4/410, 'Central Province and Districts: Annual Agricultural Reports, 1952', L.H. Brown's Central Province report, especially the section on Agricultural Betterment Funds.
66. KNA DC/FH 1/26, 'Fort Hall Annual Report, 1947', pp. 1–6, 15; DC/FH 1/27, 'Fort Hall Annual Report, 1948', pp. 4–5, 11, 12, MAA 8/68, 'Chief Waruhiu, 1948–52', passim; and Ag 4/410, 'Central Province and Districts: Annual Agricultural Reports, 1952', G. Gamble's Nyeri District report.

223

Ten

The Drift to Mau Mau

By 1950 rumours of a subversive organisation called 'Mau Mau' and reports of secret oathing ceremonies had begun to disturb the field administration in the Kikuyu reserves and the White Highlands. The millenarian sects became more and more vociferous and anti-European, while attacks on chiefs and agricultural instructors, which had declined since the peasant revolt, increased in frequency until the Othaya Division of Nyeri was virtually abandoned. Settler cattle were maimed and crops set on fire. In January and February 1952, for example, there were numerous cases of arson in Nyeri, both in the reserve and on the neighbouring European farms, until a collective fine of £2,500 was imposed on the local Kikuyu.[1] Settler farms in Timau were attacked and barns destroyed. Indeed, during the royal visit to Nanyuki on 7 February 1952, five grass fires could be seen. During the next five weeks another 58 fires were started around Nanyuki and thousands of acres of grazing were destroyed. A Turkana herdsman, who had worked in the area for 25 years, reported that 'I have never before seen fires like this year. I am getting very frightened, as I know these fires are the work of Mau Mau who have come here to destroy the white man'.[2] Meanwhile, in Murang'a James Beauttah resumed his campaign against the chiefs and disrupted the anti-rinderpest campaign, while hundreds of women from seven locations destroyed eleven cattle crushes in November 1951. Eventually 500 of them were arrested and many were sent to prison. In February 1952, Beauttah, Andrew Ng'ang'a and the Rev. Petro Kigondo, the leader of the independent churches in Murang'a, were all sentenced to two years hard labour for their part in the troubles. Order was only restored in Locations 6 and 7, the centre of the demonstrations, with the arrival of a large police levy.[3]

Mitchell and the myth of multiracialism

Despite this mounting violence. Mitchell remained confident until the end of his governorship on 21 June 1952 that his policies would succeed. He was not alone in this view. Although he was soon to be bitterly criticised for his failure to take action against Mau Mau, on the day of his retirement the *East African Standard* praised him for having been an able governor who had resolutely tackled the problems of African agriculture created by the 'ignorant man and his wife with a hoe' and for having reduced the threat of land degradation. The editorial concluded by saying that Mitchell 'has left not all the answers, but the wisdom and the thought and the high example which will give him his well-earned place in the historian's record as the most able public servant and personal influence in the remarkable story of East African progress'.[4]

This high praise did not, however, survive for long the deteriorating situation in the reserves and on European farms. On 10 July, Michael Blundell, the new leader of the European Elected Members demanded that the government arrest Kenyatta and declare a state of Emergency. There was, he warned, a 'subversive organization which is like a disease, spreading through the Colony, and the leaders have a target, and that target is the overthrowing of the Government, and my information leads me to believe that target may well be within nine months'.[5] Four days later the Commissioner of Police forwarded a long memorandum to the Secretariat on 'Kikuyu Political Activity'. It was the second attempt by the police to warn that the reserves were getting out of control. Violence had reached such a level, Police Commissioner O'Rorke observed, that it could not be dismissed as:

> . . . one of their periodical manifestations of discontent . . . (but) something far more dangerous to the peace and good order of the Colony. I am forced to the conclusion . . . that something in the nature of a general revolt among the Kikuyu people against European settlement and the policy of Government has been planned and that the plan has already begun to be put into effect.[6]

The Commissioner also reported that there had been a mass oathing ceremony in Nairobi, which had been attended by over 800 people. He suggested that the Mau Mau oath had become a killing oath, directed against Europeans and loyalists. Within three weeks of Mitchell's departure, therefore, a mass of evidence was presented to the Secretariat warning it of the serious situation among the Kikuyu and of the prospect of an imminent revolt. Why had Mitchell failed to take resolute action; was it from ignorance or from a willfull refusal to accept the evidence presented to him by the field administration?

Most informed opinion had been unhappy about the deteriorating situation for some time. The *Kenya Weekly News*, which reflected opinion among the settler farmers in the White Highlands, categorically refuted the governor's optimistic assessment. His statement, it observed, 'must have surprised many who read it. In truth, the political situation is now more disturbing and the prospect more anxious than it has been since 1936'.[7] Many settlers shared the paper's view. At an election meeting at Londiani, Hubert Buxton, a retired District Commissioner, warned that virtually the whole Kikuyu tribe had been 'contaminated' with Mau Mau. Wilfred Havelock, the Legislative Councillor for Kiambu, shortly afterwards led a delegation of Thika settlers to see O'Rorke, the Commissioner of Police, and the member for Law and Order, Whyatt, They left extremely dissatisfied with Whyatt's refusal to detain suspected Mau Mau leaders and with O'Rorke's assertion that they were being alarmist since at the most, only 10 per cent of Kikuyu had taken any Mau Mau oaths.[8]

The settlers and many members of the administration, by early 1952, were already seriously dissatisfied with the attitude of the member for Law and Order. Whyatt's legal duties as Attorney General hampered his effectiveness as the enforcer of public order. He not only was responsible for drafting the law but also acted as the Director of Public Prosecutions, deciding which cases should be brought to court. As such, his primary function was as guardian of the law rather than as defender of public order and security.[9]

Until the declaration of Emergency on 20 October 1952, Mitchell continued to insist that Kenya was more peaceful than ever before and that the policy of multiracialism was beginning to work.[10] An African élite was emerging, which could one day play a prominent role in the political and economic life of the colony in collaboration with the settlers. Although exhausted, Mitchell clung to office until after the royal visit to Kenya in February 1952, which was to be his great moment. He could ill afford to have this cancelled because of rumours of Kikuyu unrest. To the end Mitchell hoodwinked the Colonial Office with his optimistic declarations into thinking that his government had tackled the problems of land degradation in the reserves, squatters in the White Highlands and the urban housing shortage. Mitchell, of course, astutely informed Whitehall that many problems remained unsolved, but definitely indicated that Kenya was now on course to become a contented multiracial society. Constitutional African politicians, for example, were being incorporated at the centre, where there were now four African Legislative Councillors, and into the reorganised African district councils, which had been granted new powers, in the localities. These men, Mitchell hoped, would soon replace the discredited Kenyatta and the self-serving agitators in the Kikuyu Central Association, who, he thought, were behind the discontent. He sincerely believed they had little popular support.[11]

Why did Mitchell reach these conclusions and inform the Colonial Office that all was well in Kenya? Was he shielded from the truth by his admirers in the Secretariat failing to forward unpalatable district reports which contradicted his hopes of a contented multiracial Kenya, or was the mentally-exhausted governor simply refusing to accept reports of increasing Mau Mau activity? The reason probably lay somewhere in between these two explanations. Isolated in Nairobi, the senior officers in the Secretariat (who after Wyn Harris's departure were not Kikuyu exprts) failed to recognise the seriousness of the threat to colonial rule which was developing in the Kikuyu reserves, in the White Highlands and in the African locations of Nairobi. They therefore suppressed or played down the field administration's reports of trouble to avoid offending Mitchell and to shield him from his critics, Clarence Buxton and S.V. Cooke.[12] Whatever the case, the conspiracy of silence in the Secretariat strengthened the governor's reluctance to heed advice. Mitchell was an opinionated man and refused to recognise that a Kikuyu rebellion was imminent. Determined to end his career on a triumphal note, he subconsciously refused to accept that his eight years in Nairobi were ending in the collapse of the colonial state.[13]

The Secretariat, however, was equally responsible for the failure to move against Mau Mau. Rankine, Davies and Whyatt lacked the courage to go behind Mitchell's back and to warn the Colonial Office of the seriousness of the situation. All three were cautious time-servers unwilling to risk their careers. Mitchell had got rid of the only man in the Secretariat who had consistently stood up to him, Wyn Harris. First as Labour Commissioner, then as Provincial Commissioner in Central Province, and finally as Chief Native Commissioner, Wyn Harris had refused to be intimidated or to conceal unpleasant truths. He was, therefore, promoted out of the way to the governorship of the Gambia in 1949. His successor, Eric Davies, was an unimaginative colonial administrator, unable to adapt to the Colonial Office's strategy of incorporating African politicians into the policy-making process. Thus, whereas Wyn Harris had liked Kenyatta, whom he recognised as a political pragmatist trying to control the various political factions inside the Kenya African Union and to unite the constitutionalists and the militants, Davies only saw him as an extremist agitator and failed to appreciate that Kenyatta was a subtle political operator. Unlike Wyn Harris, he failed to realise that Kenyatta should not be judged too harshly as he needed room to manoeuvre politically to reconcile the rival factions inside the Kenya African Union, not to mention the trades unions and the Mau Mau Central Committee, the *Muhimu*.[14]

Shortly after Wyn Harris's departure, the liberal wing in the Secretariat suffered a second blow when Cecil Penfold was promoted from the post of Director of Intelligence and Security in 1950. The new director, who came from the Gold Coast, lacked his predecessor's understanding of the complexities of Kenya African politics, which was based upon twenty years of work in the colony and five years as Director of Intelligence. Penfold had acquired a sophisticated knowledge of the rivalries in the Kenya African Union and in the trades unions.[15] Unlike the field administration, which received most of its information from chiefs wanting to discredit African politicians who threatened their authority, the Special Branch had its own independent network of informers and received hundreds of detailed reports from its agents, who had penetrated into the inner councils of the Kenya African Union. There was, for example, a police informer inside the *Muhimu* until his cover was blown by an unsuccessful police raid on Senior Chief Koinange's home at Banana Hill, where they had expected to discover members of the *Muhimu* assembled for one of the early oathing ceremonies.[16] The new director lacked Penfold's ability and was unable to stand up to the field administration's simplistic interpretation of African politics. Unlike the Special Branch, most District Commissioners had little understanding of Kenyatta's moderating influence upon the Kikuyu militants. Instead they stigmatised the Kenya African Union as a subterfuge behind which Mau Mau operated.[17]

Windley, the Provincial Commissioner in Central Province, for example, denounced the Kenya African Union during his opening speech to an agricultural conference organised for primary-school teachers. 'The Kenya African Union and Mau Mau', he declared, 'were synonymous terms for the evil influence which was undermining the social structure and initiating a rule of force by gangs of thugs'. Coutts's reaction was symptomatic of the inability of the field administration and the Secretariat to adjust to the abrasive criticism of the post-war generation of African politicians. Most District Commissioners regarded all political activity as subversive and dismissed African politicians as agitators, whom they saw as undermining the government's authority and outside the accepted limits of political life in colonial Kenya. Coutts, for example, who had been a liberal himself when first appointed District Commissioner in Murang'a just before the peasant revolt in 1947, had never forgiven Kenyatta for his speech against compulsory female labour, which had destroyed the *ngwatio* terracing campaign in the district.[18]

When Eliud Mathu, Thuku and Senior Chief Waruhiu organised an anti-Mau Mau campaign in Kiambu, which culminated in a meeting at Kiambu township attended by 30,000 people, Kenyatta, ex-Senior Chief Koinange and James Gichuru, the former President of the Kenya African Union who had recently been appointed a chief in the area, had all been present. Yet, despite Kenyatta's denunciation of violence and warning that it would prejudice the newly-appointed Royal Commission, the field administration refused to believe in his sincerity. It complained that speeches by Kenyatta, as well as those of Chiefs Koinange and Gichuru, had been politically ambiguous and cleverly constructed to avoid any outright denunciation of Mau Mau. This was probably true, but their caution stemmed as much from fear of assassination by Mau Mau as from passive support for the movement. For any of them to condemn Mau Mau would have dealt it a major blow. They were therefore under intense pressure to moderate their attacks, Kenyatta having been warned that an outright condemnation would bring a swift response from the militants and would not be tolerated. In fact Kenyatta went as far as he dared to satisfy the authorities; if he was to retain any influence over the militants he could not go as far in his denunciations of Mau Mau as the administration wanted. In private he informed Kennaway, the District Commissioner in Kiambu, that he had little influence over the radicals and warned him that if the government banned Kenya African Union meetings following the great rally in Nyeri in July, it would play into the hands of the extremists and weaken the restraining influence of the moderates. The administration, however, ignored these warnings.[19]

The Government's response

Faced with mounting criticisms from the press and settler politicians and by even more disturbing reports from the field administration, the Secretariat began to take Mau Mau seriously in July 1952. Following Blundell's warning in the Legislative Council and O'Rorke's report, the acting Chief Secretary convened a meeting to consider the situation as outlined in the Police Commissioner's report of 29 July. The Member for Law and Order, the Chief Native Comissioner, all the Provincial Commissioners and several other senior officials were present, but neither O'Rorke nor the Director of Intelligence and Security were invited to attend, since 'matters of higher policy, which would be discussed, were not the concern of the police'. Thus the administration's prejudice against the police prevented the Secretariat from consulting the Special Branch about the political divisions inside the Kenya African Union.[20]

Berman has rightly criticised the field administration for 'a preoccupation with technique over the substance of policy and by an absorption in the exigencies of short-run control'.[21] This meeting clearly revealed that even the Kenyan Secretariat had failed to recognise that the collaborative base of the state would have to be broadened to include the proto-capitalists, who supported Kenyatta's faction in the Kenya African Union, if the colonial régime was to withstand the strains of the post-war era, and its increasing demands upon the African peasantry. Eric Davies's attitude typified the limited understanding of the political situation on the part of even the higher echelons of the Secretariat. The Chief Native Commissioner did not recognise that Kenyatta was a moderate: a constitutionalist, albeit of an unorthodox variety, who was waiting to be recruited as a new collaborator in the colonial order. Davies never got beyond denouncing him as the evil genius behind Mau Mau. He declared that:

> Although there was as yet no concrete evidence to prove that Jomo Kenyatta was behind the Mau Mau movement, there was every reason to believe that he was one of the leaders of this society. This conviction was strengthened by the fact that Mau Mau activities increased sharply in areas which he visited, and also by the display of Mau Mau emblems on the platform from which he addressed a crowd of 20,000 at Nyeri on 26 July. Moreover, all efforts to persuade him to publicly denounce the society had failed and there could therefore be no doubt that he intended to pursue his hundred per cent programme, which was designed to secure the eviction of the European Government and Settlement from Kenya.[22]

But apart from such assertions, the Chief Native Commissioner could not provide any evidence to link Kenyatta with Mau Mau. The member for Law and Order insisted that there was insufficient evidence to convict Kenyatta and refused to detain him and his lieutenants under the Deportation (Immigrant British Subjects) Ordinance. When they met again to discuss the question four weeks later on 17 August, Davies and Whyatt still could not agree. While the Chief Native Commissioner insisted that 'the utmost should be done to have Jomo Kenyatta put away by some means or other under the present law', the member for Law and Order remained adamant that this was impossible. He resisted any suggestion that the Emergency Powers Ordinance should be invoked since 'there was, in fact, no Emergency, and the measure at this time was unncessary'.[23]

While these discussions were under way Potter, the acting governor who had only recently arrived from Uganda where he had been Chief Secretary, received two delegations from the European members of the Legislative Council on 8 and 18 August. They urged that emergency powers should be taken in Kikuyuland and that the leaders of the Kenya African Union should be arrested. They also demanded that the British government should make it quite clear that Kenya could not follow the Gold Coast's path to African majority internal self-government. Potter rejected these demands and observed that although the situation in Central Province was grave, it did not yet warrant declaring a state of Emergency. The Kenyan government would not stifle the emergence of African nationalism, but would seek to divert it towards accepting multi-racialism. Both the British and Kenyan governments would, he promised, ensure that the European community retained an important role in the Kenya of the future.

John Whyatt, the Attorney General, who came in for much criticism at these meetings, forwarded a dramatic account of the proceedings to the Colonial Office. He observed:

> I have been present on one or two occasions in other Colonies when the Governor has received a deputation but I have never seen the like of this one before. All the European Elected Members (with two exceptions) rolled up at Government House in their cars and seated themselves at the long table in the Executive Council room facing Potter, the Commissioner of Police and myself. They then proceeded to state their views, Blundell acting for the most part as spokesman though the others joined in from time to time. When I say that they put forward their views, that is an understatement; it would be more correct to describe them as being in the nature of 'demands'; and as I sat there listening to them the thought flashed through my mind, 'This must be what it is like to be present at a coup d'etat'.[24]

The settlers demanded the immediate proclamation of a state of Emergency in the Kikuyu areas, the detention without trial of all 'political agitators', the appointment of a Commander-in-Chief (like General Briggs in Malaya) to supervise the destruction of Mau Mau, and the appointment of a European Elected Member as member for Law and Order forthwith. They also demanded that the Kenyan government issue a statement 'to the effect that African nationalism would not be tolerated' and anyone who remained politically troublesome should automatically be prosecuted for sedition.

The settler associations were restless at the government's inaction. Humphrey Slade, the Legislative Councillor for the Aberdares, and the Provincial Commissioner for the Rift Valley both attended a meeting of the executive committee of the Thomson's Falls Association, where the level of violence had escalated alarmingly. The local District Commissioner had already recommended imposing a collective fine in the Laikipia area to stop cattle maiming and the firing of crops, stopping bus traffic between Laikipia and Kikuyuland, closing the independent schools, which were seen as centres of subversion, and giving the District Commissioner summary powers to hear Mau Mau cases. Following this tense meeting the Provincial Commissioner reported that emergency powers should be taken to arrest all the local malcontents; and on 27 August he imposed a curfew on the Narok Marmanet and Ol Joro Orok wards and on the African locations at Thomson's Falls and Rumuruti.[25]

Meanwhile, Potter had informed the Colonial Office about the deteriorating situation. He warned that the Kenya African Union was simply a front for the subversive activities of Mau Mau. Potter reported:

> The main overt Kikuyu political organization is the Kenya African Union which, while purporting to represent all Africans, does not do so, but is in fact Kikuyu controlled, under the leadership of Jomo Kenyatta . . . The covert organization is the proscribed Mau Mau

secret society, the terms of whose illegal oath include the killing of Europeans when the war horn blows and the rescue of Kenyatta should he ever be arrested, and there need be little doubt, though there is no proof, that he controls this revolutionary organisation in so far as it is still susceptible to control.[26]

Unlike Mitchell and Rankine, Potter was prepared to heed the warnings of the field administration and had taken immediate action to warn the Colonial Office and to regain control in Kikuyuland and the White Highlands. Warnings from the police and the district administration were no longer ignored and even before the new governor, Sir Evelyn Baring, arrived in September, Whitehall had been fully apprised of the situation. Whether Potter and his advisers identified the real leaders of Mau Mau is, however, a different question.[27]

On 9 September, the Commissioner of Prisons was appointed to investigate subversion and the role of the Kikuyu independent schools. He prepared dossiers on leading African politicians suspected of being Mau Mau leaders. By that time the member for Law and Order had finally been persuaded to prepare legislation to restrict movement at night and to license printing presses to reduce the flow of subversive literature. Plans were also prepared to restrict the movement of suspected Mau Mau members. This legislation was forwarded to the Colonial Office and, on 16 September, the member for Law and Order and the Chief Native Commissioner went to London to explain the crisis. On their return, these Ordinances were rushed through a special meeting of the Legislative Council on 23 September and approved by the new governor on 3 October.[28]

When Baring finally arrived on 29 September, he was faced with reports of escalating violence. On 25 September, attacks on European farms in the Timau area, north of Mount Kenya, had reached new heights when four gangs had disembowelled 146 cattle and 380 sheep and set fire to five maize cribs. Baring was immediately given a detailed report on Mau Mau by Eric Davies and within a week of arriving in the colony, began a tour of the trouble areas in Central Province. Shortly after his return to Nairobi, the government's staunchest Kikuyu supporter, Senior Chief Waruhiu of Kiambu, was murdered on his way home from an interview with Baring at Government House.[29] After attending the funeral, Baring informed the Colonial Office that the Kenyan government was facing a planned revolutionary movement, controlled from Nairobi, and that a state of Emergency would have to be declared. The Kenyan government carefully considered the consequences of arresting Kenyatta and other African politicians. It was, they decided, essential to preserve international confidence in the colony's stability and Kenyatta's detention as the leader of Mau Mau would provide the most effective means of reasserting control. They anticipated that there would be violent opposition to his detention, but that this would be a short-term reaction and that, deprived of direction, the Mau Mau movement would quickly disintegrate.[30] In fact, exactly the reverse happened. There was little immediate response to the declaration of the Emergency, but the panic expulsion of thousands of Kikuyu squatters from the White Highlands by the settler-controlled district councils brought thousands of dispossessed young males with nothing to lose into Central Province, where they joined the landless Kikuyu in the reserves and entered the forests of Mount Kenya and the Aberdares to fight for *Uhuru* and land in the Land and Freedom Army. Once again the administration's advice proved to be dangerously wrong.[31]

Oliver Lyttelton, the Conservative Secretary of State, approved the declaration of the Emergency and the detention of the Kenya African Union's leaders on 14 October 1952. During the next six days careful preparations were made; 'Jock Scott Operation', the code name for the swoop, was timed for midnight on 20 October, by which time a battalion of the Lancashire Fusiliers would have arrived in Nairobi to support the King's African Rifles should there be widespread resistance or an uprising. In the event there was little opposition and by eight o'clock on the morning of 21 October 1952, 186 African politicians and trade unionists, including Kenyatta, Kubai and Kaggia, had been detained. The Mitchell government had failed. Metropolitan resources would now be increasingly needed, not merely to repair the fabric of the Kenyan state but to reconstruct it more radically than ever Mitchell had dared.[32]

Notes

1. KNA DC/FH 1/31, 'Fort Hall Annual Report, 1952', pp. 1-6, 11-18; DC/FH 2/1/4, 'False Prophets: *Watu wa Mungu*, 1934-60', report from the Presbyterian Church of East Africa, Tumutumu, 2 May 1952; Ag 4/410, 'Central Province and Districts: Annual Agricultural Reports, 1952', G. Gamble's Nyeri District report; and *East African Standard*, 26 February 1952.

2. F.D. Corfield, 'Origins and Growth of Mau Mau', pp. 125-6.

3. KNA DC/FH 1/30, 'Fort Hall Annual Report, 1951', pp. 1, 4: Ag 4/107, 'Veterinary Department: Annual Reports, 1940-53' R.D.G. Wachira's Fort Hall Veterinary report, 1951; and MAA 2/5/146, 'Kenya African Union, 1948-52', acting Native Courts Officer to P.E. Mitchell, 16 November 1951; and P.E. Mitchell to O. Lyttelton, 19 November 1951, for evidence of the Kenyan government's exasperation with Beauttah's activities. J. Spencer's *James Beauttah*, pp. 73-6 records Beauttah's account of the events of July 1947 in Murang'a; p. 102-3 suggests that the first oathing ceremony in Nyeri had been held in February 1947, (Kenyatta, Mbiyu Koinange and Beauttah had been present). The first ceremony in Murang'a was held at Rev. Petro Kigondo's house in July 1947. Kigondo had earlier administered the KCA oath to the

youthful Kenyatta at CMS Pumwani in December 1928. See also D.M. Feldman's thesis, 'Christians and Politicians', pp. 219-20 for details of Kigondo's involvement with the Kikuyu Central Association in the early 1920s when he was the District Commissioner's clerk and a leading businessman in the district. In 1928 Kigondo had been one of the Kikuyu Central Association candidates elected to the Local Native Council before the controversy over female circumcision.

4. Editorial, *East African Standard*, 21 June 1952.
5. Legislative Council Debates, second series, vol. xlviii, 1952, first session, second sitting, 10 July 1952, cols. 172-98; and 11 July 1952, cols. 281-349.
6. M.S. O'Rorke to J. Whyatt, 'Kikuyu Political Activity', 14 July 1952, quoted by F.D. Corfield, 'Origins and Growth of Mau Mau', p. 141.
7. *Kenya Weekly News*, 14 March 1952.
8. RH Mss. Afr. s. 596, Box 38 (A) File 1, 'European Elected Members Association', ff. 53, Kendall Ward's memorandum, 'The Rise of Mau Mau: European Warnings', 17 March 1953; and KNA MAC/KEN 33/1, 'Kenya State of Emergency: Church Missionary Society, Weithaga, Fort Hall, 1947-50', Canon M.G. Capon's reports, and MAC/KEN 33/2, 'Kenya State of Emergency: The Electors Union', Kendall Ward's memorandum, 7 August 1952; and Kendall Ward to M. Blundell, 7 August 1952.
9. F.D. Corfield, 'Origins and Growth of Mau Mau', pp. 32-7.
10. P.E. Mitchell, *The Sunday Times*, 19 October 1952.
11. CO 533/566/8 (1951), 'The Kenya African Union', P.E. Mitchell to J. Griffiths, 3 May 1951; CO 533/543/38086/38 (1949), 'Kikuyu Central Association', P.E. Mitchell to Creech Jones, 28 February 1949; and KNA MAA 2/5/146, 'Kenya African Union, 1948-52', P.E. Mitchell to O. Lyttelton, 19 November 1951.
12. RH Mss. Britt. Emp. s. 390, 'C.E.M. Buxton', Box 3, File 4, ff.1-4, C.E.V. Buxton to P.E. Mitchell, 15 August 1948; and ff. 32-9, C.E.V. Buxton's memoranda about the Emergency, undated, but probably February 1953; RH Afr.s. 596, 'European Elected Members Organisation', Box 38(A), File 1, 'Mau Mau 1947-53', C.E.V. Buxton's memorandum on 'The Kikuyu Association', February 1947; C.E.V. Buxton to Kendall Ward, 22 September 1947; C.E.V. Buxton to P.E. Mitchell, 15 August 1948; Kendall Ward's memorandum, 'The Rise of Mau Mau: European Warnings', 17 March 1953; and KNA MAC/KEN 33/2, 'Kenya State of Emergency: The Electors Union', *passim*: MAA 8/102, 'Intelligence and Security: Miscellaneous Press Cuttings, 1948-50', *East African News Review*, 22 January 1948, for report of S.V. Cooke's speech on African discontent and MAA 8/108, 'Intelligence and Security: Daily Chronicle, 1947-49', 14 January 1948 for Cooke's criticism of the chaos in the Secretariat, See also CO 537/3588/38696 (1947-48), 'Activities of Mathu', S.V. Cooke's speech in the Legislative Council, 9 January 1948.
13. RH Mss. Afr. r. 101, P.E. Mitchell's diaries, *passim*, especially 1 January 1952. Any qualms he felt about the future were blamed upon the poor quality of the European Elected Members and their opposition to multiracialism: see the entry for 31 December 1951. See also *The Sunday Times*, 19 October 1952, and his press statement while in London for King George VI's funeral, 20 February 1952.
14. KNA CS 1/14/14, 'Chief Native Commissioner: Speeches, 1949-52', Notes for collective Punishment Debate, 7 December 1951; CO 537/3646/47272/1 (1948), 'Political Intelligence Reports: East Africa', Kenya Political Summary, September – October 1948, dated 6 December 1948. Contrast Wyn Harris' observations on Kenyatta in CO 537/3591/38733 (1948), 'Petitions to the United Nations', minutes of meeting with Kenyatta, 15 October 1948, with Mitchell's fears in CO 537/4317/14332/10, 'Communism in the Colonies: East Africa', *passim*. For the opinion of an African conservative see KNA MAA 2/5/146, 'Kenya African Union, 1948-52', T. Mbotela to E.R. St. A. Davies, 28 April 1951; and E.H. Windley to E.R. St. A. Davies, 1 September 1951.

15. KNA MAA 8/106, 'Intelligence and Security: Mumenyereri, 1947–50'; MAA 8/102, 'Intelligence and Security: Miscellaneous Press Cuttings, 1948–50'; MAA 8/109, 'Intelligence and Security: African Workers Federation, 1947–48; MAA 8/108, 'Intelligence and Security: Daily Chronicle, 1947–49'; MAA 8/8, 'Intelligence Reports: Confidential Information, 1946–47'; MAA 8/105, 'Intelligence and Security: Radio Posta, 1947–48'; MAA 8/71, 'Communism, 1948–49'; MAA 2/5/146, 'Kenya African Union, 1948–52'; Secretariat 1/12/6, 'Coast Province Labour Unrest: Correspondence, 1947'; and Secretariat 1/12/8, 'Labour Unrest: Intelligence Reports, Central Province, 1947', are the most important Intelligence files which have been consulted and contain many reports by Penfold and his agents. See also CO 537/4336/14335/6 Part ii (1949), 'Colonial Intelligence Summary'; and CO 537/4715/47272/A, 'Political Intelligence Summaries: Kenya'.
16. B. Kaggia, *Roots of Freedom*, p. 10.
17. B.J. Berman, 'Bureaucracy and Incumbent Violence', pp. 147–52, and N.S. Carey Jones, *The Anatomy of Uhuru*, footnote p. 84.
18. KNA Ag 4/410, 'Central Province and Districts: Annual Agricultural Reports, 1952', report of teachers' agricultural training conference, Fort Hall, 1–6 September 1952, and interview with D. O'Hagan, Coutts's predeccessor as District Commissioner in Murang'a, in Nairobi, June 1981. For detailed reports of Kenyatta's speech see KNA Secretariat 1/12/8, 'Labour Unrest: Intelligence Reports, Central Province, 1947', C. Penfold to P. Wyn Harris, 22 and 25 July 1947.
19. F.D. Corfield, 'Origins and Growth of Mau Mau', pp. 152–3; and interview with N.F. Kennaway, the District Commissioner in Kiambu, February 1948 to November 1950, and July 1951 to February 1953, in Nairobi, September 1979. Corfield on pp. 301–8 reprints the report by the Assistant Superintendent of Police, Nyeri, of Kenyatta's mass meeting on 26 July 1952, as a damning indictment of his involvement in Mau Mau. In fact, the report can be read as a valiant attempt by Kenyatta to undermine the power of the militants despite considerable opposition from militants in the audience. This was not the speech of a radical, but of a Kikuyu moderate who wished to avoid a violent confrontation with the authorities. J. Murray-Brown, *Kenyatta*, pp. 290–2, analyses Kenyatta's speech at Kiambu on 24 August 1952. See also Mahtu's warnings in CO 537/3588/38696 (1947–48), 'Activities of Mathu', E.W. Mathu's memorandum, 'The Freedom of Assembly', July 1947.
20. F.D. Corfield, 'Origins and Growth of Mau Mau', p. 143.
21. B.J. Berman, 'Bureaucracy and Incumbent Violence', p. 147.
22. Quoted in F.D. Corfield, 'Origins and Growth of Mau Mau', pp. 142–3.
23. *ibid*, p. 144–5.
24. CO 852/437, 'Proposals to Deal with Disturbances Arising from the Activities of the Mau Mau Secret Society: Kenya', J. Whyatt to P. Rogers, 2 September 1952.
25. *ibid*, pp. 149–50. For details of the subversive activities of the independent schools and churches, see KNA DC/FH 1/31, 'Fort Hall Annual Report, 1952', pp. 11–18; MAA 6/634, 'Intelligence Reports: Central Province, 1948–53; W.H. Cantrell to D. O'Hagan, 'Report on the Position of African Anglican Church Schools and Churches in the Fort Hall District', 15 July 1953; and MAC/KEN 33/1, 'Kenya State of Emergency: Church Missionary Society, Weithaga, Fort Hall, 1947–50', Canon M.G. Capon's reports to the Church Missionary Society headquarters, London, September 1949 – August 1950, and September 1950 – August 1951; and the report of the Fact Finding Committee on Independent Schools and Churches of the Standing Committee of Synod, March 1950; and Rev. N. Langford-Smith to Synod, June 1950.
26. H.S. Potter to P. Rogers, Colonial Office, 17 August 1952, quoted in F.D. Corfield, 'Origins and Growth of Mau Mau', pp. 150–1. For similar warnings see KNA MAC/KEN/33/1, 'Kenya State of Emergency: Church Missionary Society, Weithaga, Fort Hall, 1947–50', *passim*; and RH Mss. Afr.s. 596, 'European Members Organi-

sation', Box 38(A), File 1, ff. 18, Canon M.G. Capon's interview with the African Affairs' Commitee of the Electors' Union, 5 March 1948; Major C.E.V. Buxton to P.E. Mitchell, 15 August 1948; and Kendall Ward's memorandum on 'The Rise of Mau Mau: European Warnings', 17 March 1953.

27. H.S. Potter to P. Rogers, 17 August 1952, quoted in F.D. Corfield, 'Origins and Growth of Mau Mau', pp. 150-1, 153-4.

28. F.D. Corfield, 'Origins and Growth of Mau Mau', p. 154. The independent schools in Murang'a were particularly associated with the political militants, see KNA DC/FH 1/31, 'Fort Hall Annual Report, 1952', pp. 11-18; and MAA 7/634, 'Intelligence Reports: Central Province, 1948-53', W.H. Cantrell to D. O'Hagan, 15 July 1953. DC/FH 1/29, 'Fort Hall Annual Report, 1950', pp. 15-21; and DC/FH 1/30, 'Fort Hall Annual Report, 1951', pp. 14-16, provide insights into the estrangement between the field administration and the independent schools in the district, and report the victory of the militants, led by Ndegwa Metho, over the more moderate Paulo Mungai, who was eventually appointed chief of location 4 in 1951. See also F.D. Corfield, 'Origins and Growth of Mau Mau', p. 154.

29. J. Murray-Brown, *Kenyatta*, pp. 294-5; F.D. Corfield, 'Origins and Growth of Mau Mau', pp. 157-8; and KNA DC/KBU 1/43, 'Kiambu District Annual Report, 1952', p. 2.

30. C.G. Rosberg and J. Nottingham, *The Myth of Mau Mau*, pp. 276-9; and R. Buijtenhuijs, *Essays on Mau Mau*, pp. 35-45. For the opinion of one militant see M. Mathu, *The Urban Guerrilla*, p. 17. See also L.S.B. Leakey, *Defeating Mau Mau*, p. 108; and B.J. Berman, 'Bureaucracy and Incumbent Violence', p. 170. Berman concluded that 'while small numbers of Kikuyu began to move into the forests on the fringes of the reserves as early as July and August 1952 in response to the demands being made by Europeans for a state of emergency, the underground movement posessed neither coherent plans, organization or training for guerilla combat nor a significant stockpile of modern arms. Moreover, the arrest of Kikuyu leaders at the beginning of the Emergency largely decapitated the movement, depriving it of virtually all of its educated top leaders, and left the situation in the hands of local leaders and the rank and file. It was not until the early months of 1953 that the bands in the forests were sufficiently organized to resist the colonial security forces which had invested the Kikuyu reserves . . . The Emergency, in reality, was a pre-emptive attack, carried out by the incumbent colonial authorities against a significant segment of the African political leadership of Kenya and its supporters'.

31. A. Thurston's draft manuscript, 'Intensification of Smallholder Agriculture in Kenya', pp. 105-7. See also R. Buijtenhuijs, *Essays on Mau Mau*, p. 41, for interesting observations on the role of squatters from Nyeri in Laikipia, and the introduction of oathing in these areas.

32. F.D. Corfield, 'Origins and Growth of Mau Mau', pp. 159-61; and B. Kaggia, *Roots of Freedom*, pp. 116-19, for an account of what happened on 20 October by one of the Mau Mau *Muhimu*.

Eleven

Conclusion

At the end of the war the Kenyan government faced three crucial problems: agricultural reform in Kikuyuland, the squatters, and the urban problems of African Nairobi. As we have seen, the government quickly abandoned Whitehall's strategic goals for mere tactical survival. Survivors from the era of indirect rule could not adjust intellectually to the subversive ideas emanating from Whitehall. Ronald Robinson's 'moral disarmament of African Empire' had not diminished their belief that African self-government was centuries rather than decades away.[1] Whereas Whitehall wanted to incorporate and secure the collaboration of educated Africans through training in local government and then to devolve power at the centre, the field administration remained committed to its allies, the chiefs, even although indirect rule had always been applied half-heartedly in Kenya. It was the field administration and the chiefs, however, who had to implement Whitehall's plans. This was the fundamental flaw in the Colonial Office's grand design; it could command but it could never guarantee that its orders would be obeyed. With Mitchell's support, these men on the spot effectively determined the pace of change and controlled the flow of information to London.[2]

Mitchell's 40 years as a colonial administrator in East Africa proved a handicap rather than the asset Whitehall had expected. His earlier career had never exposed him to the problems of African nationalism he had to face in Kenya. Some exposure to the more radical politics of West Africa would have provided him with a more useful experience for post-war Kenya than having dealt with the supine Tanganyika -African Association.[3] The Colonial Office, in contrast, had perforce to deal with this assertive populist nationalism and to incorporate its leaders. After the war, Britain's African collaborators were under attack from their people. In East and Central Africa, however, the search for new allies was not as imperative as in the West, since the colonial state could depend upon settler support. But in the new international climate settler political ambitions were an embarrassment and, in East Africa, Uganda had demonstrated that peasant producers could serve Britain's purposes more cost effectively than European farmers if a reliable group of African collaborators could be found.[4]

Such subversive thoughts had already begun to cross the official mind in Whitehall during the Attlee government. Although Creech Jones's beliefs became somewhat tarnished after he became Secretary of State in October 1946, this was perhaps more because of pressure from senior Cabinet colleagues, who simply wanted to use the colonies to finance Britain's trade deficit with the United States and to use colonial resources to rebuild the British economy, than because he was captured by the Colonial Office. It could equally be argued that Hinden's Fabian strategy swept through the Colonial Office between 1945 and 1950 and captured the official mind. Certainly Andrew Cohen shared most of Creech Jones's and Hinden's ideals.[5]

Mitchell and the field administration in Kenya, in contrast, failed to adapt to post-war circumstances and to the growth of African politics. Kenyatta was quite unlike any other African they had met; he was an educated, devious, professional politician, whom Creech Jones and Hinden knew better than most administrators. Kenyatta was also a spellbinding orator with complete control over his Kikuyu audiences. Mitchell, the paternalist indirect ruler, was completely unqualified to deal with such a rousing nationalist leader, who proved to be a much more subtle politician than the settlers.[6]

The Kenyan administration's ultimate failure, therefore, should be set against the transformed political scene in Kenya and in Whitehall. By 1947, the government's paternalist policies had virtually collapsed amidst widspread African opposition. For the last five years of Mitchell's governorship, the Kenyan state drifted aimlessly while the field administration and agricultural department fought over what direction the second colonial occupation should take in the reserves, and the settler district councils and the labour department were locked in conflict over the squatters' fate. Moreover, little attempt was made to reassert control over African Nairobi or to tackle the capital's acute housing shortage. Kenya's industrial policy discriminated against local Asian entre-preneurs, who might have created jobs, and vainly concentrated upon attracting international capital to invest in the new industrial area near the railway station. These international corporations, however, were only interested in investing in Kenya because of the colony's low wages. Low wages, however, prevented the stabilisation of the labour-force and the creation of a pool of skilled manpower. This economic strategy failed to produce any industrial 'take-off' or to ease the plight of 'outcast Nairobi'. Between 1945 and 1952 the city nevertheless attracted peasants from the reserves and dispossessed squatters, who joined the growing number of unemployed and destitute, depressing wages further and exacerbating Nairobi's social problems.[7]

Agricultural policy in Kikuyuland and the failure of incorporation

The government, encouraged by Humphrey and Lambert, moved against the proto-capitalists in 1945. It discovered that although it had been relatively easy to encourage African production during the depression and the war, it was impossible to staunch the flow. In post-war Kenya, the administration's paternalist policies and opposition to the peasant option quickly alienated the Kikuyu and drove them into the arms of the African politicians. By attempting to restrain and, indeed, to reverse the process of African accumulation, which had been let loose in the 1930s, the administration spurned the advances of the aspiring traders and commercial farmers, who in the first years of Mitchell's governorship had tried extremely hard to break into the magic circle, with its access to government patronage. Just when incorporation had seemed about to be attained, they were blocked by an alliance between the district administration, the settlers and the chiefs.

The administration saw these proto-capitalists as a threat to its continued control of rural Africa. It also feared that economic individualism would have disastrous ecological consequences and result in the dispossession of *ahoi* and other junior lineages from the *mbari*, which would shatter the social fabric of Kikuyuland. Humphrey's alarmist report on the situation in Nyeri had provided the administration with justification for its atavistic attack on the Kikuyu proto-capitalists.[8]

The settlers and chiefs had less altruistic motives. They saw the large-scale wattle and maize cultivators as a threat not to the social equilibrium of the reserves, but to their own privileged position. The settlers recognised that Kikuyu cultivators in the reserves and squatters in the White Highlands posed a serious challenge to their economic hegemony and that Africans could produce high-standard cash crops with less state support than many settlers. Moreover, if the settlers' economic primacy were questioned, their wartime political advances would disappear. The Kikuyu chiefs were equally hard-headed about the challenge to their power from the Kenya African Union. Their economic advantages over the alternative élite depended on the continued domination of the Local Native Councils by the chiefs and their clients. If this were broken and members of the alternative élite, like Beauttah and Ng'ang'a, were allowed some government patronage, then they would soon be able to mount a challenge to the established economic power of the chiefs. Thus, while the settlers were using their strong economic position to defend their wartime political gains, the chiefs, even more successfully, used their privileged political access to the district administration to bolster their economic dominance and to exclude the challengers, who attempted to use the Kenya African Union as a battering ram to gain incorporation into the colonial state.[9]

While the colonial state in West Africa was, therefore, at Whitehall's insistence, being weaned from its dependence on the chiefs and, in the Gold Coast and Southern Nigeria, induced to allow greater participation by the educated alternative élite and, in the last analysis, was even willing to incorporate the radicals of the Convention People's Party once they had demonstrated they had popular support, in Kenya the government responded to the 1947 crises by rushing to prop up the faltering authority of the chiefs. Indeed, when the struggle was at its fiercest, in the Kikuyu reserves during the peasant revolt, the Kenya African Union irreparably damaged its chances of incorporation because of its confrontation with the chiefs over terracing and was discredited in the eyes of the government.[10] Without the ability to mobilise sustained support even in Kikuyuland, the Kenya African Union was unable to force the authorities to abandon the chiefs, or more importantly the settlers, who controlled the political 'levers' the African politicians were denied. Unlike Nkrumah or the Kenyan settlers, Kenyatta could not translate political discontent into seats on the Legislative Council. Thus, instead of destroying the chiefs, the agricultural disturbances of 1947 cemented their alliance with the government.[11]

By 1947, the government's agricultural strategy had disintegrated. District Commissioners and agricultural officers could no longer take solace from the governor's persistent declarations that all was well and that Kenya was gradually becoming a multiracial society in which educated Africans could participate in the economic, political and social life of the colony. These men in the districts knew that this was palpably untrue and that frustration, especially amongst the Kikuyu, was threatening to erupt into violence.[12] The agricultural campaign, with its compulsory communal terracing two mornings per week, had provided the Nairobi militants with a ready-made constituency with which to challenge the African moderates' rural power base. Even by 1952, the benefits of the agricultural department's new strategy of encouraging peasant cash-crop production had not yet filtered down, while terracing continued unabated and the various agricultural regulations were enforced with even greater intensity as the number of European specialists in the technical departments grew to supervise this second colonial occupation. In his discussion of the origins of decolonisation, Ronald Robinson perceptively noted that the 'nationalists had to contrive a situation in which their rulers ran out of collaborators'.[13] The agricultural campaign in Kikuyuland had made this task easy by undermining the authority of the chiefs. But the moderates had lost control of the campaign to the militants who were not afraid of provoking the colonial régime, while the proto-capitalists had begun to draw back from a violent confrontation. Equally many poor peasants recognised that their interests were not the same as those of the alternative élite, who merely wanted to gain recognition from the district administration and a share in local patronage. Indeed, many of the proto-capitalists in the Kenya African Union were themselves seizing the land of the poor or former *ahoi* and were asserting private land rights over the commonage.[14]

The struggle in the reserves, therefore, was not simply a two-way contest between the loyalists and the alternative élite, but also included the mass of Kikuyu peasants, who, after the failure of the anti-terracing campaign in 1947, began to desert the proto-capitalists and to turn to the militants who had close ties with Nairobi. It was therefore extremely difficult for Kenyatta and his associates to translate the anti-colonial nationalism of the small modern élite 'into broader terms of indigenous, neo-traditional politics . . . [so that] it could challenge and overthrow the imperial collaborative system and set up a rival system of non-collaboration', as Ronald Robinson postulated. Instead, the rural radicals formed an alliance with the urban activists who wanted not to be incorporated into the colonial state but to destroy it. Increasingly the African moderates were squeezed between the chiefly establishment and the urban *nihilists* and could exercise little influence over the course of events, which escalated into violent conflict.[15]

The fate of the Kikuyu squatters

By 1952 the government's policies had also collapsed in the Rift Valley, where the settler-controlled district councils were allowed to rush ahead with their anti-squatter policies and to reduce squatter cultivation and stock rights, regardless of the effects upon the food supplies and incomes of squatter families. Despite warnings from the labour department and the administration in the surrounding reserves that the district councils were going too far too fast, the Secretariat refused to intervene and allowed the settlers to obstruct the labour department's attempts to devise a policy that would gradually, over the course of a generation, transform squatters into wage labourers. Yet, despite the provocative behaviour of the district councils, the mass expulsion of squatters from the White Highlands and Olenguruone was, in itself, insufficient to precipitate a major revolt. Squatter discontent was only one of several ingredients in Mau Mau.

Ranger has pointed out that 300,000 Ndebele squatters were moved from European estates in Matabeleland under the Land Apportionment Act in the late 1940s and early 1950s, which was far more than the number of Kikuyu affected by district council orders in Kenya.[16] In Kikuyuland, however, land was a scarce resource and when the dispossessed squatters returned to the reserves they discovered that their *githaka* land rights had been reapportioned among the senior lineage of the *mbari*. It was, therefore, impossible for the squatters to be reabsorbed into the Kikuyu reserves, where social divisions, based primarily on restricted access to land, were already causing conflict. The former squatters, therefore, could not be co-opted by the chiefs and the *mbari* leadership as a new group of dependents. Instead, they clashed with the rural landowners, intensified social tensions, and became a rural 'proletariat', denied access to land except as wage labourers for the African accumulators of the established élite around the chiefs and their rivals in the Kenya African Union.[17]

In contrast, Kalenjin squatters were able to fit back into life in the reserves. As Tabitha Kanogo shows, most squatters in western Kenya had not irreparably cut themselves off from their relations in the African Land Units.[18] They regarded squatting more as a form of migrant labour than as an opportunity to continue the peasant option on settler farms, away from the overcrowded reserves. The Kikuyu risked much more with the squatter option and, when their comparatively prosperous existence was curtailed after the war, their resentment was much greater than among the Kalenjin and Abaluhya.[19]

The response of the squatters in the Nyanza, Trans Nzoia and Uasin Gishu districts was also less militant because the settler alliance of anti-squatter forces had dissolved. The settler maize and wheat farmers and the plantation interests had delayed moves against the squatters until 1947 or 1948, by which time squatter resistance in Naivasha and the Aberdares had already been defeated. The western Kenyan district councils, disturbed by the conflict in the Kikuyu squatter areas, had therefore moved with great caution. Another crucial factor was that in the west, where the Kikuyu comprised only a small proportion of the squatter population, most of whom were Abaluhya, Nandi or Elgeyo, the majority of squatters still had aceess to land in the reserves.[20] These squatters, therefore, were able to challenge a divided settler community, and could shatter the tenuous agreement between the anti-squatter dairy and stock farmers and the apprehensive cereal farmers and the plantation sector by threatening to return to the reserves and thus exacerbate the existing labour shortages. This would have had serious repercussions as the squatters provided over 50 per cent of the local farm labour force and were indispensable during the harvests.[21] Thus, by 1951 the squatters in the three western district council areas had so alarmed the cereal farmers that they had compelled the settler cattle interest to back down and to accept a much more limited and slower reduction of squatter stock and cultivation in exchange for higher wages as the labour department had consistently advocated.

The squatters' access to land in western Kenya had also ensured that, despite the fears of the field administration, for a short time it had been possible to absorb large numbers of squatters and their cattle into the North Nyanza, Nandi and Elgeyo reserves without provoking an ecological crisis. This sojourn in the reserves, however, turned out to be a temporary move and, before the resulting tensions had time to surface, the pressure on the reserves was eased. Following the declaration of the Emergency, the panic-striken district councils bordering on Central Province quickly expelled their remaining Kikuyu squatters, who were forced to return to Kikuyuland where they joined the Land and Freedom Army in the forests.[22] Western Kenya, however, benefited from the Kikuyu's plight, because this mass expulsion of the Kikuyu enabled Abaluhya, Nandi and Elgeyo squatters to flood back into the White Highlands to fill the deficiencies in farm labour created by the Kikuyus' enforced departure. Mau Mau therefore eased the pressure in the non-Kikuyu reserves and, paradoxically, forestalled the development of potentially militant protest movements, such as Elijah Masinde's *Dini ya Msambwa* among the southern Abaluhya of Bukusu, and helped to ensure that the revolt would remain a purely Kikuyu fight against the British.[23]

Outcast Nairobi

In Nairobi, the militants' control over the locations and shanty towns was virtually absolute; the police seldom ventured into the area after dark. Thousands continued to sleep in the open and to scrounge a meagre living in the informal sector or from crime. The destitute, with nothing to lose, posed the most serious challenge to the government. They looked first to Chege Kibachia and the African Workers' Federation and, after his arrest in August 1947, to Fred Kubai, Bildad Kaggia and Mwangi Macharia for leadership. The Kikuyu, who formed over half the city's total population, were particularly resentful. Many of them had only recently been squeezed off their land by the proto-capitalists or been forced to leave the White Highlands because of the new restrictions on squatters. Nairobi offered them their only refuge. Full of thousands of unemployed vagrants, Nairobi was the centre of militant opposition and provided the required anonymity for the militants to co-ordinate protests in the reserves and the White Highlands and to control the introduction of the Mau Mau oath to unite the Kikuyu against the colonial régime.[24]

The militants suffered a heavy blow with the collapse of the Nairobi general strike in May 1950 and the arrests of Makhan Singh, Fred Kubai and Mwangi Macharia, but they quickly recouped their position because of the intransigence of the City Council and other employers, who dismissed thousands of Kikuyu strikers when they returned to work. This peremptory behaviour bolstered support for the militants when they were at their weakest.[25] During the next few months they reassessed their strategy and, within a year of their defeat by the government, Kubai and Kaggia captured control of the Nairobi branch of the Kenya African Union from Mbotela and the educated élite and began to use it as a power base from which to challenge Kenyatta's control over the nationalist movement and to usurp the position of the aspiring alternative élite, who were Kenyatta's main supporters. Trades union activity, centred around Kubai's semi-skilled followers in the Transport and Allied Workers' Union, became less important as the militants switched to nationalist politics, behind the facade of which they continued their mass oathing campaign, which they expanded beyond Nairobi into the Kikuyu reserves and the White Highlands.[26]

African politics

The Indianists have taught us that the British had little to fear from the politics of the locality.[27] Peasant revolts provided little threat to the stability of the empire provided they were restricted to one region. This was equally true in Africa. The Second World War and the second colonial occupation, however, transformed the scale of African political activity. Local disturbances, such as those in Murang'a during 1947, threatened to engulf neighbouring Kiambu and Nyeri as the effects of peasant protest rippled from one ridge to another. But even more important, as was clearly shown during the general strike of September 1947 in Tanganyika, the roads and the railway provided a trail along which the flame of resistance could travel between the centre and the locality.[28] Once the second colonial occupation had disturbed rural Africa, linkages were quickly established between the reserves and Nairobi as the reverberations of trouble in the districts were registered throughout the colony. Indeed local action was increasingly directed from Nairobi. The capital's taxis and country buses, as well as the railway, provided the arteries along which African politics flowed as urban militants began to organise rural resistance.[29]

Gallagher has described this process in India and West Africa, but the same holds true for Kenya, particularly after the Second World War when African politics began to take over from settler politics as the main cause of government apprehension. He observed:

> In Africa, as in India, much of the impetus behind the mass parties came from the policies of the government itself. It was the government which pushed ahead with economic development; consequently it had to intervene more continuously, more forcefully, inside African society than it had done before . . . The government . . . furnished the structure for mass parties. It produced the grievances; it also provided the way in which these grievances could find a vehicle for their expression. As it busied itself more in the affairs of its subjects, so it had to seek support (or at least acquiescence) from larger numbers of them.

Conclusion

Perforce it had dragged them out of the politics of localities and districts into wider arenas, into the politics of provinces and finally of the nation.[30]

In particular, he pointed out that the weakness in Whitehall's local government strategy, whether as designed by Lord Hailey or later in Cohen's famous despatch of 1947, was that concentration on local institutions did not 'divert attention from the centre . . . Instead it allowed the feared African politician to turn his locality into his bailiwick, and then to bond together one bailiwick with another in wider arenas of political action'.[31]

The Murang'a disturbances of 1947 mark the beginnings of this process in Kenya. The colonial régime could no longer isolate one district from its neighbours. The politically conscious élite seized on local problems to browbeat the field administration by complaining to the Secretariat or Whitehall. Even the Colonial Office did not escape unscathed, for the Russians could be relied upon to give publicity to any attack on British imperialism in the United Nations.[32] Under Kenyatta's leadership, the Kenya African Union mastered these political devices, but, by arousing peasant opposition, played into the arms of the chiefs and militants, for the peasant revolt had simply alienated the government and foreclosed any possibility of co-opting the moderates. Mitchell and the field administration reacted to the peasant revolt by concluding that Kenyatta and the Kenya African Union had shown themselves to be unscrupulous demagogues who refused to work within the limitations of the colonial system and were, therefore, unworthy of patronage. This refusal to incorporate the African proto-capitalists, of course, simply strengthened the influence of the militants who could argue that moderation and constitutional politics had failed to produce any reforms.[33]

This saga was repeated at the district level where the new politicians sought acceptance by the chiefs and district officials. The administration's alliance with the chiefs and traditional elders, however, precluded it from reaching any agreement with these rival elements. Moreover, its commitment to the communalist ideology of organic development and the preservation of 'traditional Africa' hindered it from recognising that the Kenya African Union, rather than the chiefs, now represented African opinion. As the effects of the second colonial occupation penetrated into the maize *shambas*, the stalwart faithfuls of the Kikuyu Central Association and the returned *askari* of a younger generation coalesced to challenge the political and economic power of the chiefs and their clients, whom they denounced as government stooges.[34]

Even in the localities the dimensions of political activity were transformed. Whereas in the 1920s, opposition to the chiefs was manifested through *mbari* solidarity, the second colonial occupation provided the African politicians with an issue around which to mobilise pan-*mbari* opposition and to organise resistance throughout the location and, indeed, the district and province.[35] The second colonial occupation in fact enabled the Kenya African Union to emerge as a nationalist movement, with support throughout the colony, not simply among the Kikuyu in Central Province. Although they remained the most politically conscious group in the movement, Kenyatta ensured that all the main tribes were represented in its leadership. Compared to the Kikuyu Central Association, or Thuku's unsuccessful East African Association, the Kenya African Union was able to tap popular discontent outside Kikuyuland to a much greater degree than any of its predecessors.[36] The confines of tribe were turned into a political resource by men like Beauttah, Awori and Ngei during the Kenya African Union's internal political bargaining. Indeed, tribalism became a tool for the new movement and ceased to be an insurmountable obstacle to nationalist solidarity. But, as Anil Seal has pointed out for India, 'what seems to have decided political choices in the localities was the race for influence, status and resources. In the pursuit of these aims, patrons regimented their clients into factions which jockeyed for position . . . However persuasive the slogans from the top, they can have made little impact upon the unabashed scramblers for advantage at the bottom'. This was equally true in Kenya. The aims of the African élite were never the same as those of the peasantry or urban unemployed.[37]

Some thoughts on Mau Mau

This book is Kikuyu-centric because the Kikuyu bore the brunt of the post-war social engineering, dominated African politics and provided most of Kenya's African traders and commercial farmers. The process of internal social differentiation was more advanced among the Kikuyu than elsewhere in Kenya because of their close ties with the international economy, both as wage labourers and cash-crop cultivators. Moreover, the second colonial occupation progressed most rapidly in Central Province. Thus, whereas the Kikuyu peasantry had already been antagonised by the demands of the terracing campaign in 1947, the agricultural development programme was still only beginning in Nyanza and did not really get under way in Machakos, despite Mitchell's 'D Day', until 1950.

However, once the agricultural campaign gatherered momentum in Machakos after 1950, it quickly aroused widespread resistance and, by 1954, the field administration had almost lost control of the district as it had in Kikuyuland. For six months in 1954, Machakos Kamba tottered on the brink of joining the Mau Mau revolt. By then, however, the

Conclusion

Kikuyu forest fighters had already been driven out of the reserve and forced to seek refuge in the forests. The Kamba, therefore, wisely waited for the outcome of the conflict and did not join forces with their Kikuyu neighbours.[38]

Settler distrust of all Kikuyu during the rebellion benefited other Africans, especially in the Rift Valley and Nyanza. We have seen how Kikuyu squatters were replaced by Nandi and Abaluhya resident labourers on settler farms, thereby averting conflict over access to land in the reserves, but the mass screening exercise of 'Operation Anvil' in April 1954 equally drastically reduced the number of Kikuya in Nairobi and provided new employment opportunities for other Africans. In the short term, Mau Mau enabled the Kenyan government to harass its Kikuyu opponents, to strengthen its alliance with the Kikuyu loyalists and to reduce the tensions created in western Kenya by the second colonial occupation and by the anti-squatter measures of the settler district councils, at the expense of suspect Kikuyu.[39] At the same time, fundamental Kikuyu land-tenure reforms were pushed through, creating consolidated smallholdings and entrenching the land rights of collaborators in Kiambu, Murang'a and Nyeri. Without the Emergency, the government would have been unable to press these reforms upon a reluctant peasantry. Mau Mau provided a useful excuse behind which the field administration and agriculturalists were able to institute the social reconstruction they had earlier contemplated but had been powerless to achieve.[40]

The different effects of the second colonial occupation and of the Emergency on particular districts therefore ensured, along with the government's ban on pan-tribal political associations, that nationalist solidarity was not yet achieved. The Emergency seemed to provide an opportunity for the non-Kikuyu to catch up and to gain greater access to hitherto Kikuyu dominated education, skilled employment and commercial opportunities. But in fact it laid the foundations for the subsequent success of Kikuyu businessmen and commercial farmers by sweeping away traditional obstacles to private tenure and bank loans, which ensured Kikuyu domination of Kenyatta's neo-colonial state and allowed the Kikuyu proto-capitalists to become Kenya's first indigenous bourgeoisie. The tribal division of power in the Kenyan state had to be reworked when the Kikuyu were readmitted to political activity and was ultimately resolved in the five-year struggle for power and access to state patronage between 1961 and 1966 – first, before independence, with the Kalenjin and the Coast Africans who supported the Kenya African Democratic Union and then, after 12 December 1963 and the attainment of *Uhuru*, in the more difficult contest with Kenya's second most powerful tribe, the Luo.[41]

Most interpretations of the origins of Mau Mau date the government's loss of control in Nairobi and Kikuyuland from 1950, but this is three years too late; 1947 was the key year. The administration never really reasserted its authority after the disturbances of September 1947. In Nairobi, Makhan Singh, the Indian communist, helped Kaggia and Kubai to create a stronger, more politically conscious trades union movement from the remnants of the African Workers' Federation. In alliance with the Kikuyu street gangs, the urban political militants quickly established a firm grip over 'outcast' Nairobi, although they alienated the non-Kikuyu inhabitants of the locations.[42]

The prestige of the chiefs, the agricultural department and the field administration never recovered from the blows they suffered in 1947 during the peasant revolt. Politics in the reserves came to be dominated by a new group of rural radicals, such as Beauttah, Gathanju and Mwangi Macharia, who had close contacts with the Nairobi militants. They continued to criticise the chiefs and the soil conservation campaign. During 1950 and 1951, oathing spread rapidly throughout Kikuyuland, cementing peasant resistance by binding the peasants not only by particularist appeals to tradition, but also by making them break their psychological acceptance of British authority in a specific act of illegality and declaration of support for the militants. Thus, the individual was subsumed within the Kikuyu community. Oathing signified the psychological acceptance of resistance and marked the first step along the path to armed rebellion. By October 1952, this step had already been taken by many Kikuyu. The divisions had been drawn.[43]

Mau Mau's uniqueness, however, should not be unduly exaggerated. Throughout British Africa, the consequences of the second colonial occupation on peasant life were a key factor in the growth of mass support for African nationalism. The Tanganyika African National Union's strength in Sukumaland during the 1950s, the 1953 disturbances in Nyasaland and the support for the Convention People's Party in the southern Gold Coast, like Mau Mau in Kikuyuland, all mobilised peasant support for the nationalist élite in the capitals because of the demands the post-war agricultural development campaign made upon rural Africans. The second colonial occupation enlarged their vision and brought many Africans, for the first time since the conquest, into sustained opposition to the colonial order. Whether the immediate focus of discontent was destocking as in Sukumaland, the uprooting of the cocoa crop because of swollen shoot disease as in the Gold Coast, or terracing and soil conservation regulations as in Kenya and Nyasaland, once the peasantry were aroused the days were numbered for colonial rule.[44]

Just as the various provinces of Kenya were disturbed by the second colonial occupation at various times, equally different British colonies in Africa experienced its impact at different moments and with different consequences. In the Gold Coast, the agricultural department's attempt to eradicate swollen shoot disease during the late 1940s generated support in the south-east of the colony for Nkrumah's Convention People's Party and discredited the chiefs. This enabled Nkrumah to gain support beyond his original urban base and to sweep the cocoa-growing areas in the 1951 election. In Nyasaland, however, the soil conservation campaign gathered momentum more slowly and only began to arouse peasant opposition after 1950, culminating in the 1953 disturbances, which were associated with the establishment of the Central African Federation.[45]

The effects of the occupation also differed profoundly in the settler-dominated colonies of Kenya and the Rhodesias. In the Rhodesias, especially in the south, the hold of the settler farmers over the state and the economy was much stronger than in Kenya. Northern Rhodesia had nearly twice as many Europeans as Kenya, and Southern Rhodesia had more than five times as many. Moreover, during the rule of the British South Africa Company before 1923, the settlers had effectively restricted African peasant production. Even the mining interests in Northern Rhodesia had been tied into the settler economy and had accepted the higher cost of settler-grown food supplies from Southern Rhodesia and South Africa in return for a guaranteed supply of cheap migrant labour. In Kenya such a bargain between metropolitan and settler capital could not be struck. The interests of the settler food producers, who had formed the Kenya Farmers' Association to gain control over the maize market and who wanted to secure the maximum return for their crops, and the large-scale employers, who wanted to minimise their labour costs, always conflicted. African peasant producers were therefore able successfully to undercut the settler farmers and to continue to supply the domestic market; they had established their independent position in the Kenyan economy.[46]

These economic differences, of course, stemmed from the fact that after 1923 the Rhodesian settlers became their own masters with complete control over their colonial state. They continued the British South Africa Company's policy of suppressing peasant production with even greater zeal. In Kenya, by contrast, 1923 saw the Devonshire Declaration of the paramountcy of African interests. Although it has long been fashionable among historians to deride this vague pledge, and although it is true that the British and Kenyan governments failed to live up to their promise, the fact that Kenya was subordinate to the metropolitan control of the Colonial Office did ensure that African interests were considered and sometimes nurtured. Thus, while African proto-capitalists were strangled in Southern Rhodesia, in Kenya the Kikuyu were allowed to become a serious economic threat to the settlers' dominant position in the colonial state during the depression and the Second World War.[47]

The settlers, however, were largely able to exclude their Kikuyu challengers from the White Highlands. This ensured that the process of capital accumulation was turned inward upon the Kikuyu reserves, which further exacerbated the growing social pressures over access to land and the problems of internal differentiation. Mau Mau, therefore, was not only a collision between settler and Kikuyu proto-capitalists, struggling to become an indigenous capitalist élite, but was also an eruption by the landless and those who had lost out in the scramble for resources in the reserves against Kikuyu accumulators. These tensions were apparent inside the Kenya African Union. The Kikuyu proto-capitalists, who were not allied with the chiefs, supported Kenyatta and the moderates who provided the leadership of the movement until 20 October 1952, but it was the dispossessed have-nots who provided the recruits for the forest fight which developed once the British had detained virtually all the leading political activists – moderate and militant alike.[48]

The reason why Mau Mau was so bloody and by far the most dramatic example of post-war African opposition to the demands of the second colonial occupation and of disillusionment with British colonialism, was that several streams of discontent coincided among the Kikuyu and precipitated the revolt. The Kikuyu were not simply deeply disrupted by the agricultural campaign and the second colonial occupation, but were also bitterly divided among themselves. In many respects Mau Mau was a Kikuyu civil war between the rich and the poor; the Christian missions versus the adherents of the independent churches; the old against the young. The Kikuyu reserves had been more fully integrated into the international economy than any other African Land Unit in Kenya and were already experiencing a three-way conflict – between the chiefs and the established traders; the aspiring commercial farmers and traders who supported Kenyatta and the Kenya African Union; and the mass of Kikuyu, who were being squeezed in the fight for land and commercial control by the two rival élites.[49]

These problems of internal differentiation were further exacerbated by the wider conflict between the Kikuyu and the European settlers, which was most blatant in the White Highlands whre they stood face to face. Outcast Nairobi, which was the militants' power-base against the settlers and chiefs (and after 1951 also against Kenyatta and the moderates in the Kenya African Union) provided a refuge for those disgruntled Kikuyu who had either been defeated in the struggle in the reserves and the White Highlands or were simply innocent victims.

The government's failure to create its vision of a multiracial Kenya and the outbreak of the Mau Mau rebellion shortly after Mitchell's retirement, were almost inevitable outcomes of this unique combination of intractable problems. Until the British government could select and support a Kenyan governor with the courage to sacrifice the settlers and to incorporate the alternative African élite around Kenyatta and the Kikuyu Central Association faction inside the Kenya African Union, long-term political stability was impossible. Despite his vast experience of East Africa, Philip Mitchell was not that man. He had never even begun to understand the problem. In the 1940s only the subtle political minds of Harold Macmillan and Jomo Kenyatta had really grasped what needed to be done. The Mau Mau rebellion, however, foreclosed the settler option once and for all and, in the early 1960s, enabled Macmillan and Kenyatta, with the help of Macleod, Mboya, Blundell and MacDonald, to reach an arrangement which satisfied the Kikuyu élites (both loyalist and Kenyatta-ite) and the British.[50] But that is another story.

Notes

1. CO 533/549/38232 (1946–47), 'European Settlement', P.E. Mitchell's speech to the Nairobi Caledonian Society, 30 November 1946; CO 533/549/38232/15 (1946–47), 'European Settlement Squatters', P.E. Mitchell to Creech Jones, 14 April 1947. RH Mss. Brit.Emp.s. 365, 'Fabian Colonial Bureau', Box 5, File 3, ff. 70, contains Rita Hinden's hostile reaction to Mitchell's paternalism. She observed to H. Beer, a Kenyan settler, in a letter dated 27 February 1948, 'I am afraid I do not admire the speech as much as you do. He is so insistent that what we have to do is to establish British values and standards in Kenya, and hardly mentions the fact that Africans may perhaps have some values and standards which they desire to keep. I agree that British imperialism may – to some people – be an expression of faith and purpose, and it is stupid to use it just as a term of abuse. But I do not like imperialism even when it is a faith, and I shall continue to work for its ending as soon as possible. That does not mean to say that we have to walk out of Kenya tomorrow – but it does mean that all our efforts are strained to achieve the day when we can walk out and leave a democracy – independent of race – behind us.' Mitchell was never able to understand such views. Africans, he considered, would for many years, perhaps centuries, be unready to receive independence.

2. CO 533/561/12 (1950), 'Petitions and Memorials: Kikuyu People'; CO 533/561/14 (1950), 'Petitions: East African Trades Union Congress'; CO 533/566/7 (1950), 'The Kenya African Union'; and CO 533/566/8 (1951), 'The Kenya African Union', *passim*, all clearly show how the Colonial Office simply reiterated the views of the Kenyan government in replies to African petitioners. Whitehall had no alternative but to accept Mitchell's advice, since it lacked any alternative sources of information. As the situation became increasingly tense in Kenya it became futile to send petitions to the Colonial Office in order to circumvent the Kenyan government. Invariably the reply simply repeated verbatim the counter-submission of the Kenyan authorities.

3. Until the last years of his Kenyan governorship Mitchell had never encountered the kind of sustained African opposition or populist politics West Africa governors had endured in the 1920s and 1930s. See J. Miles, 'Rural Protest in the Gold Coast', pp. 152–70; and M. Crowder, *West Africa under Colonial Rule*, pp. 454–78.

4. C. Ehrlich, 'The Uganda Economy', pp. 397–475.

5. CO 533/547/38132/465 (1947), 'Visit of Mbiyu Koinange to the United Kingdom', P.M. Koinange to Creech Jones, 24 June 1947, records the concern of one political activist at the failure of Creech Jones and the Labour Government to fulfil their promises. See also R.E. Robinson, 'Sir Andrew Cohen', pp. 353–63, and 'Andrew

Conclusion

Cohen and the Transfer of Power in Tropical Africa', pp. 50–68. For an account of American economic pressure upon the Attlee government, see E.A. Brett, S. Gilliatt and A. Pople, 'Planned Trade, Labour Party Policy and US Intervention', pp. 130–42.

6. Negley Farson, Mitchell's journalist friend, provided an unusually sympathetic account of Kenyatta in his book on Kenya, *Last Chance in Africa* pp. 113–31, as did Wyn Harris in CO 537/3591/38733 (1948), 'Petitions to the United Nations', minutes of meeting with Kenyatta, 15 October 1948. Mitchell, in contrast, came to believe that Kenyatta was the organiser of opposition to the government and an avowed communist. This view was encouraged by reports such as CO 537/3646/47272/1 (1948), 'Political Intelligence Reports: East Africa',· Kenya report, September–October 1948. J. Murray-Brown's semi-official biography, *Kenyatta*, pp. 264–96, avoids controversy and fails to provide an adequate account of Kenyatta's political activities between his return in Kenya in September 1946 and his arrest in October 1952.

7. A. Hake, *African Metropolis*, pp. 53–63; S.D. Stichter, 'The Formation of a Working Class in Kenya', pp. 34–44; and her 'Workers, Trade Unions, and Mau Mau Rebellion' pp. 259–75. See KNA Lab 9/30, 'Colonial Cooperation: African Labour Conference, Elizabethville, July 1950', E.M. Hyde-Clarke, 'Notes on Efficiency of Labour', undated; Lab 9/452, 'Minimum Wage Ordinance, 1947–51', T.G. Askwith, 28 December 1946 Lab 9/644, 'Labour Exchange: General Policy, 1944–56', P. Wyn Harris to the Executive Council, 15 February 1944; and Lab 9/1090, 'Report of the Central Minimum Wages Advisory Board, 1947', E.M. Hyde-Clarke, 10 April 1947; and A. Hope-Jones, 16 April 1947, for various attempts by the Kenyan government to overcome the problems of Kenya's inefficient, low-wage economy.

8. CO 852/662/19936/2 (1945–46), 'Soil Erosion: Kenya', N. Humphrey, 'The Relationship of Population to the Land in South Nyeri', *passim*; KNA DC/NYI 2/1/20, 'Mr Humphrey's Report on South Nyeri, 1944–47', N. Humphrey to D.L. Blunt, 'A Preliminary Report on Agricultural Conditions in South Nyeri', 22 Sepember 1944; and DC/NYI 2/2/4, 'Mr Humphrey's Report on Agriculture in South Nyeri, 1945', *passim*, but especially D.L. Morgan to C. Tomkinson, 28 March 1945.

9. KNA Secretariat 1/1/12, 'Report of the Joint Agricultural and Veterinary Services Sub-Committe of the Development Committee', *passim*, for settler attitudes to the peasant option; and J.M. Lonsdale's unpublished paper, 'African Elites and Social Classes in Colonial Kenya', pp. 10–14, for one account of the struggle between the chiefs and the alternative élite around Kenyatta and the Kikuyu Central Association for political and economic power. See also B.E. Kipkorir, 'The Educated Elite and Local Society', pp. 254–68.

10. Creech Jones, 'The Place of African Local Administration in Colonial Policy', pp. 3–6; R.E. Robinson, 'The Relationship of Major and Minor Local Government Authorities', pp. 30–3, and his article, 'The Progress of Provincial Councils in the British African Territories', pp. 59–68; R.A. Stevens, 'The Application of English Local Government Principles in Africa', pp. 68–73; Earl of Listowel, 'The Modern Conception of Government in British Africa', pp. 99–105; and the African Studies Branch of the Colonial Office, 'A Survey of the Development of Local Government in The African Territories since 1947', pp. 1–83. For developments in Kenya see D. O'Hagan, 'African's Part in Nairobi Local Government', pp. 156–8; the African Studies Branch of the Colonial Office, 'Local Government Reorganisation in the Eastern Provinces of Nigeria and Kenya', pp. 18–19, 25–9; and KNA DC/FH 1/26, 'Fort Hall Annual Report, 1947', pp. 1–6, 15; and DC/FH 1/27, 'Fort Hall Annual Report, 1948', pp. 1–2, 4–5, 11. See also S.D. Mueller's thesis, 'Political Parties in Kenya', pp. 1–7, 22–40.

11. KNA DC/FH 1/26, 'Fort Hall Annual Report, 1947', pp. 1–6; and MAA 8/68, 'Chief Waruhiu, 1948–52', *passim*.

12. *ibid*. Wyn Harris was particularly concerned about the government's loss of control over the Kikuyu reserves, see P. Wyn Harris to P.E. Mitchell, August 1948.

Conclusion

13. R.E. Robinson, 'Non-European Foundations of European Imperialism', p. 138.
14. J.M. Lonsdale's unpublished paper, 'Explanations of the Mau Mau Revolt', pp. 4–6, 8–10; and KNA Secretariat 1/12/8, 'Labour Unrest: Intelligence Reports, Central Province, 1947', C. Penfold to P. Wyn Harris, 25 September 1947 and 10 October 1947.
15. R.E. Robinson, 'Non-European Foundations of European Imperialism', p. 138; F. Furedi, 'The African Crowd in Nairobi', pp. 282–9; and S.B. Stichter, 'Workers, Trade Unions and the Mau Mau Rebellion', pp. 260–75.
16. T.O. Ranger, *Peasant Consciousness and Guerilla War in Zimbabwe* pp. 99–132.
17. G. Kitching, *Class and Economic Change in Kenya*, pp. 128–30, 144–6, 288–97.
18. T.M.J. Kanogo's unpublished paper, 'Comparative Analysis of the Aspirations of the Kikuyu, Luo and Luhya Workers in the White Highlands', pp. 10–17, and CO 533/549/38232/15 (1946–47), 'European Settlement: Squatters', J.H. Martin, 'The Problem of the Squatter: Economic Survey of Resident Labour in Kenya', 24 February 1947. Martin discovered that 72% of squatters surveyed in the Uasin Gishu, 51 per cent in Trans Nzoia and 52 per cent in Naivasha claimed to have land in the reserves, but while the claims of Kikuyu squatters were probably based only on a vague claim to *githaka* land rights, those of Nandi, Luo and Abaluhya squatters in the Uasin Gishu and Trans Nzoia were based on hard fact and frequent periods of residence in the reserves.
19. T.M.J. Kanogo's thesis, 'The History of Kikuyu Movement . . .', pp. 245–379; and F. Furedi, 'The Social Composition of the Mau Mau Movement in the White Highlands', pp. 492–504. See also T.M.J. Kanogo, 'Rift Valley Squatters and Mau Mau', pp. 243–51 and M. Tamarkin, 'Mau Mau in Nakuru' pp. 228–37. B.A. Ogot, 'Politics, Culture and Music in Central Kenya', pp. 277–86, which remains one of the few serious studies of Mau Mau's ideological aims, has emphasised the centrality of the land issue to the rebellion. See also J.M. Lonsdale's unpublished essay, 'Kenya's Civil War and Glorious Revolution'.
20. CO 533/549/38232/15 (1946–47), 'European Settlement: Squatters', J.H. Martin, 'The Problem of the Squatter; Economic Survey of Resident Labour in Kenya', 24 February 1947.
21. KNA Lab 9/326, 'Resident Labour: Trans Nzoia, 1945–57', F.R. Bancroft to T.C. Colchester, 7 November 1946; and Lab 9/598, 'Resident Labour: Trans Nzoia, 1943–56', A.C. Hoey to F.W. Cavendish-Bentinck, 12 February 1946. See also Lab 9/247, 'Labour for Pyrethrum, 1953', *passim*; and Lab 9/351, 'Supply: Labour Shortage, 1946–49', A.T. Wise to E.M. Hyde-Clarke, 5 February 1947, 'Special Labour (Native) Census, 1946'.
22. C.G. Rosberg and J.Nottingham, *The Myth of Mau Mau*, pp. 285–6.
23. KNA Secretariat 1/2/2, 'Nyanza Province, 1949–50', P. Wyn Harris to the Executive Council, 13 July 1949; and minutes of meeting to discuss the *Dini ya Msambwa*, Kakamega, 6 September 1949; and C.M. Deverell to K.K. O'Connor, 12 October 1949. See also C.G. Rosberg and J. Nottingham, *The Myth of Mau Mau*, pp. 328–30; G.S. Were, 'Politics, Religion and Nationalism in Western Kenya', pp. 92–103; and A. Wipper, 'Elijah Masinde – a folk hero', pp. 157–81.
24. J. Spencer, *KAU*, pp. 208, 211–13, 221–4, 227–8.
25. KNA MAA 8/22, 'City African Affairs Officer: Correspondence, 1947–50', G.R.B. Brown to E.R. St. A. Davies, 23 May 1950.
26. J. Spencer, *KAU*, pp. 202–32; and B. Kaggia, *Roots of Freedom*, pp. 79–83, 108–9. R. Buijtenhuijs, *Essays on Mau Mau*, pp. 12–35; and R.M. Githige's thesis, 'The Religious Factor in Mau Mau', pp. 149–244, discuss the origins and significance of Mau Mau oaths.
27. J. Gallagher, *The Decline, Revival and Fall of the British Empire*, pp. 145–9; J. Gallagher, G. Johnson and A. Seal, *Locality, Province and Nation*; and especially A. Seal, 'Imperialism and Nationalism in India', pp. 3–6, 15–27. See also A. Seal, *The Emergence of Indian Nationalism*, pp. 341–51.

28. J. Iliffe, *A Modern History of Tanganyika*, pp. 402-4, and his article, 'The Creation of Group Consciousness among the Dockworkers of Dar-es-Salaam, 1929-50', pp. 63-4.
29. J. Spencer, 'Kenya African Union and Mau Mau', p. 205; and *KAU*, pp. 202-32, 239-40; M. Singh, *History of Kenya's Trade Union Movement*, vol.1, pp. 240-5, 268-9 for information about the long struggle between the Nairobi City Council and the Transport and Allied Workers' Union over the taxi-cab bylaws, which may partly explain the militancy of Nairobi's taxi drivers and their prominent role in Mau Mau oathing.
30. J. Gallagher, *The Decline, Revival and Fall of the British Empire*, p. 148.
31. *ibid*, p. 147.
32. CO 537/3591/38733 (1948), 'Petitions to the United Nations', A.B. Cohen to J. Galsworthy, 12 October 1948; J. Galsworthy to J. Fletcher-Cooke, 14 October 1948 and A.B. Cohen to P.E. Mitchell, 14 October 1948. See also CO 537/4661/38733 (1949), 'Petitions to the United Nations', P. Wyn Harris to A.B. Cohen, 23 February 1948; and CO 537/2545/96038/1 (1947), 'Soviet Propaganda in Colonial Newspapers', *passim*.
33. CO 537/3588/38696 (1947-48), 'Activities of Mathu', *passim*; CO 533/543/38086/38 (1949), 'Petitions: Kikuyu Central Association', P.E. Mitchell to Creech Jones, 28 February 1949; and CO 533/540/38032 (1949), 'Legislative Council', P.E. Mitchell to Creech Jones, 11 December 1948; CO 533/566/7 (1950), 'Kenya African Union', P.E. Mitchell to Creech Jones, 31 January 1950; and CO 533/566/8 (1951), 'Kenya African Union', T. Mbotela to P. Rogers, 28 April 1951; and P.E. Mitchell to J. Griffiths, 3 May 1951.
34. KNA DC/FH 1/25, 'Fort Hall Annual Report, 1946', pp. 7, 9-10; MAA 7/2, 'Nyeri Ex-Soldiers Association, 1945-47', D. O'Hagan to W.S. Marchant, 6 July 1946; and Secretariat 1/12/1, 'Manpower and Civil Reabsorption, 1946', A.L.B. Perkin to G.M. Rennie, 'Manpower, Demobilisation and Reabsorption', pp. 18-57, 28 February 1946.
35. KNA DC/KBU 1/38, 'Kiambu Annual Report, 1947', pp. 1-6; DC/KBU 1/43, 'Kiambu Annual Report, 1952', pp. 1-4; DC/FH 1/26, 'Fort Hall Annual Report, 1947', pp. 1-6, 15; DC/FH 1/27, 'Fort Hall Annual Report, 1948', pp. 1-2, 4-6, 11; DC/FH 1/31, 'Fort Hall Annual Report, 1952', pp. 1-5, 11-18. See also MAA 8/68, 'Chief Waruhiu, 1948-52', P. Wyn Harris to K.K. O'Connor, 30 July 1948; and to P.E. Mitchell, August 1948; and Secretariat 1/12/8, 'Labour Unrest: Intelligence Reports, Central Province, 1947', *passim*.
36. J. Spencer, *KAU*, pp. 224-5. In November 1951 the Central Committee of the Kenya African Union consisted of:

President	Jomo Kenyatta	Kikuyu
General Secretary	J.K. Otiende	Abaluhya
Assistant General Secretary	Paul Ngei	Kamba
Treasurer	Harry L. Nangurai	Maasai
Assistant Treasurer	William Kioko	Kamba
Trustees	R. Achieng Oneko	Luo
	Mbiyu Koinange	Kikuyu
	Gideon Nzaka Rimba	Giriama
Auditor	Peter Okondo	Abaluhya
Committee Members	Fred Kubai	Kikuyu
	Bildad Kaggia	Kikuyu
	James Beauttah	Kikuyu
	Senior Chief Koinange	Kikuyu
	Charles Wambaa	Kikuyu
	Jonathan Njoroge	Kikuyu

Conclusion

Jessie Kariuki	Kikuyu
James Njoroge	Kikuyu
Isaac Kitabi	Kamba

Thus while the main offices were distributed among the main tribes, the Kikuyu still dominated the committee. Overall there were ten Kikuyu members, three Kamba, two Abaluhya, and one member each from the Luo, Maasai and Giriama.

37. J. Gallagher, *The Decline, Revival and Fall of the British Empire*, p. 148. Many obstacles to nationalist solidarity, of course, remained. The moderate Coast African, Tom Mbotela, who served as Superintendent of African Locations in Nairobi, and who was ousted by the militants from the Vice Presidency of the Kenya African Union at the elections in November 1951, had earlier complained that: 'As regards the Kikuyu, the time has also come when they should abolish this deplorable idea of thinking that everything good in the city should be for the Kikuyu and nobody else'. This view was shared by many other non-Kikuyu inhabitants of the city, and partly explains why Mau Mau was unable to gain the support of Africans from Nyanza and the Coast, and remained a Kikuyu dominated movement. See CO 533/562/7 (1950), 'Information on Trade Unionism in Kenya by Tom Mbotela', Tom Mbotela, 'Memorandum on African Interests in Nairobi', 20 July 1950. Mbotela was assassinated by Mau Mau on 27 November 1952. A. Seal, 'Imperialism and Nationalism in India', p. 3, examines the same process in India.

38. KNA DC/MKS 1/1/33, 'Machakos Annual Reports, 1955–56' and MAA 7/112 'Policy: Kamba in Nairobi and Mombasa, 1954–56'.

39. D. Mukaru-Ng'ang'a, 'Mau Mau, Loyalists and Politics in Murang'a', pp. 366–83; M. Omosule, 'Kiama Kia Muingi', *passim*; and C.G. Rosberg and J. Nottingham, *The Myth of Mau Mau*, pp. 303–8.

40. A. Thurston's draft manuscript, 'The Intensification of Smallholder Agriculture in Kenya' pp. 123–204; M.P.K. Sorrenson, *Land Reform in the Kikuyu Country*, pp. 97–252; and M. McWilliam, 'The Managed Economy', pp. 257–69.

41. G. Wasserman, *Politics of Decolonization*, *passim*; D. Goldsworthy, *Tom Mboya*, pp. 131–46, 166–93, 232–46; and C. Gertzel, *The Politics of Independent Kenya*, *passim*.

42. C.G. Rosberg and J. Nottingham, *The Myth of Mau Mau*, pp. 262–76; R. Buijtenhuijs, *Essays on Mau Mau*, pp. 17–35; B.J. Berman, 'Bureaucracy and Incumbent Violence', pp. 165–72; S.B. Stichter, 'Workers, Trade Unions and the Mau Mau Rebellion', pp. 269–70; M. Singh, *History of Kenya's Trade Union Movement*, vol. 1, pp. 161–287; and S.B. Sticher, 'Trade Unionism in Kenya', pp. 155–72. See also CO 533/561/14 (1950), 'Petitions: East African Trades Union Congress', East African Trades Union Congress to E. Parry, Assistant Labour Advisor to the Secretary of State, 23 November 1949; and J.D. Rankine's note, 20 October 1950; CO 533/562/7 'Information on Trade Unionism in Kenya by Tom Mbotela', *passim*; and CO 533/566/6 (1950), 'Temporary Removal of Undesirable Natives Legislation', J.D. Rankine to Creech Jones, 18 January 1950.

43. J. Spencer, *KAU*, pp. 204–10, 239–40, and his article, 'Kenya African Union and Mau Mau', pp. 207–12, 214–18. R.M. Githige's thesis, 'The Religious Factor in Mau Mau', pp. 76–116 analyses Kikuyu traditional oaths; pp. 117–59, Kikuyu Central Association oaths. Mau Mau oaths and the 'Oath of Unity' are discussed on pp. 160–210; and the Batuni oath on pp. 211–38.

44. G.A. Maguire, *Towards Uhuru in Tanzania*, pp. 27–31, 59–78, and his article, 'The Emergence of the Tanganyika African National Union in the Lake Province', pp. 639–66; Wendy Sykes's draft manuscript on 'Sukumaland', *passim*; D. Austin, *Politics in Ghana*, pp. 58–66, 159–61. For information on opposition to soil conservation measures in colonial Nyasaland, I am grateful to William Beinart, Richard Grove and Megan Vaughan.

Conclusion

45. D. Austin, *Politics in Ghana*, pp. 58–66, 159–61. Oral information from William Beinart and Richard Grove. See also R.I. Rotberg. *The Rise of Nationalism in Central Africa*, pp. 257–62.

46. The following essays from R. Palmer and N. Parsons (eds), *The Roots of Rural Poverty in Central and Southern Africa*, reflect the influence of under-development theory on African historiography in the late 1970s: M. Muntemba, 'Thwarted Development', pp. 345–61; R. Palmer, 'The Agricultural History of Rhodesia', pp. 227–45; I. Phimister, 'Peasant Production and Underdevelopment in Southern Rhodesia', pp. 255–64; and B. Kosmin, 'The Inyoka Tobacco Industry of the Shangwe People', pp. 279–85. See also C. Van Onselen, *Chibaro* pp. 74–127. It should, however, be noted that recent work by Wolfgang Dopfke and T.O. Ranger has cast some doubt on the destruction of the peasantry thesis so fashionable in the 1970s.

For the Kenyan peasantry see P. Mosley, *The Settler Economies*, pp. 71–143; D. Mukaru-Ng'ang'a, 'What is Happening to the Kenyan Peasantry?', pp. 10–13; and M.P. Cowen's unpublished papers, 'Patterns of Cattle Ownership and Dairy Production', pp. 23–43 and 'Differentiation in a Kenya Location', *passim*. For an assessment of what has happened to the Kenyan peasantry since independence see P. Anyang'-Nyong'o, 'What the Friends of the Peasant are', pp. 17–26 and 'The Development of a Middle Peasantry in Nyanza', pp. 108–20; A.L.N. Njonjo 'The Kenya Peasantry', pp. 27–40; and M.P. Cowen, 'The Agrarian Problem', pp. 57–73.

47. R.E. Robinson, 'The Moral Disarmament of African Empire', pp. 92–93; and R.E. Gregory, *Sidney Web and East Africa passim*, for the Colonial Office's agonising over African interests.

48. R. Buijtenhuijs, *Esays on Mau Mau*, pp. 49–51 and H.K. Wachanga, *The Swords of Kirinyaga*, pp. xv–xvi; until he entered the forest Wachanga was the General Secretary of the Mau Mau Central Committee, the *Muhimu*.

49. B.A. Ogot, 'Revolt of the Elders', pp. 136–145; and MAA 7/634, 'Intelligence Reports: Central Province, 1948–53', W.H. Cantrell to D. O'Hagan, 15 July 1953, 'Report on the Position of African Anglican Church Schools and Churches in the Fort Hall District.' J.M. Lonsdale's unpublished paper, 'Explanations of the Mau Mau Revolt', pp. 5–6, 8–10, considers these questions. For the socio-economic background to Kikuyu differentiation and political conflict , see G. Kitching, *Class and Economic Change in Kenya*, pp. 117–21, 128–130; and M.P. Cowen's unpublished paper, 'Differentiation in A Kenya Location' *passim*. Maina wa Kinyatti, 'Mau Mau', pp. 292–3 provides a radical perspective on the struggle between the moderates, led by Kenyatta, and the Mau Mau militants for control over the Kenya African Union in 1951 and 1952.

50. For Macmillan see CO 967/57/46709 (1942), 'Sir Arthur Dawe's Memorandum on a Federal Solution for East Africa and Mr Harold Macmillan's Counter-Proposals', H. Macmillan to Sir George Gater, 15 August 1942. The fullest account of Kenyatta's activities during this period is J. Murray-Brown, *Kenyatta*, pp. 261–96, but it lacks a theoretical framework to organise 'mere events' and ignores important questions. One suspects that he deliberately chose to avoid controversy. D. Goldsworthy, *Tom Mboya*, pp. 93–146, 166–93; G. Wasserman, *Politics of Decolonization, passim*; Sir Michael Blundell, *So Rough a Wind*, pp. 261–318; D.F Gordon, 'Mau Mau and Decolonization', pp. 329–45; B.E. Kipkorir, 'Mau Mau and the Politics of the Transfer of Power in Kenya', pp. 314–26, provide some useful insights. See also D.W. Throup, 'The Origins of Mau Mau', pp. 399–433. R.F. Holland, 'The Imperial Factor in British Strategies' and J. Darwin, 'British Decolonization since 1945', pp. 165–86, 187–209, provide interesting assessments of Britain's imperial decline. For a brief discussion Mau Mau's role in the ending of empire see R.F. Holland, *European Decolonization*, pp. 144–9, 236–48.

Biographical Appendix

Official Members of the Executive Council

The Governor
Sir Henry Moore	1940-1944
Sir Philip Mitchell	1944-1952
Sir Evelyn Baring	1952-1959

The Chief Secretary and Member for Development
Sir Gilbert Rennie	1939-1948
Hon. J.D. Rankine	1948-1952
Hon. H.S. Potter	1952-1954

The Attorney-General and Member for Law and Order
Hon. S.W.P. Foster-Sutton	1945-1949
Hon. K.K. O'Connor	1945-1952
Hon. J. Whyatt	1952-

Financial Secretary and Member for Finance
Hon. J.F.G. Troughton	1944-1950
Hon. V.G. Matthews	1950-1952
Hon. E.A. Vasey	1952-1959

Chief Native Commissioner and Member for African Affairs
Hon. W.S. Marchant	1944-1947
Hon. P. Wyn Harris	1947-1949
Hon. E.R. St. A. Davies	1949-1953

The Member for Agriculture and Natural Resources
Hon. F.W. Cavendish-Bentinck	1945-1955

The Member for Education and Labour and Deputy Chief Secretary
Hon. C.H. Thornley	1948-1952

The Member for Health and Local Government
Sir Charles Mortimer   1946–1952

The Member for Commerce and Industry
Hon. A. Hope-Jones   1950–1960

Heads of Technical Departments

Director of Agriculture
D.L. Blunt   1945–1948
S. Gillett   1948–1951
G.M. Roddan   1951–1956

Director of Education
C.E. Donovan   1945–1947
R. Patrick   1947–1952
W.J.D. Wadley   1952–

Director of Medical Services
Dr N.M. MacLennan   1945–1950
Dr T.F. Anderson   1950–

Director of Veterinary Services
R. Daubney   1944–1947
E. Beaumont   1947–1951
R.A. Hammond   1951–

Labour Commissioner
P. Wyn Harris   1944–1946
E.M. Hyde-Clarke   1946–1951
F.W. Carpenter   1951–

Field Administration Central Province

Provincial Commissioners
C. Tomkinson   1943–1946
P. Wyn Harris   1946–January 1947
A.C.M. Mullins   February1947–April 1948
E.H. Windley   April1948–December 1948
A.C.M. Mullins   January1949–May 1949
E.H. Windley   May1949–March 1950
C.M. Johnston   April1950–November 1950
E.H. Windley   November1950–January 1953
D. O'Hagan   January1953–September 1953

District Commissioners Embu
I.R. Gillespie   1943–1946

R.E. Wainwright	1946–February 1950
J.H. Chandler	February1950–October 1950
R.E. Wainwright	October1950–September 1951
R.A. Wilkinson	September1951–1954

District Commissioners Kiambu

A.C.M. Mullins	May1944–January 1945
W.F. Coutts	January1945–March 1945
A.C.M. Mullins	March1945–February 1947
E.H. Windley	April1947–February 1948
N.F. Kennaway	February1948–November 1950
M.E.W. North	November1950–July 1951
N.F. Kennaway	July1951–February 1953

District Commissioners Kitui

R.D.F. Ryland	July1944–August 1947
F.R. Wilson	4 August1947–24 August 1947
K.W. Simmonds	August1947–January 1948
W.F.P. Kelly	January1948–March 1949
J. Pinney	April1949–October 1949
W.F.P. Kelly	October1949–July 1952
P.J. Browning	July1952–September 1952
R.A.M. Birkett	September1952–1953

District Commissioners Machakos

G.R.B. Brown	May1944–1946
R.J.C. Howes	1946–June 1948
J.W. Howard	June1948–December 1949
J. Pinney	December1949–August 1950
J.W. Howard	August1950–May 1951
J. Pinney	May1951–July 1951
J.K.R. Thorp	July1951–November 1952
D.J. Penwill	November1952–1953

District Commissioners Meru

V.M. McKeag	1943–July 1945
C.M. Johnston	July1945–June 1947
N.F. Kennaway	June1947–February 1948
C.M. Johnston	February1948–April 1950
R.G. Brayne-Nicholls	April1950–October 1953
F.D. Homan	October1950–April 1953

District Commissioners Murang'a

P.S. Osborne	July1944–April 1945
D. O'Hagan	April1945–May 1947
W.F. Coutts	May1947–January 1949

F.A. Loyd	January1949–February 1950
F.D. Homan	February1950–October 1950
F.A. Loyd	October1950–August 1953

District Commissioners Nairobi
D. O'Hagan	November1944–April 1945
E.G. St C. Tisdall	April1945–December 1945
J.D. McKean	December1945–December 1948
P.J. de Bromhead	December1948–January 1949
J.D. McKean	January1949–October 1949
C.F. Atkins	October1949–1953

District Commissioners Nanyuki
J.B.S. Lockhart	1947–June 1951
A.D. Galton-Fenzi	June1951–January 1952
J.B.S. Lockhart	January1952–March 1952
A.D. Galton-Fenzi	March1952–July 1953

District Commissioners Nyeri
D.L. Morgan	1943–September 1945
P.S. Osborne	September1945–June 1948
F.A. Loyd	June1948–January 1949
P.S. Osborne	January1949–September 1950
A.C.C. Swann	September1950–March 1952
O.E.B. Hughes	March1952–September 1953

District Commissioners Thika
E.D. Emley	1943–1946
H.A. Carr	1946–June 1948
G.E. Noad	November1948–June 1950
C.J. Denton	June1950–September 1950
R.S. Winser	September1950–March 1951
D.G. Christie-Miller	March1951–July 1951
M.E.W. North	July1951–September 1952
R.S. Winser	September1952–1954

Biographical Appendix of Administrators and Politicians

Askwith, Thomas, G.
b. 1911; ed. Haileybury and Cambridge University; District Officer, Kenya 1936; Municipal African Affairs Officer, Nairobi, 1945–49; Principal the Jeanes School, Kabete, and Commissioner for Communal Relations, 1950–54; served in the Secretariat 1954. Askwith was a former Olympic oarsman and Diamond Sculls champion. At Kabete he proved

Biographical Appendix

to be too paternalistic and did not get on with the 18 year-old Tom Mboya, who was president of the students' council.

Awori, Wyclife Work Waswa
b. 1925 in Nambale, Western Kenya; ed. Kakamega High School and Mulago Hospital, Kampala, to train as a health inspector with the Nairobi Municipal Council; resigned 1945; journalist and editor of *Radio Posta, Habari za Dunia, Tribune*, which were kept afloat by Ernest Vasey, the settler politician; a close associate of Henry Gathigira, Pio Gama Pinto and E.K. Shaldah; Treasurer of the Kenya African Union, 1946; Vice President, 1946–47, but could not co-operate with Kenyatta, who forced him to resign; in 1947 was closely associated with the African Workers' Federation and nearly succeeded Chege Kibachia as its General Secretary; retired from politics and became a successful businessman and large farmer in co-operation with his father Canon Jeremiah Awori; appointed as Legislative Councillor for North Nyanza, 1952–56; died Nairobi, 5 May 1978.

Baring, Evelyn
1st Baron Howick of Glendale; GCMG (1955), KCMG (1942), KCVO (1947). b. 1903; younger son of 1st Earl Cromer, Consul-General in Egypt; ed. Winchester and New College, Oxford; 1st Class Hons in Modern History; entered Indian Civil Service, 1926; Secretary to the Agent of the Government of India in South Africa, 1929; retired 1934; Merchant Banker, 1934–42; Governor of Southern Rhodesia, 1942–44; High Commissioner in South Africa and to Basutoland, Bechuanaland and Swaziland, 1944–51; Governor of Kenya, 1952–59; Director Swan, Hunter and Wigham Richardson 1960; Chairman Commonwealth Development Corporation 1960–72; Chairman Nature Conservancy, 1962. He was a devout Anglo-Catholic and an authority on Swahili literature; and a boyhood friend of many senior Conservative politicians such as the Earl of Home, the Secretary of State for Commonwealth Relations, 1955–60. An aristocrat, he was the complete antithesis of Mitchell. His appointment appealed to the snobbish prejudices of many Kenyan settlers.

Battershill, William Denis
KCMG (1941), CMG (1938); b. 1896; ed. King's School, Worcester. War service in India and Iraq, 1914–19; Cadet Ceylon 1920; clerk to the Legislative Council, Ceylon 1928; Assistant Colonial Secretary, Jamaica, 1929–35; Colonial Secretary, Cyprus, 1935–37; Chief Secretary, Palestine, 1937–39; Governor of Cyprus, 1939–41; Assistant Under-Secretary of State, Colonial Office, 1941–42; Deputy Under-Secretary of State, Colonial Office, 1942–45; Governor of Tanganyika, 1945–49.

Biographical Appendix

Battershill was the Colonial Office's 'spy' among the East African governors, but he was much less successful than Mitchell in Kenya and Hathorn Hall in Uganda at implementing the second colonial occupation. His behaviour became increasingly erratic and he retired to Cyprus, aged 53, in 1949.

Beauttah, James
b. c. 1888; originally called Mbutu wa Ruhara; raised at Lower Muhito in Mukuruwe-ini Division of Nyeri District; his parents died while he was still a child; houseboy in 1900 to a Mnyamwezi policeman in Fort Hall town; moved to Nairobi in 1903. ed. Rabai mission school, Mombasa, and Buxton High School. Trainee telegraphist, Rabai, 1910. In 1911 posted to Bombo in Uganda; resigned from the Post Office in 1932; helped form the Kikuyu Central Association in Nairobi in 1924; settled Maragua, Murang'a in 1936; elected to the Murang'a Local Native Council with Job Muchuchu in 1937; founded the Murang'a Land Board Association to fight for the alienated Kikuyu lands, and the Kenya African Traders Association; 1945 joined the executive committee of the Kenya African Union; Vice President of the Kenya African Union in Central Province, 1947–51; a member of the Labour Trade Union of East Africa 1946. Sentenced to two years imprisonment 12 February 1952 for organising anti-inoculation protests in Murang'a; detained 1952–58; defeated in 1963 general election.

Beecher, Leonard James
CMG b. 1906; ed. St. Olaves School, Southwark, and Imperial College, London, and Institute of Education, London. Physics and mathematics master with Church Missionary Society at Alliance High School, Kikuyu, 1927; headmaster Kahuhia Teacher Training College; married 1929, Gladys Leakey, second daughter of Canon Leakey, the first Anglican missionary at Kabete; ordained 1930; Archdeacon 1945; Member for African interests on the Legislative Council 1943–47; and on the Executive Council, 1947–52; Bishop of Mombasa, 1953–64; Archbishop of East Africa, 1960–70; retired to Karen, a Nairobi suburb.

Blundell, Michael
KBE (1962). b. 1907; ed. Wellington College, where he was a friend of Patrick Gordon Walker, later Secretary of State for Commonwealth Relations, 1950–51. Became a farmer in Kenya in 1925, starting as a farm manager; Second Lieutenant, Major, Lieutenant Colonel, and Colonel with the Royal Engineers, 1940–45, in Ethiopia and South East Asia; Chairman of the Board for European Settlement 1946–47; European Legislative Councillor for the Rift Valley constituency, 1948–63; Leader

of the European Legislative Councillors 1952–54; Member of the Executive Council, 1952; Minister on the War Council, 1954–55; Minister of Agriculture, 1955–59 and 1961; Leader of the New Kenya Group, 1959; Director of Barclays Bank, Kenya and sixteen other companies; retired to Muthaiga, Nairobi. Blundell left Kenya for two years in the early 1930s to train as an opera singer in Vienna. He became politically more liberal as he grew older; an astute political operator. Publications: *So Rough a Wind* (London 1973).

Blunt, Denzil Layton
CMG (1945). b. 1891; ed. Shrewsbury and King's College Cambridge. Indian Education Department, 1912–14; European War, Royal Army Signals Corp, 1915–19; farming in England 1919–22; agricultural research at Cambridge, 1922–26; Senior Agricultural Officer, Kenya, 1926–33; Director of Agriculture, Cyprus, 1933–37; Director of Agriculture, Nyasaland, 1937–39; Director of Agriculture, Kenya, 1939–49. Retired to his Limuru farm.

Brown, Leslie H.
b. 1917; ed. St. Andrews University and the Imperial College of Tropical Agriculture, Trinidad. Nigerian Agricultural Service, 1940–46; transferred to Kenya, November 1946; Assistant Agricultural Officer; Embu, 1947–51; Provincial Agricultural Officer, Central Province, 1951–56; Deputy Director of Agriculture, June 1956. Brown was a dynamic and far-sighted character, but was abrasive and could not get on with his colleagues. Fortunately his superiors recognised his abilities. He had a searing tongue which he frequently employed on the field administration. Became a noted authority on African ornithology.

Buxton, Clarence E.V.
Served European war, wounded, became a Major and won the Military Cross. Assistant District Officer, East African Protectorate, October 1919; District Officer, Kenya, 1922; acting District Commissioner, Narok, January–June 1923; District Officer, Murang'a, 1925; District Commissioner Kajiado, October 1928–April 1931; District Commissioner, Kisii, 1933; District Commissioner, Narok, March 1935–April 1937; Officer-in-Charge, Maasai, May 1937–May 1938; seconded· to Palestine, September 1938; retired to his coffee farm in Kiambu, 1939. Buxton was the exact opposite of Mitchell; as a District Commissioner he was loyal to his subordinates and critical of his superiors. A former war hero, he cut a dashing figure with the ladies. From 1947 Buxton was extremely critical of Mitchell for ignoring the subversive threat posed by the African political ogranisations in Kikuyuland and persistently warned him that Kenyatta should be arrested.

Biographical Appendix

Caine, Sydney
KCMG (1947), CMG (1945); b. 1902; ed. Harrow County School and the London School of Economics. Assistant Inspector of Taxes, 1923–26; transferred to the Colonial Office, 1926; Secretary of the West Indies Sugar Commission, 1929; Financial Secretary Hong Kong, 1937; Assistant Secretary, Colonial Office 1940; Member of the Anglo-American Caribbean Commission, 1942; Financial Adviser to the Secretary of State, 1942; Assistant Under-Secretary, 1944; Deputy Under-Secretary, 1947–48; Third Secretary, the Treasury, 1948; head of the UK Treasury Delegation to Washington, 1949–51; Chief World Bank Mission to Ceylon, 1951; Vice-Chancellor of the University of Malaya, 1952–56; Director of the London School of Economics, 1957–67; Member of the Independent Television Authority, 1960–67; published *The Foundation of the LSE* and *British Universities: Purpose and Prospects*. Caine was a fierce exponent of *laissez-faire* policies and was highly critical of Mitchell's attempts to secure guaranteed prices for tropical cash crops; he consistently attempted to minimise government participation in colonial development.

Cavendish-Bentinck, Ferdinand William
Eighth Duke of Portland 1977–80; KBE (1956), CMG (1941), MC; b. 1889; ed. Eton, and RMC Sandhurst. Served in Malta and India, severely wounded in European war 1914–18; Staff Officer, War Office; Assistant Adjutant, RMC Sandhurst; Liberal candidate South Kensington, 1922; worked for Vickers Ltd 1923–24; private secretary to the governor of Uganda, 1925–27; Hon. Sec. Kenya Convention of Associations, 1930; Legislative Councillor for Nairobi North, 1934–45; Legislative Councillor, 1934–60; Member of the Executive Council, 1938–60; Member for Agriculture, 1945–55; Speaker of the Legislative Council, 1955–60; leader of the Kenya Coalition, a right-wing settler party opposed to Blundell's New Kenya Group, 1960; retired in Muthaiga; died aged 91 in December 1980. Cavendish-Bentinck was the Eamon de Valera of Kenyan politics; a tall, gaunt figure with a will of iron, totally dedicated to Kenya as a 'White Man's Country'; a die-hard imperialist, but personally charming. As a minister he was, however, indecisive, often agonising over minor decisions. He epitomised the settlers' capture of the colonial state during the war when he served as chairman of the Agricultural Production and Settlement Board, 1939–45; as Timber Controller for East Africa, 1940–45; and as a member of the East African Civil Defence and Supply Council, 1940–45.

Cohen, Andrew Benjamin
KCMG (1952), CMG (1948), KCVO (1954), OBE (1942); b. 1909; ed. Malvern and Trinity College, Cambridge; double first in Classics. Inland

Revenue 1932; transferred to the Colonial Office, 1933; seconded to control food supplies in embattled Malta, 1940–43; Assistant Secretary, Colonial Office, responsible for East Africa, 1943–47; Assistant Under-Secretary for Africa (the 'King of Africa') 1947–51; Governor of Uganda, 1952–57; Permanent British representative on United Nations' Trusteeship committee, 1957–61; Director General of the new Department of Technical Co-operation, 1961–64; Permanent Secretary of the Ministry of Overseas Development, 1964–68. On his father's side, Cohen was descended from the *haute juiverie* of business, and on his mother's, from a radical Unitarian family. Cohen was a large, exuberant man, with an enormous appetite for food and work. He was intellectually aggressive, extremely untidy, physically unattractive, and a brilliant and far-sighted colonial administrator. Cohen married in 1949. During the 1950s he tried to become a Labour Member of Parliament. Had been expected to become Permanent Secretary for the Colonies; published *British Policy in Changing Africa* (1959).

Cooke, Shirley Victor
Assistant District Officer, East African Protectorate, January 1917; Somalia patrol against the 'Mad Mullah', 1917–18; Political Officer, Turkana, 1921; District Officer, Kajiado, January–April 1923; District Commissioner, Kenya, 1928; Assistant District Commissioner, Kisumu, 1930; transferred to Tanganyika, 1931–38; resigned from the Colonial Service, 1938; elected settler Legislative Councillor for the Coast, 1938–63; settler Member of the Executive Council 1952, but unseated by his colleagues. Cooke was a vituperative Irishman; his tongue often got him into trouble as an administrator and he was often out of step with his settler colleagues; resigned from the African Settlement Board with Mathu in 1947 because of the government's failure to reopen the White Highlands' question. Mitchell considered appointing him as Member for Education in 1950, but gave the job to Ernest Vasey instead.

Coutts, Walter Fleming
KCMG (1961), CMG (1953), Kt. (1961), MBE (1949); b. 1912; ed. Glasgow Academy, St Andrews University and St John's College, Cambridge. District Officer, Kenya, 1936; Secretariat, 1946; District Commissioner Murang'a 1947–49; Administrator St Vincent, 1949; Minister for Education, Labour and Lands, Kenya, 1958–61; Special Commissioner for African elections, 1955; Chief Secretary, Kenya, 1958–61; Governor of Uganda, 1961–62.

Daubney, Robert
CMG (1939), OBE (1937), M.Sc., MRCVS. b. 1891, ed. Manchester Grammar School, Liverpool University, George

Washington University, Cambridge University, and Royal Veterinary College, London. Served European war, 1914–18; Helminthologist, Ministry of Agriculture 1920; joined Colonial Veterinary Service 1925; Director Veterinary Services, Kenya, 1937–46; Director of East African Central Veterinary Research Institute, 1939–46; Veterinary Adviser to the Egyptian Government, 1946–53. Daubney was a brilliant scientific researcher, but not a very practical supervisor of his staff. The veterinary department was more concerned with safeguarding settler-owned stock and with devising new serums for exotic stock than with devising a veterinary policy for the African reserves.

Davies, Eric Reginald St. Aubrey
OBE (1945); b. 1905; ed. Felsted School and Corpus Christi College, Cambridge. Cadet, Kenya, 1928; District Commissioner Nairobi, 1940; Information Officer, 1943–45; deputy Provincial Commissioner 1946; Provincial Commissioner, Coast Province, 1947–49; Chief Native Commissioner, September 1949–1953. Later served as Lieutenant-Governor of the Isle of Man where he retired. When Davies visited the Colonial Office in 1953 to discover where he was to be transferred, he was initially told that he should visit the labour exchange around the corner; eventually the Colonial Office relented and he was 'sentenced' to the Isle of Man.

Dawe, Arthur James
KCMG (1942), CMG (1938), OBE (1932); b. 1891; ed. Berkhamstead School and Brasenose College, Oxford. War service, 1914–18; joined the Colonial Office, 1918; Assistant Principal, 1920; private secretary to Leo Amery, 1920; and to E.F.L. Wood, 1921; Principal, 1921; secretary of the Commission of Enquiry into the affairs of the Freetown Municipality, 1926; Secretary to the Malta Royal Commission, 1931; Assistant Secretary, 1936; Assistant Under-Secretary for Africa, 1938–45; Deputy Under-Secretary for Palestine, 1945–47, when he retired.

Deverell, Colville Montgomery
KCMG (1957), CMG (1955), CVO (1953), OBE (1946); b. 1907; ed. Portora School, Enniskillen and Trinity College, Dublin, where he read law, and Trinity College, Cambridge. District Officer, Kenya, 1931; clerk to the Executive and Legislative Councils, 1938–39; Civil Affairs Branch, East African Command, served in Somaliland and Ethiopia, 1941–46; Secretary of the Development and Reconstruction Authority, Kenya, 1946–49; acting Financial Secretary 1949 and acting Chief Native Commissioner, 1949; Administrative Secretary, Kenya, 1949–52; Colonial Secretary, Jamaica, 1952–55; Governor of the Windward Islands, 1955–59; Governor of Mauritius, 1959–62.

Biographical Appendix

Francis, Edward Carey
b. 1897; ed. William Ellis School, London, and Peterhouse, Cambridge; Senior Wrangler. Lieutenant, Royal Artillery, 1916–19; Fellow of Peterhouse and University Lecturer in Mathematics, 1922–28, and as Bursar of Peterhouse, 1924–28; served with the Church Missionary Society in Kenya, 1928–62; Principal of Maseno School, 1928–40; Headmaster of Alliance High School (the Eton of Kenyan schools for Africans), 1940–62; assistant master at Pumwani Secondary School, 1962–66. Carey Francis was a brilliant maths master, a devout Evangelist and an unrelenting paternalist. At Maseno he quarrelled with the young Oginga Odinga, and as the new headmaster of Alliance High School soon drove his three senior African masters, E.W. Mathu, J.S. Gichuru and J.D. Otiende, from the staff.

Gater, George Henry
GCMG (1944), KCB (1941), Kt. (1936); b. 1886; ed. Winchester and New College, Oxford; 2nd class in Modern History; Diploma in Education. Oxfordshire Education Committee, 1911–12; Assistant Director of Education, Nottinghamshire, 1912–14; served in the war in Gallipoli, Egypt and France, was twice wounded; awarded DSO and bar, Commander Legion of Honour, and *Croix de Guerre*. Director of Education, Lancashire, 1919–24; Education Officer, London County Council, 1924–33; Clerk of the London County Council, 1933–39; Permanent Under-Secretary for the Colonies, 1939; Joint Permanent Secretary at the Home Office, 1939–40; Permanent Secretary at the Ministry of Supply, 1940; Permanent Secretary, Ministry of Home Security, 1940–42; Permanent Under-Secretary for the Colonies, 1942–47; Chairman School Broadcasting Council, 1948; Member of the Advisory Council of the BBC, 1952; Warden of Winchester, 1951–59.

Gichuru, James Samuel
b. 1914 at Thogoto in Kiambu; ed. CSM Kikuyu, Alliance High School, and Makerere College, 1933–34. Master at Alliance High School, 1935–40, but quarrelled with Carey Francis; Headmaster of CMS Junior Secondary School, Kikuyu, 1940–50; secretary of the Kenya Union of Teachers throughout the 1940s; President of the Kenya African Union, 1944–47; Vice-Chairman of Kiambu Local Native Council, 1948–50; Chief of Dagoretti location, Kiambu 1950–December 1952; restricted 1955–60, but allowed to continue teaching; acting President of the Kenya African National Union, 1960–61; MP Kiambu 1961–63; and Limuru 1963–82; Minister of Finance, 1962–69; Minister of Defence, 1969–79; and Minister of State, Office of the President, 1979–82.

Biographical Appendix

Gillett, Stuart
b. 1903; ed. Faversham Grammar School, Bedford School and the South Eastern Agricultural College, Wye, 1928. Assistant Agricultural Officer, Kenya, 1928; Agricultural Officer and Experimentalist, 1932; senior coffee officer, 1946; Commissioner for European Settlement, 1947; Director of Agriculture, 1949–51; Chairman of the Overseas Food Corporation, 1951.

Griffiths, Rt. Hon. James
PC (1945). b. 1890; ed. Bettws Council School, Ammanford, and Labour College, London. Coalminer; secretary of the Ammanford Trade Council, 1916–19; Agent Llanelly Labour Party, 1922–25; Miners' Agent for the Anthracite Mines Association, 1925–36; President South Wales Miners' Federation, 1934–36; executive committee of the Miners' Federation of Great Britain, 1934–36; Labour MP Llanelly, 1936–70; Minister of National Insurance, 1945–50; Secretary of State for the Colonies, 1950–51; Chairman of the Labour Party, 1948–49; Member of the National Executive, 1939–59; Deputy Leader of the Labour Party, 1955–59; Secretary of State for Wales, 1964–66.

Hall, George Henry
PC (1945), 1st Viscount Hall, 1946. b. 1881; ed. Penrhiwceiber Elementary School, Glamorganshire. Coalminer from the age of twelve at Penrhiwceiber colliery; check-weighter, local agent of the South Wales Miners' Federation, 1911–22; Labour MP Aberdare, 1922–46; Civil Lord of the Admiralty, 1929–31; Parliamentary Under-Secretary, Colonial Office 1940–42; Financial Secretary to the Admiralty, 1942–43; Parliamentary Under-Secretary at the Foreign Office, 1943–45; Secretary of State for the Colonies, 1945–46; First Lord of the Admiralty, 1946–51; Deputy Leader of the House of Lords, 1947–52.

Hall, John Hathorn
GCMG (1950), KCMG (1941), DSO, OBE, MC, *Croix de Guerre*. b. 1894; ed. St Paul's, and Lincoln College, Oxford. Military Service, 1915–18; Egyptian civil service, Ministry of Finance, 1919; Assistant Principal, Colonial Office, 1921; Principal, 1927; British representative to the Permanent Mandates Committee of the League of Nations, 1926–37; seconded to the Foreign Office, 1932; Chief Secretary, Palestine, 1933–37; British Resident, Zanzibar, 1937–40; Governor of Aden, 1940–44, Governor of Uganda, 1944–51.

Hammond, Robert Alston
OBE (1950), MRCVS, b. 1906; ed. Plumtree School, Southern Rhodesia, University of Liverpool, and the Royal Dick Veterinary

College, Edinburgh. Veterinary Officer, Kenya, 1930; Deputy Director of Veterinary Services, Kenya, 1947–52; Director of Veterinary Services, 1952.

Harris, Percy Wyn
KCMG (1952), CMG (1949), MBE (1941). b. 1903; ed. Gresham's School, Holt, and Gonville and Caius College, Cambridge; 2nd class Hons in Natural Sciences. District Officer, Kenya, 1926; Settlement Officer, Kikuyu Land Claims, 1939–40; District Commissioner, Nyeri, 1941–43; Labour Liaison officer, 1943–44; Labour Commissioner, 1944–46; Provincial Commissioner, Central Province, 1946–47; Chief Native Commissioner, 1947–49; Governor of the Gambia, 1949–58. 1929 made second ascent of Mt Kenya; first visit to North Island, Lake Turkana, 1931; member of the Mt Everest expeditions of 1933 and 1936. In 1933 took part in first assault with L.R. Wager and reached 28,000 feet. In retirement sailed a yacht around the world.

Hobson, (John) Basil
Q.C. (1950), b. 1905; ed. Sherborne; solicitor, 1929; Deputy Registrar, Supreme Court, Trinidad, 1936; Middle Temple, 1938; Crown Counsel, Uganda, 1939; served in the King's African Rifles, 1939–41; Deputy Judge Advocate, East African Command, 1941–44; Solicitor General and Legislative Councillor, Kenya, 1947–51; Chairman Labour Advisory Board, 1948–49; Attorney General, Nyasaland, 1951.

Hope-Jones, Arthur
KBE (1964), CMG (1956), b. 1911; ed. Kirkby Lonsdale and Christ's College, Cambridge; 1st class Hons in History; Columbia University (Commonwealth Fund Fellow), Brookings Institute, Washington DC. Fellow of Christ's College, Cambridge, 1937–46; war service 1939–46; economic adviser to the Anglo-Iranian Oil Company in Iran, 1944–46; economic adviser to the Kenyan government, 1946–48; Member of Commerce and Industry, 1948–60; Director and adviser to various companies since 1960; Chairman, London Sumatra Plantations Ltd since 1978. Publications: *Income Tax and the Napoleonic Wars* (1939).

Howes, Richard John Clyde
MBE; b. 1906; ed. King Edward VII School, Lytham, and Jesus College, Cambridge. Military service, King's African Rifles, 1941–42; Cadet, Kenya, 1929; District Officer, 1930; private secretary to Sir Joseph Byrne; Assistant Secretary, East African Governor's Conference, 1942; Secretary to the High Commissioner, Kenya and Uganda Railway and Harbours, 1944–45; Secretary, Development and Reconstruction Authority, 1945–46; Secretary to the Member for Health and Local

Government, 1946; District Commissioner Machakos, 1946–48; acting Commissioner for Local Government, 1949.

Hughes Rice, Thomas
b. 1907, Assistant Agricultural Officer Nyanza, 1939; served King's African Rifles, 1941–44, became Lieutenant Colonel; Assistant Agricultural Officer, Nyeri, 1944–45; Murang'a, 1945–47; 1947–51; Machakos, 1951–53; Provincial Agricultural Officer, Nyanza, 1953–56; Assistant Director of Agriculture, 1956.

Humphrey, Norman
b. 1897; ed. Haberdashers' Hampstead School; Military service, 1915–16; Agricultural Officer, Kenya, 1930: agricultural course at Cambridge, 1933; Senior Agricultural Officer, Kenya, 1940; sociological research in Kenya, 1944.

Hyde-Clarke, (Ernest) Meredyth
MBE. b. 1905; ed. St George's School, Harpenden; the London School of Economics and Wadham College, Oxford. Coffee farmer in Kenya, 1926; Cadet, Kenya, 1927; Assistant Secretary in the Secretariat, 1939; Personal assistant to the Chairman Agricultural Production and Settlement Board (Cavendish-Bentinck) 1944; Civil Reabsorption Officer, 1945; Deputy Labour Commissioner, 1945–46; Labour Commissioner and Legislative Councillor, 1946–51; chairman of the sub-committee of the Labour Advisory Board on African Registration, 1948.

Johnston, Carruthers Melvill
b. 1909; ed. Shrewsbury and Brasenose College, Oxford. Cadet, Kenya, 1933; District Commissioner, Meru, July 1945–June 1947 and February 1948–April 1950; Provincial Commissioner, Rift Valley, February 1951–July 1951 and March 1952–August 1953; Provincial Commissioner, Central Province, April–November 1950 and September 1953. Nicknamed 'Monkey'.

Jones, Arthur Creech
b. 1891; ed. Whitehall Boys' School. Civil servant in the War Office and the Crown Agents' Office, 1907–16; secretary of Camberwell Trades Council and Borough Labour Party, 1913–22; member of the No-Conscription Fellowship, 1915; imprisoned, September 1916–April 1919; Secretary to the National Union of Docks, Wharves and Shipping Staffs, 1919–22; national secretary of the administrative, clerical and supervisory section of the Transport and General Workers' Union, 1922–29; Executive Committee of the London Labour Party, 1921–28;

organising secretary of the Workers' Travel Association, 1929–39; defeated Labour candidate, Heywood and Radcliffe, 1929; Labour MP Shipley, 1935–50 and Wakefield, 1954–64; Chairman of the Labour Party's Advisory Committee on Imperial Affairs, 1943; Member of the Colonial Office's Advisory Committee on Education, 1936–45; Chairman Fabian Colonial Bureau, 1940–45; Vice Chairman of the Commission on Higher Education in West Africa, 1943–44; Parliamentary Private Secretary to Ernest Bevin, 1940–44; Under-Secretary for the Colonies, 1945–46; Secretary of State for the Colonies, 1946–50. Published *Trade Unionism Today*, *The Ruhr*, and ed. *Fabian Colonial Essays*.

In 1926 he instructed Clements Kadalie, general secretary of the South African Industrial and Commercial Workers' Union on trade union organization and this marked the beginning of his interest in colonial affairs. Creech Jones, however, did not visit Africa until 1944 when he went to West Africa; as Under-Secretary he toured East Africa with Andrew Cohen in August–September 1946. Creech was an ineffective performer in both Cabinet and the House of Commons and his relations with Attlee were distinctly cool. He would probably have been dropped from the Cabinet had he not lost his seat at Shipley in the 1950 general election. He was a protégé of Ernest Bevin. Creech Jones was a civil libertarian and less interested in colonial development.

Kaggia, Bildad Mwanganu

b. 1922 at Dagoretti; ed. Kahuhia School, Murang'a, where he was a classmate of B.M. Gecaga. Clerk District Commissioner's Office, Murang'a 1939–42; joined the army, and served in Egypt, Libya, Syria and Britain, 1942–45; rose to become staff sergeant. Refused to join the Kenya African Union as it was too élitist and conservative. Formed his own independent Anglican Church, the *Dini ya Kaggia*, 1945. Joined the Kenya African Union when Kenyatta became President in 1947; President of the Clerks' and Commercial Workers' Union, 1948; President of the Labour Trade Union of East Africa, 1950; General Secretary of the Nairobi branch of the Kenya African Union, 1951–52; arrested 20 October 1952; detained 1952–61; Assistant Minister of Education, 1963–June 1964; Deputy Leader of the Kenya People's Union, 1966–69; Chairman of the Cotton, Lint and Seed Marketing Board, 1970–71; Chairman of the Maize and Produce Board, 1971; published *The Roots of Freedom* (1975). MP for Kandara, 1963–66.

Kennaway, Noel Frederick

b. 1908; ed. Oundle and Clare College, Cambridge. Cadet, Kenya, 1931; District Commissioner, Kwale, 1945–46; Meru, June 1947–February 1948; Kiambu, February 1948–November 1950 and July

1951–February 1953; Provincial Commissioner, Coast Province, February 1953. Retired to Karen, Nairobi.

Kenyatta, Jomo
b. 1889; ed. CSM Kikuyu, London School of Oriental and African Studies, and London School of Economics. Carpenter;· interpreter in the Kenya Supreme Court; worked for the Nairobi Water Board, 1921–26; joined Young Kikuyu Association, 1922; General Secretary of the Kikuyu Central Association, 1928; editor of *Muigwithania*, the Association's newspaper, 1928–29; left for Britain, February 1929; visited Moscow; visit to Britain to submit evidence to the British government, 1931, remained until 1946; attended Quaker College, Woodbrooke, Birmingham, visited Moscow again and attended the Negro Workers' Congress in Hamburg; 1933–36 assistant in phonetics, London School of African and Oriental Studies; at the London School of Economics with Malinowski; published *Facing Mount Kenya* in 1938; organiser fifth Pan-African Congress in Manchester, 1945; married Edna Clarke, 1942; returned to Kenya, September 1946; elected President of the Kenya African Union, June 1947; detained 20 October 1952 until 1961; elected to the Legislative Council in January 1962; Prime Minister 1963–64; President 1964–78.

By 1952 Kenyatta had lost his influence over the political militants, he was becoming depressed at their reckless behaviour and had begun to drink heavily. He found it difficult to adjust to Kenya's racist society after 15 years in Britain; few Africans shared his intellectual interests, while the Europeans regarded him with profound suspicion as a dangerous communist agitator. Detention made him a political martyr and restored his reputation among the Kenyan masses as the leader of the nationalist movement, which had become tarnished between 1946 and his detention in 1952.

Khamisi, Francis Joseph
b. 1913 at Rabai near Mombasa; ed. Catholic High School, Kabaa. Employed by the East African Meteorological Service, 1937–39; editor of *Baraza*, 1939–45; General Secretary of the Kenya African Union, 1944–47; chief clerk with African Mercantile, Mombasa 1948–58; member of the Nairobi African Advisory Council, 1939–48; appointed member of the East African Central Assembly, 1957–61; elected Legislative Councillor, Kenya, for Mombasa, 1958–61; member of the Nairobi Municipal Council, 1946–47; member of the Mombasa Municipal Board, 1950–60; editor of *Baraza*, 1961–79.

Kibachia, Chege
b. 1920 in Kiambu; ed. Alliance High School, 1939–42, where he was taught by Eliud Mathu and James Gichuru. Worked with the Kiambu Chicken and Egg Sellers Co. 1943–45; then with the East African Clothing factory in Mombasa, 1945–47; emerged as President of the African Workers' Federation during the general strike in Mombasa in January 1947; detained because of his trade union activities, August 1947; detained Baringo 1947–57; 1964 appointed Industrial Relations Officer in the Labour Department in Mombasa; Senior Labour Officer, Mombasa, 1964; member of the Industrial Court of Kenya since 1979. Even after his detention the Kenyan government contemplated sending Kibachia on a course of trade union affairs at Ruskin College, Oxford; he was far from regarded as a hopeless militant, but they chose Meshak Ndisi instead.

Koinange, Peter Mbiyu
b. 1907 at Njunu in Kiambu; ed. CMS Kiamba, Kabete Primary School, Buxton High School Mombasa, and Alliance High School; Hampton Institute, Virginia, 1927–31; Ohio Wesleyan University, 1931–35; Teachers' College, Columbia University, 1935–36; St John's College, Cambridge, 1936–37; and Institute of Education, London University, 1937–38. He refused to serve on non-European terms in the Kenya Education Department; founded and was Principal of the Kenya Teachers' College at Githunguri, 1939–48; failed to be selected as the first African Member of the Legislative Council in 1944 despite campaigning for the job; a founder of the Kenya African Union in 1944, but became more closely involved after Kenyatta's return in 1946; delivered Kenya Land Petition to London with Achieng Oneko in 1951 and was still in London when the Emergency was declared; worked with the London Co-operative Society, 1951–59; the Kenya African Union's representative in London, 1951–59; Director of the Bureau of African Affairs in Ghana, 1959–60; Secretary General of the Pan African Freedom Movement for East, Central and South Africa in Dar-es-Salaam, 1961–62; MP for Kiambu, 1963–79, Minister for Pan African Affairs, 1963–64; Minister of Education, 1964–66; Minister of State, Office of the President, 1966–78; Minister for Water Development, 1978–79. Kenyatta married Koinange's sister in 1947; she died in childbirth in 1948. Koinange was Kenyatta's closest political associate from 1936 when they met in London until 1978.

Koinange wa Mbiyu
b. 1870s to 1881; a member of the *mbari ya Njunu*, which owned large tracts of land in southern Kiambu; appointed headman under his father Mbiyu, who was a government chief, in 1905; succeeded as chief in 1908;

Biographical Appendix

Senior Chief of Kiambu, but without locational responsibilities in 1938; retired as Senior Chief in 1949; President of the Kikuyu Association in 1919; dominated the Kiambu Local Native Council from the mid-1920s until the 1940s; one of three witnesses appointed by the government to give evidence to the Joint Select Committee on Closer Union in London; active in raising funds for the Kenya Teachers' College at Githunguri; a member of the Executive Committee of the Kenya African Union, 1947–52; detained 1952–60. Koinange became increasingly radical after the Kenya Land Commission report, which was published in May 1934; by 1940 the government no longer trusted him because of his close relations with the Kikuyu Central Association. Became close friend and father-in-law of Kenyatta after 1946. Father of Mbiyu Koinange.

Kubai, Fred

b. of a Kikuyu father and a Giriama mother in Mombasa in 1915. Worked as telegraphist and became active in trades unionism; organizing secretary of the Kenya African Road Transport and Mechanics' Union, which became the Transport and Allied Workers' Union, in 1947; acting General Secretary in 1948; formed the East African Trades Union Congress in 1949, of which he was the President; organised boycott of the Nairobi Royal Charter celebrations in 1950; arrested but acquitted for attempting to assassinate Muchohi Gikonyo; Chairman of the Nairobi Branch of the Kenya African Union, 1951–52; editor of *Sauti ya Mwafrika*, 1951–52; arrested 20 October 1952; detained 1952–61; Member of the Mau Mau Central Committee, the *Muhimu*, 1948–52; failed to oust Tom Mboya from the leadership of the Trade Union movement after his release; MP Nakuru East 1963–74 and since 1983; Assistant Minister of Labour, 1963–74; since July 1985 has been Assistant Minister in the Office of the President. Between 1948 and 1952 Kubai was perhaps the most feared man in Kenya because of his close contacts with the Nairobi Kikuyu criminal gangs, such as the Forty Group, the *Anake a Forty*, and Mau Mau; Kubai controlled oathing in Nairobi from 1949–52; and was the leader of the militants.

Lloyd, Thomas Ingram Kynaston

GCMG (1951), KCMG (1947), CMG (1943), KCB (1949). b. 1896; ed. Rossall, RMA Woolwich, and Gonville and Caius College, Cambridge. Served in the Royal Engineers on the Middle Eastern front, 1916–19; Assistant Principal, Ministry of Health, 1920; transferred to the Colonial Office, 1921; Principal, 1929; Secretary of the Palestine Commission, 1929–30; Secretary of the Royal Commission to the West Indies, 1938–39; Assistant Secretary, 1939; Assistant Under-Secretary, 1943; Permanent Under-Secretary, 1947–56. Lloyd was a keen gardner, and *Country Life* referred to his garden at   Radlett as 'probably the most

274

beautiful in Hertfordshire'. In his memoirs, Lyttelton observed that 'Tom Lloyd was an example of the best in the Civil Service, wise and salty in his judgements, never in a panic or a hurry, enlightened and broad-minded on colonial policy, a good judge of men . . . Some said that he did not allow his imagination to walk abroad but only took it on a lead for a short time. If this were true I should be far from saying that it was a fault in the permanent head of a department . . . With all this, he had perhaps too much loyalty for some of his particular swans who had turned, in the stress of colonial affairs or under the erosive influence of Government Houses, into geese.'

Lyttelton, 1st Viscount, (Oliver)

PC (1940), DSO, MC. b. 1893; ed. Eton and Trinity College, Cambridge. Grenadier Guards, 1915–18; Managing Director, Metal Box Co. Ltd; Conservative MP Aldershot, 1940–54; President of the Board of Trade, 1940–41; Minister Resident in the Middle East, 1941–42; Minister of Production, 1942–45; President of the Board of Trade, 1945; Chairman Associated Electrical Industries, 1945–51; Secretary of State for the Colonies, 1951–54; Chairman Associated Electrical Industries, 1954; Chairman of the N. Ireland Development Council, 1955; Chairman of the National Theatre, 1962; President oft he Institute of Directors, 1954. Published *Memoirs of Lord Chandos* (1962). Lyttelton was an unreconstructed right-wing Conservative imperialist, and had had little previous experience of the colonies when he was appointed Secretary of State; he had hoped to be Chancellor of the Exchequer.

Maher, Alfred Colin

b. 1905; ed. Cambridge University and the College of Tropical Agriculture, Trinidad. Assistant Agricultural Officer, Kenya, 1929; Agricultural Officer, 1931; Secretary of the Board of Agriculture and the Maize Enquiry Committee, 1932; agricultural experimentalist on coffee and cereals in Trans Nzoia, 1933; Head of the Soil Conservation Unit, 1938–50. Resigned and farmed on the Kinangop. Maher was an intellectual, uninterested in sport or heavy drinking, and did not get on with his colleagues. After his appointment as experimentalist in 1933, he worked alone and kept his relations with other agricultural officers to the minimum. He did not suffer 'fools' gladly; a theoretician who was not interested in *ad hoc* reforms. Maher resigned in 1950 when he was passed over in the reconstruction of the agricultural department. Three weeks later his wife committed suicide, leaving him with four young children to raise. He failed to get a job with the Overseas Food Corporation in Tanganyika, or as a professor at the College of Tropical Agriculture in Trinidad. Maher was a frequent contributor to the Kenyan press on agricultural subjects; his wife was, for many years, the Trans Nzoia correspondent of the *East African Standard*.

Marchant, William Sydney
CMG (1942), OBE (1937), b. 1894. Served European war, 1915–18; Cadet, Kenya, 1919; Deputy Provincial Commissioner, Zanzibar, 1935–37; Deputy Provincial Commissioner, British Solomon Islands, 1939–43; Chief Native Commissioner, Kenya, 1943–47; Labour Adviser to the Overseas Food Corporation, 1947–50.

Masinde, Elijah
b. 1910; ed. Church of God Mission School, Kima, in Western Kenya; a keen footballer; became a physical instructor; Native Tribunal Court Process Server, N. Nyanza, 1937–42; formed the *Dini ya Msambwa* in 1942, an anti-European cult; sentenced to prison, 1945–46; detained at Lamu, 1948–61. Masinde has been imprisoned several times since independence for preaching defiance of authority.

Mathu, Eliud Wambu
b. Riruta in Kiambu in 1910; ed. Riruta Primary School, CSM Kikuyu, Alliance High School, Fort Hare University in South Africa, Exeter University, and Balliol College, Oxford. History master at Alliance High School 1940–43; Principal of Dagoretti High School, 1943; President Kenya Union of Teachers in the 1940s; nominated to the Legislative Council, 1944–57; nominated to the Executive Council, 1952; member of the East African Central Assembly, 1948–60; served with the United Nations Economic Commission for Africa, 1960–64; Chairman of the Council of the University of East Africa, 1963–69; Private Secretary to the President of Kenya, and Comptroller of State House, 1964–77; Chairman of Kenya Airways, 1977–80.

Mathu was Kenya's leading African politician from 1944–57. His relations with Kenyatta and Koinange were strained, but during the late 1940s Mathu became increasingly critical of the government. Despite his abilities, the British ceased to trust him and in 1954 appointed Ohanga instead of him as the first African minister. Three years later they engineered his defeat in the first African elections for the Legislative Council by the Meru politician, Bernard Mate. Mathu, however, was too moderate a figure, tainted by his colonialist past, to emerge as a powerful politician in independent Kenya, although he probably exercised considerable influence behind the scenes as Kenyatta's private secretary.

Mitchell, Philip Euen
GCMG (1947), KCMG (1937), CMG (1933), MC. b. 1890, fifth son of Capt. Hugh Mitchell of the Royal Engineers, who was working as a railway engineer in Spain; ed. St. Paul's School, and Trinity College, Oxford; 2nd class in Classics. Assistant Resident, Nyasaland, 1912–15;

Lieutenant, King's African Rifles, 1915-18; ADC and private secretary to the Governor of Nyasaland 1918-19; Assistant Political Officer, Tanganyika, 1919; Assistant Secretary for Native Affairs, Tanganyika, 1926-28; Provincial Commissioner, Northern Province, 1928; Secretary for Native Affairs, 1928-34; Chief Secretary, Tanganyika, 1934-35; Governor of Uganda, 1935-40; deputy Chairman of the East African Governors' Conference, 1940-41; political adviser to General Wavell, 1941-42; British Plenipotentiary in Ethiopia and Chief Political Officer to East Africa High Command, with the rank of Major-General 1942; Governor of Fiji and High Commissioner in the Western Pacific, 1942-44; Governor of Kenya, 1944-52. Retired to his farm at Subukia, 1952-63; and to Gibraltar, 1963-64. Published *African Afterthoughts* (1954).

Mitchell refused to remain in Kenya when Kenyatta came to power since he still believed him to have been the leader of Mau Mau. Mitchell's personal ideology reflected his inter-war experiences in Tanganyika and Uganda, where the chiefs had been the cornerstone of the colonial state and African politicians had hardly existed or could easily be dismissed as agitators – half educated men in trousers misleading the noble men in blankets. Although Fiji had provided Mitchell with a vision of a multi-racial society, which he hoped could be created in Kenya as well, he was unwilling to co-opt Mathu, let alone Kenyatta. The Colonial Office, as we have seen, had selected him to reassert metropolitan authority in Kenya, because not only was the he their most experienced East Africanist, but he also had a reputation for being anti-settler. This was probably true – he never got on socially with the settler politicians or businessmen in Nairobi, who ostensibly came from a similar background. While he was willing to accept that the settlers had captured certain key positions within the state during the war and had quickly recognised that it was politically inadvisable to dislodge Cavendish-Bentinck from his position as a 'virtual Minister of Agriculture', he refused to make any major concessions to the Kenya African Union, even when the moderate constitutionalists were firmly in command during 1945 and 1946. Throughout his years in Kenya, Mitchell remained conceptually stuck in the mud of indirect rule and his successes in Tanganyika and Uganda in the 1920s and 1930s. To him (and many other senior administrators) African politicians were by definition 'agitators', against whom the *wananchi* had to be protected. As their demands became increasingly strident, paternalism and 'a firm refusal to be rattled' were even more essential. For this kind of blinkered mind, the rumours of discontent among the squatters in 1946, the violent disturbances in Murang'a in 1947, or the continual troubles in Olen-guruone, simply provided further proof of the irresponsibility and short-term, selfish aims of these troublecausers. Now was the time for the colonial government to stand firm and to push ahead with its agricultural development programme in Central Province and to prevent further land degradation. The men in blankets had to be protected from their unscrupulous leaders. Indeed to Mitchell's paternalist mind, the demonstrations against terracing and dipping stiffened his resolve. He was convinced that the agitators knew, like himself, that the agricultural campaign would eventually succeed, raise African living standards and create a contented peasantry. These politically inspired protests were their last desperate throw, before the benefits became evident to the *wananchi*. If only the government stood firm and the agricultural department pressed ahead, Kenya would soon emerge out of the tunnel of despair into a future of organic development and political tranquility, well on the way to a stable, multiracial future. The late 1940s might be a difficult time, but if only he could hold on, the alarmists would be discredited, African opposition would subside, and Philip Mitchell in the early 1950s would be justified, and confirmed as a great colonial governor.

Mitchell therefore refused to lose his nerve and clung to office, despite his increasing exhaustion and ill health. Next year, if not this, he was firmly convinced, would prove him right. The governor obstinately refused to heed warnings about Mau Mau or the deteriorating position in the reserves or the White Highlands and convinced himself, in his lonely isolation, that they would wither away. The ship of state would sail through the present storm into a peaceful, sunny anchorage, with the governor at the helm. As his views became known in the administration, District Commissioners who after 1950 were already having to fight to keep control of their districts, found that their warnings were watered down in the Secretariat, who knew what the governor wanted to hear, and Mitchell refused to warn Whitehall of the impending doom. As African resistance grew in the 1950s, during the last two years of Mitchell's governorship, there was a loss of political will and self-confidence in the field administration.

Moore, Henry Monck-Mason

GCMG (1943), KCMG (1935), CMG (1930). b 1887; ed. King's College School, Cambridge and Jesus College, Cambridge. Cadet, Ceylon, 1911; Assistant Colonial Secretary, 1914–16 and 1919–20; Salonika campaign, 1916; Private Secretary to the Governor of Ceylon, 1919–20; Colonial Secretary, Bermuda, 1922–24; Principal Assistant Secretary, Nigeria, 1924–27; Deputy Chief Secretary, Nigeria, 1927–29; Colonial Secretary, Kenya, 1929–34, Governor of Sierra Leone, 1934–37; Assistant Under-Secretary, Colonial Office, 1937–40; Governor of Kenya, 1940–44; Governor of Ceylon, 1944–48; Governor-General of Ceylon, 1948–49; retired to Cape Town, 1949–64. Moore never got over the experience of serving as Byrne's Colonial Secretary when he bore the front of settler criticism during the depression. When he returned as governor he wanted a quiet life, and allowed the settlers to make considerable political gains during the war.

Morgan, David Loftus
CMG (1952), MBE (1943). b. 1904; ed. Harrow and Trinity College, Cambridge; gained upper second in History. Cadet, Kenya, 1926; District Officer, 1928; District Commissioner Nyeri, 1943–45; Provincial Commissioner, Rift Valley, 1946 to February 1951; Resident Commissioner, Swaziland, 1951–56. Morgan had little time for African opposition and had no understanding of the complex problems which faced the field administration in post-war Kenya.

Mortimer, Charles Edward
Kt. (1950), CBE (1943). b. 1886; ed. Hartley College, Manchester. Son of Joseph Mortimer, Mayor of Nairobi in 1930 and 1937; Methodist Minister, 1910–16 in Britain; clerk Land Department, Kenya 1917; Land Assistant, 1920–27; Lands Secretary, 1928–38; Commissioner for Lands and Settlement, 1938–39; Commissioner for Local Government, Lands and Settlement, 1939–46; Member for Health and Local Government, 1946–50 and 1952–54.

Mullins, Aubrey Charles Madgewick
b. 1903; ed. St Andrew's College, Grahamstown, South Africa, and Keble College, Oxford. Cadet, Kenya, 1926; Assistant District Commissioner, 1926; District Commissioner, Kiambu, May 1944–January 1945 and March 1945–February 1947; Deputy Provincial Commissioner, 1946; Provincial Commissioner, Central Province, February 1947–April 1948 and January–May 1949; and Provincial Commissioner, Coast Province, 1949–52.

Odede, Fanuel Walter
b. 1912 at Uyoma, Central Nyanza; ed. Maseno Secondary School, Alliance High School, Veterinary Training Centre at Maseno, and Makerere College. Assistant Veterinary Officer at Maseno, 1941; appointed temporary member of the Legislative Council during Beecher's absence in 1945; advanced study in Britain; appointed lecturer in Veterinary Science at Makerere; Director of the Associated Press of East Africa Ltd, 1952; acting President of the Kenya African Union following Kenyatta's detention, October 1952–March 1953; detained 1953–October 1960; MP 1961–63 and October–December 1974.

O'Hagan, Desmond
CMG (1952). b. 1909 at Nyeri, where his father was a coffee planter; ed. Wellington College and Clare College, Cambridge. Cadet, Kenya, 1931;

Inner Temple, 1935; private secretary to the British Resident in Zanzibar, 1937; District Commissioner, Kenya, 1940; District Commissioner, Nairobi, November 1944–April 1945; District Commissioner, Murang'a, April 1945–May 1947; Native Courts' Adviser, 1948–52; Provincial Commissioner, Coast Province, 1952–January 1953 and September 1953–1959; Provincial Commissioner, Central Province, January–September 1953; head of the Passenger Transport Board in Tanganyika, 1959–62, Retired to his wife's family's coffee farm at Kiambu. O'Hagan was a firm paternalist who encouraged African entrepreneurs, but would not tolerate opposition; he was a popular District Commissioner with the Kikuyu in Murang'a between 1945–47, and was very successful at encouraging terracing.

Ohanga, Benaiah Apolo
b. 1913 at Gem, Central Nyanza; ed. Maseno School and Alliance High School. Teacher, 1933–45; in 1949 went on courses in primary education and local government in Britain; member Central Nyanza District Education Board, 1943–48; secretary of the Luo Language Committee and a member of th Kenya Language Board, 1945; nominated Legislative Councillor, 1947–57; 1954 appointed first African Minister, served as Minister of Community Development and Rehabilitation, 1954–57; Nairobi City Education Officer, 1958–63; Secretary and Executive Officer, Kenya Overseas Scholarship Committee, 1963; Member Nairobi City Council, 1961–63; Inspector of Children in the Ministry of Home Affairs, 1963–66; Vice President of the Central Organisation of Trade Unions, 1966.

Osborne, Paul Stanley
b. 1908; ed. Christ's Hospital, and Sidney Sussex College, Cambridge. Cadet, Kenya, 1931; District Commissioner, Murang'a, July 1944–April 1945; District Commissioner, Nyeri, September 1945–June 1948, and January 1949–September 1950; and District Commissioner North Nyanza, September 1950–1952.

Penfold, Cecil
b. 1906; ed. Lancing and Oxford University. Police Constable, Kenya, 1930; Assistant Superintendent, 1933; Superintendent and Director of Intelligence and Security, 1946–50; Assistant Commissioner of Police, 1950.

Potter, Henry Steven
KCMG (1955), CMG (1948). b. 1904; ed. Shrewsbury and Queen's College, Cambridge; 3rd in Law. Cadet, Kenya, 1926; District Officer, Kenya, 1928; Deputy Financial Secretary, 1944–45; Financial Secretary,

Uganda, 1945–48; Chief Secretary, Uganda, 1948–52; Chief Secretary, Kenya, 1952–54; British Resident, Zanzibar, 1954–60. Potter acted as governor from Mitchell's departure in June until Baring arrived in September. Unlike Mitchell, he immediately informed Whitehall that the situation in the Kikuyu areas was getting out of control.

Rankine, John Dalzell
KCMG (1954), CMG (1947), KCVO (1956). b. 1907, son of Sir Richard Rankine, Chief Secretary, Nyasaland, 1920–27, Chief Secretary Uganda 1927–30, and British Resident, Zanzibar, 1930–37; ed. Christ's College, Christchurch, New Zealand, and Exeter College, Oxford; 2nd in History. Cadet, Uganda, 1931; District Officer, Uganda, 1933; Assistant Secretary of the East African Governors' Conference, 1939–42; Assistant Colonial Secretary, Fiji, 1942–45; Colonial Secretary, Barbados, 1945–47; Chief Secretary, Kenya, 1947–52; Resident Zanzibar, 1952–54; Governor of Western Nigeria, 1954–60. Rankine was Mitchell's protégé from 1935–52 and went in awe of him.

Rennie, Gilbert McCall
KCMG (1949), CMG (1941), Kt. (1946), GBE (1954), MC. b. 1895; ed. Stirling High School, and Glasgow University. Military service, 1915–19, acting brigade major. Cadet, Ceylon, 1920; police magistrate, 1923; District judge, 1925; Controller Finance and Supply, 1932; Secretary to the Governor, 1934; Financial Secretary, Gold Coast, 1937–39; Chief Secretary, Kenya, 1939–48; Chairman of the Development and Reconstruction Authority, 1945–48; Governor of Northern Rhodesia, 1948–54; High Commissioner in London for the Federation of Rhodesia and Nyasaland, 1954–61; Chairman UK Freedom from Hunger Campaign, 1965.

Ryland, Richard Desmond Fetherston-Haugh
b. 1904; ed. Sedbergh and Lincoln College, Oxford. Cadet, Kenya, 1928; District Commissioner, Kitui, July 1944–August 1947; District Commissioner, Nyeri, April 1948–December 1950 and March 1952–January 1953; Provincial Commissioner, Rift Valley, November 1948–January 1949 and July 1951–March 1952.

Scott, Lord Francis Montagu-Douglas
b. 1879, sixth son of the sixth Duke of Buccleuch; ed. Eton and Oxford. Served in the army, 1899–1919, ADC to the Viceroy of India, 1905; settled in Kenya, 1919; Member of the Legislative and Executive Councils in the 1920s and 1930s; following Lord Delamere's death was the leading settler politician throughout the 1930s; severely injured in the leg during the First World War; his leg was amputated just before his

Biographical Appendix

death in 1952. Mitchell hated him, because Scott viewed the governor as a middle-class upstart and treated him as such.

Singh, Makhan
b. 1913 in India; came to Kenya in 1927; ed. Government Indian High School, Nairobi. Formed Labour Trade Union of East Africa, 1934; led two month strike in Nairobi in 1937; formed Labour Trade Union of East Africa, 1939; interned in India, 1940–45; returned to Kenya on 22 August 1947; worked for the East African Indian National Congress, 1947–49; took over the African Workers' Federation in 1949; formed East African Trade Union Congress, 1949, with Fred Kubai as President, and Makhan Singh as Secretary; organised boycott of the Nairobi Charter celebrations, 1950; arrested during the Nairobi general strike on 15 May 1950; detained May 1950–October 1961; tried unsuccessfully to re-enter the trade union movement; retired to write a history of the Kenyan trade unions. Published *History of Kenya's Trade Union Movement to 1952* (1976), and *History of Kenya's Trade Union Movement, 1952–56* (1980). Singh was a member of the Indian Communist Party and embarrassed Kenyatta and Mathu by calling for immediate independence for Kenya at a joint meeting of the Kenya African Union and the East African Indian National Congress in April 1950.

Tempany, Harold Augustin
Kt. (1946), CMG (1941), CBE (1933), D.Sc., FRIC, FCS. b. 1881; ed. privately and University College, London. Assistant government chemist, Leeward Islands, 1903; JP Antigua, 1910; Legislative Councillor, Antigua, 1912; Director of Agriculture, Mauritius, 1917–29; Director of Agriculture, Malaya, 1929–36; Assistant Agricultural Adviser to the Secretary of State, 1936–40; Agricultural Adviser to the Secretary of State, 1940–46. Published *Principles of Tropical Agriculture*.

Thornley, Colin Hardwick
KCMG (1957), CMG (1953), CVO (1954). b. 1907; ed. Uppingham and Brasenose College, Oxford; read Jurisprudence. Cadet, Tanganyika, 1930; seconded to Colonial Office, 1939–45; Private Secretary to the Secretary of State, 1941–45; Administrative Secretary, Kenya, 1945–47; Deputy Chief Secretary, Kenya, 1947–52; Member for Education and Labour, 1947–52; Chief Secretary, Uganda, 1952–55; Governor of British Honduras, 1955–61; Member of the Regional Boundaries Commission, Kenya, 1962; Director of Save the Children Fund, 1965–74.

Biographical Appendix

Thuku, Harry
b. 1895 at Kambui; ed. Gospel Missionary School, Kambui. Compositor, *Leader of British East Africa*, a settler newspaper, 1911–17; telephone operator at the Treasury, 1917–21; founded East African Association, 1921; detained February 1922–December 1930; President of the Kikuyu Central Association, August 1932; disagreements with Jesse Kariuki and Joseph Kangethe; formed Kikuyu Provincial Association, 1935; President Kenya African Union, 1944–45. By 1945 Thuku had become a loyalist; he was a strong opponent of Mau Mau and in 1952 organised meetings with Chief Waruhiu against the movement.

Troughton, John Frederick George
MBE (1936), b. 1902; ed. St Andrew's College, Dublin and Trinity College, Dublin; gold medal in mental and moral philosophy. Cadet, Kenya, 1926; District Officer, 1928; Secretary to the Kenya Land Commission, 1933; clerk to the Legislative and Executive Councils, 1933; seconded to the Colonial Office, 1936; and to BBC News, 1936; Deputy Financial Secretary, Kenya, 1939–44; Economic and Development Secretary, Kenya, 1944–46; Financial Secretary, 1946–49; Member of the Kenya Legislative Council, 1943–49; Controller of Finance, Overseas Food Corporation in East Africa, 1949–50; Member East African Central Assembly, 1949–50; Director Uganda Development Corporation, 1950. Troughton quarralled with Mitchell when he was Deputy Chairman of the East African Governor's Conference, 1940–41 and their relations between 1944 and 1949 were always strained.

Vasey, Ernest Albert
KBE (1959), CMG (1945). b. 1901; left school aged twelve at Bromley. Served on the Executive Committee of the National Conservative Association, the West Midlands Unionist Association and the Junior Imperial League; active in West Midlands' Conservative politics, 1929–37; migrated to Kenya in 1937; elected for Westland to the Nairobi Municipal Council, 1938–50; Mayor of Nairobi, 1941–42 and 1944–46; succeeded Cavendish-Bentinck as Legislative Councillor for Nairobi N. 1945–50; Member for Education, Health and Local Government, 1950–52; Minister of Finance and Development, 1952–59; Tanganyika Minister of Finance, 1959–62; economic adviser to the World Bank, 1962–66; Resident representative of the International Bank for Reconstruction and Development, Pakistan, 1963–66. Vasey was a liberal in settler politics; indeed he financed W.W.W. Awori's newspaper, *Radio Posta*, in the late 1940s.

Vincent, Alfred
b. 1891; ed. Russell Hill, Purley. Vincent was a prominent Nairobi businessman, Managing Director of Motor Mart and Exchange; Chairman, International Airadio (EA) Ltd.; Chairman, Greenham (EA) Ltd and of the Savings and Loan Society Ltd; Member of the Legislative Council, 1942–48; Member of the Executive Council, 1944–48; Member of the East African Central Assembly, 1948–53; Member of the inter-territorial Supply and Production Council; Chairman of the East African Airways Corporation. Vincent was the leader of the settler elected members from 1944–48. Mitchell was disappointed with him when he failed to support multiracialism during the Closer Union controversy and merely followed the diehards. He was a weak and ineffective politician and retired in 1948 to concentrate on his business activities, which were based on his position as East African representative for General Motors and the Ford Motor Co.

Windley, Edward Henry
b. 1909; ed. Repton and Cambridge University where he read anthoropology. Cadet, Kenya, 1931; District Commissioner, Kiambu, April 1947–February 1948; Provincial Commissioner, Central Province, April 1948–December 1948, May 1949–March 1950, and November 1950–January 1953. A man of considerable private means.

Bibliography

Archival sources

1. Kenya National Archives, Nairobi
A large number of files from central government ministries were consulted as well as a selection of District and Provincial correspondence. These included:
Government House Deposit Four
Secretariat
Chief Secretary Deposit One
Chief Secretary Deposit Two
Labour Deposit Two
Labour Deposit Nine
Labour Deposit Eleven
Agriculture Deposit One
Agriculture Deposit Two
Agriculture Deposit Four
Member for African Affairs Deposit One
Member for African Affairs Deposit Six
Member for African Affairs Deposit Seven
Member for African Affairs Deposit Eight
Member for African Affairs Deposit Nine
Member for African Affairs Deposit Ten
Member for African Affairs Unclassified, i.e. files from the old catalogue which had not been
    reclassified when I left Nairobi in September 1981.
Commerce and Industry Deposit Six
Commerce and Industry Deposit Seven
Defence Deposit Nine
Defence Deposit Ten
Defence Deposit Fifteen
Education Deposit One
Attorney General Deposit One
Central Christian Educational Association
The Murumbi Archive
Provincial Commissioner Central Province
Provincial Commissioner Nakuru
Provincial Commissioner Rift Valley Province
Provincial Commissioner Nyanza Province
District Commissioner Nakuru
District Commissioner Kiambu
District Commissioner Fort Hall (Murang'a)
District Commissioner Nyeri
District Commissioner Machakos
District Commissioner Kajiado
District Commissioner Narok

Bibliography

District Commissioner Teita–Taveta
Some Annual Reports, Political Record Books, Handing Over Reports and Intelligence Reports concerning Central Province, Kiambu, Fort Hall and Nyeri were consulted on microfilm at the Seeley History Library, Cambridge.

2. Public Record Office, London
Series C.O. 533 Kenya Original Correspondence
Series C.O. 537 Colnial General Supplementary Original Correspondence.
Series C.O. 543 Kenya Miscellanea, 1901–1946
Series C.O. 544 Kenya Sessional Papers
Series C.O. 822 East Africa Original Correspondence
Series C.O. 852 Economic Original Correspondence
Series C.O. 967 Private Office Papers
Series C.O. 968 Defence Original Correspondence
Series W.O. 276 East Africa Command, 1936–1954
Series Cab. 134 Cabinet Committees: General Series, 1945 onwards.

3. Rhodes House Library, Oxford
Collections of private papers:
Records of the Fabian Colonial Bureau (RH Mss.Brit.Emp.s. 365)
Records of the Electors' Union and the European Elected Members' Organisation (RH Mss.Afr.s. 596)
Thomas G. Askwith (Rh Mss.Afr.s. 1170)
Clarence Edward Victor Buxton (RH Mss.Afr.s. 1103)
Arthur Creech Jones (RH Mss.Brit.Emp.s. 332)
Colin Maher (RH Mss.Afr.s. 1741)
Philip Euen Mitchell (RH Mss.Afr.r. 101)
Stephen Howard Powles (RH Mss.Afr.s. 1121)

4. Private Collections
The Standard Newspaper Group, Nairobi, allowed access to their press-cuttings library which contains many extracts not only from the *East African Standard*, but from a wide range of other Kenyan and British newspaers and includes many original documents such as official reports and election manifestos.

Unpublished theses

Anderson, D.M., 'Herder, Settler and Colonial Rule: A History of the Peoples of the Baringo Plains, Kenya, circa 1890 to 1940', (Ph.D., Cambridge, 1982).
Barnes, C., 'An Experiment with African Coffee Growing in Kenya: the Gusii, 1933–1950' (Ph.D., Michigan State, 1976).
Behrmann, C.F., 'The Mythology of British Imperialism', (Ph.D., Boston, 1965).
Berman, B.J., 'Administration and Politics in Colonial Kenya', (Ph.D., Yale, 1973).
Breen, R.M., 'The Politics of Land: the Kenya Land Commission 1932–33 and its Effects on Land Policy in Kenya', (Ph.D., Michigan State, 1976).
Cowen, M.P., 'Capital and Household Production: the Case of Wattle in Kenya's Central Province, 1903–64', (Ph.D., Cambridge, 1978).
Feldman, D.M., 'Christians and Politics: the Origins of the Kikuyu Central Association in Northern Murang'a, 1890–1930', (Ph.D., Cambridge, 1979).
Githige, R.M., 'The Religious Factor in Mau Mau', (M.A., Nairobi, 1978).
Hay, M.J. 'Economic change in Luoland: Kowe, 1890–1945',(Ph.D., Wisconsin, 1972).
Horowitz, D., 'Attitudes of British Conservatives towards Decolonization in Africa during the Period of the Macmillan Government, 1957–63', (D.Phil., Oxford, 1967).
Kanogo, T.M.J., 'The History of Kikuyu Movement into the Nakuru District of the Kenya White Highlands, 1900–1963', (Ph.D., Nairobi, 1980).
Kennedy, D.K., 'A Tale of Two Colonies; the Social Origins and Cultural Consequences of White Settlement in Kenya and Rhodesia, 1890–1939', (Ph.D., University of California, Berkeley, 1981).

Bibliography

Mosley, P., 'The Settler Economies: Studies in the Economic History of Kenya and Southern Rhodesia, 1900–1963', (Ph.D., Cambridge, 1980).

Mueller, S.D., 'Political Parties in Kenya: Patterns of Opposition and Dissent, 1919–1969', (Ph.D., Princeton, 1972).

Mukaru-Ng'ang'a, D., 'Political History of Murang'a', (M.A., Nairobi, 1978).

Redley, M.G., 'The Politics of a Predicament; the White Community in Kenya, 1918–1932', (Ph.D., Cambridge, 1976).

Westcott, N.J., 'The Impact of the War on Tanganyika, 1939–49', (Ph.D., Cambridge, 1982).

Unpublished papers and reports

Berman, B.J., 'Provincial Administration and the Contradictions of Colonialism: "Development" Policy and Conflict in Kenya, 1945–52', Cambridge Conference on the Political Economy of Kenya, 1975.

Cowen, M.P., 'Concentration of Sales and Assets: Dairy Cattle and Tea in Magutu, 1964–1971', Institute of Development Studies, Nairobi, Working Paper No. 146.

—— 'Differentiation in a Kenya Location', Paper No. 16, Eighth Annual Conference of the East African Universities Social Science Council, December 1972.

—— 'Patterns of Cattle Ownership and Dairy Production, 1900–1965', mimeo, 1979.

—— and K. Kinyanjui, 'Some Problems of Class Formation in Kenya', mimeo, Institute of Development Studies, Nairobi, March 1977.

—— and F.Murage, 'Wattle Production in the Central Province: Capital and Household Commodity Production, 1903–1964', mimeo, Nairobi, July 1975.

—— 'Notes on Agricultural Wage Labour in a Kenya Location'.

Furedi, F., 'Olenguruone in Mau Mau Historiography', Paper presented to the Conference on the Mau Mau Rebellion, Institute of Commonwealth Studies, London, 29 March 1974.

Kanogo, T.M.J., 'Comparative Analysis of the Aspirations of the Kikuyu, Luo and Luhya Workers in the White Highlands, 1900–1930', History Department, Nairobi, Seminar Paper.

—— 'The Kikuyu Squatter Phenomenon in the Nakuru District of the Rift Valley: An Interpretation', History Department, Nairobi, Seminar Paper No. 21, May 1977.

Lonsdale, J.M., 'The Growth and Transformation of the Colonial State in Kenya, 1929–52' History Department, Nairobi, Seminar Paper No. 17, August 1980.

—— 'African Elites and Social Classes in Colonial Kenya', for the Round Table, Elites anciennes et nouvelles et colonisation, Maison des Sciences de l'Homme, Paris, July 1982.

—— 'Explanations of the Mau Mau Revolt, Kenya 1952–56', University of Cape Town African Studies Seminar, 27 July 1983.

—— 'Kenya's Civil War and Glorious Revolution: Notes Towards a Peasant Ideology', unpublished essay.

Maher, A.C., 'Soil Erosion and Land Utilisation in the Kamasia, Njemps and East Suk Reserves', Agricultural Department, Nairobi, mimeo, 1937.

Mutiso, G.C.M., 'The Creation of the Kitui Asomi', mimeo, Institute of Development Studies, Nairobi, Working Paper No. 304, October 1977.

Omosule, M., 'An Assessment of the Role of the Kenya Land Commission Report in the Mau Mau Outbreak', Historical Association of Kenya Annual Conference, August 1981.

Sykes, W., 'Sukumaland', report for the Oxford Development Record Project, 1983.

Thurston, A., 'The Intensification of Smallholder Agriculture in Kenya: the Genesis and Implementation of the Swynnerton Plan', report for the Oxford Development Record Project, 1983.

Westcott, N.J., 'The Politics of Planning and the Planning of Politics: Colonialism and Development in British Africa, 1930–1960', Development Studies Association Conference, 1981.

Bibliography

Official publications

1. **United Kingdom Government: Parliamentary Papers and Colonial Reports**

1934 Cmd. 4556 *Report of the Kenya Land Commission* (Chairman Sir Morris Carter)
1934 Cmd. 4580 *Kenya Land Commission: Summary of Conclusions Reached by His Majesty's Government*
1936 Col. 116 *Report of the Commission Appointed to Enquire into and Report on the Financial Position and System of Taxation in Kenya* (Sir A. Pim)
1946 Col. 191 *Inter-Territorial Organization in East Africa*
1946 Col. 193 *Labour Conditions in East Africa* (G. St. J. Orde-Browne)
1947 Col. 210 *Inter-Territorial Organization in East Africa: Revised Proposals*
1950 Cmd. 7987 *The British Territories in East and Central Africa, 1945–1950*
1952 Col. 290 *Land and Population in East Africa: exchange of correspondence between the Secretary of State for the Colonies and the Governor of Kenya on the appointment of the Royal Commission*
1955 Cmd. 9475 *East Africa Royal Commission, 1953–55: Report* (Chairman Sir Hugh Dow)
1960 Cmd. 1030 *Historical Survey of the Origins and Growth of Mau Mau* (F.D. Corfield)

2. **Kenya Government Publications**

1941 *Report on the Housing of Africans in Nairobi*
1941 *Interim Report of a Committee Appointed to Advise as to the Steps to be taken to deal with the Problem of Overstocking in order to Preserve the Future Welfare of the Native Pastoral Areas* (East Africa Pamphlet No. 293)
1943 *Report of the Food Shortage Commission*
1943 *Report of the Sub-Committee on Post-War Employment of Africans*
1945 *The Kikuyu Lands: the Relation of Population to the Land in South Nyeri* (N. Humphrey); and *Memorandum on Land Tenure in the Native Lands* (H.E. Lambert and P. Wyn Harris)
1945 *Post-War Settlement in Kenya: proposed schemes*
1945 *Report on Native Tribunals* (A. Phillips)
1945 *Report of the Committee of Inquiry into Labour Unrest in Mombasa* (Chairman A. Phillips)
1945 *Proposals for the Reorganization of the Administration in Kenya* (S.P. No. 3)
1946 *Report of the Development Committee*, 2 vols. (Chairman J.F.G. Troughton)
1946 *General Aspects of the Agrarian Situation in Kenya*, Despatch No.44 (17 April 1946) from Sir Philip Mitchell
1947 *The Agrarian Problem in Kenya* (Note by Sir Philip Mitchell)
1947 *Report of the Taxation Enquiry Committee*, Kenya, 1947 (Chairman R.P. Plewman)
1947 *The Liguru and the Land: Sociological Aspects of some Agricultural Problems of North Kavirondo* (N. Humphrey)
1948 *Nairobi, Master Plan for a Colonial Capital* (L.W.T. White, L. Silberman, and P.R. Anderson) (London, 1948)
1948 *An Inquiry into Indian Education in East Africa* (A.A. Kazimi); and *Report of Committee on Educational Expenditure*
1948 *A Ten Year Plan for the Development of African Education*
1949 *Report of the Select Committee on Indian Education*
1949 *African Education in Kenya: Report of a Committee Appointed to Enquire into the Scope, Content, and Methods of African Education, its Administration and Finance, and to Make Recommendations* (Chairman Rev. L.J. Beecher)
1950 *Report of Committee on Agricultural Credit for Africans* (Chairman J.H. Ingham)
1950 *Report of a Commission of Inquiry Appointed to Review the Registration of Persons Ordinance 1947* (Chairman B.J. Glancy)
1951 *Agricultural Policy in African Areas* (P.E. Mitchell)
1951 *African Education: a Statement of Policy*
1953 *Report of the Inquiry into the General Economy of Farming in the Highlands* (L.G. Troup)
1954 *The Psychology of Mau Mau* (J.C. Carothers)
1954 *Report of the Committee on African Wages* (Chairman F.W.Carpenter)
1954 *A Plan to Intensify the Development of African Agriculture in Kenya* (R.J.M. Swynnerton)

Other publications

1. Books

Aaronovitch, S. and K., *Crisis in Kenya*, (London 1947).

African Land Development Board, *African Land Development Board in Kenya 1946–55: Report by the African Land Development Board*, (Nairobi 1955).

Allan, W., *Studies in African Land Usage in Northern Rhodesia*, (Rhodes–Livingstone Papers, No. 15, Oxford 1949).

Andaya, B.W. and L.Y., *A History of Malaysia* (London 1982).

Asad, T. (ed.), *Anthropology and the Colonial Encounter* (London 1973).

Austin, D., *Politics in Ghana, 1946–1960*, (Oxford 1964).

Barnett, D.L. and K. Njama, *Mau Mau From Within*, (New York 1966).

Bell, J.B., *On Revolt: Strategies of National Liberation*, (Cambridge, Massachusetts 1976).

Bennett, G., *Kenya: A Political History*, (Oxford 1963).

Bernard, F.E., *East of Mount Kenya: Meru Agriculture in Transition*, (Munich 1972).

Berque, J., *French North Africa: the Maghrib between Two World Wars*, (London 1967).

Blundell, Sir Michael, *So Rough a Wind* (London 1964).

Brett, E.A., *Colonialism and Underdevelopment in East Africa: the Politics of Economic Change, 1919–1939*, (London 1973).

Bromley, R. and C. Gerry, (eds), *Casual Work and Poverty in Third World Cities*, (Chichester 1979).

Buijtenhuijs, R., *Essays on Mau Mau: Contributions to Mau Mau Historiography*, (Leiden 1982).

Cagnolo, C. *The Akikuyu*, (Nyeri 1933).

Cliffe, L. and J.S. Saul, *Socialism in Tanzania*, vol. 1, (Nairobi 1972).

Cohen, A.B., *British Policy in Changing Africa*, (London 1959).

Crowder, M., *West Africa under Colonial Rule*, (London 1968).

Darwin, J., *Britain, Egypt and the Middle East: Imperial Policy in the Aftermath of War, 1918–1922*, (London 1981).

Dewey, C. and A.G. Hopkins, *The Imperial Impact: Studies in the Economic History of Africa and India*, (London 1978).

Farson, N., *Last Chance in Africa*, (London 1949).

Fisher, J.M., *Anatomy of Kikuyu Domesticity and Husbandry*, (London 1964).

Frost, R.A., *Race Against Time: Human Relations and Politics in Kenya before Independence*, (London 1978).

Gallagher, J.A., *The Decline, Revival and Fall of the British Empire: the Ford Lectures and Other Essays*, (Cambridge 1982).

Gallagher, J.A. and G. Johnson and A. Seal (eds), *Locality, Province and Nation: Essays on Indian Politics, 1870–1940*, (Cambridge 1973).

Gann, L.H. and P. Duignan (eds), *African Proconsuls: European Governors in Africa*, (London 1978).

Gertzel, C., *The Politics of Independent Kenya, 1963–1968*, (London 1970).

Ghai, Y.P. and Y.P.W.B. McAuslan, *Public Law and Political Change in Kenya*, (Nairobi 1970).

Goldsworthy, D., *Colonial Issues in British Politics 1945–1961: From 'Colonial Development' to 'Wind of Change'*, (Oxford 1971).

—— *Tom Mboya: the Man Kenya Wanted to Forget*, (London 1982).

Gregory, R.E., *Sidney Webb and East Africa*, (Berkeley 1962).

Gupta, P.S., *Imperialism and the British Labour Movement, 1914–1964*, (London 1975).

Gutkind, P.C.W., R. Cohen and J. Copans (eds), *African Labor History*, (London 1978).

Hailey, Lord, *An African Survey*, 1st edition, (Oxford 1938).

—— *Native Administration and Political Development in British Tropical Africa*, (Nendeln/Liechtenstein 1979).

—— *Native Administration in the British African Territories*, 4 vols. (London 1950).

—— *Native Land Tenure in Africa* (printed for the Colonial Office, London 1945).

—— *An African Survey*, (revised edition, London 1957).

Hake, A., *African Metropolis: Nairobi's Self-Help City*, (London 1977).

Harlow, V., E.M. Chilver and A. Smith (eds), *History of East Africa*, vol. 2, (Oxford 1965).

Harris, J.E. (ed.), *Recollections of James Juma Mbotela*, (Nairobi 1977).

Hennings, R.O., *African Morning*, (London 1951).

Bibliography

Hillmer, N. and P. Wigley (eds), *The First British Commonwealth: Essays in Honour of Nicholas Mansergh*, (London 1980).

Holland, R.F., *European Decolonization 1918-1981*, (London 1985).

—— and G. Rizvi, (eds), *Perspectives on Imperialism and Decolonization: Essays in Honour of A.F. Madden*, (London 1984).

Hollis, A.C., *The Nandi* (Oxford 1909).

Hughes, L. (ed.), *An African Treasury* (New York 1960).

Humphrey, N., *The Kikuyu Lands: The Relation of Population to the Land in South Nyeri*, (Nairobi 1945).

Humphrey, N., *The Liguru and the Land: Sociological Aspects of Some Agricultural Problems of North Kavirondo*, (Nairobi 1947).

Iliffe, J., *A Modern History of Tanganyika*, (Cambridge 1979).

Jeffrey, R. (ed.), *Asia: the Winning of Independence*, (London 1981).

Jones, N.S. Carey, *The Anatomy of Uhuru*, (Manchester 1966).

Kaggia, B., *Roots of Freedom, 1921-1963*, (Nairobi 1975).

Kennedy, P., *The Realities Behind Diplomacy: Background Influences on British External Policy, 1865-1980*, (London 1981).

Kenyatta, J., *Facing Mount Kenya: the Tribal Life of the Gikuyu*, (London 1953).

Kimambo, I.N., *Mbiru: Popular Protest in Colonial Tanzania*, Historical Association of Tanzania, Paper No. 9, (Nairobi 1971).

Kirk-Greene, A.H.M., *A Biographical Dictionary of the British Colonial Governors: Africa*, (Stanford 1980).

Kitching, G., *Class and Economic Change in Kenya: the Making of an African Petite-Bourgeoisie*, (London 1980).

Lambert, H.E., *Systems of Land Tenure in the Kikuyu Land Unit*, (School of African Studies, University of Cape Town, Paper No. 22, February 1950).

—— *Kikuyu Social and Political Institutions*, (London 1956).

Leakey, L.S.B., *Defeating Mau Mau*, (London 1954).

—— *The Southern Kikuyu before 1903*, 3 vols., (London 1977).

Lee, J.M., *Colonial Development and Good Government*, (Oxford 1967).

—— and M. Petter, *The Colonial Office, War and Development Policy*, (London 1982).

Leys, C., *Underdevelopment in Kenya: the Political Economy of Neo-Colonialism, 1964-1971*, (London 1975).

Little, K., *West African Urbanization: A Study of Voluntary Associations in Social Change*, (Cambridge 1970).

Louis, W.R., *Imperialism at Bay: the United States and the Decolonization of the British Empire, 1941-1945*, (Oxford 1977).

Low, D.A. and A. Smith (eds), *History of East Africa*, 3 vols., (Oxford 1976).

Madden, F. and D.K. Fieldhouse (eds), *Oxford and the Idea of Commonwealth*, (London 1982).

Maguire, G.A., *Towards Uhuru in Tanzania: the Politics of Participation*, (Cambridge 1969).

Maina wa Kinyatti, (ed.), *Thunder from the Mountains: Mau Mau Patriotic Songs*, (London 1980).

Mathu, M., *The Urban Guerrilla*, (Richmond, British Columbia 1974).

Middlemas, K., *Politics in Industrial Society: the Experience of the British System since 1911*, (London 1979).

Mitchell, P.E., *African Afterthoughts*, (London 1954).

Moore, S. Barrington, Jr., *The Social Origins of Dictatorship and Democracy* (Boston 1966).

Morgan, D.J., *The Official History of Colonial Development: Origins of British Aid Policy, 1924-1945*, (London 1980).

—— *The Official History of Colonial Development: Developing British Colonial Resources 1945-1951*, (London 1980).

Mosley, P., *The Settler Economies: Studies in the Economic History of Kenya and Southern Rhodesia, 1900-63*, (Cambridge 1983).

Mungeam, G.H., *British Rule in Kenya, 1895-1912: the Establishment of Administration in the East African Protectorate*, (Oxford 1966).

Munro, J. Forbes, *Colonial Rule and the Kamba: Social Change in the Kenya Highlands, 1889-1939*, (Oxford 1975).

—— *Africa and the International Economy, 1800-1960*, (London 1976).

Murray-Brown, J., *Kenyatta*, (New York 1973).

Mwangi, M., *Kill Me Quick*, (London 1973).

Bibliography

—— *Going Down River Road*, (London 1976).
Newman, *The Ukamba Members Association*, (Nairobi 1974).
Ngugi wa Thiong'o, *Detained: A Writer's Prison Diary* (London 1981).
Ogot, B.A., (ed.), *Hadith*, vol. 2, (Nairobi 1970).
Ogot, B.A., (ed.), *Hadith*, vol. 3, (Nairobi 1971).
—— (ed.), *Hadith*, vol. 4, *Politics and Nationalism in Colonial Kenya*, (Nairobi 1972).
—— (ed.), *Hadith*, vol. 5, *Economic and Social History of East Africa*, (Nairobi 1975).
—— (ed.), *Hadith* vol. 7, *Ecology and History in East Africa* (Nairobi 1979).
Owen, E.R.J. and R.B. Sutcliffe, (eds), *Studies in the Theory of Imperialism*, (London 1972).
Palmer, R. and N. Parsons, (eds), *The Roots of Rural Poverty in Central and Southern Africa*, (London 1977).
Parkin, D., *The Cultural Definition of Political Response: Lineal Destiny among the Luo*, (London 1978).
Pearce, R.D., *The Turning Point in Africa: British Colonial Policy, 1938-1948*, (London 1982).
Perham, M., (ed.), *Ten Africans*, (London 1936).
—— *Colonial Sequence, 1930-1949*, Vol. I (London 1967).
—— *East African Journey: Kenya and Tanganyika, 1929-30*, (London 1976).
Peristiany, J.G., *The Social Institutions of the Kipsigis*, (reprinted London 1964).
Ranger, T.O., *Peasant Consciousness and Guerrilla War in Zimbabwe*, (London 1985).
Ricklefs, M.C., *A History of Modern Indonesia*, (London 1981).
Roelker, J.R., *Mathu of Kenya: A Political Study*, (Stanford 1976).
Rosberg, C.G. and J. Nottingham, *The Myth of 'Mau Mau': Nationalism in Kenya*, (New York 1966).
Rosen, I. and F. de F. Stratton, *A Digest of East African Criminal Case Law* (Durban 1957).
Rotberg, R.I., *The Rise of Nationalism in Central Africa: the Making of Malawi and Zambia, 1873-1964*, (Cambridge, Massachusetts 1965).
Rotberg, R.I and A.A. Mazrui (eds), *Protest and Power in Black Africa*, (New York 1970).
Routledge, W.S. and K., *With a Prehistoric People: the Akikuyu of British East Africa*, (reprinted, London 1968).
Sandbrook, R. and R. Cohen (eds), *The Development of an African Working Class: Studies in Class Formation and Action*, (London 1975).
Seal, A., *The Emergence of Indian Nationalism: Competition and Collaboration in the later Nineteenth Century*, (Cambridge 1968).
Shanin, T. (ed.), *Peasants and Peasant Societies*, (London 1971).
Shepperson, G.A. and T. Price, *Independent African: John Chilembwe and the Origins, Setting and Significance of the Nyasaland Native Rising of 1915*, (Edinburgh 1958).
Singh, M., *History of Kenya's Trade Union Movement up to 1952*, (Nairobi 1969).
Sorrenson, M.P.K., *Land Reform in the Kikuyu Country: A Study in Government Policy*, (Nairobi 1967).
Spencer, J., *KAU: The Kenya African Union*, (London 1985).
—— *James Beauttah: Freedom Fighter*, (Nairobi 1983).
Stichter, S.B., *Migrant Labour in Kenya: Capitalism and African Response, 1895-1975*, (London 1982).
Storry, R., *Japan and the Decline of the West in Asia, 1894-1943*, (London 1979).
Swainson, N., *The Development of Corporate Capitalism in Kenya, 1918-1977*, (London 1980).
Swynnerton, R.J.M., *A Plan to Intensify the Development of African Agriculture in Kenya*, (Nairobi 1954).
Thomas, H., *John Strachey*, (London 1973).
Thorne, C., *Allies of a Kind: the United States, Britain, and the War Against Japan, 1941-1945*, (London 1978).
Tignor, R.L., *The Colonial Transformation of Kenya: the Kamba, Kikuyu and Maasai from 1900 to 1939*, (Princeton 1976).
Tosh, J., *Clan Leaders and Colonial Chiefs in Lango*, (Oxford 1978).
Trapnell, C.G. and J.M. Clothier, *The Soils, Vegetation and Agricultural Systems of North-Western Rhodesia*, (Government Printer, Lusaka 1937).
Van Onselen, C., *Chibaro: African Mine Labour in Southern Rhodesia, 1900-1933*, (London 1976).
Van Zwanenberg, R.M.A., *Colonial Capitalism and Labour in Kenya, 1919-1939*, (Nairobi 1975).
Von Albertini, R., *Decolonization: the Administration and Future of the Colonies, 1919-1960*, (New York 1971).

Bibliography

Wachanga, H.K., *The Swords of Kirinyaga: the Fight for Land and Freedom*, (Nairobi 1975).
Wasserman, G., *Politics of Decolonization: Kenya Europeans and the Land Issue, 1960-1965*, (Cambridge 1976).
Wolf, E.R., *Peasants*, (Englewood Cliffs, New Jersey 1966).

2. Articles
Abrahams, P., 'The Blacks', in L. Hughes, (ed.), *An African Treasury*, (New York 1960), pp. 50-62.
African Studies Branch of the Colonial Office, 'Local Government Reorganisation in the Eastern Provinces of Nigeria and Kenya', *Journal of African Administration*, vol. 1, no. 1, January 1949, pp. 18-29.
African Studies Branch of the Colonial Office, 'A Survey of the Development of Local Government in the African Territories since 1947', Supplement to the *Journal of African Administration* vol. 4, no. 1, January 1952, pp. 1-83.
Anderson, D.M., 'Depression, Dust Bowl, Demography and Drought: The Colonial State and Soil Conservation in East Africa during the 1930s', *African Affairs* vol. 83, no. 332, July 1984, pp. 321-43.
Anderson, D.M. and D.W. Throup, 'Africans and Agricultural Production in Colonial Kenya: The Myth of the War as a Watershed', *Journal of African History*, vol. 26, 1985, pp. 327-45.
Anyang'-Nyong'o, P., 'The Development of a Middle Peasantry in Nyanza', *Review of African Political Economy*, no. 20, January-April 1981, pp. 108-20.
—— 'What the "Friends of the Peasantry" are and How they Pose the Question of the Peasantry', *Review of African Political Economy*, no. 20. January-April 1981, pp. 17-26.
Atieno Odhiambo, E.S., ' "Seek Ye First the Economic Kingdom": A History of the Luo Thrift and Trading Corporation (LUTATCO), 1945-1956', in B.A. Ogot, (ed.) *Hadith 5: Economic and Social History of East Africa*, (Nairobi 1975), pp. 218-56.
Bennett, G., 'Settlers and Politics in Kenya, up to 1945', in V. Harlow, E.M. Chilver and A. Smith (eds), *History of East Africa*, vol. 2 (Oxford 1965), pp. 265-332.
Berman, B.J., 'Bureaucracy and Incumbent Violence: Colonial Administration and the Origins of the Mau Mau Emergency in Kenya', *British Journal of Political Science*, vol. 6, pp. 143-75.
Bowles, B.D., 'Underdevelopment in Agriculture in Colonial Kenya: Some Ecological and Dietary Aspects', in B.A. Ogot, (ed.), *Hadith 7: Ecology and History in East Africa*, (Nairobi 1979), pp. 195-215.
Brett, E.A. and S. Gilliatt and A. Pople, 'Planned Trade, Labour Part Policy and U.S. Intervention: the Successes and Failures of Post-War Reconstruction', *History Workshop*, no. 13, Spring 1982, pp. 130-42.
Bujra, J.M., 'Women Entrepreneurs of Early Nairobi', *Canadian Journal of African Studies*, vol. 9, no. 2, 1975, pp. 213-34.
Cell, J.W., 'On the Eve of Decolonisation: the Colonial Office's Plans for the Transfer of Power in Africa, 1947', *Journal of Imperial and Commonwealth History*, vol. 8 no. 3, May 1980, pp. 235-57.
Cliffe, L., 'Nationalism and the Reaction to Enforced Agricultural Change in Tanganyika during the Colonial Period', in L. Cliffe and J.S. Saul, *Socialism in Tanzania*, vol. I, (Nairobi 1972), pp. 17-23.
Cowen, M.P., 'The Agrarian Problem: Notes on the Nairobi Discussion', *Review of African Political Economy*, no. 20, January-April 1981, pp. 57-73
Darwin, J., 'British Decolonization since 1945: A Pattern or a Puzzle?', in R.F. Holland and G. Rizvi, (eds), *Perspectives on Imperialism and Decolonization: Essays in Honour of A.F. Madden*, (London 1984), pp. 187-209.
Ehrlich, C., 'The Uganda Economy, 1903-1945', in V. Harlow, E.M. Chilver, and A. Smith (eds), *History of East Africa*, vol. 2, (Oxford 1965), pp. 395-475.
Fosbrooke, H., 'Public Opinion and Changes in Land Tenure', Special Supplement on Land Tenure to the *Journal of African Administration*, October 1952, pp. 28-36.
Frost, R.A., 'Sir Philip Mitchell: Governor of Kenya', *African Affairs*, vol. 78, no. 313, October 1979, pp. 535-53.
Furedi, F., 'The African Crowd in Nairobi: Popular Movements and Elite Politics', *Journal of African History*, vol. 14, no. 2, 1973, pp. 275-90.
—— 'The Social Composition of the Mau Mau Movement in the White Highlands', *Journal of*

Bibliography

Peasant Studies, vol. 1, no. 4, (1973), pp. 486–505.

—— 'The Development of Anti-Asian Opinion among Africans in Nakuru District, Kenya', *African Affairs*, vol. 73, no. 292, July 1974, pp. 347–58.

—— 'The Kikuyu Squatters in the Rift Valley, 1918–1929', in B.A. Ogot (ed), *Hadith* 5: *Economic and Social History of East Africa*, (Nairobi 1975), pp. 177–94.

Gadsden, F., 'The African Press in Kenya, 1945–52', *Journal of African History* vol. 21, no. 4, 1980, pp. 515–35.

Gordon, D.F., 'Mau Mau and Decolonization: Kenya and the Defeat of Multi-Racialism in East and Central Africa', *Kenya Historical Review*, vol. 5, no. 2, 1977, pp. 329–48.

Hailey, Lord, 'The Land Tenure Problem in Africa', Special Supplement on Land Tenure to the *Journal of African Administration*, October 1952, pp. 3–7.

Hennings, R.O., 'Some Trends and Problems of African Land Tenure in Kenya', *Journal of African Administration*, vol. 4, no. 4, October 1952, pp. 122–34.

Holland, R.F., 'The Imperial Factor in British Strategies from Attlee to Macmillan, 1945–63', in R.F. Holland and G. Rizvi, (eds), *Perspectives on Imperialism and Decolonization: Essays in Honour of A.F. Madden*, (London 1984), pp. 165–86.

Horowitz, D., 'Attitudes of British Conservatives towards Decolonization in Africa', *African Affairs*, vol. 69, no. 274, January 1970, pp. 9–26.

Hyam, R., 'The Colonial Office Mind, 1900–1914', in N. Hillmer and P. Wigley, *The First British Commonwealth: Essays in Honour of Nicholas Mansergh*, (London 1980), pp. 30–55.

Iliffe, J., 'The Creation of Group Consciousness among the Dockworkers of Dar-es-Salaam, 1929–1950', in R. Sandbrook and R. Cohen, (eds), *The Development of an African Working Class: Studies in Class Formation and Action*, (London 1975), pp. 49–72.

Johnson, D.H., 'Evans-Pritchard, the Nuer, and the Sudan Political Service', *African Affairs*, vol. 81, no. 323, April 1982, pp. 231–46.

Jones, A. Creech, 'The Place of African Local Administration in Colonial Policy', *Journal of African Administration*, vol. 1, no. 1, January 1949, pp. 3–6.

Kamunchulun, J.T.S., 'The Meru Participation in Mau Mau', *Kenya Historical Review*, vol. 3, no. 2, 1975, pp. 193–216.

Kanogo, T.M.J., 'Rift Valley Squatters and Mau Mau', *Kenya Historical Review*, vol. 5, no. 2, 1977, pp. 243–52.

King, K.J. and R.M. Wambaa, 'The Political Economy of the Rift Valley: A Squatter Perspective', in B.A. Ogot, (ed.), *Hadith 5: Economic and Social History of East Africa*, (Nairobi 1975) pp. 195–217.

Kipkorir, B.E., 'The Educated Elite and Local Society: The Basis for Mass Representation', in B.A. Ogot, (ed.), *Hadith 4: Politics and Nationalism in Colonial Kenya*, (Nairobi 1972), pp. 250–69.

—— 'Mau Mau and the Politics of the Transfer of Power in Kenya, 1957–1960', *Kenya Historical Review*, vol. 5, no. 2., 1977, pp. 313–28.

Kirk-Greene, A.H.M., 'Margery Perham and Colonial Administration: A Direct Influence on Indirect Rule', in F. Madden and D.K. Fieldhouse, (eds), *Oxford and the Idea of Commonwealth*, (London 1982), pp. 122–43.

—— 'On Governorship and Governors in British Africa', in L.H. Gann and P. Duignan, (eds), *African Proconsuls: European Governors in Africa*, (London 1978), pp. 210–257.

—— 'The Progress of Pro-Consuls: Advancement and Migration among the Colonial Governors of British African Territories, 1900–1965', *Journal of Imperial and Commonwealth History*, vol. 7, no. 2, January 1979, pp. 180–212.

—— 'The Thin White Line: the Size of the British Colonial Service in Africa', *African Affairs*, vol. 79, no. 314, January 1980, pp. 25–44.

Kosmin, B., 'The Inyoka Tobacco Industry of the Shangwe People', in R. Palmer and N. Parsons (eds), *The Roots of Rural Poverty in Central and Southern Africa*, (London 1977), pp. 268–88.

Lee, J.M., 'Forward Thinking and War: the Colonial Office during the 1940s', *Journal of Imperial and Commonwealth History*, vol. 6, no. 1, October 1977, pp. 64–79.

Listowel, Earl of, 'The Modern Conception of Government in British Africa', *Journal of African Studies*, vol. 1, no. 3, July 1949, pp. 99–105.

Lonsdale, J.M., 'Some Origins of Nationalism in East Africa', *Journal of African History*, vol. 9, no. 1, 1968, pp. 119–46.

—— 'European Attitudes and African Pressures: Missions and Government in Kenya between the Wars', in B.A. Ogot, (ed.), *Hadith 2*, (Nairobi 1970), pp. 229–42.

Bibliography

—— and D.A. Low, 'Introduction: Towards the New Order, 1945-1963', in D.A. Low and A. Smith (eds), *History of East Africa*, vol. 3, (Oxford 1976), pp. 1-63.

McCracken, J., 'Experts and Expertise in Colonial Malawi', *African Affairs*, vol. 81, no. 322, January 1982, pp. 101-16.

McWilliam, M., 'The Managed Economy: Agricultural Change, Development and Finance in Kenya', in D.A. Low and A. Smith, (eds), *History of East Africa*, vol. 3, (Oxford 1976), pp. 251-89.

Maguire, G.A., 'The Emergence of the Tanganyika African National Union in the Lake Province', in R.I. Rotberg and A.A. Mazrui, (eds), *Protest and Power in Black Africa*, (New York, 1970), pp. 639-70.

Maina wa Kinyatti, 'Mau Mau: the Peak of African Political Organization in Colonial Kenya', *Kenya Historical Review*, vol. 5, no. 2, 1977, pp. 287-311.

Mair, L., 'Anthropology and Colonial Policy', *African Affairs*, vol. 74, no. 295, April 1975, pp. 191-5.

Masefield, G.B., 'Farming Systems and Land Tenure', Special Supplement on Land Tenure to the *Journal of African Administration*, October 1952, pp. 8-14.

Meek, C.K., 'The Amsterdam Land Tenure Symposium', *Journal of African Administration*, vol. 4, no. 3, July 1952, pp. 113-14.

—— 'Some Social Aspects of Land Tenure in Africa', Special Supplement on Land Tenure to the *Journal of African Administration*, October 1952, pp. 15-21.

Miles, J., 'Rural Protest in the Gold Coast: the Cocoa Hold-Ups, 1908-1938', in C. Dewey and A.G. Hopkins, (eds), *The Imperial Impact: Studies in the Economic History of Africa and India*, (London 1978), pp. 152-70.

Mukaru-Ng'ang'a, D., 'What is Happening to the Kenyan Peasantry?', *Review of African Political Economy*, no. 20, January-April 1981, pp. 7-16.

—— 'Mau Mau, Loyalists and Politics in Murang'a, 1952-70', *Kenya Historical Review*, vol. 5, no. 2, 1977, pp. 365-84.

Muntemba M. 'Thwarted Development: A Case Study of Economic Change in the Kabwe Rural District of Zambia, 1902-70', in R. Palmer and N. Parsons, (eds), *The Roots of Rural Poverty in Central and Southern Africa*, (London 1977), pp. 345-345-64.

Nelson, N., 'How Women and Men Get By: the Sexual Division of Labour in the Informal Sector of a Nairobi Squatter Settlement', in R. Bromley and C. Gerry, (eds), *Casual Work and Poverty in Third World Cities*, (Chichester 1979), pp. 283-302.

Newton, S., 'Britain, the Sterling Area and European Integration, 1945-50', *Journal of Imperial and Commonwealth History*, vol. 13 no. 3, May 1985, pp. 163-82.

Njonjo, A.L.N., 'The Kenya Peasantry: A Reassessment', *Review of African Political Economy*, no. 20, January-April 1981, pp. 27-40.

Ogot, B.A., 'Politics, Culture and Music in Central Kenya: A Study of Mau Mau Hymns, 1951-1956', *Kenya Historical Review*, vol. 5, no. 2, 1977, pp. 275-86.

—— 'The Revolt of the Elders: An Anatomy of the Loyalist Crowd in the Mau Mau Uprising, 1952-56', in B.A. Ogot, (ed.), *Hadith 4: Politics and Nationalism in Colonial Kenya*, (Nairobi 1972), pp. 134-48.

O'Hagan, D., 'African's Part in Nairobi Local Government', *Journal of African Administration*, vol. 1, no. 4, October 1949, pp. 156-8.

Omosule, M., 'Kiama Kia Muingi: Kikuyu Reaction to Land Consolidation Policy in Kenya, 1955-59', *Transafrican Journal of History*, vol. 4, nos. 1-2, 1974, pp. 115-34.

Palmer, R., 'The Agricultural History of Rhodesia', in R. Palmer and N. Parsons, (eds), *The Roots of Rural Poverty in Central and Southern Africa*, (London 1977), pp. 221-54.

Pearce, R.D., 'Governors, Nationalists and Constitutions in Nigeria, 1935-1951', *Journal of Imperial and Commonwealth History*, vol. 9, no. 3, May 1981, pp. 289-307.

Pedler, F., 'The Contribution of Lord Hailey to Africa', *African Affairs*, vol. 69, no. 276, July 1970, pp. 267-75.

Philip, A.J., 'Nutrition in Kenya', *East African Medical Journal*, July 1943.

Phimister, I., 'Peasant Production and Underdevelopment in Southern Rhodesia, 1890-1914', in R. Palmer and N. Parsons, (eds) *The Roots of Rural Poverty in Central and Southern Africa*, (London 1977), pp. 255-67.

Rathbone, R.J.A.R., 'The Government of the Gold Coast after the Second World War', *African Affairs*, vol. 67, no. 2, 1968, pp. 209-18.

—— 'Businessmen in Politics: Party Struggle in Ghana, 1949-57', *Journal of Development Studies*, vol. 9, no. 3, 1973, pp. 391-401.

Bibliography

Robinson, R.E., 'The Relationship of Major and Minor Local Government Authorities', *Journal of African Administration*, vol. 1, no. 1, January 1949, pp. 30–3.

—— 'The Progress of Provincial Councils in the British African Territories', *Journal of African Administration*, vol. 1, no. 2, April 1949, pp. 53–68.

—— 'Non European Foundations of European Imperialism: Sketch for a Theory of Collaboration', in E.R.J. Owen and R.B. Sutcliffe, (eds) *Studies in the Theory of Imperialism*, (London 1972), pp. 117–142.

—— 'The Moral Disarmament of African Empire, 1919–1947', *Journal of Imperial and Commonwealth History*, vol. 3, no. 1, October 1979, pp. 86–104.

—— 'The Journal and the Transfer of Power, 1947–51', *Journal of Administration Overseas*, vol. 13, no. 1, 1974, pp. 255–258.

—— 'Andrew Cohen and the Transfer of Power in Tropical Africa, 1940–51', in W.H. Morris-Jones and G. Fischer, (eds), *Decolonization and After: the British and French Experience*, (London 1980), pp. 50–72.

—— 'Sir Andrew Cohen: Proconsul of African Nationalism', in L.H. Gann and P. Duignan, (eds), *African Proconsuls: European Governors in Africa*, (London 1978), pp. 353–63.

Rowlings, C.W., 'An Analysis of Factors Affecting Changes in Land Tenure in Africa', Special Supplement on Land Tenure to the *Journal of African Administration*, October 1952, pp. 21–8.

Saul, J. and R. Woods, 'African Peasantries', in T. Shanin, (ed.), *Peasants and Peasant Societies*, (London 1971), pp. 103–13.

Seal, A., 'Imperialism and Nationalism in India', in J. Gallagher, G. Johnson and A. Seal, (eds), *Locality, Province and Nation: Essays on Indian Politics, 1870–1940*, (Cambridge 1973), pp. 1–27.

Singh, M., 'The East African Trade Union Congress, 1949–50: the First Central Organisation of Trade Unions in Kenya', in B.A. Ogot, (ed) *Hadith 4: Politics and Nationalism in Colonial Kenya*, (Nairobi 1972), pp. 233–249.

Spencer, I.R.G., 'Settler Dominance, Agricultural Production and the Second World War in Kenya', *Journal of African History*, vol. 21, 1980, pp. 497–514.

Spencer, J., 'Kenya African Union and Mau Mau: Some Connections', *Kenya Historical Review*, vol. 5, no. 2, 1977, pp. 201–24.

Stevens, R.A., 'The Application of English Local Government Principles in Africa', *Journal of African Administration*, vol. 1, no. 2, April 1949, pp. 68–73.

Stichter, S.B., 'Trade Unionism in Kenya, 1947–1952: the Militant Phase' in P.C.W. Gutkind, R. Cohen and J. Copans, (eds), *African Labor History*, (London 1978), pp. 155–74.

—— 'The Formation of a Working Class in Kenya', in R. Sandbrook and R. Cohen, (eds), *The Development of an African Working Class: Studies in Class Formation and Action*, (London 1975), pp. 21–48.

—— 'Workers, Trade Unions and the Mau Mau Rebellion', *Canadian Journal of African Studies*, vol. 9, no. 2, 1975, pp. 253–75.

Tamarkin, M., 'Mau Mau in Nakuru', *Kenya Historical Review*, vol. 5, no. 2, 1977, pp. 225–41.

Throup, D.W., 'The Origins of Mau Mau', *African Affairs*, vol. 84, no. 336, July 1985, pp. 399–433.

Trapnell, C.G., 'Ecological Methods in the Study of Native Agriculture', *East African Agricultural Journal*, vol. 2, 1937, pp. 491–4.

Van Zwanenberg, R.M.A., 'History and Theory of Urban Poverty in Nairobi', *Journal of Eastern African Research and Development*, vol. 2, 1972, pp. 165–203.

Were, G.S., 'Politics, Religion and Nationalism in Western Kenya'. in B.A. Ogot, (ed), *Hadith 4: Politics and Nationalism in Colonial Kenya*, (Nairobi 1972), pp. 85–104.

Westcott, N.J., 'Erica Fiah: An East African Radical', *Journal of African History*, vol. 22, 1981, pp. 85–101.

—— 'Closer Union and the Future of East Africa, 1939–48: A Case Study in the Official Mind of Imperialism', *Journal of Imperial and Commonwealth History*, vol. 10, No. 1, 1981, pp. 67–88.

Wipper, A., 'Elijah Masinde – a folk hero', in B.A. Ogot, (ed.) *Hadith 3*, (Nairobi 1971), pp. 157–91.

Index

Abaluhya, fear of Kikuyu gangs in Nairobi, 171, 191–2; prosperity of maize growers, 65; squatter resistance among, 111–13, 242–3, 247

Aberdares, squatter policy of district council, 7, 110–12

Administration, blames Kenyatta for opposition, 52–3; careers of Secretariat officials, 43–4; condemns Beuattah for Murang'a protests, 153; controls information to Secretariat, 161–2; expansion of, 25; fears of squatter resistance in Nandi and North Nyanza, 111–13; failure to respond to situation in Nairobi, 182–3, 195–6; growing isolation of, 27, 53–4, 75–7; implementation of Whitehall's plans, 237; influence on Mitchell, 25, 37–8, 52–6; influenced by chiefs, 239–40; Mau Mau, warnings from District Commissioners, 231; myth of de-tribalised urban Africans, 171, 175–6; muhirig'a, reliance on, 71–2, 203, 209–11; Olenguruone policy, 122–6, 128–32; opposition to African individualism, 5, 25–7, 34–5, 44, 68, 72–7, 79, 203–4, 207; opposition to Kikuyu interpenetration, 122–3; O'Rorke excluded from policy meeting, 229; prejudices of, 2; quarrels with Attorney General over Olenguruone, 131–2; reliance upon chiefs, 45, 72, 145–64; reluctant promotion of individualism, 203; resolve strengthened by Murang'a troubles, 204; spurns African elite, 239; subverts Colonial Office policies, 4, 6, 25–7; views on Mau Mau, 227–8; weak in Nairobi, 174–5

African Advisory Council, Nairobi, 176–7

African Workers' Federation, 9–10, 173, 243

Agricultural Department, abandons communal terracing, 209–14; agricultural betterment campaign, 209–14; divided over individualism, 204; expansion of,

25, 215; Mitchell's policies, 38–43, 67–81; reluctance to take over control of squatters, 109–10; reorganisation of, 206; supports second colonial occupation, 214

agricultural policies, acreages terraced, 79–81; betterment campaign in Murang'a, 139–64; cattle destocking, 4, 64–5, 67–81; Creech Jones impressed by muhirig'a, 81; effect of Olenguruone on other settlement schemes, 132–3; Kikuyu agricultural incomes, 69; origins of muhirig'a terracing system, 79–81; promotion of communal controls, 72–7; settlement scheme at Olenguruone, 123–8; soil conservation, 4, 38–43, 63–72, 79–81, 94, 126–8; stock diseases, 95

ahoi, basis of squatter community, 92–3; movement to Nairobi, 8; relations with senior lineages, 8–9, 77–9, 140–1; support for Mau Mau, 11, 163–4

Anderson, Dr. T.F., Kikuyu nutrition, 67

anthropology, and the Kenyan administration, 26; encourages opposition to individualism, 73–4

Anti-Slavery Society, criticism of White Highlands, 24

Armitage, R.P., support of social engineering, 208

Asians, investment in Kenya, 46–7; response to Closer Union debate, 50

Askwith, Tom, career of, 260–1; lack of effective administration in Nairobi, 175; mob-rule in Nairobi, 172–3; social conditions in Nairobi, 182–8

Awori, W.W.W., career of, 261; spokesman for Nairobi elite, 175–7

Baring, Sir Evelyn, arrival in Kenya, 11; captured by Secretariat, 11–12; career of, 261; declares Emergency, 233; informed of Mau Mau threat, 231–2; Waruhiu's assassination, 12

Index

Baringo, ecological crisis in 1930s, 64–5

Battershill, William, career of, 261–2

Beauttah, James, arrested, 224; career of, 262; opposed by the administration, 75; opposition to terracing, 6, 153; political exclusion of, 239; President of Murang'a KAU, 75, 145; relations with Administration, 161–2; supported in vernacular press, 159

Beecher, Archdeacon Leonard, career of, 262; crime in Nairobi, 177–8

Benson, Jack, agricultural policy in Meru, 6, 141, 203; promotes individualism, 208, 211–12

Berque, Jacques, effect of the Depression on the Maghreb, 17

black market, African production for, 26, 65–6; trade routes from Kiambu to Nairobi, 66; trade routes from Nyeri and Murang'a, 65–6

Blundell, Sir Michael, career of, 262–3; demands action against Mau Mau, 225; Independence compromise, 251

Blunt, Denzil, career of, 263

Bourdillon, Sir Bernard, plans for colonial development, 20

Brooke-Popham, Sir, as governor of Kenya, 23

Brown, G.R.B., class and ethnic divisions in Nairobi, 192

Brown, Leslie, agricultural policy in Embu, 6, 203; career of, 263; criticises Maher, 143; policy contrasted with Humphrey's, 69; promotes cash crop production, 204–8, 210, 213–14; relations with Maher, 205

Buxton, Clarence, career of, 263; as District Commissioner Maasai, attitude to Kikuyu, 122; warns Mitchell of African opposition, 27, 56

Byrne, Sir Joseph, as governor of Kenya, 23

Caine, Sir Sydney, career of, 264; influence on colonial economic policy, 20

capitalism, development of in Central Province, 8–9

Capon, Canon, warns Mitchell of Kikuyu subversion, 56

Carpenter, F.W., administrator of Olenguruone, 128–30; conditions in Nairobi, 187–8;

cash crops, exports to Ukambani, 66; Brown's policy contrasted with Humphrey's, 69; expansion of, 216–17; incomes from, 210–11; cattle, opposition to dipping, 7; policy of agricultural officers in Embu and Meru, 6, 141, 203–10, 213–14

Cavendish-Bentinck, Ferdinand, appointment as Member for Agriculture, 37–8; career of, 264; concerned about Kenyatta's criticism, 108; obstructs Hyde-Clarke's squatter policy, 108–10; squatter policy, 92, 103–6

Central Province, acreage protected by terracing, 66, 79–81; development of capitalism, 8–9; return of evicted squatters, 111; social differentiation, 140–1; soil exhaustion, 66–8

Chief Ignatio, relations with Beauttah, 6–7, 155–6; criticised in vernacular press, 158–9; succeeds Muriranja Mureithi, 147; terracing protests in his location. 153–7, 159–60

Chief Koinange wa Mbiyu, career of, 273–4

Chief Makimei, allegations against, 161

Chief Muhoya, 140, 159; agricultural progress, 212

Chief Nderi, 140, 157

Chief Parmenas Mockerie Githendu, supporter of KAU, 150

Chief Waruhiu, allegations against, 159–61; assassination of, 12, 232; organises anti-Mau Mau meeting, 228

chiefs, as accumulators, 76, 144–6; administration's reliance on, 45, 145–64; attacks on chiefs, 155–62; compulsory terracing, 4–5, 6–7, 145–64; control Local Native Council, 144–6; criticised by Coutts, 153; criticised in vernacular press, 159, in Murang'a, 146–64; influence administration against KAU, 239; political legitimacy of, 2, 6, 11, 144–62; relations with KCA and KAU, 6; second colonial occupation, 5, 72, 139–64; social background of, 6; spokesmen of African opinion, 44–5; tenure of office, 145–51; terracing, 141

Closer Union, 48–52

coffee, demand for Kikuyu squatter labour, 95; policy of agricultural officers in Embu and Meru, 6

Cohen, Andrew, career of, 264–5; Closer Union debate, 49–51; cirticises Kenyatta, 127; decolonisation policies of, 6, 17–18; defence of Kenya Land Commission and White Highlands, 41–2; ideals of, 238; Oleguruone, reaction to 126–7; private secretary to Sir John Maffey, 51; reaction to Accra riots, 18; reaction to Mitchell's reform of Kenyan Secretariat, 38; settlers as agents of economic development, 46–8; visit to Kenya, (August 1946), 51;

Colonial Development and Welfare Act, 18; colonial sterling balances, 20–21; finance for agricultural betterment campaign, 39, 141–2

Colonial Economic Development Commit-

Index

Index

The Broken Peace

The Broken Peace

Disorder

Martha Adele

To order additional copies of this book, contact:
Xlibris
1-888-795-4274
www.Xlibris.com
Orders@Xlibris.com
792390792390

CONTENTS

PART TWO

Broken Peace

CHAPTER ONE

Sam

Finally.

After weeks of working in the kitchens and weeks of packing things to take out of the mountain, Mavis, the rest of the workers, and I all get to leave Bergland.

Most of the Bergland citizens had left to go help rebuild the streets, buildings, houses, and farmland in Bestellen after Bergland won the war, but a few people had to stay here in the mountain to help pack everything into the helicarriers and cargo cars. Mavis, Sarah, and I were three of the workers who stayed behind.

We got our new schedules for the week yesterday and have been riding in one of the final helicarriers leaving Bergland ever since. Mavis and I have been assigned to work under Sarah in culinary aid in what has been declared as the "new capital" of this nation.

According to Sarah, Janice and all of Bergland's other teachers are spread throughout the new nation and are talking with all the Bestellen people to catch them up on everything and teaching them how this new government will work.

"It will be the same setup as Bergland, government-wise," Sarah tells us as we wait for the helicarrier to land, "but the economy and new businesses will be fun to see working outside of a strict schedule."

"What about the states?" I ask her, looking around the humid steel-lined room with many of the other workers strapped into similar seats as myself. "Are we going to have the same state lines? Same state names?"

"No," Sarah guffaws at the idea, "definitely not, Sam! They won't have the same occupations either. I don't think."

One of the other workers leans forward, past Sarah, and looks at Mavis and me. "What I heard was that they would be remaking and redefining every state's borders, which will make it much more travel friendly."

"Me too!" another one of the workers cheer. "I think they are going to try to split the land of the old states up and divide it so that no single state remains the same, owning the same land."

"Meaning what?" I ask. "That they would give half of Bouw and half of Bloot to a new state?"

Sarah shrugs. "I guess so."

Mavis and I remain quiet for the remainder of the helicarrier ride as we listen to the rest of the workers discuss what their hopes and dreams are for this new nation. Each person seems to have a different idea of their own utopia. Some want to live in a very rural and provincial state with gorgeous farmlands and houses far away from each other while others want to live in a tight-packed city with sky-high buildings and busy streets. Everyone seems to have an idea of where they want to live and what they want to do.

All I know is that I want to see my mom and to know if Logan is okay.

As I sit and think, my mind can't help but wonder how Mavis feels. At this point, she only has Logan and Derek, and both of them had been sent off to fight. She has no idea if either of them are alive, just as I have no idea if my mom is alive.

Mavis and I may be the only one each other has left.

The helicarrier engines whir loudly as the machine lowers itself to the ground. It lands on a brand-new clearing that has obviously just been paved. Everyone unbuckles themselves, and we help roll off the equipment and pack it into a large van. Once everything is loaded up, the vehicle carries us all to a new location. When we exit the van, I find myself slowly looking up, allowing my eyes to follow one of the elevators on the outside of the building as it rises to dozens of floors.

"Woah," I mutter under my breath, earning a nod of agreement from Mavis.

"Follow me, everyone," Sarah tells the group. As she leads us outside, the freezing wind meets my face and reminds me of one of the only reasons I hate going outside. The bitter cold almost instantly dries out my skin, as well as many of the other workers. Sarah quickly leads us into a much smaller kitchen than we originally had in Bergland and cheers. Opening her arms wide to our new culinary station, she announces loudly, "Welcome to my new kitchen!"

A lot of the workers chuckle as they roll the equipment past Sarah and make comments about how it is *their* kitchen rather than hers. I wait for Sarah to stop messing with the other workers and make my way over to her.

"Hey." I tap her shoulder to get her attention. "What are the other floors on this building for?"

"Oh, I'm glad you asked that!" She turns to the rest of the kitchen crew and claps to gather everyone's attention. "Hey, guys!"

No one stops, moving equipment and clashing pots and pans.

"Hey!" she shouts louder. "Guys!" This time, a few people stop long enough to help everyone else notice that Sarah was trying to get their attention. "If you were paying attention, you may have noticed the height of this building on your way in. I was just alerted and told that this building is not only for cooking, but also for storing and growing some of Bergland's superfoods. Instead of planting those foods in the ground, we had some workers prepare a similar setup to the ones we had back home so that we would always have some at hand for our use."

One of the workers in the back groans loudly, allowing their complaint to echo through the room. "Does that mean we have to be the ones to deal with them?"

Sarah chuckles as the rest of the workers all chime in to answer and make smart-aleck comments. "All right, guys, whatever. Let's get to work."

Mavis and I share a look as we scurry back over to Sarah.

"Excuse me, Sarah," Mavis says as she taps her on the shoulder just as I did earlier, "all the Bestellen citizens got to be reunited with their families before they were forced to work."

"Yeah," I chime in. "What about us? How do we find out where our family is?"

Sarah points back in the direction that we just came from. "Go ask one of the men up at the front of the building. They should know."

Mavis and I speed back through the building. When we finally do find someone, he is at the front desk and talking on the phone.

"Um," I say, not knowing when to chime in. "Excuse me."

He gives me an annoyed look and holds up one finger.

Yes, I realize you are on the phone, but you probably know whether or not your family and friends are dead. We don't.

He hangs up after a few moments and fakes a smile. "What can I do for you two?"

Mavis looks at me and waits for me to answer, but I'm not sure I can do it nicely. I take a moment and force up an equally fake smile as the man behind the desk. "We need to know where to go or who to talk to, to find out where our families are."

"You are looking for the AO." He looks back down at his desk and scribbles something down on a small square piece of paper. "Wave down one of the cars with a bright-blue stripe on the side of it and tell the driver to take you to the Administrative Office. When you get there, ask the person at the desk about what you want and who you want." The man looks up from his desk and tears off the piece of paper. Handing it to me, he simpers, "I wrote it down for you just in case."

I clench my teeth and make another effort to smile. "Thanks."

Mavis takes my arm and pulls me out to the street where we wait for one of the blue-striped vehicles to come. I glance down at the paper he gave me to see that he has scribbled down "Administrative Office," as if I would be incapable of remembering "AO."

When we finally flag down one of the cars, I hold the door open for Mavis and look back through the glass doors of the building to see that the man has left his position behind the desk. I doubt this is the first time he has left his post while "on the clock."

"Where would you two fine-looking young people like to go today?" the driver cajoles.

I smile back at him from the rearview mirror. "The Administrative Office please."

"All right, all right." He shifts the vehicle's gears and begins down the road. As we ride, Mavis and I see many rebuilt apartment complexes, along with many roads leading to houses and other buildings. Not to my surprise, there is a construction site almost everywhere I look. The sidewalks, perfect roads, a few cars, many pedestrians, and workers all perfectly functioning together seem to give me hope for the future.

But the only hope I really have right now is the hope I get to see my mom again.

I distract myself from any and all horrible thoughts by shifting my attention back to the driver. "Have you been here long?" I ask him, still not knowing his name.

"Yep." He nods and glances back at me through the mirror. "I grew up in Bestellen. I was one of the people who supported Bergland in Minje."

I pause for a moment, not knowing what to say. "That's nice," I finally answer. "I'm originally from Bouw, and Mavis here is from Bloot."

"Oh really?" He chuckles. "That's great! So tell me, have either of you ever seen people build cities, or even buildings for that matter, this quickly?"

I shrug back. "No, sir. I haven't."

"Me neither," he replies. The conversation is quickly taken over by this man as he fills the car with a sort of joy that comes from hearing people tell their stories, even if you don't really care.

As we pull up beside the AO building, he parks the car and turns back to Mavis and me. "Well, I am really enjoying having you two ride with me today! Would you like me to wait on you so I can finish my story?"

Mavis looks at me and shrugs, obviously not wanting to hurt the man's feelings. I get the idea that we may need a ride back to where we just were, so I nod to the man and ask him to wait.

"Okay! I will." He extends his hand to me and gives me a firm shake. "My name is Chuck by the way."

"Sam." I return the shake and nod back at him as we exit the car. "Thank you very much, Chuck."

When Mavis and I enter the building, we find a small line of people leading to the front desk. My ears immediately cut through the silence and focus in on the woman at the front of the line.

"Jodie Vaughn, Lisa Vaughn, and Rebecca Hurtz." The woman brings a tissue up to her eye with her left hand and reveals a small rectangular strip of randomly placed dots on her wrist. "Please." The woman sniffles and whines something that I cannot make out.

The man working behind the desk answers the woman quietly, causing her to storm out of the building in hysterics. As the reality of it all slowly sets in, my eyes widen as we take a step forward in line.

Allowing my eyes to dart around the room to keep myself busy, they fall upon multiple different paintings hanging on the walls of the building. Some of them are paintings of the old mine shafts that started Bergland; others are paintings of the river that flowed through the mountain, the same river I never got to go and see. Janice explained to us that they had turbines powered by the river, which provided a lot of Bergland's power, but that this river was also blocked off to the public for safety reasons.

When my eyes meet a man's who has just come around the corner of the room, I turn away and focus on the person in front of me, who happens to have the same sort of black dotted code tattooed on their wrist as the woman who just left the building. I look past the man in front of me and notice that everyone in this room, other than Mavis and me, seems to have one of these tattoos.

Much quicker than expected, the two of us make it to the front of the line, where the words seem to jump out of my mouth. "Bonnie Beckman. I need to know where Bonnie Beckman is, please."

After typing into his hologram computer, he looks at me and smiles. "She is in a hospital in State Five." The man prints off a sheet of paper and hands it to me with the address of the hospital and a small map of the new town. "If you give this to one of the cabdrivers, they should be able to take you, but since—"

"Wait." Shocked, I stop him in midsentence. "Hospital? Why is she in the hospital? What happened?"

"If you go to this address, you can find out, but I can't tell you from what information I have here." The man gives me a genuine smile and looks at Mavis. "Next?"

Mavis steps up to the man and gives him names or asks him questions. My brain switches over to panic mode, and I don't pay attention to what Mavis asks him.

Why is she in the hospital? I mean, she is alive, but for how long?

Is she even conscious? Will she remember me? What if she already died in the hospital?

Mavis taps my arm and snaps me back with a look of horror in her eyes.

"What happened?" I ask her.

She stumbles to find her words for a moment before she lets out quietly, "Logan is in a hospital too." She pulls out a sheet of paper with Logan's hospital address on one half and Derek's address on the other.

Mavis

The man told me that Derek and his mom are in the capital with Sam and me and that he is working as a builder.

Of course, I want to go see him, but I need to go see Logan first.

"He is in a hospital in the capital, not too far from here. He is staying at the same place where all of the other injured Taai members are being kept," I tell Sam. "Do you want to go with me to see him, or do you want to go see your mom first?"

"Mom," he tells me. "I have to go see my mom."

"Okay. How far away is your mom's hospital? Do you want me to come with you?"

He shakes his head. "You need to go see Logan and Derek. I don't want to keep you."

We head out of the building and back into Chuck's car, where we see him in the driver's seat reading a newspaper.

"Hey, that was pretty quick!" He laughs, tossing the paper onto the seat beside him. "Where to now? I'll finish my story once we get going."

Sam and I share a look as we realize we can't both go in the same car. After a moment of silence, Sam looks back down to his paper and tells me, "We should probably go talk to Sarah first."

I nod, and Sam tells Chuck to take us back to where he picked us up.

After a minute or so of driving, Sam interrupts the story of how Chuck learned to swim. "Excuse me," Sam apologizes. "I'm sorry, but can I ask you a question?"

"Me? Oh sure!" Chuck cheers.

"What is that on your wrist?"

Chuck lifts up his right hand and looks at a mole. Before he has the chance to say anything, Sam corrects him, "The other one."

"Oh!" Chuck flashes a dotted code tattoo on his wrist at us and places his hand back on the wheel. "This here is how they are keeping track of everybody. It makes everything so much easier, and it will continue making things easier when we all get new careers or try to buy things."

"What do you mean?" Sam asks him, giving me a confused look.

"It's a bar code." Chuck answers. "All the money we earn can be given to us in credits or cash money. Credits will be scanned directly onto the code and will be usable at most all places, but you can turn it into cash if you'd like by going by an office or bank to get it."

"So it—"

Sam is interrupted by Chuck, continuing to explain, "And when we choose our jobs, they'll scan us on over to it instead of doing a bunch of paperwork like we used to have to do. It'll be so much easier to keep track of things too. Like . . ."

Chuck rambles the rest of the ride about how wonderful these new bar codes will be, never finishing his story and never answering our other questions, not that I was going to ask anyway.

Once we get back to the kitchen, Chuck drives off. We speed past all the people as they unload the helicarrier and make it straight back to Sarah.

The moment Sarah sees us, she hobbles excitedly past the rest of the workers and over to Sam and me. "Hey, guys! What's the news? Is everyone okay?"

Sam shakes his head in a frenzy. "No. No, my mom. She is in the hospital." He pulls out his paper and points to it, showing Sarah the map. "She is in State Five."

"State Five?" Sarah takes the paper from him and looks it over. "Really? Is she okay?"

Sam continues shaking his head and muttering, "No, I don't know. I don't know."

I set my hand on his back and try to get him to calm down while looking over to Sarah. "Can he take a trip to see his mom if I do his work?"

Sam jerks his eyes over to me as Sarah locks her eyes with mine.

"How long would it take him?" she asks me.

Sam shrugs. "I don't know."

Sarah looks back down at the map and analyzes it. She sighs. "It'll probably take two or three days to get there, spend a day with her, and to come back." She hands Sam his paper back and nods. "Just make it back here within three days. Got it?"

Sam nods to Sarah. "Thank you." He turns to me and gives me a quick hug. "Thank you."

I nod and let him go. Sam turns on his heel and is quickly called back by Sarah. "Hey!" Sam turns back around and looks at both of us, confused.

"Can't I go?" Sam asks her.

Sarah nods and shows us her newly coded wrist. "Yes, but first, you will need to go and get the code tattoo."

"When did you get that?" Sam asks her.

"When you all left, a truck came by to code all the newly arrived workers. They told me to tell you guys to go and get your code as soon as you get back. You can get them at the Administrative Office."

Sam rolls his eyes and thanks Sarah as he scurries out of the building.

"What about you?" Sarah asks me. "Did you find your friends?"

I nod and pull my paper out of my pocket. With Derek's address on the top half and Logan's on the bottom, I hand it over to Sarah.

She stares at it for a moment before handing it back to me. "You can come back tomorrow morning. Go ahead and visit your friends and get your code." Before I get to say anything, Sarah asks me, "Do you have a place to stay tonight?"

I shrug. "I may. Worse comes to worse, I could probably stay with Derek."

"Some of the first things that were built when we won were houses," Sarah tells me. "Once everyone gets their bar codes, they will be given a house to share for the time being. If you can't find a place to stay, come back here before nightfall and you can stay with me and a few of the other workers."

"So we are just going to be given houses?" I ask.

"No, next week—" Sarah is interrupted by a loud crashing sound as someone knocks over the racks where the pots and pans were being held, followed by an almost equally loud concoction of laughter and jeering. Sarah rolls her eyes and looks back at me. "Next week, everyone will meet with a career officer, and they will help you decide what you are qualified for and what you want to do. After that, they will help you find a house within your pay grade or set you up on a payment plan or whatever. It varies depending on what you want to do, who you want to live with, and a lot of other things."

I thank Sarah, and she tells me to "scurry off." When I make my way out of the building, I find Sam still waiting on a cab. Just as I approach him, Sam flags one down and jumps in. The second he sees me, he scoots further in and waves me over.

This cabdriver is nothing like Chuck. He asks us where to go, takes us both to the AO, and drops us off. No stories, he doesn't offer to wait on us, and he speeds off after we get out of the car.

I actually kind of prefer him over a chatty driver.

As soon as we step back onto the familiar concrete sidewalk, Sam almost sprints into the building and up to the man at the desk.

"Didn't I just speak with you two?" he asks us, holding a confused expression.

Sam nods. "We need to get our codes. We were told to come here."

His head tilts back and he smiles. "Ah, I see. One moment." He grabs his desk phone and dials up. Holding the phone to his ear, he exchanges glances with Sam and me. "Hi! I have two people here who need to come up and get their codes . . . Yeah . . . Yeah . . . Got it. Okay. Bye." He hangs up the phone and points down the hall. "The elevators are right down there. Go up to the third floor and someone will take you back."

I follow Sam back in silence as we head up to the third floor. The moment the elevator doors open, we are greeted by one man and one woman. The woman looks at me and waves me out after Sam approaches the man without any sort of hesitation.

The man looks at both of us. "Are you two here for your codes?"

Sam and I nod.

The woman smiles at us. "One of you will need to come with me"—she gestures to Sam and the man across from us—"and the other can go with Walter."

"One second please." Sam turns back to me and pulls me aside. "After I get my code done, I am going straight to my mom. Okay? So I may not see you again until I get back."

I nod and Sam pulls me into a hug.

"Ready to go?" Walter asks us both, earning a slight glare from Sam.

We part ways, and the girl takes me back to a small room with one seat and one counter with a drawer. I take a seat, and the woman pulls up my name, face, and account on a hologram computer that seems to pop up out of nowhere.

"Okay." She pulls out a small black pad with a plastic covering. Connecting a wire from the desk to the pad, she smiles at me. "I am going to set this on your wrist, and it will print the code. You will feel a small pinching when it places the dots, but it shouldn't hurt, okay?"

Shouldn't? I think, not willing to ask the woman.

"Okay," I say.

She peels off the plastic and places the pad onto my writs. It is surprisingly covered in a squishy and sticky substance that binds itself to my skin as the woman turns on the machine. The moment I see her press the button, I hear a whirring noise and feel the slight pinching she told me about.

It takes about three minutes for this process to complete. Once the machine beeps, the pinching stops, and the woman peels the pad off my arm. She wipes my wrist with a wet napkin and cleans off all the goop with a smile on her face. "That wasn't too bad, right?"

I nod in agreement as she runs a small handheld scanner over the code and types some stuff into the hologram. Next thing I know, she is waving me goodbye and I am outside of the building, waiting for a cab to take me to Logan's hospital.

CHAPTER TWO

Logan

"That's it," my physical therapist tells me as she helps me off the examination table. "You did great today, Logan."

I nod to her and move my aching body one inch at a time. "Thank you."

When I woke up after the jet crashed into the hospital, two weeks had passed. My eyes flickered open as I tried to move any part of my body. Only I couldn't. The drowsiness from the medication they had me on greatly restricted my movement, causing me to wait in that room, listening to my heart rate monitor for what felt like hours, waiting on someone to come in and help me get the IV out.

After the doctors explained to me that I was in a coma and my ability to move and speak returned, my first question was, "Where is Eric and Werner?" My question was quickly answered when Eric rolled into the room missing his left leg.

"Werner is out doing his job," Eric told me as he rolled past the doctor. "He is fine."

I froze. Eric wheeled his way over beside my bed as I stammered and stuttered, struggling to find the right words.

Eric put the brakes on and folded his hands in his lap. "All the equipment he had on him that day, along with how far he had run, saved him from any serious damage. Just a few bumps and bruises along with a minor concussion."

I remained frozen, not being able to find the right words. When I finally did manage to get them out, they whimpered, "What happened to you?"

He looked down at his leg, or where it used to be, and touched it with one of his hands, seemingly still in disbelief. "Shrapnel. They couldn't save it."

"What about me?" Using all of my energy, I forced the blanket off to find scars strewn across my legs, causing me to notice the same scars on my arms. "Why didn't they have to do that to me?"

"That?" Eric asked me. "You mean amputate?"

I nodded.

A long pause filled the room as Eric looked over his shoulder to the doctor.

The doctor took this cue and stepped forward to me. "Mr. Barnes lunged on top of you when the jet crashed. He took the large chunks of the blast."

That day, Eric and I were placed to live together at this rehabilitation center until we reach a certain point of recovery. We have been roommates ever since. In this center, we have unlimited access to any and all medical care we need, and almost every day, we come down and have physical therapy sessions free of charge. They even have a game center where we can play board games and card games with some of the others who are in the same boat as we are.

Though we have the option to play games with other people, Eric prefers to keep to himself and would rather play me than anyone else. Before this whole incident, I had no idea how to play chess. Eric taught me last week and has been challenging me to it every day since.

Every now and then, Werner would drop in and play a few games with us as well when he had time. He always makes it a point to come in and sit with us at least once every other day. I don't know if it is because he feels bad for us, if he feels guilty for it, or if he genuinely enjoys spending time with us. Either way, I am not going to complain. I am just happy to be getting beat at chess by someone other than Eric.

As I sit at this table, playing another one of the injured soldiers who happens to have no right arm, I watch him put me one move closer to checkmate.

"Check," he tells me for the fifth time in a row.

I scan over the board at my remaining moves and try to figure out which would be best. Though I have the slight feeling that my defeat is imminent, I push back any competitive feelings I may have and accept his victory.

I move my king over one space to the right, only to have this man move his queen over one space also, never letting my king flee from its wrath. "Check," he tells me again.

As his pieces chase and steal mine throughout the board, I think back to how Gramps used to try to teach me this game. He would snap at me for not paying attention and tell me that chess is one of the best board games ever invented. After about three tries, Gramps gave up on me playing chess and let me go back outside to play and, at the time, go back home to Mom and Dad.

Gramps died back in Minje during the war. Even though I prepared myself for the news, it still hurt to hear the words. At least I know for a fact that he fought for what he thought was right until his last breath.

"Checkmate." The man slides one of his remaining pieces, the last rook on the board, over five spaces and puts my king into an inescapable situation.

I lean back in my seat and smile at the man. "Good game."

"How does it feel being beaten at chess by someone who has only ever played once?" he asks me with a delighted look on his face.

"Once?" I spout, surprised at how horrible I must really be at this game. "How in the—"

My question to the man is interrupted by a sight I catch out of the corner of my eye. The long blond hair immediately grabs my attention and somehow seems to offend the man I played with.

I turn my head from him to see Mavis standing at one of the desks asking the secretary something.

I rise to my feet, leaving the man in front of me baffled at what has my attention. He turns to look in that direction and chuckles. "Boy, you better calm yourself or you'll scare her off."

I haven't been able to stop thinking about Mavis or Sam this entire time I've been away. Has she come to visit me? Someone else? I have no clue, but having her this close has lifted such a weight off my shoulders I can barely feel the aching in my back.

After a few steps over to her, she glances this way, and her eyes grow as big as mine. Somehow, we make it over into each other's arms and stay intertwined.

"Are you okay?" she mumbles into my shoulder as our bodies stay pressed against each other's.

I place my hand on the back of her head and wrap my other arm tighter around her waist. "I'm fine," I whisper. "I'm fine."

"Obviously not! Or else you wouldn't be in here!"

"Well . . ." I chuckle. "I may have gotten blown up . . . twice."

Neither of us let go of each other, even though I can feel too many pairs of eyes watching us. I dismiss their attention and give mine back to Mavis. "What about Sam? Is he okay?"

"Yes." Mavis pulls back from the hug but leaves her hands around my waist. When she realizes how much attention we've drawn, she pulls back completely. "He's visiting his mom in a hospital in State Five."

I look around the room to see the man I was playing chess with snickering while a bunch of others join him in the jeering.

"What happened with his mom?" I ask Mavis, pulling her aside and out into the hallway so that the others will stop staring.

"I don't know. Neither does Sam. He won't know until he gets down there."

I close the door behind us and usher Mavis to one of the vacant benches in the hallway. "That is awful. I can't imagine the suspense."

The bench squeaks as I take a seat beside her. She turns her body to me and crosses her legs, making herself comfortable.

"So," I continue, "what's going on? Are you living in the capital right now? When did you get here? When did Sam get here?" I pull myself back and force myself to question her more slowly and give her a chance to speak.

Mavis's focus shifts from my arm to all the scars back up to my eyes. Our gaze locks upon each other, and we sit for a moment before she answers. "Sam and I got here this morning. We will be working at a kitchen about fifteen to twenty minutes away from here until we meet with the career counselor. What about you? When will you be leaving the hospital?"

"This isn't a hospital," I correct her, just as I have been corrected hundreds of times. "This is a rehabilitation center."

"Ah." She chuckles. "I see. When will you be leaving the rehabilitation center?"

"They told me I should be getting out soon. My therapist told me that once she thinks I am ready, she will sign some discharge papers and send me on my way that day."

"What will you be doing after you get out? Where will you live?"

I shrug. "I don't know exactly. I won't know until I go to the career counselor."

"You don't have any ideas? I mean, I don't, but I figured you'd want to go back into the Taai or something."

A group of a few men and women come down the hallway, all with different visible injuries. One of the women has been shaved bald and has had her head wrapped in white bandages. One of the men has his arm in a brace and the other arm missing. One of the men, with obvious burn scarring on his face, pushes one of the women who sits in a wheelchair similar to Eric's. Each one of them give us a different look as they pass. The looks range from sour, to happy, to confused.

I wait for them to pass before I turn back to Mavis and answer her question. "John came to visit Eric and me last week. He told us both that we will forever be remembered as part of the Taai, whether we come back or not, and will be treated with 'the same level of respect as any other member.'"

"Eric?" Mavis asks me. "Barnes? The one that, the one with, you know, Sam?"

I nod.

"What happened to him?"

"He was in both of the explosions I was in."

"Is he okay?"

I pause, not knowing how else to phrase it. "He lost one of his legs. His left one, actually." Mavis freezes and stammers the same way I did when I first saw Eric. I explain, "When the second explosion hit, Eric jumped on top of me and got the worst of the shrapnel."

"What? Where is he? Is he here?"

"Still in bed," I tell her. "He doesn't like getting out of bed much anymore."

Mavis sighs. "I'm sorry."

"Me too."

After we sit for another moment and listen to the light chatter throughout the hallway and in the game room behind us, I rise to my feet, fighting the urge to groan with the movement, and turn back to Mavis. "So do you want to go back to the game room with me?"

She rises with me, looking back at me with her emerald-colored eyes and flashing her flawless smile at me. "Why not?"

We make our way over to the door as I hold it open for her, and my eyes fall upon an empty board game table. "Do you know how to play chess?" I ask her.

She chuckles back at me and nods. "I used to play it all the time with a friend back home."

"Oh," I answer, ready for my imminent defeat. "Finally, a challenge."

Mavis

Exiting the "rehabilitation center," I flag down a cab and hop in.

"Where to, ma'am?" the driver asks me.

I hand him the paper with Derek's address on it, and he punches it into his guidance system on the dashboard. We take off almost immediately, and I watch the rehab center disappear into the mass of buildings taller than it.

Though I am ready to go see Derek, and though it is getting late, I still feel bad about leaving Logan right after I won the chess match. I'm sure he understands. He knows I need to go see Derek before I head back to the kitchen, but leaving right after winning in chess? It feels kind of rude.

As we drive, I see people setting up their night gear and turning on all the streetlights so they can continue construction work even after it gets dark.

I guess to them, working around the clock makes sense. This entire time, I have been wondering how they have rebuilt this entire country so quickly, but I guess the answer is never-ending labor.

"Those people up there"—the cabdriver takes one hand off the wheel and both eyes off the road to point out all the construction workers toward the top of the skyscrapers' skeletons—"they change from day shifts, to night shifts, to morning shifts in case you were wondering."

"How did you know?" I ask him, not feeling too comfortable with someone paying that close of attention to me to know what I am wondering.

"The paper you gave me, it is the same paper they give people who are looking for other people. Most times, people in the city who hand me those papers are first-time visitors."

"Oh okay." A slight feeling of relief comes over me, followed by a slight amount of panic. "Thank you."

I hope he doesn't want to keep talking.

I *really* hope he doesn't want to keep talking.

I also really hope Derek doesn't have the night shift for what he does. Even if he does, I will get to see his mom, who has been a mother to me since my mother passed.

I only hope that she will recognize me.

We continue to drive through the city, passing some completed buildings, but many are still being worked on. The driver keeps giving me facts about this city, about what used to be where, what is being built, and so much more. I refuse to be rude, so every time he says something, I acknowledge him with a "huh" or "okay," but it seems my telepathic messages aren't getting through to him. I really wish he wouldn't expect me to keep talking.

"You know what else? The new capitol building is being built just a few miles from here. You should go check it out one day. It looks like it will be spectacular." He continues to drive and describe how he imagines the beautiful gardens, along with exquisite fountains, and I assume that he must have been from Verwend, where they don't ever really think about money unless it's theirs.

He continues talking as he drives me through the town and down a few back roads that have not been fully developed yet. The driver slows down and parks the car right in front of a small wooden bridge that is over a creek. If there wasn't a mailbox out a bit closer to the road than the bridge, we both would have completely missed it, for the trees hang too low and the sun has fallen too far for it to be completely visible to the passerby.

"Well." The driver chuckles. "This is it. Do you, um, want me to stay here?"

My stomach turns as I look into the woods. Not necessarily in a bad way, but more with excitement. Of course, Derek would make sure to get the most secluded house he can in the capital. I know this has to be the way to his house, so I turn back to the driver. "No thank you."

He gives me an odd stare. After a moment of silence between us, he says to me, "I will wait here for a while just in case you decide to come back."

I chuckle at how protective he is and nod. "Thank you." Exiting the cab, I make my way over the bridge hidden by the trees and into the woods. The cold air becomes even colder as the wind bounces off the creek and splashes me. Once I get over the bridge, I find that the path has been lined with stones on both sides, just as Derek's mother always talked about having for her dream house.

Down the dirt path I go, walking, walking, walking, until I see a light in the distance. I quicken my pace and find a small wooden cabin with smoke coming through the chimney. Each step I take up onto their porch, the wooden stair steps squeak alive, causing me to make much more noise than I mean to.

I knock on the door and hear shuffling from inside. The muffled talking between the inhabitants quickly comes to an end as the door is slowly opened by Derek's mother. Her hair has become almost completely gray, and her skin has somehow sagged much more than I expected.

"Can I help you?" she asks me, looking me up and down as if I am a stranger.

"Ms. Page," I say to her like I always have, "it's Mavis."

She continues to stare at me in confusion with her now grayish-blue eyes. I feel my heart slowly tearing as I realize how bad it's gotten. The smell of her favorite scented candle, apple cinnamon, hits my nose and almost causes tears to fall.

The gut-wrenching feeling is pushed aside as Ms. Page's face lights up with joy. "Mavis!" she cheers as she pulls me into a hug. Our arms find their way around each other, and we squeeze each other tight. She kisses me on the side of my head as my whole body warms up from her love.

I hear her sniffle as she weeps into my shoulder. "I thought you were dead. I thought you were dead."

Derek enters the room, having just washed his hands, and throws the hand towel down as he rushes over to us both with joy. He wraps his arms around us and gives the huddle a quick squeeze, but is interrupted by his mother who turns to him with tears running down her face.

"Look! It's Mavis!" She grabs my face and continues to sob with joy. "It's sweet little Mavis! I thought she was dead."

I look back over to Derek with one eyebrow raised. I have to wonder whether or not he told his mom that I was alive. Sure, we haven't got to spend much time together since the draft, but still.

She pulls me back into a hug, and I look back at Derek, glancing down at his still bandaged arm. "Did you tell her?" I mouth.

He nods as reality sinks in.

It's getting worse.

Ms. Page pulls away from the hug and grabs my face once again. "Derek was just about to make dinner! You should stay! We have enough, right, Derek?"

He nods again as Ms. Page releases my face.

"Can I help?" I ask, earning a smile from them both.

Derek bends down and picks the towel up off the floor, throwing it back onto the wooden countertops. "Sounds good to me."

"All righty then!" Ms. Page cajoles. "I am going to go and take a shower, but I will be back soon." She chuckles as she walks out of the room. "It is so nice to have a functioning shower."

"And a wall phone too," Derek adds, pointing to the red block on the wall with a wire dangling from it.

I chuckle and make my way over to Derek. We hold each other and stand in silence, listening to Ms. Page's shower turn on from the other room. I want to ask him about the war, about what happened, about where he was assigned, about the revolt, about his arm, about what happened with my dad, and so much more.

I settle and try to ask him about his mom, but manage only a stutter. "So, you, how is, you know . . . your mom?"

He chuckles. "Yeah."

"Yeah what?" I ask him into his shoulder.

"Yeah, it's gotten worse."

I freeze, not knowing what to say.

"I missed you," Derek tells me, turning around and pulling out a pot and a few cans of stew for the fireplace.

I back away from him and look around the living room. Though it is mostly taken up by the fireplace in the center of the building, it seems much bigger on the inside than it does on the outside.

Derek brings the pot and cans over to the small ledge on the bottom of the stone fireplace and sets them all down. "We could have either had a working shower or a stove, and since we already had a fireplace, I found no need to get a stove."

I smile back at him, knowing he would have it no other way. "Good choice." Looking around the house, I ask Derek, "Are you two planning on staying here permanently, or temporarily?"

"Well"—he pulls the top of the cans off and pours them into the pot—"I got the offices to buy this house for me under my name. I will finish paying it off with my job in construction pretty quickly after we start getting paid." He picks up the pot and places it on the hook in the fireplace. "Because believe it or not, this house wasn't anyone in the 'new capital's' first pick."

"I can see that." I chuckle. "This really is a nice house though, and I especially like how you lined the path with stones."

He chuckles back. "Yep. Mom practically begged me to do it."

My smile slowly fades as I brace to ask him the questions I want to ask about his mom. I shuffle through them all and force out the least difficult one to ask. "Are you planning on continuing to live with her? Until . . .," I pause, not knowing how else to say it, "you know."

He pulls his lighter out of his pocket and lights a piece of lint against the rest of the kindling. Once the fire really starts burning, he turns back to me and sits against the fireplace. "Yeah. I don't really have a choice." The light from the fire glistens and reflects off his pale face, causing the portion of his profile untouched by the light to seem much darker.

We sit in silence, watching the small fire turn into a larger one. "So," I interrupt the crackling, "how is she?"

"There are good days and bad days." The crackling interrupts him, and he pokes at it with one of the stokes. "She tries to play things off as if she remembers, but I know she doesn't, and I definitely don't push the issue with her because of how scared she already is of the disease."

We listen to Ms. Page talk to herself in the shower through the wall and sit in silence. The phrase "I'm sorry, Derek," finds its way out of my mouth, only to be lost in thought by the person it was addressed to. "Does talking about it help?" I ask him.

He nods. "It does, but I don't like talking about it."

I nod back and point to his forearm where the bandage covers his wound. "How is it?"

He looks down at it and looks back at me. After a moment, Derek unwraps the bandages and shows me the long scar running up his forearm.

"What . . .," I stammer, "what exactly happened?"

"Are you sure you want to know?"

I chuckle nervously, knowing that I am going to learn something I don't want to. "Why else would I ask?"

Derek sighs. He takes a few moments to think, which causes the suspense to grow even more. "There were riots," he begins, his voice deep with pain and angst. "People were setting houses on fire, throwing bottles of flaming liquor at officials, shooting . . . killing. It was terrifying." He pauses to clear his throat and looks from me to the fire. "After one of the Taai members got us all together, he told us to run and follow him once they took care of the wall. As he addressed the group, I realized I couldn't see your dad anywhere. I saw Randy, but not your dad.

"I ran back to your house as soon as I could and found your dad in the living room, which was absolutely wrecked. There were bottles and trash in every direction. The entire house stunk like urine and had become home to hundreds of flies.

"When I went in, I immediately called to your dad. I heard some rustling in the back of the house, and after a few moments passed, he stumbled out more drunk than I have ever seen him before. He . . ." Derek's fists clench together, along with his jaw. "With a bottle in his hand, he spit on the floor and growled at me, 'What do you want?'

"I asked him if he had heard anything outside or knew what was going on. He told me he heard the riots, but he didn't want to go." Derek pauses again, but looks away from the fire and back at me. "He told me he 'just wanted to die.'"

"What?" I ask him.

"Without your mom, Steven, and you, he had nothing left to live for. He told me, 'Mavis was all I had, and she was drafted.' I tried to convince him to come out, but he got angry at me. He said that I drove you away from him while you were here, so it's my fault that you didn't like him." He pauses again and looks back at the fire. "He said you were happy to be drafted to get away from him."

Derek rises to his feet and grabs a large spoon from the kitchen. "I continued to try to get him to come and follow, but he threw the bottle in his hand at me. He missed the first time, which made him even more upset." Derek comes back to the fireplace and stirs the stew, keeping his eyes averted from mine. "He picked up every bottle and piece of trash he could get his hands on and threw it at me until I left. I only left after one of the bottles shattered on the wall and cut me. When I left the house to get back to the rally, I ran into Randy."

Derek heads back to the kitchen and brings a plate back to lay the spoon on after he finishes stirring. "I tried to convince him to come with me. I tried to tell him that your dad didn't want to leave, but Randy wouldn't listen."

Shocked.

That's all I am.

That's all I feel.

Not because of the drinking, that was normal for Dad. Not because of the anger, that was normal too. I am shocked because I had no idea that Dad loved me. After Mom died, he stopped telling me that. I always figured he hated me because I reminded him of Mom.

Derek finishes stirring and comes to sit back down beside me. "Are you okay?"

I hesitate. What do I say? How am I okay? How is this okay?

"I'm sorry, Derek."

He places his arm around me and pulls me into a hug. "Don't be. It's not your fault."

"I . . .," I sniffle as I realize I will never get to see my dad again. I take a shaky breath as I realize I never told him I loved him either. "I didn't know he loved me."

"I'm sorry." He sits close beside me, trying to console me. "I'm sorry."

The tears fall down my face as I think back to my brother. Steven never knew how much Dad loved him. If he would have known how Dad felt, would Steven have killed himself? Dad beat Steven almost every day. The only days Steven wasn't beat were the days when Dad was at work or blackout drunk. The only day that I wasn't verbally abused were those same days.

How could Dad have loved us and treated us that way? Sober or drunk, that is inexcusable . . . Right?

Derek's hold on me becomes tighter as he speaks to the top of my head. "I know your mother knew that your dad loved her, and I'm sure somewhere in his heart Steven did too."

I continue to sob as Derek tells me that it's okay.

Everything is okay.

My mom's last thoughts were not about how much her husband loved her, but more likely, "Why is he beating me?"

The moment the incident occurred, he was immediately consumed with even more guilt than he originally had from selling Sander the bad fruit. After the fruit, he started drinking. After Mom, he became a nightmare.

He drank to forget, but the more he drank, the more the guilt seemed to grow. The more the guilt grew, the more the anger did too.

How much worse was it for Steven than it was for me? The beatings ranged from one slap across the face to having Steven slammed down onto the ground. Every time Dad would sober up, he would apologize profusely for what he had done, but that never made things better.

I don't ever remember Dad apologizing to me for anything he ever said. He would only ever apologize to Steven, and that was only if there were visible injuries.

It's pointless to sob now. It is pointless to think about it.

Pointless to dwell.

I feel weak. There is no reason to shed a tear. It is done.

There is nothing I can do.

I sniffle and apologize into Derek's chest, wiping my tears before I show my face. "I'm sorry."

"It's fine. I understand."

I pull away and rise up. "There's no reason to cry. It's done with."

He follows me to a standing position and looks into my eyes, letting me know he sees through my lie. Derek takes the hint and heads back to the stew.

"So what happened after I left?" I sniffle, holding back everything, pushing it as far down as I can. "After I was drafted?"

Derek stirs the stew and tells me about how just after I left, the word of the revolt began spreading like wildfire. As I listen to Derek tell me about everything that happened, I continue pushing back the tears and the pain. I ignore how awful I feel and focus on the fact that I still have Derek.

Just listening to him makes me feel better. His calming voice mixed with the crackling of the fire, the same color as his loosely curled hair, helps the tears stop forcing themselves down my cheeks.

"We had been preparing for the revolt for weeks, so when the time came, almost everyone was more than willing to fight," he tells me. "You know everything that has happened since. We went from Bloot, to Bergland, back to Bestellen." He sighs and turns back to me. "What about you? What happened when you were drafted? Where did you go?"

I give him a smile and a slight chuckle. "Where do I begin?"

I tell Derek about everything that has happened since I was drafted. I tell him about the woods, the rats, the van, Bergland, the vials, Logan, Sam, and even about Eric. We go back and forth just like old times. He tells me that the moment the new government set up, they set up vial distribution stations at every hospital and ran everyone back through the system, diagnosing and prescribing the vials as needed.

He turns his wrist over, and we compare our codes side by side. His code seems to have a few large dots while mine has twice the amount of small dots.

As we continue to compare and count the marks, Ms. Page emerges from the hallway in warm clothes and her hair tied up in a towel. She comes over and takes a seat in the living room at the dining table.

"So"—she turns to me and crosses her legs—"where are you going to be staying for the night?"

"I actually don't really have a place yet. My boss told me that—"

"Oh," she shouts with joy, "that's perfect! You can stay with us! Isn't that right, Derek?"

I turn to see him with a goofy smirk rising on his face. "Sure? I guess so. I, I mean I don't have a problem with that."

I smile back and chuckle. "I don't want to be a bother."

"It's no bother! No bother at all!" Ms. Page rises to her feet and scurries out of the room. "I will go find you some sheets."

We both chuckle as Derek rises to his feet and heads back into the kitchen to get the bowls and spoons for the stew. All the utensils and bowls clink against each other as he brings them over. His blue and purple eyes meet mine as he smiles down at me. Handing me my bowl and spoon, his smirk grows. "Welcome home, roomie."

CHAPTER THREE

Sam

My head smacks the side of the door as my car hits a bump. I wake up immediately and wipe my eyes until I see a swirling of a million different-colored dots. I have changed cabs every two to three hours and have been riding for almost sixteen hours now. Lucky for me, two of the cabdrivers took me to get food when I told them what I am doing. I made a promise to myself after we arrived at Bergland, and that promise was to never skip another meal. Since I ate breakfast with Sarah and Mavis on the helicarrier on our way here, I have technically kept my promise and had three meals today.

Well, yesterday.

When we finally cross into State Five, I see newly renovated streets, buildings, sidewalks, and streetlamps. I never thought that any Bouw land would ever look like this. The old streets and sidewalks of my hometown always had tree roots growing under it, through it, and sometimes over it. I loved walking down the sidewalk and being able to see where exactly the tree roots are under the concrete. I loved seeing the grooves of the roots forcing their way to the top of the ground.

My mom used to love that too.

We keep driving for another half an hour before the driver drops me off at the base of a hospital I do not recognize. Immediately, I thank him and take off running into the building. I head to the front desk and notice that the hospital seems to be empty other than the man typing into the desk hologram.

"I'm here to see my mom," I tell him. "Bonnie Beckman."

The man nods to me and types something into his hologram. He picks up a box with a wire connecting it to the hologram and holds out his hand. "Can I see your code first?" I shoot him a confused look, and he chuckles at me. "Just to check and make sure."

I hold up my wrist, and the man presses a button on the box. A red line shoots out and scans the code by swiping up and down over the splattered dots, causing the man to smile at me. Typing something into his hologram, he points to a set of doors a few feet over from him. The man smiles at me and types back into his computer. "All right, Mr. Beckman, she is in room 206 on the second floor. If you can't find her, just ask one of the nurses up there and they will tell you."

I nod and zip past him.

"Mr. Beckman," he calls out to me, stopping me in my tracks. "Please try to be as quiet as you can. It is very early and most of our residents are sleeping."

I nod again and take off up the stairwell and onto the second floor. I walk around the large loop of rooms and look for 206. I notice that some of the rooms are actual rooms with hardwood doors while other rooms are just walls with curtains blocking them off from the hallway.

I continue roaming around until I finally have a run-in with a nurse. In a frenzy, I try to explain to her the situation, but only manage to get out "Mom" and "206."

"Yes. Hey, it's okay." She puts one of her hands on my back and leads me in the opposite direction I was heading. "The man at the desk called me and told me that you may need help finding your mom."

She ushers me through the loop and down a hall I missed the first time around. She gives me a smile and places her hand on the curtain. "Now, she may be asleep and she needs her rest, so do me a favor and be as quiet as you can, okay?"

I nod. The woman pulls the curtain back to reveal my mother sleeping peacefully in her bed, cocooned in multiple white blankets. I step in and approach her slowly, not knowing exactly how to approach. The curtain behind me falls back to its resting position as the nurse leaves me alone with my mom.

Her breathing is slow and steady, like it normally is in her sleep. Other than being in a hospital bed, swaddled to the point of no movement, she seems fairly unrestricted. I see nothing wrong with her.

The curtain rises once again as the nurse brings in a small chair and sets it beside Mom's bed.

"Here," she tells me.

I sit down and thank her. Just as she turns around to leave the room, I blurt, "Can I spend the night here?" Quickly realizing how loud I am, my shoulders seize up and I clench my teeth, hoping I haven't woken her.

The nurse pulls me out of Mom's room as quietly as she can. When we exit the curtained area, I find myself being glared at by one of the patients as he walks by in his gown.

The nurse whispers to me, "Do you have somewhere else you need to be?"

"No, ma'am. My boss gave me a few days off to be with her."

She nods to me. "Then you can stay with her as long as you want."

"Thank you," I tell her.

"I'll go get you a pillow and a blanket." The woman quickly turns and heads down the hallway, leaving me to go back to my seat. The moment I shift the curtain to go back in, Mom's eyes meet mine.

With tears welling up in her eyes, her lip quivers as she tries to form words. I take a step forward and feel the tears rise in my eyes as well.

"Sam?" she whimpers. "I thought you were dead." She fixes her bed into an upright position and frees herself from the cocoon.

Rushing over to her, I fall into her open embrace, just as she does mine. I pull back after a moment and realize her right arm is being held in a white wrap, along with a blue sling.

"What happened to you?" I ask her. "Are you okay?"

She continues to sob. The tears don't stop pouring as she sniffles, "I thought you were dead. I thought I'd—" She coughs, choking on her emotions and the overwhelming amount of tears and mucus coming from her. "I thought I wasn't ever going to see you again!"

I pull her back into me and hold her close. "I know," I whisper to her. "I know." Mom slides over in her bed and pulls me onto it. She sits me beside her and holds me by my side until she calms down.

"So what happened to your arm?" I finally ask her after she regains her normal breathing pattern.

She sniffles, "I'm fine. I got shot in the arm, but I'm fine."

"What?" I shout, quickly regretting my volume. I correct myself and whisper back to her, "What happened?"

"It's nothing. I'm fine. What happened to you? They said that you were thrown into the woods? For a disorder?" She squeezes me tighter and presses her head against my chest. "I had no idea any of this was happening. I promise you. I would not have let them take you if I knew."

"Hey." I rub her back, trying to calm her back down. "I know. No one knew. No one could've known."

She sniffles back all of her sobs and sits back up straight, still resting in my arms. "So what happened to you? How long were you in the woods before they came and found you?"

"Not long," I tell her, "just a day or two." I don't want to make her feel any more guilty than she already does. There's no reason for her to feel guilty, but knowing her, she will feel guilty no matter what. As my mind does cartwheels, trying to figure out what to say next, it lands on a new question. "How did you know I wasn't actually drafted?"

"What?" she asks me.

"You just said 'they' told you that I was thrown into the woods for a disorder. Who told you that?"

"No, no. No one actually told me that. When we were being prepped and having everything explained to us, we were told that some of those who were drafted for our military were thrown out into the woods to use as bait rather than actually being drafted."

"Yeah? And how did you know that I was one of the ones thrown out?"

"Well, I thought back to what little training you received. You would always come home and tell me that everyone else who was assigned to be in the military had to do a lot more than you, so I connected the dots." She pulls me into another awkward hug. "I couldn't figure out what was worse. The idea of you fighting for Bestellen, most likely being killed during the war, or you being thrown into the woods to fend for yourself."

Chuckling, I pull away. "I guess we have our answer."

Mom sniffles again and wipes the edges of her eyes. "I guess you're right. So . . ." She takes one long and large deep breath and wipes her eyes.

"Tell me. What has happened since the draft? How was it in Bergland? Do you have a job? Do you—"

"Mom," I interrupt her, "how did you get shot?"

She pauses and clears her throat. The pause she takes is so long, it is almost as if she is trying to ignore the question.

"Mom," I repeat.

She clears her throat again and looks at the ceiling, trying to keep the tears in.

I don't want to make her cry. She never cries, but once she starts, she can't stop.

"There was a kid," she whispers. "A kid in the field. He went out to go look for his mother, but there was no one else out there." She takes another deep breath and chuckles as a few tears escape her eyes. She wipes them away and turns away from me. "I'm sorry."

"Hey no." I rub her shoulders as she composes herself. "It's okay. You don't have to tell me if you don't want to."

"No." She sniffles again and clears her throat once more. "It's fine. The kid was in the field alone. I went in after him, and there was an official. Next thing you know, the kid's blood has splattered over me, and my arm feels like it had been blown off." Her free hand finds its way onto her shoulder and down her arm slowly. "I lay down, I played dead, and the official ran past me and onto others." She glances over to me then back down to her lap. "The kid didn't make it."

I pull her close and kiss her on the head as she adjusts her position. She whispers into my chest as I feel the tears soak through my shirt. "He wasn't even five years old. He was just a baby."

I watch as she holds her wrapped-up wound with her free hand. When my hand falls on hers, she winces.

"Does it hurt?" I ask her, already knowing the answer.

"I'm fine."

"That's not what I asked. I know you can handle it, but I asked if it hurts."

She clears her throat and coughs a bit, trying to play it off. "It is sore and it throbs, but it isn't nearly as bad as a lot of the other injuries in this hospital."

"I'm sorry," I whisper.

"It's fine. I'm fine. What about you?" She looks up to me from my chest. "What happened to you? You know, after the draft? Tell me everything."

I sigh and rub her arm up and down, the same way Dad used to do for her to get her to go to sleep. "After I was forced into the officials' van, everything went dark. Next thing I know, I woke up in the woods."

"Wow, really?"

"Yes. And you know what, when the officials dropped me off, they laid me on a rock. I woke up barely able to walk because of that stupid stone. After I managed to stand, I was stalked by this giant catlike beast. It was almost as large as one of the official's vehicles."

"What?"

"Yeah, and guess what, I only managed to get away after some guards on the wall shot at me."

"Oh my! That's horrible!"

"That doesn't even cover all of day one . . ."

Logan

I move my horse up and around, capturing a pawn of Eric's. "Aha," I say, happy to finally have captured one of Eric's pieces.

He stays silent, just like he always does when we play chess.

Mavis has come in to visit me every day since she arrived, and every day we play chess. I hoped that by playing chess as often as I do, I would be getting better, but it seems my hopes are just that—just hopes.

As Eric and I continue our game, I catch a small grumble coming from Eric. His face winces as he adjusts his position in his seat.

"Hey." I move one of my pieces forward. "Are you okay?"

Eric takes his piece that looks like a castle and slides it forward, capturing my last little horse in the process. He doesn't respond to me verbally, but he nods.

After a while of playing back and forth and listening to the surrounding card players whoop and holler, I finally speak up. "So do you know what kind of job you want to get? You know, once we get out of here?"

Eric moves one of his pieces forward. Keeping his eyes on the board, he sighs. "I don't know of any jobs I can qualify for without a leg."

I hesitate for a moment, not wanting to make him any more upset, but the words come out of my mouth in a chuckle. "Cabdriver?" Eric glances up to me then back down to the board as I continue. "Or any desk job, really."

I move one of my pointy pieces that moves diagonally and capture Eric's castle. I can't help but smile as I feel the sense of victory nearing. As the smile finds its way onto my face, I ask Eric, "Do you have any ideas on what you would like to do?"

After Eric steals my pointy piece with one of his pawns, I hear him grumble, "Grow my leg back."

My stomach is immediately shot with an immense feeling of guilt. I feel the blood drain from my head, and the pounding find its way back into my brain.

It's my fault that Eric lost his leg. If I wasn't there, Eric wouldn't have used himself as a human shield. He would have kept running and probably got far enough to escape from any serious wounds.

I want to tell Eric how sorry I am, but I don't want to tell him I feel guilty. I don't want to make his pain about me.

"So," I continue, trying to shift his focus, "what about me? What do you think I should get a job as?"

I move my last castle across the board, not really paying attention to the rest of the pieces. Eric immediately uses one of his pointy pieces and takes my castle. "You can do anything," he tells me as he slides my piece off the board.

I shake my head. I can't to "anything" anymore. I know there are limitations. The doctors told me that I need to take it as easy as I can until they tell me otherwise. And last time I asked them, they told me it would be a year or two before I regain normality, but I'm not going to say that around Eric. Eric has more limitations than I do.

And I caused them.

We sit here, playing chess in silence for another moment, listening to the hologram screen in the back of the room talk about the new capitol building and how it "will be finished in just a few weeks."

Everyone in the room quietly chatters about whatever they are doing, ranging from card games, board games, supervising, to listening to the news.

Eric, never looking up from the board, asks me, "Did you get an invitation to the inauguration ball?"

"Ball?" I ask him. "What ball?"

"You know"—Eric moves one of his pieces and yawns—"the ball. The large gathering of 'important people' for the new chancellor's inauguration."

"The chancellor hasn't been elected yet."

Eric chuckles. "I know. The capitol building hasn't been finished yet either. I was just wondering if you had gotten an invitation yet."

"No, why would I?"

"You were part of the Taai, remember?"

I think back to John telling us how we were and still are valued members of the Taai and "will always be treated as one."

"Are the Taai members being invited?" I ask Eric.

He nods. "As far as I know."

I move one of my pieces and give into the urge to yawn. "What about you," I moan as my yawn comes to an end.

"Not yet, but John told me that all the high-ranking military members would get invited, along with most of the government officials and politicians."

"And you and I are high-ranking military members?"

He nods. "The Taai is the highest rank. It is our elite force, and I doubt John would let the team go by without getting recognition."

A few moments of silence between us pass as we stare at the board and try to plan out our next moves. As I listen to our surroundings, I have slowly become convinced that some of the men in here have smuggled in booze.

I hear them whisper between each other to "put it away, put it away" and "give me some." When I look over my shoulder, I see one of them taking a swig of a bottle with a towel wrapped around it. He chuckles as he passes it around his circle of card players.

My attention is brought back to the game when Eric calls out to me, "Check."

I look down and realize this game is coming to an end. As I try to figure out what to do, Eric crosses his arms and leans back into his wheelchair. "So have you beat Mavis at chess yet?"

"Me? Beat Mavis?" I snort. "I don't think so. She is even better at this than you are."

"I see." He pauses for a moment and looks over the board. "So are you and Mavis a, um, 'thing'?"

A confused smirk rises on my face as I look at Eric, who is finally making eye contact. He chuckles when he sees my confusion, but doesn't say anything.

"What? A 'thing'?" I ask him. "What are you talking about?"

"You know what I'm talking about."

"Well"—I move one of my pieces in front of my king—"if you mean a couple, then no. We are not."

Eric looks back down at the board and resumes his silent thinking position. After a few moments pass, Eric moves another one of his pieces and calls, "Check."

I know I am about to lose, but I shan't give up easily.

"Why not?" he asks me.

Again, a confused smirk rises on my face. "Why not what?"

"Why aren't you two a thing?"

I shrug as I move my king over one space. "I don't know."

Placing me in checkmate, Eric returns with, "It's pretty obvious you like her."

"Yeah right." I chuckle as we reset the board.

"It's okay. It's not a big deal, but denying it won't make any difference." He winks at me. "I won't tell anyone."

We reset the board without another word. I think about how Eric has never spoken of anyone he fancies. The only girl I have ever really seen him interact with was Janice, somewhat Mavis, and Mandy. The only one out of those three that I would even consider an option for him is Mandy, and that is because she is obviously smitten with the "elite force member."

The more I think about it, the more I realize that Eric has never spoken about his family or his past at all.

"Eric," I say to him as he moves his first piece, "do you, um, do you know, um . . ."

He looks up at me and shoots me an almost annoyed look.

"Your family," I continue. "Do you know where your family is?"

I move my piece as he looks back down at the board. "I don't have a family anymore." He moves another piece. "Both of my parents died during the epidemic, and my younger brother was in the military. He died during the war."

"I'm sorry." I move another piece. "How old was your brother?"

"Eighteen." Eric clenches his jaw and moves his horse in front of one of the many pawns. "He signed up to help at the last minute." I move one of my horses and do the same thing that Eric did. "He wanted to be a doctor." He continues, choking back his emotions. "I was so sure he was going to be one. He was so smart and determined." Eric chuckles. "Even more than me."

A few moments of silence pass as we play the game. The room seems to become much calmer as the news about the capitol building echoes through the room.

"It should have been me," Eric whimpers.

I stay quiet, not knowing what to say. The woman on the news switches over to a male announcer whose shirt looks to be the same color as snot yellow.

"Thank you, Laura. Good afternoon, everyone, today I am here in front of one of the new career buildings where everyone will be going next week to decide on their new profession! Bestellen used to force their citizens to take whatever career they were assigned as a baby, even if they were no good at it, but this all changes as we enter a new age of prosperity . . ."

Since everyone is now out of Bergland, most of the cities are almost fully repaired, which means in a few days, the week of career choices will begin. Many people will choose to be builders because of how needed they are and that they don't have much education for anything else. They will take a few classes before they start, but with the technology Bergland has brought over, building isn't going to be one of the harder jobs.

The man on the screen continues and tells us which career options are the best-paying ones, the most-needed ones, the ones which will require the most education, and so on and so forth.

After everyone chooses their new career path and is assigned to a new job, they will get to select a house and a payment plan to pay off the house. The real estate officers will make sure that everything is chosen according to need, meaning, if one single man decides he wants to be a florist, but chooses to live in the biggest house in town by himself, they can refuse to sell him that house because it would take too long for him to pay it off.

Once everyone gets a job and a living arrangement set up, the following week will have one day where we can go and cast our vote for the chancellor, who comes along with a set of advisors.

The council members, such as head of education, head of health, and all the other leading positions from Bergland will be transferring over here to continue in their given positions. The thing the people will be voting for is a new chancellor, who will then choose a group of people to help guide himself and the council members.

I am somewhat upset about the fact that we have to be twenty years old to vote. If we are old enough to fight in the war at eighteen, then why aren't we old enough to have a say in who runs the country?

Along with the fact that there is nonstop coverage on the news about each candidate, there are pamphlets in every office building about all contestants for chancellor, so I am hoping that everyone will do their research before voting. There are many hologram screens in the capital, so most everyone here will be exposed to the news coverage in one way or another. From what I've heard, there is at least one in every building.

This fact baffles me just to think about. Just a few months ago, I would never have expected all of this to be where Bestellen once was.

I look up at Eric as he moves another one of his pieces. "Will you be voting next week?" I ask him. Eric is twenty-three, so I figure he will take advantage of it.

Eric's eyes are squeezed closed, his fists are clenched, and he squirms within his seat, seemingly trying to escape from pain.

"Are you okay?" I ask him. "Do you want me to—"

"I'm fine," he snaps at me. Eric quickly adjusts his posture to a perfect position and moves his queen forward. "Check."

I look at Eric with confusion as I take his queen with my queen. "Check?" I say to him, wondering how he could have missed this setup.

Eric grunts in pain and squeezes his eyes closed again.

"Are you okay?" I reiterate. "Do you want me to go get a nurse?"

Eric sniffles, clears his throat, and shakes his head. He takes my queen with a pointy piece. "Checkmate," he tells me as nonchalantly as he can.

I raise one eyebrow at him and hesitantly begin resetting the board.

Eric winces once more as I move the pieces and reaches down below the table, kicking one of the table's legs in the process. With one swift grunt of pain, he quickly takes the brakes off his wheelchair and rolls backward.

"I'll play later," he tells me, rolling faster than I've ever seen him roll. Without stopping, Eric rolls through the crowd, weaves through the tables, and hits the side of the door on the way out. He hesitates for a split second before continuing out of the room as quickly as possible.

CHAPTER FOUR

Sam

Back to the capitol's administration offices I go. I wave to the woman who drove me and make my way in to find myself at the end of a very long line of people. I can't help but get slightly annoyed. Shouldn't there be more people working at this desk?

After a few minutes, I realize there are three separate people at the desk helping whoever is next in line. They just happen to be taking much longer than I wish. Once my turn arrives, I am called over to the woman at the far right.

"How can I help you?" she asks me.

"I'd like a transfer request."

The woman gives me a confused chuckle. "What kind of transfer?"

"Sorry." Realizing the vagueness of my request, I elaborate. "A hospital transfer. One of the nurses at my mother's hospital said to ask this office for a transfer sheet."

"Under what grounds do you want the transfer?"

"Grounds?" I ask her. "What do you mean?"

She gives me another chuckle, this time seeming more rude. "Meaning, why do you want the transfer?"

"Oh, um, so that my mother can be closer to me."

"You are going to need a better reason than that." She sighs and leans forward to me. "Do you mean so that your mother can be near you, the person who provides for the family"—she clears her throat—"the meat bearer?"

My head finds its way into a slow nod as I catch her hint. "Yes. That is what I mean. I am the family provider. I need her, I mean, she needs to be here with me."

The woman nods to me and holds out a scanner. I place my wrist under and the red line scans up and down my code.

"Okay, Mr. Beckman, you will be called back to these offices soon to review what all a transfer requires and entails." She smiles at me and turns to the next person in line. "Next please."

Before I can thank her, someone pushes past me and steals my spot. I take that action as my cue and head back to Sarah and Mavis at the kitchen. Once I make it outside, I flag down one of the many cabs roaming the street. On our way to the kitchen, I can't help but let my mind drift back to the time I got to spend with my mother. Why did she feel like she needed to act as if she was okay?

I mean, she survived, and I am superhappy she did. I remember the anxious feeling of not knowing whether or not she was even alive, but just because others have it worse does not mean that she isn't allowed to feel bad.

She is allowed to request medicine if she is in pain, just like I am allowed to take a vial if I need to calm down.

The thing is, when I am with her, I don't feel the need to take the vials. The whole time I was with her, I never even had to think about taking the vials.

I will do anything, get any job that I need, to make sure I can get Mom up here and get her the medical attention she needs.

When I finally make it to the kitchen, it is almost an hour after the morning shift started and the breakfast rush has come in full swing. There are very few restaurants and produce stores in the capitol right now, so this cafeteria is busy. This isn't the only cafeteria in the city, but it is the largest and happens to be toward the center.

The moment I step into the building, I am consumed by the crowd. A woman to my right, with red hair, shoves past me to get in line before me even though I wasn't planning to get in line. She continues to shove past people until she bumps into a large man who stands his ground. As soon as she elbows him to get in front, I see him bow up as his eyes meet hers. As much as I desire to watch this unravel, I scurry through the crowd and back to the kitchen, which is now set up to look exactly like the one back in Bergland.

My eyes fall upon Sarah, who is at the front, working in the serving lines as always. Making my way over to her, I catch a glimpse of Mavis in the back of the room cutting vegetables and decide to not bother Sarah. I wash my hands, head back to Mavis, and immediately get to work.

As the knife slides into my hand, Mavis turns to me and sets hers down. "Sam!" She throws her arms around me without using her juice-covered hands. I do the same to her, and we chuckle as we retract.

"How's your mother?" she asks me, scooting back to her cutting board.

"Fine," I tell her. "She was shot in the arm trying to save a kid, but she is okay now. How is Logan?"

She rolls her eyes. "He says he is fine, but he was blown up twice."

"Blown up?"

"Twice!" she reiterated.

I can't help but chuckle. "Is he okay?"

Mavis nods. "He can walk and talk like normal. There is no permanent damage. No limbs were lost or anything." She turns back to the cutting board and picks up her knife to continue. "At least not on him."

"What? What do you mean 'at least not on him'?"

She continues cutting and glances over to me. "Eric was in both explosions too."

I pause, not sure what to say. I begin cutting and stare at the vegetables as I ask, "Is he okay?"

She shrugs. "He was after the first explosion. The second one did some damage."

"What happened?"

"He lost one of his legs." She clears her throat and places her chopped vegetables into the large pot. "He lost it saving Logan from the explosion."

I pause again.

Saving Logan from the explosion? Is this the same Eric that stood by and watched me get bullied?

Or is it the same Eric who stood up for me when no one was watching?

"Is he okay?" I ask her.

She nods. "He will be."

After a few moments of silence, I jump back into the conversation. "How about you? I'm sorry, I should have asked that first. How are you? What have you all done in the last few days? Where have you stayed?"

She smiles. "I stayed at Derek's house with him and his mom."

"Oh, you did, didn't you?" I elbow her in her arm and chuckle as she elbows me back. "I'm kidding, how was it? Was there much room? What was the house like? How is his mom? How about him?"

"Sam"—she looks over and holds her hands up toward me—"one question at a time please."

"Okay," I scoff at her. "What kind of house are they staying in? No." I pause my chopping. "Where is their house? Is it in the city or what?"

"Again, those were multiple questions, but I'll answer anyway. It is a small cabin-type house, and it is in the middle of the woods a few dozen miles away from here."

I nod to her. "That sounds like something you'd like. Are you going to keep staying with them?"

She shrugs. "I don't see why not. Derek will be needing some help taking care of his mother, and I think I can help when I'm not working."

"What's wrong with his mom?"

I realize the bluntness of this question the moment it leaves my mouth. Mavis turns from the vegetables and looks at me with what seems like a light glare.

"Wait, no, scratch that, new question," I tell her as she turns back to the veggies. "Do you know where I can stay? You know, to sleep?"

"Sarah said that some of the workers in the kitchen are all sharing a place until they find their own homes and get different jobs." She throws the cut veggies into the pot. "I'm sure you can stay with them too."

I nod. "I will ask her when I get the chance, but I need to catch up on some work first before I ask for any favors."

She chuckles and looks at a man who is wearing a small messy smock and appears to be in his thirties. He comes over to us and plops down a large tub of more vegetables to cut.

"Hi, Mavis." He glances at me and forms a guessing smirk. "Hi, Sam?"

I nod as Mavis smiles back at him. "Hi, Aiden." She turns to me and gestures to the man. "Sam, this is Aiden. Aiden, this is Sam."

As I shake his hand, Mavis continues to cut her vegetables and introduce us. "While you were gone, he and I worked together. Aiden is actually from Bloot too."

"Yeah, just a few precincts away from hers." He wipes his hands on his smock and crosses his arms. "I am so happy that I got out of there when I did. The rest of my family along with most of my friends wanted to stay there when the revolt came, but I couldn't understand why."

"It's home to them," Mavis tells us. After a short moment of silence, Mavis clears her throat, looks back at us, and sets her knife down. "I am going to go and grab another pot for the cut vegetables."

I find myself watching her leave as I shift back to the cutting table. Once she is out of sight, I turn back to the man. "It's nice meeting you, Aiden. She hasn't given you any trouble while I was gone, has she?"

He chuckles. "Only a bit." Aiden looks around the room and leans in toward me. "My name is actually Hayden, with an *H*."

Confused, I shoot him an odd, squinty look. "What?"

"Mavis heard it wrong when we first met, but I never corrected her because it was so loud in the kitchen, that I thought she was saying it right"—he shrugs with a goofy look on his face—"and now it is too late."

His little story causes me to cackle and guffaw, just as Sarah does. "I'll tell her," I say. "It's no problem."

"No," Hayden tells me. "It's been days. It's too long now."

"It'll just get even more weird the longer you wait! I mean—"

He shushes me as Mavis rounds the corner with a pot half her size. When she sets the pot down, I can't help but snicker, causing Hayden to leave.

"What?" Mavis asks me, knowing something is going on.

"Oh nothing," I tell her. "*Aiden* just had to get back to work."

"Got it." She nods back to me. "You know, this is Aiden's chosen career. He chose it as a permanent job this morning."

"Oh yeah?"

She nods again. "Yeah. And you know what else? I get to go and choose my job tonight after my shift ends."

"Really? What kind of career are you going to choose?"

She shrugs. "I don't know."

"You don't know? Is that not the sort of thing that you need to know before you go in?"

Mavis gets back to cutting. "Yes, but I am not really prepared for anything. I don't have any real 'education' for anything other than being thrown out into the woods, remember?"

"Well, most people from Bestellen are not really prepared for any jobs besides the ones they were originally assigned to, but thanks to the technologies Bergland has brought over, many of the jobs we now have are going to be a lot easier."

She scoffs. "Like what?"

"Eh," I pause, "like a, um, road paver or a construction worker?"

Mavis chuckles. "Good job. Those may be the only two I can think of." She throws some of the chopped vegetables into the pot. "Derek is a construction worker. He told me that they have machines that build all the buildings and that all he has to do is load them up with the proper tools and then his managers will punch in the instructions."

"See?" I nudge her in the arm. "Easy, right?"

"Sure, but I don't want to do that."

"Why not? The machines really do all the work."

She looks back at the cutting board and continues chopping.

I know I was joking with her when I told her that the machines do all the work, but that claim sits with me. It is true.

Having machines help build a new nation quickly is great, but what about after that? Do we keep improving upon these machines until they can do the work by themselves? Why haven't they made robots that can help make food, do the gardening, do the cleaning, and do the driving all by themselves?

If we do, won't that take jobs away from people who need them?

I shake off the thought of robots making humans obsolete and get back to cutting carrots when all of a sudden, a large crashing sound echoes through the room. Mavis and I both look for the source of the sound to find Hayden standing over a bunch of metal pans that he knocked over.

"Good old Aiden." I chuckle at Mavis.

Logan

I fold one of my final shirts and shove it into my bag. Eric and I are finally being dispatched today.

I don't have much to pack. Just a few clothes that the hospital and John have provided me.

Once I finish putting them all in my bag, Eric and I head out. Since we were both injured working for the Taai, our benefits are extremely gracious compared to most. Along with the fact that we share the same benefits, neither Eric nor I have any family left except for each other.

Over the period of time that Eric and I have spent together in recovery, we have become close. About as close as you can get when one person won't speak very much. Though Eric speaks every now and then, I catch him muttering things to himself more than actually speaking.

John came by earlier today and told us both that he has set up a small house for the two of us. He said, "It is completely handicapped accessible, and once we get Eric up and moving with his prosthetic leg, we can take off any and all ramps."

Though this was supposed to be comforting, I noticed Eric roll his eyes when John told us. Usually, when John sees disrespect like that, he will snap, but he can tell that scolding Eric won't help anything.

Other than McCullough and the others in our van who died during the first explosion, no other Taai was killed. A few of them were hurt, but Eric and I took the worst hits, which is why I assume John pulled all the strings he could to get us a house to ourselves without having to force us to pay for it just yet.

He wanted the new house to be a surprise, so neither of us have seen it yet. All we know is that the only people who have keys to our house are Eric and I, and that is because John came by and dropped them off earlier.

I can't help but be excited about the new house, but just as Eric does, I play it off as if it is nothing. Though I say "play," I don't know if Eric is playing or not. I figured he would be excited to move into his first house outside of Bergland, out in the real world, but he hasn't made any real effort to show enthusiasm.

Neither of us are one hundred percent sure that leaving the rehabilitation center will be the best thing, but I know for a fact that we both want to get out of there and stop feeling like victims.

As Eric and I get into the cab, I chuckle. "I'm actually going to somewhat miss this place."

Eric scoffs as he takes a seat and tries to scoot inward. "I'm not."

"That's too bad, because you will be coming back quite often for physical therapy." I elbow him as I take my seat beside him. "It'll be like you never left."

Eric rolls his eyes. "You'll be back here too."

I nod. "Yes I will, but at least I am not going to be crabby about it."

Eric finishes scooting over and looks out of the window with nothing to say.

"So"—I sit in beside him and hand the driver the piece of paper with the address of our new house—"are you happy to be getting a prosthetic leg?"

Eric shrugs. "I'll be happy if it works."

With Eric ending the conversation, the driver gets us to buckle up, and we take off. Eric and I look around to see how much the city has changed. I haven't gotten out much, and I don't think Eric has gotten out at all since the hospital explosion. The number of new finished buildings is baffling and extremely impressive. The roads are beautiful, the structures are gorgeous, and there are bronze-colored streetlamps lining the roads, along with the occasional raised decorative box clock on a street corner.

As we drive and see all these magnificent structures, I am reminded that by tonight, I need to have a career chosen. John has submitted a list of careers that I can do to the career officer I will be meeting with. After submitting the list, he made sure that the officer understood that those were the only jobs I am allowed to do, all because John wants me to take it easy for a while.

Out of the jobs John gave me, I can't decide what I want to do. I know I don't want a job where I will be working a lot. I am too sore to even think about working all day, but the main reason I don't want to have a full-time job is I don't want to leave Eric alone for too long. He is already depressed enough; leaving him alone won't help anything.

After driving for a few miles, we turn down a road, lined with freshly planted trees, looking like they have been planted less than a month ago. We keep driving to find a small circle of houses at the end of the street. The house the driver pulls up to is a small fancy-looking stone building with a red shingle roof. Compared with all the other houses in this area, it is extremely small, but it is still much bigger than the house I grew up in in Bestellen.

"Here we are," the driver tells us. He gets out of the car, just as I do, and he pulls Eric's wheelchair out of the trunk. After setting it in front of Eric, we watch him deny help and struggle to get back into his chair.

Once he is settled, the two of us pull out our small bags, thank the driver, and wave him goodbye. He takes off and pulls out of the neighborhood just as quickly as he pulled in. Eric and I wait and stare at our new house from the front in awe. The windows are perfectly square and clean, the grass appears to have the same deep shade of healthy green coloring as the grass from the woods outside the wall, and lining the sides of the house are fancy bushes with pink flower buds frozen closed on them.

I take a few steps forward to get out of the chilly air, following Eric's lead up the perfectly paved driveway. When he gets to the door, he pulls out the house key and unlocks the door. Assuming he was about to head in, I bump into Eric who remains parked in the doorway.

Before I get the chance to ask him if he's okay, he sighs. "I figured the first house I got to live in, the first real house, the first time I entered it, I wouldn't be wheeling myself in."

CHAPTER FIVE

Mavis

As my shift comes to an end, Sarah hobbles over to me with a pained expression on her face.

I set down my rag and turn to her. "Are you okay?"

"My feet." She places one of her hands on my station and leans, trying to relieve some of the pressure. "I've been on them all day every day, but something about being out of the mountain is making them hurt worse."

"I'm sorry." I lean against the table as well and look down at her feet. She wears closed toed shoes that cover her entire feet, but it is obvious that her ankles are swollen. "Is there anything I can do to help?"

"No." She shakes her head and straightens her posture. "I'm sorry to whine. I was actually coming over here to tell you that once you are done cleaning your station, you can go home. I'll see you tomorrow."

I nod. "Thank you, Sarah."

She nods back and hobbles over to Sam, where it looks like they have the same conversation we just had. I pick my rag back up and wipe all the crumbs off the table, onto the floor, and begin to spray down the stainless steel surface.

Just before I get the chance to start wiping, a familiar voice echoes through the room, causing both Sam and I to jerk our heads toward the kitchen entrance. My eyes quickly fall upon Janice as she makes her way into the kitchen.

"Mavis! Sam!" Her smile grows as her joyful voice bounces off the walls and she makes her way over to the two of us. She wraps her arms around us both and squeezes us tight. "How are you two? I missed you both so much!"

"We missed you too," Sam tells her as he pulls out of the hug. "Where have you been? We haven't seen you in weeks!"

"I am the assistant secretary of education, remember?" She chuckles. "I have been having to sort things through and organize a bunch of stuff. I have had so many different tasks since I got here that I can't count them all. The main thing that Hash and I have been doing is prepping everyone from Bestellen."

Sam's jaw drops in a smile. "You two did all of that? You two were the ones who prepped everybody and explained stuff to them?"

Janice shakes her head with wide eyes. "No, no. Oh wow, no. We have teachers from Bergland who have spread out and have been teaching for us. They have also been gathering up the citizens and helping them set up school schedules. It is a lot of work. The two of us couldn't do it all."

"Oh yeah, is everything going okay?" Sam asks her. "Meaning, you haven't had too many people fight you on all this?"

She shrugs. "Most everything is running smoothly. A good sixty-five percent of Bestellen fought with Bergland during the war, and most of the thirty-five percent that was against Bergland was either an official or a citizen of Metropolis or Verwend."

Before Sam can speak, I chime in and ask Janice, "Where are all the people who didn't agree with Bergland?"

"General Wilson is taking care of that." She smirks. "I wasn't trying to sound menacing. Wilson and the new government has them labeled as traitors, so they will be spending time in prison."

Sam's face makes the expression that it makes just before he chimes in, so Janice speeds her speaking up. "They aren't being tortured or abused or anything, they are just being held until they are no longer considered a threat."

"How long will that be?" Sam asks her. "And what exactly will deem them fit to come back to society?"

"Once they have a full understanding of Bergland, they should be ready to submit." She crosses her arms as someone in the back sprays someone else with the sink hose. I can almost hear Sarah's frustration with these immature beings. Janice brings her attention back to us after a moment of watching the madness unfold. "Some have already been released. It was mainly people who only fought with Bestellen because they were scared that if they didn't, they would die."

Sam raises his finger to interject once again, but Janice jumps in. "They are still being monitored though."

Sam's finger lowers as he nods with an impressed look on his face.

"So," I say, "the extremists are staying in prison?"

She nods as we all listen to Sarah scold one of the new workers. This is the first time that I've ever actually heard or seen her angry. I can't help but turn around and watch as her face turns bright red and she tries to calmly tell the workers not to do that.

Janice pulls us aside and gets our attention away from the mess. "So careers! Is this the one you guys chose?"

"Nope," Sam tells her. "I haven't chosen yet."

I wave them back to come with me so I can finish wiping down my table. "Nor me. I am actually going to go and choose my career right after I finish my shift."

"Oh really?" Janice grows with excitement. "That's great! What are you going to choose?"

I shrug. "I don't know yet. I am not prepared for anything."

Janice watches me wipe the table down for a moment and sighs. As I throw the rag back into the cleaning bucket, she asks me, "Do you want to keep working with food?"

The water from the bucket splashes back up at me, getting a small chunk of the vegetables, from earlier today, on my arm. "No," I tell her, flicking the chunk of food off me, "not really. I have had enough of it, but if I can't think of another career, I will come back to do this until I figure something else out."

As I place the bucket back on its little hook, I grab the broom and dustpan and bring it over to sweep all the trash and crumbs from my table.

"Well, that's okay. The counselor you will meet with can help you find something." Janice kicks out a small piece of trash from the side of the table. "They can figure out what you are best suited for and what you would probably enjoy the most."

I nod as I continue to try to get the trash from every corner and area as I can. If this career officer can help me like Janice says they can, then I am actually kind of excited for this.

"So"—Janice turns from me, back to Sam—"do you know when you are going to go and choose a career?"

"Not yet, but I will be going back to the offices soon for a meeting about a hospital transfer for my mom. I will ask them then."

"Okay." She gives him a smile. "I'm happy to hear she is okay. One of the first things I did when I got here was check and see if your mother and Logan's grandfather were okay."

I nod as we all look at each other with a silent acknowledgment that Logan's grandfather is dead.

The awkward moment passes, and Janice looks back at me. "So how are you two adjusting to the new country?"

I finish sweeping my area and force all the junk into the dustpan. "It's okay. I am enjoying my time so far." I rise back up to a standing position and take the mess over to the trash can. "I'm staying with my friend Derek and his mother. They will be living in the capital for a while, but I don't know how long."

Most likely they'll be staying here for the rest of Ms. Page's life. Derek told me the other night that he would make more money staying in the capital and working as a builder than he would in any other state. He said that he has to stay here so that he can afford a caretaker for his mom.

Derek was not made to live in the city. That is why he bought the most secluded house in the entire capital, but he is making sacrifices for his mom. Another reason that he lives just outside the city is so that his mother can visit. She has always wanted to live in or near a city, so he is making sure that happens.

"That's nice," Janice tells me. "Are you planning to move back to where Bloot was? State Four?"

"No. I will be staying with Derek to help him care for his mother."

I don't have very many good memories in Bloot anyways.

"What about you, Sam?" Janice asks.

"I want my mom to live in the city with me," he immediately blurts. "Everything is fine, but I don't want to be away from my mom. I want to give her the best, and the new capital will be the best."

She chuckles at his optimistic claim and nods her head. "That sounds logical." Janice looks around the room and takes another deep breath. "All right, kids, I am very happy to see you both, but I really need to go get back to work." She opens her arms and gives us both one last hug. "Once things settle down, we will have more time to talk."

"How will you find us if we change jobs?" I ask her.

She smiles at me and begins backing out of the kitchen slowly. "I can ask the offices where you guys are. They'll tell me." She pauses and looks at us with a slightly serious expression. "Speaking of which, you guys can go to the AO and request that your information be private. This way, no one can ask about you and then get your address and where you work unless you put them on your list of people who can access that information."

Sam interjects, "Why haven't we heard about this before?"

"I don't know. Did you listen to your briefing on your way out here?"

Sam looks back at me and makes another goofy face, this one more of a "whoops" expression.

Janice chuckles. "I have already done it. I told the person in the AO that I don't want anyone but a select few to be able to contact me. You two, Logan, and a few others are on my list." Janice winks at us as. "I will see you guys later, okay?"

We nod as she heads out of the kitchen. I turn to Sam who places his hands on his hips and lets out a deep breath. "Well, time for me to finish cleaning my mess."

I smile at him as I back away, just as Janice did. "I have already finished, so I'm going to go ahead and head down to the offices for my career meeting."

Another crashing noise echoes through the kitchen as one of the new workers slips in some of the water he had sprayed earlier and drops all the pans he was holding. Sam throws his head back in disappointment as the laughter echoes throughout the room.

I chuckle to him. "Have fun."

He squints at me and gives me a sarcastic smile. "I will." Sam turns around and struts back to his station.

I let him finish his work and leave the building, hop in a cab, and ride down to the AO office. When I get there, I am forced to navigate my way through the people in the waiting room in order to get to the front desk. I listen to all the conversations blur together as I come through.

"I want to be a fireman. Wouldn't that be so amazing? I'd like to get to go in and save people from burning buildings!"

"Right, like that would be fun. That is dangerous, Kevin, and you aren't built for it. The only reason you want to do that is because you think it would be cool."

"What do you want to do?"

"I want to be a farmer. Is that weird?"

"Playing in dirt and poop all day, only to hope that food grows and your animals don't die? No. Not at all."

"I want to train to be a grief counselor."

This last statement I hear in between all the madness that is around me catches my attention. I turn to see a red-haired woman with countless freckles, brown eyes, and scars on her wrist that she shows to the person she is sharing with. I can't help but hope that this woman gets to have the career she wants.

Most everyone from Bergland has their job already carried over from the mountain or are still in school preparing for future jobs, so I assume what I am seeing in here are mainly the Bestellen citizens. Throughout each of the conversations I grasp a bit of, I manage to hear them say something about being happy no longer being a slave.

I feel the same way, but I still don't know what I want to do.

I think back to the many pamphlets that I have looked through. I saw hundreds of different career options, but I couldn't really find one that I was prepared for, and I don't desire to go through tons of training for something my heart really isn't in.

When I get to the front of the line, the lady at the desk asks me my name.

"Mavis Wamsley," I tell her.

She smiles at me as she types into her hologram. "Go to the third floor, and a woman will meet you in the waiting room."

I nod. "Thank you."

Once I find the elevator down the unnaturally chilly hallway, I press the button and hear a ding. The light above the elevator comes on, and I wait for what feels like minutes for it to actually make its way down to me.

As it opens, I take a step in, but am clobbered by an unnecessary number of people as they stampede out, not even acknowledging that I was there.

I didn't even get a chance to say sorry, but I guess that's okay.

I'm not anymore.

Once I get in, the elevator takes me to the third floor without any interruptions. I take my seat in the waiting room down the hall and watch as people come out of the maze of doors, hallways, and desks.

The lady that brings people from their meeting back to the waiting room so that they can leave looks as if she has had a very long day. She has bags under her eyes, her facial expression is constantly holding a sour look, and she gets louder every time she comes back into the room to call another name.

"Rebecca Thomas," she says the first time.

"Taylor Jennings!" she semishouts the second time.

"Randy Fipps!" she roars as she comes out the third time.

At this point, I'm not sure if choosing a career right now is worth dealing with her. I can feel my stomach becoming upset as my breathing quickens.

I hear the lady's footsteps as she comes out with another person; this time, she has a smile on her face and a kind voice as she speaks to the man. She turns to the waiting room and looks around with the sweetest expressions I've ever seen on an office worker. "Mavis Wamsley?"

I rise to my feet as the man with her spins around. "Mavis!" Logan calls out to me as he makes his way away from the worker. "Hey!"

He wraps his arms around me before I can really do anything, so I return the hug awkwardly. "Hey, Logan!"

I feel the slight sense of anxiety leave the longer we are embraced, but it soon returns when I realize how many people are staring at us.

I pull away and look up to him. "So the house? How is it?"

"It's even bigger than the one I used to live in, and in better condition! I feel that to get that house, Young may have had to pull a lot of strings. It is really nice." He chuckles. "Well, I mean, it is not as nice as all the others around it, but to me, it is all I could ever ask for."

"That's great," I tell him.

"Do you want to come see it?" he asks me. "It isn't but a fifteen-minute drive from here."

I nod. "I do, but I actually have to go into my career meeting." I gesture back to the woman, who has allowed the sour look to return to her face.

"Oh yeah, sorry. Do you know what you are going to choose?"

I shake my head. "No. I still can't figure it out. What did you choose?"

"Well, Young really limited my choices due to the fact that I need rest, so I chose the career that he suggested."

"Yeah? What is it?"

Logan's arm comes up as he scratches the back of his head. "Um, cleaning the training rooms?"

"Ah." I find my head slowly lifting back in acknowledgment. "Fancy."

"Yes yes, it is." He holds his finger up and straightens his posture. "It looks like we have a 'bright future' ahead of us," he mocks.

"Considering we heard that nonstop in Bergland, I figured you could have done it a little better."

He sarcastically scoffs and holds his chest. "Ouch."

The sour woman clears her throat and calls out my name again. "Wamsley. Mavis Wamsley."

I nod to Logan, and he nods to me as we part ways. I follow the woman down the hallway and am shown to another office, where a short bald man awaits with a hologram. The moment I step in, the woman slams the door shut behind me, scaring the man into pausing whatever he was typing.

"Hello!" He stands and reaches out for my hand. "My name is Rhegan Garrett. Pleased to meet you."

I shake his hand, and we sit down in adjacent seats. His office is all painted one bland color that reminds me of a dying leaf, and there are no pictures or paintings anywhere. It is just him, his desk, and his hologram.

After he finishes typing, he turns to me and folds his hands. "So, Ms. Wamsley, do you know what you want to do for a career?"

"No, sir." I chuckle, trying to make it not seem as pathetic as it feels. "I was kind of hoping you would help me with that."

He nods and leans back in his chair. "Let me think." Mr. Garrett looks me up and down, seemingly scanning me for answers. "You look like you are an artist. Very creative."

I look around the room for someone else that he may be focusing on, but when I look back to him, he is still staring at me.

"Um no, sir. I'm really not."

He folds his hands and points at me, still leaning back in his seat. "Cooking. How do you feel about cooking?"

I shake my head. "I have been cooking nonstop for the past few weeks and would really like a change."

He holds his position for a moment before sitting back up and typing something into his computer. "I think I have the job for you." Mr. Garrett turns back to me and folds his hands again. "I think you would make an amazing news photographer."

"News photographer?"

"Yes!" he shouts with joy. "Your boss would give you a camera and an assignment. You would then go and take pictures of said assignment."

"You," I stammer, "you think that's a good job for me?"

"Well, do you like looking at things?"

I shrug. "I guess so."

"Then why not? This is just like that! You just point and shoot. You seem creative to me, and I feel like you can take a decent picture. Does that sound okay?" He begins typing on his hologram before I can answer.

"I guess so."

"Wonderful!" A ding noise, followed by a hum, echoes through the room. The man looks down and tears a sheet of paper off his desk printer and hands it to me. On the top of the sheet lies an address.

"Go to that address tomorrow at nine in the morning and meet your new boss, Mr. Vincent Trolly." Mr. Garrett rises from his seat and takes my hand and gives it a quick shake. "Have a great night!" He leaves his desk and opens the door for me. Calling out into the hallway, he smiles at me. "Rhonda!"

The sour woman returns to me with a fake smile and escorts me out of the office.

CHAPTER SIX

Sam

After rising from my spot on the floor, folding my blankets, sliding a vial into my pocket, and trying to get the crick out of my neck, I leave the house that Sarah, myself, and the other workers stayed in last night.

The sun rose about an hour ago, blinding me as it peaks over the trees in front of our house. I try my best to close the door as quietly as I can so that I won't wake anyone, but I can't help but feel like I am much louder than I need to be. After escaping the house and walking a mile or so until I find a cab patrolling, I head to the Administrative Office.

Last night, after Mavis left the kitchen, we got a call from the AO. The woman on the phone asked me if I could come in this morning for the transfer meeting, and I happily told her I could.

When the cabdriver drops me off at the front of the building, I head in and find myself almost running to the front desk.

"Good morning," I tell the woman at the hologram. "My name is Samuel Beckman. I was called in for a meeting about a hospital transfer."

The woman slowly looks at me as if she is still half asleep and takes a sip of her tea. "Go up to the fifth floor and speak to Mr. Jamison at the desk."

I nod to her and take the elevator up. I do the same thing the moment the elevator opens up on the fifth floor, I run to the front desk to see a man typing on his hologram.

"Hi, are you Mr. Jamison?" I ask him.

Unlike the woman downstairs, he turns to me with a large and bright smile. "Why, yes I am! How can I help you today?"

"The woman downstairs told me to come talk to you. My name is Samuel Beckman, and I was called in for a hospital transfer meeting."

"Ah yes." Mr. Jamison turns from his hologram to me and gives me a goofy smile. "Mr. Beckman, I can take you."

"Thank you. Can I also do my career scheduling thing today?"

He rises from his desk and waves me to follow him. "Yes, sir, that sounds perfect."

I thank him again, and he drops me off in a small bland office with a man who is slightly taller than me and much skinnier.

"Hello, Mr. Beckman!" He gestures to one of the two chairs in front of his desk. "Please, have a seat."

I sit in the seat closest to me. "So have you reviewed my request?"

"Wow, getting right down to business, I see."

"Yes, sir," I answer. "So?"

He smiles at me, though it seems like he is trying not to. My heart sinks as I hear his words leave his mouth. "I have. I am sorry to say that I cannot transfer your mother to any of the hospitals in or near the capital."

My stomach twists into knots, and I feel all the blood seem to force itself to the back of my head as the fear of not being able to bring my mother here sets in. "What?"

"I'm sorry. I just can't do that."

"You . . ." I feel my face get hot as I realize he is telling me that he can't do it. What does he mean he can't do it? Does he mean someone else can? "You can't do it?"

He shakes his pale scrawny head as a crooked tooth and squinty smile rises up on his face.

"What? Are you happy about that? My mother needs me, and you can't bring her to the same place I am working?" I try to keep calm, but I find myself jumping up from my seat. "You won't bring a woman to be near her son in her time of need?"

The man smiles again. "Mr. Beckman—"

"Why are you smiling?"

Is he laughing at me?

Is he getting a kick out of this?

I find myself stepping forward to him with my fists clenched as I hear my name called from behind. Immediately, all the anger drips out of me.

I turn around to see my mother in the hallway with her arm all tied up like it was at the hospital, along with a suitcase by her side. "Surprise!" she cheers.

She and I embrace once again and wrap our arms around each other. I feel the anger melt away and the fear of not getting to be with her slowly fall out of my body.

"What are you doing here?" I ask her. "The man told me he couldn't get the transfer."

"Actually," the man chimes in, "I told you I couldn't get a hospital transfer. I couldn't get a hospital transfer because your mother has been discharged."

I let go of my mother and look back at the brat of a man who thought it would be funny to trick me like that, and I try to let the anger go.

"He's right," Mom tells me after scooting by and sitting in one of the chairs. "I am as free as a bird now!" She looks down at her arm. "Well, as free as a bird with a broken wing."

I can't help but smile and take a seat beside her. "Don't you need to continue to rest?"

"Oh no! I have been resting for weeks. It's time for me to get out and do some work."

"Are you sure?" I ask her.

"Of course. So have you chosen a career yet, Sam?"

I shake my head. "No, ma'am. I actually was told I can choose it during this meeting."

"Wonderful!" she cheers. "Do you know what you want to do?"

"No, ma'am." I avoid eye contact with the man, but look back over to him. "I was going to ask and see what kind of thing would be best for me."

"Well," the man says as he types into his hologram, "do you have any sort of idea as to what you'd like to do?"

I shake my head.

"What about you, Ms. Beckman?"

Mom looks at me, then back at him. "Right now, I think I should probably just stick with what I know, which would be—"

"Farming," he interjects.

Mom nods with a smile on her face as she looks at me. "I enjoy it, and it is something I have always found simple."

"I agree." I nod back to her and turn to the man. "Can I do that too? Work with my mom? I know how so I won't need any training."

"Sounds perfect." The man smiles as he types into his hologram. "There is actually a small house available on a farm owned by James Gohaki just outside of the city. You two fit the description of the type of people he wants to rent it out to. All you have to do is work on the farm and pay the utility bills."

"That sounds lovely!" Mom cheers, looking back to me. "How does that sound to you, Sam?"

I nod. "That sounds great, Mom."

Whatever makes you happy.

The man prints off our new address, along with the contact information and address of Mr. Gohaki. "Go ahead and go to Gohaki's house. I will give him a call, and he will be ready for you two."

"Thank you," my mother and I say in unison.

As we rise, the two of us race to the suitcase. I smile at her as I beat her to it and wheel it out of the building, making it easier for her to make it down to the cab. On our way out to Gohaki's farm, Mother and I comment on almost everything we pass.

"Logan, the guy I told you about that was in the woods with me is staying in a recovery center right down that road."

"What? Really? What happened?"

"He got blown up."

"Really?"

"Twice."

The cabdriver laughs at us almost every time we comment on a building.

"I have been working at a kitchen right down that road."

"You? Cooking?" She laughs at me. "But you hate cooking."

"But I know how, so that was my job."

"You were never very good at it though." She chuckles as she looks out the other window. Mom oohs and aahs at the buildings we pass in the new and beautiful capital for what feels like the entire ride. She points out the different designs on each of the new buildings, talks about what good choices they made designing them, and how they are the prettiest buildings she has ever seen.

"These are amazing! You know, I've always wanted to visit a city with big buildings, but I have never really wanted to live in one." She turns to me and grabs my hand. "And now, we will be close enough to get to see the beauty of it while still living far enough away that we aren't drowned by the madness."

I can't help but smile as I watch her eyes widen every time she sees something new. After about twenty minutes of driving, we finally make it out onto an open street with large fields lined with barbed wire fences to keep the cattle in. Trees line the road we turn onto, and the patches of sunlight produce a strobe-light pattern as we drive through the tunnel of dead winter branches hanging overhead.

"I imagine that come springtime, this will be one of the most beautiful places we've ever seen." Mom gives my hand another squeeze. "Can't you picture it? The luscious green leaves with whatever flowers bloom, creating a tunnel above us to block out the heat of the sun, but still allows us to see the thick green grass as the cattle graze?"

I nod. "I imagine so, Mom."

We drive for another minute or so and turn right onto a gravel road or driveway, leading up to Mr. Gohaki's considerably large house. It is painted a light pastel pink with a gray tin roof. This house has the largest white columns lining their porch and decks that I've ever seen.

The moment we pull up to his house, a man hobbles out wearing a long-sleeved button-down shirt, along with a pair of brown worker pants that look as if nothing could cut them, not even a knife.

He makes his way down the stairs as Mom and I exit the cab. "Hello there," he says to us, "you two must be the Heckmans."

Mom and I exchange a glance. "Actually," she corrects him, making her way in for a handshake, "we are the Beckmans. Bonnie and Samuel Beckman."

She finishes shaking his hand and I follow. His hands are rough like sandpaper and yet plump like plums. "You can call me Sam though."

"Ah." He releases my hand and chuckles. "Why, thank you, Sam." He passes us both and pulls our suitcase out of the trunk of the cab and waves the driver off. "You can go ahead and go. Thank you very much."

The driver takes off, and Mom and I exchange another glance.

"So . . ." He carries the suitcase over to us and sets it on the ground. Pointing to my mother's wrapped-up arm in a sling, he continues. "What happened?"

"Oh, um, I was shot a while back around the time the war first started. I'm fine though." Mom smiles at the man and chuckles nervously. "I can still work."

He nods with a smile. "The man who called me just a bit ago told me you are both very hard workers. Is this true?"

We nod.

"Okay then." Mr. Gohaki smiles again. "Wait here for a moment, and I'll take you out to your new house. We can talk more there."

"Thank you," Mom and I say in unison.

Gohaki walks around the side of his house and whistles a tune that I cannot identify while Mom and I stand in the cold and try not to shiver. It looks like no snow has dropped in a while, but it is still a bit too cold for my liking.

After a minute or two, Gohaki comes around the corner of the house with a small doorless car with eight seats, a front screen, and a red roof and hood. "Come on over. Take a seat and I'll drive you guys out there."

I pick up our suitcase and throw it on, ready to get out of the cold. Mom follows and we sit in the seats right behind Gohaki.

Almost immediately, Gohaki takes off and we begin riding down another dirt path. The cold air becomes even colder as it blows with force against my face. Mom must notice the redness of my nose because she takes her free hand and holds it in front of my face as a shield.

"Thanks." I chuckle as I return the favor and hold my hand in front of her face.

"No problem," she tells me as we ride with our hands held up like weirdos.

After about half a mile, I see a house arrive on the horizon.

"Is that ours?" I ask him.

The man chuckles. "No. Those are your neighbors. I suggest you go talk to them sometime because they are also your coworkers."

We continue driving for another mile or so and come upon another house. Before Mom or I could ask if it was ours, Gohaki confirms. "Welcome home."

We pull up into the driveway of our small house to find that it has an even smaller garage attached to the side. The brown-stoned house seems oddly comforting as I walk my mother and our suitcase to the door.

Mr. Gohaki chuckles as he scoots by us. "Sorry about that." He pulls out a large set of keys and sorts through them. After listening to the keys clinking against each other much longer than they should have, he unlocks the old wooden door and ushers us in.

This house is actually about the same size as our old one, but so much nicer. The windows are perfectly shaped, no broken glass, and no dirt covering the walls around it.

"Oh, Mr. Gohaki!" Mom scurries into the building and spins around, admiring her new home. "This is wonderful!"

He chuckles. "I'm happy you like it. What about you, Sam?"

I nod and set the bag down. "It is certainly something." I turn back to him. "Thank you very much, Mr. Gohaki."

"Oh, no problem. I'm happy to have two hard workers." He chuckles again. "Just remember, I reserve the right to fire you if I think you are slacking."

Mom turns back to him and makes her way over. She shakes his hand once more. "Don't you worry, Mr. Gohaki, both my son and I will work as hard as we can. We wouldn't want to spoil an opportunity like this."

"Well, I'm happy to hear that, but I don't want you working yourself too hard, Mrs. Beckman."

"No, no," she tells him, "I'm fine, but I don't need to do too much, I will admit. The doctors did tell me I can go back to work as long as I don't overwork myself."

"Um," I interrupt, "excuse me, but, Mom? Working already? You still have your sling on."

She waves me off with her free hand. "I'm fine."

"Mom," I reiterate, "you don't need to do too much yet."

Her voice shifts into a slightly more serious tone. Her eyes meet mine as she tries to get me to stop. "Sam, I am okay. I can do work. I already spoke to the doctors about this."

"I'm not saying you can't do some, but farm work can be rough. I don't think you—"

She looks back at me and glares. "We can talk about this later, Sam."

I take a step back as I let Mother continue to speak with Mr. Gohaki. He outlines what all she and I will be doing and tells us the plan. I listen as he explains and boil as I watch. Mother won't even look my direction.

A great way to start our new lives.

With an argument.

Why doesn't she understand that I'm just trying to help her? Why did she feel the need to shut me down like that in front of Mr. Gohaki? She made me look like a kid who didn't know what he was talking about, when in reality, I think I know more about this than she does.

I just don't want her to get hurt.

"Okay, Sam," Mr. Gohaki grabs my attention, "so tomorrow, I will need you to start and clean out the horse stall. All the supplies you will need are in the barn, and you can carry them around by taking the cart in your garage."

"Cart?" I ask him. "What kind of cart?"

"It's like the one I drove you in, but smaller and more powerful. It's in your garage. I'll take you two out to the barn in a bit and show you guys around the land so you won't be too terribly lost." He winks at me and chuckles.

Creepy old man.

If he starts winking at my mom, I don't know what I'll do.

"So any questions?" he asks us.

I raise my hand so as to not offend my mother by speaking out of turn.

He chuckles. "Yes, Sam?"

"How many other workers are there?"

"We have quite a few that live off campus and that one family that lives up the road, the one we passed earlier." Mr. Gohaki takes a seat at our dining table. "The mother of the family should come over and introduce herself any time now."

"Oh"—Mom looks at us both with a giddy grin—"this should be fun!"

Mr. Gohaki nods and rises to his feet just as quickly as he sat. "So if you guys need anything, you call me on that phone on the wall over there, okay? There is a list with all the phone numbers you may need taped beside it."

"Thank you," Mom tells him.

I catch him just as he heads to the door. "Do you know when you'll take us out to show us everything?"

He nods. "I'll be back in an hour or so. That way, you guys will get to settle in a bit."

"Thank you," we tell him again.

Mr. Gohaki leaves the building, and the first thing I do is head into the kitchen and open the small white refrigerator. I open it to find a small bout of chilly air floating to me.

I've never had my own refrigerator before. Neither has my mom. Though I've seen larger and better refrigerators in Bergland, this fridge is still amazing. As I explore, I see that this house comes with two bedrooms, one bathroom, one refrigerator, some plates and silverware, and a fireplace. It is all either of us could ever ask for.

I mean, it even has a wall phone! Our phone number is written at the top of the list, so I can write it down and give it out. Now I can call Logan and Mavis.

"Isn't this great?" Mom asks me as she takes out a few of her clothes and places them into her new dresser. "And we won't even have to make house payments! As long as we do our work and pay utility bills, we have a perfect setup."

I nod. Still slightly upset with her for snapping at me, I try to push down the anger and remain calm. "You're right."

"Now all we really have to do is buy some food and pay off my hospital bills!"

I nod again. "Everything is perfect. I have to go back to the place where I stayed last night and get a few of my clothes and my bag."

"Okay, but you should probably wait until after Mr. Gohaki comes back to give us the tour."

"Yes, ma'am."

I head out of the room and sit on the couch. Our new couch.

My couch.

I sit and fold my hands, intertwining my fingers with each other. I didn't think I'd need the medicine anymore. I never really felt like I needed it when I was with my mom. When the man in the office tricked me, all I wanted was the medicine, but that desire slowly went away the longer I was with my mom.

Until she snapped at me in front of Mr. Gohaki, I felt fine. I know it shouldn't be a big deal, but it is. She snapped at me and treated me like a child when all I was doing was trying to keep her from having to go back to the hospital. And what makes it worse is the fact that she did it in front of my new boss. He probably thinks of me as a child now.

He probably thinks that I am someone who won't be capable of making decent decisions.

All because she snapped.

I reach into my pocket and pull out one of my miniature vials, which happens to be the only vial I packed for today. I inject it into my leg before things get out of control and feel a slight sense of calm wash over me.

The miniature vial definitely doesn't have the same effect as the regular-sized dose, but it does seem to help.

Now, I wait for Mr. Gohaki to come back.

Mavis

Click.

I take another photo of the voting booths.

Click.

I take another photo of people looking at the pamphlets just before voting.

Click.

I take pictures of people coming into the building.

Click.

I take pictures of people leaving.

An old lady smiles at me as she waits in line to vote.

I smile back at her, somehow inviting the woman to pinch my elbow and pull me close.

"Who are you voting for, sweetie?"

I give a nervous chuckle. "I am not old enough to vote yet."

The woman's face drops, and she lets go of my elbow. She says nothing else to me and never even looks my way again. I shake off her attempt to get me to vote for her candidate and make my way back to the other end of the room. I continue taking pictures, angling the camera and each shot to be the most aesthetically pleasing as I can.

Though I feel like my "career counselor" was really just trying to get me in and out of the office as quickly as he could, I think he made the right choice. I actually enjoy taking these pictures.

I stay at one of the voting buildings for eight hours and leave as soon as my assignment is up. I drop the camera off at Trolly, my new boss's office so that he can use them for the news, and then head over to Sam's new house.

Derek and Ms. Page are out voting tonight, so I've decided to take it upon myself to drop by and surprise the Beckmans. On my way, I have my cabdriver stop at a flower shop, and I buy a small bouquet of lilies, the favorite flowers of Sam's mother.

Though I have just started working, I have the flower shop woman scan my code and charge my account. She tells me it is all taken care of, which makes me wonder whether I got money for working at the kitchen or if my new boss has already paid me for this last week of work.

Once I get back into the cab, the purple-haired driver smiles back at me. "Those are gorgeous. Are they for someone special?"

I smile back at the woman as she takes me to Sam's address. "Yes yes, they are." Before the woman can really react, I pull the pink lilies out of the arrangement and hand them to the driver.

"Oh!" she cheers as she stops at one of the traffic lights. "These are beautiful! Are they for me?"

I nod. "Thank you for driving me."

She smiles again. "Aw, thank you." She giggles and holds them up to her head. "They match my hair!" After a minute or two of silence, she looks into the rearview mirror back at me. "You do know you'll still have to pay me though, right?"

I nod and laugh. Once we get to Sam's new place, she scans my code, and it pays her through the car. We wave each other goodbye, and I walk to the large house at the front of the property. Just as I begin climbing up the stairs of the porch, I catch someone's attention.

"Excuse me." A young man approaches me with hedge clippers in his hands. "Can I help you?"

I look around, somewhat trying to avert from eye contact and stumble to find my words. "Yes, sorry, I um, I am here to visit the Beckmans."

The man looks me up and down. After a moment, a small smile rises on his face. "Then why are you looking in there?"

"I'm sorry, I've never been here before. I figured that knocking would—"

He rolls his eyes with a smile. "I'm just messing with you. Follow me, I can take you out to their house."

Squeezing the bouquet tighter, I take one final look over the porch and follow the man back to a small red cart.

He hops in the driver's seat after tossing the clippers in the back. As he turns the keys to start the vehicle, he looks over his shoulder. "Their house is a mile or two back that way. I can give you a ride."

I can't help but begin to rethink my visit.

The man drives the cart over to me and pats the seat beside him. "Come on. I won't bite."

After hesitating for a moment or two, I give into the pressure and take a seat. We drive for about five minutes or so when a house comes into focus. The large amount of joy I feel when I think I will be able to get out of this cart is surprising, but short lived when we drive right past the building.

"There are three houses on the property. One is Mr. Gohaki's, the house you were at originally. This is the second one, where some of the other workers live. The Beckmans' is the next house we will come up to."

The rest of our ride is in silence. Once we pull up to Sam's new house, I get out of the cart, thank him, and the man drives off. Making my way up the porch's steps, I am startled by Sam swinging open the doors. "Mavis!" He leaps forward toward me and wraps me into a bear hug. "I saw you coming up the driveway!"

"Yeah" I gesture over my shoulder. "I had to hitch a ride. Next time, I will call before I show up."

"Come in, come in." He pulls away and ushers me into his home, pointing at the flowers. "Are these for us?"

I nod.

Sam smiles and calls out, "Mom!"

A woman slightly taller than me, but shorter than Sam comes into the room. Her bright-blue eyes are even brighter than Sam's and her skin much tanner.

"Who is this?" she asks Sam. "Is this—"

She pauses and points to me with a smile and Sam nods. "It is."

"Mavis!" she squeals, making her way over to me and wrapping me in a one-armed hug. "Oh hello! I'm Bonnie Beckman, Sam's mom, but you can call me Bonnie."

I can't help but smile at how similar the two are. "Thank you, Bonnie."

"So what brings you to . . ." She pauses again as she looks at the flowers Sam holds in his hands. "Are those . . ."

Sam nods. "Yes. These are from Mavis."

Bonnie turns to me with a giddy smile. "You are the sweetest thing! How did you know I loved lilies?"

I look back to Sam and smile.

Bonnie's smile turns even sweeter as she lets out a little "Oh you."

"Here." Sam places the lilies at the center of his new dining room table. "Perfect."

I continue to stand, not knowing what to do, and feeling very awkward as Sam's mother praises the flowers and me. Sam takes notice and chuckles as he ushers us both over to the couch. "Mom and I were listening to the voting results. They were just about to announce them."

"Okay," I say, taking a seat on the end of the couch, and watching Bonnie as she takes a seat right beside me.

Sam heads back to the kitchen and calls out to us both. "Do either of you want something to drink?"

"No thank you," I tell him.

Bonnie shrugs and looks back to him. "I'll take a water." Before anyone can say anything else, Bonnie continues. "I was just telling Sam about my new friend Carrol. She is so wonderful, and she lives less than a mile away. She works with Sam and I." She leans in and puts one hand beside her mouth to keep Sam from reading her lips. "And between you and I, Carrol has a daughter that I think Sam will like."

"Mom." Sam brings her a cup of water and takes a seat in one of the separate chairs near the couch. "What are you telling, Mavis?"

"Oh nothing." She smiles at me and winks. The longer I sit here with Bonnie, the more and more she reminds me of Sam.

Sam rolls his eyes at her and chuckles. Before any of us can say anything, he silences us, "Sh! It's on!"

The three of us listen as the radio on the fireplace mantel calls out, "And that wraps it up, folks! The polls are in! Grab your family, grab your friends, the votes are in!"

We look around to each other as the announcer tells us about how big and important this is, and I think to myself, *If this is so important, why don't you just spit it out already?*

He must be able to hear my thoughts because as soon as I finish the thought, his voice echoes through the room. "This new nation of the free and hardworking has been given a name, and that name is Frieden. Yes, you heard it here first, Frieden. The home of the freed Diligent workers. The home of two nations combined as one. Frieden.

"The new capital, located toward the outside of Frieden, has also been named. It's new name is Kern. Kern, the capital." The announcer chuckles to the other announcer. "You know, that's kind of funny."

"Wayman," the other announcer says to him, "I think I'll take it from here. Listen up, guys, the new state lines have been finalized. What used to be Verwend and Metropolis has now been combined into State One. What used to be all of Meer and part of Hout has now been combined into State Two. The rest of Hout and part of Bouw has been combined to make State Three. What used to be all of Bloot and part of Bouw have now been combined into State Four. And what used to be the rest of Bouw and all of Minje is now State Five. All of this will be repeated throughout the next couple of days, and I imagine the rest of this month, so don't worry if you didn't catch all of that."

"All right, Benson, since you got to announce all of that, I feel that it is only fair that I get to announce Frieden's new chancellor." A pause floats throughout the room as the three of us wait for the two announcers to figure out who is doing what. "Wayman" continues. "All right, citizens of Frieden, your new chancellor has been chosen. And you know what?" He chuckles out. "It wasn't even a close call. The new chancellor of Frieden is . . . Thomas Ronan Oswald!"

The announcers continue to chat between themselves and comment on everything as the three of us stay silent in the house. Oswald was the only real candidate that said he would do everything that the Diligents believed in. Most of the others seemed to want to compromise. I didn't do as much research as I probably should about this election, but I wasn't one of the ones who got to vote.

Oswald was the candidate whom Derek and his mom voted for, and by the smile on Bonnie's face, it looks like that is who she voted for too.

I can only hope that they all made the right decision.

CHAPTER SEVEN

Logan

I sit on the couch, watching Chancellor Thomas Oswald address the nation.

He waves to the crowd, thanking everyone for this wonderful opportunity. "I will not let you down, Frieden. My trusted advisors and I will take our jobs seriously. We promise to think of the people first in all cases and do what will be best for them rather than best for us."

On the hologram screen that the news coverage is being broadcasted on, the camera changes viewpoints to the crowd. There are people crying with what seems like happiness and others who are stone faced, never showing how they feel.

I am somewhere in the middle. I care about this, I do, but not enough to cry. From what John told Eric and me, Oswald was the obvious choice.

About halfway through his speech, a few knocks on my door scare me. None of our neighbors have ever come to visit, and John didn't say he would be dropping by. I rise to my feet and head to the door, only to be surprised by two of my favorite faces.

"Mavis! Sam!" I cheer. "Hey!"

Sam springs forward and wraps me in a bear hug. "Logan, man, it's been so long." He pulls away and enters my house without any hesitation. "Wow. Your new place is fantastic! It's even bigger than mine!" Sam turns back to me with wide eyes and looks me up and down. "Sorry, I shouldn't have started with that. How are you? Mavis said that you got blown up!"

"Twice," she corrects.

I chuckle as I look back to Sam. "Yeah, I'm fine. It's sort of a long story."

"Well, we have time." Sam looks over to Mavis and smiles. "Mavis and I are done working for the day. Is this a good time for us to hang out? Catch up? Maybe eat some of your food that I assume you are hiding in your brand-new ginormous refrigerator?"

I nod, still chuckling at the fact that Sam seems to have gotten back to normal. Last time I saw him, he was red-eyed, angry, and barely had anything to say. Now, he is back to the nonstop chatter and focused on food.

"So," I say to Sam, leading both him and Mavis over to the couch, "how are you, Sam?"

"I am actually doing great! My mom and I are now living together right outside of the city on a farm, where we also happen to work, and now that I have a job, I can afford to come and visit you! Not that the cabs are superexpensive or anything." His face falls, and his eyes widen as he looks over to Mavis then back to me. "Oh, man, I'm sorry. Mavis told me about your granddad. I didn't mean to—"

"It's fine," I tell him. "It's fine. I'm just happy that your mom is okay."

Sam smiles at me. "Me too. So go ahead, tell me, how exactly did you manage to get blown up . . . twice?"

A smile rises on my face and leaves just as quickly as I hear a door squeak open from across the house. The three of us turn to the source of the noise to find Eric crutching out of his room. With his hair and clothes in disarray, he clears his throat and straightens his posture to try to make himself look less of a wreck.

Mavis and I look at Sam, whose jaw is clenched. Though I expect Sam to seem angry or for him to become irrational, he is remaining calm.

Eric gives a slight chuckle and runs one of his hands through his hair, trying to comb it back. "You didn't tell me we had company." He pauses and looks from me to Mavis, to Sam. Without another word between the four of us, Eric turns around and crutches back into his room.

A moment or two of silence after Eric closes his door, Sam turns to me. "Can I go in there to, um, to talk to him?"

I shrug hesitantly. "I guess so."

I really hope he won't lose his cool.

I really hope neither of them will.

Sam rises to his feet and takes a deep breath. He heads back to the room Eric just entered and gives the door a knock. Mavis and I hear Eric say, "Come in," and Sam listens.

Mavis scoots over beside me as Sam closes the door behind him. "Do you know what really happened between them?"

"Yes," I whisper back. "Eric told me the same day that he and Sam met in the cafeteria. He told me that this dude who was part of the Taai was messing with Sam and Eric got them to stop."

Mavis nods. "Yeah. What else did he tell you?"

"That he confronted the others after Sam was safe, and he paid the price."

"He told you that he got beat up?" she asks me.

"He showed me too." I think back to the horrid bruising he showed me. "I don't think Eric was lying."

"Neither do I. Janice told us what Eric told her, and it sounds like he told you the same thing."

"Meaning he kept his story straight," I say.

"That's not easy to do when you tell a lie."

I nod. Mavis smiles back to me for a moment before her eyes flit away and look at our hologram where Oswald continues to give his speech.

"You know," she says, chuckling, "Sam's mom has a crush on him."

"What?" I laugh. "Really?"

"Yeah, she says his jawline and cheekbones are her favorite thing, along with his 'gorgeous blue eyes.'"

"Oh yeah?" I laugh again. "What about you? What do you think about him?"

"Eh." She shrugs and looks back at me. "I prefer brown eyes."

A small flutter of joy finds its way into my stomach. I don't know what exactly to say, so I look back to Oswald as he introduces his advisors.

Eric's door swings open, and Sam comes storming through the room. "Thank you, Logan, for letting me go back there, but I think it is time for me to leave."

"What?" Mavis rises to her feet. "Already?"

Sam gives her an annoyed, and yet a pleading, look.

"Okay." She turns back to me. "Thank you, Logan, for having us over, but I'm going to go with Sam."

"Oh okay." I walk Mavis to the door as Sam heads down the driveway. "I'll call a cab for you guys."

Speed walking over to Sam, Mavis looks over her shoulder to me. "Thank you, Logan. I'll see you later, okay?"

I nod to her and give a wave as I head to the wall phone. I call the cab company and have them send one our way, but by the time I hang up, Mavis and Sam have already left the cul-de-sac. I assume Sam decided to go ahead and walk to the nearest cab, so they should be picked up shortly.

After a brief moment of considering to ask Eric what happened, I brush it off and sit back down to listen to the news. If Eric wants to tell me, he will tell me. I don't want to cause any more problems.

The next morning, I wake up with an alarm blaring in my room. The annoying repetition of the same beep drives me nuts, to the point that if I hear the beep once, I want to go and break my alarm clock.

I take that anger and shove it deep within me, hopefully never to be seen again. After swallowing the rage against my alarm clock, I rise to my feet and wipe my crusty eyes open. After shutting off the clock, the sounds of the chirping birds outside my window catch my attention. They call out to each other, back and forth, over and over, until my attention is diverted by another noise, this one in the house.

A light weeping.

I head out of my room and follow the sound to the outside of Eric's bedroom door. Slowly, I enter to see Eric sobbing in pain. He squeezes his pillow as he lies on his stomach and holds his head down. "It hurts . . ."

"Eric?" I say, trying to see if he needs help. "Are you okay?"

He twists his body and throws his pillow at me. "Get out!"

I dodge the shot and make my way over to his nightstand. I pull out one of his vials and hold it out to him. "Here, take it."

"No!" He turns his head away from me so that I can't see his eyes. "Get out, Logan. Now!"

Just as I set the vial down onto his nightstand, I remember Grayson and Caine administering the vial to Sam, our first night in Bergland. If they can do that to someone they don't even know, I can do this to my friend, who needs my help.

I stick it into the back of his leg right before the amputated portion. Eric shouts once more as the medicine kicks in. "I told you I didn't want it. I was fine." He takes a deep breath and wipes his eyes, trying to play it off as if he is okay. "I could take it. I didn't need the medicine."

"You did," I tell him. "You are allowed to take medicine. You don't have to tough it out."

I don't want to go in to work today. I can't leave Eric.

"Please," he whimpers. "Please leave."

I take a moment and continue to stay beside him. I know I need to work, but Eric needs me.

"Please?" he reiterates into his bed.

I slowly move away, retrieve his pillow for him, and leave the room.

I know Eric could take it, but he didn't have to. He takes the medicine when it is most needed, and sometimes, not even then.

I leave the house and obey Eric's wishes. I call a cab and take it to work, but am unable to think about anything other than about how Eric's prosthetic leg is going to be ready tomorrow. I really hope that Eric will take it. I really hope it will make him feel better. The nurses told me that walking around on it should help his body release much more of the "happy hormone" than it is releasing right now.

Eric could use some happy hormone.

Last time I spoke with one of the nurses, she told me that it has been measured and designed to fit Eric's leg and every specific need he has or may have. I don't know all the mechanics of it, but I do know it will be very high-tech so that Eric will be able to get back on his feet as soon as possible.

Every day, I go with Eric to physical therapy or help him do physical therapy at home. Never once has Eric admitted how he feels about his new prosthetic. Other than "I hope it works," he hasn't said anything about it. Not even to John.

As I continue disinfecting the small hand weights, John enters the room and calls my name loudly and proudly. "Forge."

I turn to him and rise to my feet. "Young."

He grabs my hand and gives it a good shake. "How are you enjoying being a cleaning lady?"

"Why," I snort back at him, "I'm enjoying it very much, sir."

"That's good, that's good. You are doing a terrific job at it too." He chuckles and pats me on the back. "It's nice seeing you up and out."

"It's nice being up and out." I return his smile, letting my resentment toward him roll off my back. "Are you happy with who won the election yesterday?"

He nods. "I am very happy, and speaking of which, the invitations to the chancellor's inauguration ball went out this morning. You and Eric should be getting yours any day now."

"Thank you, sir." I take a seat back down on the bench beside the weights. "I just hope that Eric will be up for it."

John takes a seat beside me. "Why wouldn't he be?"

"I don't know." I shrug it off, not wanting to embarrass Eric. If I told John what happened this morning, I don't think Eric would ever forgive me. "He is just in a lot of pain and won't let anyone help."

John shakes his head and chuckles. "Eric is about as stubborn as they come. He is a tough kid, but his pride has always been something he has had trouble overcoming."

I nod in agreement, not knowing what else to say.

John takes my silence as a hint to continue the conversation. "When does he get his leg?"

"Tomorrow," I answer.

"Wonderful." John grabs one of the disinfecting wipes, along with one of the weights I have not cleaned yet. He wipes the handle, but misses the corners between the actual weights. I stare at his missed spots, hoping he would wipe them down, but he misses them and sets the weight back in its spot.

I make a note in my head to go back and reclean that one when John leaves, but try to continue the conversation as normal. "So what exactly should I be expecting for the ball?"

John grabs another weight and attempts to clean it off as well. "What do you mean?"

"Like, what sort of clothes do we need to wear? Who will be there? What will be happening at the ball?"

He chuckles as he wipes off the ends of the weight. "Don't worry about any of that. I'll get the clothes for you and Eric, and I will arrange your ride. It'll be just a large social gathering of fancy people. Most of them will be political officers or affiliates. Some will be high-ranked military."

I nod as I track which weights John fiddles with. "Will anyone else be there?"

"Yes. Everyone gets a plus one."

I turn to him. "Really? Everyone?"

He nods. "That's the deal." John quickly brings his watch up to reveal a vibrating cuff. He clicks its screen a few times and clears his throat. "Young."

"Young, the prison! It's been blown."

"What?" he asks the cuff.

"The prison! A bomb went off."

Mavis

Click.

I take a picture of what is left of the brick building.

Click.

I take a picture of the rescue team looking through the rubble for any survivors.

Click.

Rolling.

I video "Jamie Jenkins," a reporter, whose assignment it is to cover the prison bombings. Her perfectly sleek blond hair is tied back in a perfect ponytail, revealing her unusually large ears. I mean, she is really pretty, don't get me wrong. It's just that . . . her ears are much too large in proportion to her head.

I shake off my rude opinions as Jenkins clears her throat and reiterates her name. "This is Jamie Jenkins, and I have just been handed the incident report from tonight's attack. It says here that a Bestellen radical was seen on the prison security cameras, planting bombs on the cells of his fellow radicals. After a miscalculation of the strength of the bombs, this radical is responsible for killing six hundred and forty-two prisoners, as well as eighty-seven prison guards.

"Wow. That is all I have to say about this situation. Wow. I have no doubt in my mind that our new Chancellor Thomas Oswald will have a lot on his hands in the next few years. He promised us that as chancellor, he will monitor and turn in any Bestellen radicals before they can cause any damage, but it looks like he is already behind. Will Oswald be able to follow through on his promises? Will he and his administration be able to keep Frieden's citizens safe? This is Jamie Jenkins." She gives me a nod and pulls her earpiece out. "Go ahead and take that to Trolly. He wants it as soon as possible."

Before I can answer, she walks off and speaks to the man who gave her the report. I listen to her instructions and walk off in the other direction. The smoke and airborne debris floats around me as I try to make my way through the fallen bricks and cracked structure, but am bombarded by people with microphones and notepads when I make it to the street.

"What happened to the prison?"

"Who caused the explosion?"

"Was it a bombing?"

"Will there be another war?"

I throw my hands over my ears and take off running through the crowds. Why bombard me? Just because I have a camera?

The people don't follow me, but turn their attention to one of the famous reporters as she walks through the crowd.

I take my chance and hop in a cab, head to the office to drop off the camera and the footage, and then make my way home. I trudge through the small woods to make it to the house, through the cold, through some mud, and over a fallen tree branch. When I finally make it inside, the warmth of the fire meets my face and thaws out my nose.

My eyes immediately fall on Derek. He sits on the couch with one hand in his hair and one hand hovering over the chessboard, with the sound of the news on the radio echoing through the room.

"Welcome home," he tells me without turning around.

I hang up my jacket by the fireplace, taking in the wonderful scent of apple cinnamon candles, and set my boots on our shoe bench. "Thank you."

He doesn't look back at me. He doesn't move his hand from his hair, nor does he move any chess piece. I make my way around the couch and over to him. He still says nothing.

"Are you okay?" I ask.

"Yes. I'm fine."

I watch him as he stares blankly at the chessboard. His irises have gotten much deeper in color. Almost all of it is now a deep purple shade.

I can tell something is wrong. I just wish he would tell me.

"Where's your mom?" I ask him.

He doesn't look away from the board, but he leans back into the couch. "She is in her bedroom taking a nap."

I nod and look around the room, trying to get my nerves to calm down from earlier. Twiddling my fingers for a bit, I wait for Derek to put himself in checkmate. He has it perfectly arranged; that one final move will win the game.

"Do you want to go check the traps?" I ask him, hoping to help him get his mind off whatever he is thinking about.

He nods and rises to his feet. I pass the board without making the winning move and put on my wet boots that I had just taken off.

We walk in silence through the woods. Without saying a word, we observe the beauty of nature that I don't think I'll ever find in cities. As we make it about a half a mile away, we see a few of our traps have been set off, but hold no game. We walk in a little farther to find that a few of our handmade traps have caught some game while only one of the metal traps Derek and I bought in the marketplace has caught something.

At the end of our trek, we take our winnings, two rabbits and one squirrel, home. We skin the three, give the meat to Derek's mother to clean, and take the pelts to the marketplace.

We walk around the tables to see many different products, ranging from beautiful fruit aligned by color, to animal pelts aligned by the animal's breeds. This marketplace is toward the outside of the city and is set up like one of the marketplaces we had in Bloot.

The only things different about this marketplace is the quality of the products, the smells of the structure, and the status of the people. When I walk in, it reminds me of home, but not enough to strike up any uncomfortable memories.

"Buy and sell your skins right here!" an old man calls out to us as he gestures to his gorgeous fox, beaver, and even deer pelts. He smiles and points to Derek as we walk by him. "You, sir, you look like a hunter."

Derek winks at me and heads over to the man's table. "Why yes, sir, I am."

"Oh yeah? What state are you from?"

"Bloot actually."

The man's eyes grow. "That's fabulous! So was I." He pets the fox pelt on his front table. "What do you say? How would you like to make a purchase from a fellow Bloot?"

"Actually, I'm in the market for a rabbit pelt." Derek leans over the table and picks up one of the man's rabbit pelts. "How much for this one?"

The man narrows his eyes and gives Derek a smile. "For you? Twenty-five."

Derek nods his head and gives him the pelt back. "Okay. Thank you, but no thank you."

"Are you sure?" the man asks us as Derek and I walk off.

We nod and head down the line. We pass a stand that sells traps, a stand that sells arrowheads, and a stand that sells different sorts of twines and buttons. Once we get to the next pelt stand, Derek makes his way over to the woman and gives her a light smile. "Hello."

She smiles back at him. "Hello. Are you interested in buying or selling a pelt?"

"We are," he tells her.

I hand Derek the bag.

He opens it up and shows the woman. "Two rabbits and one squirrel."

She nods. "Well, you came to the right place. We sell the cheapest here and buy for the most. What kind of offer are you looking for today?"

He tilts his head and runs his hand through his hair. "Well, we were looking for thirty for each rabbit pelt and ten for the squirrel."

"Thirty?" she exclaims. "That is quite a lot for a rabbit pelt. The squirrel pelt I can do for ten, but the rabbit pelts?"

Derek nods. "You're right. That guy down there was only going to offer me twenty for each."

"Well . . ." The woman looks down at her table then back into our bag of pelts. "Would you accept sixty for the whole bag?"

Derek looks back at me for an answer. I nod, trying not to be too enthusiastic. Derek turns back to the woman and accepts sixty in bills.

He places them in his pocket, thanks the woman, and comes back over to me. "Remember when we'd barely get anything for these pelts?"

Smiling back at the money as Derek hands me half, the two of us begin walking around the maze of tables and spend the money we just made on canned goods, fruits, and vegetables. As we spend the last bit of our cash on canned meat, we hear Derek's name called out joyfully.

Derek and I turn around to find an older man coming toward us with a large smile strewn across his face. "Mr. Page! How are you?"

Derek extends his hand to the man and smiles back. "Mr. Gregory, I'm wonderful. How about yourself?"

The man nods. "I am doing pretty good actually. It's nice to see you outside of work."

Derek nods back. "I agree."

After an awkward pause where Derek clearly lied to the man, Mr. Gregory turns to me and smiles. "Well hello, dear." He turns back to Derek. "Aren't you going to introduce me to your friend?"

Derek looks back at me, as if asking if it was okay. I nod and hold my hand out to Mr. Gregory for a handshake. "Sorry about that. I'm Mavis, Derek's friend."

He takes my hand and holds it for a moment. "Just a friend, huh?"

Derek nods. "Yes, sir."

Mr. Gregory smiles at me. "Ah. I am Walter Gregory, Derek's boss." He brings my hand up to his mouth, and just before he can kiss it, I pull it away.

"Excuse me," I say to him, feeling a rush of embarrassment and uneasiness flood over me.

"No!" He takes a step back. "Excuse me! I am so sorry, I meant no disrespect. That was something I was brought up to do to beautiful women."

I nod, trying to hold back my cringe. "It's fine. It may just be me, but that isn't something I'm okay with."

He nods as Derek takes a slight step in front of me so that he is in between the two of us.

"Again, I am sorry." Mr. Gregory pulls out a card from his jacket pocket and hands it to Derek. "Here. I was coming over to give this to you and invite you to a group pheasant hunt tomorrow. All the information is on the card, and the guns will be provided by the people who are running the hunt."

"Thank you," Derek tells Mr. Gregory, "but I don't think I can afford it. These 'group hunts' cost a lot of money."

"No," the man tells us, "no, you two would be coming as my guests. I will make sure you two are partnered up so that you won't have to do much with anyone else. Consider it a treat for one of my best and favorite workers." He turns to me and gives a slight smile. "And an apology for my action."

Derek looks at me, then back to his boss. "We'll think about it." He extends his hand and shakes Mr. Gregory's once again. "Thank you very much, sir. Have a great day."

Mr. Gregory nods to us both and walks off.

Derek turns to me. "Do you want to head out?"

"Yeah." I rub my arms and play my uncomfortableness off. "It's getting a little cold."

We head out of the marketplace and find a cab. Neither of us say anything until the cab drops us off by the bridge across the creek. Once we make our way across the bridge, Derek clears his throat and pulls out the card he got from Mr. Gregory.

"Do you want to go?" I ask him.

Derek doesn't say anything as we continue toward the house. He waits until we have to step over a fallen branch. "Do you?"

I shrug. I don't want to see Mr. Gregory again, but this is Derek's boss. If I turn it down, Derek won't go. If Derek doesn't go, he may offend his boss.

"I mean, we get to keep the birds we shoot, right?" I ask him, trying to sound okay with this.

"That's what it says on the card. It is pretty much a free hunt that guarantees we leave with meat."

"Well . . ." I look at Derek as the house comes into sight. "I guess that means I better call Mr. Trolly and ask for tomorrow off."

Sam

"She really is great," Mom continues, "I mean, she came over today to hang out on our break, and she brought this little casserole that was just heavenly! And you know what else? She—"

I zone out as Mom fangirls about her new best friend for the millionth time today. My mind wanders back to an earlier event, one that I can't forget.

I didn't want to make Eric uncomfortable. It was Eric's house too. If he didn't want me to be there, I shouldn't be there.

I wouldn't want to be there if he didn't want me there.

So I went into his room to apologize. He stayed quiet as I spoke to him.

I told him, "Thank you for what you did."

I told him, "I'm sorry for lashing out on you."

And all he did was stay quiet.

He wouldn't look at me, he wouldn't speak to me, and he wouldn't even breathe in my direction. I came in, pushed aside my pride, and apologized while Eric couldn't even look at me.

No.

He *wouldn't*.

I had to get out of there when I could. I had to get out of there before I got too angry.

"You two should really meet sometime," Mom tells me as she finishes placing a pan into our oven.

I nod. "Sure."

The phone on the wall between Mom and me rings. I rise to my feet from the couch and run over to answer it before Mom can. "Hello?"

"Hey, Sam? This is Mr. Gohaki. I'm just calling to let you know the mail is here."

"Okay, thank you, Mr. Gohaki."

We hang up and I slide on my jacket. "Mom, I'm going out to get the mail. I'll be back soon."

"Take as long as you need, honey!"

I will. I don't know if I can handle another Carrol story.

I wave her goodbye and exit the house with the keys to my own individual cart. When I drive it out to the three mailboxes that are all held together by the front of the property, I park right beside it. The chilly air seems to take a break long enough for me to get out from behind the windshield without freezing to death.

When the mail finds its way into my hands, I discover that they are all the same. Five envelopes, all addressed from the same place, and to my mom.

Upon opening them, the moment my eyes fall on the numbers, my heart rate skyrockets and I feel my body become weak.

They're bills.

Over thirty thousand dollars' worth of bills.

No. This can't be. This is too much.

I can't let Mom see these.

I head up to Mr. Gohaki's house and borrow the phone on his porch. I call a cab and head to the address listed on the bills. When I arrive, the building is taller than any I've seen before, and the entire building seems to be made of glass.

I step out of the cab after having him scan my code and wave him goodbye.

Everyone seems to be using the cab service. On the road in front of me, I can count twenty-three cabs either parked or driving at this moment.

I wonder what all you have to go through to become a cabdriver. It doesn't seem that hard. All you have to do is follow the guidance system it has in the car once you put the address in.

"Sammy boy!"

I turn my head to find a familiar tattoo of the contorted Diligent symbol making his way through the crowd and over to me. "Bram?" I say as he pats me on the back.

"How are you doing?" He grabs my shoulder and pulls me with him as he walks down the sidewalk. "What have you been up to since you escaped the mountain?"

"Oh." Feeling rushed, I look around at the people shoving past us. "I-I'm working on a farm." I realize how pathetic this sounds as the words make their way out of my mouth. "But my boss provides me with an awesome house, rent-free." We continue down the sidewalk, and I catch a large and strong whiff of what smells like a man's cologne dumped on a sweaty boy to try to cover his original scent.

It didn't work.

"Really?" he exclaims. "I wish my boss would do that."

"Where do you work?" I ask him, bumping into a woman, as the two of us continue to weave through the crowds.

"I'm self-employed," he snorts and speeds up. "But hey, that means I make my own hours. Speaking of which, I really have to go. I'm on the job right now."

"Oh okay."

"But I'll see you later!" He zips through the crowd, weaving like he probably had to do, every day in Bergland. He looks back over his shoulder to me as I fail to do the same. "Where do you work?"

"Um"—I speed up to try to keep up with his pace—"do you know where Gohaki Farms is?"

"I do, that's great! I'll see you later, Sammy."

With those final words, I lose Bram in the crowd of people and find myself lost as well. Lucky for me, the building I have to go to stands out like a sore thumb. I head back through the crowd toward the tall glass building and go through the same process that I've been going through every time I enter one of these buildings. I ask the person at the desk, they reroute me to a different floor, and I wait to be called back into an office.

When my name is called, an extremely short woman comes out from behind her desk and waves me back. Her feet move twice as fast as mine, and yet I can easily keep up. I am so mesmerized by watching her speed through the office that I become lost by the time we make it to my destination.

She points me over to a desk where another woman, this one taller than me, is standing, waving me over. I thank the vertically challenged woman and head over to the new one.

"Mr. Beckman, how are you today?"

"Well, I was doing great until I made my way to the mailbox." I set the bills down on her desk and take a seat. "How about you?"

She chuckles. "I'm doing good. Thank you for asking." She picks up the mail and sorts through it, all with narrow eyes as if she needs glasses. "I'm sorry, but these are addressed to your mother, Bonnie Beckman."

I nod. "Yes, ma'am, they are, but I was wondering if I could pay them off for her. She doesn't have much money right now, and I figure I have some saved up from working back in Bergland."

"Bergland?" The woman looks back to her hologram with a confused expression, showing how horribly done her makeup is. "It says here in your file that you and your mother are from Bouw."

"Yes, but . . ." I take a breath as I realize I don't want to explain once again that I with two others made it through the woods before the war. "It's a long story. Let's just say I have money saved up."

The woman gives me a little smile and pauses a moment. "Okay. Hold your code under the scanner." She points to a little upright box connected to her desk.

I hold my wrist to it, and we go through the motions of the little red line scanning.

"Okay," the woman tells me as she types into her hologram.

"How much do I have now?"

Her face scrunches up, and she looks back to me. "A little less than two thousand dollars."

I take a deep breath. "Before or after paying the bills?"

"Before." She turns to me and folds her hands. "How would you like to handle this?"

Mom is making money. She is making enough to pay for food and the utilities.

I clear my throat and look around the room to see many people who seem to be in similar situations as I am. "Would you be able to, um, use all but one hundred or two hundred dollars of my money for the bills?"

"What?"

"Well, I'd need money for cab rides. My mom makes enough to cover our other needs, so I can use the rest of the money I make to pay off the hospital bills."

The woman lets a smile rise up on her face. "You are a good kid, you know that?" She types something into her hologram. "But are you sure you want to do this?"

I nod. "Yes, ma'am."

She prints off a receipt and hands me the small yellow paper. I look it over and it shows me she left two hundred dollars on my account, and transferred the rest over. I now have a little over twenty-nine thousand dollars left to pay off.

"The longer these bills aren't paid off, the more money will be added for you to pay." The woman tells me, "But as long as you make regular payments, the interest won't be much."

"Interest?"

"The extra you have to pay if you wait too long."

I understand that this is an incentive to keep people from skipping out on payment, but I can't help but hate it, no matter how rational. "I don't think I can afford to pay it off quick enough. Is there anything else I can do?"

"Just," she shrugs, "pay it off as soon as you can."

I think and think about a way out of this and find only one solution.

I guess it's time to get another job.

CHAPTER EIGHT

Logan

I force my overly sore body off the ground and finish wiping off the handles of the weight machine. The muscles in my back ache terribly, and it feels as if each of my lower back bones are grinding against each other. I assume that this is a result of me working so hard cleaning and brush the pain off.

After finishing the handles, I put my rag and the spray back into its bucket and look around the room. The amount of sweaty men surrounding me becomes more apparent as the smell sinks in.

A waving hand catches my attention from the gym entrance, and I make my way over. John finishes up his conversation with a man with a clipboard and shakes his hand. "Remember that," John tells him.

The man nods to John and marches off, writing something on his paper.

"Forge." John waves me over to follow him, and I do. We head out into the hall and begin walking. "You have been doing a great job cleaning. I've never seen this equipment as clean as they are when you are done with them."

"Thank you." I shrug. "I do my best."

"Good. That's good. We need more people like you." He points down the hallway. "I'm going to go and clear out Course A for you to clean next."

"Okay."

A man walks by the two of us and nods to John, who returns the gesture. Without looking back at me, John asks, "So how are you feeling?"

"Feeling?"

"Yes. Feeling. Are you sore? Is it hard to move around?"

I shrug. "Somewhat. My legs and back have not regained normality yet, but I'm doing better."

"That's good. I am happy to hear it." John clears his throat and taps a few of the buttons on his cuff. "I was actually going to see if you would be interested in rejoining Taai."

"What?" My mind stumbles over his offer. "You were the one who told me to take it slow."

He nods. "I was. I was also the one who got you this job. Do you know why I was wanting you to take this one?"

I shake my head.

"I wanted to keep an eye on you. Make sure that you were getting around okay."

"Okay?"

John chuckles. "I have been able to see that though you are sore, you should be getting back to normal anytime now. I just wanted to let you know that once you are, you are welcome to rejoin the Taai."

We make it to Course A and enter the room. John and I stand together and watch people run a course I have never seen before. They have to climb up a wall, swim through some sort of artificial rapids, carry a body dummy over their shoulders, and so much more that seems too physically painful and tiring for me to even consider.

"Thank you, Young," I tell him. "But no thank you. I like the job I have right now. It gives me more time to be home with Eric, who needs me a lot more than the team does."

John nods. "I can respect that." He smiles at me and pats me on the back. "Just remember, you can come back whenever you feel like it. Pending a few tests, of course." He winks at me and walks off into the room, observing his students.

"Young," I call out to him, catching his attention before he leaves. "I actually need to ask a favor. Eric is getting his new prosthetic today, and I was wondering if I could get off early to—"

"No problem," he interrupts. "You can get off after the course is clean."

"Thank you."

Why is he being so nice to me? I have never really liked John. I assumed the feeling was mutual with the way he treated me. But we seem to be okay now.

I would never show John that I don't like him. I would never show anyone that I don't like them. What good would that do anyway?

But I can't help it. I don't like John Young. Just speaking to him annoys me. The moment his voice hits my ears, I want to shoot myself.

Or him.

I will never let him know how much I don't like him. There are times I can tolerate him, but there will be times I can't.

When those times come, we will see what happens.

Mavis

I hold the back of the gun to my shoulder as tight as I can. I look down the barrel and line up the two small dots that this gun has for sights. I point the gun into the air and wait.

Wait.

Wait.

"Pull," I say to Derek.

He presses a button on a small controller the host of the hunt and owner of the lodge gave him. A bright orange clay skeet flies through the air from my right, and I swing the barrel of the gun over. Following its path for a moment to track its pace, I quickly aim a few seconds in front of it.

I pull the trigger, my shoulder is forced back, and the corner of the skeet cracks.

"Wow." Derek chuckles. "You hit it."

I can't help but turn to him with a scoff. "Why do you sound so surprised? I'm a good shot."

"Bows and guns are nothing alike."

I hand him the gun and take the controller. "Apparently they are."

"What are you doing? Here." He hands the gun back to me and reclaims the controller. "There are still four more shots in there. Don't be so eager to take my controller."

I roll my eyes at him and prepare myself for the rest of the skeets.

"Pull."

I shoot, missing the second skeet.

"Pull."

I shoot, barely hitting the third skeet.

"Pull."

I shoot, missing the fourth skeet. Without hesitating, I shoot my last shot and disintegrate the skeet just before it falls into the large valley of trees.

I put the gun on safety, not addressing the fact that I didn't before I handed it to him last time, and give it to Derek. "Your turn."

He nods and hesitantly hands me the controller. "Don't rapid fire on me again, okay?"

"I promise nothing."

We both practiced with another shotgun before practicing with this one. Our plan is to see which one suits each of us better and then use our favorite during the hunt.

Derek pulls his five bird shot shells out of his pocket and loads the gun. Within seconds, he brings it up to his shoulder and has it ready to shoot.

"Pull," he tells me.

I press the button labeled "right," and a skeet flies from the large wooden machine about twenty-five meters to our right.

Derek shoots and hits the skeet perfectly. It didn't disintegrate like my last shot, but it definitely did more than my first.

"Pull."

I press another button, and a skeet flies from another machine to our left.

Derek pulls the trigger and disintegrates this skeet even more than I thought possible. I see nothing but dust float from where it last felt the sun's touch.

"Pull."

"Pull."

"Pull."

Derek hits all but the last skeet, making me feel somewhat better about my skills.

"Four out of five isn't bad," he tells me, pulling out his earplugs.

"No. Not at all." I make my way back to the picnic table provided under the overhang and take a seat. "How much practice have you had at this?"

He follows my lead and sets the gun down on the table as he sits adjacent to me. He looks over to our other gun, propped up against the side of the overhang and looks back to me. "Some. Me and a bunch of others practiced for an hour or two in Bergland before we went to fight."

My jaw drops. "Only an hour?"

"Don't worry, they only gave guns to people who were actually good marksmen. Everyone else, they assigned a different job." He runs his hands through his hair, trying to get it out from in front of his face. "They actually offered me a spot in the special forces group. What was that called, the Tay? Or something—"

"Taai?" I ask.

"Yeah, that, but I couldn't complete the physical tasks necessary to be accepted."

I look down to his arm. It's covered by his jacket, but I can still picture the bloody bandage wrapped around it. Could he not be a part of the Taai because of what my dad did to him?

The old bus, parked up in front of the lodge, honks a joyful tune to let everyone know it is time to go. Derek and I rise, each with a shotgun, and head up to the bus. We watch as over fifteen old men in camouflage file onto the bus with their guns and backpacks filled with cases of ammunition.

Derek hands the controller to the lodge owner, who is standing by the bus and passing out boxes of ammo.

"Thank you very much, Mr. Page," he says as he slides the controller into his pocket. "What all do you need?"

He looks at me and shrugs. "Three boxes?"

The lodge owner nods and smiles. "Good choice." He hands me one box and Derek the other two. We slide them into our bags and file onto the bus.

The large men in puffy hunting jackets fill up almost all the seats toward the front, causing Derek and I to have to scoot through the small and tight-fitted bus to get to the back. Once we do, we share a bench and watch as all the men talk among themselves.

"So"—he leans over to me and whispers—"how many of these guys do you think are business owners?"

I look through the crowd and count nineteen people on the bus, including the two of us and the bus driver. I take a wild guess. "Thirteen."

Derek chuckles. "Once my boss gets onto the bus"—he points out the window to Mr. Gregory taking two boxes of ammo from the lodge owner—"you will be right. Apparently, Mr. Gregory rented out this party and invited his business associates. Everyone else on the bus besides the two of us had to pay a hefty fee to come."

"Why do you think he invited us?"

"A guess?" Derek tilts his head and squints. "Probably to try to make me not sue him for 'sexually harassing' my friend."

I snort, "What?"

"Yeah. I could have ruined him if I wanted. So could you."

I watch as Gregory gets onto the bus. He tilts his hat at the two of us and takes a seat in the front with one of his friends.

I shrug. "We are getting free meat out of this, so I'm okay."

Derek chuckles as the bus driver honks his cheerful horn once more. The doors close, and the bus squeaks and creaks as we take off. We ride the brakes down a steep hill, out of a fence gate, through some woods on a dirt path, and into a large open field with a wooden tower in the middle of it.

The wooden tower scares me by just looking at it. It has a rickety old set of wooden stairs spiraling up to the top, its entire foundation tilted, and the whole thing looking to be a previous meal to termites. It looks as if, with one kick, I could take out one of its four legs, causing the whole thing to come down.

We park directly beside it, and Mr. Gregory rises to his feet. Everybody else on the bus stays seated as Gregory addresses us. "Good morning, everyone! I am so happy that you all could make it today. We have just a few safety points we need to go over before you are given your partner. Okay? Okay."

He goes on to tell us that we will have bird dogs that will be running out into the field to retrieve whatever we shoot, so never shoot into the grass. He also tells us that there are a total of ten stands located around the field in a circular pattern. Each group will be at one stand per term, and there will be ten terms. The beginning of each term will be announced by a horn being blown five times. The changing of a term will be announced by that same horn being blown three times. Each change of a term, every team will need to shift one stand to their right. If the hunt for some reason needs to stop, there will be an announcement from the tower.

"So remember to listen. Okay, now that safety has been taken care of, let's get to the fun bits. There will be three trophy pheasants during today's hunt. The announcement of a trophy pheasant being thrown out will be one swift blow of the horn, so be listening. This trophy pheasant will have a purple tag around its foot. We will know who shot it because there will be a dog's keeper at every post to retrieve the birds. These keepers will be looking out for who shoots the trophies."

"What do we get if we shoot the trophies?" one of the men in the middle calls out.

"Give me a moment." Mr. Gregory holds his hands up to the man and scoffs playfully, earning laughter from everyone in the bus but Derek and me. "I was just about to get to that. Whoever shoots the trophy birds gets fifty dollars knocked off their bill for coming."

One of the men says something that I can't make out, earning another large sum of laughter from the bus. Mr. Gregory finishes up the instructions and lists who will be in each group. The group sizes range from one to three. Derek and I are paired together by ourselves, which make us both a little giddy, even though we were expecting it.

When everyone exits the bus, Gregory points them in the direction of their stand. When he gets to us, he doesn't say as much as I expected him to. "You two can head directly to my left and take the stand right there." He nods to us both once again and smiles. "Thank you for coming."

"Thank you for inviting us." Derek shakes the man's hand and heads back to our stand with me.

There is a small worn-down path within the large field of dried grass that comes up to my waist, but it isn't worn down enough that I can make my way through it easily. Once we finally get out of the grassy field, there is a large ring of dirt that paves the path for us to go to each stand after every term. It is much easier to walk on and through than the field, but it still somehow makes me question these people who set up the hunt.

After a few minutes, Derek and I stand behind the wooden pallet that is supposed to help us somehow and wait for the horn. We watch the black dog fidget with excitement as its keeper holds it by the collar and scratches it behind the ears.

"Good girl. Just wait a little longer," the man tells the dog.

Derek adjusts his grip on the gun and looks over the pallet. "How old is she?"

"Two years old next month."

"Oh wow." Derek gives him a small smile. "She is wonderfully trained."

"Thank you. I think so too." He gives her a treat and increases the rate at which he pets her. "Good girl." The brown-eyed black dog looks up at her owner and sits as calmly and still as she can, trying to earn another treat, but is interrupted as the hunt begins.

The horn blows three long blows, and Derek and I hold the shotguns up to our shoulders and aim at the tower. We watch as a pair of hands toss out a bird to our right. The feathered being squawks and flies in the opposite direction it was thrown. We lower our guns and listen to whoever is on the other side of the ring shoot repeatedly, only to miss the bird and watch it fly over them to freedom.

"This is what we're doing?" I ask Derek, "Shooting at birds that are flung off the top of a tower?"

"I didn't know."

The two of us stay at our stand, watching the birds get flung off in all directions, only to fly in whatever direction they please. Bird after bird, shot after shot, almost every bird thrown from that tower goes down.

"Don't worry," the dog keeper tells the two of us, "one will come this way."

Just as he says that, a bird is flung off the tower and flies our direction. Derek and I immediately aim the guns and wait for it to get into range.

Derek fires. He misses.

I fire. I miss.

We both shoot once more, and the bird goes down about ten yards in front of us. The sound of the bird hitting the ground is much louder than I originally expected.

The man beside us releases the dog, and it takes off into the field. I watch as the grass parts for the beast as she scurries around in circles looking for the bird. She emerges from the grass with the animal's living body in its mouth and brings it to her owner, who then grabs its head and spins it around until the body becomes lifeless.

Derek and I look at each other. A smile rises up on his face and he chuckles. "I got that one."

I can't help but scoff, "No way. I got that."

"Right," he sarcastically smirks. "You shot a second before me, and the bird went down when I shot, but you got it. Okay."

I nudge him in the arm as the tower throws another bird.

This hunt seems sick. They raise these birds to early adulthood just to throw them off a tower, forcing them to evade gunfire from every direction.

But I can't help but aim and shoot every time a bird comes our way. It is almost instinct.

Derek is enjoying himself. Every time he shoots something, a large smile finds its way onto his face, causing me to return the expression.

Whenever we change terms and arrive at our next stand, we see a pile of the dead pheasants beside the dog keeper. When we change to our third term, one of the pheasants in the pile stands out from the rest. Most of the birds are a mixture of browns and some white, but this bird is larger than the others and much more beautiful. Its entire body is covered in this sort of sheen. Its head is a deep purple, and his eyes are surrounded by red feathers. Directly beneath the purple is a set of bright white feathers, leading to more purple and beautiful auburn colors running down his chest. The feathers on his back have what looks like a yellow oval outlined by a dark brown, which pops out against the auburn, and his wings are almost a grayish teal color. Each and every feather on his back has a different pattern than his chest, and his chest has a different pattern than his wings, and yet they all go together beautifully. Even his tail, which is an array of different purples, blues, and browns, has a sort of sheen to it. Over all, this is the most gorgeous bird I have ever seen.

Derek nudges me as the round starts. "Hey, you may want to pay attention to the birds that are still flying."

"Don't worry about me," I tell him. "It's your aim you need to focus on."

"Right. Like I haven't been hitting every bird that comes our way."

"There have literally been eleven birds that have come our way. I hit seven of them. You hit three."

"No way." He snorts back at me. "Stop right there. You seem a little mixed up."

One horn sounds quickly, and the trophy bird is thrown in our direction. Almost immediately, the pheasant drops down to the ground and flies right into the grass. I watch as the dogs are released and they run through the grass, searching to scare the bird. When it finally jumps up to fly away, it flies in the opposite direction it was thrown.

No one shoots at first, not wanting the shot to get near the dogs, but after a few moments, all the guns on the opposite side of the field sound off. One shot after another, none take the bird down before it makes it into the tree line.

Just as we hear the horn sound off three times to signal the next term, I notice something above us circling.

"A hawk," the dog keeper of the next stand tells me as we arrive. "It's circling 'cause of the piles of birds. It attracts them."

"I see." I turn back to the toothless man with his small fluffy dog and nod. "Have you ever had any problem with them? The hawks?"

"Not yet I haven't."

I nod again and turn back toward the tower as the five blows of the horn echo through the air. Derek and I go through the hunt and hit every bird that comes in our direction. One after the other, I watch as the dogs bring the birds to their keepers to have their necks wrung.

We are at the last stand in the last term when I hear the dog keeper beside us call out, "George. What are you doing?" He rises to his feet and walks through the little patch of trees beside us and follows the dog. "George! Get back here."

Derek and I chuckle as another bird is thrown off the tower.

"It's coming our way," Derek says as he throws the gun up.

I follow his action and line my sights up, watching the bird soar right toward us, when something steps on my foot. My first guess by its weight is *it's a cat,* but the guess is quickly overridden by my thought, *It can't be a cat. A cat would be nowhere near this many gunshots.* My curiosity takes over, and I am shocked when I look down to see a terrified, young, and obviously wounded pheasant sitting on my right foot, cornered behind the stand.

"Derek." I nudge him as he sets his gun down. "What?" His eyes quickly fall down to my foot and he steps back in shock. "What?" He laughs. "Why, I mean, what happened?"

I set my gun down and hesitate. I have half of me who wants to pick the bird up, to get it off the ground and make it feel safe, but I also have the other half who doesn't want to touch it. Before I get a real chance to do anything, the dog keeper comes out of the trees, following his dog, and makes his way back to his seat, seeing the pheasant on my foot on the way. I look around to see "George" running around giddily, looking for the bird, and can't help but ask, "Is he still in training?"

The dog's keeper nods at me, reaches down, grabs the pheasant before I can say anything, and wrings its neck until its body becomes lifeless. "Sorry about that, ma'am."

I become speechless as the hunt comes to an end, and we are called in to come back to the bus. Derek squeezes my shoulder and pulls me a bit to try to get my attention away from the bird.

He came for help.

He had been raised with humans and came to me for help.

Only to have me let him be killed.

He came to me for help.

When we finally make it back to the lodge, it is late in the afternoon, and the lodge owner offers us all lunch. They serve it cafeteria-style and let everyone pick what they want. Derek and I both choose the foods we are most familiar with and pick a table to sit at by ourselves.

"You know what's funny?" Derek asks me, stabbing his meat with a fork and lifting it up to his mouth. "The fact that we just went pheasant hunting, and they are serving us beef."

I give him a chuckle and go back to eating. Once we are done eating, Derek and I clear our plates, put them in the sink they provide for us, and head to Mr. Gregory, who is speaking with the lodge owner.

"Mr. Page!" he calls out to Derek as we make our way over. "How did you two enjoy the hunt?"

I wouldn't call it much of a hunt.

"We enjoyed it a lot, sir," Derek tells him. "Thank you for inviting us."

"It was my pleasure." He waves us out, and we follow him away from the owner and out the front door. "You two are getting ready to go, I assume."

"Yes, sir," Derek answers him.

"Well then"—Gregory bends over and opens a cooler that sits up against the side of the entrance. He pulls out two bags of meat and hands them to us—"here you two go."

Derek opens his bag. "Is this—"

"Pheasant, yes. It's from a previous hunt. We prepare it this way so that everyone leaves with meat at the end of their hunt, whether they shot it or not."

I chuckle and look at Derek, but hold back my sarcastic comment.

Derek somehow telepathically gets my joke and rolls his eyes. "Shut up." He turns back to Gregory and shakes his hand one last time. "Thank you very much, Mr. Gregory. We enjoyed today, but we do have to get going."

"I understand, I understand." He pulls his hand away and opens the door back up for himself. "I will go call a cab for you two."

"Thank you," Derek tells him.

Mr. Gregory nods and heads inside. Derek and I take a seat in the decorative swinging bench and enjoy the slight warmth of the late winter months until our cab arrives.

Sam

Why does sheep poop look like this?

The first day I had to clean a stall and saw this poop, my first thought was, "What are these black beans doing in here?"

My question was shortly answered when I scared the sheep out of the stall and the poop fell from them as they ran.

If only I could get them to leave the stall now. For some reason, a few of the sheep will run from me, but others just assume I have food and scream at me until I scream back. At one point, Big Mamma, one of the oldest sheep of Mr. Gohaki's farm, and I had a screaming contest. She screamed at me for food over and over, and that day I couldn't take it anymore so I turned back to her and shouted in her face, "Bah!"

She quickly returned my shout with a loud and booming "Blah!" Her tongue extended out toward me as if it made her shout more powerful, so I did the same.

We went back and forth. That was the day a few of the sheep realized they shouldn't be scared of me. Now, I have to continuously run them out of the stall so I can clean it.

My scooping of the thick manure is interrupted as a bucket in the barn's hallway topples over, scaring me in the process. I look to my right through the hole in the horse stall where the horses' heads stick through to see Bram's head pop up. "Sammy boy!"

My shoulders relax and I roll my eyes. "Did you just trip over a bucket?"

"Nah, man." Bram throws his arms over the hole and leans against the wall. "Hey, you didn't tell me there was a bombshell working here."

"What?" I walk over to him and lean the shovel up against the wall. "What are you talking about?"

"You know what I mean. That girl?"

I look around the stall and out to Big Mamma. I can tell she is about to jump back into the stall, so I run over to her and spook her and her followers. The sound of all of their hoofs stomping and stampeding away is almost louder than Bram was with the bucket.

"Dude," Bram snorts, "what are you doing?"

I rise back to my standing position and realize how stupid I probably look. "Nothing," I tell him. "So what brings you by?"

"I was in the neighborhood. I have a meeting to get to in a bit and wanted to drop by."

"How'd you find me?"

He snorts again. "That girl that I was telling you about."

"I still don't know what you are talking about."

Bram rolls his eyes. "Whatever, dude." He clears his throat and smiles at me cockily. "I'm actually here with a proposition."

"Yeah?" I look back over to the sheep out in the paddock to make sure they aren't inching their way over.

"Yeah. I actually was going to offer you a job. You know, if you're up for it."

My head jerks back toward him. In surprise, I ask, "A job? What is it?" I need a job.

"A"—his head sways as he looks around—"salesman of sorts."

"Of sorts?"

"It's more a deliveryman. I make all the deals, and you meet the people."

A smile finds its way onto my face. "Oh yeah?"

"Yeah. The only real catch is that it, well, isn't something that needs to be made public."

"What?"

Bram looks around the barn and turns back to me. "Nobody is here, are they?"

I shake my head.

"Good. I trust you, Sammy. You and I have similar issues. We are both on the vial system, right?"

I nod.

"Right. So if I tell you my job, you won't tell anyone, right?"

"Well, it doesn't hurt anyone, right?"

"No way! In fact, it is the opposite."

I inhale and take in a floating piece of hay. I blow my nose out in disgusted and violent puffs and turn back to him. "What is it?"

"And you won't tell anybody?"

"No." I jolt back to the sheep as Elsa hops into the stall. I chase her out and turn back to Bram.

"I sell vials."

"Sell them? To who?"

"You know, to people who aren't prescribed the same dosage as we are or to people who can't get their hands on it at all."

I grab the shovel and continue to scoop the poop. "Isn't that illegal? Didn't we sign something when we got the vials, saying we wouldn't share them or give them out?"

"Well, think of it this way." Bram enters the stall and looks around. "You aren't sharing your vials, nor would you be giving them out. You are distributing vials that I have given you so you wouldn't be doing anything illegal."

I take in a deep breath and quickly realize it was a mistake. The poop smell gets three times worse when I hit a pocket of wet poop beneath the hardened surface.

Bram winces and exits the stall. Holding his shirt over his nose, he hands me a messenger. "Here," he says to me through the fabric, "it's good pay. Just consider it. Message my contact when you have an answer." The little clear plastic screen folds open and closed. When I open it, a small glowing keyboard pops up, along with a place to insert the number to message.

I need the money.

Mom needs the money.

"I will think about it," I tell him, sliding the messenger into my pocket.

"Message me if you decide you want to do it. I have to go. I will see you later." Still holding his shirt over his nose, Bram takes off out of the barn.

I pull the messenger out of my pocket and stare at its screen. I scroll through it and find only one contact listed: "Bram."

I need the money. If I don't pay the bills soon, they will double in size. I can't let that happen, and I can't let Mom find out.

I have to take this job.

It's not like Bram has a problem keeping his job a secret. I'm sure I could do the same.

After hours of working in the barn, I finally finish the stall and head home, covered in hay, wool, and bits of manure that had been floating through the barn. "Mom, I'm—"

I turn to the dining room table when I enter the house and find Mom looking at me with a smile, an older woman sitting beside her, and the girl from Bergland that I couldn't take my eyes off of. Her dark and silky hair looks even better in this light, and her eyes are so much more stunning up close.

". . . home?" I finish.

"Sam!" Mom rises to her feet and gestures to the two guests. "I'm so happy you're home! This is Carrol and her daughter Aspen."

Carrol rises to her feet and takes my hand. "Hi, Sam! Your mother has told me so much about you."

I give a nervous chuckle as I look at the three women, trying not to blush when I look at Aspen. "I hope they were all good things."

"Oh, they were," Aspen confirms with a smile. "All good things."

CHAPTER NINE

Logan

The air in the room that the physical therapists takes Eric and I to is much colder than I expect. I assume it is kept in this temperature because the patients will be working up a sweat. That is definitely Eric's case.

I watch as they slide his new leg on and realize it is much more of a robot leg than it is anything else.

"So as you know," the therapist tells Eric, "above-the-knee amputees have it worse than below-the-knee amputees, but this specific piece of prosthesis was made specifically for you and your needs. Okay?"

Eric nods, giving her a little smile.

"What I mean by that is we took your measurements so that this would fit perfectly and be able to hold you up just as your real leg did, but that isn't all this will do." She finishes strapping it onto his leg and rises to her feet. "This attaches itself to your nerves through the skin and reads your brain signals, just as your leg did before. Go ahead, lift up your leg."

Still sitting, Eric holds on to the arms of his chair and looks at his new limb. I stand across from him, watching, waiting, and hoping he will do it.

Slowly, but surely, he moves the foot. He lifts his foot up and down and looks at me with wide eyes. After he moves his foot, he slowly lifts the bottom portion of his leg to a completely lifted position.

"This is weird," he tells the therapist. "I'm not using any muscle, but it feels like I am, but at the same time, it feels like I'm not."

She chuckles. "I know. It will take some getting used to. Do you want to go ahead and try to stand?"

Eric nods and forces himself off the chair using the arms. He gets to a standing position, but it is obvious he hasn't put any weight on the new leg yet.

"It's okay," the therapist reassures him. "Go ahead."

He leans a little bit onto the new leg and doesn't fall. Looking down at the two different feet, he regains his normal standing position. "This is so weird."

"Yeah, I know," she reassures. "It will get better, but for now, isn't this great?"

He shrugs. "Can I walk?"

"Do you want to find out?" She looks over to two rails standing side by side that they use for people who are learning to walk again.

Eric nods, and the therapist goes to his side. She wraps her arm around him as he does to her, and they slowly make their way over to the rails. Though Eric is in pain, I can tell he somewhat enjoys her attention.

Once Eric gets between the poles, he grabs on to them and stands for a moment. He stares at the chair on the other end of his new obstacle course and takes a deep breath. One step with his new leg, and one half step with his real leg. His new leg gives out, and he falls onto the rails, shaking, holding on as if his life depends on it.

"It's okay, it's okay." The therapist makes her way to his side and places her hand on his back. "That's expected until you get used to it."

Eric, with his eyes squeezed closed and his whole upper body wrapped around the rails, nods. "I know." He forces his way back to his feet and takes a few more deep breaths. With his eyes still closed, he croaks out, "Logan, can you please leave?"

"What?" I ask him.

"Please?"

The therapist looks at me and nods. After a moment of taking one final look at Eric, I leave the room and head into the waiting room next door, where the atmosphere is completely different. In the room where Eric is working, it is slightly dim, and all the walls are painted a deep blue. It has a cold and darker feel to me, but this room? The lights are bright, the air-conditioning is even stronger than before, and the light-colored walls seem to reflect the light into my eyes.

I take a seat in one of the red foam-covered chairs and watch Eric through the door's window.

"Was it too hard to watch?" the woman behind the desk asks me.

"What?"

"Your friend. The one who is trying to walk. Was it too hard to watch?"

I shake my head and continue watching him through the window. "No. He just didn't want me in there with him."

"I can understand that," she tells me. "Don't take it too hard though. Everybody reacts differently."

I nod. "I just wish he would let me help, you know?"

"Pride is a dangerous thing." She stops her typing and looks at me. "Is he having trouble at home with pain?"

I nod again. "Yes."

"Well"—she gives me a sad smile—"sometimes a knife is really the best thing to turn to."

Mavis

When Derek and I get into the cab from the lodge, he tells the driver our address, and we watch her type it into the navigation system.

"Thank you," we tell her.

Almost immediately, the purple-haired woman turns around and gives me a curious look. We recognize each other at the same time, and she calls out to me with a squeal, "You're the flower girl!"

I chuckle and nod, slowly letting my hand find its way back onto my arm to scratch. "Yes, ma'am."

"Flower girl?" Derek asks us. "What are you talking about?"

The woman's smile grows as she turns almost completely around in her chair. "Your friend here is the sweetest little thing. Just the other day, she gave me some flowers from a bouquet that she was taking to someone."

"Oh really?" Derek asks her with a smirk on his face.

"To this day, it is my favorite ride that I have ever given."

"That's nice," Derek tells her. "Really cool."

The woman smiles back at us once more and turns back around. "Okay, off we go!"

The whole car ride, this woman tells the two of us about the other rides she has given and how rude they have been. She tells us that I am one of the only reasons that she keeps this job. "Well, that and the fact that I need money and don't know how to do much else."

When we finally make it home, we wave the driver, Laurie, goodbye.

"Bye, Derek! Bye, Mavis! I hope to get you two again sometime!"

"I hope so too." Derek waves her off, and we make our way over the bridge and through the woods, heading back home. I can feel the temperature dropping as the sun sets, and the shade of the trees consumes us.

"Well, she was nice." Derek chuckles.

"Yes. Yes, she was." I continue to scratch my arm, not wanting to stop.

"So who were the flowers for?"

"Sam's mom. That was the day I went to visit them at their new house."

"Ah. I see." We are hit by a gust of wind that makes it feel even colder than it really is. "I think the only time I appreciate cold weather like this is when we are carrying home frozen goods." He lifts the bag to indicate the individually packaged pheasant meat.

"Agreed," I tell him, "but considering this is the only time I have ever had to transport frozen meat, I don't think the cold weather is worth it."

I can tell we are getting closer to home by the smell of the smoke. One of the only things I find that I love about winter is the nonstop fire in the fireplace. I enjoy the smell of the smoke when it is from a distance like this. It reminds me of back when my mom was around. She always kept our fireplace stocked, so whenever Steven and I would come home, there would always be smoke coming out of the chimney.

Though there is something different about the smell of this smoke. It doesn't smell like dinner. It doesn't necessarily smell like the light and airy smoke I am used to either.

"Mavis." Derek nudges my arm as my eyes fall upon our house, glowing with the fire that is consuming it.

The two of us take off toward the house as fast as we can and find that the fire has covered half of the kitchen, but hasn't spread anywhere else.

"Go find Mom!" Derek shouts at me as he turns on the sink and uses a dirty cup to splash the fire.

The immediate blast of heat from the fire helps my fingers and nose, seemingly thawing them, but burns everything else. The smoke somehow blows into my eyes and blinds me as I speed through the house, shouting, "Ms. Page! Ms. Page!" But there is no answer. I go into her room and find her bed made. I run into Derek's room to find his bed the same, but neither of them have any sign of Ms. Page. As Derek continues to try to fight the fire that has spread all over the counters and into the cupboards, I break into the bathroom and find Ms. Page in the shower with the tub semifilled.

"What? What is happening? Why are you in here?" she shouts at me, grabbing a towel to wrap around herself.

"Come on! There's a fire! We have to get you out!"

I grab her by the arm and pull her out, past the kitchen and Derek, and outside into the cold. The feeling of her warm-water-covered body against the heat of the fire, followed by the abrasive cold outside of the house, shocks us both. Just as I get her out, she forces her way back inside. "No! My baby is in there!"

She stands in the living room soaking wet, watching Derek in horror. She tries to go over to him to help, but he shouts at her, "Get out! Go!"

"No! I'm not going!"

I watch them fight for a millisecond near the fire, but quickly sprint away from their bickering to run into the bathroom. I take a bucket from under the sink and fill it with the bathwater, grab a towel and stick it into the bucket, and run back into the kitchen. I throw the wet towel at Derek and dump the water onto the hanging cabinets, letting the water drench everything below it. Most of the fire is put out, except for some that is at the top of the cabinets. Derek throws the towel onto them and rubs it around, trying to get the fire to stop, and slowly succeeds before the ceiling catches fire.

After the fire is out, the three of us stand around, out of breath, looking at each other all in shock and at the counters, which are all black and charred now. Derek and I look back to Ms. Page, who is still dripping from her shower.

Following a moment of Ms. Page's and Derek's eyes locking, he heads over to her and gives her a hug. "I'm glad you are all right."

Shakily, she answers, "I'm glad you and Mavis are okay too."

"What happened?" Derek pulls away from her and heads back to the kitchen, looking around.

"I don't know," she tells us. "I was in the shower when this happened. Do you think one of you set a hot pot on a towel or something?"

Derek and I exchange a look. We know it was Ms. Page's fault. We were out all day, so she must have done something and forgot about it.

"I . . ." Derek rubs his forehead and winces. "I'm going to call the fire services to make sure this part of the house is safe." He lowers his hand and moves over to the wall phone. He dials the number, and Ms. Page adjusts her towel.

"I think I am going to go and finish my shower really quickly." She walks back to the bathroom, still shaky from this whole incident. "I'll be out shortly."

"Hey," Derek says into the phone, "I need to report a fire . . ."

I walk over to the counter and pick up the plate that Ms. Page always burns her apple cinnamon candles on.

With his eyes closed, Derek continues. "Um, yeah, everyone is okay, but I was told when I bought this house to call if anything like this happened."

I hold the plate up and show Derek, earning a look of pain. "Yeah," he tells them. "Okay. Okay. Thank you." He hangs up the phone and places his head against the wall. "Someone will be out in a bit to check and make sure the structure is fine."

I set the plate down and look around at the slightly singed ceiling. "I think it is."

"So do I," he says into the wall. After a moment, he turns around, and we both stare at the damage done.

I open up the cabinets carefully so as not to knock them down and find all the plastic dishes to be somewhat melted, but the metal ones to be fine. "Lucky for us, the fire didn't burn the cabinets with the food."

I turn back to Derek to see him still staring at the burned cabinets.

"It's time," he whispers.

I make my way over to the dining room table and sit.

He follows and takes a seat beside me. "What do you think?"

"I don't know." I take a deep breath and twiddle my thumbs.

"I'm going to have to quit my job and stay home with Mom or hire someone else to do it. We . . . I can't leave her by herself anymore."

"You wouldn't need to stay home. I can do it, no problem."

He looks over his shoulder and back to the kitchen. "I can't ask you to do that."

"You aren't asking, I am offering."

"No," he tells me, "you have a job you're enjoying. You're not quitting."

I lean back into my seat as he looks back to me. I can tell he is scared, I can tell he is worried, but I can also tell he won't ever let me quit my job to help his mother. "Hiring someone isn't necessarily the worst option. I can think of quite a few pros. Not very many cons."

"Well, I mean—"

I am interrupted by Ms. Page coming out into our view. "What?"

"Mom"—Derek rises to his feet—"why haven't you gotten back into the shower?"

Tears of rage well up in her eyes. "I was coming back out to the closet to get another towel." She becomes unable to form her words as her lower lip quivers. "Why would I need a babysitter? I am perfectly capable of taking care of myself!"

"Hey, Mom . . ." He steps closer to her. "It's okay. It's fine. We were—"

"The fire wasn't my fault!" She sniffles and growls at Derek. "If you are going to call me senile for something that wasn't even my fault, then I raised you wrong. That is my fault." Derek takes another step toward her, and she steps back. "No! I'm not losing it!"

"No, Mom, I was just suggesting getting some extra help around the house. Someone to keep you company since you aren't working anymore."

She sniffles back her terror and tries not to cry. "I know what that means."

The room is silent for a moment, except for the sound of Ms. Page's angered breathing.

Storming out of the living room, she snarls at Derek, "I hate you."

Derek and I remain frozen without saying another word. We listen to her sob in the bathroom, cursing Derek to hell, until the fire services show up.

Sam

With practice, most everything becomes easier.

This is one of those things.

We met in an alley, right behind a coffee shop. He came up, handed me the cash, and I gave him the case. The eight hundred dollars he gave me is broken up into fifties and twenties and held in an envelope.

According to Bram, I take him three-quarters of what I am given for the vials, and I can keep the rest. Before every deal, he gives me the vials that I'll be selling and tells me exactly how much the buyer should give me.

"If they don't give you the full amount, they don't get any vials," Bram told me.

I always count the money before giving them the vials. In order to keep them from stealing it from me before I can do anything about it, I hide the case wherever we are supposed to meet up. He gives me the money, I count it; and if it is enough, I tell him where the case is. Tonight's case was behind the garbage bins.

Just by doing that simple task, I made two hundred dollars in minutes. It is such an easy job. I never thought I would make this much money by doing something so easy. I will be able to pay off our bills in no time.

As I stroll through the city, looking for a cab, I admire the streetlights, the beautifully made stores, perfectly paved streets, and the white stringed lights that dangle above me, running from roof to roof across the streets. The city at night is somewhat of a dream, especially as the spring weather approaches.

I make my way down the sidewalk and catch a glimpse of something I can't tear my eyes from. I enter the boutique, allowing the vanilla-scented air fresheners to fill my nose with their scent, and try to look around, attempting to make my staring less obvious. My efforts are proven worthless as Aspen immediately sees me and strolls over.

"Hey, Sam."

"Hey, Aspen." I smile back, not really knowing what to say.

She chuckles and continues sorting through the dresses on display. "Are you trying to get out of the cold?"

"No. Are you?"

Stupid. She is looking for clothes.

"No." She moves over one section and looks at a long floral dress filled with pastel colors. "I'm here picking something out for my mom."

"Me too," I tell her.

She turns to me with a surprised smile. "Really?"

"Yeah," I lie. "I'm looking for a dress for her."

"That's so nice. Do you know what kind you are looking for?"

"No, not at all." I pull out one of the dresses closest to me. It's dark and long, made for the winter months. I grab the lower part of the dress to feel the fabric, when the bottom portion splits into two pieces, looking more like pants. "What?" I ask the dress, wondering if I broke it.

Aspen laughs. Not just a chuckle, she grabs her stomach and leans backward laughing. "That is what we call a jumpsuit. That's not a dress."

I nod. "I know." I hang the jacked-up dress back on its rack and walk around a bit more.

"How about this?" Aspen holds up another dress that is full length. "I think your mom would look nice in this."

Its purple coloring reminds me a bit too much of the lilies she is opposed to. "I don't think she likes that color. Do you see anything in an orange or yellow?"

Aspen looks around the room with an overly concentrated expression. "Yeah, I saw something earlier. Come with me."

I follow her around the store, looking at multiple different dresses, not really knowing what the best thing to get Mom would be.

The more I think about it, the more I do want to get something for my mom. She has been working hard. She has dealt with a lot lately. Why shouldn't I treat her? I have the money with me, and it's not like I need to pay off the bills by tomorrow.

Aspen and I continue to look around the store until she finds something that she can't tear her eyes away from.

"Here." She hands me the long-length light-blue and orange-patterned dress. "How about this? I really think that your mother would love this."

"Yeah?" I pull it away from my body for a moment to get a better look.

Running her hand down the pattern, she nods. "Yes. Definitely. I am one hundred percent sure that your mother will absolutely adore it."

"How do you know?"

"I'm just good at judging these sorts of things. Trust me." She folds it over her arm and gives me a little shrug. "And if worse comes to worse, she won't tell you she doesn't like it. She will wear it anyway because it was a gift from you."

I can't help but snort, "Oh yeah, right."

After we agree on my gift, I help her look around for her mom's gift.

And by help, I mean I watch her look around for her mom's gift, pull out random things, and get shot down kindly by the all-time best-looking person I have ever seen.

It is a great night.

CHAPTER TEN

Logan

One step, two steps, three. All on his own.

Eric's first unassisted steps since the incident cause everyone in the room to cheer. I watch as people stop their physical therapy and pause their conversations to turn to Eric and watch him continue to walk around the room. For the first time in a long time, Eric looks happy.

He goes through his whole session and does exercises with the leg. He stands on his toes, does a small squat, and for the final exercise, stands on the one new leg alone.

"Wonderful, Eric!" His therapist has him sit down so that she can make sure the leg is properly secured. "I think it would be okay for you to take the leg home today. Would that be okay with you?"

"Like wear it out?" Eric asks her.

"Yes. I think it would be best for you to go ahead and use it a while today. Just don't walk around too much. You have to give your thigh muscles time to adjust to being used again."

I take a few steps over to the two. "How much is too much?"

"I don't know. You probably don't want to walk around for any more than two miles today. With the physical therapy we've been doing, I do believe that your muscles are ready for activity, just not excessive. Okay?"

Eric and I nod.

"So you know how to take this off? Right?" she asks Eric.

He nods.

"Show me."

Eric looks down to the leg and unfastens the straps, unclips one clip, and slides it off the sock they have over his amputation.

"Good. Now put it back on."

Eric repeats the process he will be doing every day and fastens it on perfectly.

"Wonderful," she says. "I think we are done for today." She rises to her feet, just as Eric does, and shakes both of our hands. "Go ahead and enjoy your new limb, but don't run around too much, okay?"

Eric chuckles and agrees. The therapist leaves us both, and we walk out of the building side by side. We flag down a cab, get in normally, and have a quiet ride home. Eric watches out the window as we drive, but I can't tear my eyes away from his new leg. The bottom of his shorts covers where his amputation is and the new leg starts, leaving it looking like he has an entire robot leg. The foot is like something I have never seen. It is like a silicone mold of a foot without toes. With it being made of a clear material, I can see the metal joints within the foot. It looks just like the structure of a real foot.

When the driver pulls into our driveway, he turns around to us and gives a little smile. "So how'd you lose it?"

Eric turns to me then back to him. "An explosion."

"You two fought in the war?"

Eric nods.

"Well," the driver gives us both a small nod, "thank you for your service."

"Thank you," I say, holding my wrist out for him to scan the code.

"No." He turns back around in his seat and messes with the car's computer screen, accepting a cab call not but three minutes from here. "This ride is on me. Have a great day."

"Thank you, sir," Eric tells him as we exit the car. Seconds after the man disappears from our sight, Eric turns to me and gives a little smile. "Do you want to go for a walk?"

I can't help but return the expression. "Yeah. That sounds nice."

I watch Eric struggle to return to the same state of comfort with walking that he was back at the therapy session, but he doesn't give up. He takes it one step at a time, and soon, he is walking as well as I am.

We walk through the neighborhood, looking around at all the houses. The longer we walk, the more we see the houses spread out from one another. Down by our house, the houses are less than fifty meters away, but now, the distance seems much greater between buildings.

As we turn a corner that I've never explored before, covered in large and mighty trees that seem to have had no problem with the winter months, Eric says to me, "You know, this is the most I have ever walked outside without a gun in my hand."

My face immediately scrunches into an expression of disbelief. The expression fades just as quickly as it comes up when I realize he is right. "I'm sorry."

"Don't be. It's not your fault."

"I know, but I'm still sorry."

Eric's silent state returns, and we continue to walk until we stumble upon a small house by itself in the midst of all the trees. Its little driveway is lined with what looks like hundreds of gorgeous flowers in overflowing flowerbeds, along with many lining the road in front of it.

"I think we've walked a little too far." I chuckle.

"Yeah. It's been a little over a mile."

I turn around, taking one last look at this little cottage in the middle of all the trees. "Come on. Let's head back."

Eric freezes as his eyes rest on the flowerbeds as well. I can see he doesn't want to go, but I know he needs to before he wears himself out.

"My back is bothering me," I tell him. "I really think I need to sit down."

He looks at me and nods. Though my claim about my back is true, I really only pointed that out so that he wouldn't feel bad about the walk ending.

The two of us slowly, but surely, make it back to our house, and I am observing once again that this is one of the best walks I've had in a long time.

When we get home, Eric and I take a seat on the couch and relax. He takes his prosthetic off immediately and rubs the area that it was latched on to. After setting up the chessboard, I turn on the news, and we listen.

"There is speculation of a new bill being put into place to return the use of the one and done medicine that Lance Meir the First and his administration used. The rumors first started before the capture of Bloot, and have spread substantially since. Oswald told us last night in an interview that the medicine's formula has been perfected, but he wants to discuss things further with his administration before anything is put into place.

"He told the interviewer, 'Yes, this medicine can cure many mental disorders that most people wouldn't want to have to grow up with, but at the same time, who gives us the right to choose whether or not they get the medicine? Some of the things we will discuss and debate is at what age our citizens are allowed to take the medicine or if your parents can elect to have you take the medicine when you are born.'"

Eric and I listen to the reporters give quotes from different people, ranging from random citizens, to people working under Oswald. Neither of us say anything until the phone rings.

"I got it," I tell him, making my way to the wall phone. I pick up the piece of plastic and hold it to my ear. "Hello?"

"Logan!"

"Sam?"

"Yeah! Hey, is this a good time?"

I look over to Eric, who is purposely keeping his eyes averted from me. "Yeah, I guess so."

"Okay, good. This won't take long. I was wondering if you want to go to lunch with Mavis and me tomorrow."

"Really? Yeah, that sounds great."

"Perfect. Jones Cafe at twelve. Does that work for you?"

I shrug, still watching Eric stare off into the chessboard. "Yes, I think so."

"Sounds great. I will see you then."

"Okay. Bye." I hang up the phone and make my way back to Eric. We play the rest of the chess game, listening to the news and not saying a word.

When I get to Jones Cafe the following afternoon, I notice Sam and Mavis immediately. Sam jumps up and waves me over to their table, where the waitress is bringing three waters.

"Hey, Logan." Sam takes his seat and places a straw in his drink. "I didn't know what you wanted, so I assumed a water was okay."

"Yeah, it's great." I take a seat and look at them both. "Thank you for inviting me."

"Oh, it's no problem. I have been meaning to get us all together." Sam picks up his menu and looks it over. "Have you guys ever been here before?"

"No," Mavis answers. "Have you?"

Sam nods his head. "I come here at least once a week to pick up a sandwich. My mom and I split it. Their sandwiches are huge here, so unless you are planning on having leftovers, get a half sized."

I chuckle. "Point taken." I pick up the menu and look through it. It seems I have my work cut out for me. They have everything from sandwiches to steaks.

"So, Logan, I haven't really gotten to talk to you lately. What's going on?" Sam looks over to Mavis, then back to me. "Mavis tells me you are working in the Taai's training building?"

"Yeah." I have seen Mavis at least once a week since they got to Frieden, but this is only the second time I've seen Sam. "But I don't know how much longer I will be doing that."

"What?" Mavis asks.

"John asked me to rejoin the Taai yesterday, even though he was the one who told me to 'take it easy.'"

"John Young?" Sam asks. "This is your boss, right?"

I shrug. "You could say that."

"Are you going to?" Mavis closes her menu and sets it down on the table. "Do you want to?"

"I don't know. I don't think I will though."

"Why not," Sam asks me, taking a sip of his drink.

"Eric," I hesitate. "Eric needs me right now."

Sam takes a deep breath and sets his drink down. "I understand."

The table goes silent for a moment, allowing the waitress to come back over and take our order. After our order goes in, we continue to chat about anything and everything, except Eric.

"Yeah, I know, I was surprised too," Mavis tells us. "I didn't think I'd like being a news photographer."

"Well, why not? 'You look artistic,'" Sam mocks the career official Mavis was given.

"Yeah yeah, whatever."

The waitress brings our food out, and we all dig in. As I bite into the steak and cheese sandwich, my mouth fills with the siliva and amazing tastes. "This is the all-time best thing I have ever tasted," I tell them, taking another large bite.

Sam, with his mouth still full of fried bugels, chuckles. "That is my second-favorite sandwich to get here." He forces the large amount of food in his mouth down his throat. "My first favorite is chicken, steak, and extra cheese."

My eyes roll with delight as I take another bite. "Whatever, man. This is the best!"

"Don't knock it until you try it," Sam tells me, popping another bit of his bugels into his mouth. "What about you, Mavis? How do you like the chicken?"

Mavis continues cutting into her meat and sliding it into her mouth. She looks up and zones out. Only after a moment of silence does she look back to me and Sam. "What?"

"I take that as you like it," Sam says.

We continue eating and talking. Sam tells us both about how his mom's arm has been sore so she is keeping it in the sling, but how she is getting better. Mavis tells us that Derek's mom has been getting worse and even caught the house on fire, but that they were figuring out a plan for what to do.

"I told Derek that I'd stay home with her, but he doesn't want that for me. He told me that I found a job I am enjoying and should keep doing it."

"That makes sense," I tell her.

"I am with Derek on that one," Sam agrees, "but I also understand that you want to help." He drinks the rest of his water and brings his watch up into sight. His eyes quickly grow, and he jumps up from the table. "Okay, guys, we've been here for three hours. I really have to go." He pulls out cash from his pocket and tosses it onto the table. "Here, pay for mine and use whatever is left for yours. I will see you guys later." With that panicked frenzy, Sam takes off out of the restaurant.

I pick up the cash and count enough to pay for his meal and both of ours. "Well, I guess lunch is on Sam this time."

"I guess so." Mavis takes another sip of her drink and places it back on the table. "This has been fun. We need to do this again soon."

"I agree."

There is a silent pause where we listen to the groups of people around us speak and wait for something to say. When the idea pops in my head, I hesitate to say it.

"So . . ." I feel my hands get slightly clammy and immediately try to brush it off. "Mavis, are you going to be one of the photographers that covers the inauguration ball?"

"No. Not that I know of."

"Oh well, that's good. Eric and I were actually invited because we were a part of the Taai, and John told me I was allowed to bring someone."

"Really?" Mavis gives a nervous chuckle, and I watch as she slowly begins scratching around her wrist.

"Yeah. Do you want to go with me?"

She hesitates. Her lack of an immediate answer makes my heart drop and my stomach twist. I really hope I didn't ruin this.

"Yeah," Mavis answers. "Sure."

Mavis

I pay the cabdriver as we park in front of the little wooden bridge over our creek. "Thank you, sir," I tell him.

He nods to me and drives off, leaving me to walk home alone.

I enjoy being alone. I really do. It's not that I like being lonely, I just enjoy not having to humor others constantly. I also enjoy being able to think by myself without having to hold conversations with others.

Lunch today was great, and I hope the three of us can do it again. This wasn't one of the times that I had to really force myself to speak. With the guys, it just kind of happens.

I hope it will continue to happen. I hope that going to the inauguration ball with Logan won't make anything awkward. I hope that I don't embarrass him in front of all the important people he will get to meet. I can hear the whispers now.

"Look at that girl. She is so scrawny. She must have been from Bloot."

"How did she even get in here?"

"I bet you someone invited her just so she could come and get a meal. So sad."

Most of everybody in Frieden that came from Bergland had some sort of extra weight on them, whether it be muscle or fat. But me? I stood out like a sore thumb, and I doubt that anyone else from Bestellen will be attending the ball.

Another thing, what am I supposed to wear? What do you wear to the first ever inauguration ball of Frieden's first chancellor? My ratty clothes?

As I come up to the house, my eyes fall upon Derek speaking with a girl. From behind, she looks as if she could be twelve, but when she turns around, she looks about his age. Her blond curly locks stand out in comparison to our dark wooden porch, and her almost perfectly white skin makes her look plastic.

"Hey." Derek steps past the girl and introduces us. "This is Mavis, the girl I was telling you about. Mavis, this is Caitlyn Learwood. She is going to be Mom's new caregiver."

Caitlyn extends her hand to me and smiles. "Caitlyn Amanda Learwood, at your service. You can call me whatever you want, as long as it's nice." She winks at me as I shake her hand then turns back to Derek. "Well, it has been wonderful, but I have to go. I will see you two tomorrow." She flips her hair over her shoulder and struts off through the woods down our path.

I turn back to Derek and can't help but scoff. Scooting past him, I head inside to find that Ms. Page's candles have returned to their normal spots around the house.

"What?" Derek follows me in and closes the door. "What's wrong? Do you not like her?"

"It's nothing." I take a seat on the couch, cross my arms, close my eyes, and lean my head back onto the cushion, trying to force myself to relax.

"Nothing? You're practically fuming."

"I'm fine." *Maybe it's because you made a major decision about your mother without me.* I look away from him and stare at one of the candles sitting on the dining table.

"What is it? Come on." Derek comes around to the front of the couch and sits on the footrest. "Tell me or it'll bug you for the rest of the night."

"Fine." I sit up and look at him, mimicking the way he is stanced. "I am a little bit upset that you hired someone without telling me."

"What?" He scoffs. "I thought you'd be happy! Less work for you, whoopee."

"No." I rise to my feet. "I'm not happy. It's not that I have anything against 'Caitlyn Amanda Learwood,' it's just that I feel like I am entitled to help in the process of choosing who cares for your mom."

He rises to his feet and takes a few steps away. "Let's focus on those last two words. She is my mom. You aren't entitled to anything."

I take a deep breath, trying to cool my cheeks as they grow even hotter. "I didn't mean entitled, I just meant that—"

"We are letting you stay here with us, I am doing all the work to find her someone, I am the one suffering the pain of watching her widdle away, and you think that—"

"You're the one suffering? I understand that you're suffering, but you need to understand that I am too! She is the only mother figure in my life and has practically been my mother since I was a kid. You think I'm not suffering?"

"I didn't say that, I am just trying to point out that you aren't entitled to anything. She is not your—"

Derek is interrupted by Ms. Page entering the room hesitantly. "Is everything okay? You guys were getting a little loud."

I feel my shaky body grow even shakier as I try to calm myself.

Derek runs his hand through his hair and closes his eyes. "Yes, ma'am. We're good."

"Okay." She takes a few steps into the room and looks back and forth from Derek to me.

"I . . ." I take another deep breath. "I need to go out."

"Oh yeah? I will come with you. I need to go grocery shopping." Ms. Page walks past us both and grabs her jacket from the coat hanger. "Ready, honey?"

I nod and look back to Derek. I want to apologize, but at the same time, I don't. I didn't want to make him mad or hurt his feelings. I know he is in a sensitive state right now, but that gives him no excuse to treat me like I have done nothing but be a burden to this family.

"I'll call you guys a cab," he tells us.

Ms. Page and I head out of the house and down the cold brown path below the roof of empty tree branches. After getting to the road, we wait for the cab. When we get in, Ms. Page tells the driver, "Take us to the town please."

"Town?" I ask her. We always get our groceries from the farmers' market.

"Yes, town. I don't really need to go grocery shopping. I could tell something was wrong with you." She pats me on the knee as the driver takes off. "So what is it?"

I give her a little smile as I see a glimpse of the past return, a past where she was without this horrendous disease. "It's nothing."

"Come on. You can tell me. Did Derek do something? Though your voices were muffled, I could definitely tell you two were having an argument."

I pat her back on the knee and give her a little hug. "Thank you for caring, but really, I'm fine."

She pulls away and looks me in the eyes. One of her eyebrows rise as she lets out a little "All right. So is there anything you want to talk about?"

I shrug. "Nothing really."

"Oh yeah?"

"Well, I mean, the only thing new is that I was invited to go to Chancellor Oswald's inauguration ball."

"What?" both her and the driver exclaim.

She and I look at him with a goofy grin.

"Sorry, continue," he tells us.

"Yeah," I say. "Logan invited me."

"Logan?" she asks me.

"Yeah, you know, my friend who was part of the Taai."

She gives me a long and hard stare. After a moment, she fakes an "Oh right!"

I nod to her and chuckle. "That's pretty much it for me."

"What? That's it? Oh my goodness. You are no fun, not wanting to talk about anything."

We continue riding, and I listen to Ms. Page comment on everything we pass and explain how much she adores the city lights and buildings. When we get out, she hooks her arm in mine, and we stroll down the sidewalks, looking at the items the stores have on display. We pass discount clothing shops, fabric stores, cafes, and a few other shopping opportunities that we can afford; but once we get to the center of the city, things get pricey.

Ms. Page stops us in our tracks to look at the clothes in a store called "Kern Physic."

"Wow," I say, gazing upon the prices. "This is crazy." One of the most simple and yet fancy dresses I've ever seen is priced at over one thousand dollars. It is such a simple burgundy dress that I think even I could make it, and I've never sewn anything a day in my life.

"Do you like it?" Ms. Page asks me.

"Like what?"

"The dress." She points at the burgundy one. "You haven't pulled your eyes away from it since we stopped."

"Oh."

"So?" she reiterated. "Do you like it?"

"Does it matter?" I ask her. "It's way out of my price range."

Ms. Page looks back at the dress and stares. I give her a little pull at the elbow, and we continue walking as an odd smile rises on her face.

Sam

I never thought that I would go straight from lunch with two of my favorite people, straight into an alley, waiting on my client. When I arrive, my eyes immediately fall on a spray-painted portion of the brick walls.

"Respect Existence or Expect Resistance," it says.

The longer I allow those words to run through my brain, the more I realize how masterfully crafted the statement is. What made the artist say this? What has forced them into this sort of passion for respect? I stare at it for a few moments, admiring the skill it took to perfectly paint these words, just before I shake it off and look around. There's nowhere to hide the case, so I don't. I just hold it in my hand and watch my six-foot-something buyer come around the corner of the building, followed by another man taller than me too.

I was only expecting one.

"You got the vials?"

I shrug. "Do you have the money?"

He and his friend look down to the case I hold by my side and back up to me.

Yes, I have the vials. You know this. They know this. They see the vials.

I really should have hid them.

"I have five hundred," he tells me.

I can't help but scoff. "This case is twelve hundred."

"Come on, can't you help a guy out?" He takes a few steps toward me.

"No. You know Bram's rules. All or nothing."

He and his friend take another step forward. I reach for my pocket to type into the messenger our panic code, but as I move my hand, the two jump me. The friend of the buyer lunges forward and stabs me in the leg with a vial while the buyer shoves me as hard as he can and takes the case.

My body falls back, and I hit my hip on the ground, followed by my elbow. I tense up, trying not to let the medicine kick in before I can type in the panic code, but it's too late. I feel the relaxation flood over my anger and cause me to have that feeling of floating on a cloud that I so much enjoy. That feeling of lying on the ground comfortably, but at the same time, sinking into it, brings me peace.

I slowly, but surely, force myself to grab the messenger and type in our panic code, along with sending him my location. Within what feels like minutes, Bram shows up and helps me to sit upright.

"What happened?"

I look at him and try to figure out what to say that will not make me sound like the horrible dealer I am. "They hit me with a vial and stole the case."

"What? You let them steal the case?" Bram stands back up and paces. Back and forth, with his hands folded behind his head. "Did you not hide it like you usually do?"

I shake my head. "No. I got here too late."

"So you got here late, got yourself hurt, and lost me twelve hundred dollars' worth of vials." Bram looks me in the eyes and scoffs. "Tell me, did I make the wrong decision hiring you?"

I shake my head again, this time noticing blood on my elbow. "No, you didn't. I'll pay you back."

"Yeah. You will." After a moment of staring at me, he rolls his eyes and helps me to a standing position. "Come on."

Bram takes me out of the alley and we go to a tea shop right down the road. I head to the restroom to rinse off my elbow and find myself the center of attention. Everyone watches me as I walk past. When I make it to the restroom, I hold a paper towel onto my cut until it stops bleeding, then come out and take a seat with Bram at one of the tables. "Until you sober up enough to walk on your own without toppling, you're staying right here." Bram orders himself some earl gray tea and puts in a splash of milk. He takes his little teaspoon and stirs, staring at me. "Are you sure you don't want to order anything?"

I nod. "I've got to save up my money, remember?"

"I didn't mean you weren't allowed to buy anything until I'm paid. I'll just take it out of your cut every deal until your debt is gone." He takes a sip and smiles at me. "Try not to look like you just took a vial. Try to look a little more normal."

I roll my eyes as the thought comes back to me. "A functioning member of society." That's what I have to act like. I straighten my posture and nod. "So why'd you order that?"

"The earl gray?"

I nod again.

"Well, I've always been a fan of earl gray."

"And the milk?"

"No. I just recently tried it. One of the waitresses suggested it when she found out that this was Chancellor Oswald's favorite tea."

"Ah, sounds nice," I answer, trying to enjoy the rest of the medicine as it finishes wearing off.

We sit for a few more minutes in silence. I listen to the conversations around us, ranging from politics, to what "Margaret" told "Julie."

After regaining my sober self, I clear my throat. "Well, thank you very much, Bram." I rise to my feet and wipe off the dust from my pants. "I think I am good now. I am going to head home. Let me know when you have any other jobs for me."

"Oh, I will. They won't be as high paying as the last one, but I will definitely give you a call." He gives me a little smile and sips his tea. I nod back to him and leave the building, flagging down a cab in the process.

The driver takes me to Mr. Gohaki's house, and I walk home from there, which is about a two-mile trek. I walk and I walk, no longer enjoying the calm the medicine gave me. I walk and I walk, looking around in the dark to see if I am truly alone.

When I enter the house, I feel another sense of calm run over me. The darkness no longer surrounds me. I am no longer prey to whatever I was scared of outside. I am no longer the darkness's toy to fool around with.

The smell of a delicious meal of sorts sitting out on our counter hits my nose and further comforts me. I turn to see what looks like a casserole sitting on our counter with a few scoops taken out of it.

"Sam!" Mom comes around the corner and runs over to me, giving me a large hug. "Where were you? I was just about to start calling people to ask them if they had seen you."

"I'm fine, thank you for worrying though." I pull away and look her up and down. "That dress looks amazing on you. Where'd you get it?" I ask sarcastically, trying to shift her attention.

"Oh, this old thing? Just from the greatest son ever." She hits me in the arm with her good hand. "Except for when he leaves without telling me."

"Mom, I'm sorry. I'm back now though, and wondering what is that." I point to the pan on the counter, still releasing steam from its contents.

"That? Oh, that was just a little something that Carrol and Aspen brought over."

"They came over?"

"Yes, and they actually just left. See? See what you miss when you don't call?"

"Yeah yeah, I'm sorry. I will let you know before I leave from now on, okay?"

She narrows her eyes at me with a smile. "Okay. Now, go get you some food. It's late. I am going to go take a shower and head to bed. Good night."

"I love you," I tell her.

"I love you too."

I watch her leave and make my way over to the food. It smells delicious. I pick up the spoon that sits in the pan and grab a plate from the counter. I take a big scoop of it and watch the steam float off. Just before I plop the scoop onto my plate, I set the spoon back into the dish.

I'm not hungry.

I put my plate back into the cabinet and head back to my room. I sit on my messy bed with the pillows unaligned and my blankets laid out in disorder, and I stare at the corner of my vial case peeking out from behind my nightstand.

I have been good.

I haven't really needed them in a while, so I haven't really taken any other than the few times I've gotten angry and felt the need to calm myself.

Right now, I need to calm myself. I can feel myself getting shaky and spazzy. I need a vial to be able to go to sleep tonight.

I grab my case, punch in the code, and open it up. My case, lined with the clear tubes with the blue jell inside of it almost causes a euphoric feeling to rise up in me just by looking at them. I pull one out and close my case, sliding it back into its corner.

One more for today, and I will get to sleep.

CHAPTER ELEVEN

Logan

My alarm goes off, waking me for another day of work. I go through the morning routines of taking a shower, brushing my teeth, getting dressed, and doing whatever else I need to do, ignoring the slightly uneasy feeling of the house this early in the morning. As I make my way through the house and into the kitchen, something stops me in my tracks.

I look over to the couch to find Eric sitting there in silence. The hologram is off, the radio is off, and the chessboard is still set for a new game. Eric never wakes up this early. I never see him before early afternoon.

"Hey," I say to him.

He says nothing back.

"Are you okay?" I make my way around the couch to look at his face and find that his prosthetic leg is on, and he is just staring at it.

Eric slowly turns his head and looks at my feet. Silence fills the air between us as I wait for his response, which comes out slurred, as if he has been drinking. "Do you know what it's like to have an itch that you can't scratch?" He scrunches his face up and nods, still staring at my legs. "I'm sure you do." Bringing his hand up, he forms a motion with his fingers as if he is pinching the air and scrunches his shoulders up. "Take that little bit of discomfort you've felt, and multiply it by a million. Take that million, and multiply it even further. It's hard when you have a cast on the spot you want to scratch or something because the itch is covered. But having an itch in a place that is nonexistent?"

He looks up to me, then back down to his prosthetic. "It's not just itching. It's shooting pains. It's cramps. It's horrid feelings in limbs that aren't even there. How am I supposed to fix it?" Eric sniffles and chokes back tears, "How am I supposed to handle pain that isn't real? But trust me, Logan, it is real, I can feel it. I'm not crazy, it's there!"

"Hey, Eric," I interrupt his rant, "no one ever called you crazy."

He whimpers, trying to keep his tears in. "There's no peace. Just when I think I'm okay, something else happens."

I take a deep breath and head into the kitchen, pulling a knife out of its block. The sound of it unsheathing grabs Eric's attention, startling him somewhat.

"What are you doing?" he asks me as I take a seat beside him.

"Look." I lift the lower half of his prosthetic up and feel the silicone-like jell covering around the metal bones. I plunge the knife into the silicone, causing Eric to panic.

"Stop!" He tries to pull away, but I pull away first. We both watch as the thick substance that surrounds the metal heals itself, causing it to look as if there was no cut in the first place.

I hand Eric the knife. "One of the women at the physical therapists told me that she knows what it feels like. She showed me a similar prosthetic to the one you have, but it's for her hand. She told me that the phantom pains for her would get so bad that she wanted to kill herself."

Eric runs his hand down the mold of his calf.

"She told me that one of the ways her therapist helped her deal with her phantom pains was by sticking a knife into the area where it hurt. It shows the brain that the body part isn't there, that this is a fake, and that the pains are all in your subconscious." I take the knife back and slide it down the mold, putting one long cut into it, and watch as it fixes itself and returns to its original position. "This was made to be able to take the damage. It was made to be cut so that you can deal with phantom pains."

Eric takes the knife, adjusts his grip, and looks at his foot. He slowly slides the knife in between the toe gears and plunges the knife all the way through. He lifts his leg and stares at the knife as it sits inside his metal foot. He pulls it out and sets the knife down on the table with tears in his eyes.

I get up and head out of the house, knowing that Eric doesn't want me to see him like this.

Mavis

I slide in our tray over the fire and place the pan on top. As the meat slowly cooks, I stir it, flip it, and move it around to make sure all the sides are cooked evenly. This is the first night this week that I've gotten to make dinner for Derek, Ms. Page, and myself.

Derek should be coming home from work soon. He got the three of us messengers a day or two ago so that we can keep in contact in case something were to happen or if plans change. He messaged us just a few minutes ago saying he is on his way home from work, which let me know it was time to start dinner.

Derek and I haven't really spoken since the fight last night. That message was the first thing he has technically said to me since. We passed by each other this morning, but all we exchanged was a glance. He left as soon as Caitlyn came in.

She entered the house, set her backpack down on the table, and gave me a quick smile and a "good morning."

I told her good morning back, and she began a happy little babble. "I am so happy that we were introduced yesterday. Wouldn't it have been awkward if you were to wake up and I was just sitting in your living room?"

Caitlyn continued for a while with what I assume was nervous babbling. She isn't too bad. Actually, I kind of like her. After I left for work, she and Ms. Page hung out all day, and when I got home, Caitlyn left immediately, not wanting to intrude.

Derek made a good choice hiring her. Ms. Page likes her too, though she doesn't know she is her senior sitter; she just thinks that Caitlyn is a house cleaner.

When Derek enters the house, his eyes fall upon me at the fire, just as my eyes fall upon him. After a moment, he hangs up his jacket, pulling out a little box. "So what's for dinner?"

"Pheasant." I continue stirring and throw in some diced parsle, a superfood from Bergland.

He nods and sits by the dining room table. "Sounds good."

What feels like minutes of silence pass before he speaks up again. "I'm sorry about yesterday."

I turn back to him. "Me too."

"Okay." He spins the little box around and looks at all of its sides. "I just didn't want to worry you. I didn't want you to pay for care or anything either."

"Derek." I turn to him, leaving the pan unattended for a moment as the meat soaks in the juice. Before I can continue, Ms. Page comes out of her room with a halfway-finished gown that looks eerily similar to the one we saw last night.

"Look at this, Mavis!" She holds it up to herself then looks over to Derek. "Hi, Derek. Look at this. I'm happy to see that I haven't completely lost my touch."

"Is . . . is that the—" I look from her to Derek then back to her. "What are you doing?"

"It's that dress! The one from last night! Caitlyn took me out to town today and I got some fabrics and tools to make this."

"What's the dress for?" Derek asks us.

"Mavis was invited to the inauguration ball next week!" Ms. Page tells him. "Isn't it great?"

He looks from his mom to me. "You were invited?"

I nod. Before I can say anything, Ms. Page interrupts again, "By her friend Lucas."

"Logan," I correct her.

"Right. Logan." She chuckles.

Derek rises from the table. "Got it." He leaves with the little box and heads to his room.

Sam

All over the news.

Nonstop.

"People are arriving from all over the country just to wait outside of the capitol building!"

"They've pulled out all the stops."

"This is the biggest event of the year, possibly of the century!"

Everything is about the inauguration ball. It has been for the past week, but now that the day has come, it is getting really annoying. Even the bank has the news up on the holograms.

I come in and make my way up to the woman to pay my bills in cash. Now that I have paid Bram back, I am able to return my focus to our debt. Though I only have two hundred in cash at the moment, every bit counts.

"Well, Mr. Beckman, are you sure that you are wanting to pay this toward your mother's bills and not your own?"

"My own?" I ask her. "What are you talking about?"

"It says here that you purchased a new case of vials two days ago."

"Yeah, but I thought that medicine was free because, you know, I need it."

"Well, back in Bergland it was, but there are some new guidelines."

"How much is one case of vials?"

She prints off a sheet of paper that outlines the prices and lists everything I have to pay. My stomach drops as I read it and realize how much I owe. I'm going to have to talk to Bram and get some more deals.

The money my mother and I make on the farm is just enough to buy us food, pay our utilities, and pay for cab rides. The small amount I have left over from that I spend paying off the bills.

I thank the woman and head home. On my way out, I find that the cabdriver is one of the ball fanatics. The entire way home, he speaks about how excited he is just to see who will come. When he finally drops me off at Mr. Gohaki's house, I am relieved.

I take my time on my two-mile walk back home and feel the beginning of spring blowing in the air. I can almost smell the warmth coming closer.

As I come up on my house, I find there to be two first-responder vans outside, Carrol sobbing into Aspen's arms beside the vans, and someone being rolled out of my house on a stretcher, covered by a white sheet.

CHAPTER TWELVE

Mavis

I finish sliding the dress on and stand for a moment. The fabric feels just like how I pictured expensive clothes would feel.

"Oh my. Mavis, you look lovely!" Ms. Page has me sit down and plays with my hair, fixing it into a fancy updo. "You're going to be the best-looking person in the entire building."

I snort, "Yeah, okay."

She grins as she continues pinning my hair up into braids. Derek knocks on her bedroom door and enters hesitantly. "Hey."

I smile back. "Hey."

After a moment or two of silence between us, Ms. Page chimes in as well. "Hi."

Derek comes in and holds out the box that he brought in last week when Ms. Page first showed us the dress. "Here." He hands me the small one and hands his mom a similar box. "These are for the ball."

I open the little box to see pheasant feather earrings. The feathers dangle from a clamp that is to attach to the top of my ears from a gold chain.

"So I got these for you the other day because I know you like pheasant feathers." Derek points at the decorative pheasant feather hair clips that Ms. Page pulls out of her box. "And I got those once I found out that you were going to the ball. The woman who sold them to me said that they are 'one of the most popular fashion items there is.'"

"These are lovely!" Ms. Page places the hairpins in my hair and takes the earrings from my hands. "I think you're going to look amazing, Mavis." She hooks the clamps onto my ear and takes a step back. "I am partially to blame for that."

Derek chuckles as I rise to my feet. "You do look great, Mavis."

I have the overwhelming urge to scratch my arm, fiddle with my fingers, or just leave, but I don't. "I feel way too overdressed," I tell them.

I don't think I want to go anymore.

"What are you talking about?" Ms. Page places her hands on her hips and smiles. "This is the first chancellor of Frieden's inauguration ball! If anything, you're underdressed."

Derek elbows her. "Not helping."

I don't feel like myself; I don't want people to look at me. And the strapless dress forces my arms to be exposed, showing off the scars on my skin from my scratching, along with the marks from other incidents.

The knocking at the front door stops me from speaking before I tell them I don't want to go. Derek exits the bedroom immediately and moves to answer the door.

He opens it up to reveal Logan wearing a perfectly fitted suit with some sort of armored chest plate underneath the jacket. It doesn't seem to look as if it is for protection, but more fit to make him look stronger than usual.

I step out as Derek and Logan look at each other.

"Hi, you must be Derek." Logan and Derek shake hands awkwardly. "I'm Logan."

"Logan!" Ms. Page rushes over and shakes his hand. "I'm Derek's mother, as well as Mavis's in my opinion. It's so nice to finally meet you!"

Logan chuckles. "It's nice to finally meet you too. I have heard a lot about you both." He looks past them and to me. "Mavis, you look great."

Looking at Logan's attire, I suddenly feel underdressed. "Thank you. You do too," I tell him.

He smiles. "Um . . ." He points over his shoulder to the darkness. "Eric is in the car. We are riding with him, if that's okay."

I nod. "Yeah." He and I head out as Derek stares, and Ms. Page waves us goodbye.

We walk through the woods, over the wooden bridge, and into the black van. When Logan opens the door for me, I see Eric sitting across from the opening, wearing a similar suit as Logan, but with a long thick red cape. The collar of the cape buttons up around his neck, seemingly keeping him warm like a jacket.

I slide into the fancy cab and greet Eric. "Hello."

"Hi. It's nice to see you again."

"You too," I say as Logan slides in beside me. The driver promptly takes off, and we begin our trip to the ball. "So how much did it cost to rent this car?"

"Oh, don't worry about it," Logan tells me. "John went all out for us. He paid for this car and bought us these clothes for the ball."

"Ah," I say, "that makes sense."

"Yeah, you think I chose to wear this cape?" Eric takes part of his cape and pulls it over his lap. "I doubt this thing cost less than two hundred dollars. I wouldn't spend that much on something I would only be wearing one night."

"I agree," I tell them. "Derek's mom made this for me when she heard that I was invited to come. Thanks again, Logan." I nudge him in the arm.

"No problem," Logan answers.

"So, Eric," I say, "how are you doing? Logan said that you've gotten a prosthetic limb."

"Yeah." He pulls up his pants leg to show his fake calf. "I've almost mastered the art of walking with the new leg. But"—he lifts up a wooden cane from beside him—"I brought this in case I would be needing it at any point tonight."

We continue to chat for about thirty minutes or so. As we near the capitol building, we notice that the streets are packed. Our windows are tinted so that we can see out of them, but the outside can't see in.

"Wow," Logan scoffs. "It is crazy how many people show up just to watch and see who enters the capitol building."

We continue through the crowds, through the traffic, and down the road. The driver shows one of the gate guards our tickets, and we drive into the high posted fence. We go down the driveway, and he stops in the roundabout. The three of us exit, and a photographer snaps our photo. Once we get out of the car, the driver takes off, and we walk farther down the path, past large and luscious gardens, fountains that are being lit up by lights, and speakers that are sounding the music from what I assume is the live band inside.

We pass what feels like hundreds of people, most of whom are wearing some sort of decorative armor. Almost every person we pass holds a small dish in one hand along with a colorful drink in another hand.

When we finally make it down the gorgeous pathway and up a few stairs, guards at the door scan our wrists and take out tickets. We enter the building, and I look around to see people chatting in their gorgeous clothing that look too expensive to even breathe on, beautiful paintings hanging on the walls, and servers walking around the building, offering people whatever is on their trays.

"Rollen Crou?" a server asks us, holding the tray in front of our faces. He smiles at each one of us. "It is truly delicious and absolutely my favorite food being served here tonight."

Eric gives a small smirk and takes a piece of the small blue bread-looking food. "Thank you."

"Do you know where exactly we are supposed to go?" Logan asks the server. "We just got here."

"The ballroom is down the hall and to the left," he tells us.

Eric swipes another piece of the food and begins walking. "Thank you again."

We follow Eric and head down the decorative carpets and follow the sound of the music and laughter to find an even larger room. On one end, two sets of stairs lead up to where the band plays, and directly underneath the band is the bar, where many people have settled. On the other side of the room, there is a step from the hardwood dance floor up to tables of desserts and other goodies. The ledge that the band is on circles around the entire ballroom, allowing people to make their way to a raised glass room on the other side of the walkway. This glass room seems to be for the most important people of the night and the most important people only.

I look around to find that almost all the people here are wearing some sort of metal armor that looks to be purely for decoration. One woman is wearing a dress, similar to mine, but with a decorative bronze vest under her chest and on her stomach that fits much like a corset. The woman she is speaking with wears a blue and flowing gown with nothing on it, but wears some sort of silver-studded gauntlet that only covers the top part of her hand and arm up to her elbow, along with a silver-armored shoulder pad on that arm. Many of the men have some sort of armored boots, armored gauntlets much like the woman's, or armored shoulder pads as well.

As I walk through the crowd with Logan and Eric, I feel eyes being cast upon me as they judge. Suddenly, I am very aware of my hair being tied up and a lot of my skin showing. Without the armor that everyone seems to possess, I somehow feel naked.

The three of us stop once we take a step off the dance floor. We stand around, being passed by dozens of servers, when one of them stops by us and holds out his tray. He pronounces a word that I can't even understand, and each of us take one. The waiter nods to us and scurries off, feeding the rest of the guests. Logan gives the small pink piece of fluff a smirk before taking a bite.

"Wow, this is actually really good." He pops the rest of the small dish into his mouth and chews. Eric and I follow his lead and enjoy the sugary softness that was the random snack.

"You know," I say to them as I swallow the last bite of the fluff, "if this is what it is going to be like in Frieden, I can't wait."

"You mean servers everywhere you look?" Eric looks around sarcastically. "I doubt this will be outside of the capitol building."

"No, I mean, just having food. Back in Bloot, there was barely any food to go around. So far, under Bergland and now Frieden's reign, I haven't been forced to go a day without food."

Logan and Eric look at each other. They give an awkward smile as they nod.

"Sorry, I didn't mean to bum you guys out."

"No." Logan chuckles. "No, you didn't bum us out, it's just—"

Everyone in the room cheers and claps, causing our attention to shift to the raised stage where the band is. A man that I don't recognize, but is obviously important, walks over to the microphone, silencing the band.

"All right, all right." He motions his hands to get everyone to simmer down. "Thank you, thank you. Before we get started, let's give it up for the band!"

Everyone in the room, including us three, claps. The string players, along with the trumpet and trombone players, give the room a real jazzy feeling, even when they aren't playing.

"Okay, so I'd like to thank you all for joining us this evening to celebrate the coming of a new age. A new time of prosperity and hope for the future. Please help me in welcoming tonight's star and Frieden's first ever chancellor, Thomas Ronan Oswald."

The entire room goes crazy. Everyone claps, but some take their liberty to scream and shout for him. When he finally gets up there, flashing his fancy armored epaulets and cape, he has this smile on that you can tell he can't hold back. It's one of appreciation, and yet embarrassment.

He stands at the microphone and gestures for everyone to calm down, but the ball reminds me of a rowdy classroom in the way that there are a select few who won't stay quiet. "Thank you. Thank you. I really appreciate the love, but it's just too much for me. Now, if you want to spread it around to all the faculty and the workers, then please do so because I would be nothing without them." He raises his hands and claps, gesturing at his administration, his advisors, and the heads of departments. "Thank you so very much for all you do, and I know that with your dedication, we will make the best society we can. Now, I am not saying we will be a utopia. I know that claiming so would be unrealistic, but let me tell you all something. We will try." A few of the people begin to clap. "We will try our best and work our hardest to achieve that goal of prosperity." Everyone in the room begins to clap, so I join in too.

Oswald waits until everyone dies down again to pick up. He continues speaking of his goals and how it will not only be his doings, but also of his entire staff. He makes sure that we understand he is not the sole owner of the power that many assume he is, but that we all know he is thankful nonetheless for being allowed to govern in that position. As he continues his speech, a server walks between Eric, Logan, and me, throwing me into Logan.

His hand falls into mine, just as mine does his. Once the server passes, neither one of us look at the other, nor do we pull our hands apart. We stand rather awkwardly, I might add, and wait until Oswald's speech comes to an end to separate and clap.

The band starts back up with its music, and the entire room returns to life with excited chatter, wonderful laughter, and drunken jokes.

"Well, well," John Young comes over to the three of us and looks me up and down. "Ms. Wamsley, you look stunning." He turns to Logan and gives a little smirk. "You, on the other hand, could use a bit of cleanup." Logan and Eric exchange a look. Just before Logan says anything, John gives a little chuckle to go with his smirk. "Kidding. It was just a joke." He turns back to Eric. "You three really look wonderful."

Eric nods. "Thank you very much for everything, John."

"Well"—he looks at me then to Logan—"it was my pleasure. I had to make sure that my two best soldiers looked their best, right?"

"Young!" a voice calls out from behind us.

The four of us look back over to the dance floor to find a small group of people with Oswald in a huddle formation. General Wilson is looking over the group and waving John over to join.

John nods to Wilson and looks at me. "Mavis, may I borrow these two for just a moment?"

I look at the three of them and give a nervous shrug. "I guess so." If I were to say no, what would happen? Would they miss getting to meet Oswald? I don't want to be left alone, but I can't hold them back.

"Thank you." John takes my hand and brings it up to his face, as if he was going to kiss it, but my facial expression changed his mind. The three Taai members walk off to the group and join in. Immediately, I see Oswald turn to them and welcome them with open arms.

I look around the room and try to brush off the feeling that everyone is looking at the unarmored girl with ridiculous feathers in her hair. Even though many people here have some sort of hair decoration with feathers, metal, or some sort of pin, I still feel as if I don't belong. I feel like they think I am a cheap knockoff of their style.

As I continue to look around the room for someone I may know, a drunk woman stumbles over to me and hooks her arm into mine. "How are you doing, doll face?"

I look at her to see an older woman with a full head of silver hair, pinned into an updo similar to mine. Her dress is a little blue one that is tight around her waist, and the bottom of it is short in the front but long in the back. Her silver hair is the only thing close to a decorative metal that she wears, leaving me to think she didn't get the memo either.

"I'm okay, I guess. How about you?" I say to her.

"Fabulous actually." She takes another sip of her colorful drink. "There is an open bar."

"Yeah? Do they taste good?"

She gives the drink an odd look and shrugs. "I don't know. I haven't been able to taste in years."

I can't help but chuckle. Her drink does looks appetizing, but I decide to brush off the desire to find out what it tastes like. "So you haven't had any of those desserts over there?" I point to the dessert table a few yards away from us. "I was thinking of getting some, but I didn't know what to try."

"What?" She pulls her head back from me and gives me a look. "You can get them?"

"I guess so."

"Really?" She continues to look me over. "Where is your armor?"

I follow her gaze down to my attire. "Armor? I'm not wearing any."

"Is there a reason for that?" Licking her lips, she gives me a curious look.

"What do you mean?"

She turns us around to the dessert table and points at a couple with the armor on as they have their codes scanned. "Look. Only certain fancy people can have the desserts at the table. Everyone else can have what the servers are serving"—she takes another sip— "but unless you are someone important, no desserts for you."

"Really?"

"Yup. I found out the hard way." She takes a large swig of the rest of her drink. "The Taai and all military who are currently employed are only supposed to eat health food and certain other things while the delicacies are only for the highest of high people." She looks at me and smiles. "And you know what, I'm okay with that because you know why? A moment on the lips, a decade on the hips." She sets her empty glass down on one of the server's trays as he walks by and picks up another drink. She takes a sip of the pink liquid and smiles at me. "I'm just happy that the drinks are free."

I smile back at her. "Did you come with someone, or are you on your own?"

"Are you kidding? Me? On my own?" She takes a step back and gestures to her body. "Do you see any armor? No, you don't. You just see the perfect body of a goddess in disguise."

I chuckle again. "What is with the armor anyway? Why are certain people wearing it and other people aren't?"

"Well, the thing is, if you are part of the administration or high-ranking military members, you are to wear the armor to show your 'superiority' to others." She continues to sip at her drink and look around. "I don't really know why. I'm just telling you what my boyfriend told me."

"Your boyfriend?" I ask her.

She points over to the corner of the room to an older man with a beer belly and a clunky gauntlet speaking to other beer-bellied men. "That's him." She nudges me in the side. "I'm his arm candy." She gives me a little side eye and smiles. "Whose guest are you?"

I turn around and point to Logan.

"The dork in the cape?" the drunk woman asks me.

"No." I adjust her head to look one person over. "Him."

"Ah, him." She looks back to me and wiggles her eyebrows. She takes another sip of her drink, never taking her eyes off Logan. "God did an excellent job with that one."

"Celeste!" her boyfriend calls out, waving her over to him.

Her smile grows, and she squeaks out a happy little "It was nice talking to you, sweetie." She tickles my shoulder and scurries off to the men, leaving me awkwardly standing by myself once again. I look around the room, this time with slightly more desperation, and find Janice in the midst of it all, walking my direction.

I immediately make my way over and walk directly toward her. It is not until I almost run into her that she recognizes me. "Mavis?"

I pause and give her a confused look. "Janice?"

"Mavis!" She wraps her arms around me, and her fancy knuckle guard sends chills down my spine the second its cool surface touches my skin. "I'm so sorry. I didn't recognize you with your hair up like this." She touches the feather pins in my hair. "And in this beautiful gown. My goodness, you look so wonderful!"

"You do too," I tell her, glancing down at her emerald dress. "I've never seen you this dressed up, I am almost shocked."

"I know. Me too." She chuckles and waves me over so we can get out of the way of the servers. "Can I tell you something?"

I nod.

"When I was a little girl, I always dreamed of this sort of moment. I wanted to go to a ball and dress up and be someone important. But now?" She looks around the room and sighs. "I just want to go home and go to sleep. I am exhausted."

I chuckle. "I'm sorry. Do you have to stay the whole night?"

A large eruption of laughter comes from Oswald's huddle. Logan, John, Eric, and the others are being surrounded by fangirls who wear no armor, just like myself. They hold little colorful drinks in their hands and try to play as if they are a part of the group.

"No," Janice answers. "I don't have to, but at the same time, I kind of need to. You know?"

"I understand. Well, I would be happy to stay with you as long as you need so that you don't have to go be with the snooty people." I chuckle as one of the women standing at a table near us looks over to me with a judgmental glare.

"That sounds nice." Janice follows my gaze over her shoulder to find the woman glaring. "Let's move somewhere else."

Janice and I speak for the next hour or two, and she introduces me to many of her coworkers, along with their spouses. The entire time we stay together, I couldn't help but continue to glance over to Logan's crowd. He, as well as Oswald, has been entrapped by the girls and new crowd members. I watch as every time they try to leave, Wilson pulls them back in and introduces them to someone new.

I stand around with Janice and talk for what feels like hours until she pulls us over into a booth. The two of us then sit and enjoy the company of Emily Hash and her sister Taylor Hash.

"So, Mavis, how are you doing?" Emily asks me. "I never really got to speak with you after that first day you moved in."

"I'm doing okay. I'm doing better now that we are out of the mountain."

"I think everyone is," Taylor tells us. "I have heard nonstop praise of the air outside, the actual sunlight, and the room. Yeah, some people miss the mountains, but those people can choose to work inside instead of outside."

Janice nods and takes a sip of her water. "I agree. Bergland was a terrific temporary home for us, but we aren't made to live inside like that."

"Can you imagine how horrible it would have been if we had not had those lights in Bergland to prepare us for the sun?" Taylor snorts. "I already wear a lot of sunscreen and still get a little burned. I can't fathom how bad it would be if we were to come out of Bergland with our skin having never felt some sort of UV rays."

I chuckle at the thought. "Has there been any consideration given to letting people visit Bergland again?" I ask.

Emily and Janice look at each other, as if telepathically connecting.

"Is that a no?" I ask.

"It's not a no," Emily tells me. "It has been thought about, but . . ."

"But," Janice takes over, "if we were to have left Bergland open, it would be a good place for radicals to hide."

"'If you were to have left it open?' You mean you guys closed it?" I ask them.

"That has been the plan this entire time," Janice tells me.

Taylor looks at me with a goofy smirk. "They did it the day everyone made it out."

"What?" I exclaim, "Really? Why didn't anyone tell me?"

"It was on the news." Emily takes a swig of her water. "But it wasn't really the talk of the town, being that most everyone was excited to be outside for the first time."

I look down at the table in shock. I had no idea. "How did you guys seal it off?"

"Key codes," Janice answers. "All entrances and exits are locked, and the key codes are safe and secure."

"Well hello," Taylor purrs at a body coming up behind me.

Emily elbows her as Logan looks around awkwardly before realizing she was talking to him.

"I'm sorry about that, Mavis. John and Wilson wanted to talk for a while."

I slide out of the booth and rise to my feet. "It's no problem."

He brings up his watch and looks at the time. "Oh man, it's getting late." He looks back to me. "I'm sorry. I really am. I promise I didn't mean to bring you just to leave."

I wave it off. "It's fine, Logan. I got to hang out with Janice for a few hours."

She leans back into her seat and waves. "Hi, Logan."

"Hi, Janice." He waves back to her then to Emily. "Hello, Ms. Hash."

She nods to him with a smile. "Logan, how are you?"

"I'm good. Thank you." He looks over to Taylor as she winks at him. Quickly, he turns back to me. "Are you ready to go, or would you like to stay a bit longer?"

"I think I'm ready to go." I turn back to the girls and wave. "It was nice seeing you all again. It was nice meeting you, Taylor."

"The pleasure was mine, Mavis." She winks at Logan again. "Nice meeting you too, Logan."

He gives an uncomfortable grin, and we take off, out of the fancy ballroom, down the fancy hall, past the fancy people, through the fancy gardens, and into a fancy car.

"Don't we need to leave with Eric?" I ask him.

"No. Eric wants to stay for a bit longer with his friends and old coworkers. There will be enough rides here for him to choose from."

After driving through the crowds that are waiting to see who comes out of the capitol building, we finally get on the street that will take me home. I look around to see the driver taking the most scenic route possible and look back to Logan. "So you met Oswald?"

He nods. "I did. He seems really nice."

"Yeah?"

"Yeah. Very gentlemanly."

I nod back. "That's good. It's nice to know that our new chancellor isn't a jerk."

"Agreed."

We ride the rest of the way and chat about Oswald and how different he seems from Meir, we talk about how great and bright the future actually looks for us, and we talk about how Eric seems to be enjoying himself like he used to.

When we make it back to the bridge, Logan asks the driver to wait for him and walks me back home. We make our way over and through the woods, and I notice that the stones on our path to the house have been realigned since we left. They are much straighter and better organized than they have ever been before.

Chatting about whatever comes to mind to prevent an awkward silence, Logan and I continue walking down the path. When we get close enough to the house that it comes into sight, we see Derek sitting on the porch steps, seemingly waiting for us to get home.

CHAPTER THIRTEEN

Mavis

"Derek?" I make my way over to the porch ahead of Logan. "What's wrong?"

"You got a call." He rushes over to me and hands me a piece of paper with an address and a phone number. "It was from a hospital."

"What's wrong?" I ask him.

"It's Sam's mom. She's dead. He called here hours ago to get you." Derek looks past me and to Logan. "He wanted you too, but he said you weren't answering your phone."

Logan and I share a stare of pure horror. Sam called us while we were at the ball without him. He needed us, and we were off doing things without him. "Is he still at the hospital?" I ask Derek.

"I don't know. It was hours ago."

Logan places his hand on my back and begins walking back down the path. "Let's go see."

"Thank you, Derek." I swiftly turn and take off down the path with Logan. We rush back through the woods and back into our cab, where the driver greets us with surprise.

"I thought I'd be waiting here a little longer. Where to now?" I hand him the sheet of paper and watch him type in the first part of the address. "Wait, hospital? I know this place." He takes off driving and looks back at us in the mirror. Seeing the horror in our faces, he nods. "I'll get you there as fast as I can."

Sam

Nothing.

That's all I feel.

Nothing.

That's a lie.

Sobbing, I took a vial when I got home from the hospital. It didn't have the effect that I needed, so I took another one. Now, my body feels nothing, and yet I can feel the weight of the world pressing down on it. The pounding in my head from my cries has gone away, but the ache hasn't.

I just sit here, fading out of my vials, trying to figure out how it happened. It can't be real. I just got her back.

A knocking at my door pulls me off the couch. I head over and open it to find Mavis and Logan dressed in clothes I never expected them to wear. I sit back down on the couch without a word and wait.

"We went to the hospital the minute we heard," Mavis tells me as they enter and close the door.

"We searched the hospital and asked around until one of the nurses told us you had already left, and then we came here immediately." Logan takes a seat at the table next to the couch. "I'm so sorry, Sam."

"Are you okay?" Mavis stupidly asks me.

I turn to her and answer her question with only my facial expression. *No, I'm not okay.*

"What," Logan hesitates, "what happened?"

I clear my throat. "The bullet wound." I clear my throat again, trying to get the words out, and only manage a croak. "Her arm had become infected from the wound or something, and it got into her bloodstream." I bring my palms up to my eyes, wiping them and rubbing them until I see another dimension of swirls, shapes, and spots. "I don't know all the details."

"Do you have anyone to stay with you tonight?" Mavis asks me.

I shake my head, pulling my palms away.

"I—" She looks over to Logan then back to me. "I could stay with you, if you'd like."

Never looking over to them, I shrug. "You can stay if you want."

After a moment of silence, Mavis and Logan both come around and take a seat on the couch beside me. With Mavis in the middle of us and Logan on the other end, I continue resting my elbows on my knees. "Why do you guys look so funny?"

They take a moment. I can feel them looking at each other.

"We were at something for the Taai," Logan answers, "but that's not important right now." A few more moments of silence pass before Logan tunes in again. "So where is she? Is she still at the hospital?"

I shrug. "I don't know. When the people asked me what I wanted to do, I told them I didn't know." I sniff what I can back inside of me and lean back into the couch. "But now I know. I called them earlier and told them." I slide a pamphlet over to them from the coffee table, the one I got back at the morgue. "I want to have her cremated and then put into a gemstone."

They pick up the pamphlet and look through it to see what sort of gem cuts and colors I could choose. After they finish, the sinking feeling of despair returns to me. This process will cost a lot. It will cost less than burying her somewhere, but more than just a cremation. After going through with this, I will then be paying off Mom's medical bills, my bills, the house bills, and the gemstone bills.

But I don't care.

My mother deserves to be turned into more than just ashes. And this way, I can have her with me all the time.

Time passes, and the clock tells us it is now within the first few hours of the morning. Logan rises to his feet and looks over to me. "I have to go. I'll see you later, okay?"

I nod to him as Mavis walks him out. They whisper something to each other before giving a hug goodbye.

I follow their lead and make it to my feet. "Would you prefer the couch or my mom's room? I can lay down clean sheets and stuff for you."

"Whatever would make you more comfortable."

"I don't care." I look down Mavis's body to find that all I can hear is my mother's thoughts. "I like your dress. Mom would have liked it too." She gives a nervous smile. Before she can say anything, I head into Mom's room. "Would you like some of her clothes to sleep in? So that you don't have to sleep in that?"

"Yes please."

I come out of the room with a pair of her pajama pants, along with an oversized T-shirt of mine that she would always steal from me to wear. "Here."

"Thank you." Mavis takes the clothes from me and smiles. "I'll take the couch." She leaves the room, changes in the bathroom, and brings out the dress folded, along with the earrings and hairpins. She sets her things on the table and looks back to me, wearing the exact same outfit I have seen my mother wear before.

I swallow back the pain and nod to her as tears begin to force their way out of my eyes. "Good night."

"Wait." Mavis stops me on my way to my room and wraps her arms around me. "I love you, Sam."

We stay embraced for moments as I try to keep the tears in, but let too many fall. I love her too, but I can't get the words out without sobbing so I pull away and head back into my room without another word.

Mavis

Wearing the dress I wore to the ball, I leave Sam's house on the cart. He drives me to the farmer's house on the edge of the property where a cab picks me up and then he heads home.

I stayed with him all night and made him breakfast this morning with what I could find in his kitchen. He told me that he would be fine, that he needed to go to work for the day, so I left.

Though Sam can work in the clothes he wore last night, I cannot. Well, I'm sure I could, but it would be a little ridiculous. Once the driver drops me off in front of my bridge, I make my way back to the house to find that Derek has already left for work, leaving his mother asleep and Caitlyn on the couch reading.

"Hey." She sets her book down and looks over the back of the couch to me. "Is everything okay? How are you doing?"

I turn to her with a curious look.

"Derek told me about Sam's mom." She rises to her feet and reiterates, "Are you okay?"

I nod. "I'm okay. Thank you for asking." I look around the house and slowly inch my way back to my room. "What time did Derek leave this morning?"

Caitlyn smiles at me and sits on the arm of the couch. "He was supposed to leave like two hours ago, but he stayed for a bit longer and we talked. Why?"

"I'm just curious." *Why are you asking me why? He is my roommate.*

"You know, you're very lucky. Derek is the sweetest thing, and he cares so much about his mom." She crosses her arms and gives me another smile. "You're lucky to have him."

"I know." I nod awkwardly. "He is pretty great."

"So you two are a couple?"

"What?" I ask her. "No, he's my friend. I'm not dating anyone."

She rises to her feet with a satisfied smile. "Really? I can't say I'm not surprised."

"What?"

"Because, you know, you're so pretty. You could have anyone you wanted, and you're not dating anyone?" She wiggles her eyebrows at me. "You should snatch up the guy you like as soon as possible."

"I don't like anyone like that." I make my way into my room to change, and Caitlyn follows.

She leans against my door frame and looks at me as I shuffle through my drawer. "Good guys won't be on the market forever."

I straighten my posture after grabbing today's clothes and look at her. "If I don't 'snatch him up,' will you be making a move on Derek?"

"No. I'd never date someone I work with or for." She takes a step back and giggles. "Or at least, I won't anymore."

I roll my eyes and try to force a smile onto my face. "It was nice talking to you, but I need to shower and get ready for work."

"Oh." Caitlyn walks back over to the couch. "Of course."

I hang my dress up, place the hairpins and earrings into their boxes, and set them on the dresser. Considering I don't accumulate so many things, the fact that I sleep in an old closet doesn't bother me. I have a bed, a small dresser, and a clock. What else could I need?

I take my shower, get dressed, tell Caitlyn as kindly as I can goodbye, and head off to work. When I get to the building, I head into Mr. Trolly's office.

"Ms. Wamsley, good morning. I trust you had a fun evening?"

I nod. "As good as it could have been." I'm not telling him what happened.

"Are you ready for today's assignments?"

I nod again. "Yes, sir."

"Fabulous." He hands me a camera. "Go and photograph the people as they arrive at the conference building for the meeting today. Come back immediately afterward with the memory chip."

"Yes, sir." I take the camera and do as I am told. When I get to the conference building, it is an hour or two before people begin showing up. I listen to the reporters scream questions at the attendees as they exit their cars and head into the building with their guards.

The reporter right beside me, as I take pictures, is screaming her questions the loudest. She shouts the same questions at every person who walks by. "Do you have any comments on the prison bombings? Do you have any plans on acting against the poisonings in State Three?"

After never being answered, she gets rowdy and begins cursing at the politicians. Her cursing is followed by her being escorted off the premises.

I can't help but be glad they kicked her out. I can tell that a few other people around me are happy too. Without her screaming in my ear the whole time, I managed to get the best pictures of the day. I even took one of a few of the politicians smiling at me.

Once I take the best shots I can and all the politicians arrive, I head back to the office and give Mr. Trolly the memory card. He takes it from me and plugs it into his hologram base.

"Though some of these are blurry"—he swipes through the pictures on his hologram screen—"and a few of them are awful, I think you managed to take a few brilliant pictures." He hands me another memory chip and slides me a box with slips of paper in it. "Go ahead and choose."

I reach into the pile and pull out a slip, hoping it isn't as bad as my job last time, which was photography of a debate. In this job, Mr. Trolly lets his photographers pick their weekly assignments and bring back what they get when they are satisfied with their work. We have individual assignments every day, but he gives us one to work on over the course of the week as well. Though some of them don't have a due date, mine does.

I have now been assigned to interview the main designer of Capitol Park's garden and take pictures of each section by tomorrow night. Mr. Trolly waves me out of the room, and I head out to the lobby. Using one of the wall phones, I call the number listed on the paper and get the garden's designer.

"Hello?"

"Hello, Mr. Smith?"

"Yes, who is this?"

"Hi, Mr. Smith, my name is Mavis Wamsley. I work for Mr. Trolly, the—"

"Yes! Trolly called me earlier today and said that I'd be getting a call from you."

I stay quiet for a moment as I realize he set me up to take this assignment. "Yes, sir. So do you have any time tonight to speak?"

"No, not tonight. How about tomorrow?"

"That works for me. What time?"

"How about sevenish at the Palace by the bar?"

"Sounds good to me. Thank you very much, sir."

"Okay. I will see you tomorrow, Ms. Wamsley. I will be the one wearing a hat."

He hangs up the phone, and I head out of the building. From what I've heard, the Palace is a restaurant just a few miles down the road from here, so it shouldn't be too hard to get to.

All I can do now is hope there is not more than one person wearing a hat.

Once I finish my four-mile walk or so to the park, I am relieved to find a nice cool spring breeze coming through the large metal arch. At the top, it has the bronze letters spelling out "Capitol Park" in a decorative font, along with metal vines and leaves making its way down the sides.

I snap a photo of the beautifully designed arch and take a step through and look around to find flower beds lining the fences, tall and thick trees that seem perfectly kept, and people walking their dogs and children.

Click.

I snap a photo of a couple swinging a little girl in between them as they walk, all with large smiles covering their faces.

Click.

I snap a photo of a little babbling brook running through the park, along with a little wooden bridge that reminds me of the one that leads to Derek's house.

Click.

I follow one of the stone paths to a large flower garden that is fenced in, one that you can only enter and exit through a gate. I enter in and snap pictures of the flowers, the people enjoying looking at the landscape, and a little girl trying to pick one of the lilies.

Click.

I take an extra picture as the girl manages to tear the flower out of the ground before her parents can do anything.

I go on and on and take pictures of everything, from the birds to the shoes I find left in the grass. Once I get toward the center of the park, following a path through the shade of the trees, I find a large chessboard where the pieces are almost as tall as me. I snap a few pictures of the kids playing around with them, even though they aren't playing the correct way.

I make my way over to them and notice that the pieces are magnetized to the board so that no one can steal them, but that you can still slide them on and off the spaces as you please.

"Hey!" One of the kids sees me with the camera and waves at me. "Take my picture!" He hops up on top of the knight and sits on the horse's head. "Look at me!"

I chuckle and snap a few photos of all the kids trying to get onto the pieces. Once I take almost thirty pictures of them alone, I wave the kids goodbye and continue down the path to find dozens of stone chess tables positioned in the shade of one of the largest trees I have seen in a long time.

I take a picture of two old men playing chess together and manage to capture the exact moment that one puts the other into checkmate. His large smile as he moves his piece makes this photo one of my favorites that I have ever taken.

I continue through the beautiful park and think. Why is the designer wanting to see me at the bar? It's not like I am going to drink. In Frieden, it is legal for eighteen-year-olds to drink, but that doesn't mean I am going to. Last time I drank was before Steven died. Sure, I snuck in a drink or two every now and then, but it was nothing serious. I promised myself I would never become as bad as my dad.

I can be around alcohol. I mean, I did great at the ball last night. I didn't have any, even though they were free and colorful. So why would I pay for some tomorrow if I don't even need it?

CHAPTER FOURTEEN

Sam

It's fitting. Very fitting.

I spend my crappy life scooping crap.

Now that Mom's gone, I will have to do both her work and mine if I want to keep the house. Mr. Gohaki told me that I didn't have to start working this soon if I didn't want to, but I told him I would. He also offered to give me a roommate to help out, but I told him no.

If I need to get a roommate, I'll ask, but until then, I can do all the work myself.

The barn door creaks open as I finish cleaning out the last chicken box and placing the old bedding into the wheelbarrow. When I turn and look, I find Aspen standing in the doorway of the coop.

"Hey," she says to me.

I turn back to the new hay bale and pull the strings off. Once I get the hay free and loose, I pull some off to make the new chicken beds. "Hey." I pull my shirt up a tad bit to cover the back of the chain of my mother's gemstone necklace that I picked up this morning. I keep it under my shirt so that it won't get dirty with all the crap I have to deal with.

"I, um . . ." She gestures over her shoulder. "I was just at your house. I came to drop off a cake that my mom baked for you last night." I look over to her without a word and she chuckles. "I mean, I would have baked the cake, but I can't bake at all. I either burn it, or it comes out too dry, or something happens and whatever I was making gets ruined." She slows herself down and takes a breath. "Also, you may want to start locking your doors."

I let a slight smile rise up on my face. "Thank you," I tell her.

She steps into the coop, tears at the hay bale, and begins to help me fix the dozens and dozens of chicken beds. "So how are you feeling?"

I shrug. What am I supposed to say?

"If there is anything I can do to help, please let me know." She shoves some of the hay into another chicken bed and fluffs it just right. "Did you have anyone stay with you last night?"

I nod. "Yeah."

"Do you have anyone for tonight?"

"No. I don't really want anyone."

She nods and stuffs another box. "Okay, but if you ever change your mind and don't want to be alone, you can stay with us."

"Thanks." As I stuff another box, I turn back to Aspen. It hits me that Carrol is really upset too. She was sobbing almost as hard as I was when she found out. "How about you? How are you and your mom doing?"

She shrugs. "My mom is really upset. She was crying all last night."

"I'm sorry."

"It's not your fault. Mom is generally an emotional person, so it isn't supershocking that she is upset." Aspen stuffs another box. "She probably wouldn't be crying as much if she wouldn't have found out that I was the one who found her."

"Wait," I say, setting my pile of fluffed hay down. "What?"

Aspen hesitates to finish stuffing her box, but forces herself to anyway. "I had gone over to your house to visit you. When I got to the door, I was about to knock when I saw Bonnie on the floor." She rises back up and fixes her posture. "I knew something was wrong, so I ran in and over to her, but it was too late."

I freeze. I have been so upset and wallowing in so much self-pity that I haven't even considered the effect that this has had on other people. "I'm so sorry, Aspen."

We stand in silence, frozen in thought. After the crow of one of the roosters snaps us back, Aspen gives me a little smile. "Let me know how you like the cake." She heads over to the coop door, brushing the hay off her hands and clothes.

"I don't know if I can eat a whole cake by myself." Yes, I could. "You and your mom should come over later and have some."

She gives me another smile and nods. As she exits the coop and heads on her way, something becomes overwhelmingly obvious.

I like her.

I don't have time to like anyone, and I definitely don't have the temperament for it, but I do.

I like her.

Mavis

When I enter the Palace for the first time, I realize it is nothing like I imagined it originally. The marble countertops of the front desk and the sleek and perfect wooden cabinets and columns make this place seem much fancier than I anticipated.

I ask one of the women at the front where the bar is, and she looks me up and down. "How old are you?"

"I'm eighteen, but I'm actually just here to interview someone."

She gives me a judgmental look and pulls me aside to one of the wall scanners. Once I scan my wrist and my picture, age, weight, and home address pops up, the woman completely changes her persona. "Well, that's great! Sorry about that." She gives me the brightest smile I have seen all day. "I have to be careful, you know. Let me show you to the bar."

As she ushers me through the crowd, I see Janice sitting with one of the other officials, along with people who look to be overdressed. I assume she is in the middle of a business meeting, so I say nothing and continue walking with the woman. She brings me over to the bar, and I see a balding middle-age man who seems to be about my height, with his hat placed down on the countertop.

"Mr. Smith?" I say as the lady walks off.

He turns around and looks at me with an even brighter smile. "Ms. Wamsley! I've been saving you a barstool." He slides it out and pats it on the cushion. "Sit, sit."

I head on over and take the seat. "Thank you."

"Would you like a drink? I'm buying."

I shake my head and pull out my notepad. "A water would be nice."

He takes a swig of his drink and turns to the bartender. "Would you please get this lady a glass of water?"

He nods and gives me the drink. I take it and turn back to Mr. Smith. "Would you mind if we get started?"

"No problem at all!"

I flip open the notepad and read off the questions that Mr. Trolly gave me to ask. "What inspired you to become a garden designer?"

"Well, I've always loved design, and I had always been into art and so this is like being able to bring art to life for everyone to enjoy."

I nod and scribble down his answer. "That's wonderful, Mr. Smith. What about time? How long did it take you to design the layout of the park?" I follow Mr. Smith's gaze over my shoulder to find a man who looks to be only a few years older than me two barstools away. He is only having a water just as I am, which strikes me as odd.

I go through a whole list of questions and get all the answers I need within half an hour. Once I finish up my final question, I look back to Mr. Smith to find his forehead becoming sweaty.

"Are you okay?" I ask him.

"Yeah, yeah," he answers. "Listen, I am really honored that you came to ask me all this, but I was just wondering if we could wrap this up."

I nod. "Yes, sir. I think I'm okay. I got everything I need." I slide my camera bag over and ask him, "Would you like your picture taken?"

His smile grows, and he hops down to the ground. "Oh no, thank you. I'm sorry, it's just that I have a date." He puts his hat on and makes his way out of sight. I can't help but chuckle at how nervous he seemed to be about being late.

I remain seated and sip my water for a bit. I watch the bartender take his glass and clean it out with soap and water, making sure not a single inch of it remains unwashed.

Everyone around me seems to be happy with their drinks. The sudden urge to try one of the colorful alcohols rises within me, but I shove it back away.

I am old enough to drink. The drinking age is eighteen, so why shouldn't I? I'm not on the job anymore. I went and did what I was supposed to.

I'm not my dad. I'm not going to go overboard. I mean, worse comes to worse, I could just get one of the nonalcoholic ones.

"Hey." The man two seats over from me gives me a small smile. "Are you freelance, or do you work for someone?"

"What?" I ask him, confused.

He chuckles and scoots one seat over to me. "The camera." He points to my bag. "Do you work for yourself or someone else?"

"Oh, I work for someone else."

"That's what I thought." He takes a sip of his water. "I assumed you were here to interview that guy rather than coming here to take pictures of the bar." He looks around and smirks. "Though it is a very nice one."

I chuckle, "Yeah. I didn't know if he wanted his picture taken or not, so I brought it just in case."

"I understand." He extends his hand to me and smiles. "I'm Werner."

I shake his hand and smile back. "Mavis."

We let go, and he looks back to his drink. "I find that I take the best shot from above rather than from below."

I nod. "Well, it depends." I take a sip of my drink and look back to him. "There are some angles that work better for certain things."

"Yeah?" He sips his water once again. "Like what?"

"Well, I mean, I like taking photos of buildings from a low angle, you know? Buildings, certain plants, and most structures, I guess."

He nods. "I see. Have you had any pictures published? Any I may know of?"

"I have had a few published in the newspaper, but not many." My eyes catch a glimpse of a man at the very end of the bar looking in our direction. Werner turns around and notices the man as well. Rising to my feet, I grab my bag and sling it over my shoulder. "It was nice meeting you, Werner." I have to go and turn in the questions and my pictures.

"It was nice meeting you too. Maybe I will see you around sometime."

I nod. "Hopefully." I look over to the man at the end of the bar to see him grab his napkin off the counter and walk away.

I head out of the Palace and walk down the road until I am able to flag down a cab. When I finally get into a car, a large thundering roar echoes through the town.

The driver spins around and looks at me as I buckle in. "What was that?"

"I don't know," I tell him. After a moment of silence, I tell him my office's address, and we take off. As we drive down the road, we are passed by what feels like dozens of first-responder vehicles heading the opposite way.

"Oh my," the driver says to himself. "I really hope everyone is okay."

I nod in agreement, but say nothing. I really hope so too.

Logan

I stand by John as everyone gathers around the hologram screen to listen to one of Oswald's advisors address the nation.

"This heartless and vicious attack on the Palace killed ninety-eight people. There were no survivors. The forensic evidence confirms that this was a homemade bomb, and as of right now, we are assuming that this attack was the result of a Bestellen extremist. The three officials that were targeted and killed in the attack were Emily Hash, Terrance Parrott, and Janice Ludley. They were having a business meeting over dinner with . . ."

Janice? First Henry, then Sam's mother, now Janice?

"Hey." I nudge John in the arm. "How do they know it was a Bestellen extremist?"

"That's classified." He looks over to me then back to the hologram with a dead expression. "Trust the system."

Trust the system? Janice was the person who actually welcomed us to Bergland, and now she is dead. Or supposedly dead. If they can't even tell us how they knew she died in the process, how are we supposed to trust them? Who would kill Janice? Why would they kill Janice?

The same type of people who killed Henry. The little boy with so many hopes and dreams he wanted to fulfill, but never could because he died fighting someone else's war.

He deserved better.

Riding home in a cab, there is nothing but silence between the driver and I. I say nothing and think about everything. I think about Sam's mom. I think about Henry. I think about Janice and Emily. I think about Mavis, and I think about Sam.

When I finally make it home, I head inside and find Eric making dinner. I am usually the one who makes our meals, but Eric seems happier than I've ever seen him. Giddy, even.

"Glad you're home. I just finished." Eric plates the fish and vegetables and hands me my dish. We sit down at the table, and Eric digs in.

I take a bite and find it a tad bland, but I ignore it and continue eating. "So what has you in such a good mood?"

Eric looks over to me with a smile on his face as he chews.

"Did you finally get a girlfriend?" I raise an eyebrow at him and pop another piece of the fish into my mouth. "Possibly your physical therapist?"

Eric mumbles something under his breath and takes a bite of his vegetables.

"What was that?"

He rolls his eyes and looks back at me. "I'll get a girlfriend when you ask Mavis out."

I scoff. "What?"

"You heard me."

"I don't like Mavis."

Eric looks at me with an unconvinced expression.

"Whatever, man."

"You know you do," he tells me, "but we both know you are too scared to ask her out."

"What are you talking about? I asked her to the inauguration ball."

He sets another bite of fish into his mouth. "Was that a date?"

"Huh?"

"Was. That. A. Date?"

I pick up a vegetable on my fork and hold it up. "Define 'date.'"

He snickers. "Yeah, that's what I thought."

I take another bite of food, and we sit in a standoff, chewing our veggies. "How about this," I tell him as I finish swallowing. "If I ask Mavis out, you have to ask someone out. Not just anyone, but someone you actually like."

He rolls his eyes and extends his hand. "I'll take that deal, only because I know you'll never do it."

We shake on it, and I take another bite of food. "Whatever, man. You never did tell me what you are so happy about."

"Oh right. Okay, so I spoke with John today." He cuts into and stabs the last bit of his fish. "And he got me a job."

"Oh yeah?" I take the last bite of my vegetables. "What's the job?"

He lifts his fish meat into the air and takes his final bite. "Fisherman. Up in State Two." Eric chews with a smile. "I'll be leaving in a few weeks."

"Um, I . . ." Baffled, I look at Eric's giddy expression as he chews. "Congratulations." He has always wanted to be a fisherman and now he will be. "Do you have a place to stay up there?"

He shrugs. "I think so. John said he has it all set up for me."

"What about a roommate?"

"I don't know all the details. John and I are going to talk about it tomorrow." Shoving another piece of food in his mouth, he smiles. "I will fill you in on everything then."

Now that Eric will be moving out, maybe I should get a roommate.

Sam.

Sam needs a roommate.

If he moves in with me, he won't have to keep working on the farm.

After dinner, I head over to Mr. Gohaki's house then hike my way back to Sam's. Once I get there, I knock on his door to find no one home. I back off the porch and make my way out to the barn half a mile away to see if I can find Sam there.

The smells of the occasional fresh pile of manure find their way to my nose and bring me back to reality.

What am I doing?

Sam just lost his mother. Should I really be asking him if he wants to move in with me? There are upsides, sure. Sam won't be alone, and he won't have to work on the farm anymore, but it is really soon.

It'll be weeks before he moves in anyways, so what's the harm of asking now?

Once I get out to the barn, I can see through the boards Sam speaking with a man who has a set of dark tattoos on his neck. I enter through the doors, catch Sam's attention, and know I can't back out now.

The two of them smile at me and make an obvious change to the subject. The tattooed man clears his throat and turns back to Sam. "So have you heard anything about the poisonings?"

I continue to approach and turn to Sam with a slight smile. "Poisonings?"

"Um . . ." Sam looks back at Bram with a goofy smile. "Our friend Markus told us that there were about fifteen people that were picked off one at a time in State Four."

"Yeah," the tattooed guy tells me. "They had holes in their backs from where someone had walked up behind them and stabbed them with some sort of lethal liquid."

"How did Markus know?" Sam asks the tattooed man.

"Markus's friend works in the hospital down there."

"Do you think that the poisonings are related to the conspiracy theories?" Sam asks us both.

"I don't know," the man answers, "but over the last week or so, Markus would say something about this every night and come up with a new theory. So he certainly thinks so."

Sam chuckles. "I actually think some of his theories are true though."

"Like what?" I ask them.

Sam looks around the barn then back to me. "There's word going around, and not just by Markus, that the bombing of the Palace wasn't by a Stellen extremist, but by the new government."

"What?" I scoff.

"Yeah, the word is that they have people out on the streets and spies in the home that monitor you." The tattooed guy gives me a little smile. "And if you feel like Frieden is gaining too much power or if you don't agree with something they believe, they will kill you."

"That's why the Palace was bombed," Sam tells me. "Janice and the others didn't agree with the chancellor on something, so he wanted them out of the picture."

I shake my head in shock and disbelief. "There's no way that any of this is true."

The tattooed man walks past me and pats my shoulder. "Maybe it is, maybe it isn't. If you want to know, you need to look further into what's going on." He makes his way out of the barn. "Rather than believing the news or what we are saying, think for yourself."

"I'll see you later, Bram." Sam waves to the man as he exits the barn and throws a bag of feed over his shoulder. "Hey, Logan, sorry about that. What can I do for you?"

"Well, first, you can tell me if you believe the theories."

"It all makes sense, and nothing the theories propose can be refuted." Sam carries the feed up a step and into what I assume is the feed room.

"It has been refuted by the news reporters and the investigators, hasn't it?"

Sam exits the room and comes over to grab another bag. "Has it really?"

After all the lies and deceit I have been fed my whole life by the news, I don't know what to believe anymore. As Sam carries one of the bags back to the room, I bend over to help and grab one of the remaining bags. As I throw it over my shoulder, I feel a horrible pain in my lower back shoot through my spine and down my legs. I immediately drop the bag of feed, spilling the corn all over the floor.

Sam exits the room and looks around the floor, seemingly growing with frustration until his eyes fall upon me. "Logan, are you—"

"I'm sorry," I tell him, grabbing my back and making my way out of the barn. "I'm very sorry. I have to go."

"Logan." Sam runs over to me. "Are you okay?"

I turn to him and nod with the only smile I can muster up.

"No, you aren't." He heads over to his little cart and helps me up onto a seat. "I'm going to take you back to my place and call you a cab. You need to go to the hospital."

"No, no," I tell him. "I don't. I just need to go home."

"But, Logan—"

"I'm fine." He takes me back to his house, calls the cab, then drives me over to Mr. Gohaki's driveway without another word.

Sam helps me get into the cab when it arrives and looks at me once more. "Are you sure you're okay?"

I can tell he is worried about me. I assume he is overly worried because of the way his mom died without warning, but I assure him once more. "I'm okay. Thank you."

With those final words, I make my way home, never getting to ask my question.

CHAPTER FIFTEEN

Sam

The sun has set.

The day is over.

I head home and take a shower to get all the crap and hay off me from work. After getting out of the shower and heading into the main area, the first thing my eyes fall upon is an orange-and-yellow frosted cake sitting on the counter in a fancy glass dish.

Being only in a towel, I turn around and head back into my room to change. Once I am fully dressed, I come back out and examine the cake more closely. Carrol seems to have made a sort of swirl pattern all throughout the frosting that blends the yellow and orange together without forcing them to become one.

I consider inviting Carrol and Aspen over to enjoy the cake with me. I have all of my work done for today, so what would be the harm?

The more I think about it, the more I realize I don't feel like having anyone over right now.

I turn away from the cake and head to the radio on the mantel. I turn it on and take a seat on the couch.

"I'm not surprised. It was just a matter of time before the New Care Act came through," one man says to the other.

"You're right. This has been a hot topic for years, and I for one am glad to hear that Oswald has taken a stand and is following through on his oath."

A woman's voice comes out of the radio following the second man. "For those of you who aren't familiar with the New Care Act, it is the proposal that will be reinstating the medicine at birth that cures certain disorders. This act has made these medicines mandatory."

Thank goodness. I don't know why it took so long to pass. They have been discussing this for years, so I guess they were just waiting until they got back out here, but still. By doing this, no one would have any more mental disorders, right? This process seems not only helpful, but it also seems like it is the moral thing to do.

But isn't that what Bestellen thought?

"After the New Care Act was passed, Jonathan Riley, one of Oswald's advisors, announced that they will be cutting down on vials. He told the crowd when he addressed this issue that 'the vials have become too addicting and, with this cure, unnecessary. There were vial dealings back in Bergland, but not nearly as many as there are now. There have been over thirty reported cases of vial overdose in Frieden since we arrived, and we don't like those numbers.'"

I head over to the radio and turn it off. I don't need to hear this. I use the vials when I need to. I use them when I can't sleep or when I can't feel any peace. I just lost my mother, and now they want to take away the only thing that can help me feel calm? The only thing that can help me feel normal, like a functioning member of society?

I wash my hands and head back over to Carrol's cake, where I plate a slice and take it over to the table. As I sit down and blankly stare at the cake, I pull my mother's gemstone necklace out of my shirt. I pull it off and find myself stroking my thumb against the orange jewel.

A bite or two of cake finds its way into my mouth as I continue to stroke.

At least while I was in Bergland, I had already prepared myself to never see her again. Sure, I held on to hope, but not so much that I believed in it. I was preparing myself to either be right or to be pleasantly surprised.

But now, I feel even worse than I would have if I would have come back from Bergland to find her dead. It is so much worse to have her practically come back to life and then be snatched away just when I think everything is great again. We were just getting back to normal. Her arm was supposed to be getting better. She just said she was sore.

I wish she would have died before I got to see her again. That way, I wouldn't feel like this.

No.

I don't feel that way. I just miss her.

I miss her so much it hurts to think that I'll never get to feel her hugs again. I'll never get to feel her warmth again and never get to tell her I love her again.

My messenger vibrates to life on the couch. I check it to find Bram wanting me over at his and Markus's house. I message him back to tell him I am on my way then sit back down at the table and finish my cake. Though it is a pity cake, it is a very good one, and it should not go to waste.

Maybe I made the right choice not inviting Aspen and Carrol over to share it.

Once I get to their house, I make my way to the door and knock. Markus swings it open and looks me up and down. "Hey, Sam." He lets me in and points over to Bram. "He's over there."

I follow his directions and make my way into their kitchen. On the counter is a vial case, which I assume is why he called me here.

"What's up, Sammy boy?" Bram says to me as he slides me the case. "Are you ready for today's assignment?"

I can't help but chuckle. "You make it sound like school."

"This is even better than school though." Bram walks around the corner and places the case in my hand. "Because you're getting paid."

I nod. Bram tells me where to meet, and I head out. Once I get behind the bakery, I look around and observe my surroundings. The easiest thing to do would have been to just hide the case in the dumpster, but instead, I come up with a more original plan.

A plan that even I am impressed with.

As I climb up on top of the dumpster to reach my hiding spot, I find a familiar mark spray painted on the back of the building. This one, though, is much smaller.

REER.

Respect existence or expect resistance. I have seen this abbreviation several times since the day that I was mugged. And every time I see it, it makes me more aware of the fact that people in Frieden seem to be upset with the way it is being run. Other than this New Care Act, what do we have to be upset about?

After placing the case, I wait and wait, and the two women finally come around the corner.

"Are you Steve's guy?" one of them asks me.

"No." I shake my head and look around.

"Bram's?" the other one asks me.

I nod.

"Good. We just needed to make sure."

One of them comes over and slides an even thirteen hundred into my hand. "Where's the case?"

I smile at them and point up. Their eyes slowly rise to find the case sitting on top of one of the thick tree branches that provide the bakery with shade.

"Pleasure doing business with you," I tell them.

By the time I make it around the back of the bakery, one of the girls has already hopped on top of the dumpster and pulled the case down, the same way I put it up there. I can't help but feel proud of my hiding skills. I wasn't a jerk and made it hard to get, but I was smart and made it hard to see.

I head back to Bram's and hand him three-quarters of the cash. He nods to me and smiles. "Thank you very much."

I nod back to him without another word.

"Do you . . ." Bram turns to Markus then back to me. "Do you want to stay here for a while?"

"What?" I ask him. "Why?"

"I don't know. We know you lost your mom, and we . . ." He looks back to Markus again. "I don't know."

Markus moves over to one of the desks in the room. He pulls out a small purple vial and hands it to me. "Here. This is a type of vial that we don't usually give out to people."

I take it and roll it around in my hand. It looks to be the exact same as the blue vials, only a different color.

"Go ahead and try it," Bram tells me. "It'll help you feel better."

I continue to stare at the vial. "Take it here?"

"Yeah," Markus says.

I look at both of them and go take a seat at the table where I did the last time I took something here. I hold the vial in my hand and look it over once more before injecting it into my thigh. The purple liquid drains just as the other vials do, and I close my eyes.

"So"—Markus nudges Bram—"did you hear about the Palace bombings?"

"Obviously, dude. It was all over the news."

"No, I mean the theory. Someone told me that they found out what really happened."

As they continue, I zone out. My mind somehow drifts to Aspen. What would happen if I ask her to dinner sometime? I don't want to ask her out right now, of course, but I can't help but think about it anyway.

Taking the time to walk slowly home, enjoying the sound and smells of nature and its breezes, I walk into my house on the farm and see Aspen. The room is warm as she has already lit the fireplace, and the smell reminds me of the store we were in when we went shopping for our mothers.

She walks over to me from the hallway and throws her arms around my neck, kissing me on every inch of open skin from my neck up. When she pulls away from me, I look down to find her wearing Mom's orange gemstone necklace.

"Welcome home," she tells me.

A smile rises up on my face as I lift her off her feet and open my eyes to reveal the dream ending.

Markus and another dude I don't know have passed out on the couch beside me, leaving Bram nowhere to be seen. I rise to my feet and shake off the haziness left over from the purple vial. No one around is awake for me to say goodbye to, so I make my way to the door to leave when I am interrupted with an idea.

I make my way back to the desk that they pulled the purple vial out of and take an extra. Heading out of the house as quickly as I can, I find myself a cab roaming the streets and head home.

When I get home to an empty house and one piece taken out of the cake, I realize how much I hate living alone.

I think back to the feeling of my mother's warm hugs. I think back to how wonderful they felt. She would always welcome me home. She was always concerned with my well-being. Now, who is? No one is worried about me. No one cares about me.

Mom would have made sure the cake was put away properly rather than letting me leave it out like I did. It is going to get stale if it isn't already.

Pulling out the purple vial, I lie down on my couch and sit in silence. I stare at the purple bubbles inside the glass tube and think to myself, *One more time.*

The medicine is injected into my thigh once again, and I watch it drain. I close my eyes and lay my head back.

My mom.

I miss my mom.

It hurts.

It hurts my chest. It hurts my head. It hurts me. The pain seems to put a million tons of pressure on my chest, causing it to hurt to do anything, including breathe.

The vials are the only thing that ever help, and sometimes they don't even work.

"Don't worry."

I jump off the couch and spin around to locate the voice.

"It's okay, Sam," she tells me.

"Mom." I feel my lower lip begin to quiver, and my eyes begin to flood. I run around the couch and wrap my arms around her, just as she does me. The warmth from her hug enters into my body, causing a calming sensation greater than all others.

I don't seem to get the chance to take my time and hold her. She pulls away and brings up her sleeve, wiping the tears off my cheeks. "Why are you crying?"

"I miss you."

A smile rises up onto her face as her piercing blue eyes meet mine. "I know. I miss you too, but I will see you again one day."

"I don't want to wait." Tears pour down my face no matter how much I try to stop them. "I miss your hugs." I chuckle and wipe the tears from my face. "I'm sorry. I'm sorry."

"Hey, hey." She pulls my arms down from my face. "It's all right." She wraps her arms around me once more. "You need to be strong. There are so many things in life to look forward to. I don't want you to miss them because you are too busy dwelling on the past." She pulls away and wipes more of my tears. "Dwelling on me."

I nod and allow her to pull me into another hug.

She kisses my forehead and takes a deep breath. "I love you." The sounds of the empty house around us seems to become more apparent as I realize how shaky my breath is.

"Don't go," I tell her. "Please don't go."

I feel her hug getting lighter as she passes once more.

The gut-wrenching feeling returns as I choke out, "I can't do this myself."

Logan

"Hey, Mavis, it's Logan."

The rain outside begins to grow in severity. "Hey, Logan," she answers. "How are you?"

"I'm good, I'm good. Actually . . ." I shift away from the wall phone and pick up the newspaper off the counter. "I was just calling you to congratulate you."

"Congratulate me? For what."

"For your picture and article being in the newspaper!" I look over the beautiful pictures of the park and read down the article where they cite her name as a large roar of thunder consumes the atmosphere. "It says right here that you took these pictures and that you coauthored the article."

"Wait, what is it about?"

"The park."

"Oh really? They gave me credit for that? Yeah, those are my pictures, but I didn't help write the article, I only interviewed the man."

"Yeah?"

"Yeah. That was two weeks ago anyways. I didn't think that he was even going to do anything with that stuff."

I toss the paper back onto the counter and chuckle. "Well, he made a great choice to use your work. It looks amazing."

"Thank you. It—" The rain outside begins pouring even harder, causing our line to break up. ". . . was—"

"Hey, Mavis, the line is breaking up."

"What? Logan, the line is breaking up."

"Wait, I can hear you now." I chuckle again and look out the window. The skies say that the rain won't be letting up anytime soon. "I think I should probably go get a cab so I can make it to work on time, but before I go, I—"

"Logan—" The line continues to break. ". . . saying."

"Can I see you tonight?" I slowly and loudly enunciate.

Laughter bounces out of the phone's speakers. "I can hear you now. Yeah, that sounds good."

"Okay, when can I?" The line goes dead. "Mavis?"

I hang up the phone and dial out for a cab. If I don't get one now, I'm going to be late for work.

I call for one and have to wait over twenty minutes before the cab arrives. When the driver finally picks me up, she speeds through the rain as if there was none. Though the windshield is covered in water, completely compromising her vision, nothing stops her.

When she drops me off at the building, I almost sprint away after paying her. I have never been so relieved to get out of a car, and that includes the first time I was blown up. I make my way into the building, have them scan my wrist to sign in, and get right to work.

Throughout the entire day, I am able to avoid John. I figured that he would have come over to me and somehow scolded me for coming in late, but he hasn't checked on me once. His neglect combined with the fact that I get to see Mavis tonight makes this the perfect day. That is, until I finish cleaning one of the training rooms.

I straighten my posture as I rise to my feet from the floor and get a shooting pain in my lower back. I shoot back down into the bent-over position I was in right before the pain came along, and I freeze. I don't want to move. If I move, I could damage myself further, but I can't stay bent over.

Slowly, I begin to rise back to a normal standing position with a small amount of pain and strain on my lower back. I squat down, never twisting or bending my back, and pick up my cleaning supplies.

After packing them all up, I look around in all the training rooms for John, but can't find him anywhere. Still as stiff as can be, I head downstairs to the front desk and ask the woman at the hologram, "Excuse me, do you know where Commander Young is?"

"One moment please." She nods and finishes typing something. "Yes, sir, he is currently in a meeting. Is there anything I can help you with?"

"Um, could you tell me where the meeting is? I need to speak with him."

"Will you wait outside of the room until the meeting is over?"

"Yes, ma'am."

She smiles and gives me a little wink. "Room 314."

I return the smile. "Thank you."

After heading up the stairs once again in hopes to loosen up my back, I wait outside of the room. I can hear slight mumbling from the men and women, but I can't make out what they are saying.

When they finally exit the room, I see many random people I feel like I've only ever seen once before, along with some of the highest-standing officers in Frieden. Werner Rhodes is one of the first people to exit, but he leaves so quickly that I miss my chance to say something to him. General Wilson is the second to last to exit, followed by John.

When John sees me, he heads over to Wilson and shakes his hand, saying something just before the general leaves, surrounded by his bodyguards.

"Forge?" John comes back over to me and looks me up and down. "Why aren't you working?"

"That's what I wanted to talk to you about. I'm not feeling too good, and I think I may need to go home and lie down."

He looks down to where my right hand is resting on my back, and his jaw clenches. "How long have you been here?"

"Since about ten minutes after my shift started. The rain slowed the cab services down." All cabs except for my driver.

He takes a deep breath and lets out an even deeper sigh. "And you finished Training Room D?"

"Yes, sir."

John nods, scratching the back of his head with what seems like annoyance. "Then go ahead. You were only supposed to be here for another hour anyway."

"Thank you." I head out of the building as quick as I can to make sure John doesn't change his mind. When I finally get out, the rain seems to have stopped, and time seems to have passed much more than I realized. It is already dark out.

I flag down a cab and give them Mavis's address. I want to stop by her house on the way home to go in and see her. Yes, I need to get home and lie down, but we already said that we were going to get together tonight. We never said where, so I assume she is probably still home. Why not surprise her?

The cab drops me off by the bridge and takes off, leaving me to trudge through the muddy path to their house in the dark. Somehow, on my way, I step on part of a stick and shoot the rest of it up, scaring me into a small jump. After my nerves partially calm, I continue and make it to their house, never fully feeling safe, and turning around every few feet to make sure nothing is going to jump back out at me.

I knock once and find myself knocking nine more times. Not trying to be excessive, I stop myself there and find some sort of relief in the even number.

The door opens up, revealing a short blonde woman that isn't Mavis. Her hair is separated into curly golden locks, and her smile seems somewhat fake at first. "Can I help you?"

"I, uh . . ." I hesitate. "Is Mavis here?"

Her smile grows less fake as she looks me over. "Not right now, but she should be home soon."

Ms. Page peeks around the corner of the door's threshold and looks at me with a slight squint. "Who are you?"

"Logan." I touch my chest with my hand and look at her. "Do you remember me? I took Mavis to Chancellor Oswald's inauguration ball."

Her eyes flicker over to the blonde girl for a moment then back to me. We stand in silence for a moment as Ms. Page slowly remembers me or pretends to remember me. "Logan!" She smiles and waves me inside. "Come in, come in!"

Ms. Page heads over to the table and takes a seat. She pats the chair next to her and smiles at me. "Come sit. You are more than welcome to stay for dinner! Caitlyn is making it, and she is a fabulous cook."

I chuckle, not knowing what to say. Why would I stay if Mavis isn't here? But why wouldn't I? I don't want to be rude.

The blonde girl heads back to the fireplace and stirs the pot. "I think that's a great idea." She winks at me and smiles.

Ms. Page rises to her feet and looks around. "Hold on one moment." She exits the room with almost a skip in her step, leaving me alone with "Caitlyn."

I take a seat at the table, where Ms. Page was gesturing for me to sit and am almost immediately joined by Caitlyn.

"So, Logan, what do you do? Or are you still in school?"

"I am working as a janitor now in the training building, but I fought in the Taai during the war."

Almost immediately, her slightly shy exterior gives way. She wiggles her eyebrows at me and leans in. "You know, I may not be a photographer like Mavis, but I can really picture us together."

I can't help but blush. What am I supposed to say to that? Lucky for me, Ms. Page walks out of one of the rooms with a few framed pictures, stopping Caitlyn in her tracks.

"Mavis is just like a daughter to me." Ms. Page sets the pictures down on the table, revealing young pictures of Derek and Mavis together in the town. Both kids in this picture hold a scowl and have their arms crossed. "Neither of them wanted this picture, but when the photographer's bus came to town, I forced them both."

She slides over another picture that looks like Mavis, just with dark hair and aged a few years. "This was Mavis's mom. She died when Mavis was no more than ten. Ever since she passed, I have practically taken Mavis in. Her uncle Randy helped some, but he was always too busy to actually do anything useful." She shakes her head and slides me another picture of Derek and Mavis.

"What happened to her mom?" I ask Ms. Page.

She slowly sits back in her chair and looks over to Caitlyn, who seems overly interested as well. "You don't know?"

I shake my head. "I don't really know much about Mavis's past."

Caitlyn looks at Ms. Page and is nodded off. She heads back to the fireplace pot and stirs as Ms. Page looks down at the picture of Mavis's mom.

"Is there something I need to know?" I ask her.

She sighs a deep sigh and places the picture in front of me. "I believe so."

Mavis

I make my way into Logan's work building and head over to the desk. A woman sits here, typing away on the desk's hologram keyboard at a speed that I find unbelievable.

"Excuse me?" I say to her.

"One moment." The woman continues to type for what feels like minutes before she finally turns around to me. "How can I help you?"

"My friend works here, his name is Logan Forge. Do you know where he is?"

"I can't tell you that, ma'am. You can ask his supervisor though." She types something into her hologram. "Commander John Young."

I nod. "Thank you. Where can I find him?"

"He should be in Training Room D." She scans my wrist to log me in and points to the elevators down the hallway. The woman describes to me where on the fourth floor it is and quickly resumes typing. I thank her and follow her directions for what feels like a mile down the hallways until I see a door cracked slightly open. I peek in as I walk to see John with a clipboard, doing what looks like taking inventory on the wall of weapons in front of him. I see guns, ammunition, and what looks like little yellow vials that could fit into a gun.

I take a small step inside and utter a little "Hello?"

"Ms. Wamsley!" He smiles at me and sets down his clipboard. "How are you doing?"

I look around the room of weapons to find we are the only ones present. "I am good, how about you?"

He nods and takes a little step closer to me. "Much better now that you are here."

I give a little chuckle and cross my arms, trying not to scratch. "Do you know where Logan is? I actually came to see him."

"No, I don't. He actually asked to leave early today."

I find myself nodding. "Oh okay. Thank you." I point back to the wall of weapons and begin stepping back. "Sorry for interrupting."

"Oh, it's no problem." John follows my pace and approaches me. "I am actually happy you decided to drop by. I meant to speak with you more at the ball."

I find myself nervously chuckling. "Ah. Sorry about that. I know you guys were busy with Chancellor Oswald."

"No no, Oswald is a friend of mine. I can speak to him whenever."

"Yeah?" I ask, trying not to be rude. "Well, that's nice. It was especially kind of you to introduce Eric and Logan."

He nods once again. "Yeah. They're good soldiers, and they deserved to meet him." Stepping closer to me, he folds his arms, mimicking my stance. "I can introduce you two, you know, if you'd like."

I shake my head and try to scoot back without making it obvious. "Oh, I'm all right. Thank you for the offer though." John stares at me, so I continue, filling the silence. "Maybe one day, but as of right now, I am okay."

"Are you sure?" Smiling at me, he steps closer. "It would be no problem. I have a lot of connections and can make the arrangement fairly easily."

Nodding awkwardly back, I shrug. "Well, again, maybe one day. I just—" I look back to John as he stares me down with an unsettling smile plastered on his face.

John takes another step closer and smiles at me. "You know, you looked amazing at the inauguration ball."

Not knowing how to take the compliment, I laugh. After a moment, my mouth finally produces words. "You looked pretty nice too."

He inches even closer toward me, and I make a half a step back. Before I can do anything, he takes my hand.

I freeze, not sure what to do. All I am sure of is that I don't like this.

John slowly brings my hand up to his mouth and kisses it. I try to pull it away without making a scene, but he doesn't let go. "You were the best-looking woman at the entire party, you know that?"

I try to pull my hand away again, but he doesn't release. "Okay. Thank you, but I think I need to get going."

"What's the rush? You should stay for a bit. We have always been too busy to ever actually have a conversation."

"Maybe another time, Commander Young, but I really have to get going." I pull my hand free and turn around to leave the room, when John grabs my arm tightly.

"Where are you going?" Squeezing my arm as tightly as he can, he growls back at me. "I am just trying to talk to you." He pulls me closer and grabs my other arm as I try to pull away. "I even offered to take you to meet the chancellor. And what? You're just going to walk off?"

Swinging my hands to the center of our bodies and swinging up, I manage to break free of his grip and try to run away. Before I make it too far, John wraps his arm around my throat and pricks me in the arm with one of the little yellow vial bullets that was hanging on the wall beside us.

Within seconds, everything goes black.

CHAPTER SIXTEEN

Mavis

No.

This couldn't have happened. No, no, no.

As I come out of the haziness, I feel a pain in my hips slowly become more apparent. I open my eyes and find myself on the floor of a bathroom stall. Forcing myself to my feet, I examine myself and find a mess.

There's blood.

There wouldn't be blood if it had not happened.

There wouldn't be bruising either.

I have to get out.

I open the stall door and make my way to the sink. I wash my face and notice redness around my throat, most likely from where John grabbed me.

I can't remember anything after that. I woke up on the floor, and that is it.

I exit the restroom and look around. No one is visible, so I make my way out of the restroom and pull out my messenger. Before doing anything with the device, I realize I have to get out of the building without being seen. I can't let anyone see my injuries.

I can't confront anyone.

I can't get caught wandering the building, hazy and dazed.

Thinking back to when the woman back in Bergland administered me a vial the moment I became upset, I realize that the vial is the only way. It is the only way to get rid of this feeling.

To get rid of this feeling of horrid violation. To get rid of this feeling that I'd rather die than face that again.

To get rid of these thoughts.

Should I have fought harder?

Could I have fought harder?

Is this my fault? Is this my fault that I let him do this?

It is my fault. I shouldn't have been in the same room with him alone.

I message Sam and ask him where he is. I need to borrow a vial, and I know he has some. I want peace. I have only a few vials back home, and I'd have to go through Derek and Ms. Page to get them first.

"Can you meet me somewhere close by the capitol building?" I message him.

Moments later, Sam responds, "I'm actually heading that way. Meet me in front of Lemon's Bakery."

I look around to see the streetlights on, but no one else out. I check the time on the messenger and notice how early in the morning it really is, forcing myself to wonder how long he had me for.

Sam

After finishing the last few chores I had to do on the farm, I began heading to Bram's house, only to be messaged by Mavis.

When I turn the street corner to meet her, I see a silhouette standing by herself. Her arms are crossed so tightly that you'd think she was wrapped by tape.

"Mavis," I call out to the figure and see her spin around to me. Immediately, I see in her eyes, expression, and mannerisms that she is upset. "What's wrong?"

She looks away from me without a word. I make my way over to her to give her a hug, but she jumps back, bursting into tears.

"What? What's wrong?" I ask.

She doesn't let up. Her breathing deepens as she backs away from me.

"I'm sorry. I didn't mean to upset you."

She sniffles and wheezes, trying to get herself under control. "I'm sorry." She rubs her eyes with her palms, seemingly trying to cause blindness. "I'm sorry."

"What happened?"

"Something." She lowers her hands and looks away from me. "I don't want to talk about it." Mavis turns her body around and begins walking away.

"Hey, wait." I follow her, quite confused as to what could have happened. I have never seen her act this way.

"I'm fine," she tells me as I catch up. Pulling her jacket up almost to her ears, she shakes her head. "I'm fine."

"Are you sure?" I think back to when I said the same thing to her and tell her what she told me. "You can trust me, you know."

"I know." She looks at me and sniffles again, wiping the tears away with her sleeves.

Slowing our pace, I ask her, "Do you want to come with me to a friend's house? They have vials you can use if you want. That is where I was heading."

Mavis takes a deep breath and nods. She follows me, and we walk in silence. We walk for miles before arriving at Bram's house. When we get there, I make my way onto the porch and turn around to see Mavis standing in the driveway.

"Are you okay? Do you want to go home?" It is obvious she is uncomfortable.

She shakes her head. "I'm okay."

I knock on their door, and Markus opens it up. "Sam, hey." He looks over my shoulder then back to me. "Who is this?"

"This"—I turn around and look at her—"is Mavis."

Bram comes around the corner with a smile on his face. "Mavis? *The* Mavis?"

I chuckle. "Yes."

"Oh, why hello, Mavis." Bram shakes her hand and looks at me. "Sammy boy here talks about you a lot."

She looks at me.

"All good things," I tell her, earning a little chuckle.

Bram and Markus look at each other and come through the door, but leave it open. Markus looks at us both with a small smirk. "Well, it was nice meeting you, Mavis, but Bram and I actually have to get going."

Bram wiggles his eyebrows at me. "We have an appointment."

"Okay, but can Mavis and I go inside for a bit?" I look at each of them. "I need to grab a vial or two."

Bram gives me a small squint. "I guess so." He shakes my hand and pulls me into a hug. Whispering into my ear, he says, "Don't use too many of the purples. I know how many we have."

I pull away. "Got it."

The guys leave us. Mavis and I enter the house, and I watch her awkwardly stand around, avoiding everything in the building.

"Go ahead and take a seat wherever," I tell her.

After a moment of hesitation, she does. She sits at the table, and her eyes follow me as I head over to where Bram and Markus keep the vials.

She clears her throat. "Are you going to want someone to stay at your place with you tonight?"

I can tell she doesn't want to go home for some reason. Mavis continues scratching her arm as I answer, "I'd be happy to have you stay over."

She gives a little nod and forces her arms to cross once again.

I pull out one large blue vial for Mavis and one purple one for me. I would give Mavis a purple one, but she doesn't seem to want the dreams. She wants the peace, and that's what I'm going to give her.

"Here." I hand Mavis the blue vial and take a seat across from her.

She holds it in her hand and stares.

"Please. Take it before we leave." I look at her and close her fingers around it. "I really want you to feel better."

Mavis looks at me with tears in her eyes as she shakes her head. I can tell she wants to say something, but she wants to stay quiet more.

I watch her as she stares at it and lets tears fall. She squeezes her eyes closed and injects the vial. Pulling it out of her leg, tears flow and she sets the vial onto the table and closes her eyes. Before she knows it, her head is lying back and she is fast asleep.

With her shoulders and body relaxed, her jacket falls. It loosens and slides down, revealing dark marks around her throat. Immediately, I lean forward and take a closer look at the marks, but realize how horrendous it would be if Mavis woke up just now. She wouldn't want me, or anyone else for that matter, to be this close to her, and I am beginning to get an idea why.

I know she is strong. I know she is trying to be strong, but I also know she doesn't have to be.

I take my purple vial and hold it close. Wrapping my fingers around it, I rise to my feet and go grab a few more vials. I place them all on the table so that I won't wake Mavis if I need to get more.

With my medicine all lined up for the taking, I inject the vial into my leg and fall asleep next to one of my favorite people.

Mavis

My eyes slowly open, and I lift my head. I have a slight crick in my neck from the way I was lying, but not one big enough to slow me down.

Sam seems to have fallen asleep as well. Neither Bram nor Markus are back, so I assume the empty vials around him are his.

As I come out of my small nap, I feel the messenger in my pocket vibrating nonstop. Looking down to my pocket, I slowly pull out the little glass and plastic machine to see Derek's messages.

They were sent hours ago.

"Where are you?"

"Are you okay?"

I wipe my eyes and message him back. "I'm staying over at Sam's tonight. Sorry to worry you."

Slowly sliding the messenger back into my pocket, I rise to my feet and stretch. My body feels much more relaxed than it has been feeling lately, but I don't care. I try to shove off the memories, or lack thereof, from last night and move over to Sam.

"Sam," I say to him, looking down at his glowing pocket as his messenger shines through the fabric. "Your messenger."

He doesn't say anything. He doesn't move.

I poke him in the arm to try to get him up. "Sam."

He does nothing.

My heart begins to race, and the short-lived peace flees. I hold my fingers to his neck to find his pulse and feel nothing. I grab his wrist and wait for a small beat, but again feel nothing.

"Sam." I grab his face and try to turn it to me, but it seems his muscles have all tensed up. "Sam, wake up." I stare into his slightly opened eyes and see an image of nightmares. His blue irises have become beadier and more terrifying than anything I've ever seen.

His face lies whiter than usual, along with the rest of his body. His messenger continues to vibrate, so I pull it out of his pocket to get it to stop and see messages from Bram.

"Get out."

"Get out now."

I shake my head in disbelief and check Sam again. His pulse still remains nonexistent, and his eyes haven't changed.

I message back to Bram, "Sam is dead."

"Who is this?"

"Mavis. Sam is dead."

Immediately, he returns with, "Get out now. Run into the woods behind the house, and keep running until you hit the street on the other side."

I try to message back to him "What? Why?" but am caught like a deer in headlights as blinding white flashlights streak across the windows and through the curtains.

I shove Sam's messenger into my pocket and stumble back. After getting to my feet, I run as fast as I can out their back door and into their woods. I don't know what is happening, but I don't want to stick around for it.

Sam trusted these guys, so I can too, right?

But Sam's dead. I didn't do it. Should I really be running from people who may be able to help me? Who may be able to help Sam?

I hear shouting from the house as I continue to run, followed by gunshots that hit the trees and ground surrounding me. The shooting only motivates me to run faster. The branches slap me in the face and I trip on weeds and briars as I push through, but nothing stops me.

I feel like I am back on the outside of the wall.

I run as fast as I can until I can't run anymore. I slow my pace down and walk for a mile or so until a branch behind me snaps, causing me to run even faster than I did before. I go and go until I make it to the road, only to find no one there.

Pulling the messenger out, I regret my decision to trust them. "Where are you," I send them. I wait for what feels like minutes before he finally responds.

"Once you come out of the woods, take a left on the road and walk until you see the road sign 'Brook Street.'"

I immediately follow his directions and walk down the forest-lined roads where if someone wanted to jump out and attack me, they could. I wouldn't be able to stop them. I can't really even see anything past the first few trees beside the road. It is all darkness.

I walk until I see the sign. When I see it, I scurry over and wait. No one is here.

Bram messages me before I get the chance to message him. "I'm coming."

I wait with my arms crossed, and look around for anything that could go wrong. Another branch snaps from behind me, but just before I take off running, Bram calls out, "Hey."

I turn around and walk over to the other side of the road to meet him. "What is going on? Sam is dead, and there are people shooting back at your house!"

Bram looks around in a frenzy and waves for me to follow him. "Markus and I saw a police team flooding the neighborhood, raiding houses, and looking for vial stashes. We knew we were screwed."

"Is that why you guys left? You framed Sam and I?"

"No! Markus and I had to leave because we were meeting with an associate. I wanted Markus there for backup. You and Sam just came at the wrong time." He pauses and we both stop in our tracks. "Is Sam really dead?"

"Yes!" I shout, immediately regretting it. I scream whisper, "That is what I have been trying to tell you! One of my best friends is dead in your house, and I couldn't do anything about it because I had to run or I would be shot! What did you get me in to?"

Bram continues walking again. "What happened to Sam?"

"I don't know." Flashes of Sam's pale face and body come back to me. "He was dead when I woke up." The image of his eyes pops back into my head, and I have to try to shove it off.

Bram continues his walk in silence, but I don't.

"Where are we going?" I ask him, stepping over broken branches.

"We are staying with a group. We are leaving Frieden."

I pause, frozen in confusion. "What?"

He continues walking. "You are involved now too. You can stay behind if you want, but it is your funeral."

Still frozen, I look around the woods and let my eyes fall back on Bram.

If I go back, I could be shot at or killed. If I go forward, I don't know what could happen. Something worse could be waiting for me if I go with Bram than if I went back.

Not knowing what to do, I force myself to follow one of the last people Sam ever trusted.

CHAPTER SEVENTEEN

Werner

In my seat, remaining perched and ready for any and every shot I take.

I sit on the roof of a building toward the edge of Kern, which also happens to be on the edge of Frieden. Right now, I sit and wait to guard the border of our new nation. I watch the river flow through the barred portion of the wall. This is where I have been assigned to sit and guard tonight.

If people try to get in, it is my job to execute them. If people try to get out, it is my job to execute them. Those who enter Frieden now are extremists who are trying to get back in after escaping to meet up with other extremists. Those who exit Frieden are the same.

The extremists are the ones who want Frieden to crumble. They are the ones who want Bestellen back. We can't let that happen. By guarding the wall, I am doing one of the highest services there, keeping the peace.

Immediately, I aim my gun and look through the scope at the flock of people trying to leave through the portion of the wall that is open for the river to flow through. The bars are too close together to let people and animals enter and escape, so I watch. It could be a group going for a late night swim.

I am quickly proven wrong as the woman at the front of the group twists one of the bars off and slides through. One of the men of the group pushes past everybody and forces himself through the poles, but falls lifeless as my first shot rings through the air.

Another shot follows, and another person goes down, floating down the river. I take another shot and another shot as the people quickly try to head through the bars. Each one I shoot at goes down.

I move my aim toward the end of the line to find one woman and one man, trying to get over the dead bodies. I aim my gun for another headshot when I see the woman turn around.

Her blond hair flips over her shoulder and out of her face long enough for me to recognize her.

It's the girl from the bar.

PART THREE

Survival

CHAPTER EIGHTEEN

Logan

My stiffness and inability to move my back becomes more apparent as I wake to the wall phone ringing. I quickly try to get to my feet, but am overcome by a sharp pain in my lower back.

Instead of heading to Mavis's last night, I should have come home and rested like I told John I was going to. She didn't even show up. Once Derek came home, we exchanged a few awkward glances, and then Caitlyn put the food on the table. After seeing that Mavis wouldn't be home for dinner, I excused myself because I felt I was intruding. Ms. Page and Caitlyn seemed upset, but Derek seemed just as confused as I was.

Maybe I should take that as a sign. Maybe Mavis and I aren't meant to be together. I mean, the first time I purposely go out of my way to be with her alone, she doesn't show. What else am I supposed to do?

Slowly, I slide off the bed and make my way into the living room to retrieve the phone.

I clear my throat, realizing that I was sleeping with my mouth open. "Hello?"

A gravelly voice answers on the other end, "Yes, is this Logan Forge?"

"Yes, sir. Who is this?"

His answer shakes me to my core. Officer Gowdy tells me something I never thought I'd hear. We end the call, and I immediately redial the phone and have a cab come get me. Within thirty minutes, I am at the police department and heading to the front desk.

"Excuse me, sir," I say to the man behind the desk, "my name is Logan Forge. Officer Gowdy called me here for—"

"Yes, sir." A police officer in full uniform, holding a clipboard, walks out of the hallway and waves me back. "Come with me, son."

The man at the desk goes back to typing, and I follow the other man back to his office. He takes a seat behind his desk and gestures for me to sit across from him. I obey.

"What's going on?" I ask him as I meet the seat.

He hesitates for a moment. "Would you care for something to drink?"

I shake my head and scoot the chair forward. "No, sir. I would like to know what is going on."

Officer Gowdy takes a few moments before setting his clipboard down in his lap. "Samuel Beckman is dead," he tells me.

"Wh—" I find myself at a loss for words, along with a loss of air. My lungs don't seem to be doing their job. This can't possibly be true. It just can't. "What happened?"

"We are unsure, but as of right now, it looks to be murder."

"Murder?" I exclaim. Dark spots flood my sight, but I try to blink them away as the effect of adrenaline and lactic acid settling take over. "Who would murder Sam? Where did this happen? When did this happen?"

"Just a few hours ago. It was in a known vial distributor's household." He sighs and slides his clipboard over to him from in between us. "I can't disclose much more information. The only other thing I can say is that there were a lot of prints at the scene. Most of them belonged to the house owners, but there was a set other than Sam's that showed up." He looks at his clipboard then back to me. "Do you know a Mavis Wamsley?"

"Yes, I do. Is she okay? What does she have to do with this?"

Officer Gowdy pauses for a moment and looks at me, seemingly unable to figure out what to say.

"What happened to Mavis?" I reiterate.

"Mavis, right now, is the main suspect for Samuel Beckman's murder. She has prints all over the scene and was seen fleeing from the back of the house moments before our men arrived."

"Where is she right now?"

"We don't know, but—"

"Why is Mavis a suspect, but the others aren't?"

He sighs. "Because her prints were the only ones found on Sam."

No, this can't be. "Mavis is not capable of that. She wouldn't be able to overpower Sam! Plus, she is too—what's the word?—nice, kind, incapable of killing! She wouldn't do that." I become unable to produce words as the shock sets in.

Henry.

Gramps.

Sam's mom.

Janice.

Sam.

Is Mavis next?

"Wh—" I stutter out the words. "Why was I called here?"

"You and Mavis were the only two left of Sam's emergency contact information."

What?

This sinks in slowly. Sam has no family left besides Mavis and I, and Mavis is nowhere to be found.

Another officer interrupts us by knocking on his door and poking his head in. "Sorry, sir. A Derek Page is here for you. He says you spoke to him over the phone."

Officer Gowdy nods. "One minute please." The man in the hallway pulls away and closes the door. Gowdy looks back at me, puts on reading glasses, and picks up his clipboard and a pen. "So, Mr. Forge, may I please ask you a few questions?"

I nod.

"How close were Sam and Mavis?"

"We just met a few months ago, but we were all pretty close. Those two were about as tight knit as you can get. They were like siblings." I pause for a moment before looking back up to him. "Which is another reason why I can't believe Mavis would do such a thing."

The officer looks up to me over his glasses and stops writing. He sets his pen down and pulls his glasses off his face. "Mr. Forge, let me tell you something. There was once a pair of brothers. The youngest kept flocks, and the eldest kept the soil. Over time, the eldest brother held resentment against the youngest because the youngest was favored by his father. Not too long after the resentment began, the eldest murdered the youngest with a rock. A rock, Mr. Forge. This was the first murder ever recorded. Sibling against sibling. And you know what? I've seen it happen many times since." He places his glasses back onto his face and continues writing.

"Now, Mr. Forge, how close were you to Mavis and Sam?"

I take a moment to think. Sam and I were friends. We weren't extremely close, but I was closer to him than I've been to a lot of people. And Mavis? After last night? After finding out about her dad, her mom, and her brother after all this time? I guess we aren't very close. "Mavis and Sam were a lot closer than I was to either of them," I answer honestly.

"But what was your relationship to each of them?"

"Sam and I were somewhat close. So were Mavis and I, but we were more distant friends, I guess. We hung out sometimes, but we didn't really know much about each other apparently."

"Apparently?" he asks me.

I shrug.

"Is there something you want to tell me?"

I shake my head. "No, sir."

"You do know I just want to help, right?"

I nod. "Yes, sir. I know."

"Okay." Gowdy clears his throat. "Do you have any information or any idea where Mavis may be?"

I shake my head again. "No, sir."

He pauses for a moment and slides me a card with his phone number on it. "If you can think of anything or want to share anything that can help us find Mavis, call this number or come in to see me. Okay?"

I nod.

"I want to point out that Mavis may not have done it, so finding her is the best way to keep her safe from the people who did."

From the way he is forcing his voice to be soft, I feel as if he is lying.

"Yes, sir," I answer. "Thank you."

He opens one of his desk drawers and pulls out a small clear bag that contains the orange gemstone necklace that Sam had made after his mom died. From what Mavis told me, he wore it everywhere and hadn't taken it off since the moment he got it. "This won't do us any good to keep to ourselves, and I figure that it was important to your friend. Would you like to take it with you?"

A brief moment of hesitation passes by just before I nod.

I rise to my feet, and Officer Gowdy shakes my hand and slides me the gemstone of Sam's mother. "Have a good day."

I thank him and exit his office, placing the bag into my pocket. When I make my way down the hall and back out to the main area, I see a familiar head of red hair. Derek sits with his elbows on his knees, supporting his upper body as he stares at the floor. His folded hands seem to be clenched together as he waits to be called.

Derek's head tilts up, and his eyes fall upon me. The moment he sees me, his eyes grow big and he rises to his feet. "What's going on?" He comes over to me in a calm and yet panicked frenzy. "What happened?"

My head shakes, and my palms find their way to my eyes. "Sam's dead. Sam is dead. And they think Mavis killed him."

I drop my hands to see Derek's jaw clenched. He pulls out his messenger and is interrupted by the person behind the desk.

"Mr. Page, Officer Gowdy will see you now." The man stands and waves him over so he can be walked back.

"One minute please." He turns back to me and runs his free hand through his hair. "Why would they think that?"

"Mr. Page," the man reiterated, "Officer Gowdy needs to see you now."

Derek shakes his head in disbelief and rubs his jaw, looking at the messenger. After a moment, he follows the desk man back, leaving me alone. I head outside and flag down a cab, noticing the light hint of sunlight on the edge of the sky. The sunrise slowly inches its way up as I make it back home and fix myself some tea.

If I am going to work today, I may as well stay up.

I stand by the teapot, waiting for the water to come to a boil, and hear something else instead.

"Who called earlier?" Eric asks me as he crutches out of his room in his boxers and a shirt. "Where did you go?"

"I'm sorry. I didn't mean to wake you."

"It's fine." He continues over to the wooden dining room table and takes a seat. The moment he sits, his whole body shimmies with chills. "The seat is cold." He looks from his legs, back to me, dropping his face into a serious expression. "Sorry. What happened?"

I take a deep breath. "I was called down to the police station. Sam is dead."

"What?" Eric stumbles to find his words. "What happened?"

My eyes fall upon the tea kettle as I wonder how much longer it is going to be until the water comes to a boil. "Mavis killed him." I would really rather not wait for my tea right now.

"What?" Eric reiterates.

"The officer told me that Mavis's prints were found all over Sam's body inside of a known vial distributor's house."

"No way." Eric scoots forward in his seat and scoffs. "And that doesn't necessarily mean that she killed him, right? Where is she now?"

"Apparently, she was seen fleeing the scene as the police showed up." Way to go, Mavis. Make yourself look even more guilty.

Are you guilty?

I turn back to Eric to see his head lowered and shaking as he mutters something under his breath.

"What?" I ask him.

"Nothing." Eric shrugs it off and straightens his posture. "Are you okay, Logan? I know that you went over to her place tonight, or last night, whatever, to be with her."

Annoyed, I growl at Eric, "Why do you do that?"

"Why do I do what?" Eric defensively growls back. "Ask if you're okay?"

"Mumble something under your breath and then change the subject. You do that all the time, and you know what? I want to know what you said."

"What?"

"Right now. Tell me what you just told yourself."

The tea kettle breaks our awkward silence by allowing its whistle to slowly grow louder until I turn the burner off and move the kettle. I shift my focus back to Eric and stare, realizing how mean I really am being, but I don't care. This is getting ridiculous, and I want to finally know what he says all the time.

Eric looks down at his lap and rubs his fingers to distract himself, causing me to go back to rubbing my fingernails. Once, twice, three times on each nail.

"I was rude to Sam," he finally tells me. "When he came over to see you, he came into my room and tried to apologize." Eric looks up to me, but refuses to make eye contact. "He told me that I was the one who stood up for him, and he treated him like trash. He told me he was sorry."

"How were you rude?"

"I didn't say anything. I didn't look at him, I didn't acknowledge him, I didn't do anything."

That's why Sam left in a small frenzy. He was trying to leave before he caused a scene. He was trying to make things right, and it came back to make him feel like trash. Eric did that to him.

I take the handle of the kettle and pour the water into my cup. "Would you like some tea?" I ask Eric.

He shakes his head and rises, grabbing his crutches. "No, I'm really tired." He slowly adjust the crutches to fit into his underarms. "I'm going back to bed. You should probably get some rest too."

I nod as Eric makes his way back into his room and I sit at the table with my steeping tea bag. The steam from my small mug spirals up in a whimsical fashion. I watch the wisp flow through the air, and I pull it close so that it hits my face and warms me.

After minutes, I pull the bag out of my pocket and set it on the table. I stare at the orange gemstone as I pull it out and rub my finger over it. It has already been swabbed for samples and cleaned, I assume, but I clean it myself anyway. Once I have scrubbed every bit of the piece thoroughly, I place it around my neck and wear it just as Sam did.

CHAPTER NINETEEN

Werner

I make my way down the street and into headquarters. Through the dull green hallways, past a million different doors, and into Issana Burris's office. The moment I open the door, she looks over her glasses at me and returns to writing.

Captain Burris works under General Wilson and beside Commander Young. Young runs the Taai, which is the special operations group of our militia, while Burris leads an even more elite group. She runs a large number of individuals, giving them each their own assignment to protect the freedom of Frieden and keep it secure. Our division is so classified that not even the members of the team know what the others are doing.

"Eventful night, Rhodes?" she asks me, never looking up from her papers.

"Yes, ma'am." I close the door behind me and enter the room. After looking around, I notice that her oil lamps have been rearranged to have one in each corner of the room. It seems that every time I enter her office, they are rearranged in a different position.

"How many?" Burris asks.

"Six."

She flips the page over and begins writing on the next one. "And you got them all?"

"There were six people, and I took six shots." There were twelve people, and I took six shots. "I hit everything I aimed for."

She nods. "How long did it take?"

"Thirty minutes or so."

She looks up to me over her glasses. "Thirty minutes? That's a little long for cleanup."

"I did what I was supposed to. The rest is on the crew." I called in the cleanup crew after the six other people fled. I made sure Mavis and the others got away.

Burris nods and looks back down to her papers. "Good job. Go home and get some rest. I will call you back when I have your next assignment, but you should be good for the next day or two."

"Thank you." I turn around and place my hand back on the door handle. There are so many questions running through my head. So many things I want to say and ask. I can't ask the wrong thing without getting myself into trouble, so I think. I can feel Burris's eyes focused on me, so I turn around and focus my eyes back on her. "Is there anything I need to know?"

She freezes. Tapping her pen on her finger, she asks me, "Like what?"

"Like the reason people are fleeing Frieden."

Burris slides her glasses off and gestures to the seat across from her.

I sit and our eyes lock for a moment.

"Have you been given any reason to believe otherwise?"

I freeze, not knowing what to say.

"We get our commands from the command center in the capitol building. Those commands, after being written out and processed, go through General Wilson himself. They are signed off, filed in a filing system, and sent to us. Nothing you've been assigned was the result of a single man's actions. Many people go through to make sure everyone is in check."

I nod as I rise to my feet with a searing feeling that I made a mistake asking. I can sense her opinion of me lowering as I walk out of the room and out of the building. Even as I am dropped off at the end of the dirt road to my house, I feel that I should not have asked that question. It is obvious that even if there was something going on, Burris wouldn't tell me. Why would she?

I hike my mile or two home through the woods and make my way inside. Being from Bloot, I don't enjoy living in the city very much. I never liked the idea of everyone living so close together. That is why when I got the job up here, I bought the most secluded house in Kern. There are a few others scattered on the outsides of the city, but this one is the most hidden. It is surrounded by the forest and about as concealed as you can get in the capital. Its size reminds me a lot of my old house in Bloot, and the fact that I live alone helps the memories too. My parents died when I was a young teenager, and I have pretty much lived on my own since. Though I miss them, I don't miss living with someone. I don't miss having to clean up after others, nor do I miss all the excessive noise in the house.

The only thing I don't like about my house is the fact that I have to walk this much to get to the road and back. I had stopped by here earlier today to drop off my gun from last night's assignment and had to walk over two miles just to drop it off and get back to the cab.

It makes sense for me to do this though because I can't walk around the city with it. I'm not allowed to unless I am heading to an assignment. Only the police force and certain clubs can own firearms. There are hunting clubs, but they are extremely exclusive, and usually the only ones who are allowed in them are the rich business owners and entrepreneurs. Plus, the background checks and psych evaluations before you can purchase a gun are rigorous. The police and my division undergo serious tests to make sure we are trustworthy and good shots while the hunting clubs seem to let whoever can afford it in.

I have to keep all of my weapons hidden, not that I suspect my house will be searched anytime soon. In the event that I am searched, or even attacked, I have hidden weapon spots throughout my house. Some rooms have guns. Some rooms have knives. All rooms have one or two hidden weapons.

My bedroom closet is where I keep my rifles along with my other weapons I take on assignment. The only other weapon I use regularly is my bow, which I keep in my spare room hanging on the wall. Legally, in Frieden, bows and arrows are the only real weapons the common folk are allowed to own. And considering this is my tool of choice in the first place, I was more than happy to purchase one as soon as I could.

I head into my spare room and pull my bow and quiver off the wall. As I head out of my house, I grab the book I am currently reading off my dining room table. Typically, when I get back from assignments, I follow a routine. I grab my hunting gear and the book, head out into the woods, walk until I grow weary, then plant myself where I please. I spend most of my time in nature. This is where I prefer to be. This is where I distract myself from reality.

The reality is that my job is to kill people.

After seeing the girl from the bar, someone I knew and someone who I don't think is a criminal, I can't help but rethink things. I know that blindly following orders is wrong. I know that there should always be a reason why you do things. I just thought that now that we are under a new government, I could trust them. Now that we weren't under a dictatorship, things would be different.

But are they?

If they are different, then I made a huge mistake. I let people go, lied to my boss, and unknowingly aided rebels who are fighting to destroy everything we've worked for.

But if things aren't different, then I am committing far worse acts than any rebel ever could.

Mavis

The cold morning breeze blows against my damp clothes as the group continues walking. I rethink and review the events of the last few hours and try to force myself out of a state of shock.

When we made it through the river, we immediately ran into the woods, following the short woman leading us.

Markus was the first one to drop dead when the gunfire started. A woman followed him, and another man followed her. We ended up losing half of the group.

Everyone who was in front of me other than the woman who opened the bars for us, Van, was shot dead. Once it was my turn, the gunfire had stopped. I made it through, followed by Bram and two others. We made it into the water and swam behind the wall so that whatever was shooting at us wouldn't be able to anymore.

We ran. We were wet and cold, but the heat we produced from running helped us keep going. After we were a safe distance away from the wall, we were able to start walking.

The sun slowly rises and gradually allows heat to fall through the roof of trees around us. The longer we walk, the more I realize that I'm back in the woods. The same woods where I met Sam and Logan. The same woods where I was chased by a pack of unnaturally large rats.

Though we walk for hours, stopping for small breaks to eat what little amount of food our guide has stashed along the path, I've noticed that we have not run into any animals. The large catlike beast that Sam described hasn't appeared. We haven't heard the animals that tore apart the boy, that ran away from Sam and Logan, and most importantly, we have not run into the rat pack.

I assume they are hiding. Since the war was full blown and we moved into Frieden, cars and carriers have been rampant throughout the woods. Once we no longer needed to move from Bergland back to Frieden, the cars and carriers ceased to make their ways out of the wall. I figure that the animals would have returned to their normal state by now.

When the sun sets after the long day of walking, Van, our guide, readjusts her dark black ponytail and takes us to a large tree. "We'll sleep here tonight. By tomorrow, we'll be where we need to go." She slides the straps of her bookbag up and shows us how to climb up the branches.

The bottom branches are much smaller and thinner, but as we continue upward, the branches extend and become much thicker than any I've ever seen, almost reaching the thickness of the trunk. When we get to the top, everyone settles in and chooses where to rest. The branches are so large that we can sit on them without really needing to worry about falling off.

Almost immediately, everyone lies back and falls asleep.

At least they act like they're asleep.

I look around, remaining ready to flee at any given moment. The animals could be back. There could be something lurking.

Something.

Worse than animals.

There's always something worse.

"Hey." Bram nudges me in my arm, causing my body to jolt. "Sorry. I didn't mean to scare you."

I look from him and his hammer tattoo back out into the familiar dome of leaves. "It's fine."

"You need to get some sleep," he tells me.

I look back at him and wonder. Why would he care? I know he was friends with Sam, but Sam is dead.

Sam is dead.

"I'm fine."

"Mavis." Bram scoots a little bit closer to me, and I immediately scoot away. Bram stops in his tracks, seeming somewhat shocked at my movement. "Sam talked about you nonstop. I know that you're always on guard, but we are up in the trees. From what Sam told me, the trees are the safest place to be out here. And plus, there are all these other people that are here to watch."

I look down at my fingers and find myself rubbing my hands.

"It'll be okay," he tells me.

I nod and lay my head back against the trunk of the tree. "I know."

I don't know. I say this to get Bram to mind his own business. He leans back against the tree trunk and closes his eyes. As he begins to rest, I try to also. My eyes fall closed, but open every time I hear more than a leaf rustle in the wind. I slip in and out of a light and headache-inducing sleep, just as I did the first time I was in these woods.

Every moment I flash back is worse than the time before. I close my eyes and remember the rats chasing me. I squeeze my eyes closed and fast-forward to the bombing in Bergland, the bombing where we lost Henry. All the horrible things come flooding back in a panic. All the people I lost, all the pain I felt, all the horrendous acts—they all come back.

My eyes open to see the dome of leaves surrounding us now, the same way they did the first time, but this time is different. I notice the leaves aren't quite as big as the leaves were when I was exiled. These leaves are much smaller and more plastic looking, but remain on the end portions of the branches.

A small shift and shake catches my attention. My eyes flicker to my right as I try to find the source of the noise when a ball of white fluff with burgundy stripes creepily inches its way onto a branch in front of me. Its face reminds me of a fox, though its skull is much more rounded and its snout is much thinner. Its tail is about double the length of its entire body and carries the red-and-white fluffy stripes.

I rub my eyes and squint, trying to get a better picture and somehow cause it to freeze in its spot. Nothing on the animal moves for moments, not even its fur. Its head slowly turns to me, and its bright yellow eyes meet mine. The needlelike pupils slowly grow and consume its iris until darkness is the only thing staring at me.

The animal doesn't move. I size it up as its body remains frozen. Continuing to stare at it, I force my overwhelming sense of uneasiness and nudge Bram in the arm slightly. He jerks awake and makes a grunting noise, causing the tree fox to seize up and scream an absolutely horrendous noise.

It bares its teeth and continues shouting a loud and high-pitched screech that wakes everyone up. Less than a moment later, the screeches multiply in number and seem to hit our ears from every direction possible.

"Get down now!" Van shouts at us over the sounds of the approaching beasts. I am the first to make my way down the branches. One after another, we all shimmy down the tree and try to get to the ground as quickly as we can. I watch as the animals chase after us, hopping from branch to branch, swiping at us with their claws and nipping at us with their long snouts.

After making it about halfway down the tree, one of the fox creatures manages to lunge at and bite the arm of one of the girls. She shouts as the foxes continue to scream, and she rips the animal off her arm and chucks him as far as she can, still scurrying down the tree. Once our feet hit the ground, we run, following the guide as fast as we can. The foxes seem to have stayed in the trees so I feel slightly safer, but I can hear them running through the branches above us, shouting their battle cries. Though they stop following after a minute or two, I continue to feel as if the danger will never leave.

There is no safe space.

We run for at least a mile before the girl with the bleeding arm finally speaks up to the guide. "Can we slow down?"

Van looks around to the group and nods. Slowing to a speed-walking pace, she wipes her forehead to remove the sweat. "Yes. We can't stop though. The creek is right up here, and we need to rinse out your wound."

The girl nods, and we all keep walking.

Bram and I continue beside each other and look around to make sure nothing else is lurking. We make sure to keep a good pace and stay toward the center of the group. I make sure to stay there because being at the end or being at the front both mean you can be an easy target. I don't know why Bram has decided to stay in the center though. I assume it is because I am the only other person in this group he knows.

When I turn to look at him, I notice he holds his forearm in a way that I can only describe as he is covering something.

"What's that?" I ask him.

He looks down at his arm and back at me. "Nothing."

I continue to stare at him until he shows me four small cuts on his arm. "One of them scratched me."

"Why didn't you say something?"

"What good would that do?" he asks me. "I can rinse it off once we get to the water, but until then, how would whining help anything?"

I shrug, knowing he is right.

We walk in silence until the sound of the babbling brook hits our ears, and Van sprints off. "Come on."

Following her speed, we make it to the small stream, and she immediately waves the girl over with the bite. Van holds her shoulder in the clear water and lets it run in and through the wound. Bram makes his way over and holds his arm in the water as well. His face immediately scrunches up, but after a moment of the cool water running over his cut, his face falls into a relaxed position.

"Hey." Van looks at me and points over to the base of a random tree, where a small hole lies in the trunk. "Can you please bring me the bag that is inside of that hole?"

I glance over to it and nod. After making my way over to the hole, I slide my hand into the opening and find that the bag is much larger than I figured it would have been. I assume it won't make it through the trunk's hole, but am quickly proven wrong when the opening expands with the bag. It acts as if it is a foam covering that moves as you move it. I stare at it for a moment, confused, but my attention is quickly diverted by Van calling out to me once more. "Hey."

I spin around and bring her the bag.

She points to it and looks up to me. "Pass out the bottles. One for everyone." Van takes a bottle from my hand and pops off the lid. "Hey, guys, watch. Hold this end of your bottle in the water, and a filter will clean it and make it safe for you to drink. After you collect enough water"—she pops the lid back on and unscrews the entire top of the bottle to reveal a cup—"you can drink. Just remember to unscrew the top. Okay?"

Everyone heads upstream from the girl and Bram. We fill our waters and drink the cool liquid, and I find this to be the second most refreshing drink I have ever had. Bram grabs his bottle and comes over to me. Sitting on the side of the stream, holding his arm, he fills his bottle.

"Does it feel any better?" I ask him.

He nods. "A little bit. It still stings though."

Van calls out from her spot with the girl, "Once we get to the bunker, I will have the nurses check you both. They will get you patched up there."

We sit in silence, listening to the two others whisper to each other and Van telling the girl who got bit that she'll be okay. Everyone other than Bram and I sit, seemingly focusing on each other, while the two of us stare off into the woods.

There's something else out there.

I know there is.

The sun is slowly rising, but the darkness is still around. We are still consumed by it.

I lean over to Bram as he drinks his water and whisper, "Why do you trust her?" I look over to her as she fixes her ponytail. "The guide?"

He lowers his cup and looks over to her, making the topic of our conversation more than obvious. "Why wouldn't I?" He looks back at me and takes a sip of his water, never breaking eye contact.

"Off the top of my head?" I ask. "Because following her got Markus shot?"

Everyone at the creek becomes silent. I realize I said my remark much too loud.

Bram's jaw clenches, and he looks away from me, revealing the sweat dripping down his face onto his tattooed neck. "Are you going to blame her for Sam's death too?"

I remain quiet, not knowing what to say. Everyone at the stream looks around, searching for the next person to speak.

Van rises to her feet and looks at me. "Are you a Bergland native?"

I shake my head.

"But you've heard Frieden's anthem? The same one Bergland held for years?"

I nod, feeling all eyes on me.

"You don't know Bergland's full history, so allow me to enlighten you." Van sits down and fills her cup with the stream water. "Back when the Diligent were in a similar situation as us, they had songs to lead them to safe havens. One of those songs held the words that Bergland used for their anthem, but that wasn't it. Bergland was always a temporary nation. It was never meant to be a permanent situation, so they took the words and modified them. They took the words that motivated people and put them into the song we would hear at least once a month.

"The songs led our people through the woods, searching for clues and rest stops on their way to safety." Van lifts her cup up and unscrews the lid. "They fled for the same reason I assume you all are. It wasn't safe where you were." She sips her water, and we all remain silent.

I want to ask questions. I want to ask why it wasn't safe. I know it wasn't. If it was, we wouldn't have been shot at.

I want to know what is happening. I want to know why Markus was shot and why Sam died. I want to know why we are being forced to flee through these woods, just as I was forced to before.

But I don't ask. I remain silent and let everyone else's conversations fill the air. When everyone is done with their break, Van rises to her feet, takes the water bottles, puts them back into the bag, and shoves the bag back into the hole.

We walk for hours upon hours, seemingly hiking the entire day, until Van finally pulls us aside. "Ready?" She takes a sharp turn and shows us to a large tree trunk. Her fingers slide through the rough bark until she somehow finds a small latch. Her hand pushes a circular cutout of the tree inward and spins it like a wheel, forcing the bark in the circle out of line. A bark-covered door slowly pops out of the tree, surprising us all. Van pulls it aside and gestures for us to climb down the hole. "Safety awaits."

CHAPTER TWENTY

Mavis

My feet hit the concrete tunnel's floor, and I spin around to look. Our entire group stands down in this stuffy dimly lit entrance waiting for Van and the girl who got bit to finish climbing down the ladder.

"Come on, Samantha," Van tells her as their feet hit the ground. "You got it."

Samantha holds her arm to her body as if it is broken and looks around to each of us. Her focus flickers past us and down the tunnel. "How much longer do we have to walk?"

Van shakes her head and waves us all to follow. "Not long."

The group makes its way slowly down the tunnel, seemingly hesitant to go any farther. The sound of our steps echoes off the walls, and it magnifies the longer we walk. When a second sound of people talking hits our ears, Van speeds up, sprinting toward the end, and we all follow.

"Hey!" she yells into the room the tunnel leads us to. Running up to one of the random people walking through the large area, she tells them, "Go get the medic."

The person nods and sprints away, down another hallway, and out of sight. The longer I look around, the more I realize that when we exited the tunnel, we seemed to have arrived back in Bergland.

The group stands awkwardly in the room that looks extremely similar to one of the Bergland common areas, waiting for Van to explain what is happening. Before she gets the chance, three people come out of one of the hallways and look at us. My eyes fall immediately upon one of them as she rushes over.

"Mavis!" Janice says to me as she wraps me in a hug.

I shove her off and stumble back as the medic rolls out one of the stretchers and brings it over to Samantha. Everyone stares at me in shock as Janice regains her balance.

"What?" I stutter out. "What are you doing here! You're dead! We were told you were dead!" My head begins to pound as a sense of anguish comes rushing back.

Samantha is rolled out of the room, and Van turns to Bram. "Go with her. You need to have them check your scratches as well."

Bram nods to her and follows Samantha, leaving the group staring at Janice and I. The two others that walked out with Janice wave the group to go with them. After a moment of continuous staring at me, they hesitantly follow.

"Mavis, I—"

"Sam's mom died while you were gone. Sam died while you were gone! Is he here to? Should I assume that he isn't dead? Should I just throw away all the mourning I did for Henry as well? Is he here too?"

Janice raises one of her hands to try to silence me. "What happened to Sam?"

The palms of my hands immediately find their way to my eyes. I rub them forcefully until all I can see is swirls of different-colored spots. "I don't know. He was there, and then he wasn't. I don't know what—"

Janice comes back over to me and attempts a hug, but quickly pulls back, knowing I don't want to be touched. "And Logan?"

My palms fall and I look back to her. "He could be dead too for all I know."

"But last time you saw him, he was okay?"

I nod, trying to calm myself down. "What happened to you? Where did you go? Where are we?" The room around me looks like and feels like Bergland. The cold air tunnels through the hallway and blows against my exposed skin, causing me to feel even colder than when I was soaked by the river and somehow reminds me that they blew all the entrances and exits to Bergland. This can't be it.

"We are in an underground bunker left over from when we were first building the mountain structures. Not many people from Bergland knew about this, only a select few. We made sure to keep this out of General Wilson's knowledge."

"Wh—" I look around and step out of the path of the wind. "Why?"

"There was always slight suspicion that something would happen and we would need this." She sighs and waves me over to some seats in the corner of the room. "But we never could have predicted anything this bad."

"What? What's going on?" I shake my head and look back to her as I take a seat. "No. First, what happened to you? You blew up! The Palace, it blew up with you in it! I saw you in there."

She nods. "I was in there. I was in there at a business meeting with some of the other officials and capital workers." She sighs and looks around the room to the people walking back and forth with papers, seemingly rushing to get somewhere. "Just before the explosion, a man walked by our table and dropped a napkin in front of me. It read, 'Get out now.' When I showed the others, we all agreed to take the hint, and we slipped out the back of the building. Less than a minute after we fled, we met with a guide and the Palace blew up. The guide ushered us through the city without us being seen and brought us here, updating us on the events that had unfolded."

"Why did you trust the napkin? What if when you exited the building, you entered a trap or something? They could have killed you."

Janice shrugs. "There had been suspicion among some of the officials that General Wilson and Chancellor Oswald have been abusing their power. None of us at dinner that day had any problem trusting the napkin due to these suspicions."

"What suspicions? That they aren't the best leaders?" I ask. "What exactly have you suspected?"

"At first, they were suspicions. Now, they are known facts."

"What?" I reiterate. "What are the facts?"

She pauses as a woman comes over, handing her a clipboard. Janice smiles at her, thanks the woman, and looks back at me. "Frieden's government is almost as corrupt as Bestellen's was."

I try to get a glimpse of what is on the papers, but miss it. Janice pulls them back to her body as I ask, "How so?"

"There are spies, Mavis. Spies everywhere. Oswald has them planted throughout the nation to gather intel. If they find people who don't agree with the chancellor, they will be executed as 'rebels' or 'Amiable sympathizers.' It is already happening. People are being poisoned, restaurants are being bombed, and people who are fleeing the nation are being shot."

"How does hiding down here help anything?"

"We aren't hiding." A smirk slowly rises on Janice's face as she looks back down at the clipboard. "We are preparing to reestablish order."

Logan

"Three weeks," Eric tells me as he makes the first move of our chess game. "Three weeks until you will have to find yourself a new roommate."

"You got the call?" I ask him, returning his move.

He nods. "I spoke to Young this morning. Three weeks from now, I'll be on a boat, performing my dream job."

I chuckle. "And I'll be living alone, never having to smell your dirty laundry again."

"Aw, don't be too broken up about it. If you want, I can leave one of my shirts for you to remember me by."

I look up at Eric as he smirks. We continue playing the game as reality sets in. I will be living alone. I've never lived alone before. I was going to have Sam move in, but there is no hope for that now.

It has been a week since Sam's death and Mavis's fleeing. Everything seems so odd. I try to go to work and forget about it, but I can't. John leaves me alone to do my job and hasn't spoken to me since they left. I doubt he even knows what happened. He is the only one I ever speak to there, so when I don't see him at all during my shift, it is a long and quiet day. I am left to my thoughts.

My thoughts.

The same thing I am left to when Eric and I play chess. The first few days after Sam died, Eric would ask me occasional questions about it, but return to his silent state after the question had been answered. Now, we just play the game in silence, waiting for each other to move.

After Eric puts me in checkmate, I rise to my feet.

"Another game?" he asks me.

I shake my head. "Not right now. Maybe later." I stretch for a bit, feeling a sharp pain in my lower back, which takes my breath away, and head over to the door.

"Where are you going?"

Looking back to him, I shrug. "To visit Sam."

Eric's head slowly bobs up in understanding. He then turns back to the board and resets it, leaving me to exit the house without any eyes on me.

I walk up the road, out of our neighborhood. I take the same path Eric and I did when he first went on a walk with his prosthetic. The familiar smell of spring thawing out of winter hits my nose and fills me with a sense of calm I haven't felt in a long time. The calm is short lived as the questions swirl around in my head.

If Mavis was Sam's killer, why did she kill him?

If she didn't kill him, why did she run?

Why wouldn't the funeral services let me cremate Sam and put him into a matching gem? He would have wanted to be in the same necklace as his mother, wouldn't he?

If I was the only remaining member of Sam's emergency contact sheet, doesn't that mean I am family? If I am the only person to receive his mother's necklace, wouldn't that also qualify me to be able to choose what happens with his body?

Apparently not. The police are allowed to give me his things, but I'm not allowed to have a say in where his body goes. Lucky for me, they buried him in the cemetery not too far from my house.

I walk and walk until I pass by the house hidden behind the trees and surrounded by hundreds of flowers, the same house that Eric and I stopped at when we went for the walk. I am immediately hit by the sweet scent of the familiar plants. The orange, purple, yellow, pink, red, and blue flowers that flood this yard give me an idea.

As I lean over and pluck a few of the flowers from the yard, a shooting pain speeds up my spine, causing me to regret bending. I straighten up slowly, taking the handful of flowers I plucked, and continue to the graveyard.

This yard was so overgrown with flowers I doubt that taking a few was doing any harm. For all I know, I was doing good. I was helping them with their overgrown lawn.

When I finally make it to the cemetery, I head directly to Sam's grave. After weaving through all the plots, I set the flowers down in front of his headstone. Since I didn't have a say in how Sam was buried, they gave him the regular rectangular-shaped clear-glass headstone. Most of the other stones in this cemetery are different colors of glass, and many of them are different shapes. Just as I set the flowers down, the sun peeks out from behind the clouds and illuminates every piece of glass within viewing distance. In the afternoons, when the sun is directly above, it looks as if each stone is glowing with pride; but in the mornings and evenings, when the sun is angled, the entire plot of land looks like a rainbow melting and flowing over the graves.

I turn back to Sam's headstone to find that his name in the stone seems to glow compared with everyone else's. Though his doesn't seem to help the colorfulness of the land, and it does not take an odd shape, his stone seems more original than anyone else's.

I guess that's just the effect Sam had.

Werner

The back of my head rests against the tree as I sit in my stand and wait. Almost twenty feet in the air, I hold my bow, ready to shoot. The afternoon heat slowly begins to find me, but is blown away by the cooling spring breeze.

I try to keep my eyes open and stay awake as I wait for an animal to pass by, but occasionally I drift off. Out here, I am safe. Out here is where I come to rest and take a break from the world.

I was assigned to watch the river again last night and the night before. I've seen no one else attempt to escape through there since Mavis's group a week ago, nor have I seen anyone attempt to enter. This means for the last two nights, I've had to sit and stare at the wall's opening and think about shooting those people.

My assignments usually don't affect me. I can usually do my job and move on. Yes, I feel somewhat guilty each time, but I get over it. I was executing criminals before they could harm anyone else. But now? I can't seem to get over seeing someone I knew, someone who seemed as if they couldn't hurt a fly.

My thoughts are interrupted as something hits my arm. I look around for a moment when another pebble flies through the air and hits me in the hip. Immediately, I swing my aimed bow down and find the arrow aimed at the head of a fellow killer.

"I have always loved your greetings, Rhodes." Mac scrunches her face up into a smile and folds her hands together. "So warm and welcoming."

I roll my eyes at her lack of action when having a weapon aimed at her and climb down the stand. "You're one to talk. You were throwing rocks at me."

She shrugs. "That's fair."

Ruth Mcaninch is originally from Hout and aided the rebels in the war. She and I, being the best shots in the business, were teamed up a few weeks ago on assignment. We were to guard the capitol building one night after Burris was given a tip that there would be an attempt at infiltration by an Amiable rebel.

"Where's your book?" Mac asks me.

I shrug. "I didn't bring one today." Every day I come out here, I bring a book to sit, read, and use to pass the time. Today was one of the first days in a long time I have not.

"I noticed. You were falling asleep up there." She gives me a smile and crosses her arms as I yawn. "Tired?"

I shrug. "I had the night shift."

"Ah." Her head bobs back a little. "I had the night shift two nights ago."

"Me too," I tell her. "Burris hasn't given me the day shift in over a week."

"Have you asked for it?"

I shake my head. How can I ask Burris for something now? She already thinks I don't trust her.

Mac looks at me and squints. "Are you okay?"

I nod. "Yeah. Why?"

"You seem a little, I don't know. Hesitant?"

I shrug.

"If I ask, would you tell me what happened? It's something to do with work, right?" She shrugs back at me. "I know we can't talk about it, but it's not like I would tell anyone."

My eyes meet Mac's. We stare for a moment as I contemplate. I know if I told her that I let people pass, she wouldn't tell anyone; and I definitely know that if I tell her I'm beginning to question the system, she would hop on board immediately.

But I also know I don't want to get her into trouble.

"Do you know any reason why people would be trying to flee Frieden?" I ask her.

She sighs. "I've heard rumors. Do you know anything?"

I pause. "No."

Mac's face allows her smile to grow as she chuckles. "Forgive me if I don't believe you. I feel as if you know something." She paces around me. "Maybe not a rumor. Maybe a fact. Maybe you know something that you need to share."

I turn back and look at her. I can tell she is just messing with me but is holding on to a slight shred of hope that I will actually confess.

"Nope. I don't know what you're talking about," I tell her with a smirk.

Another sigh comes out of her mouth. "That's the thing about having friends in our line of work. There's always going to be secrets that won't be shared."

CHAPTER TWENTY-ONE

Logan

Walking through the same woods that Mavis walked through nearly every day causes me to second-guess my plan to visit the Page family. I make my way down the stone-lined path and to the small cabin to see smoke rising from the fireplace. My first thought is, "Thank goodness someone is home." My second thought is, "Who is home?"

I knock on the door and am immediately greeted by the curtains on the window beside the door sliding open and Caitlyn giving me a large and giddy smile. She closes the curtains and scurries over to the door, pulling me in.

"Logan! Welcome back! Long time no see." She closes the door behind me and tucks her hair behind her ear. "Should I go get Derek for you?"

As she finishes her question, Derek comes out of one of the back rooms. He looks at me for a moment before speaking. "Hey, Logan."

"Hey." I give him a small smile.

"Is there something I can help you with?" he asks me.

I shrug. "Not particularly. I—" I turn to him and slide my hands into my pockets. "I was just coming to check on you guys. You know, to see how you are doing."

Derek returns my slight smile. "Thank you." He walks over to me and sits at the dining table. "My mom is wondering where Mavis is. I haven't told her yet." He looks past me as I sit across from him. "She is in the other room. Please don't tell her anything."

I nod. "I won't."

Caitlyn looks at me, then at Derek, and sits at the end of the table. "Have you thought about what she will say when she comes out and sees Logan?"

Derek looks around the room and back at me. "She may not remember you. If she does, just excuse yourself, okay?"

I nod. "Okay. I will." After a moment of silence, I speak up. "So how are you?"

He shrugs. Leaning back in his chair, Derek takes a deep breath. "Confused. Still very confused."

"Me too," I answer. "It's been over four weeks, and the police haven't told me anything else even though they told me they would."

"Me too." Derek cracks his knuckles and continues staring at the table. "I still don't believe it. Mavis wouldn't do that."

"I know. She couldn't kill anyone, especially Sam."

Derek looks back up to me and quickly corrects, "Wouldn't. She *wouldn't* kill him. Believe me when I say, if Mavis had to, she'd kill."

"What?" I ask him in disbelief.

"If she had to kill someone, she would. But that doesn't change the fact that she wouldn't kill Sam without a good reason." He puts his hands on the table and looks at Caitlyn and I. "She had no motive. That's what bothers me. The police just say she killed him because they needed someone to blame it on. They have no proof! No evidence!"

"Well," Caitlyn interjects. "From what you've told me, Derek, they found her fingerprints all over Sam and saw her fleeing the scene when the police showed up."

Derek shoots her a look of anger and annoyance. "That doesn't mean she did it. What if she found him dead and then ran when she heard the police because she didn't want to be accused?"

The three of us remain silent for a moment. Caitlyn clears her throat and rises to her feet. "I'm going to go and finish dinner."

Derek's eyes close, and he takes another deep breath. "Caitlyn, I'm sorry. I didn't mean to snap."

She nods and heads over to the fireplace. "I know. It's okay." She ties her blond curls back with a hairband and stirs the pot.

Ms. Page's bedroom door creaks open as she hobbles out. Her disheveled clothing looks as if she has been wearing them for a week, and somehow the moment she exits her room, an odd smell exited with her. "Derek, what were—" She pauses as her eyes fall upon me.

Before she can say anything, I rise and head to the door. "I'll see you later, Derek."

He nods and Caitlyn follows me out before Ms. Page can comprehend what's happening. The door closes behind us, and Caitlyn looks at me with a smile. "Sorry about that. I know it can't be a short trip from your place to here."

I shrug it off. "It's fine. It was on my way home from work."

No, it wasn't.

"Well"—she gives me another smile—"thank you for stopping by. Maybe you can stop by more often. Derek doesn't have many friends who would do that for him."

I shrug. "I mean, it wouldn't be a problem to drop by every now and then. It just seems like he is a little agitated."

"Wouldn't you be?" She looks back through the window beside the door and sighs. "He is dealing with a lot right now, more than I ever could."

"I know. I just don't want to be another problem for him."

"Well, you wouldn't be stopping by just for him, right?" Caitlyn gives me a small side smile, one that I don't know what to do with. She extends her hand to mine and gives it a shake. "I will see you later, Logan."

I release her hand and nod again. "Goodbye, Caitlyn."

As I quickly make my way off the porch, she calls out, "You know . . ." I freeze and turn around. "You can call me Amanda if it's easier. That's what my friends call me." She winks at me, forcing me to feel even more awkward than before.

"Okay, Amanda," I tell her with an uncomfortable smile as I scurry down the path back to the road.

I doubt I will be going back there anytime soon.

Mavis

Bram and I sit at a table together as we finish our lunches. He had to have shots when we first arrived in order to fight off any disease he may have gotten from the tree foxes, and he hasn't taken the bandages off his arm since.

The first few days of us being here, he stayed in the hospital section of the bunker and remained medicated. He was so extremely worried that he was infected with something that the doctors have decided to keep him on a vial schedule. He has begun to wean off the vials, but as of right now, he still takes them at least twice a day.

Neither Bram nor I say anything as we slowly eat what's left on our trays. The food certainly tasted better in Bergland, but I am not going to complain. Not about the food anyways.

I have many things to complain about. Many things I want to whine about. One of which is my chest. It hurts. It's sore. Not in a way that makes me think my muscles are being overworked, but more in a way that feels as if sandbags are weighing me down. Another thing I want to complain about is the weariness that I feel. It has hit me this week how exhausted I really am. In order to try to cure that, I eat. Food is supposed to be energy, right? I am hungry most of the time anyways, so I assume that is why I am tired. I'm not eating enough.

Grayson Andrews walks by my table and gives me a small smile and a nod. He was brought down here last week by a special request of "Mrs. Ludley." When he first came down, I was more shocked than he was. It turns out that he had been spreading the word up in Frieden about what was really happening, and it was no longer safe for him to stay there.

His first words to me were, "It's nice to see you again, Mavis."

I told him, "You too."

Those were the only real things we have said to each other since his arrival. I want to ask him what all he has been doing. I want to ask him if he knows where Caine is. I want to ask him so many different things, but I don't want to speak to him enough to actually do it.

Janice comes over to our table and takes a seat. She folds her hands in front of her and looks at both of us. "Good afternoon, you two. How are you doing?"

She hasn't really spoken to me in a week. Not really since Grayson arrived, and now she wants to speak?

Bram shrugs. "I'm good, I guess. How's Samantha? Is she still, you know?"

Janice nods. "Yes. They are taking her off the medicines right now to see how she will react. If she shows no sign of improvement, they will put her back on."

"And if she does?" I say. "Show signs of improvement?"

Janice twiddles her thumbs. After a moment of silence between us, she says, "I don't know. The doctors don't think she will."

Bram nods and takes another bite of his food. "Can I go and visit her? Are we allowed yet?"

Janice slightly winces. "I don't know. I wouldn't suggest that you do. You may not like what you see."

"I don't care," he tells her. "I got scratched. She got bit. It could have been the other way around." He swallows what was left of his food. "I'd like to see her."

The sound of the dozens of others filing into and out of the room becomes more apparent with this pause. I can hear three different conversations going on around us, which all happen to be about their new schedules. Apparently, one of the girls behind me doesn't like the janitor job she received.

Looking around the room, Janice nods. "Once you finish your food, I can take you to see her. Just this once."

He nods back as I speak up. "May I come too?"

Janice releases a sigh, as if she now wishes she had not agreed to let Bram go. "Are you sure you want to?"

I clear my plate with one last bite. "Yes."

Janice rises to her feet. "Just don't tell anyone I let you guys come. Okay? This is not to leave the three of us."

We nod, put away our trays, and follow her out of the room, down the halls, up the stairs, and to the outside of a completely sealed-off room with one window. Janice heads over to a man in scrubs and whispers something to him, causing him to exit the hallway.

She waves us over to the window with a worried and sympathetic look on her face. Bram and I quickly see the cause of her expression lying lifeless on a white hospital bed. What used to be a slightly chunky woman who may have been a little older than me is now almost a skeleton. Her body is as thin as it could possibly get and looking worse than a starved Bloot. Her hair has gotten so thin that it is almost completely gone, and her eyes have become bloodshot. It seems that the only thing that is keeping her alive is an IV cord that is connected to her wrist from the ceiling of the room.

As soon as we step into her line of sight, her whole body jerks to life with more power than I expected. I watch as she thrashes to get out of the bed, only to reveal her wrists and waist tied down. She screams and shouts at the three of us nothing that I can understand and causes Bram to have to take a step back. We watch as she becomes uncontrollably angry, followed by the descent of a blue liquid down the IV.

"The doctors just administered her more medication," Janice tells us. My eyes flicker up to the IV as we watch Samantha slowly return to a comatose state. "I doubt she will get any better."

"What are they going to do?" Bram asks, obviously shaken. "Are they just going to let her continue to be eaten by whatever those animals gave her? She is obviously in pain and discomfort." He gestures to her and stammers, "I-I mean, look! In the last four weeks, she must have lost over one hundred pounds."

Janice sighs and turns back to the two of us. "I don't know what they're going to do. They may choose to euthanize her, but I don't know."

Bram nods. The three of us fall quiet as Janice walks back to where the man went a few minutes ago, leaving Bram and I alone.

This wouldn't have happened if Frieden wouldn't have been so corrupt. This wouldn't have happened if we didn't have to flee for our lives again.

If there is a plan to bring Frieden down, if there is a way to restore order and bring peace into our lives, I want to be the one to do it. I want to help.

Janice walks back from one of the rooms and ushers us out of the halls. I am the first one of us to speak. "What exactly is the plan to bring down the government?"

"Bring it down?" Janice chuckles. "We aren't going to bring it down. We are going to be fixing it."

"And how do you plan on doing that?" I ask with extreme skepticism.

She turns and looks over her shoulder to me. "Why?"

Bram's eyes follow hers, and they both wait for me to answer. The only thing I can really think to say slips out. "I want to help."

Janice gives a little chuckle. "Oh. How do you want to help? Do you want to help out and make the food again? It really tasted so much better when you actually were doing it."

I shake my head as we continue. "No. I want to help." I shoot her a look, trying to get her to understand I actually want to do something. I want to go out and help.

Janice pauses as we reach the commons area. She turns to Bram. "You know your way around from here, right?"

He nods and heads off, leaving Janice and I alone.

"What exactly do you mean?"

The more I think about it, the more I realize how stupid my request is. How am I supposed to ask to go on missions?

She sees that I am having second thoughts about asking and squints at me with amusement. "Do you want to help plan? Or what?"

I take a breath and look at her. "I want to go back to Frieden. I want to help there rather than sit in the bunker and watch everyone else help."

Janice slowly nods her head, allowing my request to sink in. The silence between us makes me almost regret asking.

Almost.

She clears her throat hesitantly. "I can take you down to the gun range and the training room. Before I send you to do anything, I need to assess your skills."

I can't help but allow a smile to rise on my face. "Thank you," I tell her.

She nods and takes me down a few flights of stairs, showing me to a large concrete room with a table of weapons, a few people shooting, and Grayson with a clipboard.

"Mrs. Ludley." With a shocked expression, his eyes fall upon me. "Mavis?"

I give him a little nod as Janice walks me over to the table. "Mr. Andrews, would you please load up 3A for Ms. Wamsley?"

He gives us a small chuckle. "Is she training for something?"

I look around the room to see that most of the eyes have fallen upon me. I am not a regular in here, and my presence has definitely gotten the others' attention.

"I guess you could say that," Janice tells Grayson as she hands me a small rectangular pistol. "Would you please have everyone exit the room for a few minutes?"

Grayson nods and presses a button on the wall, causing the lights to flicker on and off slowly. Everyone takes off their headphones and sets their guns down on their table. After looking me up and down, they all leave the room and head through the hallway.

Grayson takes notice of my confused look and smiles at me. "They'll be in the training room until I give them the signal to come back. This way, you'll be able to shoot without anyone else in here."

I follow Grayson over to a marked-off spot for me to stand. He shows me how to hold the gun, how to load it, and tells me what to expect. "This is one of the easiest shooting pistols you will ever deal with. Don't worry, but keep a tight grip. Got it?"

I nod once more as he backs away. I aim the gun and place the sight accordingly. Everything is all lined up with the metal body-shaped target at the end of the range when I pull the trigger.

I lower the gun and squint to see that I hit the target on the top-right corner.

"Good job, Mavis," Grayson tells me. Before he can get his next instructions out, I bring the gun back up and shoot again, this time hitting the center of the target, right where I was aiming. Quickly, I empty the clip, hitting every target I aim for but one and feeling very good about myself.

I clear the pistol and turn around to Janice and Grayson to see them whispering something to each other. I pull the headphones off and ask them, "What?" I know they weren't speaking to me, but I still want to know.

"That was excellent, Mavis." Janice gives me a confident smile. "Do you want to try a moving target?"

I shrug. "I guess so."

Yes, I do want to try it. I am pretty good with moving targets according to my last hunt.

Grayson steps behind his desk and tells me to get ready. I place the headphones back on and aim the pistol. Moments pass by with nothing moving. I wait and wait until the metal man in front of me slowly moves toward me. I pull the trigger, and it slides through the floor, disappearing. Immediately after, another one of the targets begins moving, this time to the side. I shoot, forcing it to the ground as well. As time goes on, the targets pop back up and begin moving faster. We continue until I use up three full clips.

"Well, well." Grayson walks over to Janice and me with a hologram board and shows the two of us my results. First, he shows me a page with the targets that were still, showing us where exactly on the target I hit. "When they are still, you seem to be able to hit them perfectly."

He swipes the page and shows me the targets that were moving. I hit only about a third of them on the marked areas on the head and chest. Most of my shots hit them in the shoulders, hips, and arms. "It looks like you may need to work on the moving targets though."

"Still," Janice says, "this is much better than what I was expecting." She smiles at me and looks at Grayson. "It seems to me that you have another soldier to train."

Werner

I sip my tea as I wait for Mac. The Marvelous Cafe's cold air makes me appreciate the drink's warmth even more than I already do. I take a deep breath through my nose and enjoy the soft scent of my surroundings. The cookies and small cakes they serve coupled with the large variety of teas makes this my favorite shop in Kern. Half of the shop is a cafe, a place for people to sit and do their business with their drinks and such, while the other half of the floor is a "lend and lease" library. If you buy a pass at the counter where you order, you can go back and read any books you want for as long as you want; you just can't take them out of the store. The book pass is only one dollar, so it isn't much. The only reason they charge is so that they don't lose money on people coming in to read and to read only.

I had bought a year's pass when I first discovered this place, and I've been coming in at least four times a week ever since.

I have just finished a futuristic novel about a utopian state and found that I am not a fan. I don't know whether it is the utopian state that I don't like or the futuristic portions where we are surrounded by machines and robots. I just find it too unrealistic to enjoy.

As I walk through the shelves to find where I originally pulled it from, a small teenage girl looks at me and smiles. "How'd you like it?"

I hold the book up and look at the starry-filled cover. "It wasn't my favorite."

"Aw well, that's too bad. What didn't you like about it?"

I shrug. "I guess I'm more of an action type of guy, and I don't really like make-believe. I find it too unrealistic."

A small smile grows on her face. "So you want the exact opposite of that?"

I nod with a chuckle as I slide the book back into its spot. "Yeah."

She scurries out of sight, behind one of the bookshelves. After one moment of muttering from her, she emerges with an excited grin. "Here."

She hands me a book with a brown cover. The picture is of a woman dressed in older clothes, walking down the road with a gun in her hand. "I feel like you'd like this."

I nod. "Thank you." The girl watches me head back to my table and pressures me into opening it. I skim over the words at the front and find that this is a series of letters written hundreds of years ago. My eyes skim through the first few pages to the first journal entry.

I read and read, feeling as if I have become the woman who is writing. Every gun she shoots, I feel is in my hands. Every word she says, I feel comes out of my mouth. Every sight she sees, breeze she feels, rock she steps on, I feel happening to me. I can tell by the end of the first journal entry that this book will be one of my favorites. I close the cover after finishing the first portion and look around to find an entire new crowd in the cafe.

After waiting over thirty minutes for Mac's arrival and filling it with the exciting life of this woman, I assume Mac isn't coming and order myself a plate of sugar cookies to enjoy with my tea and new storybook. Just as my waitress brings the plate out, Mac comes in the front door and makes her way over.

She snickers and takes a seat across from me. "You couldn't wait on me, I see."

I shrug and take one last glance over the book. "You were late. Naturally, I assumed you got caught up with something."

"I did." She picks up the tea bag I ordered for her and shakes it back and forth before ripping the paper covering off. "I was busy learning about something I feel you would be very interested in." Mac pours the water from the pot into her cup and dips the tea bag.

I take a bite of one of the cookies, feeling its warmth and ooey gooeyness melt in my mouth while remaining sweet and chewy. After a moment of letting my eyes roll back into my head, I ask her, "What do you mean?"

She takes some milk and adds a splash of it into her cup. "Let's just say that one of the rumors I heard is true."

"Which one?" I ask, taking another bite of the cookie.

She stirs her tea and stares for a moment. I wait on her to say something, but she just blows on her drink.

"Mac?"

She takes a sip and speaks into the mug. "There was speculation that people were being taken."

"Taken?" I eat the rest of the cookie and swallow too soon to allow myself to enjoy it.

"Taken. Taken somewhere downtown. I think in the training center."

"Taken for what?"

Mac looks up from her tea and swallows. "Torture."

"Torture?" I whisper back to her. "People are being tortured? For what?"

"Answers."

"How do you know?"

She looks around the room and takes another sip. "I can't tell you. Just trust me, all right?"

I sigh and take a sip of my tea. Our eyes lock as we finish with our drinks and place them on the table. "We were told when we first signed up that no one was being tortured," I say.

"I know."

"They told us that they believe torturing is inhumane," I reiterate. "They lied."

"I know."

"And if they would lie about that . . ." I pause, not wanting to finish the thought. Mac and I stare at each other, realizing we may be in the business of killing innocents. I take another cookie and slide the plate over to her.

After I finish my treat, I set cash down on the table to cover my order and leave Mac with the rest of the cookies. "I have to go," I tell her.

She nods and picks up the pot to refill her cup. "I will see you later."

I head out of the shop and begin my walk to the capitol building. When I finally arrive, I am scanned in through multiple security areas and head through. Down the halls, up some stairs, scanning into other security areas, I scope out the building.

After about twenty minutes of searching, I finally find my way to the "command station" Burris was speaking of. I enter the locked hallway and walk down, looking through each doorway until I find a large file room. Each file drawer is black steel, lined with a luminescent blue paint, forcing the entire room to look quite odd and dreamish without the lights on. A large touch screen table that matches the file cabinets rests in the middle of the room and lights up when I walk in. The entire room comes to life with a click and a whirring noise as my hand finds its way onto the table tablet.

No one other than me is in the room, which allows me to do the task I came for. I walk up and down the aisles of file cabinets and find a whole section marked "Burris." There seems to be a drawer for each month that Frieden has been a nation.

I slide open the drawer for last month and look through the names of the files. There are large files with the week dates on the tab, smaller files with each of our names, and even smaller files within our names with the jobs we were assigned to do. My finger runs across "Rhodes, Werner" first, but slowly finds its way to "Mcaninch, Ruth." I take my time and consider what I am about to do. In order for Mac to have found out that we are taking and torturing people, she would have had to be there, right?

She would have had to be assigned something along those lines, right? Would she have done it? Did she do it?

The sound of footsteps entering the room forces me to close the drawer as quickly as possible without retrieving any of the files. I am immediately greeted with a familiar melodious voice that has never been so threatening.

After bouncing off the metal cabinets and walls, Chancellor Thomas Oswald's voice meets my ears. "Hello . . ."

CHAPTER TWENTY-TWO

Werner

After a moment of silence between us, Oswald looks around the room and slides his hands into his suit pockets. "Not to be rude or anything, but what exactly are you doing?"

If I say I am retrieving files, and he asks for my code, I will be caught. If I make up a story and he asks for my code, I will be caught. I play this the only real way I know how.

"You"—I clear my throat and force myself into a giddy manner—"you're Chancellor Thomas Oswald!"

A small and embarrassed smile rises on his face. "I am."

"I am a huge supporter. Thank you so much for everything you do for us!"

He clears his throat and blushes. "Well, thank you, but it's not just me. It is the entire staff and faculty. We . . . we all have a part in it."

"But you," I continue to slowly shift around him toward the door, "you are the man who makes it happen. On behalf of me and all of Frieden, thank you."

Oswald chuckles and rubs the back of his head as if he is more embarrassed and surprised by my reaction than he can handle. "Please, I am just doing my job."

I nod. "Me too." I look down to my watch and back to him. "Speaking of which, I actually have to go." Before he can say anything, I rush over to him and shake his hand. "It was a pleasure meeting you, Chancellor Oswald."

He releases my hand and smiles at me as I exit the room. "You too."

Quickly, I weave through the halls and head out of the building without another interaction.

Mavis

I run my hands through my hair, trying to push it out of my face as I force myself onto my feet in the bathroom stall. The constant nauseous feeling in my stomach has found its way into my head. The last few weeks haven't been bad, but the stomach bug has now hit me full swing. I am not throwing up as much as I feel I need to. The nausea comes in waves and picks and chooses when it wants to force food out of me.

When Bram asked me if I was okay, I told him how I felt. He reassured me that it is just a stomach bug.

"I felt sick my first few days here," Bram told me. "You probably caught what I had."

I choose to believe his statement and exit the restroom. When I get back to the training room, I notice that only one other person is in here; and he is fighting one of the training bots. I follow his lead and stand back in front of the training dummy I had just left and reset it to easy. Its eyes light up green, and we begin. The man-shaped bot and I circle around each other on the mat, never breaking eye contact. Within seconds, it leaps forward, throwing a punch at my head. I dodge and give it a swift kick to the side.

The lifelike machine grabs its side as if my kick actually hurt and attempts to regain its balance. Before it gets the chance, I end the fighting session with one punch to the jaw of the machine, causing it to fall onto its side.

The machine resets, and its eyes change to yellow. It is now on its medium setting.

I fight it, this time with more effort, and realize how tired I really am. I have felt worse this last week than any other week of my life. I have been hungrier than I ever have been before, wanting to eat everything in sight while never getting any energy from the food I do eat. Because of how much I have been exercising and training lately, I have allowed myself to eat the large amounts of food I want. Nonetheless, my body now holds more fat and muscle than it ever has before.

The bot throws a punch at my head. I dodge and grab its arm. Before I get the chance to react, its arm twists, grabs mine, and throws me onto the ground. My legs immediately fly upward, and I wrap them around its head. Its arms reach up and grab my thighs, but I swing it to the ground before it can force itself free. I reach down and use my body weight to make one quick jolt and snap the bot's neck.

My body relaxes as I shift my weight back and sit on the bot's stomach. The machine becomes limp, and the lights in the eyes die out. I reach down to press the button on the bot's neck to have it return to the starting position but accidentally press something else.

Its eyes light up red, and its body jerks to life, throwing me off. I lie there and watch as the bot launches itself onto my body.

"Off!" I shout at it before it gets the chance to hit me again. The eyes die out, and the machine rises to its feet. It freezes in a standing position and turns off, leaving me on the ground to lie and take a few deep breaths.

I need to continue training.

But I am so tired I don't even want to get up.

The man in the corner of the room looks to me for a split second before he continues fighting his bot as if nothing is wrong. A feeling of relief floods over me as I realize this won't be made into a big deal.

"Mavis?" Grayson comes into the room and rushes over to me, causing the relief to be short lived. "Are you okay?"

I immediately force myself off the ground. "Yeah, I was just taking a break."

"On the ground?"

I nod.

Grayson scans me up and down before returning my nod. "Okay."

I try to wait until most everybody has left this training room before I use it. When shooting, I don't care who watches because they are all focused on their own targets. But when it comes to hand-to-hand combat, there are only three bots in the room for people to use. Everyone else will be watching us. I'd rather not have anyone see me try to fight a bot while also trying not to throw up.

I nod to him again, this time much more rushed and awkward as I run out of the room.

"Mavis," he calls out to me again, "what's wrong?"

My voice bounces off the walls as I quickly exit the room and run to the restroom. "Stomach bug," I answer.

Logan

"Who gets the chessboard?" Eric asks me, folding up one of the last boxes for his move. "It was a gift from Young, so that means it was both of ours, right?"

"Yes, but"—I step in front of the game with my arms crossed—"it was a gift that came with the house."

Eric snorts at my defense, "What are you trying to say?"

"It came with the house, so it stays with the house," I tell him jokingly.

"Ah, well, if we are going by that logic, doesn't that mean I get it since you get the house?"

I roll my eyes. "You're getting the new fancy job, *and* you want the chessboard? Who do you think you are?"

He shrugs. "The better chess player."

"Exactly. That means I need to keep it so that I can practice."

Eric grabs his box and walks over to set it on the table. "Valid point." He looks to me and rests his elbow on the box. "How about this, joint custody?"

I can't help but laugh at Eric's suggestion. It sounds exactly like something Sam would say. My immediate response is to say, "Okay, Sam" in a joking manner; but I can't seem to do it. It hurts too much. If Sam was still with us, I would have said it, but now that he's gone?

"Are you okay?" Eric removes his elbow from the box and looks at my face, which accidentally dropped back into a blank expression.

I nod. "I'm okay. Do you need any more help?"

"No. All my boxes are ready. The movers will be here in the morning."

"Okay. I'll be back in a bit then." I make my way over to the door and point to the chessboard. "That better be out on the table when I get back."

Eric nods. "Ready to lose one last time before I go?"

"You bet."

With those words, I exit the house. My lower back continues to remain sore. The sharp pain aches with every step I take. It feels as if each individual vertebra is grinding against one another as I move.

I brush off the pain and continue to walk. The afternoon heat steadily becomes more apparent the longer I stroll up the road. When I finally make it to the house overgrown with the flowers, I take a moment to enjoy the shade provided by the trees surrounding the land. The spring breeze blows the hair out of my face and the sweet scent of the flowers into my nose. Just as I squat down to grab a few that hang out into the road, the door of the small house squeaks open.

"Well, well, I finally get to meet the flower thief."

I look up to see an older lady with long white hair tied back in a low ponytail. Her glasses make her squinted eyes look much larger than they are, and her age doesn't seem to slow her agility one bit. She makes her way down her brick stairs and over to me, revealing how short she really is.

"I've been meaning to talk to you." She smiles at me as I drop one of the flowers in my hand. "I see you at least twice a week taking some of my flowers." She bends over and grabs the blue-and-yellow plant that I dropped and sticks it back into my small bouquet. "I think it's time for me to meet this girl of yours. I need to see if she is worth all this trouble you go through to steal my babies." The woman winks at me as she hobbles up the road. "Come along, dear. You always go this direction after taking them, but I don't know the way."

I look down to the mixture of flowers in my hands and speed up, trying to match the woman's pace. "I'm sorry, ma'am. I didn't know if anyone lived there, and I only ever took the ones dangling off into the street."

She waves it off. "Oh, it's fine. At first I was a little upset, but then when I saw you hold your back and squat down to grab them, I figured they had to be for something important. Or else, you wouldn't have gone through all that trouble."

"Well, I mean—"

"And the fact that you come by so often makes me think she is really special." The woman stops in her tracks and looks to me. "Oh! I'm sorry.

I forgot to introduce myself." She extends her hand to me, and we shake. "My name is Evelyn Zook."

"Logan Forge. It's nice to meet you, Ms. Zook."

We continue walking, and she chuckles. "So what's the story behind you and the flowers? What made you want to take them?"

I can't help but remain silent. What am I supposed to tell her? She seems so happy about me and the "special girl." Am I supposed to just drop the depressing news on her that they are for my dead friend who was supposedly murdered by the only girl I have ever really found myself infatuated with?

"Ah"—she chuckles again—"embarrassed, are we? That's okay. You don't have to tell me." She looks at me and smiles. "I'm going to follow you anyways. I will just see what's what then."

I continue to remain silent. We walk for a few minutes, only listening to the sounds around us before Ms. Zook speaks up again, "So tell me about yourself, Logan."

I shrug. "What do you want to know?"

"Tell me about your family."

We continue and make our way to the top of a hill, revealing the cemetery about a mile away. "The only living family I really have as of right now is my roommate, Eric. He and I have been through a lot together, and even though we aren't really siblings, we are brothers, you know?"

"Ah, yes." She smiles at the thought. "I understand. How long have you two known each other?"

"Less than a year. Our time together is about up actually. He just got a job in State Two. He's leaving tomorrow."

"Aw, that's too bad, Logan. What will he be doing?"

"He's going to be a fisherman. It's his dream job, so him moving isn't a bad thing."

She smiles again but slowly allows it to die out. "These flowers aren't for your girlfriend, are they?"

I shake my head as we continue approaching the cemetery. "No, ma'am."

She nods. "Who are they for?"

"A friend of mine. He died a few weeks ago."

"What happened?"

I take a moment to think about how to answer and realize this woman has made me more comfortable in her presence than I have been in anyone's since Mavis's and Sam's. "You want the full story? Or the quick and painless one?"

She shrugs. "I like stories, and I have the time, but only tell me if you are okay with it."

"I'm okay with it. I just hope you will be. It's kind of a lot."

Ms. Zook smiles at me and nods as we make our way into the cemetery. I start the tale of our story when we were first exiled from Bestellen. I tell her about us meeting, about our disorders, about the Taai, about Sam and Uri, the guy who beat him up, about Mavis and her family, about the Page family, about Eric and I and the explosions, about us settling in with the new chancellor, about the ball, about Sam's mom, and then about Sam's death and Mavis's disappearance.

Throughout the entire story, she remains silent, not commenting on anything but staring at Sam's clear gravestone. I would glance around the cemetery to see a person walking every now and then; but other than that, it has been pretty lifeless.

And now I'm here, standing in the cemetery, telling a woman I barely know my troubles. I turn to look to her, but she continues staring at Sam's grave. "I'm sorry for all that. I'm sorry about stealing your flowers too."

Ms. Zook, after a few more moments of staring, turns to me and holds up her finger. "I want to take you somewhere." She immediately turns around and begins walking out of the cemetery. "Come on."

I look around to see the sun glowing through all the different-colored headstones and decide to listen to the woman. "Where are we going?"

"You'll see. It's my favorite spot in all of Kern."

We hike for what feels like miles through trees and down a small dirt path, lined with large stones, luscious green grass, and wildflowers. We walk until through the trees; I see a large lake, surrounded by the dirt path and a few wooden benches. Ms. Zook walks over to the sandy shores of the lake and stands in the saturated mud. Placing her hands on her hips, she proudly gazes out into the lake and looks around to see the gorgeous cabins on the other side. "Welcome to Grand Lake."

She steps out of the mud and heads over to the nearest bench. Just before taking a seat, she bends over and picks up a smooth stone. "Have you ever skipped one of these before, Logan?"

I shake my head and pick up one of the other stones on the ground.

Ms. Zook snickers at me, takes the rock out of my hand, and replaces it with the one in hers. "You need a large and flat one, honey." She lays it out in the palm of my hand, showing me the stone is nearly as large around as my palm but almost as flat too.

She picks up another stone and shows me how to force it to skim across the water. "Twist back like this and shoot."

Her rock bounces off of the water twice and falls to the lake's floor.

"Let me try that again." She chuckles. picking up another stone. This time, it skips three times and seems to make a smile grow on her face. "Your turn."

As Ms. Zook sits down on the bench, she watches me twist and throw. I watch the rock skip once and then sink. I bend over to pick up another rock and feel a sharp pain in my spine, causing me to let out a grunt of pain.

"Are you okay?" Ms. Zook rises to her feet and rushes back over to me.

"I'm fine," I slowly rise up and make my way over to the bench with her.

"Are you sure?"

I nod as she sits beside me. "Thank you, though."

"Okay. I'm just making sure. With what all you've told me, you don't need anything else going wrong."

I shrug, not knowing what to say. We sit in silence and watch the birds fly overhead, listen to their songs, and let the lake's aroma meet our noses. The fresh breeze cools us off from the walk and somehow refreshes my energy.

"So what do you think"—she clears her throat and looks back out to the lake—"about your friend's death. Do you think Mavis did it?"

I watch the sunlight shimmer across the top of the lake and sit quietly, enjoying the sun's warmth. "I don't. But what do I know? According to Derek, she was fully capable of murdering someone."

She nods.

"And, I mean, I did *just* find out about her past. It's not like I knew everything about her."

Ms. Zook pats me on the leg. "I'm sorry, Logan. I'm sorry about Sam, I'm sorry about Mavis, and I'm sorry about Eric."

I titter at the thought. I had no idea things were taking this much of a turn in my life. "At least I have you, Ms. Zook."

She gives me another smile. "I'm glad. I enjoy your company, Logan."

I rise to my feet and squat down to grab another stone. "I enjoy your company as well." I toss the stone in the air and catch it once. I rub my thumb over the surface, covering every part of it twice, including a small dent; and I take a few steps forward to the lake.

I twist my arm and body back quickly to get ready to skip the stone when all my surroundings become dark and nonexistent.

CHAPTER TWENTY-THREE

Werner

With tensions high between us, I sit with my newly assigned partner and wait. We watch from the rooftop of a building near the river exit, the same river exit that I am usually assigned to do alone.

Neither of us has really said anything since we got ourselves situated. I assume that the reason Burris assigned me a partner this time around is because she has become wary. She most likely thinks that I am no longer 100 percent loyal to her and her orders, all because I asked a simple question.

Well, the truth is, I'm not.

This is the same river exit that originally made me doubt my allegiance. When I saw the innocent faces forcing their way out of Frieden, a nation I thought to be safe, all my beliefs came into question. With what Mac has been telling me, I am right to be doubting.

I look over to the man to see a scowl. He has held this facial expression since we arrived. The squinting and disgusted frown causes his nose to look almost pear shaped and his eyebrows to appear even thicker and bushier. His bleached-blond hair falls flat on his head as he raises his gun and looks through the scope.

The sound of laughter and cavorting catches my ears and forces my focus down by the river. A group of kids who seem to be no older than fourteen frolic out from the woods and toward the flowing play area.

"Hey," I whisper to my partner, "Jones."

He doesn't move from his ready-to-shoot position.

"They could just be playing."

Never looking away from the scope, he whispers back to me, "If they get any closer to the wall, I'm going to do my job, and you should too."

I look to him and then through my scope at the kids. The leading boy takes off his shirt and jumps in. Jones clicks off the safety setting of his gun, causing my heart to jump.

"No!" I shout in a hushed tone at him. "They are just playing. They got closer to the wall because the river is close."

He looks over to me and growls, "You don't know that. If they pass that rock, the large stone between them and the wall, I'm pulling this trigger."

I sit and watch in anticipation as the rest of the kids follow the boy's lead and hop in. Most of the girls keep their shirts on, but one of them decides to take hers off. I continue to watch them play and skip around in the water, splashing one another and letting the current sweep them away from the wall. Just before my nerves settle completely down, one of the kid decides it will be fun to run in the opposite direction of the current.

I find myself on the edge of my seat, watching Jones's finger tighten on the trigger and the boy forcing his way as hard as he can toward the wall, followed by the rest of the kids. They go and they go until the leading boy is only a foot away from the rock. His arm reaches out to touch the top of the large stone, peeking out above the water in the middle of the river. Moments before he does, a flash of light sweeps over the group of kids.

My body relaxes almost completely with the adrenaline and lactic acid buildup as three watchmen walk over to the group of kids with their flashlights. I feel a large and overwhelming tingling sensation come over my body and weigh me down like sandbags as the adrenaline wears off.

"What are you kids doing?" one of the men shouts at them. Before the watchmen can do anything, two of the boys sprint out of the river and take off into the woods without their shirts or shoes. One of the men attempts to run after them but is obviously outgunned in the area of speed.

The two other men get the rest of the girls and boys out and walk them out of sight, probably to the police station.

I find myself relaxing and sitting back in my seat, watching Jones release his finger off of the trigger and lower his weapon. I can almost feel the anger from him.

Though his scowl has grown worse, I cannot tell what it is about: me being right or the fact that he didn't get to shoot.

Logan

The smell is the first thing I notice.

The smell of cleaners and fresh linen.

The sound is the second thing I notice.

The sound of the news over the radio.

I force my eyes open and look down to see the thick heavy white blanket that I know too well lying over me. I pull my arms out from under it and find something different. There is no bruising.

"You're awake."

I turn to my left to see Eric in a reclining leather seat.

He gives me a little smile. "I was wondering how long it would be."

I clear my throat and notice how dry it can become when you sleep with your mouth open. "What happened?"

Eric looks away from me over to the radio as one of the newscasters speaks about the new vial policy.

"Eric?" I use my arms to force myself back on the bed enough to try to get to a better sitting position and realize my legs feel much heavier than they usually do.

He slides me a water bottle on the little side table the bed has attached. "Here."

I take the bottle and twist the cap open. I am too thirsty to ignore it but becoming quite desperate as I realize I don't see my toes wiggling, my feet moving, or even my legs shifting. "Eric, what happened?"

I continue to try to move my feet as he sighs. "When you were at the lake with that woman, something happened." He looks down to his hands and then back to me. "You twisted wrong. The doctors said that as a result of improper care from the explosions, your spine, um"—he clears his throat again and squeezes his hands together—"you're paralyzed, Logan, from the waist down."

I find myself at a loss for words. Immediately, I continue my attempts to move my legs. Nothing happens. It is as if they are just lying there.

Limbs that aren't mine, connected to my waist, holding me down in the bed.

How could this have happened? The doctors cleared me. They told me to take it easy, but they cleared me. I could walk.

The explosions were weeks ago. How is it just now coming to affect me?

I'm going to be unable to walk, unable to run, unable to move! That was all I was. I had nothing special going for me. Sam was funny. He had that. Mavis was kind and caring. That was her thing. Me? I was the person who could do obstacle courses. That was it. After the explosions, I had that taken away from me, but I could still walk around. I could still move.

But now?

My bottom lip begins quivering, and my cheeks seize up as tears flood my eyes. Anything and everything I aspire to do, or was ever going to aspire to do, is now just another lost dream.

I weep. I try not to, but I do. Eric just sits here with me as the tears fall.

I force my eyes closed, still allowing a few drops to pass, and sniffle the rest away. I force myself to stop and lie back, waiting for the flooding to die down.

"How long have I been out?" I ask Eric.

"Just overnight. It's pretty early in the morning."

Keeping my eyes squeezed closed, I clear my throat. "Aren't you supposed to be home? You're supposed to leave in a few hours for State Two?"

"It's okay."

"What?" I turn to him. I feel my cheeks burning from the salt of my tears and my eyelashes weighed down with saturation. "What do you mean it's okay? You have to be there for the movers."

He shakes his head. The corner of his mouth rises slightly as he looks from his folded hands, back to me. "I'm not going."

"What?"

"I'm going to stay here."

"What? Why?"

Eric gives me a small chuckle. "I couldn't bear parting with the chessboard."

My head falls back into the bed's pillow. "You're staying for me."

He remains silent.

"Barnes, you don't need to do that. I will be fine."

"Hey"—he scoots his chair a little closer to me—"you were here when I needed you even when I wouldn't accept help. You didn't let my whining or depression or anything else affect your actions. You just did it because you felt you needed to, right?"

I look over to him with a slight scowl on my face, one that is unintentional, but is slowly scrunching as the tears reflood. "I don't want you to miss out. You just got your dream job, and now this."

He shrugs. "Hey, this way, I get free housing, I get to play you in chess, I have a roommate that I know I can tolerate—"

I sniffle with a forced smile and use my blanket to wipe the tears from my face. "Thanks."

Eric smiles to me and leans back in his chair. "No problem."

We sit, not saying another word, and listen to the news channel flip through instrumental music and commercials. I try to remain strong but continue silently weeping throughout the rest of the morning.

Mavis

A large amount of mashed food is dropped on my tray as Bram and I pass through the food line.

"Thank you," I tell the worker, earning absolutely no acknowledgment from her.

Bram chuckles at the lack of response, and we make our way over to an empty table.

A scoop of the fluff finds its way into my mouth. I let it swoosh around as I try to chew and find it has a hardy satisfaction. I swallow and look to Bram, who is eating the same fluff. "How's Samantha?" I ask him.

He shrugs. He has been going to visit her a lot just to watch her sleep. "She isn't waking up. They're keeping her medicated."

I nod as a group of people on the other side of the room bursts into laughter. "Are you happy about that?"

"What do you mean?"

I take another bite of my food and shrug. "Do you think they should just end her misery or keep her on medication until she. . .you know?"

"I don't know. If you were in her situation, what would you want to be done?"

The silence between us grows. I don't know if she is in pain. I don't know if she can feel what is happening to her. If she can't feel it, then yeah. If she isn't aware of what's happening, then yeah. But what if she is? If she is fully aware and can comprehend what is going on but can't act on her own will, would she rather live sedated, or would she rather not live at all?

"I don't think it will be much longer anyway," Bram tells me. "She is all skin and bones now. She honestly looks as if she is already decaying."

"Have the doctors said anything?"

He shakes his head. "Not to me."

"Has Janice told you anything?"

Bram shakes his head again. "No."

I look to her as she walks out of the food line with her tray. She tends to sit with some of the other officers or government officials who are down here; but every now and then, she'll come and sit with us.

Both Bram and I look at her, hoping to catch some sort of eye contact; and we wait. Never looking over to us, she walks over to her table with the other workers. Bram looks back down at his tray to continue eating, but I keep my gaze fixed on her. The woman she takes a seat beside glances over to me and is a little confused at first. I point to Janice, and the woman does the same.

She mouths, "Ludley?"

I nod.

She smiles at me and nudges Janice in the arm. Janice turns to the worker and then to me. After she sees me staring, she says something to her table and rises to her feet, leaving her tray with her friends.

"Mavis"—Janice comes over to us and takes a seat—"did you need something?"

"Samantha—how is she doing?"

Janice's face falls, and she looks to Bram. With his head still pointed at his tray, his eyes look up and focuses on her. She clears her throat and looks back to me. "Not good. I don't think she'll be with us much longer."

I set my fork down and stare back at Janice. "Are the doctors going to euthanize her? Or are they just going to leave her unconscious and wait until she dies?"

Bram's eyes flicker over to me. After a moment of them both starting with a hurt facial expression, I realize how blunt I was.

I don't apologize.

"Well, I think they are going to probably give her a few more days before they make any decisions like that."

I nod and take another bite of my food. My stomach gurgles as I swallow, and my free hand slides across my waist. After listening to the people around us sit and socialize with their food, I look back to Bram to see him staring at his mashed substance. My eyes then make their way over to Janice, who hasn't taken her eyes off me.

"Yes?" I ask her.

"Mavis"—she gives me a small and unsure smile—"you look really well today."

"Yeah?" I ask again. "What do you mean?"

"I don't know." She sighs. "You're just . . . glowing." Just as the word leaves her mouth, her eyes grow. She rises to her feet and waves me over to her as she begins walking. "Come with me please."

Bram and I share a confused look as I exit the room with Janice. "What? Where are we going?" I ask as I follow two feet behind her.

Without looking back, she continues, "Nowhere special."

"What?"

We get out of the commons area where we were eating and make it into an empty hallway. She turns to me and crosses her arms. She quickly rethinks her stance and folds her hands in front of her seemingly more nervous than usual. "Mavis?"

"Yes?"

Janice clears her throat and looks down to the ground for a moment. "Would you, um, tell me the truth if I asked you a question?"

"Is this the question?"

She shakes her head and clears her throat again. "Um, no. The question is, um, well, it isn't meant to be insulting. And there is a large chance that I'm just taking a leap here, but you are showing some signs, and I—"

"Janice," I interrupt her, "what is the question?"

The lack of words between us allows me to hear into the commons area much more clearly. The commotion in there is a soft mixture of a dozen or so conversations. It is almost soothing to hear from this far away.

"Are you pregnant?" she asks me.

I scoff, "Pregnant? Why would you think I'm pregnant?"

"Well, you have a sort of glowing to your skin. That, and you seem to have gained a bit of weight, which, I mean, isn't bad. It's just—"

"It's just what?" The longer I think about it, the more I, the more— I can't breathe.

"Pregnant? I'm, I'm not, I can't, no." My breath becomes heavy and yet light. Too light to be able to get enough air in but too heavy and deep to feel as if I am getting all the air in around me.

"Mavis, I could be wrong." Janice places her hand on my back. "Have you slept with anyone?"

A large wheeze finds its way into my lungs. My brain skips around to all the different horrendous thoughts. If I have a child in me, it is John's.

John's.

He did this to me.

If I have a child in me, it is the child of a rapist.

"Mavis?" Janice tries to get closer to me, but I immediately place my back against the wall.

"No, no, no, no." I shove her off and slide down. I sit on the floor of the hall and run my hands through my hair, clenching my fists and pulling at each strand I hold.

Janice quickly sprints out of sight; and as I continue to panic on the floor, unable to breathe or really even speak, she sprints back. My head begins to pound and panic. The room becomes hard to see as the pounding in my head creates the illusion of the room becoming darker.

Janice administers one large vial into my leg and waves two nurses over. I watch them scurry over to me with a bag but slowly lose sight of them as the vial takes effect. I watch them run over to me in slow motion, and that is it.

When I wake up, I am on a hospital bed; and Janice is sitting beside me, reading some paperwork.

"What?" I mumble as I try to sit up.

"Hey, hey"—Janice places her hand on my arm—"everything is fine. You're all right."

My eyes close again, and I try to regain my ability to speak. I clear my dry throat and force myself to a sitting position. The drowsiness I feel overcomes my willpower, causing me to slowly turn my head to Janice. "What did you give me? I thought it was a vial."

She nods. "It was a vial, but it has a different reaction to, um"—Janice looks to me and sighs—"those who are pregnant. It doesn't do any harm. It will just have a stronger effect."

Tears quickly make their way into my eyes. They flood and fall out. I try to stop them. I throw my hands over my eyes and try to hold them in, but they squeeze out anyways. "What?"

"I'm sorry, Mavis, but you're eight weeks pregnant."

CHAPTER TWENTY-FOUR

Logan

I stare at the chessboard. The more I look at it, the more I realize how detailed each game piece is. The perfectly crafted wood seems to have been hand carved almost it is so detailed.

"Are you going to play?" Eric asks me as he brings me a cup of tea from the kitchen. "I'm not trying to rush you. Take your time. It's just that you usually don't take this long."

I turn my head and look at him for a moment. I look down to his leg and find that he has gotten so skilled at working with the prosthetic that I almost forget he is wearing it. He was so down and depressed when he lost one of his legs, not knowing he was going to be able to walk again. With how developed the technology of his new limb is, he can actually do pretty much everything he wants to. He can do obstacle courses, run, squat, and lift.

But me? I can't walk. I can't do anything by myself anymore.

I move one of my pawns and take one of his. He moves one of his knights to steal my pawn, and I take it with one of my rooks.

"Whoops." He chuckles. "I didn't see that."

I shrug and wait for him to play me back. The steam from my tea is rising at a rapid rate. I watch it and wait to enjoy the warmth and taste of one of the only things that seem to soothe me. Eric and I play the game with the occasional side comment but no real conversation.

Our game is interrupted toward the end by a knocking at the door. When Eric swings the door open, a smile grows on his face. "Young?"

"Good morning, Barnes." John walks in with a sympathetic look on his face, which becomes even more pity struck when he sees me. "Good morning, Forge."

I look from him and back to the chessboard.

"So"—Eric closes the door behind them and ushers John over to the seating area—"what brings you by?"

"I can't just come by and visit two of my favorite veteran soldiers?" Smiling, he looks over to me. I continue staring at the board. "Apparently not."

I don't want your pity visit.

"I came by to check up on you two. I heard what happened." John waves Eric over, and the two of them sit across from me. "I wanted to speak with you both."

"About?" I ask him.

"Well"—he looks around the room and smiles—"I got this house for you two because you were both injured during your services in the Taai. I wouldn't have done that for just anyone. I did it for you two, though, and I don't regret it. Since Eric was leaving, I was going to come and speak to you about rooming with another Taai member, but it seems now we don't have to worry about that."

"Meaning, you're happy I'm stuck in a wheelchair?" I ask him, slightly ticked off at the fact that he is pointing it out.

"No, no. I am definitely not happy about that at all." He clears his throat and looks to Eric. "I was actually going to come and let you both know that because Logan has been injured to the point of no return, the members of this household will have all necessities paid for."

"Really?" Eric asks almost giddily. "Meaning, what?"

"I have your codes marked on all the scanners. If you are buying food, up to a certain amount a week, or paying bills, your codes will automatically be accepted because of an account I have set aside for you."

"Wow." Eric smiles at me and then back at John. "Thank you, Young. This is really appreciated."

He nods. "That's not all I came to say. I actually"—he looks over to me and rises to his feet—"would you mind speaking to me in private, Eric?"

They leave the room and head outside on what I assume will be a long walk. They stay outside for enough time that my tea has time to cool down, and I am able to drink it all. I continue to stare at the chessboard and wait for Eric to come back. I have calculated every move I could make and have found the most productive one.

By the time he and John come back into the house, the air-conditioning has already cooled my mug completely.

They are quiet as they enter. Eric and John look to me as John waves me goodbye, leaving me in an awkward staring position.

"What was that about?" I ask Eric as he closes the door.

"Well, a few things actually." He sits across from me and moves one of his pieces, allowing me to immediately take it and put his queen in jeopardy. "Wow, you were ready for that."

"You gave me enough time to prepare."

He moves a piece in front of his queen to protect her. "Yeah, I'm sorry about that. We were going over some things."

"Like what?" I take the piece protecting her.

He takes my piece with the queen. "Well, he offered me a job. Not the same job you had but one where I would be back working in a special forces group."

"Yeah?" I ask him. "And you can do all that with your leg?"

I have never once said anything about limits to Eric before. I was always the one encouraging him to do whatever he wants and never letting anything stop him. It is obvious that when I asked him this instead of letting him know how proud of him I am, I hurt him.

"No," he tells me, "I will be fine."

I play a pawn and bait the queen to take it, but Eric steals the pawn with his rook.

"One of the other things Young was telling me was that after a certain period of time, you will need to get a job in order for him to be able to keep us in this house. You won't have to support us or anything. It's just that the government needs to make sure you aren't mooching off them, you know."

I look back up to him with a slight scour. "What kind of job am I supposed to get with no legs?"

A small smirk grows on his face as I realize what he is about to say. "Any desk job really."

Werner

I flip the page, earning myself a small papercut and pulling me back to reality. I look around the tea shop as I suck on my cut and realize there is barely anyone in here today. The storm outside must be pushing the regulars back into their homes. I've noticed that most people who have come to enjoy the Marvelous Cafe are very introverted and rarely go anywhere but here. I doubt that getting out during the storm is something they'd like to do. That, and it is midafternoon, a time when it is usually not crowded.

My eyes fall back upon the book, and I find myself fading back into her body. I am now eight chapters into the story and am loving every moment of it.

After over an hour of continuous and uninterrupted reading, I find myself having to look away from the book. I have just hit one of those moments in the story where a character does something so embarrassing that it hurts *me* to read it. I give myself a few seconds to roll my eyes and chuckle before turning the page to find a piece of paper hidden within the crease. I pull it out and unfold it to reveal a familiar set of handwriting.

Skimming over it, I read words I never before thought I would have to read.

"Burris caught me. I went through things I wasn't supposed to and found orders to execute her employees that have become wary. She has a list, and I am at the top of it. I'm sorry, but I have to go before she sends someone after me. I doubt that I will see you again anytime soon, but maybe in the future when this all dies down. I know you will see what's going on, and I know you will make the right choices. Don't follow orders blindly, Rhodes. Those acts will be the death of this new nation and cause the deaths of many more. Be careful. Burris knows a lot more than you think."

I skip to the bottom-left corner to see Mac's grandiose signature. "With best regards, Ruth Mcaninch."

I immediately rise to my feet and leave a tip on the table. I shuffle toward the door and am beeped at by the scanners.

"Sir." My waitress comes over to me, ignoring the customers she was just with. "You can't take that book with you."

Looking down at the colorful front, I hand it back to her and scurry out of the Marvelous Cafe with a nervous twisting in my stomach. I manage to flag down a cab and go for a ride to the apartment building Mac was staying in. Running up the stairs, through the halls, and past a few of her neighbors, I finally make it to her door. I turn the handle to find the door unlocked and the room completely empty. No furniture, no pictures, no electronics. I have only been to her apartment once, but I know it was furnished better than that.

If what she said in the note about Burris being on to her is true, then she wouldn't have stopped by here on her way out of the state. Mac is too smart to make those sort of mistakes. Too smart to have taken time out of her escape to warn me. Why would she have risked going back to the cafe and leaving me a note?

The only reason she would have done that is if Burris was on to me too. Does she know that I let people go by that night at the river? Would she have known how much I hesitate to shoot people if she hadn't assigned Jones to work the river with me the other night?

Am I on the list?

CHAPTER TWENTY-FIVE

Logan

Days have passed.

And I am still broken beyond repair.

For the first few days, Eric stayed pretty close to me. He would ask me if I needed anything or if I wanted to do anything or even go outside, hail a cab, and go to town. He is being much more attentive with me than I was with him.

Yes, I tried to help him with everything. Anytime I thought he needed something, I would offer my assistance. He would always turn me down and try to get it himself. Most of the time, he needed no help. The first few days were hard for him because he was just sitting around the house and pouting. After he stopped the whining and realized he could do things for himself, there were no other problems. He got his new leg; and from then on, he has been fine.

But me?

No. If I stop my stream of self-pity, it isn't going to help anything. I won't be able to just stand up and do things myself. I'm not sad that I lost one of my legs. I'm not sad because I have to wait for my prosthetic. I am sad because I will never be able to walk again.

"Are you sure you're okay?" Eric asks me for the millionth time before he heads out to work. "I put some water bottles on the counter, and I put some hot water in a thermos for you if you decide you want tea. Is there anything else you think you'll want while I'm gone?"

I shake my head with a bitter attitude that has become natural for me. "I can reach the bottom section of the refrigerator. I think I'm okay for a few hours."

Eric nods. "Okay. Call if you need anything."

I nod and roll through the room, away from the door. Eric exits the house, gets into a cab, and rides off to his perfect new job, leaving me at home, alone, to fend for myself.

It's not like it is that hard. I have pretty much mastered it. Just put the things I need where I can reach them. Eric acts as if he has to baby me. He doesn't. I can handle myself. I can help myself.

I roll the chair over to the kitchen counter and stare. I pull a mug over to me, grab a bag of honey green tea, and fix myself some liquid joy. Otherwise known as hot tea without any added cream or sugar.

I take my scalding hot mug and set it on a plate. With that plate, I pull the tea off the counter and place it in my lap. Before I begin my journey that promises not to end well, a knock at the door startles me.

I clear my throat and slowly make my way to the table to place my tea down. "Who is it?"

"Logan? It's Derek. Derek Page?"

"Come in." I continue slowly rolling myself to the table and holding the mug with one hand and wheeling with the other. "The door should be unlocked."

He slowly enters the house and looks down at me. After a moment of hesitation, he walks over toward the table. "Would you like some help?"

I look from my tea mug, my plate, and my dead legs up to him. I look into his eyes and note their purple centers before I give him a small smile. "Hello, Derek. How are you?"

He takes a step back as I continue toward the table, pretending not to have heard his question.

In hindsight, I probably should have filled up my tea once I got to the table.

Derek chuckles and takes a seat beside me as I set my tea down successfully. "Good I guess?"

"Good. I'm happy to hear that." I blow on my tea and wait for it to cool. "It's been a while since I've seen you."

He nods. "It has. And I'm sorry about that. I've been meaning to come and visit."

I smile at him. "I assume you knew of my condition?"

He nods again, this time with less enthusiasm. "I called a few days ago to talk to you, and Eric answered the phone."

I roll my chair back from the table and into the kitchen. "Would you like anything to drink? Anything to eat?"

Derek chuckles. "I guess so. I'll take a water."

I pull off a water bottle and toss it over. "Here you go."

He smiles at me as he catches the bottle and twists open the cap. "Thank you." He takes a few sips of the water and looks down to me in the chair. "I'm sorry, Logan."

"I'm fine."

Derek nods back. "I know, but I'm still sorry. And you know what, I'm here to help you with whatever you need."

I find myself slowly scowling at him. "Do you mean the only reason you are here is to babysit me?"

"What?" Derek closes his water bottle and shakes his head. "No no no, I am here to visit a friend, and if I happen to be able to assist in some way, then so be it."

"I'm fine, really. Thank you, but you have enough to deal with on your own." I scoot my chair up to the table and take a sip of the tea. "How is your mom?"

Derek remains quiet. He runs his hands through his hair to reveal a much darker red than I remember. He stares at his water for a little bit before looking back to me. "I don't really know if you'd want to hear about it. It's kind of depressing."

I smile and roll out from the table. With a sly smile on my face, I gesture to the wheelchair and earn a snicker from Derek. "Don't worry about depressing," I tell him. "I think I have you beat."

He looks at me with a small smile. "There are good days, and there are bad days. But within most of those days"—Derek sighs and opens his water bottle again—"she has trouble recognizing who I am."

As he sips his water, his eyes remain averted from mine.

I give a nervous chuckle and roll back to the table. "Well, you have me beat." After a moment of quiet, I adjust my teabag in the cup and speak up, "I'm so sorry, Derek."

He shrugs.

I can't imagine what it's like to have your own mother, especially one you are so close to, not recognize you. She cared for you half of your life, and then you care for her the rest of hers; and yet, she can't tell you apart from anyone else. I can't imagine the feeling of looking into her eyes and not having her recognize you. My mother died for me, and she knew what she was dying for. I know that she loved me so much at that moment, that she was willing to take a beating. But Derek? Derek and his mom? He can't even call her mom anymore and have her respond.

The two of us sit in silence as I drink my tea and he sips his water. We both know we have horrible things going on in our lives, but we both want to act as if it is nothing. The only way I know how to deal with that is to do the same thing I would do with Eric.

"Do you know how to play chess?" I ask him.

He nods. "Do you have a board?"

I point over to the coffee table where the game I played this morning with Eric is still set up. Derek walks over to it and analyzes the pieces as he brings the board over to the dining table.

"Who lost?"

I roll my eyes. "Let's just play, all right?"

Derek snorts with a pleased facial expression I have never seen from him. "This should be easy."

We go back and forth for about ten minutes, and I find that he is even a better player than Eric.

"So"—I take the last sip of my tea—"are you the person who taught Mavis how to play chess?"

He nods. "Yeah. Why?"

"I could never beat her either."

Derek lets a smile grow on his face. "She was always a really good player."

I nod as he puts me into checkmate. Before he gets the chance to say anything, I begin resetting the board. "Yeah yeah yeah, good job. Let's go again."

He chuckles as we reset the pieces. "So you played with Mavis?"

I nod. "And lost every time."

Derek remains silent for a moment.

"What about you? How often did you win against her?"

He shrugs. "We were about even. She won half of the time. I won half of the time."

I hesitate for a moment. The question that continuously flies through my head, flies through my head once more, and finds its way out of my mouth. "Were you and Mavis ever together?"

Derek looks to me with a puzzled look. "What? You mean a couple?"

I nod, finding that my question has seemed to make the atmosphere slightly awkward.

"No, we weren't. She was more like a sister to me than anything. I don't think I could ever even think of her that way."

I roll out from the table and go refill my tea.

"So what about you?"

I turn to look back at Derek as he finishes setting up the pieces. "What?"

"Were you and Mavis a couple?"

I roll over to him slowly and contemplate. "I don't know. I don't think so."

"She spoke of you and Sam a lot. When she spoke of Sam, it was like she was speaking of a friend." He moves his piece first. "But when she spoke of you, I could tell she felt a little bit different."

"Yeah?"

Derek nods. "And when you asked her to the inauguration ball, I thought you were sealing the deal. I thought you were going to actually make your move, but you didn't."

"Well, I mean"—I clear my throat as I pour my tea—"what was I supposed to do?"

"I don't know. You could have said, 'Hey, Mavis, it is obvious that I like you, and I was hoping that you felt the same way. Would you like to go to the inauguration ball with me?'"

"What? But it's not like I . . . well, I—" I move one of my pieces and run my hands through my hair, not knowing what to say. "I came to your house one night to actually talk to her about this, but that was the night that she wasn't there."

"Wait." He looks up from the board to me. "You mean the night that she supposedly killed Sam?"

I nod. "I had called her earlier that day, and we agreed to meet up. The rain cut us off before we were able to decide where, so after work, I made my way over."

Derek shakes his head and looks down to the board. He moves another piece. "It looks like you two just weren't meant to be."

"You think so?"

He shrugs. "Maybe. Maybe not. Maybe you just tried to make your move too late."

I shrug back. "Maybe."

We play the rest of this game of chess, and Derek decides it is time for him to head home. He does me the favor of refilling the thermos with hot water from the tea kettle before he leaves.

Finding that I enjoy Derek's company, I am excited to have him over again. I guess I was just getting sick of having Eric around me all day every day, trying to cheer me up and trying to baby me. I can do things for myself, and Derek seems to get that. He didn't offer to help me every five seconds but instead did one thing he knew I couldn't do without asking me if I wanted him to. He just did it without making me feel helpless.

About twenty minutes after he leaves, I hear the paper boy on his bicycle ride by. I roll out onto the driveway to retrieve the paper and feel the sun's warmth for the first time in a long time. I sit in my chair and look around the neighborhood, soaking in the vitamin D.

Our bushes have begun blooming a deep-pink flower of some sort, along with a deep violet, which looks really stunning together in front of our house. I reach into my shirt and pull out Sam's necklace. I really wish he was here to get to see the first spring of Frieden. I feel as if he would have enjoyed it.

Picking up the newspaper, I feel the sun's warmth on my back and find that I don't want to straighten up. I dangle here for a moment before rising and looking around to see if anyone saw me. Nobody seemed to have taken notice, so I casually roll back to the house and toss the paper down on the table.

My honey and lemon tea meets my lips as I flip through the large pages to read about Oswald and his administration being praised for cutting back on illegal vial distribution, making sure that the transient population of Frieden is less than 1 percent, and continuing to create jobs for those in need.

I then flip to the next page to reveal that there has been another explosion in a restaurant, this time in State Three. One clip of the article says, "Though the casualty count is only seven persons, there is more mental and emotional damage here today than we can tally."

The pictures shown are of the outside of the restaurant, which looks perfectly fine; but the people being pulled out by emergency response vehicles seem to be in shock. There is a little bit of smoke coming out of the windows and doors of the restaurant but not much. I assume that the bomber had a very specific target; and rather than blow the entire restaurant to bits, he managed to only hit what he was aiming for.

Another set of knocks at my door brings me back to reality. Somehow, after reading about the bombing, this knock seems much more intimidating. The fact that anyone could be behind the door waiting makes me a little bit anxious.

But then again, if they wanted to do any harm, they probably would have just barged in.

"Who is it?" I call out.

A joyous voice echoes from behind the barrier, sending a small shiver up my spine. "Amanda Learwood!"

I wasn't ever planning on visiting them again because of her; and now, she comes here?

"May I come in?" she asks through the door. "I bring ye fresh food! Just came out of the oven."

I sigh and wish I hadn't asked who it was. I should have Eric install a peephole down where I can see through it. "Come on in. The door is unlocked."

She slowly peeks by the side of the door and smiles at me. "Good afternoon, Logan!" Amanda enters the house with a large glass dish of what looks like dog food from the sides and a sort of mold on the top. "I brought you some meat lasagna."

"I see that. Thank you very much." I clear my throat as she sets it down on the counter.

Amanda rummages through my cupboards and drawers, pulling out eating utensils as she goes. "I'll go ahead and put some on a plate for you, not that you have to eat it right now but just so that you can eat it when you're ready, you know?"

"I see." I clear my throat. "Hey, um, Amanda, not to be rude, but why exactly did you bring food over? Again, I'm appreciative, but your visit was completely unexpected."

She shrugs and opens the lid off the dish, releasing one of the best smells I've ever experienced. "I don't know. I made some extra food over at the Pages' house and didn't want it to go to waste, so when Derek got home and told me he was just over here, I got the idea to come and surprise you!"

"Oh, um, thank you." I roll back over to the table, following her as she sets my food down with the fork already in it. I look at it to see the white cheese on top has hardened enough to where it isn't falling off but is still gooey looking. There are layers of meat and cheese throughout the entire slab of food she gave me, and every bit of it smells and looks more appetizing the longer I stare at it.

"Go ahead." She heads over to the cupboards and pulls out a plate and fork for herself. "You look like you're hungry."

I chuckle at the fact that I didn't want anything to do with her, but now I'm shoveling in the food she brought me. The taste is not near as good as the smell, but it still tastes decent. "It's very good," I tell her. "Thank you again."

Amanda nods and takes a bite of the food as well. "No, thank you for having me over. I didn't mean to just barge in like that, but I felt like you could use a nice home-cooked meal."

I don't say anything. I just eat.

"So you look like you're doing well."

I nod. "I am. I'm doing much better than I was when this first happened."

She looks back down to her food. "I am sorry, Logan. I can't imagine how it felt to lose—"

We both pause.

"Yeah." She continues eating and picks up the newspaper on the table that I had left. "I see you were reading about the bombing in State Three."

I nod. "It's crazy, isn't it?"

She nods with me, swallowing a mouthful of food. "Yes. These rebels are getting out of hand. They are bombing people who are just trying to make our country better or who are taking part in keeping the peace. It drives me nuts." Amanda plops another piece of the food into her mouth. "Some people just can't accept change."

I shrug. "I've heard some theories that say these bombings aren't rebels. Well, not Amiable rebels anyway."

Her blue eyes pierce into my soul the way she stares at me. Her face drops into an expression of pure seriousness, and her perfect skin and teeth, now seem somewhat threatening in the way they rest. "What do you mean?"

"Well, I, um"—I swallow the bit of food in my mouth and take a sip of tea—"someone told me that they heard Frieden's government is sending people to bomb people who don't agree with them in order to remain in charge."

"Well"—Amanda gives me a little smile—"you don't believe that, do you? It is obviously some crazy conspiracy theory."

I shrug. "I'm from Bestellen. When I believed everything the government and the news was telling us, I was believing lies. Who is to say we aren't being subjected to the same type of lies now?"

She wipes her mouth with her napkin and clears her throat. "Well, I don't know about that." Amanda looks to my clock behind me and quickly rises to her feet. "I actually have to go, Logan. Sorry about this."

"Wait." I swallow the large chunk of food in my mouth as she heads to the door. "Do you want your dish back?"

She shakes her head. "I can come and get it later. I have to go."

Amanda closes the door and walks outside, pulling out her cell phone to call a cab I assume, leaving me with a few sets of dishes to clean and an icky feeling that I said something wrong.

Werner

Sitting up in my favorite spot to hunt, I look around and watch for more than just squirrels and birds. Now, I feel as if I am the one being hunted.

Ever since I read Mac's note yesterday, I have been on edge. I feel as if I am just waiting for a sign for me to leave. Maybe I'm not on the list that Mac was on. If I was on it, wouldn't she have told me in the note? But if I wasn't on it, why would she have said, "Burris knows a lot more than you think"?

As I sit and prepare myself for the worst, it actually happens. My messenger buzzes in my pocket, and I pull it out to see a message from Burris.

"Come to my office. We need to talk."

I slide the messenger back in and take a few deep breaths. The cloudy afternoon weather makes me think rain is imminent and that I could get away if I needed to. I know all the exits in that building, and I know how to not leave a trail. I decide it would be best to go in to see what she needs first, and I climb down the tree.

I stop by my house, put my bow away, call a cab, and head to my offices. I walk through, never making eye contact with anyone, and notice that no one is making eye contact with me. I get into Burris's office to find her sitting at her desk as she always is, reading the paper in front of her. I look around to see that she has redecorated and moved her tacky oil lamps to where you can see them even better now.

"Rhodes," she says without looking up, "thank you for finally joining me."

"Yes, ma'am." I step into her room and continue looking to her, trying to read some of what she is reading. "What can I help you with?"

"No, sir, it is what I can do to help you that we are here to talk about." She looks up to me and gestures to the seat in front of her. I sit, and she folds her hands in the boss-like way that makes me think she is about to confront me about letting those people pass. "Tell me, Rhodes, how have you been?"

"Been?" Her question catches me off guard. "I've been decent. How about you?"

"Not too good. I actually have some bad news for you." She leans back and pulls out a file with pictures of Mac in it. She spreads them out on the table for me to see and shows me all pictures of Mac that look as if she had no idea they were being taken. "Do you remember this woman?"

I nod. "That is Ruth Mcananich. We were partners at one point."

She nods back. "That's right. I regret to inform you that Ms. Mcaninch is now on a list of top-priority fugitives."

I look over the pictures, and my eyes get caught on one specifically. This photo of her must have been taken as she exited the Marvelous Cafe. "What did she do?"

"That is not your concern, Rhodes." She slides all the pictures back into her folder. "I am telling you this because I know you and her were friends. I want to know if she told you where she was going."

Without hesitation, I tell Burris, "I don't know where she is going."

"Are you sure?"

I nod. "We were friends. Yes, that much I can tell you, but we were agents above that. We never shared intel, we never shared our mission assignments, and we never spoke of anything we weren't supposed to speak of."

Burris's eyes narrow on me.

"You can check the security footage at her building. I went to go visit her today, but her door was unlocked, and her apartment was completely empty. That's all I know."

Her eyes continue to stare into mine, but I don't give in. I don't look away, and I don't let up. Burris stares at me for what feels like minutes until someone enters her office and interrupts us.

"Excuse me," the short blonde girl says over me to Burris, "I have something I think you might be interested in."

CHAPTER TWENTY-SIX

Logan

I continue staring at them. Their limp and lifeless ways drive me insane. Losing my legs isn't something I would have chosen; but the more I think about it, the luckier I am. I could have lost the use of my arms. I could have been paralyzed from the neck down.

I could have died.

But instead, I just lost my legs. Not even the full limb, just the use of it. Don't get me wrong. I am not happy about it. I am just forcing myself to look at the bright side. At first, all I was doing was wallowing in self-pity. Yes, I had the right to. I lost my grandfather, who was my only living family member left; my two best friends; my job; and my legs. I had many reasons to be upset; but since Derek came over this morning and Amanda this afternoon, I have realized I still have people who care about me. Eric certainly does. He stayed back from his dream job to help me.

I force my mind off the fact that I can't walk and keep my focus on the things I can do. I can move around myself, I can feed myself, and I can do so many different things.

I roll myself out of my room and back into the living room where the scent of the meat lasagna has dissipated and become much less apparent. Making my way over to the table to clean off the dishes, I bump into the corner of one of the side tables. The lamp topples over, and I manage to catch it before it hits the ground. I place it back onto its spot and slow my roll to the table.

Nice and easy now, Logan, I tell myself. I was rushing too much to try to do things myself.

I get to the table and analyze its contents. Two plates, one with food still left on it, two forks, my thermos, and my tea mug. I slide the two plates on my lap, along with the forks and roll into the kitchen. I set them on the counter and stare at the side of the sink. I can't do anything to clean the plates without the imminent threat of breaking them, so I just leave them there.

It'll be fine. Eric won't be mad. He will be okay with doing them.

I roll back over to refill my tea with the hot water still left in the thermos and hear a noise from the back of the house. I stop pouring, set the thermos down, and turn around to hear no other noises. The house is still and silent with only the noise of my breathing.

"Hello?" I call out like an idiot.

A few moments of silence pass, and a loud noise booms through the house. Three men rush over to me from my room.

"Hey! Stop!" I shout at them and throw punches, squirming and thrashing about, trying to get them to release me. One grabs my legs, and the other two grab my arms. A fourth man runs out from another room and stabs me in the leg with a large vial as I scream for help. My body quickly becomes weak and relaxes as their grip on me tightens.

Mavis

Every shot I take, I hit my target. I hit the steel dummy in between the eyes. I hit him in the chest, right where his heart would be; and I hit him in the throat, forcing the bot down onto the ground, clutching his neck.

I pull back and reload my gun and do it all over again.

I practice and I practice because it's the only thing I want to do. Anything else leaves me too free to think about what is inside of me.

It's a child.

It's a baby.

Not my baby.

I don't want it. I don't want to keep it. I don't want to raise a child. This world is too harsh for one, so why would anyone want to bring one into this mess?

I don't want to keep it. Every time I look at its face, I will see the monster who did this to me. I don't want to keep it, but I don't want it to have a bad life. It isn't its fault it was made. It shouldn't pay the price of having a mother who can't even look at it just because of what its father did.

What if I have it in the bunker? Will someone else raise it? I mean, I will step up if I need to, but I want the kid to have a good life, and a life with me won't be good.

I take down every target I hit with one shot, except for my last one. I look at the target in the back of the room and realize I shot too low. With my streak being broken, a small amount of anger bubbles up within me. I spin around and head back to Grayson to ask for more ammunition when our eyes meet.

He looks down to my gun and grabs three more boxes of ammunition for me. "With the way you go through these, we might need to get you to come help refill the bullets."

I take the three packs and shrug. "That sounds fair to me. I wouldn't be opposed."

He chuckles. "I was just joking, but if you're really up for it, I will talk to Ludley."

I nod and head back to empty the next three boxes. After my allotted amount of time for the gun range is up, I head out of the room and into the commons area for lunch. When I get in line and have the lady behind the food plop mash onto my tray, I can't help but smile at the fact that I didn't have to help prepare it. The only reason I ever slightly enjoyed working in the kitchen was because of Sam.

And now he's gone.

I don't ever want to go back to working in the kitchen.

When I make it to my usual lunch table, I am soon joined by Bram, who sits quietly in front of me.

Without looking up from my food, I ask him, "What's wrong?" He is quiet a lot nowadays, but this is a different sort of quiet.

When he doesn't answer, I look up to see him clenching his jaw and staring at his food with a large mixture of emotions.

"Bram," I say to him, not knowing what to do.

"Samantha died this morning."

"Oh." My shoulders relax as I stick my fork back into the mash. "I'm sorry. I know that must have been hard on you."

"Why?" He looks me in the eyes almost angrily. "Because you think I think it should have been me? Because you think I look at her and draw lines between us and think, 'We're the same'?"

I shrug and snap back at him, "I don't know why exactly this was hard on you. I just know it is by the way you looked just now."

Bram looks back down to his food.

Neither of us says anything. Moments of silence pass before I speak up, "So if you weren't drawing lines between the two of you"—I clear my throat—"why was it so hard on you?"

Bram looks up to me and licks his teeth as if thinking about answering me or not. After a moment of silence, I look back down to my food, thinking he won't answer, but am proved wrong. "Because she suffered."

I look back up to him.

"She was in there for weeks, almost ten, and the doctors did nothing. They knew she was going to die, and they knew she was suffering. They did nothing."

"So," I say, "you wanted them to euthanize her?"

He takes a moment to think but quickly answers, "If she were a dog going through that much pain and suffering, knowing there would be no return, no one would have blinked. They would have put her out of her misery immediately."

"Well, she is not a dog, Bram," I tell him, slightly ticked off by his comparison.

"I know. I am saying that if we would immediately help an animal like that, why wouldn't we treat a human with the same sense of respect?"

Grayson walks over to our table with his tray and gives the two of us a smile, allowing a subject change to appear. "Good afternoon."

I nod back to him. "Hey, Grayson."

Bram looks back down to his food and continues eating in silence.

"So"—Grayson sticks his fork in his beans and stirs them around—"I spoke with Ludley earlier about you working in the ammunition hall."

"Yeah? What did she say?"

"She said you can. I have to give you the training first, obviously, but then you'll be good to go."

"Perfect," I tell him.

"I do have a few questions for you, though, you know, before you start working."

I swallow one of my last bites. "Go ahead."

Grayson clears his throat and glances over to Bram before asking me, "Do you have any restrictions physically?"

"Huh?"

"Because of your pregnancy? Anything I need to know about before you start working in order to ensure an easy job for you?"

I look to Bram, who has looked up from his food to see me answer. I turn back to Grayson with a slight amount of anger. "No. Nothing I am aware of. Why?"

"Well, I know morning sickness is an issue for some women—"

"Yeah, well, that's natural. All I will need is permission to leave as I need."

He nods. "Okay. Sounds good to me."

The three of us go back to our trays and eat in silence. I take the last bite of my food as Bram sits back up straight and gives me an odd look.

"What?" I ask him, trying not to sound too ticked off.

He shakes his head and returns his focus to his food. "Nothing."

"It was obviously something," I say to him. "Go ahead."

"You seem a little angry. I don't want to make you any more upset."

I look to Bram with a slight scowl but let up immediately. "I'm fine. Go ahead."

He clears his throat nervously just as Grayson did before asking me. Bram looks to Grayson, who chews with an equal amount of nervousness in his eyes. He takes another bite of his food and swallows. "Does Logan know about the baby?"

"What?" I ask. "No. Why would he know if I just found out?"

"Well, I sort of meant does he know that, or did he know that you could have, maybe have been, possibly pregnant?"

I look to Grayson who is chewing with wide eyes, not knowing what to say. "What are you talking about?" I ask Bram. "Why would he have known?"

Bram's eyes grow larger than Grayson's as I realize what he is insinuating.

My breathing becomes shaky as I try to get the question out. "Do . . . do you think this is . . . that—do you think that Logan is the father? Is that what you're saying?"

Bram and Grayson exchange looks. Grayson remains quiet as Bram clears his throat again. "Well, isn't he?"

"What?" I snap. "That is none of your business!"

"I'm sorry. I wasn't trying to be rude. It's just that the way Sam always spoke of you two, I figured that when you—"

"Stop." I rise to my feet and look to Grayson. "What about you? Did you think this was Logan's too?"

Grayson swallows his food. "I never assumed it was, but if I had to take a guess—"

"What? A guess?"

"Well, it was obvious at one point that you and Logan had a thing for—"

Before Grayson can finish his statement, I storm off.

Did they really assume the child inside me was Logan's? Did they really assume that just because Logan may have liked me at one point that I slept with him? They don't know anything.

I make my way through the bunker and back into the simulation room with the fighting bots. No one else is in here, which makes it much better for me. I hop onto the platform and set the bot to medium.

Its eyes light up yellow, and it whirrs to life. Its arms bend as it readies itself to fight, and its knees pop into a higher-functioning mode than they are usually set on. I wait for it to begin, and it takes one swift lunge at me.

I dodge and elbow it in the back of the neck, causing it to almost tumble.

The first shot it takes is always the easiest.

The next act it does is lunge at me again; but this time, it takes me down. I take its arm and twist it to the point that the bot falls off me and has to recoup. I rise to my feet and hop onto its back, wrapping my arms and legs around it to the point that it can't move. I hold my arm around its throat and hold until the bot simulation dies out.

I rise to my feet and prepare myself for the next mode. Its eyes light up orange as it changes modes to something between medium and hard.

The bot's head slowly turns to stare at me as I hold my position. We both run at each other at the same time and end up dodging each other's shots while also managing to land a few. Toward the end of our fight, I find myself becoming dizzy. The room slowly becomes much heavier as the bot swings its knee up and hits me hard in the stomach, causing me to lose all the air in my lungs.

Its hit somehow gives me another boost of angered energy that I then use to tackle it to the ground and beat it until my knuckles begin to bleed. I do nothing that I am supposed to do to take it out. I don't snap its neck. I don't strangle it, break its joints, or anything that I was prepped and trained to do.

I only beat the bot until the dizziness takes over.

Werner

Hours after Burris called me into her office, only to abandon me and leave to speak with some blonde girl, I am finally ushered out of Burris's room by two large men.

I am taken across town to a tall office building that I've never stepped foot into. I look around the lobby to find it bland and quite cheap looking but brush it off as I realize I recognize some of the faces.

The two men walking me through the building haven't looked me in the eyes once. They are looking forward and yet manage to keep me in a position between them so that I don't think I could ever get out without drawing extra attention.

We walk through the building, up some stairs, and down a hall until we make it to a small side door. One of the men opens the door for me; and my eyes immediately fall upon Burris, Eric Barnes from the Taai, and another large man, standing in the corner of the room.

"It's nice to have you finally join us, Rhodes." Burris waves off the two men who walked me here, and they close me in. I look to Eric, who seems just as surprised to see me as I am to see him. "I'm sorry about leaving you in my office, I truly am, but I do feel that we have now reached a place of no return."

"What do you mean?" I ask her.

"You seem to have begun doubting the system you swore to follow. All our wishes and all the assignments we have ever asked you to do were necessary actions, and you now question them. I can't have someone who doesn't trust me fully be assigned these important tasks." Burris waves me over to the table against the wall in front of a large mirror. She stands beside me and looks at me through my reflection. "Rhodes, this task I am about to give you could be your final task depending on how you handle it." She points down to the tilted table in front of us to one of the dozens of buttons, switches, and nozzles on it. Her finger lands on the little red button between us, and she looks me in the eyes. "This button causes an electric shock to be sent into someone on the other side of this mirror. I don't have to tell you why we are doing this or why I am asking you to do this. I just need to know that you can follow orders."

Burris steps back and looks to Eric for a moment. After she looks to Eric, she looks back to me with a blank expression. "Press the button."

My eyes fall to the table and look to the large sum of gears as I sort through the million thoughts going through my head. Is there really someone on the other side of this mirror? How much of a shock will be sent through them? Will Burris have me killed if I don't press the button? What is Eric doing here?

"Press the button," she repeats.

I step away from the table and look back to her, knowing I am not going to get an answer. "Why? What did the person do?"

She slowly steps to me, remaining only inches away from my face and looking me in the eyes. With a soft and yet harsh voice, she calmly states, "You failed your test." Burris presses a small button on the side of the table, and the two men who ushered me here rush me. "Take him to the cell," she tells them.

They grab my arms and begin pulling me out of the room as I watch her turn to Eric. She says something to him as I begin thrashing to get the men to loosen their grip, but I can't hear it. Just as the door closes behind me, I see Eric nod his head and press the button.

CHAPTER TWENTY-SEVEN

Logan

Another severe burning jolt is sent through my sides. With the two small metal prods jamming into my hips as I sit in the empty room with nothing staring back at me but my own reflection, I beg them to stop once more.

"I don't know anything!" I shout at them, screaming at the top of my lungs. I look down to the wooden chair and stare at the leather straps they have around my wrists and my waist. The small metal sticks being held into my hip bones slowly begin to heat up, causing me to shout at the mirror again, "I don't know anything!" After having them pull out my fingernails one by one as slowly as they could, and me still not telling them anything, why do they still think I know? They even ripped a few of them in half and bent them backward as they forced me to watch! Why would they think I know something worth going through that for?

I watch the blood dripping slowly from my fingertips. The puddles created on the ground from my new wounds drive me insane as I watch the nails sit in their own blood. I would rather sit through one hundred more electric shocks than have to have them pull out my fingernails like that again. At a time like this, I would be rubbing them each three times over. But now? All I can do is watch them lie on the floor, covered in my blood, and try not to think back to how they got there.

After a moment, the overhead speaker comes on again, "You told one of our sources that Frieden's government was the one responsible for the bombings. True or false?"

I pant, trying to catch my breath from the last shock. I feel my heart slow down an abnormal amount as my head pounds. "True."

"Okay, good. Now, where did you hear that from?"

"My friend Sam. Samuel Beckman," I whine, letting my head fall back against the chair, "and his friend Bram. I don't know his last name."

"You see, that's the thing," the voice from the speaker says. "This is where I don't believe you. It just seems too perfect of a story. Your friend Sam is dead, and his friend Bram is nowhere to be found. I mean"—the voice gives a sarcastic snort—"Sam and Bram? You even chose names that rhyme. How does that help anything?"

I feel the sticks in my sides warm up drastically. I can't help but shout out, "No! No no no!" They send a large volt and electricity through my sides, down my legs, up my torso, and down my arms to the open wounds on my fingertips. The burning and shock sensation is one of the worst pains I've ever felt. It makes me rethink saying I'd rather do this than have my fingernails pulled out again. I can't even scream as the electricity flows through me. I have no control of my body.

The moment the shocking stops, I feel myself become saturated below my waist.

"Aw, look at that," the voice says. "You peed yourself. How does that feel, Logan?"

I watch the urine spread through my pants as I soak in my own embarrassment.

"The only way to stop this is to tell me who you heard those things from."

I bang my head against the back of the chair again and find myself whining out, "I told you everything I know. It's not my fault Sam died."

"Well, too bad then." He clears his throat and chuckles. "Logan, let me introduce you to my friend. His name is Maynor Leishman, and he will be dealing with you today. It was nice working with you."

The sound cuts off for a moment in the room before another voice appears, this one much smoother in tone. "Hello, Mr. Forge."

There is a silence that sits between us for a moment. I don't say anything.

"I said," the man repeats, "hello, Mr. Forge."

The sticks on my sides begin to warm up, but I shout out before they shock. "Hello! Hello, Mr. Leishman!"

The sticks whirr back down and cool themselves as the man comes back onto the speakers. "That's more like it. So today I've watched my associate try to deal with you for a few hours. Nothing he seemed to do worked, but then again, that was him. I have a different way of dealing with you, people."

The screen in the top-right corner of the room clicks to life as a picture of a man in the same seat I am sitting in comes up. The angle of the picture is from the back right corner of the room. I look back there to find a small video camera and fear what comes next.

"I don't play games. If you don't answer my questions, it is because you don't know. And you know what? If you don't know, I have no use for you. I can't let you leave now that you've been questioned, so there is really only one way to save your skin. You tell me something I want to hear."

A click echoes through the room from above me. I look up; and immediately, gallons of some sort of clear liquid are dumped on me from the ceiling. I keep my head down to keep the liquid out of my face, but it splashes off my legs and into my nose anyways. I cough and choke, spitting it out as the liquid stops pouring, and look around the room. I watch it slowly disappear as the drains beneath me swallow the remaining drops up, and I look back to the mirror to see a soaking wet me.

"What is this?" I shout, trying not to let any more of the liquid into my mouth or nose.

"Let's just say it's not water." The giddy manner of the man's voice sends a gut-wrenching feeling into my stomach that I can't ignore. "If you don't tell me something I want to hear in the next ten seconds after the video ends, you will have the same fate as this man."

The picture on the screen in the top-right corner begins playing a video of a man in this seat, screaming, thrashing, begging to get out. The same liquid that was just dumped on me is dumped on him, but he seems to have a worse time choking on it than I did.

"What is this?" he shouts at the window just as I did.

Another click echoes through the room, this time releasing a red gas in the video. The gas floats toward the man from all angles as he screams for help. I look around the room to see small holes on the walls where I assume the gas was released and am immediately scared back into watching the video from the man's screams. His horrid voice echoes through the room as the gas touches his saturated skin, causing immediate boils and welts to form, seemingly burning him alive. The man thrashes around in a spastic manner, worse than I have ever seen before, and continues thrashing until his body falls lifeless to the side of the chair. The gas continues to float through the room on the video as the man dangles from his seat, and I look back to the mirror to see the horror I feel staring back to me.

Werner

I finally got one of the goons to tell me something. They said that I will be executed tomorrow. After they told me that, my immediate reaction was to flee. They ended up calling in another man as backup, and the three of them threw me in here and beat me.

They beat me for what felt like an hour. I got a lot of good hits in; and for a moment, I thought I was going to win. Sadly enough, one of them pulled out a vial and took me down before I got the chance to escape.

So now, I sit in my cell with a million bruises and possibly broken ribs, waiting for tomorrow to come. Hours have passed, but I don't know the time. The darkness they have left me in is causing my head to spin.

I hate being in captivity. I've never liked being trapped. That is one of the reasons I prefer to be outside. It feels as if there is more space. But in here? There is too little space. Too little air.

I don't even know where I'm being held.

I know there are guards outside of my cell, but that is all I know. I can hear them walking around. I've listened to them for hours.

Or however long I've been awake.

A thud snaps me out of my thoughts and back to reality.

Are they here? Is it time?

I brace myself to bolt out of the door as I listen. A few guards shout, but the shots of a surpresor meet my ears.

I loosen up for a moment, listening to the silence behind the cell door, but almost immediately tighten back up as I hear the lock on the door click open.

Sprinting at the woman who opened it, I lunge forward to take her down but am grabbed by the wrist. My arm is twisted behind my back, and I am shoved onto the ground.

"Stop!" she loudly whispers at me as she leans on my back, "I'm here to get you out."

"What?" I whisper-shout back at her.

The dark-haired girl releases my arm and helps me up. My eyes try to readjust to the light as she leads me through the hallways. "The people who are locked up in here tend to be the people who are on our side. You just happen to be one of the lucky ones I got to before the morning." We continue running and stop against the edge of one of the hallways. She peeks around the corner and takes out two more guards with her pistol.

"Whose side?" I ask her, stealing one of the guns from the guards.

"The people who support the real Frieden, not the one Oswald and his council have made it."

"What are you talking about?"

"I read your assignments," she tells me. "You didn't shoot everybody that night at the river. Why?"

"What?" I stop in my tracks. "How did you know that?"

She smiles at me and extends her hand. "Nice to meet you, Werner Rhodes. My name is Van. I was that group's guide that night. You spared us."

I take a step back for a moment as I scan her size. The only real thing I recognize is her hair. The darkness of it seems slightly familiar but still. "You were the guide?"

"Yes." She drops her hand, and we continue walking. "Tell me, why didn't you finish your assignment that night?"

I hesitate for a moment. "I saw someone I recognized."

"And that made you start questioning your orders, correct?"

I nod.

"Long story short, that is how you ended up here, right?"

I nod again.

"All right, then you're on our side too. You want what Frieden was supposed to be about, right? Freedom?"

"Yeah, but I—"

Van grabs my wrist and pulls me aside and into a cleaning closet. She looks around the room and climbs up one of the shelves and pops out one of the ceiling tiles. "Follow me."

I watch her climb up with ease and try to follow her steps exactly.

"Van," I call out to her in a hushed tone. She turns around and places her finger on her mouth to silence me, but I grab her wrist to get her attention. "There's someone else we need to get."

"What?" she asks me.

"There's someone being tortured in one of the rooms on the third floor. It's a small door leading to the—"

Van nods and shushes me again. She raises her wrist to her mouth and speaks into her cuff, "Q, I need you to go to room 3667. Someone is in there." Van holds her cuff up to her ear and listens for the man's or woman's muffled response. When it finally mutters something back, she points to the ceiling tile beside my foot. "Close it up and follow."

I place the tile back and mimic her quick and quiet crawls out of the building without another word. We slide out of the back through a small opening I don't think was there originally and climb down the small indents made into the brick wall. Once our feet hit the ground, we sprint off through the back side of the city and into the woods.

Logan

The gas continues to float throughout the room in the video as the man behind the window chuckles. "You have ten seconds before you are given the same fate as this man."

Leishman doesn't count down. He simply lets me do it myself, which is even worse. What if my ten seconds are longer than his ten seconds? What if mine are shorter? What if I waste all my ten seconds thinking about this?

"I don't know what you want me to tell you!" I thrash about, trying to get my arms and waist untied but realize, even if I did that, I still couldn't get out. I can't stand up. I can't run away. "I heard it from my friend Sam, and he is dead. He heard it from his friend Bram, and he is gone! What do you want?"

Click.

A low hissing noise begins to fill the room. I look to my right to see the red gas slowly floating toward me. I look to my left and see the same. The liquid on my skin has begun to heat up already, causing me to thrash about as much as I can.

"No! Stop!" I shout. "I've told you everything. I will tell you anything!"

The gas floats forward. It doesn't float up to the ceiling or down to the ground but forward to me.

"Stop! Please! I will tell you anything!"

A large amount of rumbling and tumbling noises come from behind the mirror. I stare at my reflection as another click echoes through the room, and the hissing stops.

But the gas doesn't.

It continues floating toward me as I shout and scream for help. I look down and watch the gas touch my right arm first. It slowly caresses the liquid, causing an even worse burning sensation than earlier as the acid causes boils to grow on my body. I watch in the mirror as the red slowly devours me, causing boils and blisters to cover my body. I watch the welts and sounds grow and explode, causing my skin to shrivel and tighten under the liquid. The open wounds from the exploded boils show blood and pus but let the liquid sink into them, causing the gas to grow more boils under my skin and inside of me.

Just as the pain becomes too great for me to handle, I watch the door in the corner of the room slide open.

CHAPTER TWENTY-EIGHT

Werner

We run.

And we run.

She seems to have an unlimited amount of energy while I am struggling to keep her pace.

"Come on, just a little bit farther," she tells me.

"Until where?"

"There's an underground rest stop just up ahead on the right." She continues running and speaking at the same time without gasping for air as I seem to be. "You'll need to rest for a little bit before I take you to the bunker outside of the wall."

"What?" I slow my pace and catch her attention.

She turns around and waves me on. "Come on, we don't need to get caught." Van continues to sprint off, seemingly not caring enough to see if I'm following.

I speed back up and find myself short of breath. "What do you mean the bunker outside of the wall?"

"Well, there's a bunker"—she takes a breath as she slows down a bit for me to catch up—"and it's outside of the wall. What else do you want to know?"

"Well, a lot of things." I wheeze, trying not to sound too pathetic; but we've been running for a good forty minutes now. I think I deserve at least one wheeze. "Who all is down there? How long has the bunker been there?" I take another deep breath. "How long will I be down there?"

"I don't know. There are some officials down there, the bunker has been there for years but not many people know about it, and you could be down there for a while depending on how long it takes us to restore order."

"Wait, what?"

"Oh no, don't worry. It's very nice down there. It's almost exactly like a little Bergland." She slows down for a moment and then speeds back up. "Oh, right. You've never been to Bergland. Well, trust me, the bunker is lovely."

"What do you mean restore order? What are your plans?"

She slows her pace again to a speed walk, one pace I am much more comfortable with. "Well, there are a lot of plans. Some plans are already in play."

"Can you tell me what they are?"

She looks to me and shakes her head. "No."

"Can you tell me what you meant by restore order?"

Van speeds up a bit into a little jog and makes her way to a random tree. She heads over to one of the small branches growing on it and twists it left three times, right once, then pulls it down like a lever. I hear a small shuffle of leaves on the ground, and she leads me around the tree to an opening on the bottom of the trunk. She slides in and waves me along. "Well, the officials who are in the bunker are some of the same officials from Bergland. They have quite a few plans on how to restore the government to the way it once was and to improve it for the better without all the corruption."

We climb down a small ladder and land on a concrete floor. She presses a button in the room that closes the tree trunk, and we walk down the hall into a slightly larger room with two beds and a trunk with an electric padlock.

"So what exactly is their plan to restore order? You still haven't clarified."

Van turns to me with a funny look on her face. "Why do you want to know so badly?"

"Considering what all has happened here, I know Frieden's government is corrupt." I make my way past her and sit down on the bed, trying to allow my aching body some rest. It seems that my entire body hurts, from my muscles to my new bruises, from my earlier beating. My body throbs and my head pounds as I rest on the squeaky and obviously worn mattress. "I mean, I was one of the men who helped make it that way by taking out those who don't believe the same."

"Yeah?" She heads over the trunk and punches in the code.

"I want to help."

Van looks over her shoulder at me and then back to the chest, finishing the code. "What do you mean?"

"I want to help. I have a lot of skills that have proved useful in the past, and I want to use them now to help."

She opens the chest and pulls out two water bottles and some protein bars. She tosses me one of each and sits on one of the chairs in the room.

I open the water bottle and watch her unwrap her protein bar. "I want to stay in Frieden and help you guys fix what shouldn't have gotten this messed up in the first place."

Van takes a bite of the bar and stares at me. After a moment of silence, she swallows. "You are a target now. You've just broken out of a holding cell and will most likely have your face plastered where people can see it. You will be labeled a criminal and have a price put on your head. I can't have you in Frieden. It's too dangerous."

"For who? For me?" I take a bite of the protein bar. "I will be fine. The worst they can do is kill me."

"No," she states, "the worst they can do is torture you. They can get answers from you. It is too dangerous for us to have you stay out here."

"Well, then maybe I can be someone else."

A small smile rises up on Van's face. "What do you mean?"

"Dye my hair. Give me colored contacts. I will grow a beard, put on some weight, lose some weight." I swallow another bite of the bar. "Just tell me what I need to do."

She takes another bite of her bar as I realize her smirk isn't going away anytime soon.

Logan

Stop.

I force my eyes open as the pain on my skin wakes me up.

The tight and horrible feeling of a blister on your hand caused by a burn is covering my entire body. That one feeling that everybody hates is covering my body from head to toe.

I can feel it in between my toes.

I can feel it on the back of my knees.

My body is lain back on a bed, spread out so that no body parts are bending, causing the blisters to rub together. I am in one of the best possible positions for this sort of pain but am still feeling an immense amount. The pressure on my backside pushes against the blisters; and the more I think about it, the worse the feeling gets.

After minutes of agony and trying to stay as still as I can, a man comes into my room and sits on the end of my bed by my feet. "Good morning, Logan." He gives me a small smile and clears his throat. His perfect hair seems to have just been gelled up, and his teeth seem to have just been bleached.

The sound of the medical machines around me comes in to focus as one particular set of beeping increases. I look around to find that I am in another sort of hospital but not the same one I am used to waking up in.

A small feeling of relief slowly comes over me, seemingly starting from the cold rush of liquid coming from my IV.

"You see this?" The man holds up a small handheld button attached to the bed by a wire. "Right now, I am in a good mood, so I am giving you some medicine to help with your pain."

I continue staring at him, unable to speak. I want to ask what is going on. Why didn't I die with the gas? Who is he? I don't recognize his voice.

I try to force out a question but barely get a wheeze out. My throat feels too tight to allow me to do anything but breathe.

"It's okay. You will get your voice back soon enough. Allow me to explain to you what happened." He rises to his feet and sets the button back in its little holster on the side of the bed, nowhere near where I can reach. "While you were in the chamber, a set of rebels broke into the room where my good friend, Maynard, was working. They killed him, broke into the chamber, and pulled you out, saving you from death. Sadly enough for you, your rebel friends took out all but three of our guards on that hallway. Those three guards grabbed your friends to take them for questioning, but they were unable to stop them from taking something to end their lives. Your friends killed themselves, Logan, for you."

I continue to stare at the man. I want to tell him they weren't my friends. I didn't know them. It was pure luck that they pulled me out.

"It is obvious that you know something, Logan. Why else would two rebels risk their lives to keep you alive? You are part of their team, and now we know that."

No. I'm not. You've got to believe me.

"So I guess we were kind of lucky they pulled you out. If they had not done that, we wouldn't have known you knew something. I will give you credit, though, Logan. You have more will than anyone I've ever seen." He chuckles at me and walks over to one of the medical machines. "Hurting *you* obviously doesn't work if we need answers."

Stop. What are you doing?

I watch him slide his finger across the screen of one of the machines. He looks to me with a small smile and pats my arm as another cold rush comes through my IV. "Get some rest, Forge. You're going to need it."

Mavis

Another nurse comes by my curtained room. She slides it open and gives me a little smile as I continue to sit in the hospital bed with my arms crossed.

"Good morning, Mavis. How are you feeling?"

I stare at her. I told them when I woke up, I am not speaking to anyone until they say I can get out of bed.

The nurse sighs at me. "You know, I can't help you unless you speak to me."

I say nothing. I just continue to stare at her. Not rudely, with an angered face, more with a facial expression that says, "I'm waiting."

"Or at least let me look at you." She steps closer to me, and I shift back. They examined me while I was unconscious and said everything looked fine. Why do they need to examine me again?

She sighs. "I won't do anything until you say it's okay, but you know that I can't really help until you let me."

I look down to my lap. I know that I need to let her help. That is probably one of the only ways I can get out of here, but you know what? I've held out for this long. I can hold out longer.

I can keep myself occupied. It's not like my brain ever shuts down. I have so many things going on in my head that I think I could last a lifetime without having to speak to anyone else.

Not that I'd want to do that.

I don't enjoy staying in the bed. I want to go and train. I want to go and prepare myself to help fix Frieden. And I can do it too if only they'd let me out of the bed.

They act as if I meant to harm myself. Why would I do that?

And even if I meant to harm myself, if I meant to really hurt myself, I could have. After all, I was the one who found my brother. I know exactly how he ended his life. If I wanted to do the same, I could have already.

I'm happy he is dead.

I'm happy Mom and Dad are dead.

I'm happy Uncle Randy is dead too.

I'm not happy they died. I am happy they aren't here. I'm happy they didn't have to go through the war and that none of them have to suffer as long as I have to.

Janice enters my curtained area with a fake smile on her face as my nurse leaves. "Hey, Mavis, how are you doing?"

I watch her take a seat beside me. I don't answer.

"You know"—Janice sighs—"if you say something to me, I will get them to let you leave the hospital." She pulls out a pair of my clothes from a backpack she brought and hands them to me.

I immediately face her with my whole body and tell her, "I want to leave the bunker."

"What?" Janice's face falls confused and yet amused. "Why would you want to leave the bunker?"

"I've seen people leave. They go and get others from Frieden and bring them back here. They go on missions and do other things that actually help. I want to leave the bunker and actually help."

"What?" Janice rises to her feet and gives me a nervous chuckle. "Mavis, you can't go while you're pregnant. It's not safe."

I follow her lead and stand as well. "Janice, I am able to help. I have gotten really good at the simulations, and I have become a very good shot. Just ask Grayson!"

"Mavis, I—"

"With these skills, plus the perfect cover"—I gesture to my stomach—"a pregnant woman, I would make one of the best soldiers you've ever seen."

"Mavis, you can't leave while you're pregnant. I'm sorry." Janice tries to place her hand on my shoulder, but I shrug it off as she continues, "You can keep training if you'd like. You will just need to take it easy on the simulations and limit the range practices, okay? Then, maybe after that, we can talk about you leaving."

My eyes roll as I take the clothes and exit the curtained room. Immediately, I head to the restroom to change followed by the gun range.

CHAPTER TWENTY-NINE

Logan

My wrists burn as the straps they used to keep me in the wheelchair dig into my skin. I'm sure they are barely touching me, but it still burns like fire. As the man who put me to sleep days ago rolls me through the empty hallways, the wind blows on my skin, causing even more pain to flare up. I try to move my fingers toward one another to rub my fingernails but find the squishy skin and exposed nerves still healing. I end up causing myself even more pain.

The gas-and-liquid mixture burned off most of the hair on my head, leaving the few strands I have left to fall out one by one. This, along with the fact that I am sitting up as straight as I can as he rolls me through the hallways, causes me to picture horrendous images.

Images of me.

I haven't gotten the chance to look in a mirror since the chamber. All I can picture is what my arms look like but all over my body. Welts and disfigured, shriveled skin covering my face and scalp as the last few strands of ugly singed hair falls out. I imagine my eyebrows are gone; my face most likely no longer looks like me. If someone came walking down this hallway and saw me sitting in this chair, they would think I was a monster. People would think I am a horrible experiment gone wrong.

People would think so many horrendous thoughts at first sight without ever giving me a second glance.

I wouldn't be surprised if my next torture session would be wheeling me out into a crowd to have them stare at me or to have them comment on my skin and appearance.

I wouldn't be surprised at all.

The man, who still hasn't introduced himself to me, loads us onto an elevator and takes us up to the fourth floor. When the elevator dings open, he then takes me through another empty hallway, this one seeming much more familiar than the others.

Through the hallway, into a room, down another hallway, and in front of another large mirror. The man stands beside me as I stare at myself.

My face is so much worse than I imagined.

The skin is even more shriveled and blistered than my arms and legs, and all my hair has fallen out. Before I can fully look over my body, the mirror shifts into a window. The two of us now look into a room that appears eerily similar to the chamber I was held in yesterday.

Though one thing is different about this chamber.

It has two chairs.

The man leans forward and presses a button on the wall beside the window. Just as he presses it, a door on the right side of the room opens; and two men come into the room, forcing Derek Page into one of the chairs as he thrashes around, trying to get out.

"Stop!" he shouts as they strap him into the chair. "What are you doing? Stop! I didn't do anything!"

The men leave as Derek continues to thrash about. For a moment, I think he is going to break the chair.

"Let me out!" he shouts, shakes, twists, and pulls. Nothing works.

After minutes of listening to him scream, I manage to turn my head to the man beside me. He looks to me with a small smile as I wheeze, forcing the words out, "What . . . are you . . . doing?"

His smile grows a small amount. "Mr. Forge, I'm impressed. I didn't think you'd be able to say anything for much longer than this." He turns back to the window. "That's why we weren't going to start yet. But now that I know you can tell us what we need, we can begin."

Derek bangs his head against the headrest of the chair, squeezing his eyes closed and whimpering, "I need to make sure my mom is okay."

I continue staring at the man, trying to block out Derek's shouting. "Who are—" I wheeze one large wheeze to continue my question. It takes almost all of my effort to force out the last word, "You?"

"Tony Leishman."

Leishman? As in Maynard Leishman? Is he punishing me because of what happened to his relative? I didn't do that. I had no part in that. It wasn't my fault.

He looks back through the window and presses another button on the wall. "It wasn't very easy for us to find someone you care about, Logan. All of your family is dead. Your best friends are gone, and your roommate works for us. Mr. Page was the closest friend we could find." The man presses a few buttons on the wall, and another buzzer sounds. "The plan today is to torture your friend Derek Page until death."

My eyes fall upon a door across from Derek as it slides open. One man walks in, gripping Derek's mother's arm tightly, and forces her down into the chair adjacent to Derek. The entire time, Derek is staring at his mother with a horrified expression.

"Hey, Mom"—he tries to get out of the chair but fails—"it's going to be okay."

"Derek, what's going on?" She wiggles, trying to get away from the man, but he straps her in too quickly and forcefully. "What are you doing?"

The man presses a button on his belt, and an IV system that looks exactly like the machine that was in my room yesterday rolls out of the wall. He pulls it over and forces it into her arm.

"Hey," Derek calls out to the man, "what are you doing?"

His mom begins questioning him at the same time, "What is this? Ouch! What are you doing?"

The two of them shout at the man in unison as he turns on the machine and leaves the room.

Tony looks to me and folds his hands behind his back. "Here is your chance to explain. How did you get involved with the rebels?"

I turn back to the Pages as they shout at each other. Derek continues to tell his mother that everything will be okay while she panics in the chair and begs to be let go.

"I"—I wheeze—"don't know anything." The more I listen to my voice, the more it just sounds like me pushing air out of my body.

Tony turns back to the wall and presses another button.

I turn to watch the two panic as a green liquid drains into Ms. Page. She looks down to the IV line as it enters into her and relaxes.

Derek looks to the window, seemingly looking through it to me and Tony. "What are you doing? Stop it!"

A minute or two pass where Tony, Ms. Page, and I watch Derek struggle to free himself.

"What," Ms. Page breaks the silence after a few minutes and looks around the room, "what's going on? Where are we?"

"Hey, it's going to be okay," Derek tells her, still trying to get out of the chair. "We're going to be fine."

"Who"—Ms. Page's eyes fall back onto her son—"who are you again?"

He leans back into his chair and closes his eyes. I can see the pain strewn across his face. "Mom, it's Derek."

"Where's Derek?" She looks around the room not frantically but more curiously. "I want to see him."

"Mom." He clears his throat and continues pulling hard on his wrist bondages, seemingly to the point of breaking his hands. "We're going to be okay."

Tony continues staring at the two. "The serum I administered to her hastens the dementia process. Every time you refuse to answer a question, I will administer another dose of the serum, causing her to forget more and more until she enters a vegetable state."

I turn to look to him as he stares, ever so pleased with himself, and realize what he meant. This serum doesn't hurt Ms. Page. It hurts Derek.

Tony said to me, "The plan today is to torture your friend Derek Page until death."

Not his death.

His mother's death.

Derek looks to the window and shouts, "What are you doing?" My eyes fall back upon the machine to see more of the serum being administered to Ms. Page.

I take another deep breath and force out, "I don't know anything."

Tony rolls his eyes at me. "The more you say that, the worse this will get."

We watch Ms. Page look at her arm as more of the liquid drains into her. She looks back to Derek and stares, not saying or doing anything. Minutes pass, and Derek continues to try to keep her calm.

He yanks his arms, trying to free himself once more. Derek clears his throat. "It's going to be okay."

"What is?" she asks him. "Who are you?" Ms. Page looks around the room as Derek squeezes his eyes closed again. "Where are we?"

Derek whimpers out, "Please stop."

She slowly begins to try to free herself from the restraints, grumbling something under her breath, while Derek frantically attempts to do the same.

Tony turns back to me. "Anything you want to tell me?"

"I don't know anything," I tell him. "I don't know the people who—" I wheeze from the overexertion and am unable to finish my statement before Tony presses the button again. My heart races as I watch more serum drain into Ms. Page.

She looks to Derek as he tells her, "Everything will be fine."

He tries to keep her calm for the next few minutes, but her eyes well up with tears. She mutters something I can't understand and closes her eyes.

"Hey, hey"—Derek leans forward to get his mom to calm down—"it's going to be okay."

Ms. Page looks at Derek angrily as he tries to calm her. Tony takes his hand off the button and steps forward to get a better look.

"Why did you?" she mumbles something as the tears fall.

Derek whimpers out to her, "What?"

"Why did you leave me?" She sniffles as bits of her hair falls into her face. Her cheeks have scrunched up, and her lips have begun to quiver uncontrollably.

"What are you talking about?" Derek shakes his head at her with a smile. "I never left you. I'm right here."

"No," she whimpers at him, "you left me the week he was born."

"What?"

"The . . . the . . . the last thing you did was leave me a note, Randy. A note!" She falls back into her chair and whines, "I had a baby to take care of!"

"Mom, I—"

"You left Derek and I, Randy! With nothing!" she sobs, trying to say things to him but is unsuccessful.

Tony looks to me as Derek begs her to stop crying and tries to convince her that he is Derek. "Do you have anything to say?"

I slowly move my arms and turn to him. I cough a tad bit to try to clear my throat but end up hurting myself worse. "I don't know anything."

Tony turns to the wall and presses the button again. We continue this process for hours, watching Ms. Page wither away and Derek panicking, shouting, and, overall, suffering more than I did in the gas chamber.

"I don't know anything," I tell Tony again as we watch Derek beg his mother to answer. "I've already told you."

Ms. Page just lies there in the chair with her mouth open, looking around the room. She looks to Derek as he begs her to answer, but she remains quiet.

"Those people"—I take a deep breath—"those people who saved me. I didn't—" I cough as my lungs cease to work for a few moments. A small amount of blood and mucus comes up, and I spit it on the floor beside me. My gravelly and hoarse voice shouts out, "I don't know them!"

"You know, Logan, you have done a very good job of not telling me anything." I watch the two in horror as Tony presses the button once more. "But now, Derek will be forced to watch his mother die in this state. After she passes, it's his turn."

"I don't know anything!" I growl at him, trying to pull myself out of my bondage, ignoring the burning pain of my skin and throat. "I was just in the wrong place at the wrong time!" I pull my wrists as hard as I can, almost freeing them from the chair, when Tony leans over and tightens the bondage.

"Now, now, Logan"—he adds another strap to my waist and looks me in the eyes—"you aren't done yet."

I stare into his eyes and growl into his face, "I don't know anything!"

"I'm sure something will come to mind." He stands back up straight and heads toward the door. "I will be back in a few hours."

"No!" I shout at him before he closes the door. "I don't know anything! Just—" I cough up more mucus and blood and choke on it, causing more and more to come up. I lean over the side of the chair and spit it all out, trying to catch my breath as Tony locks me in.

My voice shakes as I struggle to breathe, "Just kill me now."

Werner

As I flip to one of the final pages of the book that I was reading from the Marvelous Cafe, I hear the hatch slide open.

I set the book down beside me on the bed and watch Van climb down the ladder with a new backpack. She turns around to me and gives me a smile. "I'm happy to see you reading. I went through a lot of trouble to get you that book." She tosses the backpack onto the table and begins rummaging through it.

"I thought you said it was no trouble at all?" I head over to her and set all our supplies on the table, lining them up and seeing what we have to work with.

"Well, I mean, I had to take out the scanner. That was pretty much it." She chuckles and hands me a box of hair dye. "All it really was, was a sticker I had to peel off so that the alarm wouldn't sound when I took it. No big deal."

I smile back at her and look at the box of dye. "Midnight black?"

She flips her dark hair over her shoulder and looks to me. "What? You don't like it?"

"No, no, I mean, it'll be a new experience for me." I set the box down and pick up the colored contact case. "What color were you thinking I needed?"

Van shrugs. "Any color but your natural brown color." She sets down a small circular silver gun with a needle on the table. "After your hair and eyes, I will need to change your code."

"My code?" I look down to my wrist at the mixture of dots. "To what?"

"I have an alias lined up for you." She pulls the chair out from the table and pats it's back. "Don't worry, Mr. Zane West."

I take a seat as she presses a button on the table, revealing a vanity station behind the wall.

She looks at me through the lit up mirror and runs her hands through my hair. "I'm kind of going to miss this color."

"Yeah?" I ask her, handing her the box of hair dye.

She opens it up and pulls out a spray can. Van gives it a few good shakes and shrugs. "Yeah, but not enough not to change it." She runs one of her hands through my hair as she sprays the black over it, seemingly covering it fully without hitting her or my skin. After about five to ten minutes, she finishes and takes the scissors to the sides of my head.

"Whoa!" I move slightly before she gets the chance to make the first cut. "What are you doing?"

"Oh, come on, we don't want the change to be too subtle. We have to give you a little trim too." She pulls my head back and begins cutting. My hair falls to the floor as she completely changes my hairstyle. After finishing with the scissors, she moves onto contacts.

Van holds up each color to my face and, after a minute, settles on a deep blue. Once I have the contacts in, she grabs my wrist and takes a seat beside me.

"This may hurt just a little bit. No more than the first time you got it, though." Van flicks a switch, and the small handheld tattoo gun hums to life. She places an outline over my original code and digs into my skin to create the new one. This process takes what feels like hours; but by the time she is done, I look like a completely different person.

Van has me stand up against the wall so she can scan my face into the system and then shows me my new identification tag beside my old one. Many of the traits are different, one of which is that Zane West is a year and a few months older than Werner Rhodes.

"You see these traits? You see these dates?" She points to the new ID. "Learn them. Study them. Know them. Be them. You are no longer Werner Rhodes. Werner Rhodes is gone. You are Zane West, previous inhabitant of Bouw, who has never even heard of Werner Rhodes."

I nod and look back into the mirror to see two people. One, someone new whom I will be getting to know a lot better soon, and the other, I still don't know the real name.

Mavis

Aim.

Pull the trigger.

Shoot.

Hit what I'm aiming for.

Aim.

Pull the trigger.

Shoot.

Hit what I'm aiming for.

Aim.

Hours pass; and I follow the same routine, hitting everything I aim for. Every now and then, a few of the other shooters will gather behind me and watch.

But I don't care about them.

If I get good enough, if I surpass all the other shooters down here, Janice will have to let me leave. She will have to give me an assignment or a mission.

One of the target bodies sprint across the room. Everybody takes their shot at it, with only me and one other person hitting it in the head. After the bot continues to run, I aim down to one of its knees and cause it to face plant.

Everyone in the room continues shooting at the bots and the non-moving targets as I set my pistol down and take a few deep breaths. A stomach cramp slowly begins to form and grows stronger within seconds.

I force myself to bring my gun back up and take down the next running target by hitting it in the knee once more but am forced to take another break. My stomach quickly begins to twist once again. I hold one hand on my stomach, and I make my way out of the room without clearing off my station. Grayson gives me one odd look, but I wave him off as I rush out past him.

The room becomes heavy as a sudden burst of nausea hits me. I make it out of the room and immediately gag, throwing up a small amount onto the floor in the hallway. Not wanting to get caught out here, I wipe my mouth and try to head farther down, looking for someone to help me to the restroom.

The stomach cramp tightens, and I feel a sudden emergency come on. "Hey," I call out to one of the women I see walking out of a room, "hey, can you help me?"

She looks at my hunched-over stance and rushes over. "What's wrong, sweetie?" She places her hand on my back as I look down and see blood.

The cramp spreads to my lower back below where her hand rests and causes an immense amount of pain. I look to the woman and tell her, "I need to get to the hospital."

Nodding to me, the woman immediately takes me to the medical center. The same nurse who tried to check me a week ago looks me over once when I enter and rushes me onto a bed. She gets me all set up, into a gown, on a monitor, and back to where I was when I passed out.

Within minutes of me getting situated, Janice shows up with a look on her face of true worry. And somehow, that look relaxes me. She actually cares.

"Mavis! What happened? A nurse called me as soon as you walked in, and I got here as fast as I could."

I shrug it off. "I'm fine. It was just a stomach cramp."

"A stomach cramp? You wouldn't have come in if it was just a stomach cramp."

I give her a little smile. "Janice, I'm fine."

I am fine.

Over the next hour or so, we find out how completely fine I am.

They run the tests.

They do the work.

My nurse sits down with me after it is all said and done, and she rests her hand on my bed. "Mavis, the baby is gone."

At first, I don't process her statement. "What?"

"What?" Janice asks with me, "What happened?"

I look to Janice's face and find she is much more hurt than I am. Why am I not reacting the same way?

"Sadly, this sort of thing isn't unusual. Most miscarriages happen before week thirteen of pregnancies." My nurse wraps both her hands over her clipboard. "I'm sorry, Mavis."

The three of us sit here quietly. I don't know what to say.

I didn't want the baby, and now I don't have to deal with it. Why am I upset?

Was it the hit I took in the stomach that did it?

Did I kill the baby while I was training?

I brush off all the pained thoughts and turn to Janice. My immediate reaction is telling her, "I'm not pregnant anymore."

Janice pauses, looking to me with a confused expression. "Mavis," she takes a moment to realize what I am saying, "you need to take your time before you—"

"You told me that when I wasn't pregnant anymore, we can talk about this. Well, guess what, I don't have to wait. I didn't have the baby, so I don't have to take care of it. I didn't grow to the full size I could have, so I am still in shape. I can do this."

"Mavis—" She tries to take my hand, but I grab hers first.

"Let me do this."

CHAPTER THIRTY

Logan

I watch as Derek holds his mother's hand in his. One of the guards lets Derek free to go and be with his mom a few hours ago, and Derek hasn't moved since.

He lays his head on her knees as he sits beside her and weeps. His mother looks so frail and so empty. She hasn't moved. She just stares with her jaw hanging.

She stares into the mirror, seemingly at me.

I haven't moved either. My skin burns as air-conditioning blows on it, but this pain hurts nowhere near as much as watching Derek with his mom.

The door beside me unlocks, and Tony comes in with a smug smile on his face. "Good morning, Logan."

I stare at him, not saying anything.

"Aw, come on, why so cold? I thought you and I have become close enough to greet each other with the bare minimum."

I continue to wheeze in his direction as he waits for an answer.

"No? Okay then." He presses a few of the buttons on the wall and looks back to me. "Logan, I have come to a conclusion."

A buzzer rings in the Pages' room. A tray of food slides through a small opening in one of the doors, and everyone seems to stare at it. Derek slowly rises to his feet as we watch in silence. He picks up the tray and looks it over for no more than a split second before chucking it at the window. The splatter of the food covers my view of Ms. Page but not Derek. He stands there for a moment more and boils.

"Ignoring that tantrum"—Tony looks back to me—"my conclusion is that you won't tell me anything, even though I know you know something."

I look to him and give a gravelly, sarcastic chuckle. "You think?" But all that comes out is some sort of mumble.

Tony smiles. "So you will become a soldier."

"What?" I ask him.

"For Frieden but, more specifically, for me."

I cough to the side of my chair. "I would never, and you know this."

He nods. "Yes, yes, I know. I expect some resistance. But you should know, Logan, I have had special bionic leg structures made for you. They will restore your ability to walk around and do everything just as you used to."

"What?"

"Along with a suit that will"—Tony leans over to me and places his hand on my shoulder with a tight grip, burning my skin—"help ease your sensitivity."

I shake him off and shout at him, "I'm not helping you with anything! Just go ahead and kill me!"

Tony rolls his eyes and pulls a vial out of his pocket. He sticks it into my arm and growls back at me, "Just wait."

Mavis

The sound of the scissors slowly cutting across my hair somehow makes me nervous. The stylist cuts it much shorter than I am used to it being. By the time she finishes it, the longest part of my hair is right above my shoulders.

"My name is June Dawson. I was a Bloot. My parents, Gary and Sharron, were both killed in the revolt."

The stylist takes a can of hair dye and begins spraying. She starts with the hair at the front of my head and makes her way back. A strand of my new brown hair falls in front of my face and shocks me.

"My name is June Dawson. I was a Bloot. I had no siblings."

The woman takes my wrist and places a piece of plastic over my old code as a guide to change it. She turns on the tattoo gun and begins her work as Janice continues to prep me.

"How old are you?" Janice asks me. "What were you originally assigned to do in Bestellen?"

"My name is June Dawson. I was a Bloot. I am twenty-three years old. I was trained to be a farmer."

We go over a million more questions until I can tell you all about my life before Frieden. When the stylist finishes my code, she scans my face into the system and makes my new ID. Janice then walks me out to the bunker's exit.

"Are you ready, June? Your guide should be right outside waiting."

I nod. "I'm ready. I am all set."

Janice nods back to me and unlocks the exit. "Are you sure? I mean, it has only been a few days since—"

I look up the ladder to see a head peek in. His brown and fluffy hair dangles down toward me as his smile grows.

"Ready?" the random man asks me. "Our hike awaits."

I look back to Janice and find myself in a hug, a warm hug that I feel I will miss when I am gone. "Thank you, Janice."

She gives me another squeeze. "I will see you soon, June. Be safe."

I give her one last smile and climb up the ladder.

Logan

The machine they have me attached to injects another dose of whatever it is they are giving me. For days now, they have been feeding me nothing but nutrients through tubes and reinforcing the same logic and the same commands to me over and over.

I can tell the difference between what they tell me and what is right, but I can't get them to stop. The men beat me, shouting that I am guilty of treason against my country for even thinking about the rebels.

Another hand slaps me across my face. My head dangles as I try to move from the bondages but can't. The stinging and burning pain on my skin has become almost nonexistent with the mixture of whatever drugs they are feeding me, along with the fact that I am too distracted by the beatings.

"You're worthless. The only time you ever actually did something good in your life was when you joined the Taai."

"It is your fault that you were put into the gas chamber. You shouldn't have associated with the rebels."

"The only way you will ever do anything worthwhile is if you listen to your commands."

Their voices all become blurred together as they attempt to condition me to believe them, but their commands are slowly shifting toward more reasonable wishes.

As I listen to their commands changing, I form a plan.

Another dose is administered through the tubes, and I let my head fall back against the chair and nod.

One of the two men continues to shout at me, "You will be one of the best soldiers in history and get your legs back if you listen to us. You will no longer be a worthless rat to the rebels but a man who will save lives if you listen to us."

I nod again.

My playing along as if they are actually getting to me is the only way for them to stop torturing innocent people. If I don't comply, they may go and get more citizens like the Pages.

Hours go on, and the two men have become much kinder and much quieter.

They press a button and have the machine administer one last thing to me before pulling me out of the bondages and sitting me in a wheelchair. Almost immediately, when we cross the threshold of the room, I fall into a deep sleep. A dreamless deep sleep that seems to last no more than three seconds. The moment I close my eyes, I can hear my surroundings shift into something much quieter. When I open my eyes to check and see where I am, I find myself back in my hospital room in a different set of clothes, with another IV in me. I look around the room to see if anyone is in here with me and find a woman sitting in the corner.

"Hello, Logan." She rises from her chair and comes over to my bed. She looks me over and allows a smile to come across her face. "How are you feeling?"

I take a few deep breaths, trying to figure out how to answer. Why would they be so nice after torturing me for days?

"My name is Elloise. I am here to help you get into the skeleton."

I sit up quickly, slightly scaring the woman. She steps back and looks over to the corner of the room. My eyes follow hers to a bunch of wires and small circular pads in a pile.

"That is the machine that is going to help you walk." Our eyes meet for a moment before she heads over and grabs the pile. When she picks it up, it looks a lot more like strings with little stickers on the ends than anything else. "I am sorry about my coworkers. I know they can be harsh, but we really need you to work with us."

What? She is in on it?

"You are one of the best soldiers we've seen, Logan, and we really need your help." She pulls my blanket off my legs and places her hands on my ankles. "May I?"

I stare at her hands and give a small shrug. I don't know exactly what she is doing, but I have a feeling I can trust her.

"We would never ask you to do anything that you wouldn't be okay with. You would only be doing the security-risk jobs, like making sure innocent people will be okay."

Elloise runs her hands up my legs, seemingly feeling for pressure points. I watch her, only listening to the sound of my horrid wheezing, and think about what to say.

"Would you be okay with doing the jobs like that?"

I nod to her again, and she sets the wires on the bed.

"Logan, I need to take your pants off in order to get these on you, okay?" Elloise pauses and waits for me to say something, but I'm not sure what to say.

I sit here in silence and watch her nod to me and place her hands on the bottom of my pants. She slowly tugs on them and gets them to slide off much easier than I thought they were going to. As I sit here in my underwear, feeling awkward and exposed, I watch her bring the wires up to my legs.

She peels off a clear plastic covering from the bottom of the cold and sticky pads just before sticking each pad to my leg. Elloise goes through all the pieces and connects the skeleton to me as I think about the job offer. If I am assigned missions to make sure innocent people live, then I am not only saving them but also helping save other innocents that they may torture if I refuse.

I can do that.

I want to do that.

Elloise connects each of the little circles to random points on my legs. She rubs the sticky pads into my skin and massages them until the ends of the pads seem to disappear. My hand glides over the first pad she did, not feeling any difference between it and my skin. The only thing that seems any different are the wires sticking out of my legs.

"What did you do?" I ask her. "How did you do that?"

She gives me a little smile and continues to massage the other pads into my legs. "I am activating the sensors in the pads so that they dissolve into your skin, allowing the wires to intertwine with your—" Elloise turns her head to me and chuckles, "I am making it so that the wires can communicate with your legs." When she finishes massaging one of the pads on the side of my knee, she looks to the IV in my arm. "It's a good thing they have you medicated right now, or this process would have *hurt*."

After minutes of watching her massage the pads into my legs, something catches my eye. I feel my heart begin to race as one of the first wires connected to me slowly sinks and becomes attached to my skin as well. The other wires follow the first wire's lead and connect themselves to my skin. The last few pads she has to do are on the lower and upper parts of my hips, along with the inside part of my thigh.

She gives me a look to make sure I know she is about to begin and then slowly places the pads where they need to be. Neither of us makes any eye contact as she does her job. We are both much happier when that part is over. By the time Elloise finishes, I have two black lines running down each of my legs on both sides, seemingly outlining the joints.

"Here." She comes over to my torso and places her hand on my back. After leaning me forward, she pulls my shirt up and places one of the sticky pads on the base of my spine, right where Eric told me my original injury that caused the paralysis was.

The moment she finishes rubbing the pad into my pack, I look down to my legs to feel the pads tingling. I watch them as they seem to vibrate forcibly, causing an odd and slightly uncomfortable cramp to form. My toes begin to curl, and my calves begin to flex as I slowly regain control of the muscles.

"Logan." Elloise heads back over to her chair and pulls a vial out of her bag. "If you feel any sort of cramp coming on at all, whether it be in your leg, your foot, or even your back, you tell me as soon as it happens, okay? The first few hours are going to be the worst. If you let the cramp get out of hand, there is no telling how long it will be before you get it back under control."

As she finishes her statement, I feel a small pain in the bottom of my foot. I can't tell at first what it is; but a moment later, the cramp begins.

I point to my foot and look to her. "There's one now."

She immediately lunges toward me and sticks me in the calf of my left leg, the one she happened to be closest to. I watch as my foot contorts and takes on a mind of its own, and the cramp dies out just as quickly as it came up.

"Are you okay?"

I look to Elloise with my face somewhat scrunched as I try to ignore the pain in my foot. I nod to her and look around the room to see where the air vent is located. It seems to have just kicked on and is greatly aggravating my skin.

Each breeze that blows shoots a burning pain over all the skin exposed while the rest of my skin is forced to deal with the fabric of my clothes rubbing against it.

Elloise tries to move in front of my gaze. "What's wrong?"

I force my face out of its contorted expression and try to bend my knees. "Nothing."

She looks to my legs, and a smile grows on her face. "Great job!" She shifts to the side of the bed and places her hands on my ankles once again. This time, she takes them and slides them off the side of the bed. "Are you ready to try to stand?" Elloise heads to the corner of the room and pulls over a walker. She sets it in front of me and waits for my answer.

I look down to my feet with the shriveled skin and wiggle my toes. After a moment of staring at my legs, I slide off the bed, ignoring Elloise's pleas to wait, and immediately fall under the weight of my upper body. I catch myself somewhat on the walker but end up having Elloise support me almost fully.

"Why didn't you wait?" She holds the walker in place as I push myself up completely with my arms.

Ignoring her once again, I slowly allow myself to put pressure on my legs and find that I can stand. The weakness of my muscles shocks me. I know I haven't used them in a long time, but this is almost unbearable. I can barely hold myself up.

But I don't care.

I am standing.

Elloise slowly releases the walker and takes a step back. "Great job, Logan! Now, before you start—"

I slide my right foot forward an inch or two, still completely dependent on the walker, and find that I have taken my first step. After that, I continue to shuffle forward slowly but surely and not listening to Elloise one bit.

After I almost fall on my face, she rushes over and gets in front of the walker. "Hey, Logan, you need to listen to me, or this isn't going to be a fun experience."

I stare at her for a moment, still wheezing, and wait for her to move. Why would she care if I fall on my face? Why would they send me a therapist that actually seems to want to help me?

I tighten my grip on the walker. Before I can try to get by her, she stares me down, much like my mother used to, and somehow puts me back in my place. The next few hours go by, and I manage to walk like I used to and even learn to run again. After getting back to a normal walking motion, Elloise tells me she has something else for me.

After pulling me out of the comforts of my isolated room, she walks me through the large hallways, allowing me to stretch my legs much more than I could in my isolation. Like a lost puppy, I follow her around, enjoying having empty hallways to roam in. After I was being tied down to the wheelchair for weeks, followed by being trapped for days and tortured, being able to walk around is nice. So nice that I never want to stop.

One of the pluses of having her for my nurse is she knows I don't want anyone to see me. So she is making sure to take me down the hallways that no one else is in. The hallways she takes me down seem to be very open, almost as if they were meant to have a lane for two hospital beds to roll down at once. I look to the walls and find that the bottom half is a light-brown wood sort of design while the top half is a light-green paint. For what reason they decorate this place this way, I don't know. I originally pictured the hallway to be dark and gloomy with a guard lurking in every corner.

But it's not.

It is much friendlier than I expected.

The two of us walk for a while, ignoring the pain of the wind on my skin, and finally make it to our destination. Elloise opens up a door to another room with her code; and just before I head in behind her, she stops me. "Hey, I need you to stay right here while I grab you something, okay?"

I look around the hallway to make sure no one is coming and give her a quick nod. She smiles at me and disappears behind the locked door, leaving me feeling exposed and anxious to see if someone will get to see me after all.

If they see me, what will they think?

At least, while I was in a wheelchair, I was a monster who couldn't hurt them. But now? A free beast who can terrorize people as he pleases? Who wouldn't be scared?

Just as I look down to my fingers where my nails used to reside, Elloise comes out of the room with a box. She gives me one big smile and waves me to follow. "Come on. Let's head back to the room so I can give you this."

Immediately, I brush off the intense need to rub my fingernails and follow her. I look around the halls as we walk and realize the pattern on the floor is like a checkerboard. I watch the pieces fly by as I walk over them and cause myself more pain.

There is a gray tile where a white tile should be. The pattern is made up of off-white and light-gray tiles. I look around the whole room to find this is the only tile out of place. It puts the pattern out of order and somehow drives my brain to twitch. I force myself to speed up and continue following Elloise as I try to forget the tile and end up focusing more on the wind hitting my skin.

When we make it back to the room, I am relieved that the air-conditioning vent seems to have turned off, and I take a seat on the bed to give my legs a rest.

Elloise sets the box down beside me and gives me one big smile before opening it to reveal a dark fabric. "Are you ready, Logan?"

I peek over and into the box as she pulls it out. A long dark suit made of some sort of spandex material. I reach in and grab the final three pieces to find two gloves and a mask.

I look to her and allow my gravelly voice to speak, "What is it?"

"It's your new suit." She waves for me to stand up. When I do, she holds it against my body and gives me another smile. "Trust me, you'll like it."

I hold the gloves in one hand and the mask in another. When I spread the mask out enough to see the face, I find no eye holes or anything. It seems to be just a big sock.

"Go ahead. Try it on."

I give her a confused look.

"You can see through the fabric. It was made just for you so that you can walk around without the pain of the wind on your skin."

I look back to the mask. One of my hands finds its way to my face, and it rubs my skin gently to feel the shriveled spots and reminds me of the pain I've been through. If I would have just kept my mouth shut when talking to Amanda, I wouldn't have had this happen to me. It's my fault; and if they are offering something to help me, I need to take it.

I slide the mask on over my bald head and find the silky substance providing me with instant relief. I can see through it, just as I can see normally, and breathe through it, just as I could a moment ago.

"How is it?" Elloise asks me with a giddy look on her face.

I can't help but smile a smile I doubt she can see from under the mask. I take a deep breath and give a hoarse chuckle. "You had something to fix my legs. You had something to help my skin." I take another breath. "Do you have something to help the wheezing?"

Elloise immediately bursts into a small fit of laughter at my joke. Though I was holding on to a small amount of hope she would offer me something to help, hearing someone laugh with me was all the help I needed.

She helps me take my clothes off with the least amount of pain she can and slide the suit on. It is one that is loose on my body, seeming to be about two sizes too big, until I press a button for it to tighten, making it much easier for me to get into compared to a suit that fits like this with no stretch. Once that button is pressed, the entire suit sucks in and outlines my body as if I wasn't wearing any clothes at all, making it one of the most comfortable and soothing things I've worn in a long time. I hadn't realized how bad the pain my skin was going through really was until I put this suit on. The relief that spreads through me makes me want to just dive into the bed and lie on my back, sprawled out and letting the air-conditioning blow on me as it pleases. The relief makes me want to go back out into the hallways and sprint off, not caring how much wind hits my skin.

With the added cover of no one being able to see what I look like under here, this suit somehow brings me more joy than I ever thought I would feel again.

And it is all because of Elloise.

I look to her as she continues to smile at me. "Thank you," I tell her.

She gives me another little smirk. "It was my pleasure." After a moment of silence between us with only the sound of my wheezing to listen to, her eyes and smile grow. Elloise reaches into her pocket and pulls out a small bag. "I almost forgot!"

She drops Sam's necklace into my hand. "I smuggled this out for you. They forgot to give it back when they brought you in here."

My fist tightens around the gem as I think back to Sam. Someone I miss so much that I have to force myself not to think about him. I spent weeks grieving and am still hurting more than I've ever hurt before.

But just because I don't want to think about him doesn't mean I want to forget him.

Just before I can tell Elloise thank you, she takes a look at her watch; and her face jumps with surprise. "Well, look at that." I try to look at the time as well, but she lowers her wrist and points back to the bed. "It's almost ten o'clock. It is getting pretty late."

I follow her finger and look to the bed. After a moment, I look back to her as she stands there awkwardly.

"I need you to, um, go to bed."

I tilt my head at her, not completely sure what she will do if I don't get into bed; but I kind of want to see.

She lowers her arms down and gives a small unsure sigh. "Um, please?"

I snicker and take a seat on the sheets.

Elloise smiles at me. "Thank you, Logan." She makes her way over to me and rolls up my sleeve. I stop her halfway by grabbing her wrist. She looks back to me and grabs the rolling table in the corner. "I have to put in your IV for the night. This will give you some more medicine to make sure you get some sleep and to make sure you don't have too much pain in your legs."

I stare into her eyes as she seems to stare into mine. Her brown eyes remind me much of my mother's, not in the sense of color but in the sense of their kindness. I release her wrist and allow her to insert the IV. After putting me back into bed, she asks me, "Can I leave you for a moment to go and get you some food? Or should I wait here with you and have someone else bring it in?"

"You can go." I wheeze. "I'll wait."

She smiles at me and gives a small pat on my knee. Elloise exits the room and leaves me to watch the fluids and medicine drain into me. It takes about ten minutes for her to come back in with a tray of white foods that I can't identify and a water bottle.

I lift up the bottom half of my mask and eat for the first time in days. The feeling of food in my mouth is one that I have missed, along with water going down my throat. I finish all my food and drink within minutes and have Elloise take my tray.

"All right Logan." She comes over to my IV line and adds a small vial to the line. "I will see you in the morning. If you feel up to it then, we have a great simulation room that you can begin practicing on."

I look to her as she clips the vial in place and watch the blue liquid drain. "Thank you," I tell her. She gives me one final nod goodbye and leaves me to rest.

Zane

I sit at a table and wait. A table in a cafe, like the Marvelous Cafe, only, this one is subpar. It doesn't even have a place where you can get a book to read.

I sit at a table and wait. I wait like I used to do for Mac; but this time, I wait for another woman. As she walks in, she gives me a small nod of acknowledgment and sits across from me.

Van pulls an envelope out of her jacket pocket and hands it to me under the table. "This is to get you through the next few weeks."

I take it and slip it up my sleeve. "Thank you."

"Have you run into any trouble recently?"

I shake my head. Last night was the final night I could stay in the little safe room in the woods. Once I got out, I had to lock the entrance, to which I have completely forgotten what the code is with the branch.

"That's good to hear." Van looks behind me with a curious expression. "I have an assignment for you."

"Yeah?"

She takes my hand and gives me an odd smile. I can't help but try to pull away, but she won't let go.

"What are you doing?" I ask her.

She rises to her feet and pulls me out of my seat. With a singsong voice, she continues, "We need to go."

Her eyes flicker behind me, and I take her hint. We walk out of the shop, hand in hand, avoiding a confrontation with two policemen.

"Werner's picture has been plastered in every police station in the country," Van tells me. "I know we changed your look and your code, but that doesn't mean test your luck."

I nod, and we continue walking down the road. "Understood. What is the assignment?"

"There is a sewing and fabric shop called Fabric Room that we run. This will be where you and your new partner will be working."

"Partner?" I look to her to see a smug smile on her face. "Who is he? Is he coming from the bunker?"

Van nods. "*She* should be arriving here from the bunker today."

We take a right and continue walking through the city, dodging every police car or officer walking we can. "What's her name?"

"June Dawson."

CHAPTER THIRTY-ONE

June

After making it through the woods over the course of two days, I still haven't been told my guide's name. We enter into Frieden through an underground pathway, taking us into some woods right on the outside of Kern, and hike into the city from there.

He continues to lead us in silence, leaving me to watch our surroundings anxiously. We pass through the same part of town where Ms. Page and I saw the dress that she made for me for the inauguration ball, causing me to have to force away those memories.

My name is June Dawson. I was a Bloot. My parents, Gary and Sharron, were both killed in the revolt.

Mavis?

Mavis Walmsley?

She is dead.

She died the same night her best friend did.

I shake my head and force the memories out. If I go down that road and think about the past, I will be proving Janice right in that she doesn't think I am ready.

But I am.

I am June Dawson. I was a Bloot.

My guide and I make it through the town, down a few backroads, and to a dark-purple brick building named Fabric Room.

"Consider this your new home, June." My guide opens the door for me, a bell above the entrance rings, and I walk in to see a familiar face speaking with Van behind the cashier counter.

I turn back to look at my new guide, only to find that he has disappeared.

"June?" my old guide calls out.

Looking back to her, I nod. "And you must be Van." We shake hands as she gives me an impressed smile, obviously remembering who I was.

"Well, June Dawson, please meet your new partner."

The man from the bar the night the bomb went off at the Palace shakes my hand. Though his eyes and hair are a different color, I can still tell it is him.

"Zane West," he tells me. We shake each other's hands and share a stare and a slight smile. I have a feeling he remembers me too. "It's nice to meet you, *June*."

We turn to Van as she gives us a small chuckle. "What? Have you two met before?"

"No," we answer casually in unison, not helping our case.

Van squints at us both, not believing the lies, and backs away. "Okay then." She heads to the door and opens it, causing the bell above to ring. "I have to go. June, you have the assignment?"

I nod.

"Go ahead and brief Zane. I will let you two handle this." She closes the door and disappears just as my guide from earlier did.

I turn back to the man whose real name I can't remember and take a seat behind the counter. "Is anyone else in the building?"

He shakes his head and types something into the hologram to pull up the security cameras. The building is as empty as it is dull.

"So I have received word that Chancellor Oswald will be going to the Capitol Park gardens today."

With my hands resting in my coat pockets, the sudden chill that comes at random points at the end of spring has returned. I sit on one of the park benches and look around, enjoying the beautiful view of the grass becoming green, the flowers slowly coming back to life, and the random person every now and then strolling by. For some reason, the garden isn't as full as it usually is. Today seems to be a slow day for this area, which actually gives me a lot more of an advantage.

I watch each individual who strolls by and find that it is mainly older women. I can hear the sound of the children screaming with joy in the background of the rustling leaves over by the playground. Though I am happy that they are enjoying themselves, I much prefer the sound of nature and light voices speaking to one another over the hyena screeching that comes with adolescent joy.

When a man wearing a long tan trench coat with black gloves emerges from the gardens, I scan him over. After noticing that he appears the same height as the six-feet-and-two-inches-tall Chancellor Oswald, I immediately rise to my feet. I pull a book out of my jacket and open it to a random page.

With my nose buried deep in the book, I find myself spoiling the plot twist of the stepfather being the killer. I pull away for one moment to reread the first section of the page and end up bumping directly into the man, somehow getting my foot caught in between his and knocking us both over.

He wraps his arms around me and spins us both, forcing me to land on his front side while he takes the brunt of the fall. We both grunt as we hit the ground and slowly realize how close our faces are to each other's.

After a moment of slight awkwardness, I force myself up and begin apologizing profusely, "I am so sorry. I didn't mean to do that. I was just reading and—"

In the middle of my apology, I realize he is reacting the same way I am. "I am so terribly sorry. Oh no! It is not your fault, dear. I wasn't watching where I was going. I mean I—"

We pause at the same time and find ourselves staring at each other once more. A slight chuckle from us both relieves the tension and allows us to breathe much easier. Chancellor Oswald gives me a small smile followed by a shocked expression. He reaches down to pick up the book, brushes it off, and hands it back to me. "I really am sorry. I know how it can be when reading. It's like nothing else around you exists."

I titter and quickly flip through the book's pages like a fan, and I am hit with that beautiful almond, vanilla, and grass smell. "To be honest, I am not that much of a reader. I accidentally just kind of spoiled the book for myself by reading ahead, and it caught me off guard." I hold up the book and point to the cover. "But now I can tell you, if you want a good read, this book seems fairly decent. You'll never see it coming."

He chuckles back to me and looks around the park. My eyes follow his, and I see dozens of secret service men standing by, seemingly wary of my presence. "I'm sorry about them. It took me months now to get them to let me walk by myself, let alone get this close to someone without them around."

"Well"—I reach up to fix his jacket collar and bend it the right way—"you and I did get a little closer than either of us expected."

He looks to me with a new expression, one that I am not used to seeing. His smile almost seems shy, but it doesn't make sense. He is Chancellor Thomas Oswald, the first leader of Frieden. The great speaker, the great mind, and the great man. Why would he be shy around me?

The both of us look into the gardens, watching a few of the men in suits come closer to us. I pull away nervously and earn a sigh from Oswald. "Again, I'm sorry about knocking you over."

"No, no, please, don't be." I take a step away and hold the book with both hands. "It was one of the best trips I've taken in a while."

He looks to the ground, blushing. As I walk away, he calls out to me, "Do you think that, um, that I'll get to see you again?"

I look back to him and shrug with a smile. "Maybe."

With that as my final word, I walk out of the park and a few miles through the city to get back to the Fabric Room. When I enter the building, the familiar chime of the bell rings; and I make my way over to Zane.

"Did you get it?" he asks me.

I nod and earn a large smile from him.

Zane points to the entrance and heads to one of our back rooms. "Go ahead and lock the doors and close the blinds."

Once I close the shop down for the night, I follow him to the back to find a room full the computer systems, with only one screen that Zane is really paying attention to. He logs into some sort of program and runs different systems and numbers, none of which I understand. After a few minutes of downloading and processing, the screen we are looking for finally pops up as a wavepad.

"Here we go." He types in a few different things as I watch the sound waves move and wonder what I am missing.

The speakers scream to life with the sound of a mob of news reporters, shouting questions at Chancellor Oswald. "What do you know about the assassinations in State Three?"

"What do you have to say about the accusations that you are part of this?"

"How do you plan to deal with this?"

"Are these the acts of Amiable rebels?"

"What about all the missing citizens?"

Oswald's voice speaks over all the others not loudly but with a quiet, confused, and concerned voice. "What? Assassinations? Missing citi—"

His question to the news reporters cause them all to shout as loud as they can, furthering their questioning. Zane and I listen to the sounds of his bodyguards forcing people out of the way so that they can take him into the capitol building, and we wait for something we can use.

"So," Zane breaks the silence between us as we listen to the guards force Oswald into the building, "where did you put the microphone?"

"Under his coat collar," I tell him.

"Yeah? How'd you get it there?"

A quick smile rises back up on my face as I think back to Chancellor Oswald catching me as we fall. As he approaches the age of forty, I never expected him to feel that firm or be that quick to react.

"Thank you," Oswald says. We listen to him march through the building and walk into a room. His coat shuffles against the microphone as he clears his throat. "Riley, Madden." Another shuffle takes over as, I assume, Oswald takes his coat off. "What is going on?"

Zane looks to me and writes down on a sheet of paper, sliding it over to me. "Jonathan Riley and Phillip Madden. Two of Oswald's advisors."

One of the voices speaks up, "What are you talking about?"

"There is a mass of news reporters outside, and they all—"

Oswald is cut off by another voice, "Yes, Ozzy, there is always a mass of news reporters outside. This is why you are asked to take a car out of the fence rather than walk it."

"No, no," Oswald resumes, "you don't understand. They were asking me about . . . about assassinations and . . . and missing citizens. Have either of you heard about these?"

We watch the sound waves disappear for a moment as the three men wait for an answer. One of the two men speaks up, "No. I haven't heard anything about that."

"Neither have I," the other voice says.

"Well, I surely haven't." Oswald's voice fades out as he finishes with the men. "I am going to go and see what is going on."

Zane and I look to each other, not sure what to make of this. Isn't Oswald the one orchestrating all this? Oswald and Wilson?

"The plan can't take place soon enough."

"Just wait, Riley," Madden says to him. "Have patience. We have waited this long. We can wait one more week."

Riley groans, "I don't know if I can stand him one more week. He is so ridiculously clueless."

"Just one more week. Seven days exactly. We'll have him then."

Logan

Third mission.

This is the third mission I've been on.

Each of them has been at night.

Night.

The only time that people can't see me.

I continue to wear my suit through the town, which allows me to move much easier than I feel I have ever been able to move before.

The only thing I don't appreciate about this suit is how it seems to trap me with myself. I can hear my wheezing much more clearly than I can without the suit on; but when I pointed it out to Elloise, she told me that I was the only one who could hear it better, which I guess is a good thing.

No one else should be subjected to my wheezing. It is a horrid noise.

I continue to follow a man through the backstreets of the city, creeping around and avoiding being seen by anyone. I have been following him for about ten minutes now, and he still hasn't noticed me. My assignment is to tranquilize him and then place the tracker they gave me on him. After doing that, they will come and get the man.

This isn't a bad mission.

I was told that I wouldn't be assigned to do any bad missions. I would only do the ones that I would be comfortable with. So Elloise gave me a choice of three missions. This was the only one that made sense. The other two choices involved me killing people. When I asked Elloise what those people did to deserve the death sentence, she said she didn't know. But when I asked her what this man did, she said that he was a child abductor and has been caught on camera multiple times abducting children. They want to find out where those children are being held, so they need me to get the man alive so they can question him.

This is something I can do.

This is a good mission.

A good assignment.

I would take on this assignment even if I wasn't being forced to. This man does horrendous things and has to be stopped.

I continue to stalk the man until he makes his way out of town. I take my time, keeping my distance as I follow him and, every now and then, reaching up to Sam's gem to make sure it is still there. I have it tucked within the suit, but the pain of it pressed up against my skin is something I only want to bear when I have to, so I leave it out dangling until I get close enough to actually finish my assignment.

When we are out of the town's main area, I tuck the jewel back into my suit and pull the pistol out Elloise gave me. I have it loaded with the tranquilizers, aimed and ready to fire, but I wait. I wait until he turns around, away from me, and toward the woods.

The moment he attempts to change his pace to a sprint, I shoot him in the spine. He falls face-first onto the ground and slides, having only his fluffy brown hair to land on as comfort. Pulling my tracker out of my pocket, I press the button, head over to him, and place it inside of his jacket.

When I get back to the headquarters, I use the ladder on the side of the building and sneak in through my window just as I have been for the last three missions. When I enter back into my hospital room, I pull Sam's necklace out and close the window. They know not to have the air-conditioning on in my room; so I pull my mask off and take a deep breath, feeling the relief of not having to listen to my wheezing magnified. When the air in the room hits my face, it hurts but not nearly as bad as it used to. With the constant strings of medication Elloise has me on, I am managing to deal with the pain.

I wait in my room for over an hour before Tony enters with Elloise. I immediately rise to my feet and face him. I know I could have completed the mission sooner, but I wanted to make sure to keep him out of the busy part of the city. I didn't want anyone who wasn't supposed to see him to find him.

Tony stares at me for a moment before a smile rises on his face, relieving the tension that was strangling me more than my shriveled skin. He comes over to me and nods. "That was exceedingly . . . adequate." He turns to Elloise and gestures to the door. "Ms. Holly, please go retrieve our new recruit something to eat and tell Young I will meet him in the commons in half an hour or so."

Elloise nods to him and leaves the room. By the time she comes back, I feel a small sense of pride and yet inadequacy. I could have done better. But at the same time, if Tony, a man who knows I'm worthless, thinks I did an okay job, then I must have done well.

When Elloise returns with a tray of food, Tony leaves the room. She straps me back into the IV machine and allows me to eat with a small sense of satisfaction.

And yet, a sense of hatred.

Hatred for myself.

I could have done better.

June

If this plan of ours doesn't succeed, there is no going back. The only way that anybody will ever be safe again is if we get to Chancellor Oswald first. His advisors have all plotted to kill him; and if they take over after he is gone, there will be nobody who can stop it.

After listening to their plan, we have come up with a plan of our own. We have run through the different scenarios and come up with answers and ways to work with each and every one of them. It has been a week since we found out what the advisors plan is, and we have finally come up with a foolproof way to save the chancellor.

"So," Zane says to Van and me once more, "Van will have already taken out the driver and taken his place. She will be waiting with the car at the designated spot. At this designated spot, there will be four buildings surrounding us. I will be waiting behind the office, and June will be waiting on top of the Laundromat with the gun, ready to take out Oswald's so-called guards. Once June takes out the guards, I will force Oswald into Van's car, and we will drive him back to our interrogation room."

"Exactly," she confirms.

"And I will meet you two in the IR after disposing the guards' bodies by dumping them behind the office and covering them with the tarp we have planted there."

Van looks down to the aerial-view map and chuckles. "Will you be able to drag them behind the building by yourself?"

I can't help but raise an eyebrow. A million snarky remarks and comments come to mind, but I swallow them all and nod.

Van looks from Zane and back to me. "Then let's get ready."

CHAPTER THIRTY-TWO

Logan

In my room, I wait. I wait, pacing back and forth. I love being able to move freely with the skeleton and my suit, but I don't like to be kept waiting. I prefer being in my room over being out where people can see me, but sometimes I just really feel the need to get out.

When Tony finally arrives, he enters the room with a serious expression, immediately causing me to think I have done something wrong. The last mission he had me do was days ago. Was that because it was only adequate? Is my adequacy something that is going to get me in trouble? I can't have them take in any more civilians to torture.

"Mr. Forge, your assignment for tonight is something much more important than any other assignment we have given you."

"What do you mean?" I take a deep breath and ask him in my gravelly voice, "Do I not get to choose?"

He shakes his head at me. "Not tonight. I have a good feeling you will be comfortable with this job." Tony holds out his cuff and brings up a three-dimensional map, starting at one of the shops in the city. "Do you know where this is?"

I nod.

"Then watch carefully." Tony slowly moves the map through the city, showing me which roads to take and how to get to my mission. When he finally stops, it lands in between four separate buildings in an obscure part of the town. "Here is where I need you stationed tonight. Your assignment is to protect Chancellor Oswald as he changes from one car to the next."

I look back to Tony. "Where is he going?"

"That is confidential. All you are being told to do tonight is to make sure he gets from one car to the other safely. Got it?"

I shrug but am slapped across the face with a terrible amount of force. Not even the suit can help mask the amount of pain his slap brought upon my skin. Holding myself off the ground with my elbow, I nod violently. "I got it."

Tony's head cocks, and he gives me a small smile. "Good."

Quickly, I scurry out of the window, down the ladder, and out of the area. With a deep burning still in my cheek, I shed a few tears, causing even more pain. The salt streams down my face under the mask and feels like acid rolling down my skin. I quickly wipe them off with the fabric on my cheek and continue to the checkpoint.

When I arrive, I hide behind one of the buildings and wait. I see no vehicles at first; but just as one of them pull up to the rendezvous point, something else catches my eye.

Something peeks off the roof of one of the buildings.

June

Everything is set and ready to go.

I have my gun perched and held on my shoulder, ready to take out the guards as soon as they exit the vehicle. So I wait.

I wait in that position for over half an hour.

When the second vehicle pulls up beside Van's, I tense up, ready for the plan to commence.

I listen to the sound of the ground crackle underneath the approaching car's tires and the whistling of the wind as it blows against my face wrap. The dark and flowy fabric blows in the wind in all directions, but never once do I let it get in the way of my sight.

When the two guards exit the van, Oswald follows. After the chancellor gets out, he is followed by two more guards. I allow my sights to find their way onto the first guard's head but am slightly startled by a noise of something moving behind me.

Someone is moving behind me.

I have to move quickly.

I shoot the driver of the first van and off every guard in seconds. I watch the horror on Oswald's face as his guards all drop dead around him followed by the shock he expresses when Zane rushes him into the new vehicle.

Spinning around, I pull the pistol out of its holster and aim it at the large black figure running directly at me.

Logan

I swing my leg up and over the person's legs, forcing the hand holding their pistol onto the ground. My boot stands on their wrist until they release the gun, but I am quickly caught off guard by the person swinging their legs behind mine and then kicking me in the torso.

I stumble back but return to the person in a matter of milliseconds. When she rises to her feet, it becomes apparent that I am fighting a woman about a foot shorter than me but seemingly almost as heavy as me. I leap forward to try to get the pistol from the ground, but I am forced to dodge her kicks and punches. The third punch she throws lands right on my throat, causing me to stumble back once more. The tightness of my skin along with its sensitivity causes me to believe I may have just had my throat torn apart.

Forcing myself to act quickly, I kick the pistol off the roof and manage to get by her to the other gun. Just as I kick it off the side of the building, I see her out of the corner of my eye coming at me; so I swing a hit at her. She manages to grab my wrist, squeezes it tightly, and twists my arm to a position I cannot return from. I immediately shout in pain as her grip burns my skin but am silenced when her leg swings up to kick me in the throat.

I manage to block her kick with my left hand and pull her leg out from under her, causing her to fall to the ground and giving me a moment to recoup from the burning. I watch her hop back to her feet and stare at me. Some of her dark hair peeks out of her face mask, along with a small amount of her cheeks and eyes.

The familiarity of this figure causes me to focus too much on trying to figure out who she is and results in her lunging at me before I get the chance to do the same. The sound of my wheezing as we throw punches and kicks and dodge each other's shot becomes more and more distracting as we fight.

She throws another punch, but I manage to dodge it and grab her arm. Immediately, I knee her in the stomach twice.

The woman wraps her free arm around my knee the second time I kick and launches herself at me, causing us both to go down but me first.

The burning on my back takes over for a moment as she forces her arm back on my throat. I swing my legs up and wrap them around her body, forcing her on her back, leaving us both stumbling again to our feet.

I ignore the intense pain and look back to the woman as she pulls a knife out of another holster on her thigh.

I have to bring her in alive for questioning. If I kill her, we may have just lost Oswald for good; but if it comes to it, and she forces me to kill her, I think I just may.

I take a step toward her as she slowly walks over and see her face without the mask. I look to my left to see the wrap blowing in the wind over the other buildings and look back to see a ghost.

No.

It can't be.

This woman is much fuller than Mavis ever was. Her hair is darker and shorter.

Mavis would never do any of this. She would never have killed those men.

She would never have done any of this.

Her pace speeds up toward me; but just before she reaches a sprint, the name croaks out of my mouth. "Mavis?"

She freezes.

But only for a moment.

She lunges forward, coming at me with the knife; and that is when I see it. The small scar on her cheek underneath her bright-green eyes, the same scar I noticed when we first met.

She swings the knife across at me, but I lean my head back and manage to keep my throat intact. Just as she swings it back, I grab her arm and force the knife out of her hand. As I toss the knife over the side of the building, just as I did to her other weapons, she elbows me in the face and puts me into a chokehold.

I reach up to pull her arm off, but she has me in a position I can't get out of. After a moment of me not stopping the struggle, she swings my body down and forces us both to the ground.

I continue to try to get out of it without hurting her but slowly start to black out. The lack of oxygen causes my head to pound an unbearable amount. I look around the roof and up to Mavis so that she will be the last thing I see, but I am released. The horror on her face as she scurries away frightens me, but it doesn't help the situation.

I lie on the ground, trying to regain all the lost air and blood flow, and hear her whisper something to me. Looking up to her, I see the same slightly panicked girl I met when we were first in the woods together.

She runs over to me and grabs Sam's necklace, pulling me forward and piercing the back of my neck where the chain was resting. It must have peeked out during the struggle.

"What is this?" she whispers to me.

I wheeze, trying to figure out what to say.

Mavis yanks me forward again and shouts in my face, "Where did you get this?"

I look her in the eyes and consider pulling off the mask.

If I take it off, would she recognize me?

No.

She would become even more frightened and confused than she is now.

I can't let her see me. She doesn't recognize my voice because of how much damage I've had, so how is she going to believe that I am me if I took off this mask? How would that help anything?

It wouldn't.

"I got it from Sam," I wheeze to her, trying to sound as normal as possible.

Her immediate reaction is tightening her grip on the jewel. "Sam is dead."

I take another deep breath. "When the police found him, they gave me this necklace because it was to go to his family, but you and I were the only people left he considered family."

Her eyes widen as she releases the necklace. She takes a step back and stares at me in silence. After moments of waiting, she finally speaks up with an unconvinced and shocked expression, "Logan?"

June

The suited figure nods to me.

I take a few deep breaths, trying to figure this out. Slowly, I begin to pace on the top of the roof and run my hands through my hair, trying to get a grip on this all. Without ever taking my eyes off this man, I force the need to scratch so far down in me that I hope never to see it again.

"Prove it," I tell him. "Take off the mask."

He rises to his feet slowly. With a deep and hoarse voice, he answers, "I can't."

"I can't trust you if you won't show me your face."

He looks around the roof, and another gust of wind blows. Looking back to me, he wheezes, "The air hurts my skin. I can't take off the mask."

"Why?" I take a step toward him and ask, "What's happened since I left?"

He takes a step toward me. "Why'd you leave?"

"I had to." We stare at each other for a moment. "I would have been killed if I didn't."

He nods, possibly believing me but possibly waiting for the right moment to kill me.

"I can't keep talking," I tell him. "I have to leave."

He wheezes once more. "I can't let you do that. It was my job to keep Oswald alive."

I snort. "Well, you did a pretty crappy job." He takes a step toward me as I finish, "If it wasn't for my team and me, Oswald would have already been dead."

"What?"

"Oswald's advisors were going to kill him."

He shakes his head at me. "I don't believe that."

"You don't have to." I take a few steps to get by him and watch him watch me. "I have to go."

"I'm coming with you."

"What?" I exclaim. "No."

"I want to help."

The two of us stare at each other. "What?"

"It was my job to protect him."

My eyes narrow to him. "And you always follow orders?"

He remains quiet.

"How about this," I continue to walk past him. "I will give it some thought on whether or not to let you come, but you have to show me your face first."

He stares at me and looks around the roof of the building. After a moment, he nods. "I will but once we get out of the wind."

CHAPTER THIRTY-THREE

Logan

I drag the final guard back behind the building, and Mavis hides them under the tarp. She tucks the edges in under the bodies so that the tarp won't fly away, but it still looks suspicious.

The two of us then get into the first car that Oswald arrived in, and Mavis drives us off into the woods. Neither of us has said anything, which makes the tension somehow greater. We drive about a mile into the trees until we can't see any point of civilization, and she parks the car.

Turning the keys and pulling them out of the vehicle, she looks back to me. "So?"

I stare at her, trying not to let my wheezing become too loud. "Are you sure?"

Immediately, she nods.

I continue to stare at her, into her eyes, and reach up for the mask. Slowly, I slide it off, feeling the cool air from the air-conditioning vents that have just stopped blowing. I force myself to ignore the burning as I watch her expression shifts from seriousness, to pure shock. How she manages to keep her mouth from gaping, I don't know.

I scan her face just as she does mine. This is Mavis. It looks just like Mavis, just with more of her. Her face has gotten slightly rounder and her body slightly thicker. The more I scan her, the more she looks healthier than she did before.

Her hand slowly rises. I watch her hesitate and try to decide whether or not to touch my face. She stares at me, and our eyes flicker from one eye to another. As I wait for her to decide, I find myself holding my breath. Just as her hand becomes less than an inch away from my face, she pulls away. "You can come."

She watches me slide my mask back on and listens as my wheezing continues. When we finally exit the vehicle, Mavis's pace quickens; and we begin speed walking away from the car. On our way back to their hideout from the woods, the quiet between us reappears. After over ten minutes of silence, I decide to be the first one to speak.

"What happened with Sam?" I ask her, trying not to sound too gravelly.

"He overdosed."

I pause. Overdosed? Sam? "The police think you did it."

She looks to me confused.

"They think you killed Sam."

Looking back ahead of us, she forces herself back into the serious stature. "Mavis never killed anyone."

"Mavis?" I ask her.

"Right. She never killed anyone." She clears her throat and continues forward. "I am June. June Dawson." Adjusting her belt and the strap that holds her gun on her back, she stares straight ahead.

"What?"

"Mavis Wamsley is dead." She looks to me but only for a moment. "She died the same night Sam did."

The two of us continue in silence. I want to ask her how she has been, where she has been, and so many other things; but I don't think she will tell me. As I shuffle through all the questions I could ask, she speaks up.

"Where do you work now? Are you still with the Taai?"

I shake my head and clear my throat. "I no longer work with them but for an individual commanding officer."

She nods. "What happened to your skin?"

This question is the one that killed our conversation. Neither of us says anything after that. We just walk the seven or eight miles through the back parts and hidden areas of the town and get to the back of a purple building. June unlocks the metal door and enters, leading me to follow.

Upon entry, we file through multiple small rows of fabric rolls and make it to a small hidden latch on the ground, which has already been opened. I follow Mavis down the stairs of the entrance, and we make our way into a room that reminds me way too much of the one Derek and his mother were in. Two other people wait on the outside of the window, just as I once did, and give us shocked looks when June comes down.

I look past the two others to the inside of the interrogation room and find what I came looking for.

Chancellor Oswald.

June

"What is this?" Zane rises from his chair and glares at Logan.

Van's immediate reaction is to raise her pistol to him. Logan braces to be attacked, but I step in front of him. Van looks to me for a split second but keeps her gun aimed on Logan. "June, you can't bring people in here."

"He can be trusted," I tell them, "and if worse comes to worse, we can kill him."

Van continues staring at Logan but lowers her pistol. "I hope we don't have to."

"I agree." Zane looks from Logan and back to me. "We were waiting for you to start." He walks past Van and into the room with Oswald. The moment Oswald sees him, a streak of fear crosses his face, causing me to feel a tad bit guilty about all this.

Van makes her way past Logan and me and over to the stairs. "I have to go. I've stayed too long already. Please be careful." She gives Logan one final glance and exits the building, leaving Logan and me alone on this side of the window. We step forward and listen to Logan's patterned breathing, along with Zane as he speaks to Oswald in a polite and calm manner.

"Good evening, Chancellor Oswald." He folds his hands on the table and looks to the blue-eyed, perfectly sculpted chancellor. "I am very sorry for tonight. I know that this can't be easy."

"Well"—Oswald chuckles nervously in his overly proper Bergland accent—"I can't say that it was."

"I know, and I'm sorry, but we had to get ahold of you."

Oswald looks to the window, seemingly right at Logan and me. "How many of you are there?"

"That's not important. What is important is that you should feel safe with us. It is not our intentions to hurt you." Zane clears his throat and leans back in his chair. "I have some questions to ask you, if you don't mind."

"Well, I, um," Oswald stumbles, "I guess I don't mind."

"Thank you. Would you please tell me, do you know anything about the missing Frieden citizens?"

"The missing citi—" Oswald leans forward on the table as well. "No, I do not. Do you?"

"What about the assassinations throughout the country?"

"No, I don't. Do you know something? I heard about these just the other day, and no one has explained to me what is going on."

"And what about the tortures?" Zane asks Oswald, earning a change in wheezing patterns from Logan.

I look to Logan and see him continuously staring at Oswald as if nothing else exists.

"Tortures?" Oswald asks. "What are you talking about?" The room is silent for a moment. Oswald speaks back up with a nervous chattering, "This is the first I have heard about any sort of torturing. Who is doing this?"

"You mean, you are unaware that your advisors have condoned torture techniques such as electric shock, beatings, and—"

"What? Unaware? Of course I am unaware!" Oswald looks at Zane with a hurt expression, one of true pain. "If I knew about this, they would all be fired immediately and all who assisted as well. This can't be true. There is no way that there is any sort of assassination or torturing condoned within my administration."

Logan immediately rushes past me and into the room with Oswald. Zane rises to his feet to get in between Oswald and Logan but is overpowered when Logan slams his fist on the table and pulls off his mask.

"Do you see this?" Logan shouts at the chancellor in a horrible, hoarse voice. "Do you see it? Do you hear it?" He growls, "This is what your administration condones. This is what your torturers do to people." Zane grabs Logan and forces him out of the room as Logan struggles to breathe. Logan coughs and gasps for air as I watch the two struggle and Oswald gapes in horror. Zane shoves Logan out of the room and slams the door behind him.

"What are you doing?" Zane shouts at Logan. "He needs to feel safe with us."

"I was helping you! I am an example of what the torturers do." Logan gets in Zane's face. "Do you see my skin? I am helping make the point that you need."

The two of their voices overlap as they shout.

"It's not like I was going to hurt him! It is my job to keep him alive!"

"Oh yeah? Whose orders are those?"

"Don't you twist my words. I am not doing anything wrong."

"Tell that to the—"

"Guys!" I stand in between them and shove them both away. "Stop." Looking to Logan, I speak calmly. "Thank you for that. I know it couldn't have been easy." I turn to Zane and head over to the door. "Please, try to get along."

I enter the room with Oswald, and the entire tone of the scene changes. This room is much better lit than outside, and the walls are a much lighter color. I turn back to the window to find a mirror and that Oswald and I are staring at each other through it.

"Hello again," I say to him kindly. "I'm sorry we have to meet under these circumstances."

"What? You are working with them?"

I shrug. "That depends. Who is them? Who do you think we are?"

He looks around. "From what has happened tonight, my first assumption was the rebels, but now I'm not so sure." A moment of silence passes between us as we stare. "Why haven't you all killed me?"

"Because that isn't what we are here to do. That isn't why we took you tonight." I sigh, not really wanting to break the news to him. "We actually took you to save you."

Oswald gives me an odd look. "What?"

"The day you and I ran into each other at the park, I slipped a small microphone underneath your coat collar." I pull out a small plastic box on which we saved the clips of his advisors. "After you left the room, we heard something. Something that is hard for me to show you." I press the button and listen to the plastic piece whirl. "You have a right to know."

The recorder plays the clips of Riley and Madden with another advisor, who we don't recognize, going over the plan.

"Just one more week."

"Everyone will assume it was a 'rebel act.' After he is gone, Riley can take over, and we won't have to go through Oswald anymore to propose acts."

"This can't be over soon enough."

As it plays through, Oswald looks to me with tears filling his eyes. None have fallen yet, but they have all formed a wall over his perfectly blue iris.

I reach my hand out to his and place mine on top. "Hey, you're okay. You're safe here."

He shakes his head, staring down at the table. The moment he blinks, two streams of tears fall down his cheeks. "They were my friends. I had no idea they thought me so idiotic. I had no idea they had plotted to have me killed." One of his hands combs through his hair as he continues to stare at the table. His voice has changed into a state of sadness but not a voice that I usually hear with tears. He sounds as if he isn't even crying. "I have been played like a pawn." He slowly flips his hand over and takes hold of mine. Oswald sits there in silence for a moment, holding my hand in his and trying to get back to his normal state.

"Please"—he releases my hand and sniffles, looking up to me and back to the mirror—"let me help you. I had no idea any of this was happening. I didn't know there were assassinations, I didn't know there were missing citizens, and I certainly had no idea there were any tortures happening. Let me help."

I give him a small smile. "Give me one moment."

Exiting the room, I head out to find Logan with his mask back on and Zane looking to me with an impressed expression.

"We have him onboard."

Zane

Rolling up the last portion of fabric to restock the shelves, I listen to the hologram screen and watch as the interview with Oswald takes place.

He is dressed in one of his nicer suits and sits across from the interviewer in a comfy chair with larger-than-life cushions and armrests. The huge red velvety seat makes him look much smaller than he actually is.

"It was terrifying. It truly was," he tells the interviewer.

She crosses her legs and brushes off her tightly fitted skirt. "It sounds terrifying. Amiable rebels are something who have been in everyone's nightmares lately. Would you be able to elaborate a little bit more of what happened last night?"

He clears his throat and folds his hands. "It was a normal transportation. Very routine. I go from one car to another and have them both drive off in separate directions. The only thing different was the atmosphere, really."

"What do you mean by that?"

Oswald looks to her with a sense of pain in his eyes. "My driver, along with the guards who went with me, none of them said anything during the drive. It was very"—he pauses and looks back to his hands—"uneasy."

"Why do you think that is?"

"I don't know." He looks back to her. "I don't know. All I know is that when we met at the rendezvous point, the first few guards got out of our car, and everything was fine. I followed them out and began heading to the next vehicle, but as soon as the rest of the guards exited the first van, I could hear hushed shots taking place. Not so much as gunshots but more of a small whistling as the bullets penetrated all the guards' heads."

"Oh my!"

"Yes. That was one of my first thoughts too, followed by, who is that man rushing toward me?"

A small wave of laughter comes from the room as Oswald chuckles at his own joke. Thinking about the fact that he is speaking of me gives me a small sense of pride. I brush it off and listen to them continue.

"Okay, okay, I'm sorry," Oswald apologizes. "This is a serious matter."

"No, no, it's okay." The interviewer giggles. "It is nice to know that the events of last night haven't taken away your sense of humor."

"Oh, yes, well, humor is one thing that I hope I never lose. I find that if you can make just one person smile a day, you have accomplished something worthwhile."

The interviewer smiles at him and chuckles again. "Well, consider your task accomplished." The room joins her in the giddy laughter as Oswald shares his famous shy smile. "Okay, okay, we were right at the part about a man rushing toward you."

"Yes, yes." Oswald scoots back in his chair and straightens up once again. He folds his hands and allows his fingers to fiddle with each other. "The man grabbed me and forced me into the van I was originally going to get into and stuck me in the arm with a vial. Next thing I know, I woke up in a, um—" Oswald looks to the side of the room. "Oh, wait, I can't tell them that?"

The crowd gives another wave of laughter as the interviewer pulls him back in. "Okay, well, that's fine. I have a few more questions for you, though, hopefully some of which you can answer."

He nods. "I will do my best."

"How did you manage to get out of the rebels' grasp?"

Oswald allows a small smile to rise up on his face. "I was aided by one of our own officers. I can't give you his name sadly because it was this officer's wish to remain anonymous. But let me tell you this. If you are listening"—Oswald looks to the camera with a deep face of sympathy— "thank you. Thank you so much for everything you have done. I know I wouldn't be here without you today if you had not shown up when you did."

The interview goes on, and I can't help but snort. I had no idea how good an actor this man was. I noticed that whenever he tells a lie, his fingers can't stay still. Like when he told everyone that I stuck him in the arm with a vial. I did no such thing. I simply sat in the back with him to make sure he stayed put.

All I can do now is hope that he wasn't lying last night about helping us. So far, he has stuck to the plan and made it seem as if the Amiable rebels were behind this. I assume that he will continue with the plan; but at the same time, he may not know whom to trust. After being betrayed by people whom he considered his closest friends, he may just be trying to do whatever won't get him killed at this point.

I just hope that June and Logan can accomplish the next part of the plan.

June

Strolling through the higher-maintenance portion of Kern is much more entertaining than I expected. Everyone dresses more expensively, except for the obvious tourists; and everything here seems to be kept by someone with extreme obsessive compulsive disorder. Everything is perfect. All the bushes are trimmed into boxes, circles, or fancy sculptures depending on where they are located; all the sidewalks seem to have been freshly scrubbed; and there is not a piece of trash on the ground anywhere to be seen. Even the fences around the capitol building are kept perfectly. The bottoms of the black metal fences that you can see through are perfectly painted and seem to have no dirt on them, even though they are stuck in the grass.

Guards are flooded around the property just as they have always been. The only difference is that the closer I get to going in, the more menacing they become.

There are signs put up all over the entrance I was told to go to. All of them say that if you ask to go in, but your name is not on the list, you will be detained and marked as suspicious personnel. You will be put onto a list that bans you from a number of spectacular events such as political rallies, parties, gatherings, fund-raisers, and other things like that.

"Name?" the guard asks me when I approach the entrance.

"June Dawson." I wipe off the bottom half of my navy dress and look around awkwardly, feeling like I stand out much more than I probably should.

He points to the scanner as a red line appears. I hold my wrist out and watch the scanner run over my code for the first time.

The guard looks to me and then back to the computer. "What state were you originally from?"

"Bloot."

He types something into the computer, leaving me waiting awkwardly as all the guards stare. The man who told me to scan my wrist looks to me with large eyes and gives me a nervous chuckle. "Oh, I'm sorry, ma'am." He presses a button in his station that unlocks the gate. "I had no idea that you were on the chancellor's list. Go ahead. I assume you know the way in?"

I nod.

"Okay, once you get to the front desk, they will have someone escort you." He gives me a large and slightly frightening smile. "Have a wonderful day."

I return his forced smile and make my way to the building. I remember which parts of the gardens to go through and which paths to go down to get to the part of the building with the front desks from the inauguration ball. I follow the same path I took that night with Logan and admire the flower blossoms that have seemed to overtake the land.

When I make it to the front desk, I notice the inside of the building looks the exact same as it did the night of the ball. The only difference is that it is missing a bunch of drunken, snooty people.

"Ms. Dawson?" An older woman comes over to me and gives me a large smile. "My name is Mrs. Ness. I am here to escort you to Chancellor Oswald."

I nod to her. I said thank you, and we head off. I am taken through many hallways, up an elevator, and through even more hallways. When we finally get to Oswald's office, she gives me one final smile and opens the large finely carved mahogany doors.

When they swing open, Oswald's eyes meet mine; and he rises to his feet. "Ms. Dawson." He comes over to me as Mrs. Ness quietly exits and closes the doors behind us.

"Hello, Chancellor Oswald." I reach out to shake his hand.

He takes it and gives me another smile. "Please, call me Tom."

"All right, Tom. I assume you will be referring to me as June as well?"

He shrugs. "If you are comfortable with that, I would be delighted."

I smile back, and the two of us share a moment or two of awkward silence.

Tom looks around the room and takes a deep breath. "You know"—he looks back to me and gives a nervous chuckle—"I am really anxious. I don't know how I feel about any of this."

"What is there to be nervous about?" I ask him. "All you are doing is bringing 'your date' over to meet your friends for the first time, right?"

He nods. "I guess so, yes."

"So why are you nervous?"

"Well, to be fair, these are the people who planned to kill me."

Another smile rises on my face as I realize this man's main goal in life really is to make the best of things. From every interview with him I've watched, he always tries to make sure the other person is doing well. He is always the first to apologize, he is always the first to crack a smile, and he is always the first to try to assume the best of people.

And yet, he has been put into a horrible situation.

The two of us sit down on the couch and talk through everything. We make sure we are on the same page about how the two of us met and realize that saying we met a week ago at the park will be good enough. Just that, we hit it off.

Sure, his friends will probably think I am a gold digger.

But you know what? I know they plotted to have Tom killed, so I will call us even.

The plan is for me to talk him up to make them see how much they need him. I will be pointing out how there was suspicion in the town that one of them tried to have Tom kidnapped. Thank goodness that isn't true, though, right?

I will make sure to have them thinking that if Tom dies, they will be blamed.

We finish talking through the plan when I see a bead of sweat dripping down his face. I reach up to him with my sleeve and wipe it off. "It's going to be okay."

He gives me a quick and unsure nod as a knock at the door surprises us both. Tom rises to his feet, wipes off his face once more, and readjusts his suit. "Come in."

Four men file into the room with obviously fake smiles on and are immediately stopped. The eyes of each fall onto me, and I can almost hear their thoughts. "Oswald has a daughter?"

"Well"—Riley chuckles at me—"who is this?"

Tom raises his hand and places it on my back. "This is my, um, friend. June Dawson."

Riley gives Thomas a curious look of slight entertainment while the others look to me in disbelief.

"Now, what exactly do you mean *friend*?" Dotson asks him, walking over to me in a way that I can only describe as unsettling.

Tom gives them all a look of embarrassment. Immediately, they come to the assumption that he and I are a couple.

"Ah," Madden approaches me first. "Hi, I'm Phillip Madden. It's a pleasure to meet you."

I nod and shake his hand. His act is followed by the other three doing the same.

The last man to greet me is James Sparrow. When he comes to shake my hand, he brings it up to his mouth and kisses it. "It's a pleasure."

The amount of hatred that rises up in me the moment he does this shocks me. I force myself to calm down and pull my hand away. "The pleasure is all mine."

Tom must be able to tell that this bothered me because just as I step back, he steps in front of me. "I'm happy you all are now introduced, but we were—"

"Yes, yes, I am too. Ozzy"—Madden steps forward and looks past Tom—"will your friend be staying for dinner?"

He turns to me with a small smile. "I don't know. Let's ask her."

Shyly, I step back. "Oh, I don't know about that."

"Well, you must at least stay for drinks," Tom says to me.

The whole room seems to freeze, waiting for my answer. I think through the plan once more just before I utter the words, "Why not?"

Logan

"Did you hear that?" one of the guards asks the other.

He answers with a mumble, and the two walk off.

Sneaking through the tunnels below the capitol building is much easier than I thought it would be. With my dark suit allowing me to blend in with the even darker shadows, I scurry through and make it into one of the bathrooms. With the clothes of a server that I have had hidden in here since last night, I slide the clothes over my suit, pull off my mask, and make my way out of the bathroom.

Wearing the large hat some of the servers wear, I keep my head down and make my way into the kitchen. Everyone is so busy with their own task that no one seems to even notice me.

When I sense the time is right, I pull out a small metal container and slide a few balls of ice out into one of the glasses. Quickly sliding the metal container back into my pocket, I prepare the rest of the glasses, putting ice in each one of them, including the one with the ice I added.

The way these cups will be set up when they get to Oswald's office is there will be six glasses. Four of them will have a blue trim around its edges, one of them will have gold around its edges, and the last will have no special trim. The advisors will receive the blue cups while the chancellor will use his gold cup, leaving the plain cup for the visitor. I still don't understand why they feel the need to make their cups different from one another. From what I hear, Oswald is actually against it; but he didn't fight it too strongly.

The special ice I put into one of the blue-ringed cups isn't something that I would prefer to drink. I mean, I have heard the tranquilizer liquid when injected doesn't hurt, but I still would rather not have its frozen substance slowly melt into my drink. I imagine that it may have some symptoms that come along with the ingestion.

"Excuse me." A woman taps me on the shoulder, startling me. I quickly turn to her as I finish loading the ice in Mavis's—I mean, June's—cup. The woman takes a step back, shocked at my face. "Um, is this cart for the chancellor's office?"

I nod and step back from the cart. "Yes."

She stares at my face for a moment more, but I can tell she won't ask. She doesn't want to be rude.

"I got these burns fighting in the war," I tell her.

Though I didn't tell her which war.

"Oh." She gives me a smile and begins pulling the cart out. "Well, thank you for your service."

I nod back at her and find my way out of the kitchen as well.

When I manage to leave the building and climb back into my own, I find Elloise waiting in my room for me.

"Well, well, well, would you look who it is?" She steps over to me and gives me a small smile. "Where have you been? I came to bring you dinner."

I shrug. Not wanting to be too suspicious, I speak up, "I like going out." "Yeah? Where?"

"Don't worry," I tell her, "I don't go anywhere where anyone can see me. I make sure to stay in the woods or in the hidden parts of the city."

Elloise gives me a look of slight disbelief but shrugs it off. "Whatever you say, Logan."

She exits the room and allows me to eat my dinner alone, leaving me to silently hope that June can complete her job.

June

"Oh really?" Madden takes another sip of his drink. "So the first time you and Ozzy actually met, he knocked you down?"

I shrug. "Well, I actually believe I knocked him down, but he won't admit it."

Tom looks to me with a squint. "What do you mean you knocked me down? I walked right into you while looking at the poinsettia trees." He thanks the woman who has just collected our plates from the table and slides her some cash. "Have a wonderful day."

"But," I say to him, smiling at the woman as she nods to me goodbye, "when I walked into you, my leg went in between yours and tripped us both."

He chuckles and wipes his mouth with the napkin from his lap. "Can we just say we both tripped up?"

I roll my eyes and take a sip of my champagne as everyone else chugs their drinks. I've noticed that Tom and I are the only two really taking our drinking lightly while the other four are taking large gulps of whatever drink they fixed themselves. As the servers finally leave the room with just the six of us, their questions and comments become more and more obnoxious.

"Well, either way, Ozzy"—Riley finishes his drink once more and heads over to the cart for another—"it sounds like you have yourself a fine young lady. Anyone who can manage to get their legs intertwined that quickly within yours has to be a—"

"What he means to say," Dotson interrupts before Riley has time to finish his obnoxious statement that was meant to be a compliment, "is that it really sounds like you two have fallen for each other." He takes a sip from his blue-lined glass and stares at us, waiting for some sort of laughter.

Tom immediately gets the joke and releases a snicker while I have to force myself to enjoy the pun. Everyone in the room snorts along, all but Sparrow.

I look to him as he holds his chest with one hand.

"Are you okay, Mr. Sparrow?"

He nods, looking like he is attempting to hold in a belch. "I'm fine. My chest just started hurting a tad bit."

"Well, you did pound down your steak." Madden chuckles.

"Oh yes," Dotson snorts, "the last time I saw something disappear that quickly was when—"

"You lost your hair?" Sparrow interrupts.

Everyone at the table laughs as Dotson glares at Sparrow. "Yeah, yeah, whatever."

"Try drinking a little bit slower." I take another sip of my drink and look to Sparrow. "It goes down better if you do that."

He nods again and returns back to the conversation.

None of our ice looks any different, but I assume that Sparrow is the one who got the tranquilizers. With him drinking it slower, it gives his ice more time to melt. I keep him talking about anything and everything throughout the next thirty minutes or so to make sure he doesn't leave or pass out.

Every time someone asks him if he is okay, he brushes it off and changes the subject. He continues to sip at that same glass the rest of the evening until it finally comes to an end.

"Well, I think it is time to call it a night," Madden announces. He rises to his feet and raises his glass to us all. The five of us follow his lead and wait. Madden stares at me for a moment and then at Tom. "I would like to make this toast in honor of Ozzy's new friend." He smiles and raises his glass once more. "To June."

"To June," the rest of them say.

I watch the four advisors all finish their glasses as Tom and I gently sip ours. Three of the advisors all exit the private dining hall cheerfully while Sparrow slowly makes his way out.

"Hey, James." Tom makes his way over to the large man and places his hand on his back. "Are you sure you are okay?"

I watch from behind as Sparrow shakes his head and collapses to the ground. Tom immediately drops to his knees and calls out his name once more. The chancellor quickly turns to me with a panic in his eyes. I point out to the door and squeal, "Go get help!"

He nods and sprints off out of the room, giving me a small window of time. I dive down and pull Sparrow's right shoe and sock off, pull the empty syringe I had on my thigh holster out, and inject three milliliters of air in between his toes. Quickly, I force his sock and shoe back on and the syringe back onto my holster and flee the room with tears streaming down my face. As I try to turn a corner to find Tom, I run directly into him at full speed. He catches me and forces me far enough away from him so that he can see my face. "I got help."

Three people sprint past us toward the private dining hall with bags and first aid patches on their arms. I look back to Tom, and he pulls me close into a hug.

With the air injected into his bloodstream, the symptoms of a heart attack are imminent. No one will know what happened. All they will know was that there were five witnesses.

He had a heart attack.

Since Tom wasn't in the room when I did my job or was told of the plan, he isn't an accomplice. He doesn't know what happened, so he can't get into trouble for it. He will also not have the guilt on his conscience.

This was what had to happen. This was what was best for the country. This was what was best for the reinstitution of justice. This was what was best for Tom.

One down.

Three to go.

CHAPTER THIRTY-FOUR

Zane

It has been all over the news for the past week.

"James Sparrow dies of a heart attack."

"Could new health acts be put forward?"

"Sparrow dies at the age of fifty-six. Could there be foul play?"

It hasn't stopped. June has had her picture taken a few times with Chancellor Oswald but none of them she knew about. It was mostly him walking her out to the fence or back into the capitol building, but either way, this isn't the most beneficial thing.

Our job is to remain hidden. I realize—and so does June—that she has a job where she will most likely have her face plastered in newspapers and on gossip channels; but that doesn't mean we need to embrace it.

I have begun to wonder, with the way she comes back talking about Oswald, if she has begun to fall for him just as every other eligible bachelorette in this country seems to have. It is not as if she is drooling over him. She is simply speaking very highly of him whenever she gets the chance. I don't think he is a bad guy, not at all, but speaking so highly of someone who lies for a living? I don't know.

She is the only one of the two of us who ever really goes out. She meets with Logan every now and then to continue discussing the plan and meets with Oswald every other day. I don't know what she does with the rest of her time, but I do feel as if I can trust her judgment.

Sometimes.

The chime at the front door rings, and I look up to see Van walking in with a smile. "How is it going, Zane?"

I shrug. "As good as it can be I guess. No one seems to really like buying fabric anymore, though, so . . ."

She nods back. "That is one of the reasons we chose this place and hid it within the city." Van pulls a file out of her jacket and slides it onto my desk. "I can't stay for too long. Go ahead and look through this and update June."

I open the file and flip through the paper-clipped pages, revealing something I find more than unsettling. I read through each page and become more and more worried about the plan.

When June walks in about an hour later, she makes sure to come through the back door. I immediately wave her over and have her read the files. "Here. Van just dropped these off this morning."

"What is it?" She lifts one of the pages up and scans over the paragraphs.

"So we know that people have been and most likely are still being kidnapped and tortured for answers, right?"

She nods.

"According to recent intel, they are also making soldiers out of them."

June looks to me with confusion and back to the file.

"By pumping the soldiers full of glucose and starving their brains of the proteins they need, they make the soldiers more susceptible to suggestion. Along with torture and old brainwashing techniques, they are enhancing the experience with vials and other medicines."

She places her finger on one of the pages, seemingly trying to block my voice out to finish reading it.

I try waiting for her to finish but can't force myself to be patient enough. "Logan was tortured. He was also assigned to 'protect' Oswald. Do we need to be concerned?"

June looks to me with a sense of pain.

"I am not saying that it would be his fault. I am just asking. He *is* one of their soldiers, and he knows about us. Do we need to be worried that he will end up telling them?"

June shakes her head and takes a step away. "Logan has a good-enough sense of judgment not to take certain missions. He is only working there so that he won't be tortured anymore."

A small moment of silence sits between us.

June turns back to the files to continue reading. "He helped us kill off one of the chancellor's advisors. Why else would he do that?"

June

I finish reading through the file and find myself slightly hesitant to meet Logan again. I head out the back of the Fabric Room and to our rendezvous point in the woods. I stand there, waiting for him, and listen to the sound of the breeze through the trees, feeling its cooling sensation on my face. I close my eyes to absorb the late-spring warmth and sniff the scent of the forest, allowing it to remind me of a better place and a better time.

The snap of a twig in the distance brings me back to the present. I look to the source of the noise and find that Logan is much closer than I thought he was. His black silhouette figure blends in with our surroundings but not enough to make me lose sight of him.

"Hey," I say to him.

I can see his cheeks rise from under his mask. "Hey."

The two of us walk through the woods toward the outside of town and talk about anything and everything that comes to mind. There are certain questions though that neither of us answers.

He asks me what happened after leaving Frieden, and I tell him. I tell him about the tree foxes, about Bram and Samantha, and about seeing Grayson and Janice. I tell him about how I trained and I trained until I became the best I could be.

But that is it.

When I ask how his back is, he tells me all about how, at one point, he was paralyzed. I can't even imagine him being paralyzed. Logan is one of the most active beings I have ever met. He tells me about Eric and how he was going to be moving to State Three for his dream job, but he stayed behind to help him instead. He also tells me that Derek came to visit him at one point but stops speaking of him after that.

I force myself to swallow my questions about the Pages and continue listening.

After telling me about Eric landing a new job with John, Logan stops. He doesn't go any further. I don't know if he stops because he senses that I cringe at the name or if he stops because that is when he was taken and tortured.

We walk in silence, just listening to the sound of whatever is around us. For me, I choose to focus on his breathing. His perfect breathing pattern is something I have always adored. Though his breathing is much more hoarse and much more of a wheeze now than anything else, I still find it lovely to listen to.

"So," I say to him, "what are the chances that you will be taking your mask off again for me?"

A small chuckle escapes his chest. "I don't know."

"I know you said the wind hurts your skin, so I wouldn't ask you to take it off now, but anytime in the future, do you think I will get to see you again?"

He shrugs. "It really depends on the situation. If we are being completely honest, even if the wind didn't hurt me, I wouldn't want to take off my mask."

"Well, I'm never going to force you to." I listen to him clear his throat and try not to disgust me. I can tell he has more he needs to cough out, but I don't push it. "But your eyes have always been my favorite trait."

Logan looks to me but glances back down to the path in front of us quickly. His eyes seem to be the only thing that didn't take any damage. Not that I wouldn't still like his eyes if they did. I just hope my pointing that out will help him feel a little better.

I break the silence between us as we continue through the woods. "So can I ask you a question about work?"

"You can ask, but I may not answer."

I nod. "What kind of assignments are you given?"

He looks to me.

"And do you always do them?"

Logan shakes his head. "I am given choices usually. They lay out three different assignments for me to choose from, and I choose the one that makes the most sense."

"What do you mean?"

He clears his throat again. "For example, just over a week ago, I was given an option to either kill one of two people, neither of which they would tell me what they did, or bring in a man who is a known kidnapper."

"A known . . . kidnapper," I restate.

He nods. "I only do assignments that I know are good, like protecting Oswald or bringing in that man for questioning. I made a deal with my officer that I will do what they ask as long as it is sensible."

I find myself silent. I don't want to offend him, but I need to know. "How do you know they are telling you the truth? Like, when they told you that man was a kidnapper, how do you know he really was? Couldn't they just be telling you that to get you to comply?"

He shakes his head at me. "No. They wouldn't do that."

I remain quiet. If he doesn't want to accept it, I don't want to push it on him and get caught in a bad situation. Not that I think he will do anything to me. I just don't want him getting himself killed.

The two of us continue our walk in silence, only asking the occasional question every few minutes.

Logan

He sent Elloise up to my room to get me. She came in and gave me the location to meet Tony and then left immediately. No other exchange was made; no other words were said.

Within half an hour of her instructions, I make my way to the building where he requested our meeting and work my way to the room I was told to meet at. When I arrive in the large concrete room with only one small entrance all the way in the back, I look to a man's silhouette.

Tony's voice meets my ears. "Thank you for finally joining me, Logan." He takes a few steps toward me when I hear a small shuffling. I look to my right to find the room fades into darkness so dark that I can't see through it to the source of the noise.

I turn to look back to Tony, and he is holding a gun to my head. "Mr. Forge, I don't want to put a damper on our relationship, but I have begun to feel as if I can't trust you anymore." Before I have the chance to say or do anything, he allows the gun to spin on its trigger forward and hands it to me. "It's time to fix that."

I take the gun, and the lights on the other side of the room switch on and reveals someone sitting in a small wooden chair, with a bag over their head, tied up with ropes.

"I need you to kill this man."

I look back to Tony. "What did he do?"

"He is an Amiable rebel."

I step forward to Tony and look back to the man as he sits, obviously drugged, in the chair. "How do you know?"

Tony takes a deep breath and stares at me. "I shouldn't have to tell you, Logan. You should just trust my word, but since I respect you, I will make you a deal." He looks back to the man and stares. "Once you kill the rebel, I will tell you how I know."

My eyes follow Tony's, leaving us both staring at the target. Dozens of thoughts run through my head, leaving me hesitating but only for a moment. I find myself raising the gun and taking out the man with a single blow to the head.

"You made the right choice, Logan." I turn back to look at Tony, and he gives me a small smile. "We know this man was an Amiable rebel because he was the one responsible for the death of Chancellor Oswald's advisor, James Sparrow."

My heart drops as his words echo through the room. I feel a sudden pounding in my head as my brain seems to become heavier and heavier. I realize it is not my brain growing in weight but my conscience as I run to the man.

"It was only a matter of time before we caught him."

I fall to my knees by the body of this man and pull the bag off his head.

"We won't put this out to the public, though. We want the rebels to think they succeeded."

His red hair covered in blood makes it appear much more orange than I ever thought it was. His eyes remain open as he lies on the ground, seemingly staring right past me. When I finally shut his eyelids, I realize I will never see the only purple iris I have ever seen again.

I rise to my feet, leaving a starved Derek Page's corpse lying beside me. I know that if I react the wrong way, they will be onto me. They will know I am no longer their soldier, so I storm toward the door so that Tony won't see my anger.

The moment I cross the door's threshold, Tony's voice echoes once more through the room, "You made the right choice."

I find myself slowly turning to stare at him and scanning him over. His perfectly coiffed hair and obviously fake teeth fall with him, lifeless, to the floor as the shot from my pistol rings through the air, blowing a matching hole through his head.

"Now I have."

June

Walking to the back room to check some of the microphones I have hidden in the capitol building, I trip on part of the carpet that has been folded back. After almost falling on my face and knowing Zane saw it, I straighten up my posture and continue forward as if nothing happened.

Listening to the high-and-mighty, all-business, super-serious Zane chuckle forces a smile to rise on my face. I've noticed that he has been tiptoeing around me since he pointed out that Logan may pose a threat a few days ago, but I don't understand why. Why would he be trying to spare my feelings? It is not as if I would take offense to him being wary.

When I make it into the back room, my eyes immediately fall upon a piece of paper folded on the desk. After making my way over to it and reading it through, I speed back out to Zane.

"Read this." I hand him the paper and watch his eyes skim over it.

"What? 'You were right'? Who is this from?"

I pull the paper back and read over the two statements made. *You were right. I am going to fix what I can.*

"Is this from Logan?" Zane asks me.

"I think so." I set the paper down on the table and look back to Zane. "I don't know exactly what this means, but I think we need to get a jump start on the plan."

CHAPTER THIRTY-FIVE

Logan

Through the halls I go, hiding behind corners whenever I need to in order to avoid contact with someone. I manage to make it undetected to Commander Isana Burris's office and surprise her.

"Excuse me." She rises to her feet when I take a step into the room. She looks me up and down, seemingly shocked at my appearance. "What do you think you're doing?"

I watch her hand as she slowly reaches underneath her desk. Before she has the chance to trigger any sort of alarm, I leap across the room, startling her backward, and snap her neck. No sound or scream was made, only the slight shuffling of me sliding her back into her chair and leaning her over her desk.

Before coming here, I went to the file room in the capitol building where they keep the papers on who runs what. All the completed assignments as far as assassinations and interrogations were signed off by this woman: Isana Burris.

I look through her office and find a list in her drawer. The same list of people who had completed tasks and assignments in the file room.

I slide this list into one of my belt pockets and lock the door to the office. She is still logged into her hologram computer, so I scroll through the information and search the keywords for each soldier's name. I go through the list and write down as many of their addresses as I can get until the computer program asks me for a checkpoint password.

Leaning back from the computer, I look around the room and find four large oil lamps. Without hesitation, I rummage through the drawers and find a box of matches. After sliding the matches into one of my pockets, I take each lamp and empty the oil on Burris, the cabinets, the desk, the walls, the door, and everything I can as I slowly back myself up to the window. I set the last empty lamp down on the floor and slide the window open.

I light one of the matches and flick it into the room. It dies out before hitting the ground, so I take another one and do the same. When the whole room finally ignites, a blast of heat strikes me in the face, causing an intense pain to flood my skin. I slide the window closed, pull out one of the hooks and lines that I took from one of Tony's supply rooms and hid in the suit's belt, and climb my way back down the side of the building.

June

"There is no way," I tell Riley.

He nods as everyone else laughs at his story. "I'm telling you, three weeks ago was the first time I had ever visited a real farm."

"And the moment you walked in, you just happen to step on a rake?" I ask.

Riley nods. "It hit me in the nose so hard that I thought I had broken it."

"That will be the last time he will ever step foot into a barn," Madden snorts.

Every time I come over to be with Tom and the others to earn their trust, I have noticed that Tom takes it into his own hands to always remain in between me and the others. Tom scoots closer to me as Dotson adjusts his seating position on the couch's armrest. I look away from him and around the room. The chancellor's office is much larger than I ever really pictured it to be; but the more time I spend in it, the more it feels regular-sized and cozy, and everything else feels subpar.

"Wasn't that the last time you did any publicity stunts?" Dotson asks Riley.

Riley nods back. "And after that, I don't think I will be doing any more anytime soon."

I roll my eyes at them and look down to Tom's knee as it rests directly against mine. His dark-gray striped suit makes him look much taller and much skinnier compared to the rest of the advisors. I look Tom up and down to find that I favor this suit of his more than any of the others I have seen.

"I really like your suit, Tom," I tell him. Looking back to the rest of the advisors, I realize each of them seems to wear a different suit every day. "How many suits do you all own?"

Dotson looks to Tom and chuckles. Each of the advisors straightens up and attempts to look proper.

"We were just having this conversation the other day," Dotson tells me. "I have over one hundred different suits, not counting all the other office clothes I own."

My jaw drops as I look to Tom. He gives me a small and shy smile. "I know. It's a bit much."

"A bit much?" Riley asks him. "That is an overwhelming amount of suits."

"Don't act so surprised," Dotson snorts at him. "You told me that you have nearly one hundred yourself."

Riley rolls his eyes back at him and takes a sip of his drink. "That isn't over one hundred, though." He swallows the last of his drink and points over to Madden. "And my count isn't nearly as many as Madden's is."

Madden rolls his eyes and looks over to me. "I have almost two hundred suits at the moment. The only time I ever rewear the suits is if I haven't been seen in one by the media."

"Which is never," Riley adds. "You are on the news at least three times a week."

Madden shrugs. "So?"

"So," Riley continues, "that is a ridiculous amount of suits, which cost hundreds of dollars each."

Madden shrugs again. "Your point?"

I force myself to keep the eye rolling to a minimum and scoot a little closer to Tom. "I actually know someone who makes suits for a living."

"Oh yeah?" Tom asks me, ignoring his advisors as they grumble insults to each other.

"Yeah! It is a friend of mine." I look to the others as they give me a small look of amusement. "Well, technically it's my friend's sister's boyfriend's uncle."

I feel Tom's small laugh against my leg as a smile rises on his face. "Yes? Are they decent suits?"

"Yes, they are. I have seen them myself." I look to the others and force myself into a giddy mood. "I think you all would just absolutely adore them."

The advisors all look at each other with an awkward smile. Dotson looks to me, trying to force the awkwardness away. "I don't know, sweetie. I just don't really see myself wearing a suit of someone whom I don't know personally."

Riley scoffs, "Yeah right, like you know every suit designer you've ever used personally."

As Dotson shoots Riley a look of "shut up," Madden turns back to me.

"What he means by that is that we are sort of suit snobs"—Madden looks to the other two—"if we're being honest."

"Yeah, no." I place my hand on Tom's leg and lean in to get a little closer to the advisors. "I totally understand. How about this. I will take your measurements and then bring in some suit jackets at no charge. If you like the jackets, you can get the rest of the suit for a great deal."

"It's not that we are looking for a great deal." Dotson tells me. "We can afford it. It's just that we don't know if we want to wear—"

"Shut up," Riley tells him. Looking back to me, Riley smiles. "Go ahead and take our measurements. We will try the jackets."

Logan

Finishing a ten-mile trek from one associate to the next, I slowly make my way up her backyard and to one of her windows.

I hold my silenced pistol up and aim through the window, right for the back of her blonde curly hair. With one squeeze of the trigger, I will take out the woman who did this to me and most likely did this to many others along the way.

The wind continues to blow outside, allowing me to listen to the leaves crackling in the sky above me and easing me in to finish what I came here to do. Just as my finger tightens on the trigger, I see someone else in the building move. I duck beneath the window and listen to a familiar voice as he walks through. Only after I hear the footsteps stop do I look back up through the window to find Amanda and Eric sitting on her couch together, watching something on the hologram.

Outraged by the sight, I find myself circling the house, breaking down the door, and holding them both at gunpoint. I enter the house with my pistol aimed at both of their heads and shout at them, "Get down. Get down now!"

Eric immediately hops off the couch and looks to me. "Hey, man, what do you think you're doing?"

"I said—" I close the door behind me and pull the trigger. The silenced bullet whistles through the air and destroys a potted plant behind both of their heads. "Get down. On your knees. Now."

Without hesitation, tears begin flowing from Amanda's eyes as she holds her hands up to me and falls to her knees. I then point the gun back to Eric and wait for him to finish getting down. I watch him slowly but surely force his way onto the ground but see he is having trouble with the prosthetic.

"What do you want?" he asks me. "Just take what you want and leave."

"Do you know this girl?" I ask him, now pointing the gun to the flustered Amanda who won't even look at me. "Do you know anything about her?"

"Who is she? Who are *you*?" Eric asks, "Why are you asking me this?"

My voice rises with hatred and disgust. I feel my scratchy voice growling at him at the top of my lungs and ignore the sandpapery feeling in my throat. "I am one of her victims!"

Amanda's tears slow as Eric looks to her. The two of us see two emotions on her face. Fear and shock. Her now-pale face seems to have drained with blood as she slowly puts the pieces together.

"What?" she asks me, looking up to my face but never really finding my eyes.

I yank off my mask and shout at them both, "Look at me! Look at this!" I point to my face with the pistol, not caring what happens anymore. "You see this? This is what you did to me. This was all because of you!"

Eric continues to stare at my face and scans me over. He rises to his feet and continues to stare.

"Get back down"—I point the gun back to his face—"now."

"Logan?" he asks me, shocking everyone in the room. "What . . . what happened? You're walking." He looks back to Amanda and then returns to me. "What happened to your skin?"

I point the gun back to Amanda. "She did this. She turned me in for asking a simple question, and the next thing I know, I am being tortured for answers I don't even have!"

"What?" he asks me.

"It wasn't just me either, no." I keep the gun pointed at her. "That family you were supposed to be taking care of? The Pages? They're both dead too. I watched them both die." I feel myself letting spit fly as I shout with a full chest of anger. "All because of you!"

"Hey, Logan," Eric takes a step toward me, but I immediately shoot him in the prosthetic knee.

He falls to the ground, and Amanda shouts back to me, "We were just doing our jobs!" She slides in front of Eric. "Don't take it out on us!"

My head jerks to Eric as her words sink in. "We?" I stare at them both and wait for an answer but don't get one. "What are you talking about?"

No one says anything, so I aim the pistol right back to Amanda. "Tell me right now what you both did, or I swear I will kill you without even blinking."

"Okay! Okay!" Her hands shake as she continues to hold them up in surrender. "You already know I was hired to tell them if I thought anyone was a problem or could know something—"

"Amanda—" Eric interrupts.

"But Eric worked there too. He even ran one of the gas chambers for a bit."

"Unknowingly!" Eric shouts. He turns to me and looks to me with a sense of pity and pleading I have never before seen. "I swear, Logan, I didn't know that is what they wanted me to do. I would never do something like that, I swear."

I aim the gun to Amanda and tilt my head. "How many times did he work in the chamber?"

"I don't know," she tells me, obviously lying, "only once."

I shoot another shot behind her and hit the hologram box, knocking out the program.

"Four times," she tells me. "He worked there four times. But he didn't know what he was doing, I swear. Neither of us knew how bad it was! We didn't—"

Both of them fall to the floor with the holes through their heads draining onto her perfectly white carpets. I stare at them for no more than two seconds before fleeing the scene and heading to my next assignment.

This time, there will be no hesitation.

Zane

As I put in the final touches on the four suit jackets, I prick myself with the needle. Looking down at the jackets I have worked on for over a week straight, I pull my finger away and go search for a bandage.

I won't ever do anything to harm these jackets, and I especially won't let my blood be on them.

"Do you need one of these?" June hands me a small sticky bandage as I rise from the hunched-over position I was in to get to the junk drawer.

"Yes, thank you." I wrap my finger up and head back to my work desk. Looking around to the stuffed torsos I have the suit jackets on, I realize that after finishing this project, I never want to make another jacket again.

"It's so sad how they will never be worn in public." June strolls over to the jackets and runs her hands over the sleeves. "They were brilliantly made and, might I add, gorgeous." Her hands slowly run around the back of the suits and find their way into the pockets.

"Well, thank you very much. And I see you like the fabric I used?"

She nods. "I love it." Pulling away from the mannequins, she watches me head back to work on the final suit. "Now that I think about it, I guess there *will* be tons of press while they wear them."

I chuckle and think through the plan. "I guess so."

The news channel we keep on in the store suddenly catches our attention as the phrase *serial killer* echoes through the room.

June and I pause for a moment and listen to the woman's voice from the radio. "Since last week, there have been a total of thirty-two victims from the Executioner. Each victim died of a single gunshot wound to the head but almost never from the same gun as a previous victim. Here is a clip from an interview with Police Chief Griffith from earlier today."

Another man's voice appears on the radio, "The killer used a variation of different guns. Some pistols, some snipers, but each shot was always execution style. It looks to us like this killer is on a mission."

"How so?"

"These killings are too random to be random. We have a slight hint that this man or woman thinks they are a vigilante."

"Meaning what exactly? Should we be scared that we could be next?"

"No, ma'am, if anything, only those who are committing crimes should be worried."

The voice changes back to the original newswoman, "From this report, it sounds to me like everyone needs to be on their best behavior, or they may be next."

I roll my eyes and go back to the jacket. "Well, that's a wonderful way to strike fear and panic into the hearts of Frieden citizens."

"Yeah," June agrees, "and what about the fact that they are trying to use the deaths of all those people as some sort of promotion for being on our best behavior?"

I shrug. "I don't know how I feel about that."

"I do," she snorts. "It is ridiculous."

"Yeah." I force one of the final stitches into the jacket and hold it up to take one last look at it. "Let's just hope that this guy isn't going to get in the way of the next plan."

Logan

The more aware the media is of my mission, the harder it becomes.

I managed to off thirty-four of Burris's employees since I started; but since I have made the news, my targets have begun to go into hiding.

With this recent development, one of my side missions has become my top priority and the next task I will complete.

CHAPTER THIRTY-SIX

Zane

Though I barely know how to drive, I feel as if I am better than most people I've ridden with.

As I drive through the woods in the car she provided me, down a dirt path that I've never seen before, I squint, looking for Van standing somewhere where I would be able to see her.

Even with my lights on their lowest setting, Van's white skin glows when they hit her. I immediately break, giving myself some form of whiplash, and exit the car.

"Are they all there?" she asks me, pointing back to the running vehicle.

I nod. "Every weapon you had stored in the basement of the Fabric Room is in that van."

She nods back. "Good." Pulling a small box out of her jacket, she smiles back up to me. "Are you guys ready to finish the mission?"

"As long as you have the ring in there, we are."

She opens the box and shows me the small golden circle with the cube on the end of it and chuckles. "I bet you didn't expect it to look this dull, did you?"

I shake my head and take the box from her. "How does it work again?"

Pointing to the mechanisms, Van leans over the box and twists the ring about. "When you have the box on the end of it against their necks, you press a trigger on the side, here, and administer the serum."

"Okay. What all is in the serum?"

"It's a form of testosterone that targets the amygdala, along with adrenaline and a few other additives that I really don't have time to get into." Walking past me to the car, Van turns around and waves me to follow her. "Ludley and the others plan on coming back tonight and should be back a few hours after the men have been arrested. Are you sure that Oswald is onboard with all this?"

"Of course," I tell her. Oswald is completely onboard with getting the corruption out of Frieden's government. He just doesn't know the full plan of how we are going to do that.

"Okay." She sits in the driver's seat of the car and looks to me through the windshield. "I will see you later tonight."

June

The cab driver scans my code and unlocks the door. I have never had a driver that locks me in before I pay, and I never want to have one again.

As I get out of the cab, I have to slowly retrieve each suit coat from the hanger provided in the car but end up almost getting my arm ripped off by the man as he begins to drive away.

"Hey!" I shout at the driver as he slams on his breaks. "Excuse me, but I still have to get my coats out."

He turns around and looks to me with an evil expression but quickly turns back to face the front and mumbles something to himself. I scoff at his rudeness and finish unhooking the jackets when I am once again startled, this time by a shadow.

"Oh, I am sorry, dear," Tom says to me as his security guards surround us. "I came out to help you bring these in." He places one of his hands over the pile of jackets in my arms, in their bags, and on their hangers. "Please, allow me."

Returning his smile, I allow him to take the jackets; and we all walk into the capitol building together. He and I, surrounded by his guards, seem cut off to the world. I almost feel bad for what he is about to witness.

This man has always been a gentleman and never done anything that I can recall to earn such horrible friends like his advisors. I only hope that what is about to happen helps bring him a better and much safer life, maybe somewhere lower in the political kingdom, somewhere where he isn't as much in the spotlight. The more time I have spent with him, the more I have realized he really only wanted to make a difference. He doesn't care who gets the credit.

When we make it up to one of the capitol building's lounge rooms, all the guards leave the two of us alone. Tom sets the suit jackets down, laying them on the back of a couch, and looks to me with another shy smile, the same one he generally gives me when we are alone.

"Would you care for some tea?" he asks me.

Taking a seat on the couch, I look back to him. "I would love some, thank you."

Tom heads over to the wall and presses a button, paging someone down in the kitchen, I do believe. "Excuse me, but would you please bring the tea cart up to the guest lounge room?"

We wait a moment before a voice buzzes back, "Of course, Chancellor Oswald. It will be up in a moment."

"Thank you very much, dear," he says to the buzzer. When he finally takes his finger off the buzzer, he comes and joins me on the couch. "So how are you doing, June?"

I look back to him. "I am good. How about you?"

He raises one eyebrow to me and crosses his legs. "You know, I ask you this because I actually care, right? Not because I am just trying to make small talk."

I look down to my folded hands and twiddle my thumbs. "I know, but I am doing good."

Tom leans forward to try to get our eyes to meet. "Are you sure? You seem a little on edge."

Looking back to him, I shrug. "I really am fine. I may just seem on edge because of that cab driver."

"Ah." He leans back onto the couch as a knock on the door interrupts us. "I saw him drive away while you were trying to retrieve the coats." Tom rises to his feet and heads to the door, opening it and taking the cart from a woman. "Thank you so much. Have a great day." He hands her some cash and waves her goodbye. After a moment, he straightens up and smiles into the hallway. "Oh, hello."

I turn to look and see who it is when I am greeted by the three remaining advisors.

"Good evening, June," Dotson says to me.

The other two greet me similarly but aren't as interested in me as they are the tea cart. Each of them fills up a cup with hot water and their favorite tea bags, leaving them between Tom and me for the first time in a long time.

"So"—Riley turns to me as he dunks his teabag—"did I hear this right? Those suit jackets are finally ready for us to try on?"

I nod and grab the jackets. "Yes, sir! Each of the bags has your names on them." I pass them out to each man, and they set their cups down on the table beside them.

As they all wait for their tea to steep, I watch them all slide their jackets out of the bags. Riley's expression shifts from cocky to surprised in a matter of seconds. "What? These are gorgeous."

I nod again. "I know. Didn't I tell you?"

Riley slides his on and moans with slight sarcasm as the comfort hits him. "This is amazing. I had no idea that I could look this good in something that wasn't designer."

As I head over to him, I spin him around and brush off his back. "It does look nice."

Riley turns to look at Tom as he slides on his jacket. "Look at this. Your girlfriend is acting more like my girlfriend."

Just as the final word of his statement falls out of his mouth, I prick him in the back of the neck with the ring.

"Ow!" he exclaims like a child. "What was that?"

"Sorry," I tell him, "the tag was sticking out."

Riley nods and rubs his neck for a moment as I go to Dotson next. I do the same to him and find much less of a reaction.

"That was the tag?" Dotson asks me.

I nod and stick Madden. "Yeah, I'm sorry about that. I will definitely tell the designer that he needs to fix them."

Madden nods back and brushes off his suit. "Yes, please. But other than that, these seem to be fairly decent suits."

Heading over to Tom, I watch him hold his arms out and observe the fabric. "I absolutely love this," he tells me. He runs his hands over the outside and looks to me with surprise. "What sort of fabric is this? It doesn't feel like any kind of suit I've ever worn before."

I shrug. "I don't know. I will ask him when I go back to"—I turn to the advisors—"order the rest of the suit?"

They all look to each other with amusement, and I realize I don't need to be pushing this so hard. It's not like it matters anyway.

"I think I would like to get the rest of it," Tom tells me. "I really do like this." He walks past me and to the tea cart. Fixing himself a cup of what looks like earl gray, he turns back to me. "What would you like to drink, June?"

"Whatever you're having will be wonderful," I tell him, earning looks of slight annoyance from the advisors.

By the time we all sit down around the seating area to enjoy our tea, I have to wonder if I did something wrong. I can tell the advisors are getting a little testy with each other, but they haven't snapped yet. The plan was for them to get into a fight, be arrested for lack of composure, and be fired for the very same reason. I think through all the controversial topics I can and spit out the best one.

"So," I say as I refill my tea cup with more hot water, "what do you guys think about the serial killer running around?"

"I wondered how long it would be before you brought that up," Tom says, sipping his tea.

Before I have the chance to ask Tom what he means by that, Riley scoffs, "The Executioner? I'm jealous, to be honest."

"Jealous?" Dotson asks him. "Of what? The name?"

"The fact that he can get the job done," Riley tells him. Looking back to Tom, he gives a fake smile. "I'm kidding, of course."

Tom tenses up a bit, and I place my hand on his. Trying to keep him calm, I give him a small look and sip on my tea.

"Sure you are," Madden says, "always making jokes."

Tom and I exchange another look as we feel the tension in the room grow. I have a feeling that we are about to witness the full effect of the serum.

"What's that now?" Riley asks Madden.

"Nothing, nothing."

Nobody says anything. Tom and I wait beside each other for someone to do something but end up causing Riley to become even more infuriated.

"Well," he shouts at us, "what are you two staring at?"

I look away from him and down to my teacup, but Tom doesn't. He continues staring at Riley. "Excuse me?"

Riley sets his cup down and looks back to Tom. "Yeah? Do you have a problem?"

"Well, I don't know if I entirely appreciate the way you are snapping at us."

"Tom." I squeeze his hand to try to get him to stop, but Riley hops up out of his seat and is forced back by Dotson.

Dotson shouts in a hushed tone in Riley's face, "What are you doing?"

"I wasn't even going to do anything! What are *you* doing? Why are you defending him?"

Madden hops in between the two and growls, "Both of you, calm down."

Riley shoves Madden off him and into Dotson. Within moments, teacups are thrown at each other, scalding water is splashed everywhere, and Tom is diving into the middle of it. "Please, gentlemen!" Tom forces the men apart but is run at by Riley.

The other two pull Riley off Tom, and we all listen to his crazed shouting. "Let me go. I am going to finish the job that should have been done a long time ago."

"Riley!" Dotson forces him down in the chair. "Stop. You're acting like a madman."

"Oh really? I'm acting like a madman? What about you? With your—"

Out of one of the lounge's hallways comes a black shadow figure with his pistol raised. He immediately drops the three advisors with a single gunshot to their heads and looks to me.

Logan holds his pistol toward me, ready and aimed; but all he does is stare. After a split second, Tom forces me behind him and is dropped just as quickly as all the others.

Logan and I stare at each other for a moment longer. As I stand there in shock, he slowly walks out of the room and disappears, leaving me surrounded by heads draining of blood and open empty eyes staring off.

Logan

I sprint out through the same route I entered through and dodge another guard walking around. I was trained to know every entrance and escape in the capitol building. This has always been one of my favorites. I never before thought I would be able to explore them.

Sadly enough, I don't have all the time I want to go down every path this tunnel offers.

Blending into the walls, I hide in the corners as soldiers and guards come running through it, trying to get to the chancellor's aid. The ease I experience completing my task concerns me for the future of our country's leaders, but knowing I helped them see flaws in their security lets my conscience rest. When I escape the building, I flee back into the woods and manage to check off four other people off my list.

June

"So you don't know anything?" the officer asks me once again.

I shake my head and continue staring straight at him. "No, sir, I don't." The interrogation room they brought me to is much larger than the one we have in the Fabric Room. It is much colder too.

It's funny. One of my first thoughts when I entered this room was *Man, I could really use one of those jackets.*

"So you just happened to be with them all for the very first time when Sparrow died," the officer restates, "and you just happen to be with them all when the serial killer came in and executed them."

"Yes, sir," I tell him, acting shocked and completely torn apart.

He stares at me for a moment and then flips a page of his notepad. "Now, tell me, why do you think that the Executioner did not kill you with everyone else?"

"I don't know," I tell him. And this time, that is completely honest. I have no idea why Logan didn't shoot me. I have no idea why he shot Tom either. I guess if he had shot the advisors, he would think he was going along with the plan, but Tom?

He had stepped in front of me to save me.

He wanted to make things better.

The officer picks up a remote, revealing a hologram screen with security cameras from the lounge. He starts the film at where the men were shouting at one another with no sound and pauses right after Logan drops everyone but me.

"Tell me." He points at the screen where Logan and I stare at each other. "Do you know who he is?"

I shake my head. "No, sir."

He leans back in his chair and rubs his eyes dramatically as if upset with me. "Tell me, if we had security cameras in the room with you the night Sparrow died, would we have seen something? Something you didn't want us to see?"

I pause. After a moment, I speak up, "Yes, sir."

"And what would that be?"

"You would have seen me cry. I don't like people seeing me cry. I never have."

The officer rises to his feet and heads to the door without another word. He holds it open and looks to me, gesturing that I am free to leave.

Zane

As I finish stocking the shelves, I pull out a broom and get to work cleaning. Sweep after sweep, I realize there is a lot more foot traffic in here per day than I realized. We only ever have a few customers in here, but they tend to buy enough to keep this store open.

I continue to clean up after the shop closes when I hear the front door unlock. The bell over the door rings its familiar chime, and I turn to see a mass of people entering the building. Its leading member is the first to smile at me.

"Good evening, Mr. West."

I smile back to her. "I'm happy to see you made it here safe, Mrs. Ludley."

CHAPTER THIRTY-SEVEN

Logan

Sitting in the house of my fifty-eighth assignment, with him lying on the floor next to me, I relax on his couch and continue watching the news. I watch Janice and Emily Hash walk back into the capitol building and listen to the news coverage of their arrival along with the deaths of Chancellor Oswald and his advisors.

After about twenty minutes of listening to the reporter talk about the Executioner, they finally flip over to Hash's speech as she addresses the nation. I watch as she stands with Janice by her side. They stand behind the famous podium Oswald used for all his speeches.

"Good afternoon, Frieden. I know for the past few days, you have all been in shock of all that has been happening. I know that almost all of you thought Mrs. Ludley and I were dead, and those of you who didn't were most likely taken in and tortured by the same government you trusted to keep you safe. Let me tell you this. The five men responsible for the tortures, the assassinations, the bombs, the executions, and all the excuses are now gone. They blamed their attacks on Amiable rebels to fool you into thinking that it was all right. They attempted to get rid of anyone and everyone who believed differently than them, but they failed. Chancellor Oswald's reign has come to an end, and you all no longer have any need to worry. We are taking a stand, and all the other government officials who supported Oswald's restrictions and choices will be found and will be taken immediately to their punishments for such treason. We will be fixing everything that has gone wrong in this government, and with your help, we will help make Frieden back into the country it was originally supposed to be."

I roll my eyes at Hash's claims and turn off the news after she announces the need for another voting session for a new chancellor. Once I turn off the news, I step over the man on the floor and head out to my next task.

June

I sit at the table and sniff the air. The smell of her cinnamon apple candles has faded out since she left, but I plan on bringing it back.

Just last week, I managed to work it out with the offices to have June Dawson as the official owner of the Pages' old residence. I am going to pay for it with the money I make with my job at the Fabric Room.

I don't know what happened to Derek and his mom, and I really don't think I want to know. Janice told me when we got together a few days ago that they both have been pronounced dead. After she told me that, I stopped asking questions.

I imagine that is one of the reasons Logan stopped speaking of Derek that night. He told me Derek had visited him, and then Logan completely shut down. He didn't say another word. He must have known Derek died and just didn't want to hurt me.

I know he doesn't want to hurt me.

That is one of the reasons he stays away from me.

At least, that is what he tells me.

Every now and then, I will get a letter from Logan without any sort of return address. Each letter tells me about the country and how it seems like it is becoming a better place already with Hash as the new chancellor. People seem happier, the towns seem safer, and he is almost giddy at the fact that they are firing so many of the old officials.

He visits all the famous landmarks on his trips through the states, tries their signature foods, and yet does his best to keep out of the public eye.

Logan tells me that he really wants to get together one day, but he doesn't want to until it is safe. He even goes on to say that he has been keeping himself busy and found that he is nowhere near as good a drawer as I am, even though I think I am complete garbage at it.

Logan goes on to write me almost a dozen letters before the one I was waiting on finally arrives.

At the bottom of his last letter lies a time and location for us to meet.

Logan

I stand out in the cold breeze. As summer comes to a close, the random bouts of cool air have decided to come at the worst possible times. With my hoodie up and over my suit, I continue to look around the woods behind the Fabric Room and wait.

This was where we had our last real talk. I figured this would be a good place to pick back up again. I tighten the strings on my hood and close off my face a little bit more, waiting on the wind to stop blowing. The thick clothes I wear over my suit helped me blend in when walking through the town, but I could feel whenever someone caught a glimpse of my face.

Without my mask, I am exposed. People can see the monster.

I hear the snap of a twig and turn around to find June walking toward me. The same butterflies I once had return as I make my way over to her, causing me to feel more nervous than I ever have before. A million thoughts go through my head as we approach each other, but the one that keeps going through is *Why won't the butterflies go away?*

I place one of my hands on my stomach to try to get it to settle down when immediately I am hit with a sharp feeling on my collarbone. I reach up and pull out Sam's necklace as the question about the butterflies repeats itself.

"Why won't the butterflies go away?"

Just as I look to the gem, I hear Sam's voice loud and clear as if he is right beside me say, "Digest them."

I snort at his advice and look around. A single leaf blows from beside me and toward her body as she approaches. My eyes follow the leaf as a smile rises on her face.

"Hey," she says to me.

I return her smile and pull my hood off, exposing myself to the wind. "Hey."

EPILOGUE

Sam

So time goes on, and it leads June and Logan right into each other's arms. They both go to work with Zane at the Fabric Room, which actually becomes a refugee center, funded by the one and only Janice Ludley.

No one knows about this center, though. Only those who fund it, those who are clients, and those who work there know.

Zane is the one who looks out and contacts new clients to protect. Whether it be abusive family members, stalkers, or anything like that, he finds out who needs their help. Mavis—I mean, June—helps them relocate, keeps contact with them, and makes sure that they are doing well. If they ever need anything or think they need to move again, June works it out. Logan keeps an eye on the abuser, whoever it may be, and does what he can to help defend the people. If he feels the need to step in and have an intervention with the abuser, he does so. There hasn't been a case yet where his intimidation has failed.

Logan and June get engaged almost a year after they begin working together at the Fabric Room. Logan gets Janice to pull a few favors and has my body dug up. They have it turned into a matching stone of the one I had made of my mother. Logan continues to wear the one of my mother around his neck while he proposed to June with a green gem ring made of me. They haven't taken them off since.

Though they both have their own demons to deal with, they seem to deal much better when they are with each other. The only time June ever lets anyone touch her is when that someone is Logan. She still has nightmares about waking up in the woods with those animals, in the bathroom the night I died, or even on that hospital bed where she saw Samantha. She only ever talks about the nightmares when she is sure she won't be falling back to sleep that night and only ever speaks of certain ones.

Logan's skin never heals. He deals with the pain constantly but finds all the peace he needs when he is with June. The only time his skin doesn't burn is when her skin is against his. He too has nightmares but is much more open to talking about them. He knows June likes to listen, and he knows it helps her trust him more when he shares. Logan continues to hold on to hope that one day, June will tell him what most of her nightmares are about.

Zane finds himself happiest when helping other people. He has decided that he would rather focus on his job than have a spouse or romantic relationship, but I just think he is afraid of commitment. I also think he likes that Van girl, but who am I to throw my opinion in?

While the three of them focus on their job almost wholeheartedly, just recently has Logan revealed his second job to June by showing her his list. When she read over all the names, he explained that he has given himself a personal assignment to hunt down the rest of the assassins, the rats, and the torturers. After sharing this with her, June tells Logan that the only way he is allowed to continue this job is if she comes with him.

They debate for a while, but June eventually convinces him to allow her to join as if he had a choice.

Not too long after Logan shares his secret with June does June share a secret with him. This act results in the two adding one more name to the list.

"John Young."

CPSIA information can be obtained
at www.ICGtesting.com
Printed in the USA
LVHW111549061120
670968LV00001B/82